Economic Analysis of Law in European Legal Scholarship

Volume 6

The purpose of this book series is to publish high quality volumes in the growing field of law and economics research in Europe, from a comprehensive theoretical and practical vantage point. In particular, the series will place great emphasis on foundational and theoretical aspects of economic analysis of law and on interdisciplinary approaches in European Legal Scholarship. Following Nobel laureate Ronald Coase's famous essay "The Problem of Social Cost" (1960) fifty years ago, law and economics has become the lingua franca of American jurisprudence. In recent decades, law and economics has also gained widespread popularity in Europe and its influence on legal scholarship is growing significantly. Therefore, the Economic Analysis of Law in European Legal Scholarship academic book series illustrates how law and economics is developing in Europe and what opportunities and problems – both in general and in specific legal fields – are associated with this approach within the legal traditions of European countries. Rather than further exploring economic analysis as such, the main focus of this series lies on the implementation of economic methods in legislation and legal adjudication from a European perspective. It takes into account the particular challenges the European legal systems face. Volumes will address law and economics research in Europe from a critical and comparative viewpoint. The studies in this series are strong and bold narratives of the development of economic analysis of law in European Legal Scholarship. Some are suitable for a very broad readership. Contributions in this series primarily come from scholars in Europe. The purpose is to provide the next generation of European lawyers with the models and skills needed to understand and improve the economic analysis of law in their own legal field. The series includes monographs focusing on specific topics as well as collections of essays covering specific themes.

More information about this series at http://www.springer.com/series/11927

Harry Bremmers • Kai Purnhagen
Editors

Regulating and Managing Food Safety in the EU

A Legal-Economic Perspective

Springer

Editors
Harry Bremmers
Law and Governance Group
Wageningen University and Research (WUR)
Wageningen, The Netherlands

Kai Purnhagen
Law School
Erasmus University of Rotterdam
Rotterdam, The Netherlands

Economic Analysis of Law in European Legal Scholarship
ISBN 978-3-030-08356-4 ISBN 978-3-319-77045-1 (eBook)
https://doi.org/10.1007/978-3-319-77045-1

Cover Design: eStudio Calamar, Berlin/Figueres

Printed on acid-free paper

This Springer imprint is published by the registered company Springer International Publishing AG part of Springer Nature.
The registered company address is: Gewerbestrasse 11, 6330 Cham, Switzerland

Contents

Regulating and Managing Food Safety in the EU: A Legal-Economic Perspective 1
Harry Bremmers and Kai Purnhagen

Private Food Safety Standards in the EU 11
Tetty Havinga

Investigating the Regulatory Structure of Voluntary Sustainability Standards: Foundations for Intervention Strategies to Increase Consumer Confidence 39
Eva van der Zee

Environmental Sustainability and the Food System 57
Alessandro Banterle, Elena Claire Ricci, and Alessia Cavaliere

EU Health Claims: A Consumer Perspective 89
Erica van Herpen and Hans C. M. van Trijp

Regulatory Compliance and Company Strategies: The Case of the Nutrition and Health Claims Regulation (EC) No. 1924/2006 105
Stefanie Bröring and Sukhada Khedkar

Foods for Specific Consumer Groups 129
Silvia L. Schmidt

Commanding to "Nudge" via the Proportionality Principle? 151
Kai Purnhagen and Ellen van Kleef

Obesity, Fat Taxes and Their Effects on Consumers 169
Silke Thiele and Jutta Roosen

Substance Over Form: A Principle for European Food Information Regulation? 195
Harry Bremmers

European Food Law and the Precautionary Principle: Paradoxical Effects of the EU's Precautionary Food Policies 217
Lucas Bergkamp and Jaap C. Hanekamp

Enforcement of European Food Laws 245
Franziska Weber

The Economics of Harmonization of Food Law in the EU 263
Michael Faure

Pre-Market Approval and Its Impact on Food Innovation: The Novel Foods Example 291
Martin Holle

Agricultural Biotechnology: Regulation in the United States and the European Union 331
Margaret Rosso Grossman

Regulating and Managing Food Safety in the EU: A Legal-Economic Perspective

Harry Bremmers and Kai Purnhagen

Abstract This chapter provides a general overview of the contents of this book. The chapter-contributions' order follows different dimensions that can be discerned for describing regulatory content and effect: public-private, mandatory-voluntary, prescription-persuasion, rules-principles, ex-ante-ex-post and centralisation-decentralisation. The book shows that the regulatory toolbox to provide food safety has become more diverse in course of time and that the insight in the social effects of the application of such tools has increased.

1 Introduction

When we consume food, we presume that it is safe. When Europeans travel in Europe, consumers can be quite certain that foods they buy and consume will not affect their health. Checking safety via smells, appeal, the seller's reputation or processing of raw eatable foods is regularly not necessary. The European Union (EU) has one of the most sophisticated food laws in the world, and many believe that it is thanks to these laws that food on the EU market is, despite some hick-ups once in a while, relatively safe.[1] This safety-orientation of EU food law is not only geared towards the provision of consumers' rights to health and safety, in the form of this 'presumption-of-safety' it is also one of the main factors determining the competitiveness of the food industry.[2] This 'presumption-of-safety' is not obvious. It is not only propagated by private businesses, but also by the institutional setting in which they operate. A key element of the institutional surroundings of our food supply

[1]Researchers have determined the EU's traceability requirements as world-leading, see Charlebois et al. (2014), p. 1104.

[2]Wijnands et al. (2008).

H. Bremmers (✉) · K. Purnhagen
Law and Governance Group, Wageningen University and Research (WUR), Wageningen, The Netherlands
e-mail: harry.bremmers@wur.nl; kai.purnhagen@wur.nl

H. Bremmers, K. Purnhagen (eds.), *Regulating and Managing Food Safety in the EU*, Economic Analysis of Law in European Legal Scholarship 6,
https://doi.org/10.1007/978-3-319-77045-1_1

chains is food law. A country with very good laws on food and a likewise rich cuisine and history of food culture is Turkey. However, Turkey is a regular number one candidate in the ranking of countries of origin of counterfeit food and beverages seized at EU borders.[3] Why does the provision of food safety work in some areas of the world better than in other parts? When travelling in the United States of America, one can likewise be quite certain that the food one consumes will not have a major health effect on the body. The provision of safe food is quite successful in the United States. Nevertheless, US consumers are among those most concerned about safety in the world, increasingly calling for stricter regulatory activity. Content-wise the norms that are accepted in a region may differ, due to among others differences in institutional and natural variables (like social habits, culture, climate etc.) and the function they perform.[4]

In the EU, next to guaranteeing the safety of foods, norms which aim at the provision of healthy and sustainable food are of key importance for the free movement of foods across national borders inside of the EU. In other words, food law is of predominant importance for the functioning of the European internal market. On the one hand, within the boundaries of social provisions such as environmental protection and fundamental rights, but also ethical considerations such as animal welfare, the rationale of the internal market (based on economic foundations as harvested from neoclassical economic theorising) determines the operation of food markets and supply chains. On the other hand, food procurement is especially vulnerable due to food safety issues involved, the credence character of foodstuffs and the tendency towards vertical and horizontal cooperation to address such issues. Without regulatory interference, the efficient and effective functioning of supply of safe food may be threatened. This induces a constant dynamics of regulation in which different considerations seem to conquest for predominance: economic allocative and distributional concerns of regulation, informational equity, cultural differences as well as fundamental rights and freedoms. Exercising economic freedoms within the ambit of the EU therefore has to be balanced with deeper concerns about long-term guarantees of food security. As a result an increasing and partly contradictory regulatory food safety framework has been put in place, and it still broadens its scope and content. Starting from the idea that economic considerations are basic to the design and functioning of the European food supply arena, and that economic effects consolidate or induce modification of the present legal structures and principles, we ask ourselves how economic, marketing and managerial theory and practice can explain and enhance the shaping and modification of the regulatory framework that fosters safe and sustainable food supply chains. In the book, generic theorising and measurement of regulatory effects (e.g. of ex-ante vs ex-post regulation, content-versus information-related regulation) is supplemented by in-depth analysis of key topics in food law (like health claims, enforcement strategies and induced risk management at the level of the food business).

[3]See Dennis and Kelly (2013), p. 26.

[4]See Bremmers et al. (2009).

2 Outline

This book addresses the effects of food law on the policies and management of actors in and around food supply chains along different dimensions: public-private, mandatory-voluntary, ex ante-ex post regulation, and regulation with rules (objective standards) or principles, prescription versus persuasion, centralisation versus decentralisation, or hybrids thereof.

2.1 *Public-Private*

Regulating markets via public law is a traditional way of interference in food supply chain activities. Due to loss of regulatory power of nation-state regulation[5] and likewise an increase of globalisation of food-related trade private regulation through standards is taking central stage in the regulation of supply chains.[6] This increasingly important form of regulation is addressed by Tetty Havinga, Eva van der Zee and Alessandro Banterle, Elena Claire Ricci and Alessia Cavaliere.

Tetty Havinga ('Private Food Safety Standards in the EU') addresses the structure of private standards and their relationship with governmental regulation. This relationship is analysed for the rulemaking, adoption, monitoring and review of private standards. The relationship is not unidirectional it seems. Private standards influence public regulation, and vice versa. The involvement of public authorities may improve the legitimacy, accountability and transparency of private standards, but carries risks also (like the risk of capture).

Eva van der Zee ('Investigating the Regulatory Structure of Voluntary Sustainability Standards') investigates the regulatory structure of standards which underlie sustainability labels. The structural regulatory characteristics of these standards are categorized in order to facilitate governments to eventually intervene in it, should consumer confidence make such intervention necessary. The assessment of such structural impediments and intervention based thereon may be necessary due to the ongoing tendency towards market-based instruments. More and more, sustainability standards are set by private parties. Accreditation could take place by private institutions also, as well as certification and the assessment of compliance. The study shows plurality in the available sustainability labels as to their structural characteristics. The present sustainability labels, using the Netherlands as case study, show that especially non-governmental organisations are involved in the setting of standards, while dominantly certification takes place by private institutions (i.e., third-party certification). This is in line with consumers' expectations, and is, in line with present consumer research, trusted and credible.

---

[5]Patterson and Afilalo (2008), pp. 35–37.

[6]Purnhagen (2015).

Alessandro Banterle, Elena Claire Ricci and Alessia Cavaliere ('Environmental Sustainability and the Food System') provide us with an overview of environmental sustainability, its connection with the food sector and the way it can be promoted. They investigate public regulation and next address private initiatives in the form of self-regulatory activities. 'Sustainable development' was among others defined in the Brundtland report 'Our Common Future' (1984) and is strongly connected to the structure of the food provision system (water and land usage, disposition of waste etc.). The authors not only go into public regulation on behalf of sustainable development (as for instance indirectly referred to in the General Food Law), but also review private initiatives in this respect (like eco-labelling and fair trade). Last, they assess the effects of measures and information on consumer choices and the preservation of human health.

2.2 Mandatory-Voluntary

Classical tools of mandatory regulation are enforced by mechanisms of public law, voluntary solutions need to persuade by appeal. In this book, the regulatory choices between the two are illustrated by three contributions that address the use and effects (for the consumer, but also for the strategies of businesses) of commercial practices on foodstuffs.

Erica van Herpen and Hans van Trijp ('EU Health Claims: A Consumer Perspective') stress the positive effects of health claims on consumer behaviour and on the effectiveness of businesses. Such effects will only occur if these claims are reliable, which was a major reason to install the nutrition and health claims regulation (NHCR) in 2006. The contribution reviews the effects of health claims from three angles: the representation of the claim in terms of text versus picture, the inferences consumers make of the representation and the consumers' motivation to choose healthy products. Legislators, as well as food businesses for their own purposes, should be aware of the mechanisms behind the differences in consumer responses to textual and visual claims.

While van Herpen and van Trijp investigate the consumer impact of health claims, *Stefanie Bröring and Sukhada Khedkar* ('Regulatory Compliance and Company Strategies: The Case of the Nutrition and Health Claims Regulation (EC) No. 1924/2006') analyse the challenges food businesses face and their strategies to deal with the NHCR. Compliance is not as self-evident as it seems. Companies can comply by submitting for a claim to be authorised if needed for an innovation (for instance a new 'functional food'). But they can also circumvent the NHCR, due to the heavy burdens connected to pre-market approval in terms of necessary scientific evidence, administrative time and resources and postponed access to the market. As to the authors, a dialogue involving all actors would be necessary to reduce the barriers to innovation due to the NHCR.

The contribution of *Silvia Schmidt* ('Foods for Specific Consumer Groups') describes the increased use of standards for vulnerable groups of consumers. From a mere market organisation the EU has developed towards balancing the freedoms in the market towards the protection of a consumer which is not 'average' but makes part of different groups with different safety and personal needs and may be vulnerable as to safety and misleading by information. This consumer is specifically protected by means of product (recipe) and process standards and mandatory food information. Regulation 609/2013, which provides protection to specific groups, is used to analyse the need for and structure of content- and information based regulation, and the trade-off between these two.

2.3 Prescription-Persuasion

Behavioural steering these days goes beyond the classical dichotomy of mandatory versus voluntary or content-related versus information-related regulation. It is increasingly supplemented by new forms of regulation, which promise to be more effective. These approaches make use of classical monetary incentivizing mechanisms such as taxing, but also increasingly use psychological findings to "nudge".[7]

Kai Purnhagen and Ellen van Kleef ('Commanding to Nudge via the Proportionality Principle?') focus in their chapter on the interplay of EU food law and nudging. Starting from the proportionality principle they look into whether nudges are less onerous but equally effective to traditional content-related and information-related regulation. If so, they hypothesize, the proportionality principle may be imperative for regulators, lawmakers and law interpreters to use nudging techniques. Contrasting recent studies on the effectiveness of nudging techniques in the food sectors they conclude that under certain circumstances, nudging techniques indeed show both, a freedom preserving and manipulative character. They argue that the proportionality principle may indeed require regulators, lawmakers and law interpreters to prefer nudging techniques over more traditional forms of regulation if certain conditions are met.

Taking tax rules as instrument to fight over-consumption, *Silke Thiele and Jutta Roosen* ('Obesity, Fat Taxes and their Effects on Consumers') focus on the effects of fat taxes. Nowadays, obesity and overweight are serious problems which have the attention of European and national authorities. Taxing unhealthy products is one instrument to change the consumers' consumption patterns. The authors describe the causes of obesity, their effects in terms of non-communicable diseases and the costs connected to them. Information deficiencies and/or externalities draw the attention of authorities at different levels of regulation. The authors review where fat taxes have been implemented (like in Mexico, or Denmark and other countries of the EU) and what the (expected) effects are on consumers and manufacturers. Next to positive effects, they also go into negative consequences (for instance budgetary impacts for low-income households). They review observation and experimental studies on the effect of fat taxes. All in all they present a comprehensive overview of the scientific work on the fight against obesity.

[7]See inter alia Jolls et al. (1998) and Purnhagen and Reisch (2016).

2.4 Rules-Principles

Regulating via rules or principles is a classic of regulatory science ever since the UK financial system started to experiment with principles-based regulation.[8] While often unspoken, EU food law relies largely on a principles-based approach. The authors in this volume will elaborate on such a principles-based approach in food law, each one from a different perspective.

Harry Bremmers contributes a chapter ("Substance over Form' – A Principle for European Food Information Regulation?') on the use of principles as a replacement of or supplement to substantive rules, to better oppose fraudulent and/or misleading practices in the food industry. He argues that the present legislative structure is not equipped to rule out such practices and a need exists to supplement the present rules with a principle like 'substance over form'. Under this principle, the created impression towards the user of a food is guiding for assessing whether he has been misled. However, notorious intentional fraudsters may not be encapsulated using this principle, since its application is based on trust in the self-governing capabilities and intentions of food businesses. Yet it may obstruct 'fraud-by-effect': the formal adherence to legislation, while materially putting the consumer on the wrong foot.

Lucas Bergkamp and Jaap Hanekamp ('European Food Law and the Precautionary Principle – Paradoxical Effects of the EU's Precautionary Food Policies') go into the adverse effects of the application of the precautionary principle to protect consumers against unidentified food risks. The principle has migrated from environmental regulation into food law and is included in Article 7 of the General Food Law (178/2002). As to the authors, precautionary policies like zero-tolerance, MRL's, or the authorisation of claims before use carry a price tag. Not only do they cost money, but they also may negatively influence the achievement of other policy goals, like innovation or food security. Then the question is whether a precautionary policy is an adequate instrument to provide safe food and if it is, at what price: not only for actors in the EU but also in other countries. The authors argue that other factors than protecting human health and costs thereof may affect the implementation of precautionary measures.

2.5 Ex-Ante–Ex-Post

While determining the effectiveness of regulation via principles-based vs rules-based regulation is a classic in regulation theory, measuring the effectiveness of regulation by determining ex-ante vs. ex-post liability is a classic in law and economics.

In this sense *Franziska Weber* ('Enforcement of European Food Laws') focuses on the preference for public ex-ante regulation versus private ex-post liability for

[8]Black (2008), p. 425.

enforcing food law. She uses the four criteria Steven Shavell has developed in 1984 to investigate the positive and negative aspects of both (i.e., information availability, insolvency risk, the possibilities to sue responsible actors and the level of administrative costs). In food law, a strong public enforcement system has been installed, which is supplemented by the possibility of private litigation. The latter is dependent on the structure of civil law per Member State. The author views the combination as strong, but notes that further studies have to be carried out to get insight in the synergies and preferences with respect to the public-private divide.

2.6 *Centralisation-Decentralisation*

In a multi-level structure such as the EU the question who regulates at what level is of prime importance.[9] Answering this question is difficult and requires a sound underlying method against which normative solutions can be presented.

Michael Faure ('The Economics of Harmonization of Food Law in the EU') asks himself to what extent and under what circumstances food law in the EU needs to be harmonized. He applies the theory of federalism to assess whether centralisation is needed and when and where a decentralised system works better. Different variables influence whether a centralized or a decentralised system of regulation is preferred on economic grounds. Can, using such theorizing, a foundation be provided for explaining the ongoing process of harmonization of EU food law? The theory of comparative federalism implicates that citizens will choose and migrate to the legal order that suits best their needs. It may be that the local level is preferred, since there the needs of citizens is understood best. However, a whole set of factors affect the level of centralisation/decentralisation, like cross-border externalities, the design of optimal jurisdictions, race-to-the bottom or top, the creation of a level playing field and transaction costs. These factors are subsequently applied to the regulation of food, with mixed results as to the preference of a centralized (harmonized) versus a decentralised (Member State) system.

A centralised approach is applied in the new novel foods regulation. *Martin Holle* ('Pre-Market Approval and its Impact on Food Innovation – The Novel Foods Example') asks himself if this piece of legislation (i.e., 2015/2283) brings alleviation to businesses that apply for access to the European market with newly developed products. The former novel foods regulation (258/97), that expired in 2018, forms with its strict and lengthy application procedure and the uncertainties in the outcome of the authorisation process a barrier to innovation. Food businesses thus are reluctant to invest in new products, which is negative for the competitiveness of the European food industry. The author systematically addresses the changes in definition, classification of products as novel, the centralisation of the application and authorisation procedure, and the imposed deadlines for the authorities and

[9]See for instance Smits (2014).

effects on administrative burdens. The evaluation results in the author's opinion that the new novel foods regulation brings about some alleviation, but still shows shortcomings that only via the implementing measures of the Commission can be dealt with.

Comparing the different regulatory approaches on genetically modified organisms and their application, *Margaret Rosso Grossman* conducts a classical comparative legal analysis of the different laws, regulations and their effect in the supranational system of the EU and the federal system of the USA ('Agricultural Biotechnology: Regulation in the United States and the European Union'). She focuses on regulatory mechanisms that govern authorization and labelling of genetically modified crops and addresses some recent legislative developments. She describes the US and EU regulations that govern genetically engineered animals and clones. Her chapter identifies some similar regulatory priorities as well as some regulatory barriers caused by significant differences in risk management in the US and the EU. Margaret Grossman suggests that innovative biotechnologies will challenge current regulatory systems, which may require new approaches both to protect human health and the environment and to encourage continued innovation and enhanced agricultural productivity.

3 Epilogue

After this endeavour, we still owe the reader an elaboration on the positive effects of the regulatory changes with respect to food safety assurance. Although the regulatory changes are still in flux, we can point at two positive influences that enhance EU food safety regulation, and ultimately food safety. One development that has been illustrated in a number of chapters, is the growth of the content of the regulatory toolbox. As there is no one-size-fits-all solution for an effective regulatory system, the number of tools that are available has increased, and probably will further be expanded. A second development that has been demonstrated is that we are permanently improving our knowledge of the social effects the tools have, as a spin-off of the bonds closed with technical and social sciences. Some tools, such as nudging, have been buried a long time underneath the known ones, mainly mandatory and voluntary interventions. Of other tools, such as pre-market approval, due to better methods to generate data on the effects, we increasingly are able to provide solid advice to policy makers. We close with a plea for a continuous and steady growth in research on the social and managerial effects of tools of regulation. Next to this, we should strive for better communication of the available tools and their effects to policy makers, so that the institutional setting for food production and procurement improves.

References

Black J (2008) Forms and paradoxes of principles-based regulation. Cap Mark Law J 8:425

Bremmers H, Haverkamp D-J, Omta O (2009) Dynamic behavioural fingerprinting: what drives the deployment of environmental information and communication capabilities? J Clean Prod 17 (8):751–761

Charlebois S, Sterling B, Haratifar S, Naing SK (2014) Comparison of global food traceability regulations and requirements. Compr Rev Food Sci Food Saf 13:1104–1120

Dennis J, Kelly S (2013) The identification of sources of information concerning food fraud in the UK and elsewhere. Report to Defra Q01R0025. Food and Environment Research Agency

Jolls C, Sunstein C, Thaler R (1998) A behavioural approach to law and economics. Stanford Law Rev 50:1471–1523

Patterson D, Afilalo A (2008) The new global trading order: the evolving state and the future of trade. Cambridge University Press, Cambridge

Purnhagen K (2015) Mapping private regulation – classification, market access and market closure policy, and law's response. J World Trade 49(2):315–323

Purnhagen K, Reisch L (2016) Nudging Germany. Zeitschrift für Europäisches Privatrecht:629–655

Smits J (2014) Who does what? On the distribution of competences among the European Union and the member states. In: Purnhagen K, Rott P (eds) Varieties of European economic law and regulation. Springer, New York, pp 343–357

Wijnands J, Bremmers H, van der Meulen B, Poppe K (2008) An economic and legal assessment of the EU food Industry's competitiveness. Agribusiness 24(4):417–439

Harry Bremmers acquired an MSc degree in business economics at Tilburg University and in Dutch law at the Erasmus University Rotterdam, in the Netherlands. Here he was employed as assistant professor till 1993. In Rotterdam, he graduated as Phd in 1994 on a legal-economic subject (Effects of environmental law on financial reporting). In 1993–2010 he occupied a full-time position at the Business Administration group of the Social Sciences department of Wageningen University, the Netherlands. Since 2010 he occupies the position of associate professor at the Law & Governance group of Wageningen University and Research, Netherlands. He participated in several national and international projects at the interplay of law and economics and has published on a broad range of legal and economic topics. He is specialized in food information law.

Kai Purnhagen is Associate Professor at Wageningen University and distinguished international visitor at the Erasmus University of Rotterdam law school. Previously, he has taught and researched at various institutions including the Ludwig-Maximilian University Munich, the University of Lucerne, the European University Institute, Wageningen University, the London School of Economics and Political Science, the University of Wisconsin-Madison, the Justus-Liebig-University Giessen, and the University of Amsterdam. He holds a PhD (European University Institute in Florence), an LL.M. (University of Wisconsin-Madison), an MJI (Justus-Liebig University of Giessen) and a State Exam in Law (Land Hessen).

Private Food Safety Standards in the EU

Tetty Havinga

Abstract Food safety regulation in the EU is a complex arrangement of public laws and private food standards. This chapter discusses the structure of private food safety standards and the complex relationship of these private standards with public regulation in the EU. Private standards are very common in the food industry in many European countries. Food safety standards such as BRC, IFC and FSSC22000 are initiated and supported by powerful retailers and food manufacturers. Although compliance with these standards is not obliged by law, food business operators in particular markets are in fact forced to join a private certification scheme. Private standards are managed by a standard-owner. Verification of compliance of the major standards is delegated to accredited third-party certification bodies. The norms of private standards are built upon public standards (Codex, EU, ISO). The EU legal framework reinforced the proliferation of private food standards. Private standards did pioneering work in modernizing food regulation. Current EU food law benefitted from the experience of standard-owners, certification bodies and food industry with private standards. The EU legal framework allows public authorities in the Member States to take account of private food safety assurance schemes in their official controls. In several countries, authorities responsible for official food safety controls are investigating ways to collaborate with private food safety assurance systems as part of their monitoring and enforcement tasks. This development raises questions about the reliability of third party certification, the exchange of information between private and public actors, and the risks of regulatory capture and conflicts of interest.

T. Havinga (✉)
Radboud University, Sociology of Law, Nijmegen, The Netherlands
e-mail: t.havinga@jur.ru.nl

H. Bremmers, K. Purnhagen (eds.), *Regulating and Managing Food Safety in the EU*, Economic Analysis of Law in European Legal Scholarship 6,
https://doi.org/10.1007/978-3-319-77045-1_2

1 Introduction

The global system of food regulation has grown into a complex arrangement of various laws and standards on different regulatory levels. These laws and standards are increasingly of a transnational nature. Currently most food laws within the Member States of the European Union are based on EU law. Next to governments, private actors also increasingly engage in food regulation. In particular corporate retailers and multinational food manufacturers have initiated and promoted private food safety standards. An analysis of food safety regulation in the EU cannot be limited to public laws and should include private standards as well. This chapter discusses the structure of private food safety standards and the complex relationship of these private standards with public regulation in the EU.

In the first section I describe the proliferation of private standards with a focus on the dominant transnational standards recognized by the Global Food Safety Initiative. In the next sections I analyse what the relationships between the private and the public regulations look like. I do so with regard to four regulatory functions: rule-making, adoption, monitoring compliance, and review. Section 2.1 deals with rule-making and analyses how public actors participate in the setting of private rules and how private actors participate in decision-making on public rules. Section 2.2 analyses whether public and private regulators adopted each other's standards and provides some examples of incorporation of private rules in EU law and incorporation of EU law in private standards. Section 2.3 deals with monitoring compliance and enforcement. Do public authorities take private certificates into account? And to what extent do private auditors check compliance with public rules? What are the subjects of discussion in this respect? Section 2.4 deals with the evaluation and review of the food regulations. Do private standards incorporate criticism from public authorities in revising the standards? Are EU institutions open to criticism and proposals from private standard organizations? Section 3 concludes.

1.1 Characteristics of Private Food Standards

Development of Private Standards

It is well documented that private standards have become increasingly important in food safety governance (as well as in other domains) over the last 25 years.[1] The use of private standards has become very common in many branches of the food industry in many European countries. Moreover, private standards did pioneering work in the modernisation of food regulation. For these reasons an analysis of food safety

[1]E.g. Bain et al. (2013), Busch and Bingen (2006), Henson and Humphrey (2009) and van der Meulen (2011a).

regulation in the EU cannot be limited to public laws and should include private standards as well.

Several circumstances made up a fertile ground for the rise of private food standards. A first circumstance is the increasing globalization of food supply chains which makes it more difficult for both food industry and national governments to safeguard the safety of food products. Food supply chains encompass places of production and trading around the globe. Some sites and processes may disappear from sight. Retailers and manufacturers sourcing globally sought ways to keep in control.[2] National governments also face a problem here because their jurisdiction is locked inside their national territory. Secondly, the increased economic power of supermarket chains contributed to the rise of private food standards.[3] Concentration in the food retail sector was the result of expansion and mergers. Several corporate food retailers operate in many countries and have a powerful market position.[4] A third development that contributed to the rise of private food standards is the growing public concern about food safety as a result of several food scandals (BSE, dioxin, E-coli, salmonella).[5] The food industry undertook all kinds of initiatives in order to restore and keep consumer trust in food. The fourth factor that has contributed to the rise of private food regulation is the perception of insufficient governmental regulation. The public response to food incidents such as the BSE crisis has been perceived as inadequate by both consumers' organizations and food industry.[6] Criticism of the regulatory capacity of governments is not limited to the domain of food regulation. The capacity of governments to regulate markets has been criticized for being ineffective, inadequate and outdated.[7] These factors constitute the context in which private food standards developed and flourish.

The rise of private food safety standards started in the 1990s. However, private standards are not entirely new in the food industry.[8] The food sector has a long history of quality controls by manufacturers, trade associations, and corporatist organizations, particularly in the production and trading of perishable food (milk, meat).[9] Systems of certification of producers, manufacturers, traders, controlling laboratories and products are common. Classic examples include kosher supervision and the French wine appellations.[10]

The new generation of private food standards differs from historical examples in several ways. The typical current food standard operates with a written normative document specifying the substantive and procedural norms and the modes of

[2]Hatanaka et al. (2005), Henson and Humphrey (2010), Oosterveer (2005) and van Waarden (2011).

[3]Burch and Lawrence (2005) and Marsden et al. (2010).

[4]Fuchs et al. (2009), ten Kate and van der Wal (2017) and Marsden et al. (2010), p. 156 ff.

[5]Ansell and Vogel (2006), Fulponi (2006), Henson and Humphrey (2010) and van der Kloet (2011).

[6]Bernauer and Caduff (2006), Henson (2011) and Vos (2000).

[7]Baldwin et al. (2012), p. 68 ff.; Majone (1994).

[8]Busch and Bingen (2006).

[9]van Waarden (1985).

[10]Lytton (2013) and Moran (1993).

verification of compliance with these norms, is international in scope, requires third party certification, covers a wide range of issues and is managed by a special organisation with formalized procedures for reviewing the standard, auditing, certification, and handling of complaints. Older private food standards were often less formalised, focussing on a single issue and a local market. Often verification and enforcement procedures were absent or less elaborated.[11]

Characteristics of Private Food Standards

A standard is a set of rules or norms about minimum requirements for products, processes or producers. A private standard is developed by private actors, such as food manufacturers, non-governmental organisations (NGOs), industry associations, farmers, retailers and food service providers. Some examples may clarify this. Several animal welfare organisations set up an animal welfare scheme to encourage firms to improve animal welfare and to enable consumers to exercise influence by buying only products with an animal welfare label. Examples include 'Freedom Food', a British farm assurance and food labelling scheme set up by the Royal Society for the Prevention of Cruelty to Animals, 'Neuland', a German animal welfare labelling scheme founded in 1988 by a farmer union and two animal welfare organisations, and 'Bioland', a private food quality scheme open for participation of agricultural and livestock producers and food processors.[12] The 'Bioland' label illustrates that private standards are not always clearly separated from public standards. The Bioland guidelines are developed by organic producer groups in compliance with European Regulations on organic production of agricultural products. The Bioland guidelines exceed the EU minimum requirements for organic produce.

The concept of private scheme usually refers to a private standard and its internal governance structure and procedures for conformity assessment and enforcement. Thus a scheme consists of not just the substantial norms and requirements (standard) but includes also a management structure and auditing protocol.

Public and private responsibilities for food governance often are not neatly delineated.[13] 'Private food standards [. . .] are better understood as part of a governance structure rather than as governmental strategies outside the state.'[14] The decisive factor for characterizing a standard as a private, public or hybrid is who decides on the rules. Animal welfare standards developed by NGOs, by farmer organisations, by fast food chains and combinations between those types of organisations are private standards. Animal welfare provisions in EU or national state laws or guidelines are public standards.

---

[11]See for example Fouilleux and Loconto (2017), pp. 5–6 who discuss the shift from community-shared value-oriented principles of organic farming to globalized auditable standards.

[12]Food Chain Evaluation Consortium (2009).

[13]Havinga (2006) and Henson and Humphrey (2010).

[14]Lockie et al. (2013), p. 289.

Private food standards cover a wide range of issues.[15] Major transnational standards such as the British Retail Consortium Global Standard for Food Safety (BRC), the International Featured Standards Food Standard (IFS), Food Safety System Certification 22000 (FSSC) and GlobalG.A.P. Integrated Farm Assurance Standard have a strong focus on food safety.[16] Other standards include quality requirements and credence attributes related to environmental and social interests. Certification may entail compliance with standards related to sustainability (e.g. Marine Stewardship Council, Rainforest Alliance), fair trading (e.g. Max Havelaar, UTZ), biodynamic agriculture (e.g. Demeter), organic production (e.g. KRAV, Bioland), religious food laws (e.g. Kashrut Division of the London Beth Din for Kosher Certification, the Halal Authority Board Standard), vegetarian food (e.g. Vegan) and requirements for a healthy diet (e.g. the Heart-Check mark from the American Heart Association). Some standards cover a broad range of issues while others just concentrate on one single issue.

Standards also differ in their geographical reach. Some standards are applied globally (BRC, GlobalG.A.P.) while others are limited to a small local area. Another distinction is that between company food standards and industry-wide standards.[17] Some food companies established their own company food standard that has to be applied by all companies in their supply chain. The origin of several food standards is an individual downstream company imposing demands on their upstream suppliers in order to prevent risks and damages (e.g. incidents, recalls, liability claims, reputation damage). There is a thin line between product requirements specified in a supply contract and arranging these requirements in a company standard. An example of a company standard is the ‘Albert Heijn Quality Assurance’, which has been abolished and replaced by industry-wide standards (first BRC and later all GFSI-recognized standards).[18] Another example of a company standard is Tesco Nurture, an exclusive independently accredited scheme to ensure that fruit and vegetables are grown according to environmental and responsible standards.[19]

Private standards fulfil two basic functions in the market.[20] The first main function is risk management. In this case private standards are used to set a minimum level of quality, safety or whatever it is that is regulated by the standard. This is a form of ex ante regulation (in contrast to ex post forms of regulation such as liability law, recall, breach of contract litigation). Setting a minimum level is the main objective of food safety standards such as BRC or GlobalG.A.P. Compliance with this type of standards is often not communicated to the public, these are so-called business-to-business (B2B) standards. Certification is a condition for entering the

---

[15]See for multiple examples of private food standards Canivet (2006), Hammoudi et al. (2015), Henson and Humphrey (2009), van der Meulen (2011a) and Wright et al. (2013).

[16]Havinga (2015a).

[17]Henson and Humphrey (2011), pp. 153–154.

[18]Havinga (2006).

[19]See http://www.tesco.com/nurture/?page=nurturescheme, accessed 1 August 2017.

[20]Henson and Humphrey (2010), p. 1639.

market, usually no price premium is included. The second function of standards is expressly differentiate products or producers meeting the standard from other products available on the market. These standards intend to signify added value, premium high quality or some special attributes. Compliance with this type of standards is usually signalled to consumers by a label or trademark. These are business-to-consumer standards (B2C). Certification may enable the access to high value markets and/or higher prices. Examples include certification to the Marine Stewardship Council standard for sustainable fish, kosher food standards, animal welfare and fair trade standards. These standards offer buyers a choice and try to seduce buyers to show a preference for products or producers in compliance with the B2C standard.

In course of time the character of a standard may change. Starting as a distinguishing standard it may develop into a minimum standard at the moment that almost all products or producers are in compliance. This development may be strived for, as is often the case for programs aiming to promote sustainability, fair trade or animal welfare. In other cases, it seems to be the result of the diffusion process of a new standard: starting small in the start-up phase and growing thereafter. GlobalG.A.P. is an example in case. In the early years farmers who were certified against this standard (called EurepGap at the time) were particularly proud of this distinguishing performance. Today almost all farmers in Western European countries including the Netherlands and Germany need to be GlobalG.A.P. certified (as the market for non-GlobalG.A.P. certified vegetables and fruits is very limited). GlobalG.A.P. certification has lost its distinguishing value in these markets. From the very start the EurepGap/GlobalG.A.P. has been a business-to-business standard. In the early years it was not allowed to communicate certification to consumers. Currently consumers can verify whether the products they buy are GlobalG.A.P.-certified by entering a number on the website.[21] The retailers that initiated the EurepGap standard did aim at a minimum standard from the very start in order to realize consumer confidence in the safety of all vegetables and fruits in their supermarket stores. They aimed also at an extensive supply of vegetables and fruits fulfilling their requirements, thus creating extensive buyer options.

Both in the literature and in public debates private standards are occasionally referred to as self-regulation. But are private standards a form of self-regulation? Most private food standards are not considered pure self-regulation. In self-regulation the regulator is also the regulatee.[22] Most of the private food standards are not initiated nor developed by the same people to whom the rules apply. In other words, the regulator is not identical to the regulatee: retailers developed standards for farmers and food manufacturers (GlobalG.A.P., BRC), an environmental organisation together with a food manufacturer developed a standard for fisheries (MSC), and a food outlet developed a standard for farmers (Starbucks Shared Planet).

Most private standards are voluntary: compliance with the standard is not made mandatory in public regulation. However, quite often the regulatee (food business) is

[21]See http://www.globalgap.org/uk_en/for-consumers/, accessed 1 April 2016.

[22]Levi-Faur (2011), p. 8.

under contract to comply with the standard. So without being legally mandatory, adoption of these 'voluntary' standards often is a contractual obligation and economically bound.[23] Regulatees might be forced by the market to adhere to the voluntary standard. In particular the large corporate retailers and multinational food manufacturers use their economic power to require certification against private food standards from their suppliers. Thus, 96% of the suppliers of own brand food products in Ahold supermarkets across Europe is certified against GFSI recognized standards.[24]

Although most private food standards are voluntary and most public standards are mandatory, this is not by definition the case. Henson and Humphrey[25] distinguish between four possible combinations of public/private and mandatory/voluntary food standards:

- public mandatory standards (regulations and laws such as the EU General Food Law and the German Lebensmittel- und Futtermittelgesetzbuch),
- public voluntary standards created by public bodies but whose adoption is voluntary (examples include Label Rouge in France, organic food labels, Codex Alimentarius standards, national HACCP (Hazard Analysis and Critical Control Point) standards such as DS 3027 and ELOT 1416),[26]
- legally mandated private standards that have been developed by private organisations and made mandatory by public bodies, and finally,
- voluntary private standards developed and adopted by private bodies, not legal mandatory (e.g. BRC, IFS and GlobalG.A.P.).

I am not acquainted with a clear-cut example of a legally compulsory private food standard. However, examples that come close include laws on organically produced food in the European Union and the United States, inclusion of HACCP provisions in Codex and EU law, a definition of fair trade in French law, and Swiss Federal law on Good agricultural practices.[27] In all these cases standards that had been developed by private organisations were included in national or federal laws. Adoption of the standard remained voluntary (organic, fair trade) or became mandatory (HACCP). This chapter deals with the private standards (the last two categories) and in particular with major transnational food safety standards. As already stated, some of the not legally mandated private standards are de facto obligatory for access to important markets.

---

[23]Cafaggi and Iamiceli (2015), Clapp (2016), p. 125; Havinga (2015a).

[24]Ahold (2016), p. 8.

[25]Henson and Humphrey (2010), p. 1630.

[26]See with regard to organic food: Arcuri (2015), Schmidt (2011), pp. 290 and 293. Henson and Humphrey (2010), p. 1630, refer to Label Rouge. Canadian FSEP is a voluntary HACCP program, Herath and Henson (2006).

[27]See for organic food Arcuri (2015), Boström and Klintman (2006), Schmidt (2011); for HACCP Bernauer and Caduff (2006), Demortain (2007); for fair trade in French law and GAP in Switzerland FAO (2014).

The status of a standard may change as the following two examples will show. Since 2003, the Safe Quality Food standard (SQF) is a US private retail-driven standard. However, SQF started as a public voluntary standard and was transformed into a private voluntary standard when the ownership of the standard changed: the Food Marketing Institute acquired the standard in 2003 from the West-Australian Department of Agriculture. The opposite happened with private standards for organic agriculture that had been developed by farmers' and consumers' organisations in many European countries. From completely private standards they have been transformed into public minimum standards. European Union regulations allow for additional requirements from private organic standards, whereas this is excluded in US regulations. As Arcuri concludes this shows 'the analytical difficulties of studying the interaction between public and private regulation in terms of binary thinking.'[28] The influence of governmental intervention on private regulatory schemes is not always either supportive or constraining but can also be both supportive and constraining.

1.2 Major Transnational Private Food Standards and Third Party Certification

The remainder of this chapter is focussed on transnational food safety standards that dominate the European market. In particular retail-driven standards are very important because many suppliers of the large multinational supermarkets are required to be certified against one of these standards. Mergers and concentration in the retail market resulted in a relatively small number of multinational supermarket chains with large economic power in global and domestic food supply chains.[29] In Western European countries these supermarkets have a large majority share of the food consumers' market. Important retail-driven private standards in Europe include the BRC Global Standard for Food Safety, the IFS Food Standard and the GlobalG.A.P. These standards have been adopted by retailer associations from the UK, Germany, France, Italy and the Netherlands and are a supplier requirement of many supermarkets and food businesses around the world. A transnational food safety standard supported by multinational food manufacturers is the Food Safety System Certification 22000 (FSSC).[30] Together these four transnational standards issued more than 200,000 certificates.[31] These standards are benchmarked by the Global Food Safety

[28]Arcuri (2015), p. 15.

[29]Fuchs et al. (2009); Retail economic power is increased through cooperation in international buying groups ten Kate and van der Wal (2017).

[30]See for a more detailed description of these standards, their development and dissemination Havinga (2015a).

[31]Figures on the website of the standards at 23 November 2016: BRC 23,000; FSSC 13,685; GlobalG.A.P. 140.000; IFS 16,800.

Initiative (GFSI). The GFSI is an industry-driven initiative providing guidance on food safety management systems and a global platform for communication to improve food safety.[32] GFSI is set up and run by representatives of some of the powerful global retailers and food manufacturers.

The process of globalization of retail-driven food safety standards for suppliers follows the pattern of bottom-up globalization of regulation. In the 1990s some retail companies changed their practice and developed a company food standard in response to food safety incidents and diminishing consumer trust. Others model this new practice and in the end this results in globalization of the new standard of practice. As Braithwaite and Drahos point out 'rather than business practice following from norms and rules, often mechanisms of modelling delivers globalization of practice which is subsequently codified in rules'.[33] Initially the collective food standards were national standards (BRC in UK, IFS in Germany). Since they have expanded fourfold.[34] (1) Geographically, the standard was adopted by supermarkets' chains in other countries. (2) Scope of the standard is no longer limited to own branded food products. (3) Scope beyond food, the organisations also developed standards for non-food, for packaging and for storage and distribution. (4) In due time other groups than the initial members gained access to technical committees and meetings and in some cases to the board of the standard organisation. This includes retailers from other countries, but also food manufacturers and certification bodies. Despite the growing openness, consumer groups and other NGOs are hardly participating in the decision-making process of any of these standards organisations. GlobalG.A.P. is the most open, BRC the most closed club.

These private standards are generally organized along the following lines (see Fig. 1). There is a standard-owner, that is a retailers' organisation or a new for-profit or not-for-profit organisation established to manage the standard. The standard-owner decides on the general regulations and management structure of the standard organisation. The standard-owner is also responsible for appointing the Board. The Board is responsible for major decisions on the standard such as provisions in the normative document, regular procedures for revising the standard document and appointing members of technical committees and working groups. Usually a technical committee or working group is responsible for the content of the standard, the review process and training programs for auditors. Often consultation rounds for all stakeholders are organized and some standards run special programs to assist small food businesses, particularly in developing countries.

Food businesses that are found in compliance with the standard are certified. Verification of compliance is delegated to certification bodies, organisations specialized in auditing and verifying compliance. Most standards only accept certifica-

[32]See on GFSI Fagotto (2017), Havinga and Verbruggen (2017) and Verbruggen and Havinga (2016).

[33]Braithwaite and Drahos (2000), p. 554.

[34]Havinga (2015a), pp. 61–63.

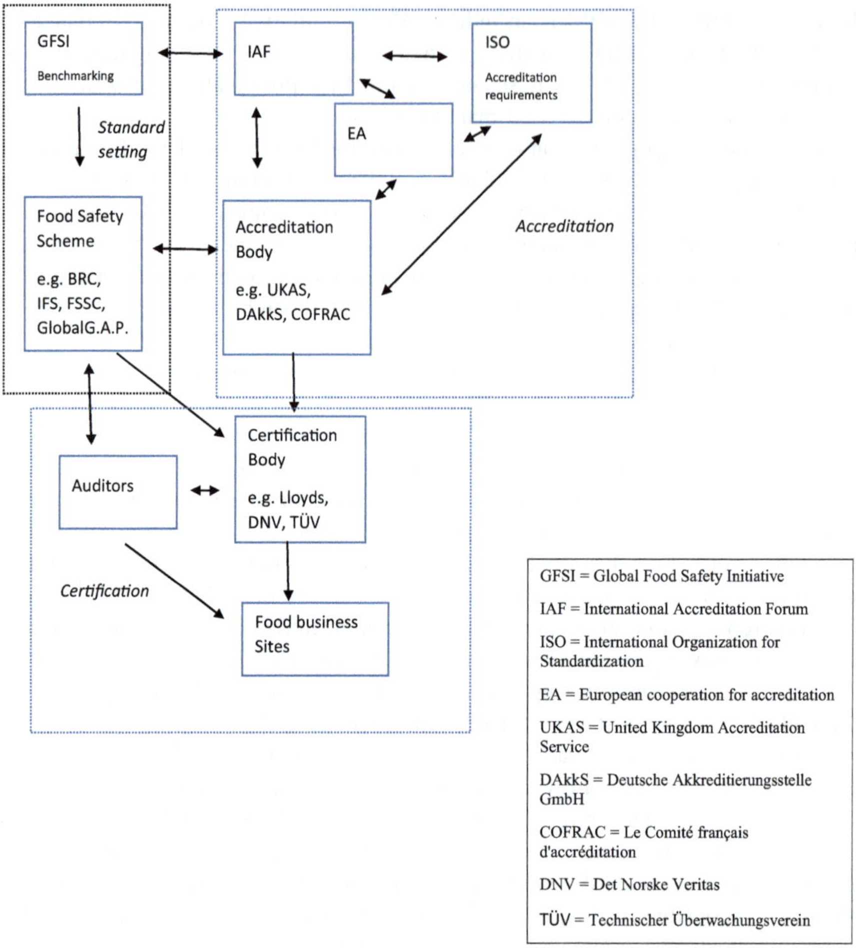

Fig. 1 System of accredited third party certification of GFSI recognised food safety schemes

tion bodies that are accredited by a national accreditation body. Some standards accept certification by all accredited certification bodies whereas other standards only accept particular selected certification bodies.

A food business that wishes to acquire a food safety certificate has to decide for a standard and then hire a certification body that will audit to verify that the firm is working in compliance with the regulations in the standard. Some standards have grades (such as one, two or three stars; level A or B), others only differentiate between compliant or not. After a successful auditing process the firm gets a certificate. After some months (often 6 or 12) a new audit visit is required to verify continued compliance. Many standards do not require unannounced inspections. However this is changing. Several standards have recently introduced (optional) unannounced audit visits to refute criticism of inadequate controls.[35] Food businesses have to pay for the auditing and certification services. This situation constitutes a conflict of interest between the auditor's financial interest in keeping the customer satisfied and its professional obligation to protect the public against food safety risks.[36]

Next to the major transnational food safety standards discussed above, several standards exist in local markets or with a focus on special commodities, particularly for primary produce. Examples include the Global Red Meat Standard and the Global Aquaculture Alliance Seafood. These standards are owned by industry associations and are GFSI benchmarked. Other standards developed by industry associations include the German 'Qualität und Sicherheit', the Dutch 'IKB' and the British 'Little Red Tractor'. National standardization organizations in for example Denmark, France, Italy and Spain have developed national standards. In these countries the national standardization organizations are private not for profit associations mandated by the government.[37] A 2010 inventory of certification schemes for agricultural products and foodstuffs marketed in the EU Member States found 441 (sub)schemes.[38] Particularly in Germany, Italy, Spain and the United Kingdom many schemes were developed.[39]

Private food safety standards cover different products and processes in the food supply chain, from farming (animals, plants, fish, grains), processing, storage, distribution and packaging to catering and retail. Private food safety standards generally include requirements related to a HACCP food safety management system, resource management, training and education of personnel, responsibilities of senior management, process control, inspection and testing, labelling, packaging, traceability, protective clothing and personnel hygiene, buildings and pest control. Recently some standards also included requirements on food fraud prevention and authenticity control.

[35]The 2017 edition of the GFSI Guidelines requires food safety schemes to ensure that unannounced audits are available as a preferred option (Article 2.5.5, GFSI Benchmarking requirements, GFSI Guidance document version 7).

[36]Lytton and McAllister (2014).

[37]E.g. Standards DS 3027, Agri confiance, UNI 10854, UNE 155000. Food safety standards are also developed by the national standardization organizations in Greece and Ireland (e.g. ELOT 1416, IS 343); these are public voluntary standards as the Greek standardization organization is state-owned and the Irish is a governmental institution. Canivet (2006), pp. 16–17.

[38]See http://ec.europa.eu/agriculture/quality/certification/index_en.htm, accessed 1 August 2017.

[39]Aréte (2010), p. 3.

2 Relations Between Public and Private Actors

2.1 Rule-Making

After the introduction of some of the widely used private food standards, we will now turn to our main question. How do private standards work: what do they do, who is involved and why. We will also investigate the relationships between the private and the public governance arrangements. Subsequently we discuss the questions for four phases in the regulatory process: rule-making, adopting, monitoring and enforcement, and review.[40] This section deals with rule-making.

Setting of private standards usually involves three parties: a technical committee preparing the draft standard, a board deciding on the standard and in most cases stakeholders. Members of technical committees are experts from the membership of the standard-owner's organisation or from different stakeholders as well as academics. Standards differ in the openness and transparency of the standard setting process. Currently many standards have public consultation rounds or stakeholders' meetings to get input for the standard and to create sufficient support. The owner of a private standard appoints the members of the board. The board has the final say in the content of the standard. Several major transnational food safety standards are owned by retailers' associations (the management may be either by the retail association or—more common—by an organisation specially established by the retailers' association to manage the standard).

Many standards started with just a few founding members and gradually included more persons in the process of standard setting, either by increased membership or by including participants from various stakeholders in a non-membership organisation. Major food safety standards such as IFS and BRC show this development. Participants include retailers, manufacturers, primary producers, certification bodies, and academics. Consumer representatives and other non-governmental organisations are hardly participating in the standard setting process of major food safety standards.[41] The active participation of NGOs is one of the important differences with B2C food standards focussing on social and moral issues. Some of these B2C standards are initiated and managed by NGOs pursuing interests such as animal welfare, ethical trading, or sustainability. The first edition of these standards often is drafted by the NGOs.

What is the relation between private standards and public regulation? There are two sides to this question:

1. How do public actors participate in the setting of private standards and schemes?
2. What is the relation between the requirements set in the private standard and legal requirements?

---

[40]See on regulatory phases Henson and Humphrey (2011), Havinga (2015b), pp. 31–33; Verbruggen and Havinga (2017), pp. 11–14.

[41]Fuchs et al. (2011).

Julia Black distinguishes four forms of self-regulation with a different role of the state,[42] that can also be applied to private food standards:

1. mandated private regulation: an industry or profession is formally or informally required by the government to formulate and enforce norms within a broad framework defined by the government;
2. sanctioned private regulation: an industry formulates a regulation which is then subjected to government approval;
3. coerced private regulation: the industry formulates and enforces the regulation in response to threats of statutory regulation;
4. voluntary private regulation without any state involvement in promoting the regulation or making its adoption legally mandatory.

The development of retail-driven private food safety standards such as BRC and IFS is a clear example of the last, voluntary private regulation. Large supermarket companies initiated this without state involvement and without the threat of statutory regulation. On the contrary, one of the drivers is the perception that governmental food regulation was inadequate and consumer confidence in food had to be reinstalled after several food safety incidents. However, the introduction of new liability legislation has contributed to the rise of private standards. The government may be involved in some voluntary standards, creating a more mixed form. Consider the participation of governmental technical experts in private standard setting. The Dutch food safety authority (*Nederlandse Voedsel- en Warenautoriteit*—NVWA), for example, participated in the development of Dutch HACCP and Riskplaza.[43]

Although these retail standards are developed without any state interference, they are nevertheless connected to statutory provisions. Private standards always operate within a legal framework. This legal framework consists of general provisions from contract law, tax law, corporate law and liability law and more specific legal provisions that both enable and constrain the development and management of private standards. Marsden, Flynn and Harrison concluded from their analysis of the British food regulatory system, that 'it is the corporate retailers who have led the way [...] also in how to regulate food quality under increasingly complex and competitive food supply conditions.'[44] From the mid-1980s till 2000 this dominance of large retailers leaves 'the State mainly as auditors rather than standard-setters and enforcers of the mainstream process.'[45] Moreover, most private food safety standards are built upon public standards such as Codex and ISO standards, and EU law.[46] A key element of private food safety standards is the practical translation of statutory requirements. Private standards lay down more specific and detailed

[42]Black (1998), p. 124.

[43]Verbruggen (2014), p. 239 ff.

[44]Marsden et al. (2000), p. 193.

[45]Marsden et al. (2010), p. 284.

[46]See for example Casey (2017) on GlobalG.A.P.; and Henson and Humphrey (2011) on the relation between private standards and Codex.

instructions as to how to comply with legal requirements. Henson and Humphrey argue this is the most important function of private standards in the area of food safety.[47] Private standards not only add detailed specifications to public regulation, many standards also set stricter requirements. They can do so by adding requirements on issues not covered by public regulation, by setting more stringent critical limits or by extending existing requirements.[48] It is particularly this characteristic of private food standards that has been contested by developing countries, international organizations such as the FAO and SME representatives for causing trade barriers.[49]

The EU General Food Law stipulates that food business operators carry primary responsibility for the safety of the food they produce or sell. Each business is responsible for taking the measures necessary to ensure compliance with food law requirements within the context of its own specific activities by applying verification procedures and quality assurance systems. One of the major obligations on food business operators in EU law is that they have to 'put in place, implement and maintain a permanent procedure based on the HACCP principles'.[50] This legal requirement reinforced the growth of private food certification schemes as implementation of a private standard helps a food business to comply with this legal requirement. A food safety management system based on HACCP principles is a core element of the private food safety standards. In fact, the legal requirement to maintain a HACCP food safety plan in place is an example of governmental rule-making using the experience of private companies and private standards. National, European and US governments included a mandatory HACCP plan in their food laws drawing upon the experiences of private food standard organizations and auditors.[51] This tended to empower the retailer-led forms of food regulation.[52] The moment national or transnational governments (such as the EU, US and Canadian government) made a HACCP food safety management system legally mandatory for (part of) the food industry, they incorporated the norms in the law.[53]

Another example of complex interactions between private and public actors in setting food safety standards is the development of industry guides to good practice

[47]Henson and Humphrey (2011), p. 160.

[48]See for example Wright et al. (2013), who assessed many private food assurance schemes operating in the UK and give an overview of correspondence of scheme requirements with legislative requirements regarding food hygiene and safety.

[49]See Henson and Humphrey (2010, 2011) and Havinga and Verbruggen (2017), pp. 196–197.

[50]Article 5 of Regulation (EC) No 852/2004 of the European Parliament and of the Council on the hygiene of foodstuffs [2004] OJ L139/1. HACCP stands for Hazard Analysis and Critical Control Point.

[51]Chatzopoulou (2015), pp. 2618–2619; Marsden et al. (2010), p. 255; Oldfield (2015).

[52]Marsden et al. (2010), p. 103.

[53]Marsden et al. (2010), p. 255. During the 1990s leading multinational food industries voluntarily adopted food safety management plans based on the principles of HACCP. Food quality systems of major retailers required HACCP from their suppliers. The large retailers were lobbying for making the operation of a HACCP food management system mandatory by law.

for hygiene and for the application of HACCP principles. Food business operators, except primary producers, are required to put in place and implement procedures based on HACCP principles.[54] This requirement is a form of enforced self-regulation (Braithwaite) or mandated private regulation (Black)[55]: food business operators are legally obliged to develop a risk management system. The option to develop industry guides to good hygienic practice was included in the law particularly to help small and medium (SME) sized food business operators to comply with this legal requirement. The guide has to be developed by a sector of the food industry or a national standards institute and approved by the government.[56] These hygiene guides are a form of what Black has called sanctioned private regulation.

The General Food Law of the European Union is committed to the involvement of stakeholder organizations in the regulatory process. Representatives of consumers, industry, retailers and farmers are consulted and informed by the Commission and EFSA.[57] Formal consultations take place in the context of the Advisory Group on the Food Chain and Animal Health. The Advisory Group has 45 members representing European associations of consumers, farmers, food industry and retailers.[58] EFSA established a Consultative Stakeholder Platform and organizes public hearings. The participation of industry, retail and farmers in rule-making and risk assessment is not undisputed as it may harm independent decision-making.

The European Commission developed guidelines for certification scheme developers and operators to help improve 'the transparency, credibility and effectiveness of voluntary certification schemes and ensuring that they do not conflict with regulatory requirements.'[59] The guidelines include recommendations regarding scheme participation and development, scheme requirements and claims, certification and inspections and mutual recognition and overlap with other schemes. The recommendations aim at the participation of all possible stakeholders, transparency and free availability of information (including disclosure of fees and providing translations), independent and effective inspections and appropriate sanctions, and the avoidance of high costs for food operators. Adherence to these guidelines is voluntary. The development of these guidelines is an attempt of the European Commission to stay in control and to influence developments in the domain of private food governance.

[54]Article 5 of Regulation (EC) No 852/2004 on food hygiene.

[55]Braithwaite (1982) and Black (1998).

[56]Havinga (2014) and van der Meulen (2017).

[57]Vos and Wendler (2006), pp. 90, 124–126.

[58]See http://ec.europa.eu/dgs/health_food-safety/dgs_consultations/advisory_group_en.htm, accessed 1 August 2017.

[59]Commission Communication 'EU best practice guidelines for voluntary certification schemes for Agricultural products and foodstuffs', 2010/C 341/04, pt. 1.2.

2.2 Adoption

After a standard is set, the standard has to be adopted by food business operators and other stakeholders. Whereas many statutory regulations are mandatory, private standards are not automatically implemented or adopted. A private standard first has to be adopted by organizations or persons: a food business or organization has to decide to strive for compliance with a particular standard or to make compliance with the standard mandatory for its trade partners.[60] A private standard that is not adopted will not be implemented and therefore remains a dead letter. Private food safety standards have been widely adopted in food supply chains. The retail-driven standards (BRC, IFS, GlobalG.A.P.) have been adopted from the start by the very retailers that initiated the standard. Currently major supermarket chains in Western European countries require from their private brands suppliers certification according to one of these private standards.[61] FSSC22000 has been developed with the support of multinational food manufacturers. Major food corporations such as Cargill, Coca Cola, Danone, Domino Pizza's, Heineken, Kraft Heinz, PepsiCo and Unilever have adopted the FSSC standard.[62] A survey revealed that more than half of SME food businesses in the EU stated they are often or sometimes asked by customers or suppliers to comply with private standards.[63] At a rough estimate, 50% of all farms and 25% of all food manufacturers in the UK belong to a third party assurance scheme; as larger firms are more often certified the proportion of the market covered is higher.[64] The purchasing power of major supermarkets, food manufacturers and caterers made private food safety standards almost mandatory in some markets. The result is a quick and broad uptake of private food safety standards in the market.

The adoption of private standards for sustainability or social interests reveals a more complicated picture. Some transnational standards have succeeded in securing considerable uptake and support. An example is the Marine Stewardship Council standard for sustainable fishery. Currently more than 250 fisheries are MSC certified in 36 countries and over 17,000 MSC labelled products are available. Several retailers and manufacturers have made commitments to 100% sustainable seafood sourcing including MSC certification. Examples include Ikea, Iglo, Dutch retailers, Sainsbury and Waitrose.[65]

Many standards operate on a national or local market only. This applies to standards for animal welfare. The British RSPCA claims that its animal

---

[60]Havinga (2015b), pp. 29–33; Henson and Humphrey (2011), pp. 155–156.

[61]Ahold, Aldi, Carrefour, COOP, Metro, Tesco (Havinga (2015a), p. 67).

[62]See http://www.fssc22000.com/documents/certifiedorganizations/complete-list.xml?lang=en, accessed 1 August 2017.

[63]Evaluation of the General Food Law: SME panel results, p. 10—available at http://ec.europa.eu/food/safety/general_food_law/fitness_check/index_en.htm, accessed 1 August 2017.

[64]Wright et al. (2013), p. 52.

[65]MSC (2015), pp. 2 32–35.

> welfare standards have had a significant influence on the animal production standards set by many major retailers for their suppliers, and on various assurance schemes in the UK and overseas. In some instances, the standards have also been used by UK and overseas governments and governmental bodies to inform legislation and associated guidance/recommendations.[66]

Supermarkets' sales in the Netherlands of products certified against the 'Beter Leven' standard of the Netherlands SPCA had a value of more than 500 million Euros in 2014.[67] The total sales with a sustainability certificate in Dutch supermarkets amounts to almost two thousand million Euro.[68] These B2C standards often have to face heated debate about the content of the standard and their strategy. The dilemma is which strategy to choose: (1) striving for improvement by developing a realistic standard and cooperating with commercial parties such as producers and retailers and risking the critique that they throw their very principles overboard; (2) no compromising for reasons of principle. In the latter case there probably will be no private standard or a private standard with only a limited number of certificates. An organisation that aims at wide diffusion of its standard in most cases will need to compromise.

Religious food standards have a less dominant position in Europe. The market for kosher products in Europe is small. The market for halal products is in some regions more substantial, but so far there are many competing private standards for halal food.[69]

Not only can food business operators adopt a standard, but governmental organizations can as well. In some cases, public agencies adopt private standards. The Belgian Food Safety Agency adopted and implemented a quality system certified ISO 9001 and ISO 17020.[70] However, these ISO standards are not food standards. Governments can also adopt a private food standard in their procurement policy, among others. International, national and local governments can make compliance with particular private standards a precondition for contracting with the government.[71] Many departments and municipalities have done so, such as in the area of fair trade coffee.

Governments sometimes facilitate or promote the dissemination of private food standards within the food industry. They may do so because governmental legislation is not feasible. First of all, the government may lack the authority to prescribe rules. This may be the case in regulation that exceeds the legislative jurisdiction (because it seeks to govern conduct outside the national borders or is not within the EU legislative competence). Secondly, governments may facilitate the development

---

[66]See http://science.rspca.org.uk/sciencegroup/farmanimals/standards, accessed 1 August 2017.

[67]Emonds (2015).

[68]Emonds (2015).This is approximately 25% of total sales of meat, fish and dairy in supermarkets over 2015. Estimation based on figures at http://detailhandel.info/index.cfm/branches/levensmiddelenzaken/supermarkten/, accessed 1 August 2017.

[69]Kurth and Glasbergen (2017) and van Waarden and van Dalen (2015).

[70]Raone (2013), p. 14.

[71]See for example ten Kate (2014) and Scottish Fair Trade Forum (2013).

and/or adoption of private standards because public regulation is not politically feasible or desirable. Governments may take various measures in order to support the adoption of private standards in the market: funding training programs or promotion campaigns, assisting food businesses in achieving compliance, publicly voicing support, and administrative or expert assistance. For example, the Dutch government has funded a promotion campaign for EurepGap, and several national governments supported and funded MSC certification of national fisheries.[72]

Do governments in their role as public regulator adopt private standards? Although public legislators do draw upon or refer to private standards, they seldom simply adopt a private standard. A related but slightly different form is incorporation of private standards in public regulation by reference. Public regulators do refer to for example the ISO/IEC 17021 standard on Conformity assessment (requirements for bodies providing audit and certification of management systems) and incorporate them in their regulatory frame. EU Regulations also refer to private standards related to analytical reference methods for microbiological food safety.[73] The new EU Regulation on official controls prescribes for example accreditation in accordance with ISO norms for delegated controls and for laboratories.[74] However, in most cases in which a government is incorporating private food rules in legislation, the state takes over completely. Except for the technical testing norms, the government does not oblige food industry to comply with substantial private standards without transforming the private established rules into public legislation. Examples of this do exist outside the food sector such as in labour relations. In the Netherlands it is quite common that collective labour agreements (the result of negotiations between employers and trade unions' collective bargaining) are declared 'generally binding', that is the provisions of the agreement are made mandatory for all employers and employees in the industry including those that were not represented in the negotiations. The negotiated rules are not changed by the government. However, in food regulation governmental organizations tend to take over the lead. Examples are the EU regulation of organic food, the inclusion of HACCP requirements and third party certification in EU law.

Private standards often do adopt public regulation by including general provisions requiring compliance with all applicable legal requirements. For example, the BRC Global Food Standard refers to legal (and legality of) products and processes in almost every chapter, 'in compliance with the law in the place of production and in the countries where the product(s) is/are intended to be sold.'[75]

---

[72] See also Lockie et al. (2013), p. 284; Kalfagianni and Andrade Roche (2017).

[73] van der Meulen (2011b), pp. 85–86. See Mendelson (2014) for a critical evaluation of the incorporation of private standards in US federal regulations by reference, focussing on transparency, accountability and potential harms.

[74] Regulation (EU) 625/2017 of the European Parliament and of the Council of 15 March 2017 on official controls and other official activities performed to ensure the application of food and feed law, rules on animal health and welfare, plant health and plant protection products [2017] OJ L 95/1, Articles 29(b), 37(4e), 40(1a), 41(a), 93(3a).

[75] BRC Global Standard Food Safety Issue 7, p. 112.

Similar provisions are included in other standards such as GlobalG.A.P. and IFS. However, Lockie concluded that compliance with relevant national legislation is expected but not part of the audit.[76]

2.3 *Monitoring and Enforcement*

This section deals with monitoring and controls. Do governmental inspectors take private certificates into account? To what extent do private auditors check compliance with public rules? What are the subjects of discussion here?

The current European Union legal framework creates several opportunities for private food standards and private auditing of food operators and has contributed to the proliferation of these standards. EU law makes food and feed producers primarily responsible for food safety and compliance with all requirements.[77] This legal framework stimulates food businesses to employ internal audits and to engage external auditing or consulting firms. Another provision that reinforces the use of private food standards is the requirement that every food business should have an operational food safety management system based on the principles of HACCP. Choosing for third party certification against a major private food safety standard might help a firm to comply with these legal requirements. To be sure, adhering to a private food standard is not legally mandatory.

EU Member States must maintain an effective legal system that requires responsible parties to take affirmative steps to ensure food safety. These include conducting food safety inspections with appropriate frequency, without prior notice and on a risk basis, which take into account the identified risks, the likelihood of consumer deception, past compliance records, private controls, and any information that might signal non-compliance.[78] The frequency of these official controls should be proportionate to the risk, taking into account 'the reliability and results of own controls that have been performed by the operators, or by a third party at their request, including, where appropriate, private quality assurance schemes, for the purpose of ascertaining compliance with' EU feed and food law, animal health and animal welfare rules'.[79] This enables public authorities responsible for official controls to ascribe an explicit role to private food safety control systems. In the Netherlands, the Netherlands Food and Consumer Product Safety Authority (NVWA) has recently developed a policy of assessing private systems of food safety

[76]Lockie et al. (2013), pp. 279–280.

[77]van der Meulen (2017).

[78]Article 9(1) Regulation (EU) 2017/625 on official controls. Article 3(1) Regulation (EC) No 882/2004 of the European Parliament and of the Council of 29 April 2004 on official controls performed to ensure the verification of compliance with feed and food law, animal health and animal welfare rules [2004] OJ L165/1had a similar provision.

[79]Article 9(1) Regulation (EU) 2017/625 and Recital 13 Regulation 882/2004/EC.

controls and integrating them in its own enforcement activities. So far, it has accepted several national private systems, and, after revision of the criteria (in the aftermath of the horsemeat fraud), the NVWA is in the process of assessing and reassigning private food quality systems.[80] In February 2017, the NVWA has found three transnational food safety schemes that fulfil these criteria: BRC, IFS and FSSC22000.[81] The UK Food Standards Agency has listed five assurance schemes to be applied when planning inspections of primary produce and is also considering other schemes on the transnational level, including BRC, IFS, FSSC22000 and GlobalG.A.P.[82] The FSA is reviewing its enforcement system and the use of private sector audit data. A change of the frequency of audits is being considered.[83]

The proliferation of private standards goes hand in hand with the establishment and growth of third party certification bodies and of accreditation bodies. Galland distinguishes between two Tripartite Standard Regimes (standardization, certification, accreditation). The European Union did foster the development of a certification industry by obliging some producers to employ third party certification in the context of the 'New Approach to Technical Harmonisation and Standardisation'.[84] The EU constructed a notification system and a list of competent certification bodies. To harmonize practices between the Member States the European Commission recommended that notified certification bodies should be accredited by an independent accreditation body and each Member State should have one single accreditation body.[85] This EU accreditation policy is framed in the context of the free market for non-foods but also had an effect on private food standards relying on third party certification. Because certification bodies tend to be not sector-specific, the EU regulations also regulate the certification bodies that verify compliance with food standards. The EU frame means that in the end a public organisation (a national accreditation body) checks the quality of the organisations that are responsible for assessing conformity with private food standards. Accreditation bodies act as carriers and enforcers of state rules.[86] Thus private food standards that rely on the process of third party certification for monitoring and enforcing conformity with the standard operate within this EU framework.

Nevertheless, public organisations still do criticize the reliability of third party certification. The Netherlands Food and Consumer Product Safety Authority concluded in 2004 and 2011 that certification of a food business operator did not

[80]Verbruggen and Havinga (2015). Comparable developments are observed in Canada and the United States, see Havinga and Verbruggen (2017), McAllister (2012), pp. 10–15; Oldfield (2015).

[81]See http://ketenborging.nl/kwaliteitsschemas-en-status/, accessed 1 March 2017.

[82]Wright et al. (2013).

[83]Regulating our Future program https://www.food.gov.uk/search?keyword=regulating%20our%20future accessed 12 April 2017.

[84]Galland (2017) and Verbruggen and van Leeuwen (2015).

[85]Regulation (EC) No 765/2008 of the European Parliament and of the Council of 9 July 2008 setting out the requirements for accreditation and market surveillance relating to the marketing of products [2008] OJ L218/30.

[86]Casey (2017).

guarantee compliance with relevant legal requirements.[87] The Netherlands authority started consultations with food standards organizations, certification bodies, and the Dutch Accreditation Council aiming at improvement of the quality of the certification process. One of the issues of discussion is that audit visits are usually announced. Critics such as the Netherlands Food and Consumer Product Safety Authority argue that most audit visits need to be unannounced to prevent the food operator to clear up before the audit. Pleas in favour of unannounced visits seem to be successful.[88] Recently several food safety schemes included unannounced visits, though mostly optional and the 2017 edition of GFSI Guidelines requires schemes to include the availability of unannounced audits as a preferred option.[89]

Another issue that has come up in the context of public-private cooperation is the need for adequate exchange of information between private certification bodies and scheme owners on the one hand and public food authorities on the other. Public agencies responsible for food safety inspections should be notified about non-conformities (and other situations) that pose a risk to public health. Moreover, public agencies should have access to actual and reliable information about the certification status of food business operators, the accreditation of certification bodies, accumulated information on audit results, and changes in the food safety scheme requirements.[90] Public agencies should inform private scheme owners and certification bodies about actual food safety risks, recalls, new legislative requirements and new scientific knowledge that might be relevant for their activities in securing the safety of food. The sharing of information is hampered by legal obstacles. Private schemes and auditors operate under the contractual condition of professional confidentiality of audit information (and the whole system is paid for by the contributions of the regulated firms). Public agencies are often not free to share information about particular firms either.

It should be noted that private auditors for food business operators that voluntary join a food safety scheme do have other obligations and responsibilities than public inspectors. A public agency that tries to get complete control over private auditors risks a failing regulatory collaboration. An example in case is the Dutch attempt to have private inspectors of egg producers control legal requirements related to eggs within a strict legal framework. The failure of this hybrid governance structure has been partly attributed to the government that regarded the co-regulatory regime as its own instrument.[91] More general 'bald displays of coercive power by the state can

[87]Havinga and Verbruggen (2017), p. 202.

[88]'A new development has been unannounced audits, arriving at the factory at 8am and entering for the inspection. In the event that access is denied for these assessments, the supplier is delisted.' Jan Kranghand, Regional Director QA MCCI Asia, Metro China at the GFSI meeting 2015 (http://www.mygfsi.com/files/Executive_Summary/GFSC_2015_Executive_Summary_HD.pdf, accessed 4 September 2015).

[89]GFSI Benchmarking Requirements Guidance document version 7, Part 2: Requirements for the management of schemes, 2.5.5 (at: www.mygfsi.com).

[90]Verbruggen (2014), p. 251.

[91]van der Voort (2015), p. 511.

undermine more normatively based motivations to self-regulate'.[92] This would jeopardize one of the key conditions for effective food safety governance.[93] The value of a strong food safety culture in a company is also acknowledged by the GFSI as they started a Technical Working Group focused on Food Safety Culture in 2015.[94] The ultimate goal of GFSI is that governments recognize or adopt GFSI third party certification as accepted tools to assist in the prioritization of food safety compliance resources and inspection.[95]

2.4 *Evaluation and Review*

This section deals with the final regulatory function: evaluation and review of the food standards and schemes. Do private schemes incorporate criticism from public authorities in reviewing the standard? Are EU institutions open to criticism and proposals from private standard organizations?

Private food safety standards that are recognized by the GFSI all have procedures in place for regular revision of the scheme. Schemes should be subject to formal internal review annually, the normative documents should be reissued at least every four years and direct stakeholders should be involved.[96] So far GFSI has shown to be responsive to criticism from international and national governmental organisations.[97] They have strengthened auditor competence requirements, requirements related to independence of scheme owners and certification bodies, requirements for stakeholder participation, public availability of relevant documents, the inclusion of unannounced inspection visits and food fraud vulnerability assessment procedures. GFSI also developed a program to assist food business operators in developing markets and SME to work their way up to certification against a GFSI recognized standard. GFSI has announced to work on the development of tools to better understand and strengthen food safety cultures within companies.[98]

The question whether EU institutions seriously consider criticism and proposals from private standard organizations requires further investigation.

---

[92]Short and Toffel (2010), p. 386.

[93]Beuger (2012) and van Wijk and Six (2014).

[94]See http://www.mygfsi.com/news-resources/news/444-call-for-participation-in-new-gfsi-technical-working-group-food-safety-culture.html, accessed 28 April 2016.

[95]Havinga and Verbruggen (2017).

[96]GFSI Guidance document, Sixth Edition, Version 6.3, October 2013, p. 63 (2.3.7, 2.3.8).

[97]Havinga and Verbruggen (2017).

[98]GFSI's Technical Working Groups are making headway, 2016-10-26. http://www.mygfsi.com/news-resources/latest-news/575-gfsi-s-technical-working-group-are-making-headway.html, accessed 1 August 2017.

3 Conclusion

Private food safety standards and other food standards have gained an important position in the European regulatory space. This proliferation raised concerns with public authorities about the legitimacy, accountability and transparency of these private regulations. Public authorities published guidance documents and formulated criteria for private food standards and schemes. In course of time private schemes are strengthened: they have been adapted to some of the main points of criticism and are tightening the requirements and adding new ones. This ratcheting up makes it harder for new food business operators to participate.

The modern food safety laws in the EU (and the US and Canada) focus on prevention and are partly built on the experience of private food schemes and food industry. Private governance structures inevitably carry the risk of capture and conflict of interest. Powerful transnational food safety schemes might push domestic public regulators to the second row in case they lack financial resources, practical experience and the best scientific expertise. For this reason or because of slow-moving wheels of political decision-making, private food schemes may be frontrunners with the risk that some public interests are neglected or that the interests of less powerful stakeholders are not sufficiently taken into account.

Acknowledgement The author benefitted very much from the collaboration with Paul Verbruggen and Frans van Waarden in several related projects and is grateful for the comments by Harry Bremmers and an anonymous reviewer.

References

Ahold (2016) Responsible retailing report 2015. Ahold, Zaandam. Available https://www.aholddelhaize.com/media/1934/ahold-responsible-retailing-report-2015.pdf

Ansell C, Vogel D (2006) The contested governance of European food safety regulation. In: Ansell C, Vogel D (eds) What's the beef? The contested governance of European food safety. The MIT Press, Cambridge, pp 3–32

Arcuri A (2015) The transformation of organic regulation: the ambiguous effects of publicization. Regul Governance 9(2):144–159

Aréte (2010) Inventory of certification schemes for agricultural products and foodstuffs marketed in the EU Member States. Data aggregations. European Commission. Available http://ec.europa.eu/agriculture/quality/certification/inventory/inventory-data-aggregations_en.pdf. Accessed 1 Aug 2017

Bain C, Ransom E, Higgins V (2013) Private agri-food standards: contestation, hybridity and the politics of standards. Int J Sociol Agric Food 20(1):1–10

Baldwin R, Cave M, Lodge M (2012) Understanding regulation. Theory, strategy, and practice, 2nd edn. Oxford University Press, Oxford

Bernauer T, Caduff L (2006) Food safety and the structure of the European food industry. In: Ansell C, Vogel D (eds) What's the beef? The contested governance of European food safety. The MIT press, Cambridge, pp 81–95

Beuger H (2012) Overheidstoezicht en Certificatie: Verhogen Betrouwbaarheid Vergt Inspanning van alle Betrokkenen. VMT:20–24

Black J (1998) Reviewing regulatory rules: responding to hybridization. In: Black J, Muchlinski P, Walker P (eds) Commercial regulation and judicial review. Hart, Oxford, pp 123–157
Boström M, Klintman M (2006) State-centered versus nonstate-driven organic food standardization: a comparison of the US and Sweden. Agric Hum Values 23(2):163–180
Braithwaite J (1982) Enforced self-regulation: a new strategy for corporate crime control. Michigan Law Rev 80(7):1466–1507
Braithwaite J, Drahos P (2000) Global business regulation. Cambridge University Press, Melbourne
Burch D, Lawrence G (2005) Supermarket own brands, supply chains, and the transformation of the agri-food system. Int J Sociol Agric Food 13(1):1–18
Busch L, Bingen J (2006) Introduction: a new world of standards. In: Bingen J, Busch L (eds) Agricultural standards: the shape of the global food and fiber system. Springer, Dordrecht, pp 3–28
Cafaggi F, Iamiceli P (2015) Contracting in global supply chains and cooperative remedies. Unif Law Rev 20:135–179
Canivet N (2006) Food safety certification. FAO. ftp://ftp.fao.org/ag/agn/food/certification_programmes.pdf
Casey D (2017) Structuring private food safety governance. GLOBALGAP and the legitimating role of the state and rule intermediaries. In: Verbruggen P, Havinga T (eds) Hybridization of food governance: types, trends and results. Edward Elgar, Cheltenham, pp 31–53
Chatzopoulou S (2015) The dynamics of the transnational food chain regulatory governance. An analytical framework. Br Food J 117(10):2609–2627
Clapp J (2016) Food, 2nd edn. Polity Press, Cambridge
Demortain D (2007) Standardising through concepts: scientific experts and the international development of the HACCP food safety standard. London CARR DP 45
Emonds R (2015) Monitor Keurmerken. Keurmerken omzetten binnen Supermarkten 2014 en YTD 2015. Iri. Available https://beterleven.dierenbescherming.nl/fileupload/Rapportage_Raad_van_Advies_BLK_2014_en_2015.pdf. Accessed 1 Aug 2017
Fagotto E (2017) Resolving gaps in third-party certification for food safety hybridization. In: Verbruggen P, Havinga T (eds) Hybridization of food governance: types, trends and results. Edward Elgar, Cheltenham, pp 54–77
FAO Food Control and Consumer Protection Group (2014) Roles of public actors in the voluntary standards. In: Meybeck A, Redfern S (eds) Voluntary standards for sustainable food systems: challenges and opportunities. A workshop of the FAO/UNEP programme on sustainable food systems. Rome, FAO, pp 215–234
Food Chain Evaluation Consortium (2009) Feasibility study on animal welfare labelling and establishing a community reference centre for animal protection and welfare. Part 1: animal welfare labelling. Final Report. European Commission Directorate General for Health and Consumer Protection
Fouilleux E, Loconto A (2017) Voluntary standards, certification, and accreditation in the global organic agriculture field: a tripartite model of techno-politics. Agric Hum Values 34:1–14
Fuchs D, Kalfagianni A, Arentsen M (2009) Retail power, private standards, and sustainability in the global food system. In: Clapp J, Fuchs D (eds) Corporate power in global agrifood governance. MIT Press, Boston, pp 29–60
Fuchs D, Kalfagianni A, Havinga T (2011) Actors in private food governance: the legitimacy of retail standards and multistakeholder initiatives with civil society participation. Agric Hum Values 28(3):353–367
Fulponi L (2006) Private voluntary standards in the food system: the perspective of major food retailers in OECD countries. Food Policy 31(1):1–13
Galland J-P (2017) Big third-party certifiers and the construction of transnational regulation. Annals Am Acad Polit Soc Sci 670:263–279
Hammoudi A et al (eds) (2015) Food safety, market organization, trade and development. Springer, Cham

Hatanaka M, Bain C, Busch L (2005) Third-party certification in the global agrifood system. Food Policy 30(3):354–369

Havinga T (2006) Private regulation of food safety by supermarkets. Law Policy 28(4):515–533

Havinga T (2014) National variations in the implementation and enforcement of European food hygiene regulations. Comparing the structure of food controls and regulations between Scotland and the Netherlands. Recht der Werkelijkheid 35(3):32–53

Havinga T (2015a) Retail driven food safety regulation. In: Hammoudi A et al (eds) Food safety, market organization, trade and development. Springer, Cham, pp 59–76

Havinga T (2015b) Conceptualizing regulatory arrangements: complex networks and regulatory roles. In: Havinga T, van Waarden F, Casey D (eds) The changing landscape of food governance: public and private encounters. Edward Elgar, Cheltenham, pp 19–36

Havinga T, Verbruggen P (2017) The global food safety initiative and state actors: paving the way for hybrid food safety governance. In: Verbruggen P, Havinga T (eds) Hybridization of food governance: types, trends and results. Edward Elgar, Cheltenham, pp 183–214

Henson S (2011) Private agrifood governance: conclusions, observations and provocations. Agric Hum Values 28(3):443–451

Henson S, Humphrey J (2009) The impacts of private food safety standards on the food chain and on public standard-setting processes. Paper Prepared for FAO/WHO

Henson S, Humphrey J (2010) Understanding the complexities of private standards in global agrifood chains as they impact developing countries. J Dev Stud 46(9):1628–1646

Henson S, Humphrey J (2011) Codex alimentarius and private standards. In: van der Meulen B (ed) Private food law. Governing food chains through contract law. Self-regulation, private standards, audits and certification schemes. Wageningen Academic Publishers, Wageningen, pp 149–174

Herath D, Henson S (2006) Does Canada need mandatory HACCP? Evidence from the Ontario food processing sector. Can J Agric Econ 54(4):443–459

Kalfagianni A, Andrade Roche T (2017) Domestic responses to transnational private governance: the marine stewardship council in Alaska, Australia and Ecuador. In: Verbruggen P, Havinga T (eds) Hybridization of food governance: types, trends and results. Cheltenham, Edward Elgar, pp 240–271

Kurth L, Glasbergen P (2017) Serving a heterogeneous Muslim identity? Private governance arrangements of halal food in the Netherlands. Agric Hum Values 34:103–118

Levi-Faur D (2011) Regulation and regulatory governance. In: Levi-Faur D (ed) Handbook on the politics of regulation. Edward Elgar, Cheltenham

Lockie S, McNaughton A, Thompson L-J, Tennent R (2013) Private food standards as responsive regulation. The role of national legislation in the implementation and evolution of GLOBALG. A.P. Int J Sociol Agric Food 20(2):275–291

Lytton TD (2013) Kosher. Private regulation in the age of industrial food. Harvard University Press, Cambridge

Lytton TD, McAllister LK (2014) Oversight in private food safety auditing: addressing auditor conflict of interest. Wisconsin Law Rev 22(4):289–335

Majone G (1994) The rise of the regulatory state in Europe. West Eur Polit 17(3):77–101

Marsden T, Flynn A, Harrison M (2000) Consuming interests. The social provision of foods. UCL Press, London

Marsden T, Lee R, Flynn A, Thankappan S (2010) The new regulation and governance of food. Routledge, New York

McAllister LK (2012) Third-party Programs to Assess Regulatory Compliance. Report for the Administrative Conference of the United States. Available https://www.acus.gov/sites/default/files/documents/Third-Party-Programs-Report_Final.pdf

Mendelson NA (2014) Private control over access to the law: the perplexing federal regulatory use of private standards. Michigan Law Rev 112(5):737–807. Available http://ssrn.com/abstract=2264321

Moran W (1993) The wine appellation as territory in France and California. Ann Assoc Am Geogr 83(4):694–717

MSC (2015) 15 years of certified sustainable seafood. Annual Report 2014–2015. https://www.msc.org/documents/msc-brochures/annual-report-archive/annual-report-2014-15-english/view

Oldfield MT (2015) Enactment of the food safety modernization act. The US FDA within the context of interacting public-private governance processes. Eur J Risk Regul 6(4):488–501

Oosterveer P (2005) Global food governance. Wageningen university, Wageningen

Raone J (2013) Revisiting Lipsky's Dilemmas: experience hybridity at the front-lines. The case of the Belgian Food Safety Agency. ISPOLE Working Paper No, 4. Louvain-La-Neuve: Institut de Sciences Politiques Louvain-Europe UCL. Available https://www.uclouvain.be/cps/ucl/doc/pols/documents/Raone_Final_Paper.pdf

Schmidt H (2011) Organic food. A private concept's take-over by government and the continued leading role of the private sector. In: van der Meulen B (ed) Private food law. Governing food chains through contract law, self-regulation, private standards, audits and certification schemes. Wageningen Academic Publishers, Wageningen, pp 289–299

Scottish Fair Trade Forum (2013) Fair trade public procurement in Scotland: a briefing. Edinburgh. Available http://www.scottishfairtradeforum.org.uk/reports/Procurement/A%20Guide%20to%20Fair%20Trade%20Public%20Procurement%20in%20Scotland%20181013.pdf

Short JL, Toffel MW (2010) Making self-regulation more than merely symbolic: the critical role of the legal environment. Adm Sci Q 55(3):361–396

ten Kate G (2014) A review of dutch policy for socially responsible public procurement. Stichting Onderzoek Multinationale Ondernemingen, Amsterdam. Available https://www.somo.nl/wp-content/uploads/2014/03/A-review-of-Dutch-policy-for-socially-responsible-public-procurement.pdf

ten Kate G, van der Wal S (2017) Eyes on the price. International supermarket buying groups in Europe. Somo, Amsterdam. Available https://www.somo.nl/wp-content/uploads/2017/03/Eyes-on-the-price.pdf

van der Kloet J (2011) Transnational supermarket standards in global supply chains: the emergence and evolution of GlobalGAP. Recht der Werkelijkheid 32(3):80–99

van der Meulen BMJ (2017) Responsibility in EU food law. In: Verbruggen P, Havinga T (eds) Hybridization of food governance: types, trends and results. Cheltenham, Edward Elgar, pp 121–136

van der Meulen B (ed) (2011a) Private food law. Governing food chains through contract law, self-regulation, private standards, audits and certification schemes. Wageningen Academic Publishers, Wageningen

van der Meulen B (2011b) The anatomy of private food law. In: van der Meulen B (ed) Private food law. Governing food chains through contract law, self-regulation, private standards, audits and certification schemes. Wageningen Academic Publishers, Wageningen, pp 75–111

van der Voort H (2015) Co-regulatory failure in the food industry. Explaining regulatory failure by means of two contrasting interpretations of governance. Eur J Risk Regul 6(4):502–511

van Waarden F (1985) Varieties of collective self-regulation of business: the example of the Dutch dairy industry. In: Streeck W, Schmitter P (eds) Private interest government. Beyond market and state. Sage, pp 197–220

van Waarden F (2011) Varieties of private market regulation. In: Levi-Faur D (ed) Handbook on the politics of regulation. Edward Elgar, Cheltenham, pp 469–485

van Waarden F, van Dalen R (2015) Markets regulating markets: competitive private regulation by halal certifiers. In: Havinga T, van Waarden F, Casey D (eds) The changing landscape of food governance: public and private encounters. Cheltenham, Edward Elgar, pp 174–198

van Wijk E, Six F (2014) De Diversiteit van het Willen. Een Onderzoek naar de Dynamiek van Motivaties achter Regelnaleving. Boom Lemma Uitgevers, Den Haag

Verbruggen PWJ, van Leeuwen BJ (2015) Europese Regelgeving inzake Medische Hulpmiddelen. Het PIP-schandaal, de 'Nieuwe Aanpak' en Consumentenbescherming. Tijdschrift voor Consumentenrecht en Handelspraktijken 3:111–121

Verbruggen P (2014) Enforcing transnational private regulation: a comparative analysis of advertising and food safety. Edward Elgar, Cheltenham

Verbruggen P, Havinga T (2015) Food safety meta-controls in the Netherlands. Eur J Risk Regul 6 (4):512–524

Verbruggen P, Havinga T (2016) The rise of transnational private meta-regulators. Tilburg Law Rev 21(2):116–143

Verbruggen P, Havinga T (2017) Hybridization of food governance: an analytical framework. In: Verbruggen P, Havinga T (eds) Hybridization of food governance: types, trends and results. Edward Elgar, Cheltenham, pp 1–27

Vos E (2000) EU food safety regulation in the aftermath of the BSE crisis. J Consum Policy 23:227–255

Vos E, Wendler F (2006) Food safety regulation at the EU level. In: Vos E, Wendler F (eds) Food safety regulation in Europe. A comparative institutional analysis. Intersentia, Antwerpen, pp 65–138

Wright M, Palmer G, Shahriyer A, Williams R, Smith R (2013) Assessment and comparison of third party assurance schemes in the food sector: a common framework. Final Report for the Food Standards Agency

Tetty Havinga is Associate Professor Sociology of Law, Radboud University Nijmegen, The Netherlands. She published on the regulation of food safety, policy implementation and law enforcement, experiences of large companies with specialized courts, equal opportunities law, and migration. Her current research deals with the development and effects of private food safety regulation, officials controls on the food industry, and the initiatives to align public and private forms of food safety governance. She co-edited *Hybridization of food governance* (Elgar 2017) and *Patterns of Interplay between Public and Private Food Regulation* (EJRR 2015).
A list of publications is available at http://www.ru.nl/english/people/havinga-t.

Investigating the Regulatory Structure of Voluntary Sustainability Standards: Foundations for Intervention Strategies to Increase Consumer Confidence

Eva van der Zee

Abstract Regulation of voluntary sustainability standards (VSSs) may increase their capacity to promote sustainable consumption. To determine if, when and where public or private institutions should intervene, an overview of the current regulatory structure of VSSs is needed. To provide such an overview the regulatory structure of 65 VSSs underlying sustainability food labels in the Dutch market was examined. This study shows a plurality of VSSs with different types of certification schemes, i.e. first-, second- or third-party certification, and with multiple actors involved. The majority of these VSSs resemble a structure where NGOs are highly involved in standard-setting and certification is mainly conducted through private, third-party certification. While these structural characteristics may be considered reliable and credible by consumers, several VSSs do not reflect this structure. The present coexistence of VSSs with different regulatory structures may negatively affect consumer confidence. Future research should aim to examine if, how and where private and public actors could intervene in the regulatory structures of VSSs to increase consumer confidence effectively.

1 Introduction

Western governments seem to consider voluntary business-to-consumer sustainability standards as instrumental to the objective of promoting sustainable consumption.[1] This fits within a shift in governance that has taken place from traditional command and control regulatory instruments used by classical government

[1]WSSD (2002).

E. van der Zee (✉)
Wageningen University, Law and Governance, Marketing and Consumer Behaviour, Strategic Communication, Wageningen, The Netherlands
e-mail: eva.vanderzee@wur.nl

H. Bremmers, K. Purnhagen (eds.), *Regulating and Managing Food Safety in the EU*, Economic Analysis of Law in European Legal Scholarship 6,
https://doi.org/10.1007/978-3-319-77045-1_3

institutions to market-based regulatory instruments used by e.g. NGOs, industry associations, and public-private partnerships.[2]

Sustainability labels have proven very popular to provide sustainability-related information to consumers. These labels often are vested on specific voluntary sustainability standards (VSSs) which a product, organisation, or product process must meet. VSSs are voluntary regulatory schemes designed and enforced by private or public bodies with the purpose of promoting sustainable development. Since the 1980s there has been a rise of VSSs on the consumer market.[3] For example, in 2014 there were around 170 different VSSs being used in The Netherlands.[4]

Despite the rise of VSSs since the 1980s the market share of sustainable food remains low.[5] Different reasons for this slow increase in market share for sustainable food may include the wide diversity of VSSs as shown by research on the credibility of eco-labels,[6] limited consumer understanding of specific VSSs,[7] and/or failure of such VSSs to trigger consumer motivation to purchase sustainably.[8]

Furthermore, VSSs may not or only hardly improve the sustainability issues they are aiming at, or the VSS may negatively impact other sustainability issues.[9] VSSs may also negatively impact trade, especially with developing countries,[10] inducing a decrease in social sustainability. As such, VSSs may fail to contribute to the effective realization of sustainable consumption.

Intervention in the regulatory structure of VSSs may be necessary to increase their capacity to promote sustainable consumption. To determine if, when and where public or private institutions should intervene an overview of the current regulatory structure of VSSs is needed. The objective of this study was to provide such an overview and to identify knowledge gaps which can induce further research.

2 Theoretical Framework

Business-to-consumer information labelling provides an increasingly important regulatory tool, promoting informed consumer choice by communicating sustainability attributes of products or production processes through logos, symbols, labels, and texts. A lack of consumer information labelling may lead to information

[2]See e.g. Tietenberg (1998), Giovannucci and Ponte (2005), Cafaggi (2013) and Purnhagen (2015).

[3]Grunert et al. (2014), Gandenberger et al. (2011), Koos (2011), Raynolds et al. (2007) and Wilkinson (2007).

[4]ANP (2014).

[5]See e.g. Dutch Ministry of Economic Affairs (2014).

[6]Fischer et al. (2005) and Teisl et al. (2002).

[7]Horne (2009) and Grunert et al. (2014).

[8]van Dam and De Jonge (2015).

[9]See e.g. Von Geibler (2013).

[10]Giovannucci and Ponte (2005).

asymmetry between consumers and producers. Producers of food products often have more or better information about specific sustainability attributes of their products compared to consumers. Information asymmetry between consumers and producers can impede the smooth functioning of markets, which in the worst case may lead to market failure. Market failure implies that consumers are unwilling to pay more for better quality, leading to a lack of motivation by producers to offer higher quality[11] Information asymmetry is especially apparent for sustainability attributes of products, as these can be considered credence attributes[12] and Potemkin attributes.[13] This is less so for search attributes which are known before purchase and experience attributes which are known costlessly only after purchase.[14] Credence attributes are expensive to determine even after purchase,[15] while Potemkin attributes, such as fair trade and animal welfare, cannot be verified by neither the consumer nor external institutions at the end-product level.[16]

The extent a labelling scheme provides relevant sustainability-related information depends on how sustainability is conceived. Numerous definitions of sustainability, or sustainable development, have appeared in international declarations, conventions, court judgments, and scholarly writings.[17] Although definitions differ, many definitions emphasise that the needs of the present must be met, while the ability of future generations to meet their own needs may not be compromised.[18] This is also known as inter- and intra-generational equity. Many definitions further specify economic, social, environmental and sometimes cultural aspects as important dimensions of sustainable development.[19] From these more abstract aspects of sustainability, more concrete sub-categories of sustainability can be determined that are potentially relevant in the context of VSSs, e.g. biodiversity, human rights and labour conditions. These categories may address several issues that could be relevant in the context of VSSs, e.g. climate change, child labour and wage levels (see also Table 1).

As many sustainability attributes of products can be expensive or impossible to determine even after purchase, consumers may question the credibility of a VSSs. Certification has as a function to provide assurance to consumers that the properties which the VSSs represents exist and so the information is credible. Certification can

[11]Akerlof (1970).

[12]Grunert et al. (2014) and van Dam and van Trijp (2011).

[13]Spadoni et al. (2014).

[14]Nelson (1970).

[15]Darby and Karni (1973).

[16]Spadoni et al. (2014).

[17]Johnston et al. (2007) and Lawn (2010).

[18]WCED (1987).

[19]Boström (2012), Conelly (2007), De Boer et al. (2004), Norgaard (1988), OECD (2008), Redclift (1992), IIED (1997), WSSD (2002) and UNCTAD (2013).

Table 1 Sustainability ideal, aspects, categories, and issues potentially relevant in the context of VSSs[a]

Sustainable development			
Ideal	Aspects	Categories	Issues
Inter- and intra-generational equity	Environmental aspects	Environmental impacts	Climate change Environment and health
		Biodiversity	Natural resources and waste Biodiversity in general One or more specific ecosystems Specific species
	Social aspects	Human health	Food safety
		Human rights	Forced labour Rights of indigenous people Freedom of association/bargaining Child labour
		Labour conditions	Wage levels Occupational health and safety standards
		Animal welfare	Working hours Free-range
	Economic aspects	Trade relations	Guaranteed price Long-term contracts Advanced payments and credit facilities Technical assistance Community support
	Cultural aspects	Geographical indications	Designation of origin Geographical indication Traditional character
		Traditional specialities	Halal
		Religion	Kosher

[a]Based on De Boer et al. (2004) and United Nations Conference on Trade and Development (UNCTAD) (2013)

be defined as the (voluntary) assessment and approval by an (accredited) party of an (accredited) standard.[20]

Certification may involve three possible parties: the certification applicant, the certification body, and the accreditation body. The certification applicant is the manufacturer or distributor that requests certification of its product or production-process. The certification body is the actor that issues the certification. The accreditation body is a formal third party that complies with the general requirements for accreditation bodies specified by the International Standard ISO/IEC 17011:2004 set

[20]Meuwissen et al. (2003).

by the International Standard Organization (ISO).[21] In general, accreditation bodies monitor certification bodies on compliance with the International Social and Environmental Accreditation and Labelling (ISEAL) alliance assurance code and/or the ISO 17065 (former ISO 65 or EN 45011).

Basically, certification schemes include public (state-run) schemes and private certification schemes.[22] Public certification schemes are assessed and approved by public bodies (Fig. 1). Three EU quality schemes are a prime example of such public certification schemes, i.e. PDO (protected designation of origin), PGI (protected geographical indication) and TSG (traditional specialty guaranteed). The European Commission examines whether a food product can be registered as PDO, PGI, or TSG.[23] Public bodies control products registered as PDO, PGI, or TSG on compliance with EU legislation.[24]

Private certification schemes can take different forms: first-party certification, second-party certification, and third-party certification.[25] First-party certification is when the manufacturer or distributor of the food product itself sets the standards and certifies compliance of the product with the set standard (Fig. 2). Many examples of first-party certification can be found with respect to seafood products, e.g. logos like dolphin-friendly tuna and fished by pole & line. In general, these standards are not externally checked. Other examples include standards such as AH Puur & Eerlijk, Fairglobe, or Bio+. These VSSs can be considered umbrella standards as the standards umbrellas for other VSSs: the umbrella standard is first-party certified but requires that the product is certified through specific third-party certification systems.

Second-party certification is conducted by an organisation other than the certification applicant (Fig. 3). These organisations are legally separate from the

Fig. 1 Public certification

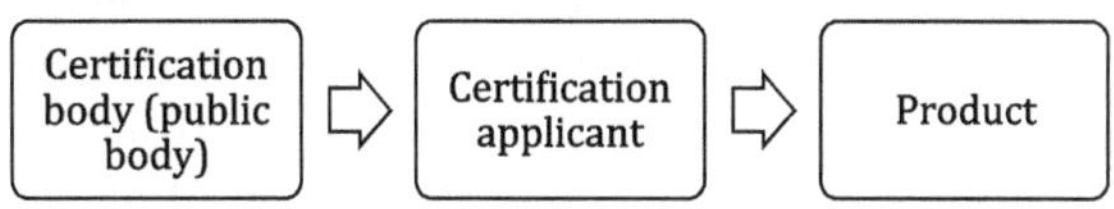

Fig. 2 First-party certification

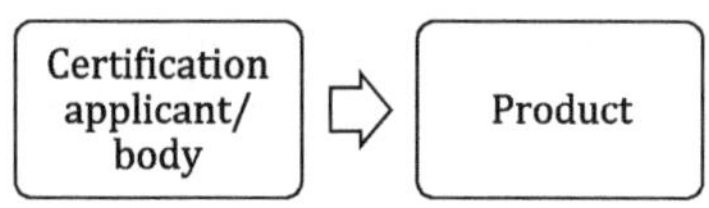

Fig. 3 Second-party certification

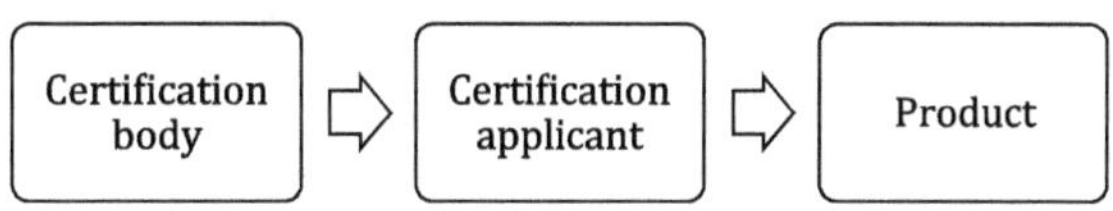

[21] https://www.iso.org/obp/ui/#iso:std:iso-iec:17011:ed-1:v2:en [last accessed 20/05/15].

[22] Jahn et al. (2005).

[23] http://ec.europa.eu/agriculture/quality/schemes/index_en.htm [last accessed 20/05/15].

[24] In The Netherlands the control bodies are: NVWA (government agency), COKZ and KCB (both government bodies). *See* http://ec.europa.eu/agriculture/quality/schemes/compliance-authorities_en.pdf.

[25] Marx (2011).

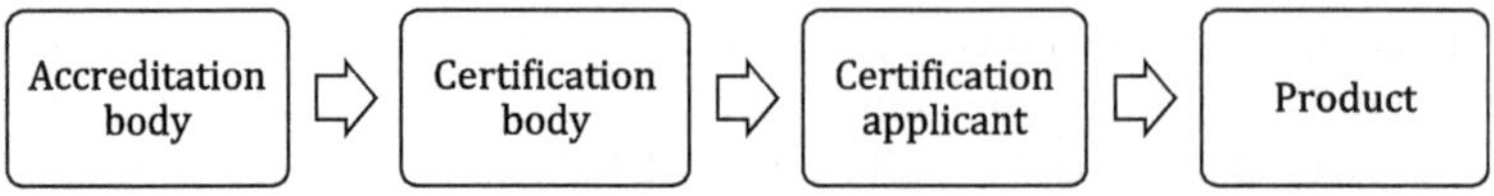

Fig. 4 Third-party certification

certification applicant. An example of second-party certification is the V-label. The V-label was launched by the European Vegetarian Union (EVU): an umbrella organisation for most vegetarian groups in Europe. The mark is checked by the different national vegetarian organization per country, i.e. Nederlandse Vegetariërsbond (Dutch Vegetarian Society).[26]

Third-party certification is conducted by a certification body that is legally separate and independent from the organisation that asks for certification (Fig. 4). The certification body needs to be accredited by an accreditation body to ensure its competence, impartiality and performance capability. An example of third-party certification is the EU organic standard. Every Member State of the EU has at least one private certification body responsible for the certification. This certification body has to be accredited.[27] Due to the independence of the certification body, third-party certification is gaining popularity on all levels of the agri-food chain.[28]

Besides the credibility of the certification scheme, the credibility of a standard may also depend on the credibility of the actors involved in setting the standard.[29] The type of actors involved in standard-setting are important as especially lack of clarity over the source of an eco-label is a key factor inducing consumer uncertainty.[30] Thus, to prevent market failure not only the type of certification but also the types of actors involved need to be considered credible.

Three types of actors can be involved in standard-setting: public actors, NGOs and firms.[31] Public actors encompass developing and developed states, as well as governmental agencies. NGOs include all private actors that are not targeted by the standard, e.g. NGO advocacy groups, labour unions, non-profit organisations student groups, and other civil society organisations, as well as socially responsible investors. Firms include those private actors that are targeted by the standard, e.g. multinationals, small firms, agricultural enterprises, and small-scale farmers. Consumer research suggests that consumers may have lower confidence in

[26]http://www.v-label.info/en/home/international.html [last accessed 15-12-2014].

[27]Article 5 (2) (c) of Regulation (EC) No 882/2004 of the European Parliament and of the Council of 29 April 2004 on official controls performed to ensure the verification of compliance with feed and food law, animal health and animal welfare rules.

[28]Auriol and Schilizzi (2003).

[29]Albersmeier et al. (2010) and Moussa and Touzani (2008).

[30]Harbaugh et al. (2011).

[31]Abbott and Snidal (2009).

company-owned standard.[32] They seem to have higher confidence in a standard-setter that is perceived to be independent.[33]

Based on the actors involved in setting standards, seven types of standards can be identified.[34] For illustration purposes examples of type of standards in the food labelling context are presented where possible. The first type of standards that can be distinguished is set by public actors only, which may include national laws and regulations, but also VSSs. Examples of VSSs set by public actors are the EU organic standard and the EU quality schemes for geographical indications and traditional specialities. The second type of standards is set by firms only, which may include self-regulative schemes, such as dolphin-safe-tuna or fished by pole and line, and brands, such as AH Puur & Eerlijk and Bio+. The third type of standards is set by NGOs only, which may include standards such as Vegan, V-keurmerk, and the Checkmark (Vinkje in Dutch). The fourth type of standards is set in collaboration with public actors and firms. The UN Global Compact is an example of such a standard, aiming at aligning business operations and strategies with principles in the areas of human rights, labour, environment and anti-corruption.[35] The fifth type of standards is set by a collaboration between public actors and NGOs. Although there are not many examples of such standards, one example is the TCO certification scheme for office equipment.[36] The sixth type of standards is set by a collaboration between firms and NGOs, which may include the more well-known VSSs, such as Max Havelaar, UTZ Certified, and Rainforest Alliance. The seventh type of standards is set by a collaboration between public actors, firms, and NGOs. An example outside the food domain is the Kimberley Process Certification Scheme focusing on conflict diamonds.[37]

3 Methodology

To identify the presence of a regulatory structure of VSSs three classes of criteria need to be examined: (1) the aim the standard is trying to achieve; (2) the actors involved in standard-setting; and (3) the type of certification scheme used. These three classes of criteria were used to benchmark VSSs on the Dutch market. These VSSs were selected from the *Keurmerkenwijzer* of Milieucentraal.[38] The

[32]Eden et al. (2008) and Sønderskov and Daugbjerg (2011).

[33]Padel and Foster (2005) and Eden et al. (2008).

[34]Abbott and Snidal (2009).

[35]https://www.unglobalcompact.org/AboutTheGC/index.html [last accessed 11/02/2015].

[36]http://tcodevelopment.se/tco_certified_story/ [last accessed 11/02/2015].

[37]http://www.kimberleyprocess.com/ [last accessed 11/02/2015].

[38]The Milieu Centraal Foundation is an independent information organisation that offers information to consumers on environmental and energy issues in daily life. www.milieucentraal.nl/over-milieu-centraal/ [last accessed: 13-11-2014].

Keurmerkenwijzer presents over 170 labels, symbols, and logos that seemingly provide information about the sustainability of food, clothes, cosmetics, detergents, appliances, wood, paper, flowers and plants. These labelling schemes could be found on products in The Netherlands in 2014. Of these 170 labelling schemes, 65 are visual representations of sustainability on food labels. For this study these 65 visual representations were selected,[39] to assess the VSSs underlying these sustainability labels. The focus of this study was on food standards, because food production bears the largest environmental costs compared to other sectors (KPMG 2012). Furthermore, current food consumption trends may negatively affect all categories of sustainable development (e.g. organic, fair trade, human health, animal welfare).

The VSSs underlying the 65 selected visual representations of sustainability on food labels were examined on the basis of three topics: (1) aim; (2) actors involved in standard-setting; and (3) types of certification. The information about these three topics was found through desk research by examining webpages of each visual representation and by consulting other websites such as www.keurmerkenwijzer.nl, www.labelinfo.be,[40] www.label-online.de,[41] and www.standardsmap.org.[42]

4 Results

4.1 Diversified Aim of VSSs

The aim of the VSSs was diverse (see Table 2). Of the four different aspects of sustainability, nine different combinations were observed. VSSs mainly focused on environmental and social aspects (24), social aspects only (11), and environmental, social and economic aspects (7). Frequently, when standards focused on social aspects, the focus was solely on the category animal welfare.

Although some VSSs focused on similar aspects of sustainability, this does not necessarily imply that the requirements are similar. These specific requirements are, however, often difficult to find and, therefore, difficult to compare. The specific requirements that could be found often differed only slightly. For example, Demeter and EU Organic aim at environmental aspects and animal welfare. Demeter sets,

[39]Beter Leven Kenmerk had three entries in de *keurmerkenwijzer* based on the Beter Leven Kenmerk ranking system: three stars, two stars, and one star. For the purposes of this study Beter Leven Keurmerk had only one entry.

[40]Website of Belgium consumers organisation Netwerk Bewust Verbruiken in cooperation with OIVO en Ecoconso, and support of Cel Sociale Economie, the POD DO, the FOD Leefmilieu and Leefmilieu Brussel. The website contains information about sustainability labels that are also present on Dutch food products.

[41]Website of independent German consumer organisation Verbraucher Initiative.

[42]Website initiated by the International Trade Centre, the joint agency of the World Trade Organization (WTO) and the United Nations Conference on Trade and Development (UNCTAD).

Table 2 Sustainability focus of VSSs

Aspects	Total	Of which social is animal welfare only
Environmental + social	24	12
Social	11	7
Environmental + social + economic	7	0
Cultural	5	N/A
No information	5	N/A
Environmental	4	N/A
Environmental + social + cultural	3	3
Social + economic	3	0
Environmental + cultural	2	N/A
Environmental + economic + cultural	1	N/A
Total	65	22

Table 3 Requirements relating to husbandry practices and housing conditions of dairy cows of EU Organic, Demeter, Duurzame Weidezuivel and Weidemelk

VSS	Type of access	Length of time
EU Organic	Open air, preferably pasture	Permanent
Demeter	Open air, preferably pasture	Permanent
Duurzame Weidezuivel	Pasture	130 days a year, 8 h a day
Weidemelk	Pasture	120 days a year, 6 h a day

however, additional production and processing requirements, e.g. as to mutilations of poultry (like forbidding cutting, trimming, or castration;[43] at least two thirds of the fodder offered to the animals must originate from Demeter production,[44] and milk may not be homogenised.[45] When EU Organic and Demeter are compared on husbandry practices and housing conditions of dairy cows with the husbandry practices and housing condition requirements of two other dairy standards that focus on animal welfare, Duurzame Weidezuivel (Sustainable Pasture Dairy) and Weidemelk (Pasture Milk), differences also occur (see Table 3).

4.2 *High NGO Involvement in Standard-Setting*

VSSs are mainly set by NGOs (24), and to a lesser extend also by firms (14), public actors (14), or through a partnership between NGOs and firms (10). Partnerships

[43]Article 5.4.4. Production Standards For the Use of Demeter Biodynamic® and Related Trademarks As of June 2014 (to be implemented by each member country by the 1st July 2015).

[44]Article 5.5.1. Production Standards For the Use of Demeter Biodynamic® and Related Trademarks As of June 2014 (to be implemented by each member country by the 1st July 2015).

[45]Article 4.1. Processing Standards for the Use of Demeter Biodynamic® and Related Trademarks As of June 2013 (to be implemented by each member country by the 1st of July 2014).

Table 4 Actors involved in standard-setting and type of certification

	Public actor	Public actor + NGO	NGO	NGO + firm	Firm
Public certification	4	0	0	0	0
Third-party	9	3	12	8	1
Second-party	1	0	10	0	0
First-party	0	0	2	1	11

between NGOs and firms generally took the form of NGOs having public consultations with firms before standard-setting. Public-private partnerships, i.e. public actors collaborating in standard-setting with firms, NGOs, or both, were rare in the sample. There were only three public-private partnerships and these were between public actors and NGOs: KRAV, Biogarantie, and Soil Association. These public-private partnerships were, moreover, VSSs regulating organic production processes that were originally founded by NGOs; later these became official national organic standards that had to meet the requirements of the EU Regulation on Organic Agriculture[46] but upheld their stricter requirements.

4.3 *Certification of Standards Often Through Private, Third-Party Certification*

Most VSSs were certified through certification schemes. For three VSSs it was unclear what type of certification scheme was used for certification. Only four VSSs, i.e. the Danish organic Ø-mark and the EU schemes PDO, PGI, and TSG, were certified through public certification schemes. The other VSSs were certified through private certification. Most VSSs are certified through third-party certification (33),[47] followed by first-party certification (14), and second-party certification (11).

The 33 VSSs that are certified through third-party certification are often set by NGOs (12), public actors (9), or a partnership between NGOs and firms (8) (see Table 4). VSSs that are certified through second-party certification are often set by NGOs only, while VSSs that are certified through first-party certification are often set by firms only.

[46]Council Regulation (EC) No 834/2007 of 28 June 2007 on organic production and labelling of organic products and repealing Regulation (EEC) No 2092/91.

[47]Ecosocial performed two types of certification: third party certification for organic produce, and second-party certification for non-organic produce. Ecosocial is, therefore, counted twice.

5 General Discussion

This study shows that a regulatory structure is present within VSSs with respect to their aim, actors involved in standard-setting, and the certification scheme used. Most VSSs have two main characteristics, which can be found within each group of VSSs, e.g. animal welfare standards, fair trade standards, or environmental standards. First, VSSs often have high NGO involvement in standard-setting. Second, certification of VSSs is mainly conducted by private certifiers, through third-party certification. Wittingly or unwittingly the majority of VSSs resemble a structure that is trusted by consumers and considered most reliable and credible by consumer research. First, private, third-party certification is generally perceived as more reliable and credible than first- or second-party certification[48] and thus more effective in ensuring food quality.[49] Second, consumer research suggests that consumers have more confidence in NGOs than in firms or governments in standard-setting.[50] Based on these insights it may seem that the majority of VSSs are on the right track.

Even though the majority of VSSs may be on the right track, several VSSs may not. Current results show that almost half of the VSSs are set without NGO involvement. Furthermore, certification of almost half of the VSSs is not conducted through third-party certification, but through first- or second-party certification. In other words, the majority of VSSs may be considered 'good', i.e. they are more reliable, credible,[51] effective,[52] and trusted,[53] while a minority may be considered 'bad', i.e. they are not considered as reliable, credible, effective, and trusted. The coexistence of a plurality of 'good' and 'bad' VSSs on the market may confuse consumers, as consumers cannot trust that every VSSs is 'good'. As this study also showed the multiplicity and diversity of VSSs on the market, it is very difficult for consumers to know every single VSSs and distinguish 'good' from 'bad' standards. As such, consumer perception towards the reliability and credibility of VSSs, even to those standards that are reliable and credible, may be negatively affected. As a consequence, the effectiveness of VSSs to increase sustainable consumption may be reduced.

To increase the effectiveness of VSSs to increase sustainable consumption, private and/or public intervention may be necessary. An example of private intervention is the merge between Rainforest Alliance and UTZ Certified by creating a single agricultural VSSs, with the aim to simplify the certification process and to increase engagement with consumers.[54] As actors are likely to commit themselves to

---

[48]Golan et al. (2001).

[49]Hatanaka et al. (2005).

[50]Padel and Foster (2005) and Eden et al. (2008).

[51]Golan et al. (2001).

[52]Hatanaka et al. (2005).

[53]Padel and Foster (2005) and Eden et al. (2008).

[54]http://www.rainforest-alliance.org/article/rainforest-alliance-utz-merger [last accessed 30-06-2017].

a system of governance when they grasp that their self-interest is served by such commitment,[55] it is not unlikely that further collaborations will emerge. Governments could induce such collaborations between private standard-setters by drafting international procedural guidelines for standard-setting.

An example of public intervention is governments setting, through command and control regulatory instruments, minimum requirements which a product or production process claiming to be sustainable should meet. For example, in the US, when energy efficiency was becoming popular, a great diversity of claims were made about the value of energy efficiency. The US government stepped in and created a third-party certified energy efficiency standard for products and buildings that meet the highest energy efficiency levels.[56] Consumers could recognise products and buildings that met this standard through the state-controlled, voluntary standard called Energy Star. Another example of governments that stepped in when a great diversity of VSSs appeared on the market with respect to sustainability issues is the EU initiated organic standard. The EU organic standard is a voluntary, third-party certified standard. Producers are legally obliged to place the stamp accompanying the standard on their product labels when they claim their product to be organic. The EU organic standard was set up to increase consumer confidence in products labelled as organic, which would ensure fair competition and a proper functioning of trade in organic produce.[57]

Through Energy Star and the EU organic standard, governments have intervened with the regulatory structure of VSSs by setting minimum quality standards. The VSSs are not checked by the government but by private, third-party certifiers. The Danish organic Ø-mark and the EU quality schemes are examples of VSSs in which the government intervened by setting minimum quality standards that are checked by *public* bodies. As such, the government is more involved in the regulatory structure of these standards compared to Energy Star and the EU organic standard.

It remains unclear, however, whether and to what extent such public or private interventions with VSSs are effective in increasing consumer confidence. Previous research concerning the Energy Star label[58] and the EU quality labels[59] have focused mainly on consumer willingness to pay, concluding that consumers are willing to pay a price premium for Energy Star or EU quality-labelled products. Whether a VSSs will be effective in motivating consumers to purchase the product may not only depend on willingness to pay, but also on consumer recognition of the label,[60]

[55] Druzin (2014).

[56] Energy Policy Act. Section 131 of the Act amends Section 324 (42 USC 6294) of the Energy Policy and Conservation Act.

[57] Council Regulation (EC) No 834/2007 of 28 June 2007 on organic production and labelling of organic products and repealing Regulation (EEC) No 2092/91, para 3.

[58] Ward et al. (2011) and Newell and Siikamäki (2013).

[59] Menapace et al. (2011) and Aprile et al. (2012).

[60] Thøgersen (2000).

basic consumer knowledge of the production standards covered,[61] and consumer confidence in the VSSs.[62] Previous research concerning the Danish eco-label Ø-mark has been very elaborate on these three factors: the Ø-mark is recognised by almost all Danish consumers, Danish consumers seem to have a basic knowledge of the production standards,[63] and Danish consumers seem to have high confidence in their national eco-label Ø-mark compared to consumer confidence of UK, Swedish and US consumers in their national eco-label.[64] Previous research concerning the EU organic standard shows low recognition of the EU organic label by EU consumers[65] and EU consumer confidence in the underlying EU organic standards and the certification systems seems not very pronounced.[66] The effectiveness of these VSSs in increasing consumer confidence in VSSs thus seems to differ. Furthermore, the Energy Star standard, the EU organic standard, and the Danish Ø-mark standard focus on environmental issues, so question remains whether a similar approach would be effective and legally possible for other categories of VSSs (e.g. fair trade, animal welfare, health) or sustainability in general.

Further research is necessary whether and to what extent public or private actors should intervene in the regulatory structure of VSSs to effectively increase consumer confidence. Consumer confidence in VSSs may depend on the number of standards in one market and to what extent these standards address similar or different issues. To assess whether and to what extent public or private actors should intervene in the plurality of VSSs, future research should focus on whether and how much consumer confidence in VSSs is reduced with different levels of plurality of sustainability claims in one market. This can be examined in an experimental study where differences in consumer confidence caused by differences in the number of standards and issues addressed are studied. This can be done by systematically varying the extent to which consumers are confronted with a single standard for each sustainability issue, or a range of standards addressing each same issue. In addition a variation can be made whether a consumer is confronted with a single sustainability issue or a range of sustainability issues. It is expected that if multiple issues are addressed by multiple labels at the same time, consumer confidence would be lowest. Furthermore, it is expected that if multiple issues are each addressed with a single standard this would lead to the highest confidence, as it gives most information with least complexity.

In addition, consumer confidence in VSSs may also depend on the actors in which consumers have confidence. Previous research has shown that consumers have higher confidence in VSSs set by NGOs[67] and that consumers do not identify or

---

[61] Hoogland et al. (2007).

[62] Thøgersen (2000) and Brécard et al. (2009).

[63] Daugbjerg et al. (2014).

[64] Sønderskov and Daugbjerg (2011).

[65] Janssen and Hamm (2014).

[66] Janssen and Hamm (2012).

[67] Padel and Foster (2005) and Eden et al. (2008).

prioritise third-party certification as more independent than other types of certification.[68] Sønderskov and Daugbjerg conclude, however, that visible and substantial state involvement in standard-setting and certification increases consumer confidence in organic standards.[69] From both studies it can be derived that consumers have low confidence in organic standards set and confirmed by firms. Both studies contradict each other whether NGOs or governments should set and confirm standards. However, they focus only on organic standards, while results may differ for other categories of sustainability. To assess whether and to what extent actors involved in standard-setting affect consumer confidence, future research should focus on whether firms, NGOs and/or governments should set and/or certify standards to increase consumer confidence and whether this may differ per dimension of sustainability (e.g. fair trade, organic, animal welfare). This could be examined with a survey where consumers are asked to compare VSSs on trustworthiness and willingness to pay. In this survey different VSSs (e.g. fair trade, organic, animal welfare) with different regulatory structures should be tested with different roles for different actors (i.e. set and/or confirmed by NGOs, governments or firms). The outcome of the experiment and the survey could be used to determine the most effective intervention strategy in VSSs.

This study provided an overview of the current regulatory structure of VSSs underlying sustainability labels in The Netherlands. The Netherlands was used as a case study as, similar to other Western countries, it struggles with the proliferation of VSSs.[70] The data collection consists of publically available information as this information is also available to consumers. A limitation was that NGO-firm partnership was assumed when NGOs had public consultations with firms before standard-setting. Such a broad interpretation of NGO-firm partnership was used to not exclude NGO-firm partnership of which publically available information was ambiguous.

Private or public intervention may be necessary to effectively reduce the impact of 'bad' standards on the trustworthiness of 'good' standards. Governments may especially have a role to play as they can induce collaborations between private standard-setters and set minimum requirements which a product or production process claiming to be sustainable should meet. As Western governments have repeatedly stated that they wish to promote sustainable consumption,[71] time has come for action rather than words.

[68] Eden et al. (2008).

[69] Sønderskov and Daugbjerg (2011).

[70] See e.g. Koos (2011).

[71] WSSD (2002).

References

Abbott KW, Snidal D (2009) Strengthening international regulation through transnational new governance: overcoming the orchestration deficit. Vand J Transnatl Law 42:501–578

Akerlof GA (1970) The market for "lemons": quality uncertainty and the market mechanism. Q J Econ 84(3):488–500

Albersmeier F, Schulze H, Spiller A (2010) System dynamics in food quality certifications: development of an audit integrity system. Int J Food Syst Dyn 1:69–81

ANP (2014) Ploumen wil 'orde' in aantal keurmerken (English translation: Ploumen wants 'order' in the amount of certification marks). Volkskrant. Retrieved from www.volkskrant.nl/binnenland/ploumen-wil-orde-in-aantal-keurmerken~a3627943/. Accessed 20 May 2015

Aprile MC, Caputo V, Nyga JRM (2012) Consumers' valuation of food quality labels: the case of the European geographic indication and organic farming labels. Int J Consum Stud 36(5):158–165

Auriol E, Schilizzi SGM (2003) Quality signaling through certification. Theory and an application to agricultural seed markets. University of Toulouse, Toulouse

Boström M (2012) A missing pillar? Challenges in theorizing and practicing social sustainability: introduction to the special issue. Sustain Sci Pract Policy 8(12):3–14

Brécard B, Hlaimi B, Lucas S, Perrau I, Salladarre F (2009) Determinants of demand for green products: an application to eco-label demand for fish in Europe. Ecol Econ 69(1):115–125

Cafaggi F (2013) The regulatory functions of transnational commercial contracts: new architectures. Fordham Int Law J 36:1557–1618

Conelly S (2007) Mapping sustainable development as a contested concept. Local Environ 12 (3):359–278

Darby MR, Karni E (1973) Free competition and the optimal amount of fraud. J Law Econ 16 (1):67–88

Daugbjerg C, Smed S, Andersen L, Mørch L, Schvartzman Y (2014) Improving eco-labelling as an environmental policy instrument: knowledge, trust and organic consumption. J Environ Policy Plan 16(4):559–575

De Boer J, van der Grijp N, Campins Eritia M, Gupta I (2004) The conceptual framework. In: Eritja C (ed) Sustainability labelling and certification. Marcial Pons, Madrid, pp 39–48

Druzin BH (2014) Anarcy, order, and trade: a structuralist account of why a global commercial legal order is emerging. Vand J Transnatl Law 47:1049

Dutch Ministry of Economic Affairs (2014) Consumentenbestedingen aan Duurzaam Gelabelde Producten. Monitor Duurzaam Voedsel 2013. www.rijksoverheid.nl/bestanden/documenten-en-publicaties/rapporten/2014/06/04/monitor-duurzaam-voedsel-2013/14094896-bijlage.pdf

Eden S, Bear C, Walker G (2008) Understanding and (dis)trusting food assurance schemes: consumer confidence and the 'knowledge fix'. J Rural Stud 24(1):1–14

Fischer C, Sedjo R, Jawahar P, Aguilar F (2005) Forest certification: toward common standards? Resources for the future. Discussion paper dp-05-10, Washington, DC

Gandenberger C, Garrelts H, Wehlau D (2011) Assessing the effects of certification networks on sustainable production and consumption: the cases of FLO and FSC. J Consum Policy 34:107–126

Giovannucci D, Ponte S (2005) Standards as a new form of social contract? Sustainability initatives in the coffee industry. Food Policy 30:284–301

Golan E, Kuchler F, Mitchell L, Greene C, Jessup A (2001) Economics of food labelling. J Consum Policy 24:117–184

Grunert KG, Hieke S, Wills J (2014) Sustainability labels on food products: consumer motivation, understanding and use. Food Policy 44:177–189

Harbaugh R, Maxwell JW, Roussillon B (2011) Label confusion: the Groucho effect of uncertain standards. Manag Sci 57(9):1512–1527
Hatanaka M, Bain C, Busch L (2005) Third-party certification in the global agrifood system. Food Policy 30:354–369
Hoogland CT, de Boer J, Boersema JJ (2007) Food and sustainability: do consumers recognize, understand and value on-package information on production standards? Appetite 49(1):47–57
Horne RE (2009) Limits to labels: the role of eco-labels in the assessment of product sustainability and routes to sustainable consumption. Int J Consum Stud 33:175–182
International Institute for Environment and Development (IIED) (1997) Changing consumption and production patterns: unlocking trade opportunities. UN Department of Policy Coordination and Sustainable Development. http://pubs.iied.org/pdfs/8851IIED.pdf
Jahn G, Schramm M, Spiller A (2005) The reliability of certification: quality labels as a consumer policy tool. J Consum Policy 28:53–73
Janssen M, Hamm U (2012) The mandatory EU logo for organic food: consumer perceptions. Br Food J 114(3):335–352
Janssen M, Hamm U (2014) Governmental and private certification labels for organic food: consumer attitudes and preferences in Germany. Food Policy 49:437–448
Johnston P, Everard M, Santillo D, Robert K (2007) Reclaiming the definition of sustainability. Environ Sci Pollut Res 14(1):60–66
Koos S (2011) Varieties of environmental labelling, market structures, and sustainable consumption across Europe: a comparative analysis of organizational and market supply determinants of environmental-labelled goods. J Consum Policy 34:127–151
KPMG (2012) Expect the unexpected: building business value in a changing world. Report. KPMG International, Amstelveen
Lawn PA (2010) Toward sustainable development: an ecological economics approach. CRC Press, Boca Raton
Marx A (2011) Global governance and the certification revolution types, trends and challenges. In: Levi-Faur D (ed) Handbook of the politics of regulation. Edward Elgar, Cheltenham
Menapace L, Colson G, Grebitus C, Facendola M (2011) Consumers preferences for geographical origin labels: evidence from the canadian olive oil market. Eur Rev Agric Econ 38(2):193–212
Meuwissen MPM, Velthuis AGJ, Hogeveen H, Huirne RBM (2003) Technical and economic considerations about traceability and certification in livestock production chains. In: Velthuis GJ, Unnevehr LJ, Hogeveen H, Huirne RB (eds) New approaches to food safety economics. Kluwer Academic, Wageningen
Moussa S, Touzani M (2008) The perceived credibility of quality labels: a scale validation with refinement. Int J Consum Stud 32(5):526–533
Nelson P (1970) Information and consumer behavior. J Polit Econ 78(2):311–329
Newell RG, Siikamäki J (2013) Nudging energy efficiency behavior, the role of information labels. Resources for the future RFF discussion paper 13–17
Norgaard RB (1988) Sustainable development: a co-evolutionary view. Futures 20(6):606–620
Organisation for Economic Co-operation and Development (OECD) (2008) Promoting sustainable consumption. Good practices in OECD countries. http://www.oecd.org/greengrowth/40317373.pdf
Padel S, Foster C (2005) Exploring the gap between attitudes and behavior: understanding why consumers buy or do not buy organic food. Br Food J 107(8):606–625
Purnhagen K (2015) Mapping private regulation – classification, market access and market closure policy and law's response. J World Trade 49(2):309–324
Raynolds LT, Murray D, Heller A (2007) Regulating sustainability in the coffee sector: a comparative analysis of third-party environmental and social certification initiatives. Agric Hum Values 24:147–163
Redclift M (1992) The meaning of sustainable development. Geoforum 25(3):395–403

Sønderskov KM, Daugbjerg C (2011) The state and consumer confidence in eco-labelling: organic labelling in Denmark, Sweden, the United Kingdom and the United States. Agric Hum Values 28:507–517

Spadoni R, Lombardi P, Canavari M (2014) Private food standard certification: analysis of the brc standard in italian agri-food. Br Food J 116(1):142–164

Teisl MF, Peavey S, Newman F, Buono J, Hermann M (2002) Consumer reactions to environmental labels for forest products: a preliminary look. For Prod J 52(1):44–50

Thøgersen J (2000) Psychological determinants of paying attention to eco-labels in purchase decisions: model development and multinational validation. J Consum Policy 23(3):285–313

Tietenberg T (1998) Disclosure strategies for pollution control. Environ Resour Econ 11 (3–4):587–602

United Nations Conference on Trade and Development (UNCTAD) (2013) Sustainability claims portal. http://www.unctad.info/en/Sustainability-Claims-Portal/. Accessed 20 May 2015

van Dam YK, De Jonge J (2015) The positive side of negative labelling. J Consum Policy 38 (1):19–38

van Dam YK, van Trijp H (2011) Cognitive and motivational structure of sustainability. J Econ Psychol 32:726–741

Von Geibler J (2013) Market-based governance for sustainability in value chains: conditions for successful standard setting in the palm oil sector. J Clean Prod 56:39–53

Ward DO, Clark CD, Jensen KL, Yen ST, Russell CS (2011) Factors influencing willingness-to-pay for the ENERGY STAR label. Energy Policy 39(3):1450–1458

Wilkinson J (2007) Fair trade: dynamic and dilemmas of a market oriented global social movement. J Consum Policy 30:219–329

World Commission on Environment and Development (WCED) (1987) Our common future (Brundtland report). Policy report. Oxford University Press, Oxford

World Summit on Sustainable Development (WSSD) (2002) Plan of implementation. United Nations, Johannesburg

Eva van der Zee is a Postdoc at Wageningen University, researching trust and contractual relations. She conducted PhD research on sustainability standards in the EU and WTO legal framework at the Law and Governance group and Marketing and Behaviour group of Wageningen University using doctrinal and empirical methods. She was a visiting researcher at the NYU and the EUI and participated in the Ius Commune research school. She obtained an LL.B. in law and economics from Utrecht University, and two LL.M. degrees: International Trade and Investment Law from the University of Amsterdam and Fundamentals of Law from Utrecht University (cum laude).

Environmental Sustainability and the Food System

Alessandro Banterle, Elena Claire Ricci, and Alessia Cavaliere

Abstract The food system and the natural environment are closely linked. Indeed, food production strongly relies on environmental resources and services, and releases outputs into the environment. This implies that food-related activities can create negative externalities for the environment, for example related to overexploitation and pollution, given that the market fails to deliver the socially optimum level of resource use and/or pollution. Given this market failure, public intervention is required to regulate such activities. Public intervention can take different forms, from no intervention to simple guidelines up to strict regulation. Indeed, regulation can follow either an approach that outlines general principles or that fixes specific standards, or that promotes information and education.

The aim of this chapter is to highlight the issues of environmental sustainability in the context of the agri-food system and to discuss current public and private initiatives that regulate the market from an environmental perspective. Thus, in this chapter we firstly introduce the concept of sustainability, including all the three pillars (profit, people and planet) and then discuss the issues of environmental sustainability related to food. Moreover, we discuss the different forms of public intervention and then we present European regulation that relates to environmental sustainability within the food system, including public and private voluntary initiatives. Furthermore, we discuss the interest of consumers for environmental sustainability and their perception of the impact of food production on the environment. Moreover, we analyse synergies between environmental sustainability and health issues. Concluding remarks follow.

A. Banterle · E. C. Ricci (✉) · A. Cavaliere
Department of Environmental Science and Policy, Università degli Studi di Milano, Milano, Italy
e-mail: alessandro.banterle@unimi.it; elenaclaire.ricci@unimi.it; alessia.cavaliere@unimi.it

H. Bremmers, K. Purnhagen (eds.), *Regulating and Managing Food Safety in the EU*, Economic Analysis of Law in European Legal Scholarship 6,
https://doi.org/10.1007/978-3-319-77045-1_4

1 The Concept of Sustainability

Even if the link between economic development and natural capital has long been known, the consequences of economic growth in terms of environmental degradation and pollution started to be debated by the scientific community in the 1950s and 1960s. An important role was played by the Club of Rome, an international and multi-disciplinary group of scientists, professionals and politicians particularly interested 'in the future of humanity and of the planet',[1] and promoting a holistic intertemporal (across generations) and system approach to the matter. The 'Limits to growth'[2] report firstly highlighted the importance of considering the limited nature of resources and of taking into account future needs:

> We are searching for a model output that represents a world system that is sustainable without sudden and uncontrolled collapse and capable of satisfying the basic material requirements of all of its people.

The concepts of limits ('imposed by current state of technology and social organisation'[3]) and of needs are also the core of the first and most recognized definition of sustainability, that dates from 1987 when the Brundtland Commission,[4] in the 'Our common future' report, defined sustainable development as:

> development which meets the needs of current generations without compromising the ability of future generations to meet their own needs[5];

This document is one of the first global 'notices' suggesting that countries and society should seek economic growth via decisions that can 'sustain this and the coming generations',[6] and that what would subsequently be called 'green-growth' can also address poverty and development issues. Indeed, sustainability is not only a recipe for developed countries:

> the goals of economic and social development must be defined in terms of sustainability in all countries - developed or developing, market-oriented or centrally planned.[7]

One of the main contributions of the Brundtland report is of having gone beyond its original call by the UN, that was related only to environmental concerns, and highlighted the need to integrate environmental, social and economic growth issues:

---

[1] See http://www.clubofrome.org/.

[2] Meadows et al. (1972), p. 158.

[3] World Commission on Environment and Development (1987), p. 16.

[4] The Brundtland Commission was the UN World Commission on Environment and Development that was appointed by the UN to discuss 'a global agenda for change', and who's chairman was Gro Harlem Brundtland (that subsequently became Prime Minister of Norway), that gave the name to the Commission.

[5] World Commission on Environment and Development (1987), p. 41.

[6] World Commission on Environment and Development (1987), p. 11.

[7] World Commission on Environment and Development (1987), p. 41.

> The environment does not exist as a sphere separate from human actions, ambitions, and needs, and attempts to defend in isolation from human concerns have given the very word "environment" a connotation of naivety [...]. But the "environment" is where we all live; and "development" is what we all do in attempting to improve our lot within that abode. The two are inseparable.[8]

The report, in its definition of sustainable development, highlighted the need to take into consideration both intra-generational issues and inter-generational issues, that are often unaccounted for when taking decisions, at all levels. Indeed, another very important concept related to sustainability is interconnectivity and seeing the world as a system, where all parts relate to each other in space and time.

This has strong implications on policies and regulation, as global societal and environmental problems often cannot be addressed by single countries alone, but need to be addressed globally. Before the Brundtland Commission, an attempt to face environmental and social issues on a global level was done in 1972 in Stockholm during the UN Conference on the Human Environment that focused on human interactions with the environment and produced the so-called Stockholm declaration.[9] This is a document that presents 26 principles on environment and development with which:

> The Conference calls upon Governments and peoples to exert common efforts for the preservation and improvement of the human environment, for the benefit of all the people and for their posterity.[10]

Such principles included considerations on human rights, natural resources, pollution, developing countries, institutions, policies, cooperation, and weapons. The conference also defined an 'Action Plan for the Human Environment' with several (hundreds) recommendations.

The next important attempt to find global and commonly agreed solutions was the Earth Summit—the United Nations Conference on Environment and Development—held in Rio de Janeiro in 1992. This event gathered 178 governmental delegations, about 2400 non-governmental representatives and over 5000 members of the press, making it the largest global event since then.

Outcomes of the Conference were: Agenda 21, the Rio Declaration on Environment and Development, the Statement of Forest Principles, the United Nations Framework Convention on Climate Change, and the United Nations Convention on Biological Diversity.

After 10 years, in 2002 another global meeting was organised in Johannesburg, the World Summit on Sustainable Development (WSSD), focused mainly on the governance issues and on political and social aspects. After another 10 years the UN organised the Rio+20 Earth Summit—the United Nations Conference on Sustainable Development—held in Rio de Janeiro in 2012.

---

[8] World Commission on Environment and Development (1987), p. 7.

[9] UNEP (1972).

[10] UNEP (1972).

Since then the concept of sustainability has evolved into a not very well defined umbrella term that can cover about everything and anything depending on the context, and thus a fully defined and accepted definition does not exist in the literature. In general, all definitions include at least three pillars: economy, environment, and society or, as other scholars refer to, people, planet, and profit. Then, depending on the context and application, these pillars can be—and have been—extended or developed.[11] Nevertheless, in all cases it defines a way to approach problems and decisions, that calls for a wide, multidisciplinary and across-generations vision, and for distrusting narrow perspectives as they are too limited and short-sighted.

At the European Union (EU) level, since 2015 sustainable development is promoted mainly via the 2030 Agenda for Sustainable Development.[12] This agenda builds on the previous Millennium Development Goals (MDGs) and proposes Sustainable Development Goals (SDGs) to be achieved by 2030. These are 17 goals aimed at tackling: poverty, hunger, health and well-being, education, gender equality, sustainable management of environmental resources, energy, sustainable economic growth and industrialisation, sustainable consumption and production, climate change, issues of equity, social inclusion, and global partnership. The EU plans to target such goals by implementing a set of coherent internal policies, but also with external action to favour global implementation.

If we focus on the food system, current regulation is set in the framework of human-rights obligations, safeguarding the fundamental freedoms, in relation to providing 'adequate' food[13] considering a high level of environmental protection. In the context of sustainable development, the inter-generational and intra-generational equity issues relate, for example, also to:

- the right to food today (for all);
- the right to food tomorrow (for all);
- the right for a liveable planet (for all).

Other important links between sustainability and the food system relate to food quality, public health, the use of resources, emissions, landscape and land use.

In the following sections we will focus mainly on environmental sustainability.

2 Issues of Environmental Sustainability of the Food System

The links between food and the environment are very strong.

---

[11]Ricci (2013), pp. 19–25.

[12]COM(2016) 740 final, pp. 3–9.

[13]van der Meulen et al. (2014), p. 2.

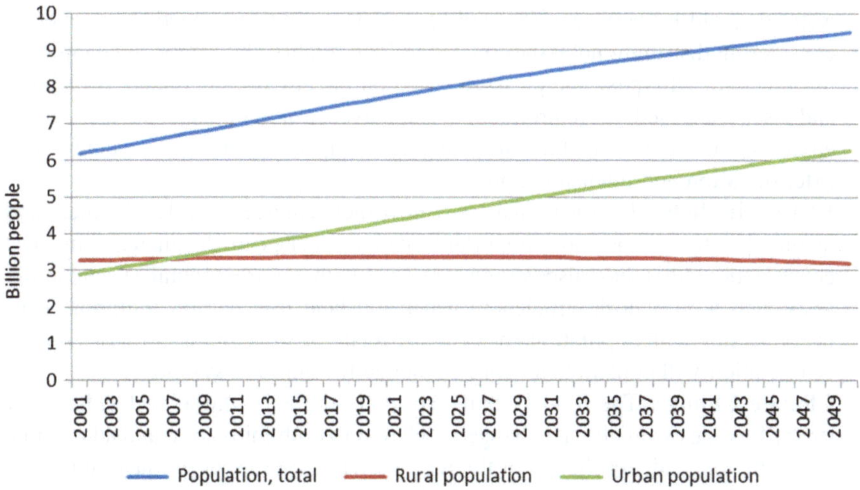

Fig. 1 Projected population growth. Source: Adapted from World Bank data

Firstly, the food system relies on the environment for most of its primary inputs, especially related to agriculture: water, land, soil, seeds, nutrients, biodiversity, fish stock, energy, etc. Inputs are taken from the natural environment at virtually all stages of the food system: agriculture, processing, transport, retailing, consumption, and disposal.

Secondly, another important link is related to the outputs of production, consumption or disposal, that are introduced in the natural environment (products, air/water/land emissions, residual water, food and other waste, drug resistance, etc.).

Thirdly, the food system also relies on ecosystem services such as 'biocapacity',[14] resource regeneration, flood control, weather control, erosion, pest control, pollination, etc. Indeed, agri-food productivity is strongly related to the environment: climate, weather, soil and water conditions, erosion, etc.

Moreover, the food system is currently facing many issues linked to environmental sustainability that relate to the following points.

- **Population growth.** World population is growing and projections suggest that it will reach nine and a half billions by 2050 (Fig. 1).[15] Moreover, the predictions indicate that most of the growth will take place in developing countries and that two thirds of the population will live in urban areas. This implies that food production will have to drastically increase, especially in specific parts of the world. Overall, food-crop demand in 2050 is projected to grow by 70–85%, and

[14]Biocapacity is usually referred to the capacity of ecosystems to produce useful biological materials and to absorb polluting materials generated by humans.

[15]http://databank.worldbank.org.

water demand by between 30% and 85%.[16] This challenge needs to be met by considering distributional issues related to food quality and safety, availability of resources (of all types), the pressure posed on the environment, land availability and use. Increased food production can have strong impacts on the natural environment and on human-wellbeing. Impacts can arise both with extensification and intensification.[17]

- **Change in diets.** Historical data show how diets change with development and income.[18] One of the most important changes relates to the increase in meat consumption, that has also strong linkages with environmental sustainability associated with: calorie efficiency; water and land use; carbon footprint. This, in connection with population growth—especially in developing countries—, and urbanisation will constitute a major challenge for the food system.
- **Climate Change.** The food system, especially the agricultural sector, has very strong linkages with climate change in relation to both mitigation and adaptation.

  On the one side, each step of the food system (from input production to final consumption and disposal) is responsible for greenhouse gas emissions. Data indicates that, for example, in the US 16% of energy use is related to food, and this has in turn an impact on the sector's emissions.[19] IPCC data show that agriculture, forestry and other land use (AFOLU) are responsible for 20–24% of global greenhouse gas emissions, 'mainly from deforestation and agricultural emissions from livestock, soil and nutrient management'.[20] This means that, globally, it is the second largest emitting sector, after the energy sector.[21]

  On the other side, agricultural productivity is projected to be strongly influenced by changes in climate in relation to temperature, floods, draught and other changes. Some areas of the world are supposed to gain from increases in mean temperature, while large parts of South America, Africa and South-East Asia will most likely incur losses in productivity, up to 50%.[22] Many of the areas that are expected to be vulnerable to climate change already have high levels of undernourished population.[23]

  Overall, in recent years yields have been declining or stabilizing. A study from UNEP estimates that 'the combined effects of climate change, land degradation, cropland losses, water scarcity and species infestations may induce a strong reduction in yields.[24] At the same time, the increase in general energy demand could lead to an increase in prices of fertilizers and pesticides. Moreover, the

[16]Millennium Ecosystem Assessment (2005a), p. 17.

[17]Smith et al. (2010), p. 2942.

[18]WHO/FAO (2003), pp. 20–22; Stranieri and Banterle (2015), p. 22.

[19]USDA (2010), p. 12.

[20]IPCC (2014), p. 9; Smith et al. (2014), p. 816.

[21]IPCC (2014), p. 9.

[22]Nellemann et al. (2009), p. 46.

[23]UNEP (2012), p. 71.

[24]Nellemann et al. (2009), pp. 6–7.

report estimates that 'if losses in cropland area and yields are only partially compensated for food production could potentially become up to 25% short of demand by 2050'.[25]

A recent report from the OECD estimates that by 2060, globally, climate change impacts on agriculture may generate a 0.8% GDP loss, which is quite significant given that the GDP share of agriculture is modest in many regions of the world.[26]

- **Resource distribution.** Studies indicate that there is enough food to feed the world's population[27]; however, FAO estimates that in 2014–16 there are still about 800 million people that suffer from undernourishment.[28] Although, the number has decreased significantly in the last decade, this is still slightly higher than the 2015 Millennium Development Goal 1 that aimed at 'halving the proportion of the chronically undernourished' from 1990 to 2015.[29] At the same time, in other parts of the world we have problems related to over-nutrition and food waste. The problem is related to resource distribution. Figure 2 depicts the areas of the world that suffer the most from hunger.[30] Undernutrition is a complex and multi-dimensional issue that needs a holist approach to be tackled. It is mainly connected to poverty and food accessibility. A crucial role is played by food self-sufficiency that has strong linkages to the use of natural resources and the environment.
- **Resource depletion and food waste.** One of the main issues that triggered the discussions about sustainability and sustainable development is related to resource depletion. The Millennium Ecosystem Assessment[31] report highlights that 60% of the ecosystems services analysed during the assessment are being exploited in an 'unsustainable' manner to meet rapidly growing demands for food, feed, fresh water, timber, fibre, fuel, and raw materials. These services include: 'fresh water, capture fisheries, air and water purification, and the regulation of regional and local climate, natural hazards, and pests'.[32] Indeed, according to this assessment, the supply of food is one of the most important causes for this degradation.[33] In addition to overexploitation also pollution is an important source for ecosystem disruption. In relation to the food system, the most relevant source is agriculture, especially when it is done in an intensive way

[25]Nellemann et al. (2009), p. 7.

[26]OECD (2015), p. 58.

[27]Leathers and Foster (2009), p. 433.

[28]FAO, IFAD and WFP (2015), p. 8; UN (2015), p. 20.

[29]FAO, IFAD and WFP (2015), p. 9; UN (2015), p. 20.

[30]'Undernourishment means that a person is not able to acquire enough food to meet the daily minimum dietary energy requirements, over a period of one year. FAO defines hunger as being synonymous with chronic undernourishment' (http://www.fao.org/hunger/en/).

[31]Millennium Ecosystem Assessment (2005a), p. 6.

[32]Millennium Ecosystem Assessment (2005a), p. 6.

[33]Millennium Ecosystem Assessment (2005a), p. 6.

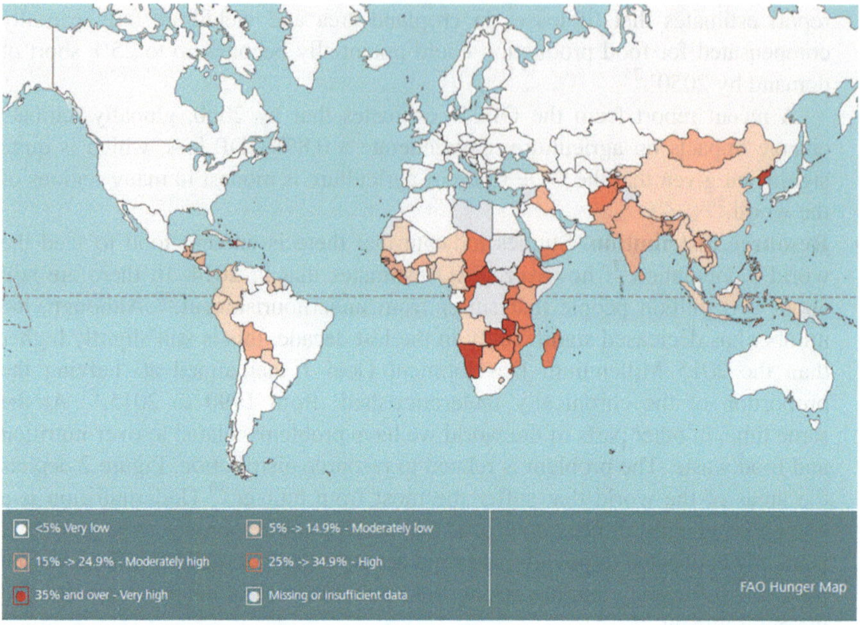

Fig. 2 Levels of undernutrition estimated by FAO for 2014–2016. Source: Food and Agriculture Organization of the United Nations, 2017, FAO hunger map, http://www.fao.org/hunger/en/. Reproduced with permission

and with a strong reliance on pesticides and fertilizers. Resource depletion could also be connected to food waste, if resources are used to produce food for human consumption that is not used for that. The result of this wasteful use of resources may then add to the environmental and land-use issues related to waste disposal.

- **Loss of Biodiversity.** The Millennium Ecosystem Assessment report on Biodiversity[34] highlights how in the last decades ecosystems have been dramatically impacted at unprecedented levels and speed, with a consequent strong loss of biodiversity. Biodiversity loss is related to habitat and ecosystems' degradation, fragmentation, climate change, invasive species, loss of coral reefs, overexploitation, and pollution.[35] Causes strictly related to the food system are catch of fish, use of fertilizers and pesticides, irrigation, change in land use, and land cover.[36] It needs to be highlighted that the challenge of preserving biodiversity is (among other things) strictly related to food security issues in the long-run.

[34]Millennium Ecosystem Assessment (2005a), p. 2.

[35]Millennium Ecosystem Assessment (2005b), pp. 8–10.

[36]Millennium Ecosystem Assessment (2005a), p. vii.

- **Land competition.** From an economic perspective, the production sectors that are more land intense are related to: food, feed, livestock, forestry, non-food crops, and the energy sector (crop and non-crop based production). Such activities are then in competition with the conservation of natural habitat[37] and other less extent land uses (residential, infrastructures, industry, etc.). In 2012, cultivated systems[38] occupied about 24% of the total earth surface.[39] Considering only land area, 38% is already dedicated to agriculture, 31% to forestry, and 31% to other uses.[40] Of the land dedicated to agriculture, 32% is occupied by arable land and permanent crops and 68% by permanent meadows and pastures. Increase in food production will have to deal with the strong competition for land, in a growing world.

Given all the issues that the food system will have to face in the next decades and the strong links between the food system and the environment and society, it is important to regulate activities considering sustainability issues. More in detail,

> actions such as the integration of ecosystem management goals in various sectors (such as agriculture, forestry, finance, trade, and health), increased transparency and accountability of government and private-sector performance in ecosystem management, elimination of perverse subsidies, greater use of economic instruments and market-based approaches, empowerment of groups dependent on ecosystem services or affected by their degradation, promotion of technologies enabling increased crop yields without harmful environmental impacts, ecosystem restoration, and the incorporation of nonmarket values of ecosystems and their services in management decisions all could substantially lessen the severity of these problems in the next several decades.[41]

Indeed, one of the most important regulatory problems to solve is the accounting of externalities and finding appropriate ways to manage common goods. Resource depletion and ecosystem degradation and the consequent loss in ecosystem services is related to the fact that markets exist for certain natural resources and their related products such as food, fresh water, timber, fibre, and fuel, but not for the conservation of the services that produce or support such rivalrous goods, and thus the value for such services is often neglected and not perceived. Therefore, there are no incentives for short-sighted private agents to protect common goods, especially when the costs are borne by future generations.

Most of the direct impacts described above are related to food production but indirect impacts are also related to food consumption and changes in lifestyles, thus policies should affect both the production and the consumption side.

At the EU level, the most relevant issues do not concern so much population growth and diet changes, in terms of large increases in animal-derived products, that

[37]Smith et al. (2010), p. 2941.

[38]That are defined as areas where at least 30 of the landscape is cultivated (Millennium Ecosystem Assessment 2005a).

[39]Millennium Ecosystem Assessment (2005a), p. 3.

[40]FAOSTAT data for 2012. Available at http://faostat3.fao.org/browse/E/EL/E.

[41]Millennium Ecosystem Assessment (2005a), p. 2.

tend to be more stable compared to developing countries, but more climate-altering emissions, resource depletion, biodiversity loss, and land competition.

The EU response to these issues is sketched—in general terms—in the 2030 Agenda for Sustainable Development[42] whose environmental-related goals will be achieved mainly by: (i) focusing on resource efficiency, sustainable consumption and production for the promotion of the transition towards a more circular economy; (ii) supporting conservation and sustainable management of natural resources; (iii) working to achieve coordinated and coherent global actions for common public goods; (iv) integrating environmental and climate objective in development cooperation strategies; (v) promoting a widespread access to clean energy.

3 Public Intervention

As highlighted in the previous sections, a market failure in the provision of environmental protection exists. Indeed, private agents traditionally do not have strong market incentives to avoid overexploitation of common environmental goods or pollution. Even if recent trends in consumer preferences show an increasing interest for the protection of the environment, especially in developed countries, the emerging market-related incentives motivating firms to adopt more environmentally-friendly measures are not enough to deliver the socially optimal levels of environmental protection, thus, public intervention is still necessary to regulate economic activities on such issues.

Regulation can take different forms that include different levels of intervention, such as outlining general principles, implementing information or education schemes, providing incentives, or fixing standards.

Focusing on principle or standard based regulation, the latter aims at defining with a certain degree of detail the restrictions for the regulated behaviour, trying to avoid regulatory gaps.[43] Such regulations reduce to the maximum the uncertainty of interpretation and allow for limited (if any) flexibility of action for the regulated agents. These, in the food context, are meant as strong warranties for consumer safety. Nevertheless, they may not be optimal alone when there is a high level of uncertainty about the possible risks and these cannot be identified at the onset of the activities and regulation.[44] For example, fixing very conservative concentration thresholds on particular substances does not protect consumers from the effects of other substances, whose negative impacts were unknown at the time the regulation was enacted. On the one side, they may provide specific guidelines that need to be

[42]COM(2016) 740 final, pp. 12–14.

[43]van der Meulen et al. (2014), p. 5.

[44]van der Meulen et al. (2014), p. 5.

followed, thus limiting interpretation or creativity-requirements and uncertainty for agents.[45] But, on the other side, it can be more cumbersome to access or comply with a large number of detailed requirements with respect to principles,[46] leaving the question of effectiveness in promoting compliance an open one. Nevertheless, a strong monitoring and enforcement effort is required from state-institutions. Fixing strict regulation unilaterally may also limit economic competitiveness of domestic economic agents, especially when standards refer to production process or facilities that do not lead to a positive change in the quality profile of the product. For example, national environmental standards imposed on production plants, with the aim of reducing pollution, generate additional costs for domestic producers, but not for foreign ones producing and exporting the same product. Other standards that affect product characteristics instead imply adequacy costs for all producers. Nevertheless, in certain cases, stricter regulation may increase the ability of companies in being competitive on the global market,[47] and also induce other countries to enact similar regulation.[48]

Principles-based regulation takes a different stand-point and defines very general principles that should be followed by the agents, leaving the details to the application of the principles.[49] Indeed, the interpretation of the principles can make them become quite precise, even if not necessarily univocal.[50] Principles compared to standards are meant to leave more flexibility to agents; nevertheless, there are real-life applications whereby compliance strategies are quite uniform.[51] In a principle-based setting, the attribution of responsibilities and liabilities becomes crucial,[52] while in a standard-based setting economic agents are not held responsible if they are in compliance with regulation, and thus may lead to 'minimalist approaches' to compliance.[53]

In the food domain, regulation takes various forms, some that are more principle-based and some that are more standard-based, depending both on the country legislative framework and on the target of the regulation. Garcia Martinez et al.[54] organise government intervention in six options: no intervention, self-regulation, co-regulation, information and education, incentive-based structures, direct command and control intervention. No intervention is a governmental stand-point whereby the regulatory institution decides not to take action on a specific issue, for different possible reasons, even though this decision is not without implications.

[45]Black (2008), pp. 452–454.

[46]van der Meulen et al. (2014), p. 8.

[47]Porter (1990), p. 88.

[48]van der Meulen et al. (2014), p. 1.

[49]van der Meulen et al. (2014), pp. 5–6.

[50]Black (2008), pp. 446–447.

[51]Black (2008), p. 447.

[52]Bremmers et al. (2015), p. 4.

[53]Garcia Martinez et al. (2007), p. 300.

[54]Garcia Martinez et al. (2007), p. 301.

Self-regulation relates to voluntary initiatives or rules that firms impose to themselves to provide quality assurance to customers, improve communication with consumers, and increase firm reputation. Co-regulation refers to public-private instruments aimed at developing shared codes of practice and action plans. For instance, in recent years, EU regulation has given to private agents an increasingly active role for what concerns food safety controls. For example, importers are asked to set up self-monitoring tools to verify that their products respect the Maximum Residue Limits (MRLs) for pesticides imposed by EU law.[55] Information and education refer to all of those initiatives aimed at informing and educating citizens and consumers. These include labelling schemes that provide more information to consumers, the publishing of scientific evidence about specific issues that are of interest to the public debate, education initiatives in schools, information and education public campaigns. Incentive-based structures include subsidy, tax, and limits on emissions based on cap-and-trade mechanisms, aimed at creating market incentives for the target behaviour. Examples may be the incentives for farmers to promote biodiversity or environmental and climate benefits set by the greening mechanism of the Common Agricultural Policy. Finally, the strongest type of intervention is direct command and control. This includes measures that indicate specific rules that agents need to follow, accompanied by public enforcement and monitoring schemes with a related sanction structure.

The above options of public intervention confirm, in the food context, the trend of including non-state actors in designing regulatory mechanisms highlighted by the literature on decentralised regulation.[56] Julia Black provides a very open and inclusive definition of regulation, identifying a set of more and less traditional actors that in some way are involved in designing regulation: state institutions (like, national or international agencies, ministries, etc.); non-state institutions (such as associations, firms, communities, etc.); economic forces (markets); social forces (among which norms, cultures, institutions, etc.); technologies (as enablers of manipulation and change).[57]

In this context, co-regulation and self-regulation are good examples of firm or network involvement in regulation. In the food sector, also consumers play an important role in defying the specific attributes deriving from self or co-regulation that can have success in the market. When dealing with consumers, an important policy instrument next to standards and principles is information measures. This can influence consumer perception, for example, with the adoption of labelling and certification schemes that can be introduced by state-institutions (e.g., Eco-label), firms (private schemes) or international and national organisations (e.g., Fair Trade, Dolphin Safe, etc.).

[55]Rouvière and Caswell (2012), p. 248.

[56]Black (2002), p. 2.

[57]Black (2002), p. 16.

4 Regulatory Framework in the EU

In the EU there is no structured comprehensive legal framework for environmentally sustainable measures connected to agri-food production. Sustainability is mentioned in a number of treaty articles and regulations, but it remains at a very general level.

For example, Article 3 of the Treaty on European Union specifies that:

> The Union [. . .] shall work for the sustainable development of Europe based on balanced economic growth and price stability, a highly competitive social market economy, aiming at full employment and social progress, and a high level of protection and improvement of the quality of the environment.[58]

Moreover, the Treaty on the Functioning of the European Union (TFEU) prohibits quantitative restrictions on imports between Member States (Article 34), unless they can (among others) be justified on the grounds of "the protection of health and life of humans, animals or plants" (Article 36).[59] Article 114 sets the principle by which:

> The Commission, in its proposals envisaged in paragraph 1 concerning health, safety, environmental protection and consumer protection, will take as a base a high level of protection, taking account in particular of any new development based on scientific facts. Within their respective powers, the European Parliament and the Council will also seek to achieve this objective.[60]

In the food context, Regulation 178/2002, that establishes the general principles of food law, calls for the adoption of the precautionary principle whenever there is scientific uncertainty about possible harmful effects on health related to food (Article 7). Moreover, the same Regulation specifies that one of its objectives is to protect "animal health and welfare, plant health and the environment" (Article 5). More in detail, the regulation indicates that risk assessment should include "societal, economic, traditional, ethical and environmental factors".[61] All of the above principles will have environmental impacts following their applications, nevertheless, there are no specific rules connected to the practices to improve the environmental sustainability dimension of food production.

In any case, within the EU agri-food regulatory framework it is still possible to highlight five fields where action related to environmental sustainability has been taken: the Common Agricultural Policy (CAP); the Common Fisheries Policy (CFP); food waste; voluntary measures related to public standards for environmental practices; and private standards. In relation to the most relevant environmental issues for the EU highlighted in Sect. 2, the CAP currently tries to tackle biodiversity loss and land competition. Resource depletion is (partly) addressed by the CFP and food

[58]Consolidated version of the Treaty on European Union, Article 3.

[59]Consolidated version of the TFEU, Articles 34–36.

[60]Consolidated version of the TFEU, Article 114.

[61]Recital 19 of the Preamble to Regulation 178/2002.

waste regulation. Whereas issues connected to climate change are not tackled by specific structured measures.

4.1 Common Agricultural Policy

The CAP is the oldest common policy and it was introduced to support the agricultural sector. During the 1960s and 1970s, the support was mainly based on a price policy aimed at keeping internal prices above the global market level through a complex system based on market intervention and border measures. This policy brought about a strong increase of production such that the EU switched from being a net importer to a net exporter of agri-food products. The strongest downside was the high levels of production surplus and the related high costs, especially during the 1980s.[62]

In the 1990s, the MacSharry reform reduced the level of the guaranteed prices and, at the same time, introduced a support based on unit of land. This reform was the first to introduce specific measures related to the environmental dimension of agricultural production. In particular, Regulation 2078/1992 provided support for environmentally-friendly agricultural practices, like low impact production systems (organic agriculture and integrated-pest-management production), active management of pastures and meadows, agronomic techniques for soil and water conservation, practices for landscape care, etc.[63] Furthermore, Regulation 2080/1992 supported the afforestation of cultivated land.

The next reform was based on the 'Agenda 2000' document, which reinforced the switch of the support from a productive view to an environmentally-conscious one, integrating environmental objectives into the CAP. Agenda 2000 divided the CAP in two pillars: the first included direct-payments to farmers and market measures, the second was focused on all measures connected to rural development.[64] The agri-environmental measures and afforestation became part of this second pillar. Agenda 2000 also introduced in the CAP the concept of 'multifunctionality', i.e., the fact that agriculture provides not only tradable goods and services, but also other benefits for society, such as environmental preservation, landscape care, employment, etc. These benefits are defined by OECD as 'non-commodity outputs' and can be considered as positive externalities or public goods.[65]

The following reforms of the CAP (Mid-term Review and Health Check) develop the aims and concepts of Agenda 2000. In particular, the Mid-term Review (or Fischler Reform) introduced the decoupling of direct payments, making them

---

[62]Segrè (2008), pp. 144–145.
[63]OECD (2005), p. 142.
[64]Segrè (2008), p. 148.
[65]OECD (2001), p. 13.

independent from production, and made 'cross-compliance' compulsory.[66] This measure, firstly introduced by Agenda 2000, establishes that direct payments are allowed only to farmers that are in compliance with regulation concerning environment, food safety, labour and so on.

In 2010, a Communication by the European Commission shaping the CAP toward 2020 specifically indicates that "to preserve the food production potential on a sustainable basis throughout the EU, so as to guarantee long-term food security" is the first aim of the CAP.[67]

The latest version of the CAP reform, published in December 2013, emerges from a complete revision of the Policy that takes into account the proposed aim. The two pillars are maintained and their linkages are strengthened, and "a more holistic and integrated approach to policy support" is adopted.[68] The new policy moves "from product to producer support and [. . .] to a more land-based approach" answering to external economic, environmental and territorial factors, the environmental ones being "resource efficiency, soil and water quality and threats to habitats and biodiversity".[69] From an environmental point of view, the main innovation introduced by the new payment-scheme is 'greening', that relates to farm practices that 'deliver environmental and climate benefits as part of their everyday activities'.[70] This is a specific payment that farmers can receive if they follow particular rules related to: crop diversification, grassland maintenance, and ecological focus areas. In this way, farmers are rewarded for the provision of both private and public goods. Another important change relates to the increased budget flexibility provided to Member States that takes into consideration the different climate, environmental and socio-economic conditions.[71]

4.2 *Common Fisheries Policy*

The Common Fisheries Policy (CFP) is the EU regulatory framework for fishing and aquaculture activities whose aim is to "ensure that fishing and aquaculture are environmentally, economically and socially sustainable and that they provide a source of healthy food for EU citizens".[72] The policy was first enacted in the 1970s and the latest version dates 2014. It sets out the rules that need to be followed by operators to, on the one side, ensure that fish stocks are harvested at a sustainable rate, and on the other side, that all EU fishing fleets have equal access. Fish

---

[66]Sorrentino et al. (2011), pp. 2–4.

[67]COM(2010) 672 final, p. 2.

[68]European Commission (2013a), p. 1.

[69]European Commission (2013a), p. 2.

[70]McMahon and Cardwell (2015), p. 453.

[71]European Commission (2013a), p. 5.

[72]EU Fisheries—CFP, accessible at: https://ec.europa.eu/fisheries/cfp_en.

stocks are a finite common resource that needs to be managed appropriately for it to be 'renewable' in the long term. The CFP is based on four main policy areas: fisheries management, international policy, market and trade policy, funding of the policy.[73] Fisheries management includes some relevant instruments for sustainability, like[74]:

(i) Total Allowable Catches (TACs), i.e., catch limits imposed for certain fish stocks, that are applied to the single EU countries by means of national quotas, that can be also exchanged between countries;
(ii) fishing effort restrictions introduced for some specific stocks over and above the TACs to limit fleet capacity and the time spent at sea by the same fleet;
(iii) technical measures related to fish measurements, net sizes, fishing gear, by-catches, zonal or seasonal restrictions.

International policy refers to the fishing agreements for fishing out of EU waters and to the initiatives to promote a sustainable international governance of seas and oceans. Other sustainability related measures concern the common organisation of the markets. This regards a set of instruments to empower economic agents:

> producers are responsible for ensuring the sustainable exploitation of natural resources and equipped with instrument to better market their products. Consumers receive more and better information on the products sold on the EU market, which, regardless of their origin, must comply with the same rules[75]

Among the different instruments developed, those more related to environmental sustainability are marketing standards and consumer information. The former define the characteristics that products sold in the EU need to have, independently from their origin. The latter establish the mandatory information that must be given to consumers (final consumers and/or mass-caterers). Article 35 of Regulation 1379/2013 imposes to specify for a set of fishery and aquaculture products several information among which: the exact species, the production method, the area where the fish was caught or farmed, and the type of fishing gear adopted. This is a useful tool to provide consumers with the necessary information to make (at least partly) informed choices in relation to fish stocks management and protection of ecosystems. In this direction the EU is also studying the feasibility of adopting a common eco-labelling system for fish products.

4.3 Food Waste

At the EU level, a specific legal framework regarding food waste has not yet been developed. Nevertheless, the Directive 98/2008 on waste establishes a general

[73]EU Fisheries—CFP, accessible at: https://ec.europa.eu/fisheries/cfp_en.

[74]EU Fisheries—Managing fisheries, available at: https://ec.europa.eu/fisheries/cfp/fishing_rules.

[75]EU Fisheries—Market organisation, accessible at https://ec.europa.eu/fisheries/cfp/market.

'waste hierarchy' indicating the priorities for waste prevention and management. Such hierarchy includes five levels of action:

- prevention;
- preparing for re-use;
- recycling;
- other recovery, e.g. energy recovery;
- disposal.

The application of this scheme to the food system can be related to the following actions. The first step concerns the prevention of waste at the source, this relates to all the measures that can be done in the different steps of the food supply chain and to a correct behaviour in planning and preparing meals at the household level. The second step can be linked to the distribution of food surplus to charities and people in need, as mentioned by the Feeding the 5000 report.[76] The part of food that is not fit for human consumption can be diverted to animal feed. The third step is related to the composting of the waste. The fourth step refers to the use of food waste for energy or heat production. Finally, the last option is for food waste to become a real waste to be disposed.

The European Commission estimated that in the EU 88 million tonnes of food are wasted yearly.[77] The policy process is still ongoing and the Commission states that "every opportunity to prevent food waste and strengthen sustainability of the food system" should be searched.[78] In the Communication 'A resource-efficient Europe – Flagship initiative under the Europe 2020 Strategy' the Commission calls for a general increase in resource efficiency, including agri-food products. This document represents a general 'framework for policies to support the shift towards a resource-efficient and low-carbon economy'.[79] In this context, agri-food products play an important role and a revision of the CAP and of the Common Fishery Policy is invoked. Food waste is also one of the issues tackled by the EU response to the UN 2030 Agenda for Sustainable Development goal concerning sustainable consumption and production (SDG12). An EU Platform on Food Losses and Food Waste will be developed to contribute to the UN target of halving per capita global food waste by 2030.[80]

Furthermore, in 2014 the European Commission promoted a 'circular economy' approach that emphasises to design the different steps of production, distribution and consumption keeping in mind the need to reduce waste.[81] In the circular economy concept the whole life of products is considered from the initial design and planning

[76] Feeding the 5000 (2015).

[77] http://ec.europa.eu/food/safety/food_waste/index_en.htm. Accessed on September 5, 2017.

[78] http://ec.europa.eu/food/safety/food_waste/index_en.htm.

[79] COM(2011) 21, p. 6.

[80] COM(2016) 739 final, p. 9.

[81] COM(2014) 398 final.

to its final destination. In this context, the opportunities for recycling represent a key step to close the circle from outputs to inputs.

More specifically related to food, there are regulations that indirectly may have an impact on food waste, for example those targeting risk material for the protection of human health. Bremmers et al.[82] discuss how general principles related to food safety requirements (like for example the precautionary principle of Regulation 178/2002) and the attribution of responsibility may induce excess precaution and, consequently, food waste in the case of durability dating. One of the arguments being that the lack of regulatory certainty may generate multiple levels of control and precautionary margins. On the other hand very restrictive standards may also generate food waste in relation to those products that do not meet the standards. For instance, Waarts et al.[83] describe how regulations concerning food contaminants for warrantying animal and human food safety can generate food waste. A similar argument can be made also for novel-food legislation and hygiene rules.[84] When very strict and complicated standards are imposed, they may generate difficulty in compliance for producers and this is particularly true for small businesses in developing countries. Considering international trade, such issues can lead to boarder rejections of food products, which often turn into waste as it is not economically viable to find a new market given the perishability problem.

Moreover, food information law can also have an impact on food waste.[85] Durability dating for example has two specifications: use-by and best-before dates. An unclear distinction between these two indications may for example induce consumers to get rid of foodstuff before it becomes unsafe to consume it. At the same time, this uncertainty in the interpretation can generate food waste also from the producer side, when producers chose the date of minimum durability not on the basis of safety considerations but on quality deterioration, for precaution or marketing reasons.[86] Other sources of food waste can be aesthetic and marketing standards, common examples of these are refer to egg size and fruit and vegetables characteristics. Products that do not fit the requirement can be diverted or discarded[87] for marketing reasons not related to safety attributes.

Labelled information about voluntary quality schemes may also generate waste. European policies aimed at protecting quality and tradition attributes of food products impose specific protocols that should be followed by producers. Non-compliance with these quality standards may indeed generate waste,[88] and affect not only firms in the EU but also firms in other producing countries.[89]

---

[82]Bremmers et al. (2015), pp. 4, 14.

[83]Waarts et al. (2011), Appendix 1.2, pp. 82–85 and Bremmers et al. (2015), p. 3.

[84]Waarts et al. (2011), Appendix 1.3 and 1.4, pp. 86–89.

[85]Bremmers et al. (2015), pp. 3–5.

[86]Bremmers et al. (2015), pp. 5–6.

[87]Waarts et al. (2011), pp. 26–29.

[88]Bremmers et al. (2015), pp. 4 and 14.

[89]Trienekens and Zuurbier (2008), p. 108.

4.4 Voluntary Measures

The EU regulatory framework also includes some voluntary measures that economic agents may adopt, but that, once adopted, must be in compliance with specific standards provided by the Commission. In this context, we can analyse two types of standards (EMAS and Ecolabel) related to environmental certification and a specific measure aimed at directly favouring environmentally-friendly (or 'green') producers (GPP).

The Eco-Management and Audit Scheme (EMAS) was developed in 1993 by the European Commission as a tool for assessing, reporting and increasing the performance of organisations in environmental terms.[90] It is applicable to all economic sectors and services with the aim of contributing to sustainable development. It is currently regulated by Regulation 1221/2009. The approach of EMAS is based on the 'Plan-Do-Check-Act' procedure. First the organisation has to carry out an environmental review and adopt an environmental policy with specific targets. Second, it has to implement such policy, establishing an Environmental Management System, and make it openly available. Third, the environmental performance needs to be assessed by independent auditors. Finally, further improving actions need to be devised.

Ecolabel is an instrument that was introduced by the EU Commission in 1992 in order to reduce the environmental impact of goods and services.[91] Its main objective was to create a common voluntary labelling scheme to signal products produced with environmentally-friendlier practices than their regular counterparts. The general idea was to increase consumer trust towards the actual implementation of such practices, by means of third-party certification. Ecolabel is regulated by Regulation 66/2010. In such scheme, products must be in line with a set of environmental criteria, with a particular attention to Life-Cycle Assessment. In this way, the environmental impacts of eco-labelled products must be lower than those of similar products. Ecolabel can be applied only to specific categories of goods, such as, for example, wooden furniture, touristic services, and so on. Food is not included among the eligible products, but agri-tourism farm stays are.

The above two voluntary standards are aimed at reducing asymmetric information between consumers and producers and at making green producers more visible on the market. The Ecolabel scheme also specifically refers to the aim to "provide consumers with accurate, non-deceptive, science-based information on the environmental impact of products".[92] Moreover, both standards promote sustainable development that is one of the aims of the EU.[93]

---

[90]See http://ec.europa.eu/environment/emas/index_en.htm accessed on 5 September 2017.

[91]See http://ec.europa.eu/environment/ecolabel/facts-and-figures.html accessed on 5 September 2017.

[92]Recital 1 of Regulation 66/2010.

[93]Consolidated version of the Treaty on European Union, Article 3; Recital 1 of Regulation 1221/2009; Recital 5 of Regulation 66/2010.

Another voluntary scheme that promotes sustainable development proposed by the EU Commission is green public procurement (GPP). This relates to public authorities purchasing environmentally friendly goods and services. The idea behind this scheme is that public agents are major consumers that can use their purchasing power to promote sustainable products and to set an example for consumers.[94] More in detail, the principles that guide GPP are value for taxpayers' money—including not only strict economic consideration regarding price but also other societal cost/benefits—and fairness, that includes non-discrimination, equal treatment, transparency and proportionality issues.[95] The EU Commission has developed specific criteria for different products, from office equipment to food and catering services. More in detail, Communication 400/2008 indicates that 'GPP relies on having clear and ambitious environmental criteria for products and services' that are also verifiable.

4.5 *Private Standards*

Private standards refer to voluntary initiatives that have arisen next to state driven regulation, with the aim of signalling and certifying environmentally-friendly practices carried out by firms. Such initiatives are proposed to fill the gap between existing public regulation and the emerging consumer demand for food production with lower environmental impacts. With respect to the public voluntary schemes, private standards are often tailored to more specific practices and/or products. Such standards can be divided in two groups: third-party certified schemes and private schemes. As environmental practices are credence attributes of food products, the former type of standards provides more guarantees for consumers, related to the level of independence of the certifying body.

As for the first form, ISO 14000 is a set of tools to manage the environmental performance of firms established by the International Organization for Standardization (ISO). More in detail, such tools relate to rules and procedures connected to environmental management systems and greenhouse gases. ISO 14001 is in some parts similar to EMAS, but it is more diffused at the international level. The subset of ISO 14020s refer to environmental labels and declarations. An example of application to the food system is that of Barilla EPD (Environmental Product Declaration) Process System that applied at the process level of pasta production the ISO 14025 standard.[96]

[94]See http://ec.europa.eu/environment/gpp/index_en.htm accessed on 5 September 2017.

[95]European Commission (2016), p. 21.

[96]Ruini et al. (2012), p. 1.

Other third-party schemes specific for the food sector include a number of labelled certifications that relate to particular products and impacts. Examples of these schemes are[97]:

- Marine Stewardship Council, which aims at protecting the marine ecosystem;
- Friend of the Sea, that supports a responsible fishing system;
- Dolphin Safe, that regards dolphin catches during tuna fishing;
- Rainforest Alliance, that relates to deforestation, biodiversity and rural communities in tropical areas;
- Global Gap, that refers to good agricultural practices;
- Biodiversity Friends, aimed at supporting biodiversity;
- Roundtable on Sustainable Palm Oil, regarding sustainable palm oil production;
- Roundtable on Responsible Soy, that aims at reducing the environmental and social impact of soy production.

Regarding the second form, private schemes, it can be noted that these are developed by companies or groups of companies that intend to adopt environmentally-friendly practices, even if not certified by third-parties. These initiatives can be found, for example, in large retailing companies that can design product lines that follow their own protocols and are marked with specific logos, like 'ProPlanet' products for Rewe group in Germany, or 'Naturama' for Esselunga in Italy.

5 Consumer Perception of Environmental Sustainability and Food

Given the role of private firms in a decentralised regulatory system,[98] it is important to verify to what extent consumers are receptive of the private initiatives and if there is convergence between private and public utility (i.e., what is good the single consumers and for society as a whole). Moreover, recent literature shows how consumers can be important for reducing the environmental impact of production and consumption of goods and services, and how they need to be actively involved to tackle global environmental problems.[99]

Several studies show that consumers are quite aware of the issues of environmental sustainability and of the relation to their own food choices.[100] More in detail, Flash Eurobarometer 367 reports that 84% of EU27 citizens declare that the

[97]Banterle et al. (2013), p. 776.

[98]Black (2002), p. 16.

[99]Seyfang (2006), p. 383; Spaargaren and Mol (2008), p. 350; Evans (2011), p. 109; Grunert et al. (2014), p. 177.

[100]Banterle and Ricci (2013), p. 153; Grunert et al. (2014), p. 184; Vecchio and Annunziata (2015), p. 338.

environmental impact of a product is for them 'very' (38%) or 'fairly important' (46%) when choosing which products to buy.[101] 26% of the respondents declared to 'often' buy environmentally-friendly products, while 54% declared to do it 'sometimes'.[102] Moreover, 89% of the Eurobarometer respondents declared to 'strongly' (50%) or 'tend to agree' (39%) that 'buying environmentally-friendly products can make a real difference to the environment'.[103] Moreover, many respondents believe that the following personal actions related to food have 'the greatest impact on solving environmental problems in their countries': recycling and minimising waste (54% of respondents); buying local agricultural products (35%); making efforts to use less water (31%); buying products by eco-friendly producers (23%).[104]

EU consumers seem to be also willing to change their diets, and in particular their meat consumption, for environmental reasons. More in detail, 80% would 'eat less meat but of certified origin', 72% would 'replace beef or pork with poultry or fish', and 50% would 'replace most of the meat they eat with vegetables'.[105] Indeed, consumers can reduce the environmental impact of their food consumption by purchasing appropriate quantities of food (to reduce food waste), and by paying attention to the impacts of food home processing (washing, cooking, storage).

Consumers may also play an important role when choosing among similar products and are able to influence production and distribution. Indeed, consumers may exert a demand pull, especially in relation to non-mandatory environmental sustainability characteristics that food products may have. Eurobarometer data indicates that 77% of EU citizen declare to be willing to pay a premium price for products that have a low environmental impact, if they are confident that they do so.[106]

As mentioned in the previous section, to convey information about the sustainability properties of food products producers or retailers usually rely on labelled information. In the absence of a strong legislation, such as in the case of environmental sustainability food product features, this may give way to opportunistic behaviour by producers induced by asymmetric information. Indeed, environmental characteristics of food products are, in general, credence attributes[107] related to production and distribution. This means that the consumer is not able to verify the presence of the labelled characteristics.

Information measures such as labels are indeed useful measures. Many EU citizen 'when buying food, check to see if (the product) has a quality label that ensures the

[101]European Commission (2013b), pp. 51–52.
[102]European Commission (2013b), p. 10.
[103]European Commission (2013b), p. 17.
[104]European Commission (2013b), p. 62.
[105]European Commission (2013b), p. 98.
[106]European Commission (2013b), p. 55.
[107]Darby and Karni (1973), p. 68; Caswell and Mojduszka (1996), p. 1249.

food has specific characteristics': 22% do it 'always', 45% do it 'sometimes'.[108] Moreover, 81% of EU citizen would like to find environmental information about products on their labels. Fewer people are interested in having such information available: on the shop shelf (55%); in product advertisement (41%); on internet (34%); on leaflets in the shop (32%); on the barcode to be scanned by personal or shop devices (24%).[109]

However, literature highlights that in the case of environmental sustainability there are issues related to confusion, lack of understanding, and barriers to the use of labels,[110] especially in relation to the large number of different symbols and logos that exist. Moreover, issues of trust and 'greenwashing' arise as the claims and certifications may be: of third-party origin; private schemes; or even only logos and images with no relation with food characteristics.[111] This because no specific regulation has been enacted to reduce the potential of opportunistic behaviour by firms. Indeed, considering the issue of confusion and lack of understanding, Eurobarometer data indicates that 47% of EU citizen do not find it 'easy to differentiate environmentally-friendly products from other products'.[112] Moreover, only 7% of EU citizen consider that 'current product labels provide enough information about products' environmental impact and (that) the information is clear for all products'; 32% consider the information to be enough but 'unclear for certain products'; and 59% declare that labels do not provide enough information (2% do not know).[113] Focusing on issues of distrust, instead, 47% of EU citizen 'do not trust producers' claims about the environmental performance of their own products'.[114]

All of the above highlight the need for unique, clear and transparent rules to avoid opportunistic behaviour by firms and confusion or distrust by consumers.

6 Environmental Sustainability and Health

As highlighted in the previous sections, food consumption can play an important role in shaping production and on the environmental impact of the food system.[115]

In recent years, worldwide we have witnessed a change in dietary patterns, with a constant shift of food consumption towards products high in saturated fat, high in sugar, meat, and oils.[116] Such changes in dietary habits pose a problem both in terms

[108]European Commission (2012), p. 24.

[109]European Commission (2013b), p. 77.

[110]Grunert (2011), p. 209; Dendler (2014), p. 74; Grunert et al. (2014), p. 183.

[111]Pedersen and Neergaard (2006), p. 17.

[112]European Commission (2013b), p. 30.

[113]European Commission (2013b), pp. 73–74.

[114]European Commission (2013b), p. 83.

[115]Garnett (2014), p. 6.

[116]Tilman and Clark (2014), p. 521.

of environmental degradation and in terms of public health.[117] Such behaviours are also associated with an increase in diet-related diseases. According to WHO, in 2014 in the world more than 1.9 billion adults were overweight and, of these, over 600 million were obese.[118] Thus, the issues of sustainable food consumption and diet-related diseases could be tackled jointly by policy makers, as they both represent central concerns.[119] Policies could be devised to change dietary patterns in order to reduce the impact on the environment and, at same time, improve public health and social well-being. FAO defines sustainable diets as:

> those diets with low environmental impacts, which contribute to food and nutrition security and to healthy life for present and future generations. Sustainable diets are protective and respectful of biodiversity and ecosystems, culturally acceptable, accessible, economically fair, and affordable; nutritionally adequate, safe, and healthy; while optimizing natural and human resources.[120]

Which are the eating patterns that are suitable both for health and the environment? Trying to answer this question, the BCFN (Barilla Centre for Food and Nutrition) developed a new construct of the nutritional pyramid, in which an additional triangle representing the environmental impact of the different food categories is placed next to the traditional one. This new construct aims at explaining that the foods placed at the base of the nutritional pyramid are also those that have a lower impact on the environment (Fig. 3). In the last years, data supporting the reliability of the Double Pyramid have increased (about 1200 citations) and this is strengthening its importance. In the scheme proposed by the Double Pyramid the impact of the food chain is quantified using three environmental markers (Carbon Footprint, Water Footprint, and Ecological Footprint). The aim of this scheme is to stress the relevance of the close link existing between environmental sustainability and health, highlighting that good practices in food consumption often correspond to good environmental ones.[121] In other words, the Double Pyramid illustrates that, very often, the food products that according to nutritional recommendations should be eaten less frequently (like meat and cheese) are the same products that are discouraged to be consumed for environmental reasons. The opposite is true for the case of cereals (important for fibre content), fruit and vegetables. These groups of products, following the recommendations of the food pyramid, have a high recommended number of daily servings for health reasons, and have also a low impact on the environment.

[117] Stehfest et al. (2009), p. 84.

[118] See http://www.who.int/mediacentre/factsheets/fs311/en/.

[119] Cavaliere et al. (2014), p. 9496.

[120] FAO/Bioversity (2012), p. 294.

[121] van Kernebeek et al. (2014), p. 89.

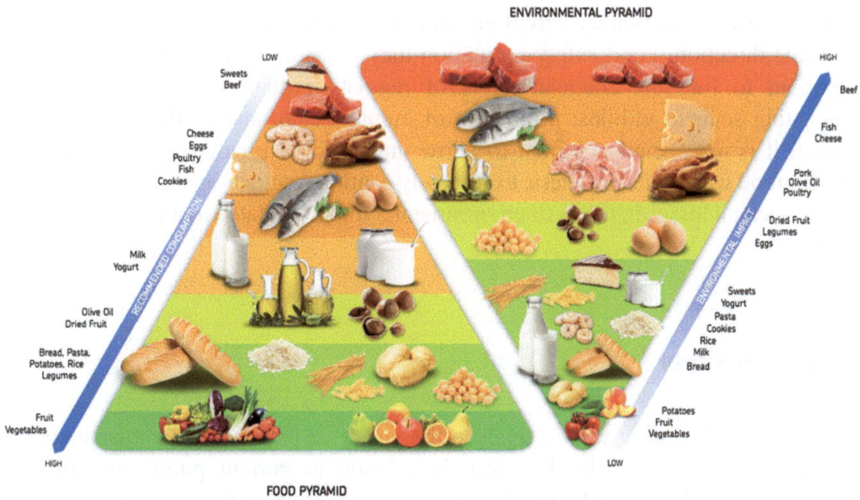

Fig. 3 Food and environmental Double Pyramid. Source: Barilla Centre for Food and Nutrition. Double Pyramid. https://www.barillacfn.com/. Reproduced with permission

Moreover, several studies compared plant-based diets with those based on meat consumption in order to demonstrate the differential impacts of these diets on the environment.[122] Results of such research show that plant-based diets are better in terms of environmental impact, as meat-based diets require more energy, land, and water resources. For instance, the production of 1 kg of animal protein requires a quantity of water 100 times more than 1 kg of grain protein.

In this context, policy intervention could be aimed at evaluating tools that can help to discourage meat consumption, with the aim of producing societal benefits related to climate change mitigation and the reduction of the incidence of certain food-related diseases.[123] Moreover, the promotion and encouragement of fruit and vegetable consumption would be effective both for the environment and for health issues. Information campaigns could be of great help in this, as through such tools consumer consciousness about these issues may be increased. Moreover, information policies could also make consumers more knowledgeable about the link between diet, sustainability and health. Being more aware during food purchasing, consumers might be able to make healthier and more environmentally-sustainable food choices.

[122] Baroni et al. (2006), p. 279; Leitzmann (2003), p. 658; Pairotti et al. (2015), p. 513; Pimentel and Pimentel (2003), p. 662; Reijnders and Soret (2003), p. 666; Vanham et al. (2013), p. 54.

[123] McMichael et al. (2007), p. 1253; van Dooren and Kramer (2015), p. 54.

In the case of food safety, environmental and health issues may instead not go in the same direction. Food safety regulation may generate food waste.[124] Thus it is important to find the adequate level of regulation that may balance the two contrasting societal utilities: protection of human health and of the environment. Indeed, it is not socially optimal to allow unsafe foodstuff on the market just to prevent food waste. Nevertheless, excessively cautious regulation of food safety may induce societal losses in terms of environmental impacts related to unnecessary food waste.

7 Conclusions

The aim of the chapter was to analyse the issues of environmental sustainability connected with the agri-food system in relation to current public and private environmental-related regulation. A general discussion about the concept of sustainability and a description of the major environmentally-related challenges that the food sector is facing and will face in the coming years was firstly provided. The chapter moved on to discuss the needs and the different types of public intervention in the context of the food market, focusing on the differences among standards, principles and information measures. Then, it focused on the EU regulatory framework presenting different initiatives that target environmental sustainability within the food context. Finally, the chapter explored consumer perceptions on the matter and the linkages between environmental sustainability and health issues.

The analysis highlighted the large set of environmentally-related issues connected to the agri-food system at the global level. This underlines the need for public intervention as the market fails to provide the socially optimal level of environmental protection. What is the EU doing to take on such challenges in the food domain?

The EU does not have a structured and comprehensive framework on environmental policies in the agri-food system. The analysis reveals that even if sustainable development and environmental protection are mentioned in several treaty articles and regulations, they are treated in general terms and the regulatory measures targeting the issues highlighted are limited. At the level of general principles, for example, the precautionary principle included in the general food law makes reference only to food safety issues, even if such a principle was originally developed and is widely adopted in the realm of environmental issues. Moreover, intergenerational equity considerations that are at the basis of sustainability are not included in the principles that govern food legislation.

Nevertheless, a number of important non-strictly-food related strategic agendas have been adopted to give long-term directions to firms and promote a change in business models. Examples are: the Europe 2020 Strategy for a smart, sustainable, inclusive growth; the "Innovating for Sustainable Growth: A Bioeconomy for

[124]Bremmers et al. (2015), pp. 4 and 14.

Europe" to promote the development of bio-based products starting from renewable resources; the Circular Economy Package to promote the shift from a linear to a circular production models; and the participation to the UN 2030 Agenda for Sustainable Development to try to achieve the Sustainable Development Goals.

Moreover, some specific interventions have been developed to tackle specific issues. For example, the CAP differently from the past, where the productive objectives played a crucial role, currently aims at favouring landscape protection, environmentally-friendly agricultural practices, and biodiversity conservation. This at least partly responds to the issues of environmental degradation, biodiversity loss and land competition related to food production. Also the common fisheries policy takes into account environmental sustainability aspects and imposes a set of rules targeting the preservation of fish stocks and of the marine environment. For what concerns more general issues of resource depletion, guidelines have been developed to reduce food waste and to promote a more circular-economy approach for consumption and production. Measures to increase the market for green food producers are promoted by means of green public procurement.

Additional types of intervention could be developed to engage consumers or producers. For example, consumers could be made more aware about the food-related environmental issues with information and education campaigns or supported while purchasing by labelling schemes. In this direction, EMAS is a voluntary scheme aimed at promoting the use of environmental management systems and policies, though it is not widespread among food firms and not well known by consumers. The Ecolabel voluntary labelling scheme is more known to consumers but it is not applicable to food products. Private standards and certifications have emerged to give indications on specific sustainability-related issues. Are these private initiatives enough to guide consumers to sustainable food consumption? Consumers are currently faced with a large variety of certifications focusing on different aspects of sustainability and characterised by different levels of protection; this may lead to consumer confusion. At the same time, the freedom left to producers to signal only what they desire could lead to opportunistic behaviour. A possible strategy for the EU to overcome such issues could be of devising a unified label with the aim of harmonising and increasing the variety of information reported on food labels to give consumers a more complete 'sustainability picture' of the product.

Other possible ways of intervention to regulate resource use and prevent depletion could relate to economic measures (e.g., taxes and/or subsidies). These may promote sustainable food behaviours and practices and deter the choice of less-sustainable products. Such policy instruments should be able to improve consumer and producer environmental behaviour, and in the case of taxes promote the polluters pay principle. Nevertheless, the design and real-life application of such measures is quite difficult in relation to the identification of the optimal level of the tax/subsidy and to possible unwanted distributional effects (Markandya and Ricci 2012). This is particularly relevant in the food domain given the low elasticities of demand (for example, an increase in price that leads to a disadvantage for the poorest segments of population).

Moreover, specific standards could be imposed, for example on energy-efficiency or energy-source; though, measures not targeting directly products but production processes—that do not impact product quality directly—tend to imply a burden for domestic firms compared to foreign ones.

Other policy measures could promote research and development to decrease the costs related to environmentally-friendly technologies and practices, and thus favour their widespread adoption. Or implement strategies and tools to change production models. The EU is developing frameworks to favour the use of bio-based products starting from renewable resources or waste and to surpass the linear approach to production and use resources to their full potential, in line with the so called bio-economy and circular economy approaches.

It must be underlined that resource use is a very difficult issue to tackle and to regulate given the wide diversity of resources that could be targeted (e.g., land, water, ecosystems, energy, etc.) and the issues related to common-pool resources that are often subject to the 'tragedy of the commons' (Hardin 1968). Co-regulation could be one of the strategies that could be implemented to reach a commonly agreed set of rules that may tackle the issue of overexploitation in an effective manner.

The issue of climate change has not been directly tackled in the context of food, except among the general targets of the bio-economy strategy, even if the food sector is responsible for a significant amount of GHG emissions, for example related to the use of energy-intense fertilizers and pesticides, production and transport, or land use change. Also in this context, policies could be devised at different levels. Concerning information and education measures, campaigns could be implemented to increase awareness about the link between food choices and greenhouse gas emissions and human-induced climate change. Changes in consumption behaviour may be made easier by the adoption of labelling schemes, for example related to the concept of carbon footprint and sustainable forest management, which for food products are currently left in the hands of non-governmental institutions. Also market mechanisms could be devised, for example imposing carbon-content taxes on food products recognised to be responsible for a higher amount of GHG emissions.

Evaluating existing measures in the EU, what emerges is that, differently from food safety issues, that are regulated by general principles but also by very specific standards, environmental issues related to agri-food are mainly addressed at a very general level by guidelines, incentives or voluntary standards. This indicates an absence of strict regulation and the presence of flexibility for the different economic agents. Even if environmental protection is a public good, the EU regulator has taken a stance of leaving a good deal of freedom of action to the individual players. This may be related, on the one side, to a certain degree of uncertainty about the optimal social level of environmental pollution and resource use and, on the other, to the will to allow consumers to adjust their food choices to their own personal preferences in terms of environmental-sustainability attributes and marketing attributes (price, brand, etc.). Additional warranty is provided, for those who wish, by public and private voluntary standards that impose more stringent requirements.

This freedom left to private agents may not lead to the socially optimal level of environmental protection. Indeed, recent studies show that while consumers are very concerned to general environmental issues, such as climate change, pollution and so on, this concern is not a strong enough motive to trigger the adoption of environmentally sustainable food choices. However, day-by-day consumer choices may have a strong impact on the natural environment. This leaves room for further public intervention to promote more conscious behaviour.

References

Banterle A, Ricci EC (2013) Does the sustainability of food products influence consumer choices? The case of Italy. Int J Food Syst Dynam 4:149–158

Banterle A, Cereda E, Fritz M (2013) Labelling and sustainability in food supply networks. Br Food J 115:769–783. https://doi.org/10.1108/00070701311331544

Baroni L, Cenci L, Tettamanti M, Berati M (2006) Evaluating the environmental impact of various dietary patterns combined with different food production systems. Eur J Clin Nutr 61:279–286. https://doi.org/10.1038/sj.ejcn.1602522

Black J (2002) Critical reflections on regulation. Aust J Leg Philos 27:1–36

Black J (2008) Forms and paradoxes of principles-based regulation. Cap Mark Law J 3:425–457. https://doi.org/10.1093/cmlj/kmn026

Bremmers H, van der Meulen B, Waarts Y (2015) Reduction of food waste – a legal-economic analysis of durability dating. SSRN Electron J. https://doi.org/10.2139/ssrn.2627650

Caswell JA, Mojduszka EM (1996) Using informational labeling to influence the market for quality in food products. Am J Agric Econ 78:1248–1253. https://doi.org/10.2307/1243501

Cavaliere A, Ricci E, Solesin M, Banterle A (2014) Can health and environmental concerns meet in food choices? Sustainability 6:9494–9509. https://doi.org/10.3390/su6129494

Darby MR, Karni E (1973) Free competition and the optimal amount of fraud. J Law Econ 16:67–88

Dendler L (2014) Sustainability meta labelling: an effective measure to facilitate more sustainable consumption and production? J Clean Prod 63(Special Volume: Sustainable Production, Consumption and Livelihoods: Global and Regional Research Perspectives):74–83. https://doi.org/10.1016/j.jclepro.2013.04.037

European Commission (2012) Special Eurobarometer 389: Europeans' attitudes towards food security, food quality and the countryside - European Union Open Data Portal

European Commission (2013a) Overview of CAP Reform 2014–2020. Agricultural Policy Perspectives Brief 5

European Commission (2013b) Flash Eurobarometer 367 - attitudes of Europeans towards building the single market for green products

European Commission (2016) Buying Green! - a handbook on green public procurement

Evans D (2011) Consuming conventions: sustainable consumption, ecological citizenship and the worlds of worth. J Rural Stud 27:109–115. https://doi.org/10.1016/j.jrurstud.2011.02.002

FAO, IFAD and WFP (2015) The State of Food Insecurity in the World 2015. Meeting the 2015 international hunger targets: taking stock of uneven progress. Food and Agriculture Organization of the United Nations, Rome

FAO/Bioversity (2012) Annex I final document. In: Sustainable diets and biodiversity. FAO, Bioversity International, Rome

Feeding the 5000 (2015) The Food Waste Pyramid. http://feedbackglobal.org/. Accessed Nov 16

Garcia Martinez M, Fearne A, Caswell JA, Henson S (2007) Co-regulation as a possible model for food safety governance: opportunities for public–private partnerships. Food Policy 32:299–314. https://doi.org/10.1016/j.foodpol.2006.07.005

Garnett T (2014) Changing what we eat: a call for research & action on widespread adoption of sustainable healthy eating|Food Climate Research Network (FCRN). Report of FCRN - Food Climate Research Network

Grunert KG (2011) Sustainability in the food sector: a consumer behaviour perspective. Int J Food Syst Dynam 2:207–218

Grunert KG, Hieke S, Wills J (2014) Sustainability labels on food products: consumer motivation, understanding and use. Food Policy 44:177–189. https://doi.org/10.1016/j.foodpol.2013.12.001

Hardin G (1968) The tragedy of the commons. Science 162:1243–1248. https://doi.org/10.1126/science.162.3859.1243

IPCC (2014) Summary for policymakers. In: Edenhofer O, Pichs-Madruga R, Sokona Y, Farahani E, Kadner S, Seyboth K, Adler A, Baum I, Brunner S, Eickemeier P, Kriemann B, Savolainen J, Schlömer S, von Stechow C, Zwickel T, Minx JC (eds) Climate change 2014: mitigation of climate change. Contribution of Working Group III to the Fifth Assessment Report of the Intergovernmental Panel on Climate Change. Cambridge University Press, Cambridge and New York

Leathers HD, Foster P (2009) The world food problem: toward ending undernutrition in the third world. Lynne Rienner Publishers, Boulder

Leitzmann C (2003) Nutrition ecology: the contribution of vegetarian diets. Am J Clin Nutr 78:657S–659S

Markandya A, Ricci EC (2012) Green taxes on aviation: the case of Italy. The proposal of the Green taxation matrix. In: Castellucci L, Markandya A (eds) Environmental taxes and fiscal reform. Palmgrave-MacMillan, Basingstoke and New York

McMahon JA, Cardwell MN (2015) Research handbook on EU agriculture law. Edward Elgar Publishing

McMichael AJ, Powles JW, Butler CD, Uauy R (2007) Food, livestock production, energy, climate change, and health. Lancet 370:1253–1263. https://doi.org/10.1016/S0140-6736(07)61256-2

Meadows DH, Meadows D l, Randers J, Behrens WW III (1972) The limits to growth: a report to the club of Rome. Universe Books, New York

Millennium Ecosystem Assessment (2005a) Ecosystems and human well-being: synthesis. World Resources Institute, Washington

Millennium Ecosystem Assessment (2005b) Ecosystems and human well-being: biodiversity synthesis. World Resources Institute, Washington

Nellemann C, MacDevette M, Mandes T, Eickhout B, Svihus B, Prins AG, Kaltenborn BP (2009) The environmental food crisis - the environment's role in averting future food crises. A UNEP rapid response assessment. United Nations Environment Programme, GRID-Arendal, Norway

OECD (2001) Multifunctionality. Towards an analytical framework. OECD Publishing, Paris

OECD (2005) Evaluating agri-environmental policies: design, practice and results. OECD Publishing, Paris

OECD (2015) The economic consequences of climate change. OECD Publishing, Paris. https://www.oecd-ilibrary.org/environment/the-economic-consequences-of-climate-change_9789264235410-en. https://doi.org/10.1787/9789264235410-en

Pairotti MB, Cerutti AK, Martini F, Vesce E, Padovan D, Beltramo R (2015) Energy consumption and GHG emission of the Mediterranean diet: a systemic assessment using a hybrid LCA-IO method. J Clean Prod 103(Carbon Emissions Reduction: Policies, Technologies, Monitoring, Assessment and Modeling):507–516. https://doi.org/10.1016/j.jclepro.2013.12.082

Pedersen ER, Neergaard P (2006) Caveat emptor – let the buyer beware! environmental labelling and the limitations of "green" consumerism. Bus Strateg Environ 15:15–29. https://doi.org/10.1002/bse.434

Pimentel D, Pimentel M (2003) Sustainability of meat-based and plant-based diets and the environment. Am J Clin Nutr 78:660S–663S

Porter ME (1990) The competitive advantage of nations. Harv Bus Rev, March 1
Reijnders L, Soret S (2003) Quantification of the environmental impact of different dietary protein choices. Am J Clin Nutr 78:664S–668S
Ricci EC (2013) An integrated assessment of super & smart grids. Nota di Lavoro 84.2013. Fondazione Eni Enrico Mattei, Milan, Italy
Rouvière E, Caswell JA (2012) From punishment to prevention: a French case study of the introduction of co-regulation in enforcing food safety. Food Policy 37:246–254. https://doi.org/10.1016/j.foodpol.2012.02.009
Ruini L, Marchelli L, Marino M, Filareto A (2012) Barilla EPD process system to increase reliability, comparability and communicability of LCA studies. In: Rennes, France. http://www.studiolce.it/Files/Pubblicazioni/2012/Barilla%20EPD%20Process%20System.pdf
Segrè A (ed) (2008) Politiche per lo sviluppo agricolo e la sicurezza alimentare. Carocci editore, Rome
Seyfang G (2006) Ecological citizenship and sustainable consumption: examining local organic food networks. J Rural Stud 22:383–395. https://doi.org/10.1016/j.jrurstud.2006.01.003
Smith P, Gregory PJ, van Vuuren D, Obersteiner M, Havlík P, Rounsevell M, Woods J, Stehfest E, Bellarby J (2010) Competition for land. Philos Trans R Soc Lond B Biol Sci 365:2941–2957. https://doi.org/10.1098/rstb.2010.0127
Smith P, Bustamante M, Ahammad H, Clark H, Dong H, Elsiddig EA, Haberl H et al (2014) Agriculture, Forestry and Other Land Use (AFOLU). In: Edenhofer O, Pichs-Madruga R, Sokona Y, Farahani E, Kadner S, Seyboth K, Adler A, Baum I, Brunner S, Eickemeier P, Kriemann B, Savolainen J, Schlömer S, von Stechow C, Zwickel T, Minx JC (eds) Climate change 2014: mitigation of climate change. Contribution of Working Group III to the Fifth Assessment Report of the Intergovernmental Panel on Climate Change. Cambridge University Press, Cambridge and New York
Sorrentino A, Henke R, Severini S (eds) (2011) The common agricultural policy after the Fischler reform. Ashgate, Farnham
Spaargaren G, Mol APJ (2008) Greening global consumption: redefining politics and authority. Glob Environ Change 18(Globalisation and Environmental Governance: Is Another World Possible?):350–359. https://doi.org/10.1016/j.gloenvcha.2008.04.010
Stehfest E, Bouwman L, van Vuuren DP, den Elzen MGJ, Eickhout B, Kabat P (2009) Climate benefits of changing diet. Clim Change 95:83–102. https://doi.org/10.1007/s10584-008-9534-6
Stranieri S, Banterle A (2015) Consumer interest in meat labelled attributes: who cares? International Food and Agribusiness Management Review
Tilman D, Clark M (2014) Global diets link environmental sustainability and human health. Nature 515:518–522. https://doi.org/10.1038/nature13959
Trienekens J, Zuurbier P (2008) Quality and safety standards in the food industry, developments and challenges. Int J Prod Econ 113(Research and Applications in E-Commerce and Third-Party Logistics Management Special Section on Meta-Standards in Operations Management: Cross-Disciplinary Perspectives):107–122. https://doi.org/10.1016/j.ijpe.2007.02.050
UN (2015) United Nations Millennium Development Goals. New York
UNEP (1972) Stockholm 1972 - declaration of the United Nations conference on the human environment. United Nations Environment Programme
UNEP (2012) Global environment outlook 5 (GEO-5): environment for the future we want, 5th edn. United Nations Environment Program, Nairobi
USDA (2010) Energy use in the U.S. food system. Economic Research Report Number 94 - United States Department of Agriculture
van der Meulen B, Bremmers H, Purnhagen K, Gupta N, Bouwmeester H, Leon Geyer L (2014) Governing nano foods: principles-based responsive regulation: EFFoST critical reviews #3. Academic Press
van Dooren C, Kramer G (2015) Food patterns and dietary recommendations in Spain, France and Sweden|CORPUS. LiveWELL for Life. http://www.scp-knowledge.eu/knowledge/food-patterns-and-dietary-recommendations-spain-france-and-sweden. Accessed Oct 19

van Kernebeek HRJ, Oosting SJ, Feskens EJM, Gerber PJ, De Boer IJM (2014) The effect of nutritional quality on comparing environmental impacts of human diets. J Clean Prod 73:88–99. https://doi.org/10.1016/j.jclepro.2013.11.028

Vanham D, Hoekstra AY, Bidoglio G (2013) Potential water saving through changes in European diets. Environ Int 61:45–56. https://doi.org/10.1016/j.envint.2013.09.011

Vecchio R, Annunziata A (2015) Willingness-to-pay for sustainability-labelled chocolate: an experimental auction approach. J Clean Prod 86:335–342. https://doi.org/10.1016/j.jclepro.2014.08.006

Waarts YR, Eppink M, Oosterkamp EB, Hiller SRCH, van der Sluis AA, Timmermans T (2011) Reducing food waste; obstacles experienced in legislation and regulations. 2011-059. LEI, part of Wageningen UR, The Hague

WHO/FAO (2003) Global and regional food consumption patterns and trends. In: Joint WHO/FAO expert consultation on diet, nutrition and the prevention of chronic diseases, 13–29. WHO Technical Report Series, No. 916 (TRS 916), Geneva, Switzerland

World Commission on Environment and Development (1987) Our common future. Oxford University Press, Oxford; New York

Alessandro Banterle is Full Professor and Head of the Department of Environmental Science and Policy at the University of Milan. He is Editor-in-Chief of the international scientific journal 'Agricultural and Food Economics'. He has been member of the International Jury for the 'EXPO Awards' of EXPO Milano 2015. He has been deputy-director of the Department of Economics, Management and Quantitative Methods. His research interests include supply chain management, behavioural economics, food policy, and environmental sustainability. He participated in the coordination of several research projects such as TRUEFOOD (2006–2010), CAPINFOOD (2011–2014), SOSTARE (2009–2011); MOSE4AGROFOOD (2010–2012), Long Life—High Sustainability (2014–2017).

Elena Claire Ricci holds a degree in Environmental Sciences from University of Milan-Bicocca, an MSc in Environmental and Resource Economics from University College London, and a PhD in Economics from the University of Milan. She is now a post-doc research fellow at Department of Environmental Science and Policy of the University of Milan. Her research field is food, environmental, and energy economics and policy, with a focus on sustainable transitions. Her research focuses on consumer behaviour and the effects of CSR-goals on food firms. Her research interests also include system dynamics, education for sustainable development, and climate-change economics. She has taken part to several national and international research projects among which: LeGeReTe (2017–2019), CAPINFOOD (2011–2014), ICARUS (2012–2013).

Alessia Cavaliere received her PhD in Agricultural Economics at the University of Milan. She is currently Assistant Professor at the Department of Environmental Science and Policy of the University of Milan, where she teaches courses in Food Economics, European Food Legislation and Food Policy. Her main research interests are related to the study of consumer behavior, the economic aspects of obesity, and information-based food policy and she is author of several academic articles on these topics. She participated as researcher to numerous national and international research projects such as TRUEFOOD (2006–2010), CAPINFOOD (2011–2014), MOSE4AGROFOOD (2010–2012), Long Life—High Sustainability (2014–2017).

EU Health Claims: A Consumer Perspective

Erica van Herpen and Hans C. M. van Trijp

Abstract Health claims can inform consumers about important nutritional qualities of food products that would otherwise go unnoticed, and influence consumer choice. This chapter reviews consumer behaviour literature related to health claims, and discusses this in the context of the EU legislation. It addresses the influence of textual as well as pictorial health claims, how consumers form inferences based on health claims, and the potential influence of health claims on consumer motivation to choose healthful products. Consumer choice is argued to be based on the fit between inferred product benefits and the goals that are accessible at the moment of choice. This relates to the dual goal of the legislation on health claims, namely information transparency as well as consumer health motivation. The scientific insights from consumer studies are confronted with the current legislation on health claims. Important bottlenecks for reaching the objectives of the legislation are a lack of attention by policy makers to the non-textual information on product packaging, a lack of ability of health claims to increase consumer motivation by themselves, and difficulty of consumers in correctly understanding health claims.

1 Introduction

The use of health claims on food products can have important consequences for consumer behaviour, marketing strategy and public health. Health claims can inform consumers about nutritional qualities of food products that would otherwise go unnoticed.[1] Health claims are also important instruments for food companies. They can enhance the level of differentiation of their products from competing brands in the market place (and hence their competitive advantage) on the basis of

---

[1]Kozup et al. (2003).

E. van Herpen (✉) · H. C. M. van Trijp
Wageningen University, Marketing and Consumer Behavior Group, Wageningen, The Netherlands
e-mail: erica.vanherpen@wur.nl; hans.vantrijp@wur.nl

H. Bremmers, K. Purnhagen (eds.), *Regulating and Managing Food Safety in the EU*, Economic Analysis of Law in European Legal Scholarship 6,
https://doi.org/10.1007/978-3-319-77045-1_5

increased healthfulness of their products. Drawing a parallel to the past, the introduction of the Nutrition Labelling and Education Act in the US in 1990 has been shown to influence the nutritional quality of existing brands as well as new brand extensions, because companies attempted to occupy distinct strategic positions in the marketplace that would be valued by consumers (Moorman 1998). Health claims and their regulation can potentially have similar effects. This implies that consumers could benefit from enhanced transparency in the food assortment, either directly because claims signal healthier options within the assortment, or indirectly because transparency may lead companies to put an extra effort in enhancing the nutrition quality of their product portfolio.[2]

However, these positive outcomes on the use of health claims will only materialise if information provided in such claims is correct, unambiguous and in no way misleading. Concerns about consumer misunderstanding and potential overgeneralizations of health benefits, has led to European legislation regarding health and nutrition claims (Regulation No 1924/2006). The aim of this legislation is to protect consumers from potentially misleading information and to help them make more informed healthful choices. The legislation distinguished between nutrition claims (predefined in the Annex of the legislation), and health claims which are the main focus of this contribution.

The present chapter discusses health claims from a consumer behaviour point of view, in the context of the EU legislation. It particularly addresses three key issues relevant to (the legislation on) health claims:

1. The influence of textual versus pictorial health claims: The legislation is not restricted to texts, and explicitly covers any "pictorial, graphic or symbolic representation, which states, suggests or implies that a food has particular characteristics". This implies that next to the textual claims themselves also symbols and other cues on the packaging are included, and insights from consumer behaviour literature on the relative effectiveness of textual versus pictorial information are relevant for legislation.
2. Consumer inference making based on health claims: A "health claim" is any claim that states, suggests or implies that a relationship exists between a food category, a food, or one of its constituents and health". (Article 2.2.5.) Health claims should be "well understood by the average consumer" (Article 13.1.ii). It is thus relevant to examine how consumers form their understanding of health claims, and which factors may prohibit them from drawing correct health inferences from health claims.
3. Consumer motivation to choose healthful products (health goal accessibility): Nutrition and health claims legislation serves a dual role, namely that of (a) protecting consumers from potentially misleading information and (b) helping them make more informed healthful choices. Whether consumer motivation is likely to be affected by the presence of health claims is thus essential as well.

[2]Roodenburg et al. (2011) and Vyth et al. (2010).

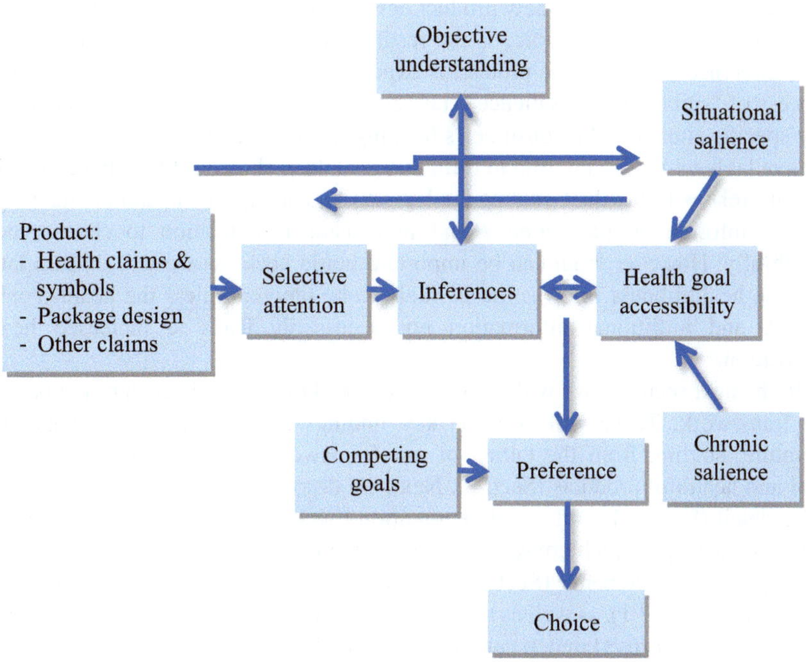

Fig. 1 Framework of the effects of health claims

In this chapter we provide a selective review of the consumer behaviour literature related to nutrition and health claims. This review is organized around a comprehensive theoretical framework that has been developed within the EU Framework 7 project CLYMBOL, a European Commission-funded research project running from 2012 to 2016, which aims "to understand better the effects of health claims and symbols on food labels, and how this affects purchase and consumption behaviour". The selective review will disentangle the relevant processes through which health claims affect consumer understanding, goal accessibility, and choice. Next, we discuss how this relates back to legislative issues. Specifically, we will confront the current scientific evidence from empirical consumer studies with the legislation regarding pictorial, graphic, or symbolic representations, which state, suggest, or imply that a food has healthful characteristics.

2 A Framework for the Role of Claims and Symbols in Consumer Behaviour

Figure 1 summarises the general framework (based on the model developed within CLYMBOL) for the role of nutrition and health claims in consumer understanding, purchase and consumption. The framework builds on van Trijp and Grunert's (2014) work on consumer oriented new product development. Essentially the model argues that, through preference, choice is the resultant of a process of "belief formation" (i.e., inferences) on what the product is expected to deliver, on the one hand, and a process of "situation need salience" (i.e., goal accessibility) on the other hand. If at any specific situation, the consumer's health goal is salient/accessible and products are available which are inferred to fulfil this goal, then choice is likely to occur. This directly relates to the dual goal of the legislation, namely that health claims play a role in information transparency and in consumer motivation to choose more healthfully. However, both can be important bottle necks as we will discuss later, because healthfulness information is likely to be ignored unless the health goal is salient, and nutritional information not necessarily leads to increased health motivation.

In the next sections, we will briefly review the key finding in each of the parts of the framework. These will describe key findings from the consumer behaviour literature, starting from the kernel of our framework, the fit between the health goal and healthful products (Sect. 3). Next, we describe health goal accessibility in more detail (Sect. 3.1) and selective attention (Sect. 3.2), before moving on to the processes through which consumers make sense of health claims in the context of other packaging elements (Sect. 4). We discuss the health claims and symbols themselves (Sect. 4.1), as well as the process of inference making (Sect. 4.2), leading to (correct or incorrect) understanding of claims (Sect. 4.3).

3 Health Goals

3.1 Fit Between the Salient Health Goal and Products (Believed to) Satisfy it

Central to the framework is a fundamental principle from the consumer behaviour literature, namely that when confronted with a choice from multiple products, consumers will strive for goal satisfaction.[3] In other words, implicitly or explicitly, they will form an assessment of how well they believe that each of the choice options will help them satisfy their goals at that particular moment in time. Products that do a better job in satisfying relevant goals enjoy a higher preference and are more likely to be chosen and consumed.

This basic principle sets challenges for policy makers and legislators, who need to both facilitate consumer demand on the one hand and provide transparent and motivating information provision on the other hand. This is complicated because consumer goals are multidimensional in nature and subgoals are not necessarily independent nor always compatible. At any moment in time, health goals and taste goals (as an example) may both be active with different intensities, and products can

[3]Bagozzi and Dholakia (1999) and Chernev (2004).

relate to multiple goals. Products can be seen as bundles of benefits (Lancaster 1966), which may, through their packaging, claims and symbols and from previous experience, appeal to multiple goals. For simplicity, within the present framework the health goal to which the health claims and symbols appeal is separated from competing goals, which are portrayed as an external factor in preference and choice.

Health goals compete and combine with other goals in the generation of preference and choice. Most academic attention has focussed on the trade-off between indulgence (taste) versus health goals, recognizing that indulgence goals provide instantaneous satisfaction whereas the benefits of health often tend to manifest themselves only in the long run. This has important implications for the process of preference formation as well as choice. Literature on construal level theory and temporal discounting suggests that (a) consumers tend to discount benefits that manifest themselves in the longer term, and (b) that although such longer-term benefits are reflected in preferences (they are important) they do not necessarily play a big role in choice (they are not decisive).[4]

3.2 *Health Goals*

The extent to which health goals are salient as a motivational factor in consumer decision making differs both between (chronic salience) and within (situational salience) individuals. Some individuals are more health oriented than others. Research on the food choice questionnaire suggests that groups which are more likely to be chronically motivated towards healthful food choice have a higher probability of containing females, people with children and with relatively high income.[5] However, irrespective of such general motivations toward health, health motivation may become situationally salient, particularly when health is at stake either for oneself or for someone one is taking care off.[6] This explains why elderly and those caring for young children are often more motivated towards healthful food choices.

Although health may not be top-of-mind as a motivation at any particular moment of choice, the choice context provides an opportunity for attempts to activate such situational salience. Health communication at the point of purchase might activate healthfulness as a choice motivation. For instance, a recipe flyer with a low-calorie recipe has been claimed to stimulate overweight individuals to buy fewer snacks.[7] For such effects to occur, conscious awareness during shopping may not be required, but initial attention is,[8] as well as enough cognitive resources (Walsh 2014).

[4]Dhar and Kim (2007) and Trope and Liberman (2003).

[5]Steptoe et al. (1995) and Kornelis et al. (2010).

[6]Ma et al. (2013).

[7]Papies et al. (2014).

[8]Papies et al. (2014).

Although health claims and health symbols on pack could in theory also activate health goals, their ability to do so may be hampered because these packaging elements may receive little attention in practice.

3.3 Selective Attention

Attention to information on pack, including information contained in nutrition and health claims and symbols, is a necessary, but insufficient, condition for correct inference making about the healthfulness of food choice options.[9] Information that is not attended to, cannot be further processed, and hence (healthfulness) inference making (as a higher order cognitive process) critically depends on attention. Attention is a limited resource on the part of the consumer and in many instances, in information rich environment, available information will be selectively attended to. There are two important implications arriving from this observation of selective attention. First, health-related information may generate limited attention as such information may compete for limited attentional resources against other information on pack. Second, whether correctly or not, other information on pack that is attended to may be used as a cue for healthfulness of the product contained in the package.

Food packages are loaded with information, including the product name, the brand name, the visuals on pack, packaging colour, and competing claims about product-delivered benefits (e.g., taste) and how the product is produced (e.g., organics claims). Eye-tracking research is often applied to verify whether any specific information on pack is attended to sufficiently to be processed further. Eye-tracking on nutrition information on pack suggests that this type of information is not necessarily actively attended to, but that health-related information processing may be enhanced if the health motivation is (made) situationally salient and/or ability to process the information is enhanced.[10] Eye-tracking research has also lead to specific recommendations to increase the chance that information is attended to. Graham et al. (2012) provide a summary, in which they advise to place labels centrally, to reduce visual clutter surrounding the labels, to use contrast to increase visual salience of the label, and to increase their surface size.

In summary, research on attention processes suggests that attention is a key bottleneck, limiting the effects of nutrition and health information. Although consumers say that claims are useful for them,[11] studies in which consumers are followed when doing their day-to-day grocery shopping generally find that the use of health claims and nutrition labels is limited.[12] An important challenge for nutrition

[9]Grunert et al. (2010).

[10]van Herpen and van Trijp (2011).

[11]Williams (2005).

[12]Rayner et al. (2001) and Grunert and Wills (2007).

and health information to be effective in guiding consumer choice behaviour thus lies in "breaking through the attention barrier".

4 How Consumers Process Health Claims

4.1 Health Claims and Symbols in the Packaging Context

Consumers generally think that products with health claims are more healthful than alternatives without such claims,[13] but the extent to which health claims are accepted differs between types of claims and product categories. Consumers appear to be more accepting of health claims on products that are relatively healthful by themselves and of health claims based on more familiar ingredients.[14] They seem to particularly prefer health claims based on ingredients that are naturally present in the product.[15] For instance, consumers believe and appreciate a calcium claim more when placed on milk than when placed on orange juice. This has relevant implications for legislation. Legislation ensures protection of consumers and instils trust, which are important for economic transactions. The insights from consumer behaviour literature suggest that the ability of legislation to instil trust in consumers is especially important when it concerns the addition of healthful ingredients that are unfamiliar and/or not naturally present in a product.

Not only the context of the product category and ingredients matters for consumer responses to health claims; the context provided by other packaging elements is relevant as well. Consumers form an impression of a product based on the integration of the various visual and textual packaging elements.[16] Pictorial elements on a package may be particularly relevant, and can provide a background for interpreting and understanding health claims.[17]

Whereas textual nutrition information and health claims have difficulty attracting consumer attention, this may hold for a lesser extent for visual elements on a product's packaging. Visual elements can draw attention to products, also when consumers are under time pressure,[18] and can help consumers remember other product characteristics (e.g., learning and remembering quality differences between products by linking these to distinctive colour differences).[19] Moreover, visual elements can obtain meaning over time, and become capable of communicating

[13]Dean et al. (2007) and Urala et al. (2003).

[14]Grunert et al. (2009), Lähteenmäki et al. (2010) and Verbeke (2010).

[15]Lähteenmäki et al. (2010).

[16]van Rompay and Pruyn (2011).

[17]Bone and France (2001) and Purnhagen et al. (2016).

[18]Pieters and Warlop (1999) and Underwood and Klein (2002).

[19]Warlop et al. (2005).

complex and sophisticated messages,[20] especially since mass media is available to teach consumers a large vocabulary of images and layer these images with meaning.[21] Finally, visual elements tend to have longer lasting effects on people's memory[22] than textual elements. Whereas both research and legislation on health claims has primarily concentrated on textual health claims, visual elements are as least as important but often overlooked.[23]

A few studies have examined the effects of visual elements in the context of health claims, and these have shown that visual elements can influence how consumers evaluate a product. Comparing the connotations of two health-related and two non-health related symbols, along with verbal information, Carrillo et al. (2014) have found that the symbols on the package were more important than the verbal information. Moreover, visual elements can influence health perceptions and serve as a context in which a health claim is interpreted. Visuals of fruit, realistic pictures, and visual suggesting that a product is more natural has been shown to lead parents to believe that a product intended for children is more healthful.[24] Of particular relevance is the study of Bone and France (2001). They investigated whether visual elements influence health inferences even when the nutrition claim on the package provides objective and accurate information. They provided participants with the package of a cola which contained a low-caffeine claim. For half of the participants this claim was supported by the picture on pack of a man lounging under a palm tree, whereas the other half of the participants saw a picture of a football player with a lightning bolt, which sends an implicit message that is inconsistent with the low caffeine claim. Results showed that which picture was used affected consumer perceptions of caffeine content. This has important implications for legislation. Although the European legislation regarding health claims specifically includes non-textual elements of a packaging ("pictorial, graphic, or symbolic representation, which states, suggest or implies that a food has particular characteristics"), court cases so far have focused on textual claims.[25] More attention to visual elements may be warranted, given their pervasive influence on consumer perception. When pictorial elements contradict textual claims, as in the study of Bone and France (2001), the pictorial elements will affect consumer perceptions. Factually correct textual claims will not be sufficient to completely prevent consumer misunderstanding. This implies that visual elements can potentially mislead consumers. Legislation needs to take this into serious consideration.

[20]Scott (1994).

[21]Scott and Vargas (2007).

[22]Childers and Houston (1984), Stenberg et al. (1995) and Hockley (2008).

[23]Purnhagen et al. (2016).

[24]Abrams et al. (2015).

[25]Purnhagen et al. (2016).

4.2 Inference Making

An important point regarding healthfulness information is that the degree of healthfulness of any particular food product cannot be personally verified by a consumer by investigating the product itself. Health is a so-called "credence" attribute, which differs on essential points from search and experience attributes.[26] Specifically, search attributes are attributes that a consumer can verify by examining a product before purchase, and experience attributes are attributes that a consumer can verify after purchase. As an example, when buying cheese, attributes such as its size and colour can be verified prior to purchase by visually inspecting and handling the product (search attributes), attributes such as its taste and texture can be verified after purchase by consuming the product (experience attributes), but its healthfulness cannot be verified at any point (credence attribute). This also implies that healthfulness information will often go unnoticed for consumers unless communicated.

Even though consumers cannot verify the healthfulness of products, they will make inferences about this credence attribute, and they can do so using two different belief formation processes. The first process is *informational belief formation*, where consumers accept information from relevant others/authorities that provide such information. This can for example be a claim, logo, symbol, or advice from a trusted stakeholder (e.g., nutrition centre). The second process is *inferential belief formation*, where consumers use their own rules of thumb in the inference making on healthfulness. Such inferences may arise from health-related claims and symbols, but also from other relevant or irrelevant cues. These could be claims and symbols related to taste, such as when a taste claim reduces the healthfulness perception of a product as a result of the tasty = unhealthy intuition,[27] value chain practices, such as when consumers infer from an organics logo that the product is healthful,[28] or cues related to packaging, such as when the colour of a packaging affects perceptions of caloric content.[29] Repeated exposure to colour codes or other symbols will stimulate such inference making and allow consumers to make quick identification of otherwise unobservable product attributes based on these colours and symbols.[30] This directly relates to the meaning of health claims ("anything which states, suggests or implies . . .") and the adequate understanding of the nutrition and health information. An important issue in terms of transparency is the extent to which such subjective inferences correspond to the objective information conveyed by the nutrition and health claim, symbol and information.

[26]Ford et al. (1988).

[27]Raghunathan et al. (2006).

[28]Hughner et al. (2007).

[29]Bilman (2014).

[30]van Herpen and Pieters (2007).

4.3 (Correct) Understanding of Health Claims

Understanding of health claims comes about as an (higher order) inference making process based on information cues on the packaging combined with personal knowledge. This not only holds for inferences regarding healthfulness, but also for the inference making with regards to other product benefit, and these benefits perception may interact (and hence are not independent of each other) as in the case of the unhealthy = tasty intuition.[31] Understanding through inference making processes involves if-then linkages, for instance between the health claim and various product benefits.[32] The process is subjective, and may or may not reflect objectively correct product characteristics. For instance, consumers have been shown to infer that products with health claims are probably less tasty and less natural.[33] The inferences that consumers draw can thus go beyond the information provided on the package, and this has implications for consumer understanding of health claims. Hence an important challenge for correct understanding of health claims lies in the regulation of information provision such that it provides best chances that the inferred meaning of health claims does not deviate from the intended true meaning of those health claims.

Research on consumer understanding of health claims distinguishes between objective and subjective understanding. Objective understanding concerns the extent to which consumers have correctly understood (i.e., inferred) the beneficial aspects of a health claim, whereas subjective understanding refers to their own experience (i.e., whether consumers themselves think they understand the health claim, irrespective of whether they are correct in their assessment or not). Objective understanding may be low when consumers overgeneralize the health benefits of a product with a claim, or when they make inappropriate inferences about other product characteristics. Overgeneralization of health benefits has been termed the 'magic bullet effect',[34] whereas incorrect inferences about product characteristics are a form of the 'halo effect' (Nisbett and Wilson 1977). An example of the latter is when consumers draw inferences about, for instance, taste or price based on a health claim.

Although such overgeneralization and halo effects may be beneficial from a commercial point of view to motivate consumers to purchase the product for healthful reasons, these processes are at odds with the ambition of information transparency and consumers' right to know. This is critical to the legislation (information should not be misleading) and the definition of health claims to which the legislation applies ("anything that states, suggests or implies …").

It can be difficult for consumers to draw correct inferences from health claims. Long claims on the front of a package, although very accurate in content, may lead

[31] Raghunathan et al. (2006).

[32] Kardes et al. (2004).

[33] Lähteenmäki et al. (2010).

[34] Andrews et al. (1998) and Roe et al. (1999).

consumers to question the believability of the claim and decrease their understanding of the claim compared to shorter claims.[35] Comprehension of health claims can also be hindered due to difficult or confusing wording of such claims.[36] Subtle message elements, such as the difference between a claim stating that a nutrient reduces a health risk versus a claim stating that a nutrient *may* reduce a health risk, are often lost in all the information that is present. This is especially true for low-literate consumers, who often have difficulty interpreting nutrition and health information.[37] Thus, although the legislation has taken great care in constructing a list of permitted health claims and the exact wording that is allowed, this does not necessarily ensure high consumer understanding among more vulnerable consumer groups.

In summary, health claims affect both how consumers perceive a product and whether they choose to buy the product. Of particular importance in consumer perceptions is the level of understanding of the health claim.[38] A serious concern is that consumers may overgeneralize health claims, leading them to believe that a product is more healthful than it actually is. As a result, such overgeneralization from a health claim could stimulate unfounded consumer expectations. A deeper understanding of consumer-level issues related to nutrition and health claims, offers opportunities for regulators and policy makers to stimulate the use of health claims on product packaging for healthful food products, to increase healthy choices. It also offers opportunities for companies to differentiate their products from competitors' products by using health claims.

5 Discussion and Implications for EU Law

The EU legislation on nutrition and health claims has two important objectives: (1) to protect consumers from potentially misleading information, and (2) to help consumers make more informed healthful choices, thereby enhancing fair competition. The present study has reviewed existing consumer behaviour information regarding nutrition and health claims, in their context, against a consumer behaviour framework of how, when and why health information may induce correct understanding and motivate healthful choices. The review has identified several factors that may undermine the sympathetic logic that "more healthful information will lead to more healthful choices on the part of the consumer".

First, health information on pack always competes with other information in the decision context. In such information-rich environments, health information may not be the first source to be attended to. Attention is enhanced when the health goal is (made) situationally accessible, either because there is a chronic disease state

[35]Wansink (2003) and Wansink et al. (2004).

[36]Grunert and Wills (2007), van Kleef and Dagevos (2015) and Lähteenmäki (2013).

[37]Viswanathan et al. (2009).

[38]Grunert and Wills (2007) and Nocella and Kennedy (2012).

(making health information particularly relevant and decisive in choice) or because situational factors (e.g. communication at the moment of choice) make health goals situationally accessible. Health information in itself might also direct consumer attention towards the health goal and hence health information could induce a context in which health goals become more relevant. Hence a first important factor of health claims on pack is that they increase relevant product differentiation at the shelf, indicating consumers that "there is something to choose" and that products on shelf differ in terms of healthfulness.

Second, a crucial factor in consumer behaviour on health claims (and nutritional information in general) is that their effect critically depends on the attention that such information attracts. This is increasingly challenging in information-rich environments and when consumers have limited attentional resources. As attention processes are essential it is crucial to "guide" consumers' attention to healthfulness at the moment of choice. This can either be achieved by stimulating consumers' health goal accessibility through, other than product/packaging related, communication at the point of purchase. Point of sale nutrition-and-health campaigns may activate consumers' health goal accessibility, thus drawing attention more easily to the search for health-related information on pack. Alternatively, and complementary, attention can be enhanced if health information "stands out" compared to other competing information on pack. This can be achieved by making health information highly salient (visible on pack), and/or by communicating it in terms of visuals rather than text, as these appear to more easily attract attention, especially in information-rich contexts.

Third, once attended to, the inference making process based on health claims and symbols is crucial. Next to purely informational belief formation about healthfulness (the objective decoding of claims and symbols), consumers also use own rules of thumb (inferential belief formation) in their understanding (inference making) of nutrition and health implications. Several packaging elements, including colour, visuals, brand names, production method, and even competing claims may, in the eyes of the consumer, be indicative for the healthfulness of the product. The major implication here is that, although the legislation accounts for other factors that may "state, suggest, or imply" a relationship with perceived healthfulness, more effort may need to be invested to truly understand potentially misleading packaging cues when it comes to healthfulness inferences on the part of the consumer.

Correct understanding of nutrition and health claims is not only a matter of selective attention to cues and subjective inferences. It is also a matter of knowledge and clarity in communication. Nutrition and health issues are complex and often suffer from lack of full consensus between expert scientists. As a result, nutrition and health claims are often expressed in complex and subtle wording, to do full justice to the current (lack of) consensus within the scientific community. This is problematic from a lay-person consumer perspective as it complicates the correct "decoding" process. One important implication is that to make health claims more effective at the consumer-understanding and -motivational level, wording may need to be simplified. This provides an interesting and challenging trade off against the state of the art in nutritional sciences, which needs to be solved to ensure that the communicated information is both market-relevant and scientifically-correct.

A related important point is that, although the legislation regarding health claims explicitly covers pictorial, graphic or symbolic representations that can suggest or imply that a product is healthful, in practice the focus is on textual claims.[39] The list of approved claims in the Annex only contains textual claims, and is not particularly suitable for pictorial representations. Moreover, court decisions up to date have also focused on textual health claims. Visual packaging elements, however, may be especially powerful in drawing consumer attention and influencing inferences about the healthfulness of food products. Regulating visual packaging elements that communicate health is more complex than regulating textual health claims. The meaning of visual elements is contextually situated,[40] implying that the same visual element may have vastly different meanings when placed on different products. A heart symbol can primarily communicate heart health when placed on a margarine product, but the same symbol may primarily communicate romantic love when placed on a chocolate product. Regulation thus needs to take the context in which such elements are encountered into account, and black or white lists are not going to be very practical in such a case.

Summarizing, EU health claim legislation serves the dual objectives of increasing information transparency and consumer motivation to choose more healthful options. The current review of relevant consumer behaviour literature has identified important bottlenecks for reaching these objectives, which can help policy makers in increasing the effectiveness of the legislation. Particularly, more attention should be paid to non-textual information on pack as these have a high potential of being attended to, and hence of influencing consumer perceptions and behaviours. Secondly, health claims and symbols alone may not suffice in increasing consumer motivation to choose more healthful options, and may need to be supported by other communication efforts. Finally, health claims should not only be scientifically correct but also communicated in an easy to understand way to consumers, if they are to be effective.

Acknowledgment CLYMBOL (*Role of health-related CLaims and sYMBOLs in consumer behaviour*) has received funding from the European Union's Seventh Framework Programme for research, technological development and demonstration under grant agreement no. 311963.

References

Abrams KM, Evans C, Duff BRL (2015) Ignorance is bliss. How parents of preschool children make sense of front-of-package visuals and claims on food. Appetite 87(1):20–29

[39]Purnhagen et al. (2016).

[40]Scott and Vargas (2007).

Andrews JC, Netemeyer RG, Burton S (1998) Consumer generalization of nutrient content claims in advertising. J Market 62(4):62–75

Bagozzi RP, Dholakia U (1999) Goal setting and goal striving in consumer behavior. J Market 63 (Special Issue 1999):19–32

Bilman E (2014) Claiming satiety: consumer perception, interpretation & subsequent food intake. Dissertation, Wageningen University

Bone PF, France KR (2001) Package graphics and consumer product beliefs. J Bus Psychol 15 (3):467–489

Carrillo E, Fiszman S, Lähteenmäki L, Varela P (2014) Consumers' perception of symbols and health claims as health-related label messages. A cross-cultural study. Food Res Int 62:653–661

Chernev A (2004) Goal-attribute compatibility in consumer choice. J Consum Psychol 14 (1&2):141–150

Childers TL, Houston MJ (1984) Conditions for a picture-superiority effect on consumer memory. J Consum Res 11(2):643–654

Dean M, Shepherd R, Arvola A, Vassallo M, Winkelmann M, Claupein E, Lähteenmäki L, Raats MM, Saba A (2007) Consumer perceptions of healthy cereal products and production methods. J Cereal Sci 46(3):188–196

Dhar R, Kim EY (2007) Seeing the forest or the trees: implications of construal level theory for consumer choice. J Consum Psychol 17(2):96–100

Ford GT, Smith DB, Swasy JL (1988) An empirical test of the search, experience, and credence attributes framework. Adv Consum Res 15:239–244

Graham DJ, Orquin JL, Visschers VHM (2012) Eye tracking and nutrition label use: a review of the literature and recommendations for label enhancement. Food Policy 37(4):378–382

Grunert KG, Wills JM (2007) A review of European research on consumer response to nutrition information at food labels. J Publ Health 15(5):385–399

Grunert KG, Lähteenmäki L, Boztug Y, Martinsdóttir E, Ueland Ø, Åström A, Lampila P (2009) Perception of health claims among Nordic consumers. J Consum Policy 32(3):269–287

Grunert KG, Wills JM, Fernández-Celemín L (2010) Nutrition knowledge, and use and understanding of nutrition information on food labels among consumers in the UK. Appetite 55 (2):177–189

Hockley WE (2008) The picture superiority effect in associative recognition. Mem Cognit 36 (7):1351–1359

Hughner RS, McDonagh P, Prothero A, Shultz CJ II, Stanton J (2007) Who are organic food consumers? A compilation and review of why people purchase organic food. J Consum Behav 6 (2–3):94–110

Kardes FR, Posavac SS, Cronley ML (2004) Consumer inference: a review of processes, bases, and judgment contexts. J Consum Psychol 14(3):230–256

Kornelis M, van Herpen E, van der Lans I, Aramyan L (2010) Using non-food information to identify food-choice segment membership. Food Qual Prefer 21(5):512–520

Kozup JC, Creyer EH, Burton S (2003) Making healthful food choices: the influence of health claims and nutrition information on consumers' evaluations of packaged food products and restaurant menu items. J Market 67(2):19–34

Lähteenmäki L (2013) Claiming health in food products. Food Qual Prefer 27(2):196–201

Lähteenmäki L, Lampila P, Grunert K, Boztug Y, Ueland Ø, Åström A, Martinsdóttir E (2010) Impact of health-related claims on the perception of other product attributes. Food Policy 35 (3):230–239

Lancaster KJ (1966) A new approach to consumer theory. J Polit Econ 74(2):132–157

Ma Y, Ailawadi KL, Grewal D (2013) Soda versus cereal and sugar versus fat: drivers of healthful food intake and the impact of diabetes diagnosis. J Market 77(3):101–120

Moorman C (1998) Market-level effects of information: competitive responses and consumer dynamics. J Market Res 35(1):82–98

Nisbett RE, Wilson TD (1977) The halo effect: evidence for unconscious alteration of judgments. J Pers Soc Psychol 35(4):250–256

Nocella G, Kennedy O (2012) Food health claims: what consumers understand. Food Policy 37 (5):571–580

Papies EK, Potjes I, Keesman M, Schwinghammer S, van Koningsbruggen GM (2014) Using health primes to reduce unhealthy snack purchases among overweight consumers in a grocery store. Int J Obes 38:597–602

Pieters R, Warlop L (1999) Visual attention during brand choice: the impact of time pressure and task motivation. Int J Res Market 16(1):1–16

Purnhagen K, van Herpen E, van Kleef E (2016) The potential use of visual packaging elements as nudges: an analysis on the example of the EU health claims regime. In: Nudging anthology. Springer, pp 134–149

Raghunathan R, Naylor RW, Hoyer WD (2006) The unhealthy = tasty intuition and its effects on taste inferences, enjoyment, and choice of food products. J Market 70(4):170–184

Rayner M, Boaz A, Higginson C (2001) Consumer use of health-related endorsements on food labels in the United Kingdom and Australia. J Nutr Educ 33(1):24–30

Roe B, Levy AS, Derby BM (1999) The impact of health claims on consumer search and product evaluation outcomes: results from FDA experimental data. J Publ Policy Market 18(1):89–105

Roodenburg AJC, Popkin BM, Seidell JC (2011) Development of international criteria for a front of package food labelling system: the international choices programme. Eur J Clin Nutr 65:1190–1200

Scott LM (1994) Images in advertising: the need for a theory of visual rhetoric. J Consum Res 21 (2):252–273

Scott LM, Vargas P (2007) Writing with pictures: toward a unifying theory of consumer response to images. J Consum Res 34(3):341–356

Stenberg G, Radeborg K, Hedman LR (1995) The picture superiority effect in a cross-modality recognition task. Mem Cognit 23(4):425–441

Steptoe A, Pollard TM, Wardle J (1995) Development of a measure of the motives underlying the selection of food: the food choice questionnaire. Appetite 25(3):267–284

Trope Y, Liberman N (2003) Temporal construal. Psychol Rev 110(3):403–421

Underwood RL, Klein NM (2002) Packaging as brand communication: effects of product pictures on consumer responses to the package and brand. J Market Theory Pract 10(4):58–68

Urala N, Arvola A, Lähteenmäki L (2003) Strength of health-related claims and their perceived advantage. Int J Food Sci Technol 38(7):815–826

van Herpen E, Pieters R (2007) Anticipated identification costs: improving assortment evaluation by diagnostic attributes. Int J Res Market 24(1):77–88

van Herpen E, van Trijp HCM (2011) Front-of-pack nutrition labels. Their effect on attention and choices when consumers have varying goals and time constraints. Appetite 57(1):148–160

van Kleef E, Dagevos H (2015) The growing role of front-of-pack nutrition profile labeling: a consumer perspective on key issues and controversies. Crit Rev Food Sci Nutr 55(3):291–303

van Rompay TJL, Pruyn ATH (2011) When visual product features speak the same language: effects of shape-typeface congruence on brand perception and price expectations. J Prod Innov Manag 28(4):599–610

Verbeke W (2010) Consumer reactions to foods with nutrition and health claims. Agro Food Ind Hi-Tech 21(6):5–8

Viswanathan M, Hastak M, Gau R (2009) Understanding and facilitating the usage of nutritional labels by low-literate consumers. J Publ Policy Market 28(2):135–145

Vyth E, Steenhuis IHM, Vlot JA, Wulp A, Hogenes MG, Looije DH, Brug J, Seidell JC (2010) Actual use of a front-of-pack nutrition logo in the supermarket: consumers' motives in food choice. Public Health Nutr 13(11):1882–1889

Walsh D (2014) Can priming a healthy eating goal cause depleted consumers to prefer healthier snacks? J Consum Market 31(2):126–132

Wansink B (2003) How do front and back package labels influence beliefs about health claims? J Consum Aff 37(2):305–316

Wansink B, Sonka ST, Hasler CM (2004) Front-label health claims: when less is more. Food Policy 29(6):659–667

Warlop L, (Ratti) Ratneshwar S, van Osselaer SM (2005) Distinctive brand cues and memory for product consumption experiences. Int J Res Market 22(1):27–44

Williams P (2005) Consumer understanding and use of health claims for foods. Nutr Rev 63 (7):256–264

Erica van Herpen is associate professor at the Marketing and Consumer Behaviour Group of Wageningen University. She received her PhD in marketing at Tilburg University. Her research focuses on consumer evaluation, use of, and choice from (food) product assortments. She examines consumer decisions in retail settings, studying how the presentation of products and of the store itself affect consumer behaviour, and how consumers can be stimulated to buy more healthful and/or more sustainable products. This includes the effect of nutrition labels and health claims on consumer decision making.

Hans C. M. van Trijp is Chair and Full Professor of Marketing and Consumer Behaviour at Wageningen University in The Netherlands. He received his PhD in marketing at Wageningen University and has combined his job in Academia with an affiliation in food industry for many years. His research focuses on marketing and consumer behaviour, primarily from a "social" marketing perspective, namely how these insights can be used and extended to the case of consumption and production of healthy and sustainable products. Research on the effect of nutrition labelling (symbols and claims) has been a part of his research portfolio for long time.

Regulatory Compliance and Company Strategies: The Case of the Nutrition and Health Claims Regulation (EC) No. 1924/2006

Stefanie Bröring and Sukhada Khedkar

Abstract The area of functional foods has seen an investment of millions of dollars and increase in interest from all stakeholders over the past years. In the EU, the Nutrition and Health Claims Regulation (EC) No. 1924/2006 (NHCR) was adopted in year 2007. This regulation is based on a premarket approval system and sets harmonized rules to govern nutrition and health claims. It aims at consumer protection, fair competition and fostering innovation in the EU food sector. This chapter investigates the topic of companies' compliance with respect to the NHCR, firstly by focusing on their perceived challenges and then by probing into their possible compliance strategies. The NHCR brings along numerous challenges related to the wording of claims, missing transparencies, financial and R&D resources etc. Companies seem to implement different strategies to deal with this regulation. Existing literature indicates that the compliance strategies that companies may adopt with respect to the NHCR could range from working on the data and reapplying for a claim, to circumventing the regulation altogether by changing communication methods or marketing products without using any health claims.

1 Introduction

Health has been considered as the most significant trend and innovation driver in the global food and drinks market.[1] Due to the rising prevalence of obesity, diabetes and cardiovascular diseases, there is increasing importance of a healthy diet in the European Union (EU).[2] Additionally, growing public interest in possible health benefits of food has created an attractive opportunity for the food industry in the

[1]Meziane (2007).

[2]Cencic and Chingwaru (2010).

S. Bröring · S. Khedkar (✉)
Technology and Innovation Management in Agribusiness, Institute for Food and Resource Economics, University of Bonn, Bonn, Germany
e-mail: s.broering@ilr.uni-bonn.de; s.khedkar@ilr.uni-bonn.de

H. Bremmers, K. Purnhagen (eds.), *Regulating and Managing Food Safety in the EU*, Economic Analysis of Law in European Legal Scholarship 6,
https://doi.org/10.1007/978-3-319-77045-1_6

form of functional foods.[3] Food companies have grabbed this opportunity by presenting a plethora of functional foods with ingredients like vitamins, minerals, antioxidants, probiotics etc. to the modern-day health aware consumers.[4] According to Diplock et al. (1999), there is no universal definition of the term 'functional food'. However, the authors state that

> a food can be regarded as functional if it is satisfactorily demonstrated to affect beneficially one or more target functions in the body, beyond adequate nutritional effects in a way that is relevant to either an improved state of health and well-being or reduction of risk of disease. Functional food must remain foods and they must demonstrate their effects in amounts that can normally be expected to be consumed in the diet which means that they are not pills or capsules but part of normal food pattern.[5]

Due to being credence attributes, health benefits of food products are difficult for consumers to evaluate before and after consumption. As a result, health claims, product labelling and packaging play a significant role in communicating and marketing the credence attributes of food products to consumers.[6] It has been found that products with scientifically substantiated and approved claims are mostly perceived positively by consumers. Consumers believe that these products help them in making healthier food choices.[7] Industries use claims as potentially powerful communication tools to convey information on food characteristics (e.g. source of vitamin D and calcium) and health benefits that might otherwise remain unknown to the consumers (e.g. calcium and vitamin D are needed for the maintenance of normal bones and teeth).[8] On one hand, the use of health claims may enable companies to achieve competitive advantage and provide an incentive for product innovation. This can be done by bridging the information gap between the buyer's knowledge and seller's information on intrinsic qualities of food.[9] On the other hand, consumers might be confused about what health claims exactly are and perceive such health claims to be a mere marketing strategy adopted by industries with a potential of misleading them.[10] Therefore, companies are forced to ascertain the trustworthiness of their health claims through scientific substantiation.[11]

Against this background, the EU Parliament and the Council adopted the Nutrition and Health Claims Regulation (EC) No. 1924/2006 (NHCR) which

[3]De Boer and Bast (2015), p. 61.

[4]Bornkessel et al. (2014) and Bröring (2010).

[5]Diplock et al. (1999), p. 6.

[6]Nelson (1974), p. 730.

[7]van Buul and Brouns (2013).

[8]Richardson and Eggersdorfer (2015), p. 10.

[9]Hobbs and Kerr (2006).

[10]Pothoulaki and Chryssochoidis (2009).

[11]Bröring et al. (2016), p. 1.

came into force on 1 July 2007.[12] According to the original proposal of the European Commission (EC) in 2003, the NHCR had the following general objectives[13]:

1. To achieve a high level of consumer protection.
2. To improve the free movement of goods within the internal market.
3. To increase legal security for economic operators and ensure fair competition in the area of foods, and
4. To promote and protect innovation in the area of foods.

The NHCR is unique and may be regarded as a positive development because it facilitates nutrition and health claims for conventional, novel, fortified foods, food supplements etc. and could help to distinguish between the food and medical market.[14] It adopts the system of premarket approval and scientific substantiation for approval of health claims on food products and supplements. The European Food Safety Authority (EFSA) evaluates if the provided scientific evidence is sufficient (Article 16 of Regulation (EC) No. 1924/2006)[15], and companies can bring products with health claims to the market only if they receive a positive opinion from the EFSA.

With regards to consumer protection against misleading claims, it needs to be considered that consumer awareness varies significantly with respect to functional food ingredients. Consumers are more likely to be aware of ingredients which are well known and have a long research history.[16] They tend to accept functional ingredients which are well established and have a broadly appealing health image rather than functional ingredients which are non-familiar, specific and require advanced nutrition knowledge. Health claims play an important role in delivering the benefits of non-familiar functional ingredients to the consumers.[17]

From the company side, the NHCR was welcomed by (especially large) companies, as it enables them to differentiate their functional food products from apparently similar products and gain competitive advantage. Also, companies that are not yet eligible for using claims on their products are given incentives to innovate. At the same time, the NHCR requires that food companies prove the effectiveness of their health claims scientifically, which might be challenging for them (especially for small and medium sized enterprises (SMEs)) to achieve due to lack of financial or R&D resources to conduct research activities,[18] or experience with regulatory approval processes.[19] Therefore, even though the NHCR is one of the few

[12]Regulation (EC) No. 1924/2006.

[13]European Responsible Nutrition Alliance (2011), p. 57.

[14]Schwitters et al. (2007), p. 29.

[15]Regulation (EC) No. 1924/2006, recital 23, p. 7.

[16]Bornkessel et al. (2014) and Mejborn (2007).

[17]Mejborn (2007).

[18]Regulation (EC) No. 1924/2006, recital 32; Khedkar et al. (2016b).

[19]Bröring (2005).

regulations that targets to protect interests of all involved actors (from producers to end consumers) in the area of functional foods, the topic of how companies cope with this regulation remains to be explored.

In view of the above presented literature on functional foods and the NHCR, this chapter focuses on the following two research questions:

(a) What are the (perceived) challenges faced by companies to comply with the NHCR?
(b) What are the strategies that companies might adopt to comply with the NHCR?

The present chapter is further structured as follows: Sect. 2 provides a brief literature background on the relationships between regulation, innovation and the NHCR in the EU and presents the current status of health claims governed by this regulation. Section 3 presents the research method employed, while Sect. 4 focuses on the challenges companies perceived to face to comply with the regulation. Section 5 explores the strategies that companies may adopt to comply with the NHCR, and finally, Sect. 6 discusses the research questions against the extant literature and concludes by highlighting the main findings and opportunities for future research.

2 A Brief Literature Review on Innovation, Regulation and the NHCR in the EU

2.1 Innovation in the EU Food Industry

According to FoodDrinkEurope (2014), the EU is the leading food and drink producer worldwide with a turnover of 1048 billion Euros. It is also the leading exporter of food and drink products with a share of 16.1% in the global food and drink trade. The EU food industry is fragmented and consists of 286,000 companies. It is dominated by SMEs with 99.1% of the food and beverage companies belonging to this category. The SMEs contribute to 51.6% of the food industry's turnover and 64.3% of the food industry employment.[20] The food industry is also the third most trusted industry in the EU.[21] It ranks first in terms of turnover in France, Spain, Belgium, Denmark and the UK, which evidently shows that it is an important sector in several EU countries.[22] With R&D investment of 0.27% in 2014 (as a share of

[20]FoodDrinkEurope (2014).

[21]Ibid.

[22]FoodDrinkEurope (2014): FoodDrinkEurope is the source for all data describing characteristics and current innovation situation of the European food industry (e.g. turnover, number of companies, share of SMEs etc.).

food industry turnover), this food industry traditionally shows a trend of lower investments into innovation and R&D compared to food industries in other countries.[23] Innovations in the EU food industry are mainly driven by consumer expectations, while its other concerns are international competition, food safety and quality and changing consumer trends.[24] Thus, food innovation plays an important role for this sector to meet consumer demands and maintain its position in the global market.

Innovation represents a source of competitive advantage for companies, allowing them to face the growing competition in both national and international markets.[25] It is at the heart of Europe 2020 and plays an important role in re-establishing the competitiveness and economic strength of the EU economy. Nutrition and health claims are important pathways towards innovation in the EU food industry.[26] Thus, the EC considers the regulation of health claims to be a stimulation for the companies to innovate and develop healthier food or food products with functional benefits, thereby improving their competitiveness.[27] It has been observed that over the last 10 years, product innovation has played a critical role in meeting changes in the demand pattern. Furthermore, both—innovations and demand pattern changes incline towards product quality attributes such as health benefits, sensory characteristics, convenience features etc.[28] Nonetheless, it is well established that the EU food industry is usually engaged in process innovations, which along with product innovations, help to increase efficiency in the global market.[29]

With respect to the degree of innovativeness (incremental-new to company or radical-new to market), in general, food industries see more of incremental innovations. This is mainly because food industries, due to low R&D intensity and shorter R&D cycles, often do not possess sufficient R&D capacities to create new products.[30] Moreover, the intrinsic nature of food related to tradition and its traditional attributes hinder product innovation.[31] The EU food industry also sees more of process innovation but considers product innovation to be more important for its overall competitiveness and growth.[32]

[23]Ibid.

[24]Ibid.

[25]Banterle et al. (2011), p. 474.

[26]European Responsible Nutrition Alliance (ERNA) (2011), p. 64.

[27]Flynn (2012) and Moors (2012).

[28]Banterle et al. (2011), p. 474.

[29]Ibid.

[30]Bröring (2010).

[31]Banterle et al. (2011), p. 475.

[32]Martinez and Briz (2000).

2.2 Impact of Regulation on Innovation in General and for the Food Industry in Particular

Regulation and innovation share an interesting relationship which has not been researched at length. According to Blind (2012), policies to improve the framework conditions relevant for innovation are becoming more important. This is particularly because it is difficult to increase public spending in R&D to promote innovation due to public budget restrictions. He also states that in sectors with strong ethical dimensions and a high importance of externalities (e.g. health), the link between regulation and innovation is obvious and close. Finally, he says that while on one hand, regulations may prohibit innovations-especially radical innovations, on the other hand these regulations might increase the acceptance of new products among consumers, since consumers can rely on a minimum level of product safety.[33]

Over the last decade, the food sector has become one of the most regulated in the EU. As mentioned in the introduction, the NHCR requires a pre-market approval before products with claims can appear in the market. Following Henson and Caswell (1999), different forms of food safety regulation can be distinguished based on the degree of intervention. This degree of intervention ranges from information requirements to prior approval, while the formulation of standards can be ranked between these two extremes.[34] At one extreme end of information measures, suppliers are needed to disclose some facts about their products, but otherwise their behaviour is not restricted. At the other extreme end of prior approval, suppliers need to obtain prior approval of a product from an official agency before they can introduce it to the market.[35] Food safety standards are in the middle of these two extremes and permit suppliers to launch new products in the market without a pre-market approval if they meet some minimum safety standards.[36]

On a general note, premarket approval requirements might have a negative quantitative effect on innovation and thereby on competitiveness. This may be illustrated by the fact that fewer than 100 innovations have been approved for the EU market between 2003 and 2008. Product innovation was the area most prone to be affected by premarket approval requirements and seemed to be obstructed the most.[37] For the case of the EU food industry, as mentioned previously, majority of food companies in the EU are SMEs. Given their resource limitations, high legislative stringency and strictness in the form of premarket approvals may pose certain compliance challenges for them, which might also hold true in the case of NHCR. The perceived challenges that companies might face to adhere to the NHCR are discussed later in the chapter.

[33]Blind (2012).

[34]Henson and Caswell (1999).

[35]Ibid.

[36]Ibid.

[37]van der Meulen et al. (2012), p. 459.

2.3 *The Current Status of the Nutrition and Health Claims Regulation (EC) No. 1924/2006 (NHCR)*

Historically, companies attempting to launch functional food in the EU have faced variety of legislative frameworks. Such legislations mainly governed the approval of products, food labelling and the types of functional claims and health claims. The way of regulating, however, was highly inconsistent between EU member states.[38] The only pre-requisite was that the consumers should not be misled by the information on food products.[39] In December 2006, the NHCR was adopted by the European Council and the Parliament, which set harmonized rules to govern nutrition and health claims in the EU (Regulation (EC) No. 1924/2006).[40]

According to this regulation, nutrition claim means any claim which states, suggests or implies that a food has particular beneficial nutritional properties due to[41]

1. the energy (calorific value) it
   (a) provides;
   (b) provides at a reduced or increased rate; or
   (c) does not provide; and/or
2. the nutrients or other substances it
   (a) contains;
   (b) contains in reduced or increased proportions; or
   (c) does not contain.

Health claim means any claim that states, suggests or implies that a relationship exists between a food category, a food or one of its constituents and health (Article 2 of the NHCR).[42]

Health claims need to be scientifically substantiated and as specified in the regulation, according to the EFSA,[43] the evidence requires to demonstrate the extent to which

1. the claimed effect of the food/constituent is relevant for human health,
2. a cause and effect relationship is established between the consumption of the food/constituent and the claimed effect in humans (such as: the strength, consistency, specificity, dose-response, and biological plausibility of the relationship),
3. the quantity of the food/constituent and pattern of consumption required to obtain the claimed effect could reasonably be achieved as part of a balanced diet,
4. the specific study group(s) in which the evidence was obtained is representative of the target population for which the claim is intended.

---

[38] Bech-Larsen and Scholderer (2007), p. 231.

[39] Patel et al. (2012), p. 15.

[40] Regulation (EC) No. 1924/2006.

[41] Ibid.

[42] Ibid.

[43] European Food Safety Authority (EFSA) (2007), p. 5.

Broadly, the NHCR governs three types of claims which are summarized under their relevant Articles in Table 1.

Based on the EU Register for nutrition and health claims as well Gilsenan (2011), one main reason for obtaining negative opinion from the EFSA seems to be insufficient scientific evidence or characterisation. For example, under Article 13.1, the claim *"(Cow's) Milk products help support dental health. (Cow's) Milk helps support*

Table 1 Current status of health claims under the NHCR

Article	Definition	Status
Article 13.1[a]	The so-called 'General Function Health Claims' referring to the growth, development and functions of the body, psychological and behavioural functions and slimming or weight-control.	(a) Up to year 2011, 44,000 Article 13.1 health claims were submitted to the EFSA from individual EU member states. Around 80% of the proposed claims have received a negative opinion from the EFSA.[b] (b) As of July 2017, according to the EU Register on nutrition and health claims, 229 Article 13.1 health claims have been authorised, while 1875 claims have not been authorised.[c]
Article 13.5[d]	New function health claims referring to newly developed scientific evidence and/or for which protection of proprietary data is requested.	(a) For these health claims authorisation is required on a case-by-case basis, following the submission of a scientific dossier to EFSA for assessment.[e] (b) As of July 2017, according to the EU Register on nutrition and health claims, 6 Article 13.5 health claims have been authorised, while 108 claims have not been authorized.[f]
Article 14[g]	(1)(a) Risk reduction claims on reducing a risk factor in the development of a disease; and (1)(b) Health claims referring to children's development (European Commission 2015)	(a) These health claims follow an authorisation procedure based on individual applications.[h] (b) As of July 2017, according to the EU Register on nutrition and health claims, 14 Article 14(1)(a) risk reduction health claims and 12 Article 14(1)(b) health claims referring to children's development have been authorized, while the number of non-authorized health claims for Article 14(1)(a) and Article 14(1)(b) was 24 and 44 respectively.[i]

[a]Regulation (EC) No. 1924/2006
[b]Gilsenan (2011), p. 538; Pravst (2012), p. 171
[c]European Commission (2017)
[d]Regulation (EC) No. 1924/2006
[e]European Food Safety Authority (EFSA) (2017)
[f]European Commission (2017)
[g]Regulation (EC) No. 1924/2006
[h]European Commission (2015)
[i]European Commission (2017)

the normal and healthy development of teeth. (Cow's) Milk contributes to dental health" was rejected on the reason *"Non-compliance with the Regulation, because on the basis of the scientific evidence assessed, this food is not sufficiently characterised for a scientific assessment of this claimed effect and the claim could not therefore be substantiated."* Similarly, under Article 13.5, a claim on Lactobacillus rhamnosus GG (LGG) such that *"Lactobacillus GG helps to maintain defence against intestinal pathogens"* was rejected due to the following reason *"Non-compliance with the Regulation, because on the basis of the scientific evidence assessed, this claimed effect for this food has not been substantiated."*[44] Lack of positive opinions from the EFSA may suggest that companies perceived to face some challenges with respect to the NHCR. Consequently, they might adopt various strategies to cope with this regulation.

3 Methods

The method employed to gather knowledge for the present book chapter is mainly desk research. The research questions presented in the introduction are explored based on reviews of existing literature. We mainly utilized external secondary sources such as books, peer reviewed journal articles, government policies, reports of government organizations, newsletters and relevant case studies for investigating the topic at hand.

4 The NHCR: Potential Challenges and Criticalities

Extant literature (e.g. Da Silva 2010; Brookes 2010; ERNA 2011; Gilsenan 2011; Moors 2012; Bröring et al. 2016; Khedkar et al. 2016a, b etc.) identified some of the main challenges that seem to be related to complying with the NHCR. These challenges are discussed as follows:

1. Changing List of Ingredients

   The NHCR states that *"there is a wide variety of claims currently used in the labelling and advertising of foods in some Member States relating to substances that have not been shown to be beneficial or for which at present there is not sufficient scientific agreement"*.[45] It also says that the labelling requirements laid down in the regulation might affect the usage of certain ingredients, thereby forcing companies to change their recipe formulations. This is also confirmed by a study conducted by Brandenburger and Birringer (2015).[46] If companies are

[44]Gilsenan (2011); European Commission (2017).

[45]Regulation (EC) No. 1924/2006, recital 14, p. 5.

[46]Brandenburger and Birringer (2015), p. 46.

unable to communicate the benefits of their products to consumers, certain products would no longer be available in the market.[47] Companies might prefer to use ingredients which allow them to use an already approved claim, so that they do not need to change their recipe formulations. For example, approval of most claims with vitamins and minerals, and rejections of claims on antioxidants, probiotics and other functional food ingredients might reduce the usage of ingredients with non-authorized claims. It might happen that companies merely choose to use established vitamins and minerals with approved claims instead of conducting new research on novel ingredients with potentially interesting health functionalities.[48]

2. Missing Transparency

   Article 1-2 of the NHCR states that *"this regulation shall apply to nutrition and health claims made in commercial communications, whether in the labelling, presentation or advertising of foods to be delivered as such to the final consumer"*.[49] However, it is argued that there are only limited guidelines about where the boundaries of commercial communication lie.[50] In addition, studies describe that companies face uncertainties with respect to NHCR,[51] particularly regarding what exactly will be accepted by EFSA. As a result, they may rethink their decisions about engaging in new research activities and bringing new products to the market.[52] In case of a rejected health claim, companies might have to invest more in promotions or advertisements to keep their product in the market without an approved health claim. Thus, they may shift R&D budgets towards marketing activities.[53]

3. Time to Comply with the Regulation

   The Commission Regulation (EU) No 432/2012 of 16 May 2012 which established the list of permitted health claims for Article 13.1 states *"This Regulation should apply six months after the date of its entry into force to enable food business operators to adapt to its requirements."*[54] The NHCR puts forward that the companies have 6 months to comply with the regulation in case of a rejected health claim for health claims which are not under Article 13.1(a) and Article 14.1(a). It also says that health claims as referred to in Article 13.1(a) may be made from the date of entry into force of this Regulation until the adoption of the community list.[55]

---

[47]Da Silva (2010), p. 166.

[48]European Responsible Nutrition Alliance (2011).

[49]Regulation (EC) No. 1924/2006.

[50]Gilsenan (2011), p. 540.

[51]Brookes (2010); Brandenburger and Birringer (2015), p. 54.

[52]European Responsible Nutrition Alliance (ERNA) (2011).

[53]Brookes (2010).

[54]Commission Regulation (EU) No 423/2012.

[55]Regulation (EC) No. 1924/2006, Article 28, recital 5,6.

As for the time taken for approval procedure, Article 16-1 of the NHCR states "in giving its opinion the Authority shall respect a time limit of five months from the date of receipt of a valid application. Whenever the authority seeks supplementary information from the applicant, such time limit shall be extended by up to two months following the date of receipt of the requested information submitted by the applicant."[56] Nevertheless, literature suggests that claim approval procedures might see a delay of up to 2–3 years, which may result in a long time to comply with the regulation.[57]

4. Wording of Claims

   Although the regulation also governs health claims in pictorial, graphic or symbolic form (Article 2-1), it only mentions examination of the wording of claim (Article 16-3) in relation to the scientific proof presented.[58] As laid down in the general conditions of the NHCR (e.g. in Article 5-2) *"The use of nutrition and health claims shall only be permitted if the average consumer can be expected to understand the beneficial effects as expressed in the claim."*[59] Thus, the wording of claim should be scientific and specific but also simple enough for the consumers to understand.[60] Using the 'official' wording is often unattractive for marketing reasons, since scientific wording might not be easily understandable for the 'average consumer'. Even after the wording of claims is accepted, whether it can achieve a balance between meeting the mandatory legal requirements, and being understandable for consumers, remains to be seen. Moreover, the meaning of what a claim is may not be immediately clear for consumers. Consumers may understand the general notion behind the claim (e.g. relatively low energy-levels contained in a product called 'lite'), but they might not understand or know how this is measured.[61] In case of more scientific claims, the use of certain terms such as 'connective tissues', 'nitric oxide', 'metabolism' could be difficult for average consumers to understand.[62]

5. Limited Financial Resources

   The NHCR requires that *"Health claims should only be authorised for use in the Community after a scientific assessment of the highest possible standard"*.[63] It may be that a submitted claim is rejected more than once, so that the funds invested in innovation of new products cannot be earned back in time. Moreover, as mentioned earlier, to keep the products with rejected health claims in the market, companies may have to invest more in advertisements.[64]

---

[56]Regulation (EC) No. 1924/2006.

[57]Moors (2012), p. 434.

[58]Regulation (EC) No. 1924/2006; Lelieveldt and Boonen (2012), p. 581.

[59]Regulation (EC) No. 1924/2006.

[60]Gilsenan (2011), p. 540.

[61]Bremmers and van der Meulen (2013), p. 100.

[62]Mariotti et al. (2010) and Nocella and Kennedy (2012).

[63]Regulation (EC) No. 1924/2006.

[64]Brookes (2010).

Compliance with the NHCR may also require companies to conduct human clinical trials, which could be a costly and risky activity for them (especially for SMEs).[65] The regulation itself mentions that the SMEs usually lack the financial capacity to carry out research activities.[66] Brookes (2010) estimated the cost of resources invested by food sector to compile entries of Article 13.1 list of submission to range between 4.51 and 7.65 million for the complete list. The adjustment costs associated with a negative opinion from the EFSA were estimated to be around 0.12 million (per company).[67] Brandenburger and Birringer (2015) also found that companies incur additional costs to conduct scientific studies, access legal experts and analyse the nutritional value of their products.[68] Thus, it might not be feasible for food companies, especially SMEs to undertake clinical trials (if required) to obtain an approved health claim.

6. Limited R&D Resources

As mentioned in Sect. 2, the food industry is generally characterized with low R&D intensity ($<1\%$ of sales) and short R&D cycles (1–3 years). It sees less of product innovation due to lack of R&D resources. Moreover, food companies usually have little or no skills in the area of regulatory approval processes and lack familiarity with safety and efficacy testing due to little or no experience in clinical product evaluation.[69]

The functional ingredient producers play an important role regarding health claims as they deliver the ingredients that include a health claim, and often take care of the health claim dossier. Manufacturers of functional foods for the supermarkets buy these ingredients and add them to their products (e.g. Omega 3 being added to a dairy drink). However, the functional ingredient producers are often SMEs and may not have the resources to submit new health claim dossiers.[70]

7. Switching Product Categories

If companies do not win a health claim, the existence of certain products might get threatened. It may happen that certain products get 'selected away' from the market by goods that have a health claim.[71] The existence of some companies, especially SMEs might get threatened, and they may have to switch to other product categories or leave the functional foods sector altogether.[72]

As demonstrated above, the NHCR seems to present certain compliance challenges to companies. A recent empirical study presented in Khedkar et al. (2016a, b) reveals that specifically, *wording of claims, missing transparency and*

[65]Brookes (2010) and Younesi and Ayseli (2015).

[66]Regulation (EC) No. 1924/2006, recital 32, p. 7.

[67]Brookes (2010).

[68]Brandenburger and Birringer (2015), p. 46.

[69]Bröring (2010).

[70]Moors (2012), p. 433.

[71]Ibid, p. 436.

[72]Ibid, p. 438.

limited financial resources seem to be the major (perceived) challenges faced by companies to comply with the NHCR. These challenges could have an impact on the companies' overall business strategies. This motivates us to investigate the compliance strategies of food companies with respect to the NHCR. Some possible strategies to comply with the NHCR are discussed in the following section (Sect. 5).

5 Possible Compliance Strategies to Deal with the NHCR

To deal with a novel regulation such as the NHCR, companies might adopt a wide range of strategies. Some possible compliance strategies with regards to this regulation are discussed as follows:

1. Work on the Data and Evidence

   For some companies, the only option to comply with the NHCR would be to work on their data and evidence. Due to investments in R&D, and building and submitting a dossier with scientific evidence, some companies might be locked-in in the approval procedures. For such companies, renewed application could be the only option. Further, it might not be possible to market certain products without a health claim, if it is the only way to bring the special characteristics of these products to the attention of consumers. In such situations, companies may have to prepare a renewed application with new scientific evidence in case of a rejected claim. This seems to hold true for most probiotics, since the markets have expanded dramatically for these products and the stakes are high.[73] Kaur et al. (2016) argue that foods bearing a health claim are only slightly healthier than those without a health claim. Considering their findings, working on the data and evidence might be necessary for some companies to legitimise the health benefits of their products.[74]
2. Collaborations with Pharmaceutical Companies, Scientific and Legal Institutions

   With respect to the food industry, intra- and cross-industry cooperation, collaborations with competitors, consultants, customers and interactions with end consumers affect the success of innovation positively.[75] Moors (2012) recognizes that cooperation between food companies will gain importance, for example in sharing the risks and costs of the research for the health claim dossiers. Many food companies also have science-based collaborations with universities and intermediaries (e.g. research institutes) to conduct clinical studies for their health claim dossiers. Collaborations also take place to gain rapid access to new scientific and technological knowledge, and to benefit from

[73]Moors (2012), p. 166.

[74]Kaur et al. (2016).

[75]Ashok et al. (2014), pp. 5–6.

economies of scale in joint R&D. Universities are a strong research partner, as functional food research is an expanding area at universities.[76]

Compared to food companies, pharmaceutical companies possess higher R&D intensity (>14% of sales) and longer R&D cycles (10–20 years). The latter also have long term experiences in regulatory approval systems, conducting clinical trials, targeting industrial clients. Food companies, however focus on consumer markets, and have better consumer orientation.[77] Hence, by complementing each other's strengths, food and pharmaceutical companies may collaborate to comply with the NHCR. Further, manufacturers may consider working closely with governments to anticipate market opportunities that arise, if and when the rules are altered.[78]

One example of a research collaboration would be the example of krill player Aker BioMarine and the Norwegian food supplement manufacturer Sana Pharma to achieve positive opinions on health claims from the EFSA. The two companies collaborated to add Aker's SuperBa omega-3 krill oil to Sana Pharma's existing range of food supplements—Vitaepro which also includes ingredients like astaxanthin, lutein, zeaxanthin and vitamins C, D, E.[79] The case of Fruitflow also presents an example of a successful collaboration to obtain a health claim. Fruitflow secured a positive opinion from EFSA for its Article 13.5 health claim *'helps maintain normal platelet aggregation which contributes to healthy blood flow'* by working together with scientists and business experts.[80]

Khedkar et al. (2016b) also found a positive relationship between the NHCR and collaborations, and between collaborations and innovation activities of companies. Thus, collaborations could be used as a compliance strategy to deal with the NHCR.[81]

3. Piggybacking Strategy or Do Not Innovate

Article 13.1 health claims can be used by anyone who fulfils the requirements of use. Thus, companies might piggyback or free ride and use the already approved Article 13.1 health claims by reformulating their products.[82] For example, some products might see certain vitamins or minerals with acknowledged effects as ingredients, although they may not be necessary ingredients for these products.[83]

Due to the challenges related to the NHCR, and particularly the lack of required financial and R&D resources, some companies might take to avoidance behaviour. This means that they might not innovate at all or reduce their

[76]Moors (2012), pp. 429, 230.

[77]Bröring (2010).

[78]KMPG (2015), p. 16.

[79]Bryne (2010).

[80]Bouckley (2011), Brandenburger and Birringer (2015), p. 49 and Provexis plc (2015).

[81]Khedkar et al. (2016b).

[82]ERNA (2011) and Koehler (2013).

[83]Hermans (2011).

innovation efforts. Smaller companies may not apply for new health claims.[84] The phenomena of not innovating and using already authorized health claims may also be referred to as the 'me too syndrome'.

As argued by Moors (2012), in theory, despite high development cost, products with new health claims are attractive, because they provide an early mover advantage to companies that market the product first. This may further result in higher sales and market leadership.[85] However, in the case of high costs for application of new health claims and uncertainties associated with the outcome of the evaluation by EFSA, it might be easier to follow the product leader, thereby making product imitation rather attractive. Product followers could use the product leader to collect more information and assess the potential of a health claim to get an approval.[86]

4. Apply a 'Small-Big' Strategy

   According to Food Valley (2010) as described by Bremmers et al. (2013), a 'small-big'-strategy entails claiming for an easy-to-get claim and then expanding the claim to a more attractive one. Although this strategy delays the full harvesting of cash flows, it may reduce the risk of loss of image and market.[87]

5. Change the Product Category

   If food companies are unable to win a health claim, they might circumvent the regulation by bringing products to the market through another regulation. An example for this case could be botanicals. Most health claim applications involving botanicals have received a negative opinion from the EFSA or are on hold. The NHCR does not consider the traditional use of botanicals, and considers them as 'other substances' within the context of food supplements, which means that the food law applies to them.[88] As mentioned by Trovato (2013), in Europe a product can be lawfully placed on the market only if it fulfils the requirements for conformity of a single specific and relevant legislation.[89] Thus, to avoid the authorisation procedure connected to claims, food companies might access the market via the Traditional Herbal Medicinal Products, adopted in 2004 (Directive 2004/24/EC). This is mostly because the only requirement of this particular regulation is to provide evidence of safe use of a 'herbal medicine' for at least 30 years and the traditional use of botanicals is recognized.[90] This strategy could also protect the product from 'free riding'.[91]

[84]Moors (2012), p. 437.

[85]Ibid, p. 434.

[86]Ibid.

[87]Bremmers et al. (2013), p. 166.

[88]Trovato (2013) and Gruenwald (2014).

[89]Trovato (2013).

[90]Ibid.

[91]Appelhof (2010), pp. 62–63.

6. Change the Method and/or Medium of Communication

   Another strategy for companies to cope with the NHCR might be to change the method of communication. Under this strategy, instead of stating the claim directly, companies could rather suggest it through hidden messages, company taglines (e.g. "*Your trusted partner in health*"), and non-commercial communication methods or implied advertising.[92] For instance, companies might make recommendations relating to healthy eating while promoting fruit and vegetable juices. They might also promote their products with messages such as *'The berry that helps protect you inside'* which lie on the border between nutrition and health claims, or what is and what is not a claim.[93]

   It should also be noted that the NHCR governs textual claims in all commercial communications. Lelieveldt and Boonen (2012) state that

   > According to Article 2-1 of the Health Claims regulation, a claim is any type of message or representation and includes "pictorial, graphic or symbolic representation, in any form" but when it comes to the actual scrutiny of such claims, the regulation only talks about a procedure to examine the 'proposed wording' of the claim (Article 16-3) in relation to the scientific proof presented.[94]

   Thus, companies might promote the health benefits of their products via non-textual methods such as advertisements on television and other digital media. Lelieveldt and Boonen (2012) present the case of Optimel Control to explain that textual health claims are a small part of marketing for producers, and that those manufacturers may largely rely on non-textual features to market their products. Firstly, they found that in the case of Optimel Control, to suggest weight control effects of the product, individual bottles as well as the four pack were shaped as slender bodies. The packaging had a ribbon carrying a *"helps to eat less"* message placed around the slimmest part of the bottle. In this manner, the presentation of the product could give the impression that the product helps consumers to reduce weight around the waist and stomach. Secondly, the link between Optimel Control and weight reduction was stressed by using illustrations and logos and video-clips both on-air and online. Thirdly, they found that consumers perceive non-textual claims differently than textual ones. Consumers do understand that images are figurative communication of a health-related claim that is not expressed in words. Finally, they say that since the NHCR does not specifically target non-textual claims, in practice producers may find alternative ways of conveying a health claim to emphasize the healthiness of products.[95]

7. Do not Rely on Health Claims

   Some studies (e.g. Binns 2009; Koehler 2013) claim that the food industry is not completely dependent on approved health claims and that owing to media

[92]Marketing without health claims (2012) and Hermans (2011).

[93]Hermans (2011).

[94]Lelieveldt and Boonen (2012), p. 581.

[95]Lelieveldt and Boonen (2012).

offerings, the appeal of products could still be enhanced by marketing of products without claims.[96] Some companies may use blurred or fuzzy claims (such as 'super fruit') thereby communicating health benefits of the product without actually claiming anything. Such a strategy might enable companies to circumvent the health claim procedures of the NHCR, and to sell products without a health claim.[97] Lelieveldt and Boonen (2012) and Koehler (2013) assert that producers could market their products using a broad range of non-textual marketing techniques. They also argue that as long as these practices are not restricted at national level, consumers will try and buy these products.[98]

8. Move the Market Outside Europe

   The EU food industry has a global market, and its worldwide internet sales are increasing in importance. Thus, even if products may not comply with the NHCR, it might be possible to purchase them from outside Europe. This is because internet sales of functional foods and health products belong to a legal grey zone, as authorities are still working on their regulation. Therefore, it is difficult to regulate products that are not on the shelves. Such regulatory situations could make multilevel marketing an attractive channel for products that may not completely conform to the NHCR.[99] Apart from this, Asian countries are developing regulations on food supplements for the first time. Regulations in Asian countries might recognize nutrition science in all its forms including tradition of use data and may not require scientific substantiation.[100] All these factors might lead to companies moving their markets and innovations outside Europe.

9. Reposition the Product: Emotional Branding

   It could be said that health claims are not a panacea for marketing the health benefits of a product. In case of a rejected health claim which was already in use before the NHCR was implemented, companies might reposition the product and build its identity differently. They might also need to change their overall image or profile in the minds of their target consumers. With the means of *emotional branding,* companies may connect with consumers at an emotional level to build brand loyalty for products which are marketed without health claims. Emotional branding might help companies to gain consumer trust and enable product differentiation, since health is an emotive and subjective topic.[101]

10. Let Others Make Your Claims

   In case of no health claims, companies might promote healthiness of their products through national food campaigns, endorsements by organizations, campaigns by member states, trade bodies, scientists (publications), press

---

[96] Binns (2009), p. 8 and Koehler (2013).

[97] Moors (2012), p. 436.

[98] Lelieveldt and Boonen (2012) and Koehler (2013).

[99] Gruenwald (2012).

[100] Starling (2012a).

[101] Marketing without health claims (2012) and Koehler (2013).

coverage etc. For example, health benefits of a product might be promoted through national campaigns like the '5 a day programme'.[102] Another example would be probiotic products. Probiotics have a 100% rejection rate and the EU lawmakers suggest that the name 'probiotic' itself may imply a health claim, especially around gut and immunity benefits. Nevertheless, probiotic health claims on boosting healthy gut microflora seem to be perceived positively by some member states to be used.[103]

The strategy of letting others make the claim could be used to communicate technical terminology of authorised health claims to end consumers through healthcare professionals, as described by De Morpugo and Botana (2016). The communication to healthcare professionals has to be through non-commercial communication or in compliance with the NHCR.[104] The authors argue that in case of non commercial communication, companies might communicate their claims only to healthcare professionals by channels which are not easily accessible by consumers.[105] Furthermore, in case of authorised health claims with technical terminology, healthcare professionals might rephrase and communicate their technical terminology to end consumers so that the latter understand the health benefits of the food products.[106] Thus, food companies might be able to communicate the health benefits of their products in a non-commercial (i.e. objective and non-promotional) manner to healthcare professionals and through them to end consumers.[107]

6 Discussion and Conclusions

Research and development in the food industry is gaining a lot of interest from public authorities. The NHCR aims at protecting interests of companies by promoting fair competition and fostering innovation in the EU food industry. This chapter delves into the following two issues regarding compliance of food companies with the NHCR:

1. (Perceived) challenges faced by companies to comply with the NHCR.
2. Strategies that companies might adopt to comply with the NHCR.

Food companies perceived to face several challenges related to the NHCR. Some major (perceived) compliance challenges faced by companies seem to be related to *lack of financial and R&D resources, uncertainties and transparencies, wording*

[102]Hermans (2011).

[103]Starling (2012b).

[104]De Morpurgo and Botana (2016).

[105]Ibid

[106]Ibid.

[107]Ibid

of claim, changing list of ingredients, changing product categories etc.[108] Companies may adopt different strategies ranging from *working on data and evidence, using already approved health claims* to *not using health claims at all* or *moving the market outside Europe* to deal with the regulation.

While the (scientific) wording of claim is a key aspect of the NHCR, literature suggests that more than how the claim is worded and what benefit it promises, two aspects: (1) familiarity about established connections between the benefit and ingredient and (2) existing knowledge and beliefs of the consumers, play an important role in consumer perception of functional foods.[109] Moreover, textual health claims have a small share in all the marketing strategies applied by companies to promote health benefits of their products.[110] Companies might find new avenues to communicate their products to the consumers by means of social media platform, indirect messages, internet sales, partnerships with other companies etc. Therefore, it might happen that the demand for substantiated health claims remains limited.[111] Also compared to scientifically worded claims, 'soft' information frames on foods or supplements appear to be more effective in creating a positive perception of a product in terms of health inference and attitudes.[112] As mentioned earlier, while the NHCR in its definition of 'claim' is open to cues other than text, it mainly refers to the 'proposed wording' in the inspection of these claims.[113] Therefore, it seems that along with textual health claims, food authorities may wish to consider other marketing material to protect consumers from misleading product information.[114]

It is to be noted that some of the most promising targets for functional food science are gastrointestinal functions, redox and antioxidant systems, and metabolism of macronutrients. The assurance of the success of these targets might need a rigorous scientific approach. Here, scientifically worded health claims might help to substantiate the health benefits and trustworthiness of the products, and simultaneously convey these health benefits to consumers in a better manner.[115] In addition, the need of scientific health claims bears the potential of an effective cooperation between different stakeholders of the food sector (government, scientists, research institutes, companies, consumers etc.).[116] Thus, scientifically worded claims could certainly contribute in building trust and proving the efficacy of emerging functional foods.

While functional foods with health claims encourage product differentiation and present an increasing opportunity for food companies to innovate as well as inform

[108]Brookes (2010) and Khedkar et al. (2016a).

[109]Lähteenmäki et al. (2010).

[110]Lelieveldt and Boonen (2012).

[111]CBI Ministry of foreign affairs (2014).

[112]Aschemann-Witzel and Grunert (2015), p. 98.

[113]Regulation (EC) No. 1924/2006, Article 2 and Article 16; Lelieveldt and Boonen (2012).

[114]Lähteenmäki et al. (2010), p. 239.

[115]Roberfroid (2000), p. 1660.

[116]Brandenburger and Birringer (2015), p. 49.

consumers about the positive effects of their products, regulatory uncertainties can hinder innovation and competition prospective of the EU food sector. Therefore, collaborations between food authorities, companies as well as consumers might benefit the assessment of the implementation and impact of the NHCR. This might help to counter the perceived challenges faced by food companies to adhere to the NHCR and facilitate compliance with this regulation.

To conclude, firstly it could be said that the NHCR affects a broad spectrum of expectations and wishes with respect to nutrition and health-related attributes of foods.[117] For companies, the most straightforward strategy to comply with the regulation might be to provide sufficient scientific evidence and obtain a health claim. In practice, however, this could be a difficult option. Secondly, even if companies apply for a health claim, the scientific evidence they submit for the authorization process might not be sufficient to obtain an approval due to various reasons. For example, currently, botanical health claims are on hold, and are tolerated if they meet the general requirements of the EU regulation, do not mislead consumers and are scientifically substantiated. However, due to lack of clinical trials and traditional use being considered as insufficient evidence, it seems difficult for companies and researchers to meet these criteria.[118] Thus, food companies might change the regulatory channel with which they bring their products to the market. Thirdly, if companies perceive compliance with the regulation to be challenging, they might refrain from innovating and investing into R&D. In addition, the importance of marketing through health claims might decrease. Companies might market products without direct health claims, in which case the possibility of conveying misleading information to consumers would still prevail. Fourthly, it is to be considered that the NHCR is a fairly new regulation. It bears the potential of significantly changing the dynamics of the EU food industry. Effective implementation of the NHCR would increase the reliability and credibility of health claims.[119] To achieve this, food authorities might benefit by addressing the relevent issues and providing sufficient guidance to food companies. All in all, public authorities might want to confirm that the NHCR functions for the benefit of its involved actors. Thus, collaborations among all stakeholders associated with the regulation might help to achieve effective implementation of the regulation. This may further enable companies to comply with the NHCR.[120] Finally, such collaborative efforts might lead to successful consumer protection, innovation and production of healthier food products.[121]

[117]Bremmers et al. (2013), p. 162.

[118]Kušar and Pravst (2015).

[119]Verhagen et al. (2010), p. 14.

[120]Khedkar et al. (2016b).

[121]O'Connor (2011).

References

Appelhof T (2010) De claimsverordening. Praktijkgidsen Warenwet. SDU, the Hague

Aschemann-Witzel J, Grunert KG (2015) Influence of 'soft' versus 'scientific' health information framing and contradictory information on consumers' health inferences and attitudes towards a food supplement. Food Qual Prefer 42:90–99

Ashok M, Narula R, Noya AM (2014) End user collaboration for process innovation in services: the role of internal resources. UNU-MERIT working paper series, 019, Maastricht Graduate School of Governance, Netherlands

Banterle A, Cavaliere A, Carraresi L, Stranieri S (2011) Innovativeness in food small business: what is its relationship with marketing? Agric Econ 57(10):474–483

Bech-Larsen T, Scholderer J (2007) Functional foods in Europe: consumer research, market experiences and regulatory aspects. Trends Food Sci Technol 18(4):231–234

Binns N (2009) Session 4: challenges facing the food industry in innovating for health regulatory challenges and opportunities for food innovation. Proc Nutr Soc 68(01):1

Blind K (2012) The influence of regulations on innovation: a quantitative assessment for OECD countries. Res Policy 41(2):391–400

Bornkessel S, Bröring S, Omta SWF, van Trijp H (2014) What determines ingredient awareness of consumers? A study on ten functional food ingredients. Food Qual Prefer 32:330–339

Bouckley B (2011) Provexis keeps fruitflow powder dry, axes UK R&D facility. http://www.beveragedaily.com/Manufacturers/Provexis-keeps-Fruitflow-powder-dry-axes-UK-R-D-facility. Accessed 11 Aug 2015

Brandenburger S, Birringer M (2015) European health claims for small and medium-sized companies–Utopian dream or future reality? Funct Foods Health Dis 5(2):44–56

Bremmers HJ, van der Meulen BMJ (2013) Opportunities, problems and pitfalls of nutrition and health claims. APSTRACT: Appl Stud Agribusiness Commer 7:93–98

Brookes G (2010) Economic Impact Assessment of the European Union (EU)'s Nutrition & Health Claims Regulation on the EU food supplement sector and market, UK. www.pgeconomics.co.uk/pdf/Impact-Assessment-health-claims.pdf. Accessed 7 May 2015

Bröring S (2005) The front end of convergence in converging industries: the case of nutraceuticals and functional foods. Gabler-Verlag, Wiesbaden

Bröring S (2010) Innovation strategies for functional foods and supplements - challenges of the positioning between foods and drugs. Food Sci Technol Bull Funct Foods 7(8):111–123

Bröring S, Khedkar S, Ciliberti S (2016) Reviewing the Nutrition and Health Claims Regulation (EC) No. 1924/2006: what do we know about its challenges and potential impact on innovation? Int J Food Sci Nutr 68:1–9

Bryne J (2010) Norwegian krill collaboration may secure EFSA claims, says Sana Pharma. 2010. http://www.nutraingredients.com/Regulation-Policy/Norwegian-krill-collaboration-may-secure-EFSA-claims-says-Sana-Pharma. Accessed 6 Aug 2015

CBI Ministry of foreign affairs (2014) CBI trends for natural ingredients for pharmaceuticals. http://www.cbi.eu/sites/default/files/study/trends-europe-natural-ingredients-health-products-2014.pdf. Accessed 2 Aug 2015

Cencic A, Chingwaru W (2010) The role of functional foods, nutraceuticals, and food supplements in intestinal health. Nutrients 2(6):611–625

Commission Regulation (EU) No 423/2012 (2012) Commission Regulation (EU) 2015/7 of 6 January 2015 authorising a health claim made on foods, other than those referring to the reduction of disease risk and to children's development and health and amending Regulation (EU) No 432/2012 Text with EEA relevance. OJ L 136, 25.5.2012, pp 1–40

Da Silva MF (2010) The EU regulation on nutrition and health claims: current and future trends. In: Eaglesham A, Bennett AB, RWF H (eds) Proceedings of the twenty-second annual conference of the National Agricultural Biotechnology Council, 2010 Jun 16–18, California. University of California, Davis, CA

De Boer A, Bast A (2015) International legislation on nutrition and health claims. Food Policy 55:61–70

De Morpurgo M, Botana PC (2016) The nutrition and health claims regulation applies to commercial communications addressed to health professionals. Eur J Risk Regul 7(3):634–641

Diplock AT, Aggett PJ, Ashwell M, Bornet F, Fern EB, Roberfroid MB (1999) Scientific concepts of functional foods in Europe: consensus document. Br J Nutr 81(1):1–27

European Commission (2015) Health claims. http://ec.europa.eu/food/safety/labelling_nutrition/claims/health_claims/index_en.htm. Accessed 10 Aug 2015

European Commission (2017) EU Register of nutrition and health claims made on foods. http://ec.europa.eu/food/safety/labelling_nutrition/claims/register/public/?event=search. Accessed 20 July 2017

European Food Safety Authority (EFSA) (2007) Opinion of the panel on dietetic products, nutrition and allergies (NDA) on a request from the Commission related to scientific and technical guidance for the preparation and presentation of the application for authorization of a health claim. EFSA J 530:1–44

European Food Safety Authority (EFSA) (2017) "New function" health claims under Article 13.5. https://www.efsa.europa.eu/en/topics/topic/article13-5. Accessed 2 Jan 2016

European Responsible Nutrition Alliance (ERNA) (2011) Nutrition and Health Claims in the EU Regulation (EC) 1924/2006. A review of the consequences of implementation. Brussels, Belgium

Flynn A (2012) Scientific substantiation of health claims in the EU. Proc Nutr Soc 71(01):120–126. https://doi.org/10.1017/S0029665111003168

Food V, Fortuyn F (eds) (2010) To claim or not to claim. Food Valley, Wageningen

FoodDrinkEurope (2014) Data & trends of the European food and drink industry 2013–2014. Brussels. http://www.fooddrinkeurope.eu/S=0/publication/data-trends-of-the-european-food-and-drink-industry-2013-2014/. Accessed 7 May 2015

Gilsenan MB (2011) Nutrition & health claims in the European Union: a regulatory overview. Trends Food Sci Technol 22(10):536–542. https://doi.org/10.1016/j.tifs.2011.03.004

Gruenwald J (2012) Health claims regulation impacts European market. http://www.nutraceuticalsworld.com/issues/2012-11/view_features/health-claims-regulation-impacts-european-market. Accessed 6 Aug 2015

Gruenwald J (2014) A stalled situation for botanicals in Europe. http://www.nutraceuticalsworld.com/issues/2014-11/view_columns/a-stalled-situation-for-botanicals-in-europe. Accessed 6 Aug 2015

Henson S, Caswell J (1999) Food safety regulation: an overview of contemporary issues. Food Policy 24(6):589–603

Hermans J (2011) Main challenges for the fruit juice industry: health claims: achilles heel of fruit juices? In: 10th international juice world conference, Moscow

Hobbs JE, Kerr WA (2006) Consumer information, labelling and international trade in agri-food products. Food Policy 31(1):78–89

Kaur A, Scarborough P, Matthews A, Payne S, Mizdrak A, Rayner M (2016) How many foods in the UK carry health and nutrition claims, and are they healthier than those that do not? Public Health Nutr 19(06):988–997

Khedkar S, Bröring S, Ciliberti S (2016a) Exploring the Nutrition and Health Claims Regulation (EC) No. 1924/2006: what is the impact on innovation in the EU food sector? Int J Food Sci Nutr:1–8

Khedkar S, Ciliberti S, Bröring S (2016b) The EU health claims regulation: implications for innovation in the EU food sector. Br Food J 118(11):2647–2665

KMPG (2015) Nutraceuticals: the future of intelligent foods: where food and pharmaceuticals converge. http://www.kpmg.com/ID/en/industry/CM/Documents/neutraceuticals-the-future-of-intelligent-food.pdf. Accessed 6 Aug 2015

Koehler I (2013) Innovative product concepts that can improve consumer appeal without using health claims. Agro Food Ind Hi Tech 24:26–29

Kušar A, Pravst I (2015) Botanical health claims on foods: minimising the risk of mis-leading consumers during the evaluation period in the EU. Planta Medica 81(16):PM_218

Lähteenmäki L, Lampila P, Grunert K, Boztug Y, Ueland Ø, Åström A, Martinsdóttir E (2010) Impact of health-related claims on the perception of other product attributes. Food Policy 35 (3):230–239
Lelieveldt H, Boonen C (2012) EU health claims regulation and the marketing of functional foods: a regulatory void? Eur J Risk Regul 3(4):577–580
Mariotti F, Kalonji E, Huneau JF, Margaritis I (2010) Potential pitfalls of health claims from a public health nutrition perspective. Nutr Rev 68(10):624–638
Marketing without health claims (2012) http://www.nutraingredients.com/Regulation-Policy/Marketing-without-health-claims. Accessed 10 Aug 2015
Martinez MG, Briz J (2000) Innovation in the Spanish food & drink industry. Int Food Agribus Manag Rev 3:155–176
Mejborn H (2007) Health claims on food and food supplements: existing practice in Nordic and Baltic countries. Technical University of Denmark, National Food Institute, Copenhagen
Meziane Z (2007) Future innovations in food and drinks to 2012. NPD, trend convergence and emerging growth opportunities. Business Insights Ltd., London
Moors EHM (2012) Functional foods: regulation and innovations in the EU. Innov Eur J Soc Sci Res 25(4):424–440
Nelson P (1974) Advertising as information. J Polit Econ 82(4):729–754
Nocella G, Kennedy O (2012) Food health claims – what consumers understand. Food Policy 37 (5):571–580
O'Connor A (2011) Nutrition and health claims–where are we with the health claims assessment process? Nutr Bull 36(2):242–247
Patel A, Smith C, Knowles T, Lin Y-L (2012) Nutrition and health claims: an enforcement perspective. Trends Food Sci Technol 28(1):15–22
Pothoulaki M, Chryssochoidis G (2009) Health claims: consumers' matters. J Funct Foods 1 (2):222–228
Pravst I (2012) Functional foods in europe: a focus on health claims. In: Valdez B (ed) Scientific, health and social aspects of the food industry. InTech, Rijeka
Provexis plc (2015) Fruitflow. http://www.provexis.org/fruitflow/. Accessed 11 Aug 2015
Regulation (EC) (1924/2006) Regulation, No. 1924/2006 of the European Parliament and the Council of 20 December 2006 on nutrition and health claims made on foods. Off J Eur Union L 404:L12/13–L12/17
Richardson DP, Eggersdorfer M (2015) Opportunities for product innovation using authorised European Union health claims. Int J Food Sci Tech 50(1):3–12
Roberfroid MB (2000) Concepts and strategy of functional food science: the European perspective. Am J Clin Nutr 76(6):1660s–1664s
Schwitters B, Achanta G, van der Vlies D, Morisset H, Bast A, Hanekamp J (2007) The European regulation of food supplements and food fortification: intended normal use? The ultimate tool in organising level playing field markets and regulations, or how to break the fairy ring around? Other substances? Environ Law Manag 19:19–29
Starling S (2012a) Go east: inside Asia's evolving health claims laws. http://www.foodnavigator-asia.com/Business/Go-East-Inside-Asia-s-evolving-health-claims-laws. Accessed 6 Aug 2015
Starling S (2012b) Probiotic health claims find an EU lifeline. http://www.nutraingredients.com/Regulation-Policy/Probiotic-health-claims-find-an-EU-lifeline. Accessed 6 Aug 2015
Trovato M (2013) Regulatory framework of "Botanical" food supplements in Europe. http://www.plantlibra.eu/web/sites/default/files/u3/Files/Trovato%20Beijing%202013.pdf. Accessed 6 Aug 2015
van Buul VJ, Brouns FJPH (2013) Nutrition and health claims as marketing tools. Crit Rev Food Sci Nutr 55(11):1552–1560
van der Meulen BMJ, Bremmers HJ, Wijnands JHM, Poppe KJ (2012) Structural precaution: the application of premarket approval schemes in EU food
Verhagen H, Vos E, Francl S, Heinonen M, van Loveren H (2010) Status of nutrition and health claims in Europe. Arch Biochem Biophys 501(1):6–15

Younesi E, Ayseli MT (2015) An integrated systems-based model for substantiation of health claims in functional food development. Trends Food Sci Technol 41(1):95–100

Stefanie Bröring is full professor for the "Chair for Technology and innovation management in Agribusiness" at the University of Bonn in Germany. Earlier she was professor for Food Chain Management at the University of Applied Sciences in Osnabrück. She is also a research fellow at Wageningen University in the Netherlands. Prior to academia she worked in the agri-food industry and gained a wide array of consulting and industry experience, working mainly in new business development-related functions as well as marketing. After her studies in Lübeck, Münster and Rotterdam she obtained her PhD on "Innovation management of functional foods" from the University of Münster in Germany, which included a research stay at the University of Quebec at Montreal and the Institute of Nutraceuticals and Functional Foods in Quebec City, Canada. Her research focuses on the challenges of technology and innovation management across agri-food chains and networks, industry convergence between foods and drugs as well as the impact of health claims on innovation and technology acceptance in the food domain (see www.tim.ilr.uni-bonn.de).

Sukhada Khedkar is a PhD student at the "Chair for Technology and innovation management in Agribusiness" at the University of Bonn in Germany. She has completed Masters in Agriculture and Food Economics at the Institute for Food and Resource Economics at the University of Bonn, Germany. Her research interests include innovation and strategic management in the context of product convergence, impact of health claims on innovation as well as diffusion and acceptance of innovations at the food-pharma interface.

Foods for Specific Consumer Groups

Silvia L. Schmidt

Abstract Conveying food information to consumers is a complex issue given both the vast array of European consumers, as well as the threefold purpose of the display of food information: it is required to communicate about the safety of a product and its ingredients, it assists consumers in making informed choices, and it is also a tool that may have an impact on the functioning of the internal market.

Food information is conveyed to all consumers. However, some more vulnerable consumers may require more targeted food information, be it because they are defenceless against certain commercial practices or be it because they have special dietary needs and therefore make use of foods for specific consumer groups. The question is how the vulnerability of consumers is protected with specific *ad hoc* legislation while maintaining and promoting the fundamental freedoms. In this chapter, we address generic and specific regulation. With regards to the latter, we will review the current European legislative framework for specific consumer groups, especially the way vulnerable consumer groups are protected against unfair practices using targeted food information.

1 Introduction

Following a certain foodstuff from the beginning of its production to the moment in which it arrives at the final consumer—from farm to fork—has become increasingly difficult in the past decades. This is partly due to an ever more globalised food chain which results in an overwhelming amount of information that consumers may be exposed to. Notwithstanding this increased complexity of the food chain, consumers expect, and rightly so, to be adequately informed about the potential purchases they make. They do not want to be misled as to the content of a certain food product, be it

The present chapter reflects the opinion of the author and not that of the institution or company she is working for.

S. L. Schmidt (✉)
IFOAM EU - International Federation of Organic Agriculture Movements, Brussels, Belgium

H. Bremmers, K. Purnhagen (eds.), *Regulating and Managing Food Safety in the EU*, Economic Analysis of Law in European Legal Scholarship 6,
https://doi.org/10.1007/978-3-319-77045-1_7

in terms of its safety or in terms of the ingredients used. Importantly, EU legislation foresees provisions aimed at protecting consumers and at attending to their expectations and needs. Specifically, European regulators have set forth provisions covering consumer protection, as well as provisions regulating the content and display of food information. Both sets of rules occupy a significant place in this chapter. Some consumer groups, such as children, the elderly and disabled people, are especially vulnerable. This chapter will explore the way in which specific consumer groups are protected against unfair information practices.

Providing adequate food information to consumers satisfies three important objectives identified in EU legislation. The first and perhaps most straightforward is self-evidently to inform consumers and facilitate them to make informed choices. For this purpose, generic provisions are laid down among others in Regulation (EU) No 1169/2011 on Food Information to Consumers (abbreviated as FIC). In addition, truthful and compliant food information is also a means to verify the safety of a certain food as outlined in the General Food Law (abbreviated as GFL; Regulation (EC) No 178/2002). Last but not least, food information is a tool necessary for facilitating the correct functioning of the internal market by protecting the commercial interest of consumers, as specified in the Unfair Commercial Practices Directive (abbreviated as UCPD; Directive 2005/29/EC[1]). Specifically, the UCPD was adopted in view of protecting consumers' economic interests from unfair commercial practices in a harmonised manner.

These general provisions apply also to foods for specific consumer groups, although there are exceptions. For instance, the rules on the mandatory nutrition declaration in the FIC are without prejudice to the rules on nutrition labelling in Regulation (EU) No 609/2013, which covers certain foods for specific purposes. This Regulation repeals Directive 2009/39/EC (also called the "PARNUTS" directive, as an abbreviation for "particular nutritional uses")[2] and contains specific rules for vulnerable consumer groups, specifically with regards to composition and information of their food.

This chapter will look specifically into the vulnerability of certain groups of consumers and how to adequately address this vulnerability by adjusting food information to their needs, as is the case with infants, sportspeople, or people intolerant to gluten. Indeed, at first glance these population groups do not seem to have much in common. When considering them in terms of consumer groups however, they share one important feature. Their diet requires particular attention, be it because of a delicate stage of development, increased nutritional needs, or a disorder that requires the avoidance of certain foods or food components.

As laid down in Articles 168 and 169 of the TFEU, the Union shall implement measures that ensure the public health of European citizens as well as a high level of

[1]Directive 2005/29/EC of the European Parliament and of the Council of 11 May 2005 concerning unfair business-to-consumer commercial practices in the internal market.

[2]Directive 2009/39/EC of the European Parliament and of the Council of 6 May 2009 on foodstuffs intended for particular nutritional uses.

consumer protection. Vulnerable consumers are protected by generic as well as by specific EU legislation. Generic legislation is included in the GFL, the FIC and the UCPD. The borderline with specific regulation is not very tight. For instance, the FIC also protects consumers that are allergic to certain food components, which are therefore vulnerable to certain foods. Moreover, the UCPD protects the average consumer of the group to which an unfair commercial practice is addressed (e.g. children in candy commercials) and not just the "average consumer".

In the following section we will review in more detail the legal framework that is aimed at protecting consumers under EU law.

2 Protecting the Consumer Under European Food Law

In Sects. 2.1 and 2.2 we will focus on the existing generic rules that protect consumers. Subsequently, in Sect. 2.3, we will both give an overview of the present legal structure as well as delve more into the specific rules that protect vulnerable consumer groups.

2.1 Generic Safety Rules for Consumers

Food regulation can be defined as the "*system which develops, implements and enforces regulatory and non-regulatory measures designed to manage food safety risks*".[3] Food regulation and food information specifically, play a fundamental role in assuring both European citizens' public health, as well as their protection. Importantly in this context, Article 168 of the Treaty on the Functioning of the European Union (TFEU), which focuses on public health, stipulates that "*a high level of human health protection shall be ensured in the definition and implementation of all Union policies and activities*". Article 169 of the TFEU focuses on consumer protection and mentions explicitly their right to information. Specifically it states that the Union must "*contribute to protecting the health, safety and economic interests of consumers, as well as promoting their right to information, education and to organise themselves in order to safeguard their interests*". Food regulation therefore plays a role in achieving both the provisions on public health as well as the provisions on consumer protection as laid down in the TFEU. The main pillar of EU *food* law is Regulation (EC) No 178/2002 (the General Food Law or GFL). It lays down *inter alia* the general principles and requirements of food law and the procedures in the matter of food safety. Article 14 specifies that "*food shall not be placed on the market if it is unsafe*", a condition which is fulfilled if the food in question is neither "*injurious to health*" nor "*unfit for human consumption*". The

[3] Wilson et al. (2015).

GFL states that in order to determine whether a certain food is unsafe, attention should be paid to the information conveyed through that food. Therefore, through the GFL, food information plays an important role in determining whether a certain food product is unsafe.

In European food law, consumers are protected by two types of provisions: content-related rules (e.g. hygiene requirements) and information-related rules (which cover among others information that is displayed on food packages, e.g. the nutrition declaration and health claims). The "hygiene package" is an example[4] of content-related EU legislation which ensures the safety of foodstuffs and subsequently the protection of consumers. It consisted of three main regulations that all became applicable in 2006.[5] Foodstuffs need to also comply with the FIC and with Regulation (EC) No 1924/2006 on nutrition and health claims. Consumers should not be misled by information displayed on the package of a certain foodstuff or in association with a certain foodstuff. As such, for nutrition and health claims to be useful to consumers they ought to be understandable and well-substantiated.[6] These two pieces of legislation determine (among others) which information should be made available to consumers.

When it comes to consumer protection and food information in the EU, there is a synergy between different pieces of legislation that have different aims. In general information has the priority over standard-setting, as it is cheaper and also less intrusive on the freedom of the individual consumer.

2.2 *Generic Commercial Protection Rules for Consumers*

A key objective of the EU is to guarantee the four fundamental freedoms.[7] Therefore the responsibility to ensure consumer protection has to be seen in the context of the functioning of markets. Consumers should be enabled to participate freely in the internal market without running the risk of being misled. Specifically on the latter point, Article 6 of the UCPD defines that a commercial practice is misleading if it "*contains false information* [. . .] *or in any way* [. . .] *deceives or is likely to deceive the average consumer*". This Article further states that "*a commercial practice shall*

[4]One of these, regulation (EU) 882/2004 on official controls is replaced by a new Regulation 2017/625 that will be applicable in December 2019.

[5]Regulation (EC) No 852/2004 of the European Parliament and of the Council of 29 April 2004 on the hygiene of foodstuffs. Regulation (EC) No 853/2004 of the European Parliament and of the Council of 29 April 2004 laying down specific hygiene rules for food of animal origin and Regulation (EC) No 854/2004 of the European Parliament and of the Council of 29 April 2004 laying down specific rules for the organisation of official controls on products of animal origin intended for human consumption (recently replaced by Regulation 625/2017).

[6]van Buul and Brouns (2015).

[7]The four fundamental freedoms: (1) free movement of goods, (2) of services and freedom of establishment, (3) free movement of persons, and (4) free movement of capital.

also be regarded as misleading if [...] *it causes or is likely to cause the average consumer to take a transactional decision that he would not have taken otherwise*".

Consumer protection in the UCPD comes into play as a reaction to market failure.[8] An EU 1985 Communication,[9] which shortly followed the White Paper on completing the internal market in the foodstuffs sector,[10] stipulated that there are two ways to address consumer protection. The first is to develop vertical legislation covering each single food product. The second is to consider that if the purchaser conveys the correct information regarding food products, it would not be necessary to draft vertical provisions for each product. In order to preserve commercial flexibility and to foster innovation taking into account that the variety of tastes and traditions, the Communication clearly advised that the Commission should take the second approach, i.e. ensuring the display of adequate information without using vertical legislation.[11]

Differences in rules on commercial practices could result in obstacles to the functioning of the internal market as well as distortion of competition.[12] As such, the main purpose of the UCPD is detailed in its first Article, i.e. to "*contribute to the proper functioning of the internal market and achieve a high level of consumer protection*". Consumers play an essential role in the context of commercial practices given that they are the receiving end of such transaction, be it a fair or an unfair one. Keeping this in mind, this Directive takes as a benchmark the notion of the "average consumer" who is "*reasonably well-informed and reasonably observant and circumspect, taking into account social, cultural and linguistic factors* [...]".[13] The priority of a rationally acting consumer and the advantage of information over standard setting is dominant in consumer protection, despite the fact that vulnerable consumers are given special attention. In the UCPD the average consumer is the "average" in the subgroup to which the activities of the seller are addressed. Just like Article 1 of the FIC it opens the possibility to recognise differences in perception of consumers.

The UCPD lays down provisions aimed at "*preventing the exploitation of consumers whose characteristics make them particularly vulnerable to unfair commercial practices*" (recital 18). It is important to highlight that the term "vulnerable" as used in the UCPD should be roughly understood as meaning "defenceless" in the

[8]Unberath and Johnston (2007).

[9]The Communication in question is "A new impetus for consumer protection policy" (Communication from the Commission to the Council 1985).

[10]"Completing the internal market"; White Paper from the Commission to the European Council, June 1985.

[11]Macmaolain (2007).

[12]Stuyck et al. (2006).

[13]This concept of the 'average consumer' is also mentioned in recital 15 of Regulation 1924/2006 on nutrition and health claims.

world of commercial practices. An example of a category of vulnerable consumers is children.[14] The UCPD stipulates that in the case that "*the economic behaviour only of such consumers is likely to be distorted by the practice in a way that the trader can reasonably foresee, it is appropriate to ensure that they are adequately protected by assessing the practice from the perspective of the average member of that group*". Recital 19 of this Directive specifies that characteristics that may make consumers particularly susceptible to a commercial practice or to the underlying product include "*age, physical or mental infirmity or credulity*".

The term "vulnerable" is also used in other pieces of EU legislation (such as Regulation 609/2013) and should in that context be understood as "unsafe" from a nutritional standpoint for that vulnerable consumer in question. As used in the UCPD the consumer is *vulnerable* to unfair commercial practices, while in other pieces of EU legislation the term "vulnerable" refers to the fact that the consumer is *vulnerable* to a certain food ingredient or food product.

2.3 Foods for Specific Consumer Groups in the EU

In addition to general provisions concerning consumer protection as per the UCPD, European legislation also foresees more targeted provisions, which are specifically intended to protect and adequately inform certain categories of consumers, e.g. consumers with special dietary needs or consumers of foods for specific groups. Despite the absence of a formal definition of "consumers of foods for specific groups", they are referred in relevant legislation as "*clearly identified vulnerable groups*", "*vulnerable consumers*" and "*vulnerable population groups*". The term "vulnerable" in this case should be roughly understood as "unsafe" for consumers who have specific dietary needs. This section will first briefly review the European market for foods for specific groups, then the legislative underpinnings of such regulation, and finally the importance of these products and their regulation in the Europe 2020 strategy.

The Market of Foods for Specific Consumer Groups

Eurostat data from 2009 recorded that there are approximately 700 businesses involved in the sector of dietetic[15] foods and homogenized food preparations and that three Member States (France, Spain, and Italy) account for about 50% of

[14]Annex I of this Directive lists the commercial practices which are in all circumstances considered unfair, among which appears the following: "including in an advertisement a direct exhortation to children to buy advertised products or persuade their parents or other adults to buy advertised products for them (. . .)."

[15]The terms dietetic foods was used under Directive 2009/39/EC as a way of defining "foods for particular nutritional uses". Given the confusion brought by this term in relation to the term "diet",

businesses and turnover in this sector.[16] Between 1994 and 2004, Eurostat reports that the most rapid import growth was held by dietetic foods and homogenized food preparations, although their total share of imports was small. Rapid export growth was also recorded for these two categories of foodstuffs when compared to other food products.[17] Data published in 2009 reveals that the output of dietetic foods and homogenized food preparations increased by 5.1% per year between 2000 and 2007, generating an added value of about 2 billion euros annually.[18] Data suggest that the sector of dietetic foods and homogenized food preparations—which could be compared to the current sector of foods for specific consumer groups—is steadily growing.

Regulating Foods for Specific Consumer Groups

Until July 2016, foods for specific consumer groups were covered by Directive 2009/39/EC on foodstuffs intended for particular nutritional uses. In this Directive, these types of foods are also referred to as "dietetic foods" or "parnuts", given that they are intended for *particular nutritional uses*. As such, Directive 2009/39/EC was also referred to as the *framework for dietetic foods*. This legal framework provides an explanation of both the consumer groups it aims to protect, as well as the foodstuffs it covers. As defined in Article 1(1), "*this Directive concerns foodstuffs for particular nutritional uses*". Recital 4 defines these foods as "*foodstuffs the composition and preparation of which must be specially designed to meet the particular nutritional requirements of the persons for whom they are mainly intended*". Particular nutritional requirements are further detailed under Article 1(3) of Directive 2009/39/EC which also provides for an understanding of the target consumers of these foodstuffs. This article stipulates that "*a particular nutritional use shall fulfil the particular nutritional requirements (a) of certain categories of persons whose digestive processes or metabolism are disturbed; or (b) of certain categories of persons who are in a special physiological condition and who are therefore able to obtain special benefit from controlled consumption of certain substances in foodstuffs; or (c) of infants or young children in good health*". Interestingly, this legislative act puts little emphasis on the specific types of products it covers. These are touched upon under Annex I (A) which stipulates that further provisions will be laid down under specific Directives for infant formulae, follow-on formulae, processed cereal based foods and other baby foods, foods for special medical purposes, foods intended for use in energy-restricted diets for weight reduction, as well as for foods intended to meet the expenditure of intense muscular effort, especially for sportsmen. Regulation 609/2013 now defines the latter category as

Regulation 609/2013 does not make reference to dietetic foods any longer, and talks instead about "foods for specific consumer groups".

[16]European Commission (n.d.) and Eurostat (2009).

[17]Eurostat (2006).

[18]Eurostat (2009).

"food intended for sportspeople", for which the European Commission decided that no additional legal act was required.

Most of the provisions laid down in this legislative framework date back to 1977. As such, shortly after the entry into force of this Directive in 2009, it was found that the concept of foodstuffs for particular nutritional uses was outdated as it no longer answered to the current legal context and market. As specified under Recital 12 of Regulation (EU) No 609/2013, "*experience shows that certain rules in or adopted under, Directive 2009/39/EC are no longer effective in ensuring the functioning of the internal market*". For instance, it was noted that the legislative framework as it was did not prevent the following issues from occurring[19]:

- Product misclassification, e.g. food supplements marketed as foods for special medical purposes (FSMPs), occurring both within and between Member States;
- FBOs taking part in "legislative shopping", e.g. cases in which FBOs use a suitability statement or a mandatory labelling statement which may be very close to a health claim that would not be allowed for a particular foodstuff.
- A too wide space for interpretation could arise from the terms "*foodstuffs for particular nutritional uses*" and "*dietetic foods*".

As a consequence, a revision of Directive 2009/39/EC was needed in order to ensure a more harmonised and effective implementation of legal acts at Community level. This new framework would have to close and prevent legal loopholes within EU legislation, thus ensuring the functioning of the internal market, as well as harmonize rules between Member States, thus ensuring that a certain product be marketed as the same type of food across all Member States.[20] These guiding lines for the revision of Directive 2009/39/EC would furthermore ensure the protection of food safety and the importance of correctly informing the consumer. The latter is even more important in the context of foods for specific consumer groups compared to foods intended for regular consumers.

Regulation (EU) No 609/2013 is applicable as of July 2016; it replaces Directive 2009/39/EC and abolishes the concept of dietetic foods. This Regulation stipulates that "*a limited number of categories of foods (...) are vital for the management of certain conditions and/or are essential to satisfy the nutritional requirements of certain clearly identified vulnerable groups*". In contrast to Directive 2009/39/EC, Regulation (EU) No 609/2013 puts higher emphasis on the foodstuffs that it covers, namely infant and follow-on formulae, processed cereal-based foods and other baby foods, foods for special medical purposes, and total diet replacement for weight control (see Article 1—subject matter).

Importantly, Regulation (EU) No 609/2013 foresees the strengthening of provisions on foods for vulnerable population groups that necessitate further protection,

[19]Commission Staff Working Paper Impact assessment accompanying the document proposal for a regulation of the European Parliament and of the Council on food intended for infants and young children and on food for special medical purposes.

[20]Press release database (2014).

e.g. infants and young children up to 3 years of age, overweight or obese people, and consumers with specific medical conditions.[21] For instance, to further prevent misleading of people suffering from gluten intolerance, provisions on products containing gluten previously set under Regulation (EC) No 41/2009 on foodstuffs suitable for people intolerant to gluten has been transferred to Regulation (EU) No 1169/2011 on the provision of Food Information to Consumers. Table 1 gives an overview of the delegated and implementing acts foreseen with the adoption of Regulation (EU) No 609/2013.

Innovation and Specific Food Products: Today and Tomorrow

Europe 2020, launched in 2010, is the EU's 10 years growth strategy.[22] Europe 2020 envisages *inter alia* more investments in Research and Development (R&D) as Europe invests less in R&D compared to the US and Japan. As a consequence, the phenomenon of "brain drain" is unfortunately well known.[23] Investing more in R&D goes hand in hand with making the European market more innovation-friendly in order to ensure competitiveness on the global market. This can be achieved, *inter alia*, by making sure that the legal framework is not a hindrance to investing in R&D. As explained under Recital 11 of Regulation (EC) No 609/2013, "*other* [. . .] *legal acts are more adapted to an evolving and innovative food market than Directive 2009/39/EC*".[24] These "*Union legal acts would adequately regulate a number of the categories of food covered by Directive 2009/39/EC with less of an administrative burden and more clarity as to scope and objectives*". Interestingly, administrative burden and an unclear scope are often flagged as being a hindrance to successful innovation.[25] In addition, implementation and enforcement of Directive 2009/39/EC differs between Member States which leads to differences in the regulation of the foodstuffs covered by this Directive in different Member States. Recital 10 of Regulation (EC) No 609/2013 specifies that "*this state of affairs undermines the functioning of the internal market, creates legal uncertainty for competent authorities, food business operators* [. . .] *and consumers*", which may in turn lead to marketing abuse, distortion of competition, and a negative impact on innovation. As such, the legislative framework covering foods for specific consumer groups undoubtedly has an impact on the role played by R&D in Europe, thus in turn playing a role in the Europe 2020 strategy.

---

[21]European Commission (2013b).

[22]European Commission (2014a).

[23]European Commission (2013a).

[24]The legal acts referred to in this Recital are Regulation (EC) No 1924/2006 on nutrition and health claims, Directive 2002/46/EC on the approximation of the laws of Member States relating to food supplements, and Regulation (EC) No 1925/2006 on the addition of vitamins and minerals and of certain other substances to foods.

[25]Albury (2005).

Table 1 Overview of the legislative stance for foods for specific consumer groups prior to and following the entry into force of Regulation (EC) No 609/2013 in July 2016

Type of food	Consumer group	Existing pieces of legislation	What will Regulation (EC) No 609/2013 change?
Infant formulae and follow on formulae	Infants and young children	Directive 2006/141/EC	Regulation (EU) No 609/2013 repeals Directive 2006/141/EC and foresees that, *inter alia*, specific compositional and labelling provisions will be adopted via delegated acts, i.e. Commission Delegated Regulation 2016/127[a]
Processed cereal based foods and baby foods		Directive 2006/125/EC	Regulation (EU) No 609/2013 foresees that, *inter alia*, specific compositional and labelling provisions will be adopted via delegated acts. These rules will repeal Directive 2006/125/EC
Foods for energy-restricted diets for weight reduction	The consumer group for which these foods are intended is not specifically mentioned in the legislation. However, the foods covered by this legislation are intended for use in energy-restricted diets for weight reduction	Directive 96/8/EC and Directive 2007/29/EC which amends Directive 96/8/EC as regards labelling, advertising or presenting foods intended for use in energy-restricted diets for weight reduction	Regulation (EU) No 609/2013 foresees that, *inter alia*, the Commission adopts a delegated act on specific compositional and labelling requirements for low and very low calorie diets. Also, statements on meal replacement products will uniquely be under Regulation (EC) No 1924/2006
Foods for special medical purposes (FSMPs)	FSMPs are intended for the dietary management of patients and to be used under medical supervision	Directive 1999/21/EC	Regulation (EU) No 609/2013 stipulates, *inter alia*, that the Commission adopts a delegated act establishing specific compositional and labelling provisions for FSMPs. Commission delegated Regulation (EU) 2016/128[b] repeals Directive 1999/

(continued)

Table 1 (continued)

Type of food	Consumer group	Existing pieces of legislation	What will Regulation (EC) No 609/2013 change?
			21/EC as of February 2019
Foods for people with gluten intolerance	People intolerant to gluten	Regulation (EC) No 41/2009	Repeal of Regulation (EC) No 41/2009 and consequent amendment of Regulation (EU) No 1169/2011 to ensure consistency[c]. Also, Commission Implementing Regulation (EU) No 828/2014 [d] lays down specific requirements
Foods for sportspeople	Foods intended for sportspeople or foods intended to meet the expenditure of intense muscular effort, especially for sportsmen	Annex I of the framework Directive 2009/39/EC stipulates that specific provisions will be laid down for such foods	Article 13 of Regulation (EC) No 609/2013 foresees that the Commission presents a report on the potential necessity of provisions covering specifically these foods

[a]Commission Delegated Regulation (EU) 2016/127 of 25 September 2015 supplementing Regulation (EU) No 609/2013 of the European Parliament and of the Council as regards the specific compositional and information requirements for infant formula and follow-on formula and as regards requirements on information relating to infant and young child feeding. This Regulation is applicable as of February 2020. *Inter alia*, this delegated Regulation prohibits the use of health and nutrition claims on infant formula in order to protect breast-feeding
[b]Commission Delegated Regulation (EU) 2016/128 of 25 September 2015 supplementing Regulation (EU) No 609/2013 of the European Parliament and of the Council as regards the specific compositional and information requirements for food for special medical purposes
[c]Commission Delegated Regulation (EU) No 1155/2013 of 21 August 2013 amending Regulation (EU) No 1169/2011 of the European Parliament and of the Council on the provision of food information to consumers as regards information on the absence or reduced presence of gluten in food
[d]Commission Implementing Regulation (EU) No 828/2014 of 30 July 2014 on the requirements for the provision of information to consumers on the absence or reduced presence of gluten in food

3 Discussion

The previous sections reviewed that the term "consumer" generally fits the definition of the "average consumer", unless, for instance, certain characteristics make the consumer more vulnerable to unfair commercial practices, or in the case of certain consumers who have specific dietary needs (i.e. "specific groups of consumers") for which specific pieces of legislation exist.

In Sect. 3.1 we address the complexities in the purchase decision making process of the consumer. In Sect. 3.2 we elaborate on specific problems food businesses experience in meeting the legal and consumer demands. In Sect. 3.3 we present a case study, focusing on elderly people, to further substantiate the previous elaborations.

3.1 Complexities in Consumers' Decision Making Process

There is much debate about conveying food information to consumers, particularly with regards to the visibility and understanding of this information. When looking at EU food legislation, it appears that conveying food information to consumers touches upon three points. Not surprisingly, (1) food information plays a role in adequately informing the consumer. It also plays a role in (2) food safety and (3) the competitiveness of the market. Safety is emphasised in Article 14 of the General Food Law which states that in order to determine whether a certain food is unsafe, competent authorities should among others look at the information provided to the consumer. Despite the fact that conveying adequate food information is covered and protected by several pieces of EU legislation, there is little scientific evidence and hardly any consensus regarding the most effective manner to convey food information to consumers, or whether consumers indeed rely upon food information when purchasing a certain food product. Nocella and Kennedy (2012) argue that there are two factors affecting the way in which food information is processed by consumers. The first factor is related to personal characteristics of individuals, e.g. socio-demographic characteristics and knowledge about nutrition information. The second factor concerns the food product and the way in which food information is conveyed. The interaction between these two factors is the birthplace of the complex process of consumer understanding of food information. The modalities of this process are not quite clear. Research shows that consumer attention to food information is positively correlated with knowledge and prior familiarity with a particular product.[26] Moreover, it seems that the perception of food information may vary depending on the product, its presentation and its use. Studies also suggest that those consumers who are particularly health-conscious or those that are searching for a specific type of information are also those that pay the most attention to food information.[27]

Informed Choice?

Therefore, in practice, food information does not seem to impact consumers uniformly. As Nocella and Kennedy (2012) argue, this may be explained by the fact that

[26]Incardona and Poncibo (2007).

[27]Ellison et al. (2013).

the concept of the "average consumer" as intended in EU legislation may not fully reflect real life consumers. For instance, let us consider a health claim displayed on a certain food product that informs consumers about the benefits for a certain condition or disorder that come from consuming that food. It is likely that the only consumers who will (1) search for this type of information and (2) be "reasonably informed" about the beneficial effects of consuming that food product, will be precisely those that suffer from the said disorder or condition. Therefore, this particular claim is useful and understandable only for a small group of the population, which is not per se in line with the concept of average consumer.[28] Similarly, certain segments of the population, which do not necessarily belong to one of the specific consumer groups as per EU legislation, may tend to behave in a more attentive way compared to others, due to their gender or age. Research shows that women of higher socio-economic status are generally more health-conscious compared to other segments of the population[29] and thus are comparatively more knowledgeable about food information. Furthermore, consumers seem to have shifted from being manageable and predictable to being "unmanageable".[30] This concept is further outlined by Gabriel and Lang (2015). These authors argue that the behaviour of consumers nowadays is not very predictable given that they, for instance, (1) have environmental and moral concerns, and (2) may quickly change their opinion about a certain food product due to social pressure and social media. As a result, the authors argue that the average consumer does not exist anymore.

In addition to the possibility that food information is potentially not relevant for all segments of the population as currently targeted, terms used in food information, and particularly in the health claims displayed on food packages, may also play a role. Generally, given that EU legislation puts the emphasis on the scientific truthfulness of food information, there are instances in which consumers are confronted with terms such as "thermogenesis", "beta-glucans", "normal homocysteine metabolism", "carbohydrate-electrolytes solutions" which are surely scientifically accurate, but not necessarily understood by all consumers. In the context of complexity and usefulness of terms, research has revealed that even people suffering from lactose intolerance are not always sure of whether "milk free" and/or "dairy free" products are suitable for them.[31]

---

[28]Nocella and Kennedy (2012).

[29]Bogue et al. (2005).

[30]Gabriel and Lang (2015).

[31]Food Standard Agency (2010).

Interestingly, Nocella and Kennedy (2012) put forth the possibility that there may be a "timewasting barrier" after which consumers give up trying to understand a certain claim, be it because they do not have the health status for which the claim is actually intended (the claim is not useful for them), or because of the complex terms used in this claim. Indeed, policy makers can hardly expect that consumers will carry out an extensive analysis of pros and cons every time that they have to make a decision about a certain food product.[32] Therefore, despite the scientific accuracy of the health claim itself, consumers may not be aware of the term used, and not understand the health claim as a result. In addition, another potential issue with the display of health claims is that these may be displayed on any product that bears a sufficient amount of a certain beneficial nutrient. For instance, if an overall unhealthy snack includes sufficient amounts of vitamin C for it to bear a health claim; the food business operator selling this snack can lawfully display a health claim that puts forward the benefits of vitamin C. In this way, consumers may be misled into thinking that the snack is actually healthy, only because they see a claim about the benefits of vitamin C, even though the product may be high in sugar, salt and/or fats. Nutrient profiles,[33] which would foresee that health claims may displayed only on nutritionally adequate products, may help solve this issue. As such, the European Commission has launched a public consultation in 2016, which aims at evaluating Regulation (EC) No 1924/2006 with regard to *inter alia* nutrient profiles.[34]

Safety of Vulnerable Consumers

Until now we mainly looked into the complexity of conveying food information to the consumer in general, without taking into account the vulnerability—in the sense of defencelessness—of certain consumers. Food information that is to be conveyed to vulnerable consumers (in the sense of consumers for which certain foods are unsafe) is addressed under Regulation 609/2013. As already mentioned, in the UCPD, a consumer is vulnerable if certain characteristics such as "*age, physical*

[32]Incardona and Poncibo (2007).

[33]Nutrient profiles of a product would entail that products are classified as per their nutritional value. Depending on their nutritional value, products may or may not bear health claims. For instance, it would not be permissible for foods high in sugar, salt, and/or fat to bear health claims. It is likely that a nutrient profiling system would foresee some exceptions, e.g. for products like salmon that are high in fats but also nutritionally very beneficial.

[34]Article 4 of Regulation 1924/2006 on nutrition and health claims foresees that the European Commission establishes nutrient profiles by January 2009. However, nutrient profiles have not been set yet. It is debated whether the entry into force of the requirement of a mandatory nutrition declaration on the 13th of December 2016 makes nutrient profiles redundant. Health advocates and NGOs are generally of the opinion that nutrient profiles should still be set given that even with a mandatory nutrition declaration, health claims about a certain nutrient can still be displayed on products high in sugar, salt, and/or fat if they contain the required amount of that nutrient. The European Commission has commissioned an impact assessment and launched a public consultation on the matter in order to gather a more comprehensive overview of the necessity of nutrient profiles.

or mental infirmity or credulity" make him/her susceptible to a commercial practice, while within the framework of Regulation 609/2013 a consumer is vulnerable if s/he has particular dietary needs. Infants and young children would be considered as "vulnerable" under both cases given their young age and the fact that they require adequate nutrition.

Nocella and Kennedy (2012) state that consumers' understanding of nutrition information may depend, *inter alia*, on ability, or "the capacity to transform perceptual stimuli into meaningful information". One may therefore argue that those people with a lower than average ability could be considered as vulnerable consumers. Therefore, the UCPD does a laudable effort in harmonizing rules related to commercial practices which apply to all business-to-consumers practices. However, Stuyck et al. (2006) argue that it is "*recommended to conduct sound empirical research* [...] *about the correlation between the characteristics of certain groups of consumers and the likelihood of being specifically vulnerable for certain commercial practices*".[35] A rather sensitive example would be that of the elderly population, which will be reviewed in Sect. 3.3. Indeed, Incardona and Poncibo (2007) argue that many elderly consumers would not deem their judgement to be so impaired that they are no longer able to make good choices. However, certain members of the elderly population may benefit from a more targeted type of food information. As such, one might question which entity is to decide upon the vulnerability of certain consumers, and how this would be assessed. It follows that the notion of the vulnerable consumer seems to be rather arbitrary and may result in difficult monitoring and enforcement.[36]

3.2 Complexities in the Businesses' Decision Making Process

The present section will review the role of an important stakeholder in this context, i.e. the food industry. The relationship between the food industry and consumers is rather simple in the sense that the former would not survive without the latter. It follows that representatives of the food industry highly value consumer protection, as they depend on consumers' trust (and ensuing purchases) to thrive.

Food business operators (FBOs)[37] are responsible for complying with EU food legislation and thus guaranteeing the correct display and truthful dissemination of

[35] Stuyck et al. (2006).

[36] Incardona and Poncibo (2007).

[37] Article 3 of the General Food Law defines Food Business Operators as "*the natural or legal persons responsible for ensuring that the requirements of food law are met within the food business under their control*".

food information.[38] Articles 17, 18, and 19 of the General Food Law lay down the specific requirements that FBOs have to comply with when it comes to their responsibilities along the whole supply chain, both in terms of the "*requirements of food law which are relevant to their activities*" and in terms of product traceability. On the latter, FBOs must be able to trace from which FBO they have received ingredients, as well as follow to which FBO they are being sent to.

If a legislative proposal that is advantageous to the consumer, e.g. in terms of additional product information, results in additional costs incurred by the food industry, it is possible that these costs may be borne by the consumer. The consumer may finally be unwilling to pay for the additional information. Therefore, policy makers have to be cautious as to which labelling requirements shall be made mandatory. On the one hand, it is important that consumers are adequately informed about the product they would like to purchase; on the other hand, they may not be willing to pay for additional information.

The food industry spends considerable amounts of money for the design and implementation of labelling that is displayed on food packages. Surprisingly, estimations of the costs incurred by the food industry for changing the presentation of a food package are not heavily discussed in the scientific literature. It seems that costs stem from three components: labelling costs, but also storage costs for warehousing additional products and shelf space charges for additional products.[39] One may hypothesise that changing the labels of a product results in considerable extra costs for the food industry, particularly in the case of small and medium enterprises (SMEs) who work with smaller quantities compared to bigger companies. Additional costs have to be reimbursed. Research shows that consumers are segmented when it comes to the willingness to pay for certain features displayed on a label. For instance, in the case of a logo for halal meat, it is the consumer group composed of young women that is more willing to pay for the costs to display a halal logo on the food package.[40] Another example is that of country of origin labelling (COOL). Given consumers' rising interest regarding the origin of certain products such as milk, the European Commission published a report[41] which looked into the feasibility of a mandatory country of origin label on certain products, as well as consumers' willingness to pay for extra information. The report shows that although consumers would like to know where certain categories of foods come from, they would not be willing to pay for this information. Several Member States have launched trial schemes that require COOL for certain food products, such as the

---

[38] Anklam and Battaglia (2001).

[39] Lesser and Lynch (2014).

[40] Verbeke et al. (2013).

[41] The report in question is "*Study on "Mandatory origin labelling for milk, milk used as an ingredient and other unprocessed meats*" published in 2014, available here: https://ec.europa.eu/agriculture/external-studies/milk-meat-origin-labelling-2014.fr.

two-year trial for dairy and meat in France.[42] This trial will be decisive in understanding whether consumers are willing to pay the extra costs in order to have more information about the origin of the food they buy. On a side-note, national COOL schemes also raise another interesting debate at EU level given that the proliferation of national schemes may undermine the efficiency of the common market.

It is therefore important to keep in mind that consumer information is not only a matter of regulation in terms of food safety and consumer protection, but it is also a matter of costs that will have to potentially be borne by the consumer itself.

3.3 Case Study: The Elderly Population

The ageing of the European population is likely to play an important role in the years and decades to come. In 2002, 16% of the EU-28 population was aged 65 and older, the proportion of older citizens increasing to nearly 18% in 2012. European citizens aged 65 and older are forecasted to represent nearly 30% of the population by 2080.[43] This steadily increasing trend is accounted for by the low fertility rates coupled with the increased life expectancy in the EU-28, and will inevitably result in the decrease of the proportion of people of working age.

Consumers at different stages of development have different needs. In the case of the elderly, advancing age is associated with changes in consumers' desires, needs, and abilities. For instance, older consumers may be dependent on external help for going to the supermarket or for carrying groceries. Another example once in the supermarket is that the access to low or high placed shelves may be difficult.[44] In addition, consumption patterns of older adults are associated with a lower and potentially insufficient daily caloric intake as well as with a loss of appetite.[45] This potentially limited access to foods may compromise the health of older adults. Studies have also shown that the elderly tend to adopt a rather preventative approach when it comes to food purchases. They will for instance be more inclined to buy healthier products such as products with more omega 3 and omega 6, cholesterol-lowering foods, and immune system boosting foodstuffs.[46] As such, the grocery shopping experience of this segment of the population should be facilitated as much as possible in order to prevent an overall insufficient food intake. This would in turn work towards preserving and maintaining the health of older citizens.

---

[42]Products containing more than 8% meat must display the place of origin, raising and slaughter of the animals used in the preparation. Products containing more than 50% milk must indicate the "country of collection" and the "country of transformation".

[43]Eurostat (2014).

[44]Meneely et al. (2009).

[45]Hughes et al. (2004).

[46]Nocella and Kennedy (2012).

Multiple initiatives at EU wide level address the particular needs of older consumers. Europe 2020 has already been introduced as EU's growth strategy until the year 2020. Under the umbrella of objectives and activities envisaged by Europe 2020, figures the European Partnership on Active and Healthy Ageing, which aims at "*(1) enabling EU citizens to lead healthy, active and independent lives while ageing; (2) improving the sustainability and efficiency of social and health care systems; and (3) boosting and improving the competitiveness of the markets for innovative products and services, responding to the ageing challenge at both EU and global level*".[47] A practical example under this initiative is the tackling of malnutrition in the elderly as a priority of the work programme for 2014–2015 of Horizon 2020.[48] This more specifically entailed developing nutritional recommendations as well as innovative foodstuffs supporting the prevention and treatment of malnutrition in the elderly population.

Despite these initiatives, EU legislation does not currently mention the potential need for further regulatory tools covering products intended for the elderly population. Regulation (EU) No 609/2013 makes reference to *older adults* once under recital 10 as one of the subgroups of the general population for which food for normal consumption and/or food for particular nutritional uses may be intended for when sold on the European market.[49] The elderly population is therefore not considered as a specific group of consumers. Legal literature seems to consider the elderly population as being part of the more vulnerable consumers as intended in the UCPD.[50] In any case, it is widely acknowledged that the European food safety system is among the best in the world—so much so that Chinese authorities took inspiration from the European system when reforming their own food safety framework.[51] Therefore potential regulatory tools covering foods targeted at the elderly population would not have to be specifically concerned with the product's safety, but rather with the product not being misleading and providing elderly consumers with foods that are adequate to their nutritional needs. Specifically, researchers have acknowledged the need for food providers to deliver tailored, healthy, and affordable options, as well as for food policy makers to take into consideration the requirements and expectations of this aging population into future program and policy developments.[52] In the realm of food law and food policy, this translates into ensuring that the nutritional requirements of the elderly population can be properly addressed, both from a theoretical perspective, e.g. knowing which nutrients should be taken in

[47]European Commission (2014b).

[48]Horizon 2020 is an initiative under the EU Framework Program for Research and Innovation aiming at ensuring Europe's competitiveness on a global level. The program foresees a funding of nearly 80 million Euros from 2014 to 2020 (European Commission 2014b).

[49]No reference had been made to *older adults* or the *elderly population* in Directive 2009/39/EC or in Regulation (EU) No 609/2013.

[50]Incardona and Poncibo (2007).

[51]Chen et al. (2015).

[52]Hunter and Worsley (2009) and Meneely et al. (2009).

increased quantities, as from a practical perspective, e.g. guaranteeing that adequate nutrition is easily accessible to this group of the population. Older consumers have identified improvements that they would deem helpful in the context of going grocery shopping. For instance, being able to purchase smaller portion sizes would prevent them from wasting food and a larger font of nutrition labels would ease the reading of such food information.[53]

In addition, in an attempt to answer to the specific nutritional needs of older consumers, the industry has developed certain products which specifically target this consumer group. These foods are currently not regulated more specifically at EU level, which may be an issue for the correct functioning of the internal market, insofar as they may be addressed and regulated differently across Member States.

Therefore, taking into account the fact that (1) the elderly population in Europe is increasing, (2) that this population has specific needs when it comes to nutrition and health, (3) that several European initiatives already address these specific needs, and (4) that food products targeted at the elderly population are already available on the European market, it may be interesting to ponder whether the importance of adequate nutrition and healthy foods and information thereon for the elderly population should be supported by proposals in the realm of food policy. This could mean that elderly consumers are to be considered either pertaining to specific consumer groups or to the vulnerable type of consumer.

Despite the fact that the *relevance* of generic information for the elderly can be doubted, that the *readability* of generic information can be questioned and that *rationality* within the context of the group is presumed when it comes to protection against unfair b-to-c practices, a rationality that may be lacking due to reduced physical or intellectual abilities, it can be stated that more specific information or segmentation of information may be necessary. However, it remains unclear how provisions would be implemented given the high costs of adjusting information to a segmented group of elderly. Food businesses might oppose further requirements to adjust the labelling, unless the costs are compensated out of public or private pockets.

4 Conclusions

Consumer understanding of food information is influenced by differences between consumers, ranging from a different educational level to varying dietary needs, their perception about food products and the interaction between these two factors. Taking this complexity into account when drafting legislation is however not an easy task due to the scarcity of scientific consensus regarding consumer processing of food information and the variability between and within different groups of consumers as well as the businesses' costs of adaptation. EU legislation has

---

[53]Meneely et al. (2009).

addressed this variability by laying down the notions of average and vulnerable consumers, as well as by creating provisions which cover products intended for certain specific groups of consumers that have specific nutritional requirements.

The previous sections highlighted that the current legislative system may not be ideal for all consumers given the extreme variability between different types of (vulnerable) consumers. Although EU legislation poses some limitations in this context, this does not mean that the market should be given the possibility to behave as it wishes. An important drawback of the latter would be that the average group member of more vulnerable consumers might not be taken into account, which would not be a viable situation.

In order to improve provisions on the display and content of food information, Nocella and Kennedy (2012) suggest moving away from the notion of the average consumer and moving towards a more segmented view of food information which would take into account that consumers are characterised by their well-being, and their own psychological and health status. The authors argue that food information should be intended for those consumers searching for certain benefits contained in health claims which are suitable to satisfy their specific needs. An additional approach may be that of focusing on the education of certain groups of consumers which may be more vulnerable than others. This educational material would be targeted to the specific needs of potentially more vulnerable consumers in order to prevent them from being misled by information which is originally intended to appeal to the average consumer.

In any case, the amendment of existing pieces of legislation in the realm of food information for the general population would perhaps first require further insight into the processing of food information in different types of consumers and across different Member States. It would also require studies of adjustment costs in specific cases, e.g. the elderly, which are still lacking. Following such analysis, researchers and policy makers alike would have the necessary knowledge to draft more targeted and efficient provisions and to solve the present regulatory challenge, i.e. the need to adjust food information to individual wishes and as a consequence the increased efforts demanded from food businesses, the costs of which have to be reimbursed.

References

Albury D (2005) Fostering innovation in public services. Public Money Manage 25(1):51–56

Anklam E, Battaglia R (2001) Food analysis and consumer protection. Trends Food Sci Technol 12 (5–6):197–202

Bogue J, Coleman T, Sorenson D (2005) Determinants of consumers' dietary behaviour for health-enhancing foods. Br Food J 107:4–16

Chen K, Wang X-X, Song HW (2015) Food safety regulatory systems in Europe and China: a study of how co-regulation can improve regulatory effectiveness. J Integr Agric 14(11):2203–2217

Commission Regulation (EC) No 41/2009 of 20 January 2009 concerning the composition and labelling of foodstuffs suitable for people intolerant to gluten, 2009, O.J. L 16/3.

Commission Staff Working Paper Impact assessment accompanying the document proposal for a regulation of the European Parliament and of the Council on food intended for infants and young children and on food for special medical purposes. https://ec.europa.eu/food/sites/food/files/safety/docs/labelling_nutrition-special_groups_food-impact_assessment_en.pdf
Consolidated Versions of the Treaty on European Union and the Treaty on the Functioning of the European Union, 2016, O.J. C 202/1.
Directive 2009/39/EC of the European Parliament and of the Council of 6 May 2009 on foodstuffs intended for particular nutritional uses, 2009, O.J. L 124/21.
Ellison B, Lusk J, Davis D (2013) Looking at the label and beyond: the effects of calorie labels, health consciousness, and demographics on caloric intake in restaurants. Int J Behav Nutr Phys Act 10:21
European Commission (2013a) Innovation Union [online]. http://ec.europa.eu/research/innovation-union/index_en.cfm?pg=why
European Commission (2013b) Legislation on dietetic foods/Food for Specific Groups (FSG) [online]. http://ec.europa.eu/food/food/labellingnutrition/nutritional/index_en.htm
European Commission (2014a) Europe 2020 [online]. http://ec.europa.eu/europe2020/index_en.htm
European Commission (2014b) What is Horizon 2020? [online]. http://ec.europa.eu/programmes/horizon2020/en/what-horizon-2020
European Commission (n.d.) Commission staff working paper impact assessment accompanying the document proposal for a Regulation of the European Parliament and of the Council on food intended for infants and young children and on food for special medical purposes [online]. http://ec.europa.eu/food/food/labellingnutrition/nutritional/docs/impact_assessment_en.pdf
Eurostat (2006) European business – facts and figures, data 1995–2004 [online]. http://ec.europa.eu/eurostat/documents/3217494/5671075/KS-BW-05-001-EN.PDF/ffc429a4-34ea-4edb-b0a7-7f655402708c?version=1.0
Eurostat (2009) European business – facts and figures, data 2009 [online]. http://ec.europa.eu/eurostat/documents/3217494/5706863/KS-BW-09-001-EN.PDF/b6e57fad-f0f8-42ae-b617-6183c6e8e5f0?version=1.0
Eurostat (2014) Population structure and ageing [online]. http://ec.europa.eu/eurostat/statistics-explained/index.php/Population_structure_and_ageing
Food Standards Agency (2010) Understanding of labelling terms "lactose free", "milk free" or "dairy free". https://www.food.gov.uk/science/research/allergy-research/allergy-labelling/understandingfoodlabellingterms
Gabriel Y, Lang T (2015) The unmanageable consumer. Sage Publishing
Hughes G, Bennett K, Hetherington M (2004) Old and alone: barriers to healthy eating in older men living on their own. Appetite 43:269–276
Hunter W, Worsley T (2009) Understanding the older food consumer. Present day behaviours and future expectations. Appetite 52:147–154
Incardona R, Poncibo C (2007) The average consumer, the unfair commercial practices directive, and the cognitive revolution. J Consum Policy 30:21–38
Lesser W, Lynch S (2014) Costs of labelling genetically modified food products in NY State. Dyson School of Applied Economics and Management Cornell University
Macmaolain C (2007) EU food law: protecting consumers and health in a common market. Hart Publishing
Meneely L, Strugnell C, Burns A (2009) Elderly consumers and their food store experiences. J Retail Consum Serv 16:458–465
Nocella G, Kennedy O (2012) Food health claims – what consumers understand. Food Policy 37:571–580
Press releases database (2014) Questions and Answers on Commission proposal replacing current framework legislation on dietetic foods. Press Release, 20 June 2011

Regulation (EC) No 178/2002 of the European Parliament and of the Council of 28 January 2002 laying down the general principles and requirements of food law, establishing the European Food Safety Authority and laying down procedures in matters of food safety, 2002, O.J. L 31/1.
Regulation (EC) No 1924/2006 of the European Parliament and of the Council of 20 December 2006 on nutrition and health claims made on foods, 2006, O.J. L 404/9.
Regulation (EU) No 1169/2011 of the European Parliament and of the Council of 25 October 2011 on the provision of food information to consumers, amending Regulations (EC) No 1924/2006 and (EC) No 1925/2006 of the European Parliament and of the Council, and repealing Commission Directive 87/250/EEC, Council Directive 90/496/EEC, Commission Directive 1999/10/EC, Directive 2000/13/EC of the European Parliament and of the Council, Commission Directives 2002/67/EC and 2008/5/EC and Commission Regulation (EC) No 608/2004 Text with EEA relevance, 2011, O.J. L 304/18.
Regulation (EU) No 609/2013 2011 of the European Parliament and of the Council of 12 June 2013 on food intended for infants and young children, food for special medical purposes, and total diet replacement for weight control and repealing Council Directive 92/52/EEC, Commission Directives 96/8/EC, 1999/21/EC, 2006/125/EC and 2006/141/EC, Directive 2009/39/EC of the European Parliament and of the Council and Commission Regulations (EC) No 41/2009 and (EC) No 953/2009, 2013, O.J. L 181/35.
Stuyck J, Terryn E, van Dyck T (2006) Confidence through fairness? The new directive on unfair business-to-consumer commercial practices in the internal market. Common Mark Law Rev 43:107–152
Unberath H, Johnston A (2007) The double-headed approach of the ECJ concerning consumer protection. Common Mark Law Rev 44:1237–1284
van Buul V, Brouns F (2015) Nutrition and health claims as marketing tools. Crit Rev Food Sci Nutr 55(11):1552–1560
Verbeke W, Rutsaert P, Bonne K, Vermeir I (2013) Credence quality coordination and consumers' willingness-to-pay for certified halal labelled meat. Meat Sci 95(4):790–797
Wilson A, Meyer S, Webb T, Henderson J, Coveney J, McCullum D, Ward P (2015) How food regulators communicate with consumers about food safety. Br Food J 117(8):2129–2142

Silvia L. Schmidt driven by a passion for studying healthy living and food in particular, obtained a Bachelor of Science in Public Health at the Amsterdam University College and a Master of Science in Food Safety at Wageningen University. During her studies she developed a keen interest in food policy and how it is shaped in the EU. She therefore subsequently worked at the Directorate-General for Health and Food Safety of the European Commission then at the European Association of Consumer Co-operatives and is currently working at the International Federation of Organic Movements (IFOAM EU) where she promotes sustainable, quality and fair food.

Commanding to "Nudge" via the Proportionality Principle?

A Case Study on Diets in EU Food Law

Kai Purnhagen and Ellen van Kleef

Abstract This chapter assesses whether nudging techniques can be argued to be a less restrictive but equally effective way to regulate diets in EU law, when contrasted to classical information-related or content-related regulation. It has been argued that nudging techniques, due to their freedom-preserving nature, might influence the proportionality test in such a way that authorities need to give preference to nudging techniques over content-related or information regulation. We will illustrate on the example of EU food law how behavioural sciences have first altered the EU food law's goal from the mere provision of safety to also steering behaviour towards healthier diets. In line with this development, the regulatory toolbox advanced beyond the traditional dichotomy of content-related vs. information-related regulation, eventually adding nudging as a third way to regulate. Drawing on previous works of legal scholars we will then present the hypothesis that nudging techniques, according to their choice preserving nature on the one hand and steering character on the other, may be less restrictive but equally effective when contrasted with information-related or content-related regulation. With reference to recent CJEU case law that such a claim would better be backed up by scientific evidence, we will evaluate several nudging studies in the area of food that test the effectiveness of this approach. We will illustrate that, while nudging indeed has a choice-preserving nature and therefore might be less restrictive, it may also be classified under certain circumstances equally effective to information-related regulation. The EU judiciary has introduced an interpretation of the proportionality principle which requires a general preference for information-related rules. The evidence presented, however, may call for a different interpretation of the proportionality principle in some cases to

K. Purnhagen (✉)
Wageningen University, Law and Governance, Wageningen, The Netherlands

Erasmus University Rotterdam Law School, Rotterdam, The Netherlands
e-mail: Kai.Purnhagen@wur.nl

E. van Kleef
Wageningen University, Marketing and Consumer Behaviour Group, Wageningen, The Netherlands
e-mail: Ellen.vanKleef@wur.nl

H. Bremmers, K. Purnhagen (eds.), *Regulating and Managing Food Safety in the EU*, Economic Analysis of Law in European Legal Scholarship 6,
https://doi.org/10.1007/978-3-319-77045-1_8

the end that it may require policy makers in the EU to primarily use nudges instead of information-related regulation.

1 Introduction

Recent switches in the scope of EU food law has opened up leeway at policy level to increasingly make use of non-legal tools, framed by law, to influence behaviour. Most prominently in the policy domain, the nudging approach takes centre stage.[1] Nudging relies on the insight that consumers do not decide in a void, but consumers' decisions for food is rather framed by the context of their decisions.[2] If a regulator understands which context design leads to which decisions, regulators can make use of these insights and steer consumer behaviour into "good" directions by altering their choice environment.[3] Legally, it was prominently argued that this development may have an effect on the interpretation of the proportionality principle. If the proportionality principle requires policy makers to always choose the "less restrictive measures," which are equally effective,[4] the proportionality principle may require preferring nudging techniques over other forms of regulation.[5] We will investigate on the example of EU food law with reference to recent studies from behavioural science whether such an effect can be observed. Drawing on these insights, we will then make normative recommendations on the interpretation of the proportionality principle.

In order to do so, we will first elaborate on how the legal framework of EU law has changed to create leeway to consider nudging techniques in EU policy making as a third way of regulation. Subsequently, we will introduce the hypothesis that this may impact the proportionality test in such a way that preference has to be given to nudging techniques over traditional content-related or information-related measures. We will then test this hypothesis by presenting various studies that illustrate that, at least in the area of food law, nudging techniques are not as effective as content-related measures. They can be, however, as intrusive but more effective than information-regulation. We will conclude with a discussion of the implications for the interpretation of the proportionality principle.

[1]Reisch and Gwozdz (2013).

[2]Reisch and Sunstein (2014).

[3]Reisch and Gwozdz (2013).

[4]CJEU, case C-262/02, Commission v. French Republic, ECLI:EU:C:2004:431, para 34.

[5]Very clearly supporting such a view is Schweizer (2016). A different approach is presented by van Aaken (2015). Purnhagen and Reisch (2016), p. 629, leave this question to a case-by-case assessment but provide criteria for this.

2 The Food Safety Goal of EU Food Law and Its Choice Architecture

Since 2002, food law in the EU has largely been designed in hasty reactions to disasters.[6] As these disasters concerned food safety-related policy questions, at the beginning of 2000 food law was mainly geared towards ensuring safety via primarily information rules such as labelling laws and, exceptionally, content-related rules such as approval procedures.[7] EU food law, however, has advanced since 2002, in particular with respect to information regulation. Increasingly more legal acts also cover the quality of information as such,[8] particularly with a view on regulating the dietary and nutrition requirements of consumers. Article 5(2) of Regulation (EC) No 1924/2006[9] for example explicitly stipulates that "the use of nutrition and health claims shall only be permitted if the average consumer can be expected to understand the beneficial effects as expressed in the claim". With this Regulation, the Union regulator acknowledges that such a consumer choice presupposes a regulatory environment, where "(a) varied and balanced diet is a prerequisite for good health."[10] One may read these provisions as an indication that EU law carefully moves to a legal system in foods which also acknowledges the pitfalls from choice architecture.[11]

This development in some areas of EU food law may be seen as a reaction to findings from research in psychology and economics. This research looked into areas where consumers make choices in a way that may not meet their preferences. Indeed, particularly when people are pressed for time and hungry, they are less motivated to deal with information.[12] Research in psychology and economics has shown that much consumer behaviour is not deliberately controlled and reasoned but rather driven by habits and automatic tendencies.[13] In particular, temptations and triggers in choice environment can greatly affect decisions. Many dimensions of the food environment have been shown to influence perceptions and food intake, such as portion and unit size, texture, shape and package images.[14] The desire for unhealthy foods is believed to be driven by the increasing occasions in which people are confronted with easy accessible and tempting food cues, such as snacks. Moreover, taste and satiety evaluations can be suggestible. Some consumers overgeneralize

---

[6]Krapohl (2007).

[7]For the priority of information regulation see Purnhagen (2014a), p. 315 ff.; for an overview of approval procedures in EU food law see Szajkowska (2012), p. 72.

[8]See Purnhagen (2015b), p. 903.

[9]For a general account from the perspective of EU food law see also Recital 41 of Regulation (EU) No 1169/2011. For a more thorough assessment see Purnhagen and van Herpen (2017).

[10]Recital 1 of Regulation (EC) No 1924/2006.

[11]For further substantiation of this claim see Purnhagen et al. (2016).

[12]Liu et al. (2014).

[13]Kahneman (2011).

[14]van Kleef et al. (2014).

nutrition claims in that they infer that the food is lower in calories which can result in overeating.[15]

As a consequence, the environment in which people make choices is winning attention in the field of policy making and health interventions, and arguably also in EU law.[16] These insights can inform lawmakers whether their laws are designed in an effective way, meaning whether the legal interventions actually reach their goal. They can also inform the EU and the Member States as policy makers where "softer" interventions based on behavioural sciences research may reach a regulatory goal more effectively.[17] It is exactly these developments that opens up EU law to consider nudging techniques as a "third way of regulation" in-between content-related and information regulation. If this is the case, this might have implications on the interpretation of the proportionality principle, which has so far mainly contrasted the two traditional types of regulatory intervention to determine which mode of regulatory intervention is "less restrictive" but equally effective. Taken this thought further, EU food law might require regulators to choose, under certain circumstances, nudging approaches over content-related or information regulation. We will investigate this claim subsequently in more detail.

3 Central Elements of the Nudging Approach

When assessing whether nudges are equally effective but less restrictive, lawyers need to be clear about the effect and regulatory potential of the nudging approach. Nudging is about inducing behaviour change. At the heart of the nudge theory is the concept of 'libertarian paternalism', where the paternalism refers to the behaviour steering nature of the nudge and the libertarianism refers to respecting personal freedom.[18] The central idea behind nudging as a behavioural approach is to build research findings of behavioural economics and psychology into nudging interventions. As a result, these research findings have quickly moved from peer-reviewed journals into policy debates. By rearranging aspects of the choice environment ('choice architecture' in nudging terminology) that people are exposed to, the aim is to help consumers make better choices without banning options or explicitly telling what is best. Examples of nudges developed to increase the chance that

[15]Provencher et al. (2009).

[16]See the claims for more inclusion of behavioural science methods into EU law and policy making COM(2015)final, Poncibò and Incardona (2007), p. 21 et seqq.; Sibony (2015), p. 71 ff.; Duivenvoorde (2015); Purnhagen (2015a) p. 51 ff.; van Bavel et al. (2013).

[17]Reisch and Gwozdz (2013).

[18]Thaler and Sunstein (2003).

consumers pick healthier foods include changes of the position of foods on menus,[19] snack assortment presentation near the checkout[20] and food order in buffet lines.[21] It has been suggested that the current popularity is driven by the attractiveness of the approach for both conservatives and progressives.[22] That is, it promises to change behaviour for the good. At the same time, as Thaler and Sunstein repeatedly stated, nudges respect personal freedom and people can and will opt out when they want that.[23] Nevertheless, opponents call nudges manipulative and use words like 'nag'[24] to make the point that nudges could be too intrusive[25] and may lead to consumers overlooking the possibility to make alternative choices.

Nudging interventions to create behaviour change are based on a variety of theories in behavioural economics and psychology. Although there is no commonly agreed upon definition of nudging, there are four central elements in nudging theory. A *first* central element is that nudging does not rely on explicit deliberation on consumer knowledge and information on 'what to do'. Rather, many decisions in daily life are highly routinised and automatic, and people use heuristics or rules of thumb in weighing choices and making decisions. Consequently, the environment in which someone lives has a strong influence on the way an individual processes information, and acts upon them. Hence, behaviour is nudged in a desirable direction through better feedback, reminders and incentives, use of defaults, or structuring choice tasks. *Second,* a nudge should benefit a more socially desirable choice (e.g. health, less excessive spending, and sustainability). In the context of food and public health, nudges are typically intended to increase desirable behaviour (e.g. eating more fruits and vegetables) or decreasing undesirable behaviour (e.g. drinking less sugary soda). Although the nudge approach often takes advantage of well-established marketing tactics, it does not have the same aim. Marketing practices are typically aimed at increasing profits without necessarily taking into account that the manipulation should be in the interest of consumers at the longer-term. *Third,* nudges do not remove choice (the contention of libertarian paternalism). Even though consumers are given a little nudge in the desired direction, they are still free to choose differently if wanted. *Finally*, nudging involves low cost solutions that can be implemented in the choice environment without must effort. They are characterised by that they are small, inexpensive and easy to implement.[26]

It is increasingly agreed that human decision making is the function of both an analytical, slow and deliberative system and an intuitive, fast and experiential

[19]Dayan and Bar-Hillel (2011).

[20]van Kleef et al. (2012).

[21]Wansink and Hanks (2013), p. e77055.

[22]Bhargava and Loewenstein (2015).

[23]See http://www.nytimes.com/2015/11/01/upshot/the-power-of-nudges-for-good-and-bad.html?_r=0.

[24]Wilkinson (2013).

[25]Gold and Lichtenberg (2012).

[26]Johnson et al. (2012).

system. The influence of the intuitive and automatic system on decision making is considered to be large which makes people susceptible to a variety of psychological biases. Research in behavioural economics and cognitive psychology has discovered a variety of these biases and heuristics (rules of thumb).[27] In this subsection, we discuss two of these 'classic' biases and the evidence on how these biases are used in nudging interventions in the area of healthy food choices.

3.1 Present Biases and Structuring of Tempting Choices

People often have good intentions, but these plans may get overruled by moments of temptation. These so-called present-biased preferences are at the heart of impulsive and less healthy (food) decisions.[28] Self-control and willpower are important abilities believed to be essential in making healthful choices in the current food environment. The idea of nudging is to design choice environments in such a way that they encourage self-control and facilitate healthy behaviours. For example, the arrangement and shelve layout of an assortment of products in supermarkets or catering outlets can be adapted to increase the likelihood that consumers purchase the healthier options. In a study on snacks near the checkout counter, sales of healthy snacks went up when 75% of the assortment consisted of healthy snacks compared to conditions with 25% healthy snack assortments, even though choices were not rated less satisfying or more restrictive.[29] A recent nudge experiment at a number of elementary and middle schools in the US examined the effect of prompts during the pre-ordering process of lunch. When students selected their meals without adding healthy items, they automatically received a personalised message to encourage adding these to the meal. As a result, students selected 27% more fruits relative to students in the control group.[30]

3.2 Status Quo and Default Effects and Associated Nudges

People are inclined to stick with the current state of affairs or default choices even when there are better possibilities. Default options have been defined as 'the choice alternative a consumer receives if he or she does not explicitly specify otherwise'.[31] One of the most known examples of this tendency to stick with the default is that of organ donation schemes. Countries who automatically register people as organ

[27]Kahneman (2011).

[28]Lynch and Zauberman (2006).

[29]van Kleef et al. (2012), p. 1072.

[30]Miller et al. (2016).

[31]Brown and Aradhna (2004).

donor unless they choose to opt out (presumed consent) see average rates of donors of more than 90% compared to countries who employ an actively opt-in system (explicit consent), where the average rate is below 30%.[32] Several explanations have been put forward to explain the strong effect of defaults. First of all, people see the default as a suggestion by the choice architect. The choice architect is perceived to be the expert and apparently it is his or her recommendation. Changing from this suggestion may feel risky and people are generally risk averse. Moreover, accepting the default requires the least effort as it requires minimal or no action.[33]

Food options in restaurants often have a default setting as well, such as the standard side dish that comes with a meal. Nudges that exploit the status quo bias make the healthiest option the default option. For example, customers of a fast-food sandwich shop were more likely to select a low-calorie sandwich when these were displayed at the front of a menu card compared to the back.[34] Default effects have been demonstrated in other food and beverage choice situations, although the power of healthy default appears limited when preferences for particular (side) dishes are strong (e.g. fries with a meal).[35] Nevertheless, the potential of changing defaults is considerable. It is not only about side dishes and menu options that indicate the default choice. Implicitly, the size of dishware, served portion sizes and packages communicates a default norm on how much to eat. Changing defaults could also be applied here as a nudge to change eating patterns for the better.[36]

4 Preference for Nudging via the Proportionality Principle?

While the Nudging approach might hence provide potential to effectively regulate food choices, it remains questionable whether EU food law may "command" policy makers to use the nudge approach. As the nudging approach preserves choice, it may indeed be a less onerous way than content-related regulation. And as it has a steering effect one may view it also a more effective way to regulate than information regulation. In EU law, when assessing which tool to choose for regulation, the principle of proportionality, which forms a general principle of EU law,[37] serves as a major benchmark. As a limitation of Union action, it is stipulated in Article 5 TFEU as follows: "Under the principle of proportionality, the content and form of Union action shall not exceed what is necessary to achieve the objectives of the Treaties." In a similar way it is also enshrined in Article 52(1) of the Charter of Fundamental Rights. When public authorities take action in the area of risk

[32]Johnson and Goldstein (2003).

[33]Kahneman et al. (1991).

[34]Downs et al. (2009).

[35]Just and Wansink (2010) and Li and Chapman (2014).

[36]Liu et al. (2014).

[37]ECJ, cases 8/55, Fédération Charbonnière, ECLI:EU:C:1956:11.

regulation, such as health and safety regulation, it is important to not only look at Union level, but into both levels of involvement – Union and Member States.[38] As a general principle, it hence limits not only Union action but also Member State action when determining their margin of discretion.[39] In EU food law, the standard interpretation as to when and how to interfere according to the proportionality principle to provide food safety relates to the Cassis-de-Dijon case.[40] This judgment stipulated that the proportionality principle needs to be interpreted in a way that in areas where consumer protection is at stake, consumer choice instead of top-down regulation guides law-making procedures and regulation in the EU's internal market, the so-called information paradigm.[41] In other words: information regulation is generally perceived by the law as a less onerous and equally effective way of regulation than content-related measures, thereby standardising the proportionality review to compare information and content-related measures to determine which is "less restrictive" but equally effective.[42] This interpretation allows, it is assumed, a proportionate balance between producers' and consumers' right to the fundamental freedoms of goods in Article 34 TFEU, producers' right to their freedom to conduct a business according to Article 16 Charter of Fundamental Rights and consumers rights to safe and healthy foods resulting from their right to physical integrity according to Article 3 (1) Charter of Fundamental Rights. It also allows balancing the different legal cultures and socio-economic settings in Member States across the EU as well as differing consumer expectations towards the level of consumer protection legislation. Indeed, Member States felt that the identity-creating culturally relevant field of food law should be left to the discretion of the respective nations. If at all, the EU hence preferably interfered with regulations that required Member States to properly inform consumers. Possibly Member States also lacked trust in the regulatory ability of the EU to ensure safety and cultural diversity of foods on the European market. This interpretation was subject to criticism, as many feared that the Cassis-de-Dijon principle would lead to a race to the bottom in terms of quality standards.[43]

When food law after the Bovine spongiforme Enzephalopathie-crisis and dioxin contaminations in Belgium[44] moved from case to codex by implementing a safety-related horizontal regulatory framework (the General Food Law, GFL) at EU level and setting up the EFSA in Parma, many viewed this also as a shift of the standard for conducting the proportionality test. Instead of deciding each and every individual case in light of Article 34 TFEU, the rules of the GFL were the outcome of a "general" balancing act once conducted in exercise of the margin of discretion vested in Article 114 TFEU, which is now to be applied to each individual case. As to the

[38]Fisher (2007), p. 211.

[39]Purnhagen (2013), p. 715.

[40]See on the Cassis de Dijon principle Purnhagen (2014a), p. 315 ff.

[41]Usher (2001).

[42]Usher (2001).

[43]Purnhagen (2014a), p. 324 f. with further reference.

[44]See to this end Casey et al. (2010), p. 1077 ff., esp. p. 1081 f.

history of the GFL, many view this balancing largely in favour of individual consumer rights, stipulating that after the BSE crisis more emphasis was given to the protection of individual rights in food law. However, a careful study of the text of the Regulation illustrates that the GFL does not deviate much from the old "Cassis de Dijon" regime. As it becomes particularly evident in Article 8(1) of the GFL, the new regime likewise preferred regulation by information in order to enable the consumer to make an informed choice. What kind of information and in what way it was presented to consumers has for a long time not been in the focus of EU legislation[45] and also did not change with the coming into force of the GFL. According to our question of whether nudging could hence be introduced as a "third way" there is very little evidence in support of this when considering the text of the GFL.

The more special Food Information Regulation (FIR), however, advanced this approach. According to Article 3(1) FIR the disclosure of food information is still warranted, but not sufficient, as the FIR also has to make sure that consumers exercise their "informed choice" in a way that consumers "make safe use of food, with particular regard to health, economic, environmental, social and ethical considerations". When food information is at stake, Article 3 FIR requires food information to "pursue a high level of protection of consumers' health and interests". While Article 3(2) FIR also requires "taking into account, where appropriate, the need to protect the legitimate interests of producers and to promote the production of quality products", the emphasis is on the protection of the consumer. This follows inter alia from the fact that taking into account business interest is conditioned to where it is appropriate, while qualified consumer choice is an unconditioned objective in Article 3(2) FIR. The drafters of the Regulation paid such detailed attention to consumer protection that they even required taking into account not only protection of the consumers but also the "differences in the perception" of consumers (Article 1 (1) FIR).[46] The pro-consumer attitude has been endorsed by the Court of Justice of the EU (CJEU). In Teekanne[47] the CJEU in a straightforward manner applied only a consumer-oriented benchmark to test whether a product labelling is in line with the average consumer benchmark without examining the business interest.[48] Article 35(1)(a) FIR even explicitly refers to the requirement to take into account

[45]Franck and Purnhagen (2013).

[46]We are grateful to Harry Bremmers to point this out to us.

[47]CJEU, case C-195/14, ECLI:EU:C:2015:361. "In Teekanne, the Court of Justice held that the labelling of foodstuffs may not give the impression that an ingredient is present in a product where it is in fact not present, and this is apparent solely from the list of ingredients on the packaging. The judgment marks a significant realignment of previous cases that had considered the behaviour of consumers regarding the list of ingredients. In prior case law the Court had found consumers to be adequately protected if they had the possibility to gather the respective information from the list of ingredients. In Teekanne, the Court stipulated that such information of the ingredients list is not able to "correct" a "consumer's erroneous or misleading impression" created by the "overall labelling" taken as a whole. The ruling is potentially the first case in a series of judgments that understands the "average consumer" in a less normative way, and opens up to arguments about the real-world vulnerability levels of consumers." (Excerpt from Schebesta and Purnhagen 2016, p. 590).

[48]Schebesta and Purnhagen (2016), pp. 590 and 593.

"scientifically valid consumer research" when determining the forms of expression of information. Article 35(1)(d) FIR refers to "scientifically valid evidence of understanding of such forms of expression or presentation by the average consumer" both sentences of Article 35 FIR arguably referring to insights from behavioural research.

With exercising the margin of discretion when initiating the FIR, the EU law-maker has hence indeed altered in a standardized manner the traditional exercise of the proportionality principle in foodstuffs in an area where the FIR is applicable. It altered the mandated disclosure rationale stemming from Cassis de Dijon towards a more inclusive approach taking into account consumer's understanding of the information presented when enacting a regulatory decision. This approach is supplemented by other food-information related acts of the EU such as the health claims regulation, which openly refers reference to regulating consumer behaviour. As hence the context of decisions and the way consumers understand information is taken into account when determining regulatory measures in food information at EU level, these developments arguably open up leeway to include nudging as a third way of regulation in-between classical content-related and information regulation. However, these developments still may only provide some benchmarks regarding how a proportionality assessment needs to be exercised when determining which regulatory intervention is proportionate. In *concreto*, regulators (and courts) still have to determine the proportionality of a legal policy tool on a case-by-case basis. Whether information or content-related measures are "necessary" in the sense of the proportionality principle or if nudging techniques rather have to be preferred rests on a case-by-case assessment taking into account the relevant legal standards determined at EU level.

In this respect, EU law has in many ways provided flesh to the bones of the proportionality principle.[49] Space constraints allow us only to highlight the most essential benchmarks which are needed for our further argumentation. The proportionality principle is divided into several tests, some categorise the Court's requirements in two main tests,[50] others in three[51] and again others in four.[52] They do not disagree on the substance of the tests, but rather on the sequence. Regardless of sequence, the proportionality principle's features are applied with different intensity depending on the circumstances at stake.[53] The standard formula applied by the Court of Justice of the European Union to test whether a provision of Union law is consonant with the principle of proportionality is whether the means it employs to achieve the aim correspond to the importance of the aim and whether they are necessary for its achievement.[54] To be able to assess most of nudging techniques

[49]See Harbo (2010).

[50]Tridimas(1999), p. 68.

[51]Tridimas (1999), p. 68.

[52]Purnhagen (2014b), chapter 7, para 23.

[53]Harbo (2010).

[54]See e.g. CJEU, case 66/82, Fromancais v Forma, ECLI:EU:C:1983:42, para 8.

we will use the categorisation that illustrates most of the features of the test best, that is, to our understanding, the four-step test.[55] In this sense, interventions at EU level have to serve a legitimate aim,[56] need to be suitable,[57] necessary[58] and proportionate strictu sensu.[59] While we will apply all four criteria, the obligation to nudge may stem particularly from the necessity test.[60] The majority of our analysis will hence focus on this test.[61] In order to determine whether a legal tool is proportionate in the Union legal system, the necessity test requires that there is no "less restrictive" but equally effective regulatory intervention available. Nudges, due to their choice preserving nature, may generally qualify as such a less restrictive measure to content-related interventions.[62] Altering the choice environment such as requiring to bow for sweets at the cashier instead of banning them entirely can be argued to be a less restrictive measure by default. Whether it is equally effective is indeed a prerequisite that has not been looked at in great detail. In the subsequent part of this chapter we will determine whether the latest research in behavioural science can provide evidence that in the food sector nudges are indeed equally effective when compared to content-related measures and can hence qualify as a less onerous measure according to the proportionality principle.

5 Available Evidence of Effectiveness of Nudging Interventions

The increasing interest in nudging approaches to change health behaviours of consumers is partly fuelled by decades of disappointing results of persuasive communication, that means traditional interventions by information.[63] At first sight, nudging seems to be very effective and promising, compared to other approaches without high costs of implementation. For promoting healthy eating, it would 'simply' require changing the way healthy and less healthy foods are located at the shelf spaces, described at labels and menu cards and ordered. Public health may be improved with substantial savings in public expenditures and regulatory costs.[64]

[55]We acknowledge that, to our knowledge, the Court has so far never applied all four features in one case.

[56]CJEU, case C-203/96, Dusseldorp, ECLI:EU:C:1998:316, para 44.

[57]CJEU, case 152/78, Commission/France, ECLI:EU:C:1980:187, para 15 ff.

[58]CJEU, case 298/87, Smanor, ECLI:EU:C:1988:415, para 15.

[59]CJEU, case 178/84, Commission/Germany, ECLI:EU:C:1987:126, para 28.

[60]Schweizer (2016), pp. 93–111.

[61]The following section is a translated and expanded version of a paragraph piece published earlier in German in Purnhagen and Reisch (2016), p. 650.

[62]Schweizer (2016).

[63]De Ridder (2014).

[64]Alberto and Salazar (2012).

Compare this with two important other policy tools for achieving better health outcomes: government regulations and health education approaches. Health education approaches have typically focused on the nutritional information route (knowledge) in an attempt to improve consumers' food choices. The assumption here is that when people are exposed to information (e.g. calorie information in food labelling) they tend to behave in their best interest.[65] In other words, awareness of the benefits of behaviour change will motivate consumers to change their behaviour. Unfortunately, it is increasingly agreed that this assumption is unrealistic and simplistic. Education has not been particularly successful in improving healthy food choices.[66]

Related to this, taxes and subsidies as government regulation to encourage healthy food consumption have received a lot of interest among policy developers. A review showed that these tools are likely to be effective in discouraging consumption of particular product groups (e.g. soft drinks), although consumers at different levels of income may respond differently, depending on the type of product being subsidised or taxed.[67] Nevertheless, the implementation of government regulations such as taxes on sugary soft drinks, but also limits on marketing to children and setting school meal standards is seen as costly and time-consuming. Partly this can be explained by the fact that this type of regulation typically meets resistance from the food industry.[68] Nudging does not seem to have these disadvantages. It has been argued that it is appealing for politicians who want to avoid forced legislation. This is related to the belief that it is less burdensome and intrusive.[69]

Although evidence on which policy route is best is hard to find as its success depends on several factors (e.g. political, socio-economic and social context), evidence on the effectiveness of specific nudges in the area of healthy eating is still relatively scarce and mixed. However, in last few years, reviews have become available. Bucher and colleagues[70] reviewed 18 studies on nudging using position alterations (e.g. shelf space allocation or order of foods in terms of more easy accessibility) and found short-term evidence that these nudges change food choices in a healthier direction. Unfortunately, data on the magnitude and sustainability of these effects on the longer-term is lacking. Another review on nudges targeting the prominence of healthier foods (e.g. with signs such as 'pick me! I am low calorie'[71]) found modest and inconsistent effects across studies.[72] Similarly, a review on nudge intervention studies encouraging teenagers to eat more vegetables found inconclusive effects.[73]

---

[65] Maziak and Ward (2009).

[66] Jeffery and Utter (2003).

[67] Thow et al. (2014).

[68] Stuckler and Nestle (2012).

[69] Hallsworth and Sanders (2016), p. 113.

[70] Bucher et al. (2016).

[71] Wilson et al. (2015).

[72] Wilson et al. (2016).

[73] Nørnberg et al. (2015).

Important to note is that several reviewed nudge studies have been investigated in well-controlled test environments, often for only limited time periods and restricted to specific groups of participants. Understanding whether short-term effects translate into better consumer habits over the course of time is essential, but cannot be extrapolated from the current available evidence. This may lead to overgeneralization of published nudging studies. Critics likewise argue that the complexity of an environment is often overlooked, and that nudges are very context specific.[74] Moreover, unhealthy high-caloric foods with a lot of sugar, salt and fat have a strong appeal to consumers due to their inherent rewarding properties. In restaurants, nudges may have limited power because eating out can give consumers a mental license to indulge. Hence, another key challenge lies in understanding whether nudges are effective in encouraging food choices that often lack inherent desirability.[75]

6 Conclusions: Applying These Insights to the Proportionality Principle

These insights allow us to dissect in more detail whether nudging can be viewed as equally effective when compared to content-related measures in the area of food. Research has shown so far that the effectiveness of nudges cannot be proven in full certainty. To a large extent, the applications of nudges show inconsistent results with regards to their effectiveness to change behaviour. The reasons for these inconsistencies remain uncertain. One may hence draw the conclusion that due to this unstableness of effects on behaviour change nudges are largely ineffective in regulating behaviour change. This would, however, only take into account the effectiveness in terms of behaviour change. In fact, nudges have two characteristics, namely behaviour change and choice preservation. It is inherent in the concept of nudging that people can and should decide against the intended behaviour change if this choice better meets their preferences. Inconsistency as to the effect of nudges on individual behaviour are no indication for their ineffectiveness, but rather a sign that nudges work according to both features, behaviour change and choice preservation. Applying this insight to the proportionality principle hence indeed depends on which "legitimate aim" will be made subject to testing the proportionality principle. If the respective measure aims at a specific regulative public goal, for instance health protection, nudges, due to their inconsistency, may be more effective than information regulation as they also include the regulatory feature of behaviour change. Content-related regulation such as prohibitions, however, may be more effective in generating behavioural change as they do not promise such a high amount of inconsistency in effects. If the "legitimate aim" of the proportionality principle

[74]Jung and Wooseong (2011).

[75]van Kleef et al. (2015).

embraces also a choice-preserving momentum which needs to be balanced against the respective public regulative goal, nudging may be more effective than content-related regulation. In Cassis de Dijon the ECJ had indeed stipulated the primacy of information rules over content-related rules when applying the proportionality principle. If nudges are choice preserving to the same extent as information rules but are more effective as they have shown at least under some circumstances to have a regulative effect, they may indeed be preferred over information-related rules. However, nudges have one important feature that is different from information-related rules. Nudges are intrusive towards addressees with a weak or non-developed preference structure.[76] While information regulation admittedly also targets at such indifferent addressees, information regulation is not as intrusive as nudging, which deliberatively points towards altering the choice of the indifferent.[77] This is also, however, the part where it is more effective than information-regulation. Judges and regulators applying the proportionality principle will hence have to answer the question on a case-by-case basis whether they value the right of individuals to stay indifferent (and hence to stay free from nudges) more than the effectiveness to achieve the regulative aim. If they do, then nudges are indeed not as effective as information-regulation. If they do not, however, nudges can be in fact a less onerous and indeed more effective way of regulation.

References

Alberto R, Salazar V (2012) Libertarian paternalism and the dangers of nudging consumers. King's Law J 23(1):51–67

Bhargava S, Loewenstein G (2015) Behavioural economics and public policy 102: beyond nudging. Am Econ Rev 105(5):396–401

Brown CL, Aradhna K (2004) The sceptical shopper: a metacognitive account for the effects of default options on choice. J Consum Res 31(3):529–539

Bucher T, Collins C, Rollo ME, McCaffrey TA, de Vlieger N, van der Bend D, Truby H, Perez-Cueto FJ (2016) Nudging consumers towards healthier choices: a systematic review of positional influences on food choice. Br J Nutr 115(12):2252–2263

Casey D, Lawless J, Wall P (2010) A tale of two crises: the Belgian and Irish Dioxin contamination incidents. Br Food J 112:1077–1091

Dayan E, Bar-Hillel M (2011) Nudge to nobesity II: menu positions influence food orders. Judgm Decis Mak 6(4):333–342

de Ridder D (2014) Nudging for beginners. A shortlist of issues in urgent need of research. Eur Health Psychol 16(1):2–6

Downs JS, Loewenstein G, Wisdom J (2009) Strategies for promoting healthier food choices. Am Econ Rev 99(2):159–164

Duivenvoorde B (2015) The consumer benchmarks in the unfair commercial practices directive. Springer, Heidelberg

[76]Purnhagen and Reisch (2016), pp. 647–648.

[77]Id.

Fisher E (2007) Risk regulation and administrative constitutionalism. Hart, Oxford
Franck J-U, Purnhagen K (2013) Homo economics, behavioural sciences, and economic regulation: on the concept of man in internal market regulation and its normative basis. In: Mathis K (ed) Law and economics in Europe: foundations and applications. Springer, Heidelberg, pp 329–365
Gold A, Lichtenberg P (2012) Don't call me "nudge": the ethical obligation to use effective interventions to promote public health. Am J Bioeth 12:18–20
Hallsworth M, Sanders M (2016) Nudge: recent developments in behavioural science and public policy. In: Spotswood F (ed) Beyond behaviour change: key issues, interdisciplinary approaches and future directions. Policy Press, Bristol, pp 113–133
Harbo T-I (2010) The function of the proportionality principle in EU law. Eur Law J 16:158–185
Jeffery RW, Utter J (2003) The changing environment and population obesity in the United States. Obes Res 11(10):12S–22S
Johnson EJ, Goldstein D (2003) Do defaults save lives? Science 302:1338–1339
Johnson EJ, Shu SB, Dellaert BG, Fox C, Goldstein DG, Hauble G, Larrick RP, Payne JW, Peters E, Schkade D, Wansink B, Weber EU (2012) Beyond nudges: tools of choice architecture. Mark Lett 23:487–504
Jung D, Wooseong J (2011) Nudge: a tool for better policy impacts and its limitations under various policy contexts. Public Adm Rev 71(4):653–656
Just D, Wansink B (2010) Better school meals on a budget: using behavioural economics and food psychology to improve meal selection. Choices 24(3):1–6
Kahneman D (2011) Thinking, fast and slow. Farrar, Straus and Giroux, New York
Kahneman D, Knetsch JL, Thaler RH (1991) Anomalies: the endowment effect, loss aversion, and status quo bias. J Econ Perspect 5(1):193–206
Krapohl S (2007) Thalidomide, BSE and the single market: a historical-institutionalist approach to regulatory regimes in the European Union. Eur J Polit Res 46(1):25–46
Li M, Chapman G (2014) Carrots by default: are healthy defaults a blessing or a curse? Adv Consum Res 42:2–5
Liu PJ, Wisdom J, Roberto CA, Liu LJ, Ubel PA (2014) Using behavioural economics to design more effective food policies to address obesity. Appl Econ Perspect Policy 36(1):6–24
Lynch JG Jr, Zauberman G (2006) When do you want it? Time, decisions, and public policy. J Public Policy Mark 25(1):67–78
Maziak W, Ward KD (2009) From health as a rational choice to health as an affordable choice. Am J Public Health 99(12):2134–2139
Miller GF, Gupta S, Kropp JD, Grogan KA, Mathews A (2016) The effects of pre-ordering and behavioural nudges on National School Lunch Program participants' food item selection. J Econ Psychol 55:4–16
Nørnberg TR, Riebeling T, Houlby L, Rohden Skov L, Peréz-Cueto FJA (2015) Choice architecture interventions for increased vegetable intake and behaviour change in a school setting: a systematic review. Perspect Public Health 136(3):132–142
Poncibò C, Incardona R (2007) The average consumer, the unfair commercial practices directive, and the cognitive revolution. J Consum Policy 30:21–38
Provencher V, Polivy J, Herman CP (2009) Perceived healthiness of food. If it's healthy, you can eat more! Appetite 52(2):340–344
Purnhagen K (2013) Beyond threats to health: may consumers' interests in safety trump fundamental freedoms in information on foodstuffs? Reflections on *Berger v Freistaat Bayern*. Eur Law Rev 38:711–719
Purnhagen K (2014a) The Virtue of Cassis de Dijon 25 years later. In: Purnhagen K, Rott P (eds) Varieties of European economic law and regulation. Springer, Heidelberg, pp 315–342
Purnhagen K (2014b) Europarecht. C.H. Beck, Munich
Purnhagen K (2015a) Why do we need responsive regulation and behavioural research in EU internal market law? In: Mathis K (ed) European perspectives on behavioural law and economics. Springer, Heidelberg, p 51 et seqq

Purnhagen K (2015b) The EU's precautionary principle in food law is an information tool! Eur Bus Law Rev 26(6):919–920

Purnhagen K, Reisch L (2016) Nudging Germany – Herausforderungen für eine verhaltensbasierte Regulierung. Zeitschrift für Europäisches Privatrecht: 629–655

Purnhagen K, van Herpen E (2017) Can Bonus Packs Mislead Consumers? A demonstration of how behavioural consumer research can inform unfair commercial practices law on the example of the ECJ's Mars Judgement. J Consum Policy 40:217–234

Purnhagen K, van Herpen E, van Kleef E (2016) The potential use of visual packaging elements as nudges. In: Mathis K, Tor A (eds) Nudging – possibilities, limitations and applications in European law and economics. Springer, Heidelberg, pp 197–216

Reisch LA, Gwozdz W (2013) Smart defaults and soft nudges. How insights from behavioral economics can inform effective nutrition policy. In: Scholderer J, Brunsø K (eds) Marketing, food, and the consumer. Festschrift in Honour of Klaus Grunert. Pearson Custom, New Jersey, pp 189–200

Reisch LA, Sunstein CR (2014) Redesigning cockpits. J Consum Policy 37(3):333–339

Schebesta H, Purnhagen K (2016) The behaviour of the average consumer: a little less normativity and a little more reality in the court's case law? Reflections on Teekanne. Eur Law Rev 41 (4):590–598

Schweizer M (2016) Nudging and the principle of proportionality-obliged to nudge? In: Mathis K, Tor A (eds) Nudging - possibilities, limitations and applications in European law and economics. Springer, Heidelberg, pp 93–119

Sibony A-L (2015) Can EU consumer law benefit from behavioural insights? An analysis of the unfair practices directive. In: Mathis K (ed) European perspectives on behavioural law and economics. Springer, Heidelberg, pp 71–106

Stuckler D, Nestle M (2012) Big food, food systems, and global health. PLoS Med 9(6):e1001242

Szajkowska A (2012) Regulating food law. Wageningen Academic Publishers, Wageningen

Thaler RH, Sunstein CR (2003) Libertarian paternalism. Am Econ Rev 93:175–179

Thow AM, Downs S, Jan S (2014) A systematic review of the effectiveness of food taxes and subsidies to improve diets: understanding the recent evidence. Nutr Rev 72(9):551–565

Tridimas T (1999) Proportionality in community law: searching for the appropriate standard of scrutiny. In: Ellis E (ed) The principle of proportionality in the laws of Europe. Hart, Oxford, pp 65–84

Usher JA (2001) Disclosure rules (information) as a primary tool in the doctrine on measures having an equivalent effect. In: Grundmann S, Kerber W, Weatherill S (eds) Party autonomy and the role of information in the internal market. de Gruyter, Berlin, pp 151–161

van Aaken A (2015) Judge the nudge: in search of the legal limits of paternalistic nudging in the EU. In: Sibony A-L, Alemanno A (eds) Nudge and the law—a European perspective. Hart, Oxford, pp 83–112

van Bavel R, Herrmann B, Esposito G, Proestakis A (2013) Applying behavioural sciences to EU policy-making. JRC Scientific and Policy Reports 2013. Available http://ec.europa.eu/dgs/health_consumer/information_sources/docs/30092013_jrc_scientific_policy_report_en.pdf

van Kleef E, Otten K, van Trijp HCM (2012) Healthy snacks at the checkout counter. A lab and field study on the impact of shelf arrangement and assortment structure on consumer choices. BMC Public Health 12:1072

van Kleef E, Kavvouris C, van Trijp HCM (2014) The unit size effect of indulgent food: how eating smaller-sized items signals impulsivity and makes consumers eat less. Psychol Health 29 (9):1081–1103

van Kleef E, Broek O, van Trijp H (2015) Exploiting the spur of the moment to enhance healthy consumption: verbal prompting to increase fruit choices in a self-service restaurant. Appl Psychol Health Well-Being 7(2):149–166

Wansink B, Hanks A (2013) Slim by design: serving healthy foods first in buffet lines improves overall meal selection. PloS One 8(10):e77055

Wilkinson TM (2013) Nudging and manipulation. Polit Stud 61(2):341–355

Wilson AL, Bogomolova S, Buckley E (2015) Lack of efficacy of a salience nudge for substituting selection of lower-calorie for higher-calorie milk in the workplace. Nutrients 7(6):4336–4344

Wilson AL, Buckley E, Buckley JD, Bogomolova S (2016) Nudging healthier food and beverage choices through salience and priming. Evidence from a systematic review. Food Qual Prefer 51:47–64

Kai Purnhagen is Associate Professor of Law at Wageningen University and distinguished international visitor at the Erasmus University of Rotterdam law school. Previously, he has taught and researched at various institutions including the Ludwig-Maximilian University Munich, the University of Lucerne, the European University Institute, the London School of Economics and Political Science, the University of Wisconsin-Madison, the Justus-Liebig-University Giessen, and the University of Amsterdam. He holds a PhD (European University Institute in Florence), an LL. M. (University of Wisconsin-Madison), an MJI (Justus-Liebig University of Giessen) and a State Exam in Law (Land Hessen).

Ellen van Kleef is Associate Professor on 'healthy food consumption' at the Marketing and Consumer Behaviour Group of Wageningen University. Originally trained in Human Nutrition and Dietetics (BSc and MSc Degree), she developed a strong interest in the driving forces behind peoples' food choices. As a PhD student, she studied how early insight in consumer behaviour can guide the development of healthy foods. In her current research she develops a deeper understanding of *how* food and eating environments influence consumption so that they can be improved in such a way that they support consumers in effectively controlling their consumption.

Obesity, Fat Taxes and Their Effects on Consumers

Silke Thiele and Jutta Roosen

Abstract Given the rise in obesity rates, regulators have started to think about new regulatory instruments. Among those are fat taxes which are discriminatory taxes charged on nutrients at risk of excess supply in modern diets. This chapter offers a discussion of the intended and unintended consequences of fat taxes. First, it gives an economic perspective on the causes and effects of obesity. In this light possible regulatory approaches are briefly discussed. The main contribution is the assessment of fat taxes, first listing recent European regulations before reviewing the literature on the effect of fat taxes. Given limited experiences with fat taxes so far, various uncertainties in the *ex ante* assessment of their effects exist.

1 Introduction

The WHO estimated in 2015 that globally 1.9 billion adults, 18 years and older, are overweight and 600 million are obese.[1] This corresponds to a share of 39% and 13% of the population, respectively. Similarly the OECD estimated in 2014 adult obesity rates to average at 18.7% among women and 17.9% among men for its 34 member countries.[2] Table 1 reports the obesity rates over time in the OECD countries as available. Rates vary from as low as 4% in Japan in South Korea to 35% in the USA. Even among European countries rates vary considerably, from 10% in Norway

[1]WHO (2015).
[2]OECD (2014).

S. Thiele (✉)
ife Institute of Food Economics, Kiel, Germany
e-mail: silke.thiele@ife-ev.de

J. Roosen
Technical University of Munich, Freising, Germany
e-mail: jroosen@tum.de

H. Bremmers, K. Purnhagen (eds.), *Regulating and Managing Food Safety in the EU*, Economic Analysis of Law in European Legal Scholarship 6,
https://doi.org/10.1007/978-3-319-77045-1_9

Table 1 Obesity among adults

	Obese (% of population with BMI > 30)					
Country	1980	1990	2000	2005	2009	2012
Australia	8.4[aa]	10.8[a,aa]	19.8[m,aa]	24.6[r,aa]	24.6[r,aa]	28.3[v,aa]
Austria		8.5[c]	9.1[b]	12.4[s]		
Belgium			12.1[d]	12.7[e]	13.8[t]	
Canada		13.3[f]	14.8[d]	23.7[aa]	24.2[t,aa]	25.4[u,aa]
Czech Republic		11.2[g]	14.0[aa]	17.0[aa]	22.0[t,aa]	21.0[u,aa]
Denmark		5.5[i]	9.5	11.4	13.4[u]	14.2[x]
Finland	7.4	8.4	11.2	14.1	20.2[r,aa]	15.8
France		5.8	9.0	9.4[e]	11.2[t]	14.5
Germany			20.3[o,aa]	13.6	14.7	23.6[aa]
Greece				16.4[s]	18.1[t]	19.6[u]
Hungary		13.2[z,aa]	18.2	18.8[j]	28.5[aa]	28.5[y,aa]
Iceland		7.5	12.4[h]	12.4[h]	20.1[r]	22.2
Ireland			15.0[h]	15.0[h]	23.0[r]	23.0[r]
Italy		7.0[f]	8.6	9.9	10.3	10.4
Japan	2.0[aa]	2.3[aa]	2.9[aa]	3.9[aa]	3.9[aa]	3.6[aa]
Korea, Republic of			3.2[d,aa]	3.5[aa]	3.8[aa]	4.6[aa]
Luxembourg			16.3[aa]	18.6[aa]	22.1[aa]	23.0[aa]
Mexico			24.2[aa]	30.2[aa]	30.0[s,aa]	32.4[aa]
Netherlands	5.1[k]	6.1	9.4	10.7	11.8	12.0
New Zealand		12.7[a,aa]	18.8[l,aa]	25.0[j]	27.8[aa]	28.4[aa]
Norway		5.0[m]	8.0[h]	9.0	10.0[t]	10.0
Poland			11.4[n]	12.5[e]	15.8	15.8[y]
Portugal			12.8[b]	15.4[s]	15.4[s]	15.4[s]
Slovak Republic		18.9[g]	16.2[o]	17.6[aa]	16.9[t,aa]	16.9[t,aa]
Spain		6.8[i]	12.6[d]	13.1[j]	16.0	16.6[v]
Sweden		5.5[a]	9.2	10.9	10.9	11.8[w]
Switzerland		5.4[p]	7.7[h]	7.7[h]	8.1[r]	10.3
Turkey				12.0[j]	15.2[t]	22.3[v,aa]
United Kingdom	7.0[aa]	14.0[c,aa]	21.2	23.2	23.0[aa]	24.7[aa]
United States	15.0[q,aa]	23.3[c,aa]	30.9	32.9[e]	34.3[t,aa]	35.3[aa]

Source: OECD Health Data from OECD. Stat (Last updated in July 7, 2015)
Note: *BMI* body mass index defined as weight in kilograms divided by height in meters squared
[a]1989; [b]1999; [c]1991; [d]2001; [e]2004; [f]1994; [g]1993; [h]2002; [i]1987; [j]2003; [k]1981; [l]1997; [m]1995; [n]1996; [o]1998; [p]1992; [q]1978; [r]2007; [s]2006; [t]2008; [u]2010; [v]2011; [w]2012; [x]2013; [y]2009; [z]1988
[aa]Denotes measured data. All other data are self-reported

(self-reported data) to 28.5% in Hungary (measured data). In all these statistics, overweight is defined by a body mass index (BMI) of 25 and above, while obesity is talked of when the BMI is equal to or greater than 30.[3]

[3]See Seidell (2005) for a genesis on definition and measure of obesity.

The epidemiology of obesity has many notable aspects. The WHO[4] estimates that obesity at the global level has more than doubled since 1980. The data in Table 1 depicts this trend for OECD countries. This rise in the phenomenon has led some people to talk of an obesity epidemic. Rising childhood obesity rates are a particular concern, because of the increased risk for early onset of chronic diseases.[5] In addition, prevalence of obesity is unequally distributed among socio-economic groups.

The importance of obesity as a factor in public health costs and individual disease burden has led to regulatory activity in this domain. Governments have focused on the regulation of the content of food, food access, food taxes and consumer information requirements. This chapter focuses on one possible intervention, namely fat taxes, that is to say taxes that are charged on nutrients at risk of excess supply in modern diets. We aim to summarize the current stage of knowledge regarding the following questions:

(a) What is the cause for the rise in obesity?
(b) What role can fat taxes play in the regulatory toolbox?
(c) What is the effect of fat taxes on food prices?
(d) What is the effect of fat taxes on consumption?
(e) What is the effect of fat taxes on health?

To address these questions, this chapter will first look at causes of obesity from an economic perspective in Sect. 2. Then it will introduce the rationale of fat taxes and review different experiences in Europe in Sect. 3. The effect on prices, consumer behaviour and health is assessed in Sect. 4. Conclusions are drawn in Sect. 5.

2 Causes and Effects of Obesity: An Economic Perspective

2.1 Causes of Obesity

At the basic level, obesity comes about because of an unbalance in energy/calorie intake and expenditure.[6] On the one hand, the issue is one of amount of food and energy density of food. On the other hand, the issue is one of energy expenditure in daily life, through exercise and base expenditure. More complex though, nutrition status and health is an outcome influenced by physiological factors and individual behaviour. Consumers' food choices and nutrition have to be seen in the individual context, determined by food prices, time pressure and habit, and in the social context

[4]WHO (2015).
[5]Deckelbaum and Williams (2001).
[6]WHO (2015).

influenced by the household, social groups and the economy, including the conditions set by technology and policy.[7]

Different models in health economics have been built on these observations. They are most often related to the health production framework by Grossman.[8] An early contribution on the phenomenon of the rise of weight and obesity by Philipson and Posner[9] was built on this health production framework. Philipson and Posner observed a rise in calorie consumption that has been accompanied by an increase in exercise and dieting. They argued that technological change to a sedentary lifestyle has lowered the real price of food and raised the cost of spending calories. In a similar vein, Cawley[10] introduced an economic framework for understanding eating behaviour and physical activity. From this economic perspective, people produce their own health by combining time (e.g., to do sports) with market goods (e. g., food or fitness club memberships). Some of these activities, such as exercise, improve health while others (e.g., cigarette consumption) do the contrary. In this framework, Cawley derived the conclusion that different measures may be taken to limit the increase in weight and obesity. One possibility is to counterbalance the food price reductions and changes in the cost of physical activity. This is a first rationale for increasing the price of *undesirable* food products by taxation or lowering the price of *desirable* foods such as fruits and vegetables. In this light, fat taxes have been introduced in the literature and in practice in addition to "thin subsidies".[11,12]

Obesity prevalence has shown an inverse gradient with regard to income and education. Hence, in more general terms, it was observed that obesity clusters in strata of individuals with lower socio-economic status. This observation is of high relevance for the discussion of fat taxes as the tax incidence will be higher for consumers of lower socio-economic status that often spend a higher share of their income on food in comparison to households of higher socio-economic status.

For example, the OECD inequality index describes the higher risk of overweight for individuals with lower education status in most OECD countries. It describes how many times as likely it is to be overweight for somebody with a low education status compared to somebody with a high education status.[13] Data from the 2012 report are given in Table 2.

The clustering of obesity in strata of lower socio-economic status has been attributed to different factors such as poor health behaviour as a determinant of

[7]Sims (1998).

[8]Grossman (1972).

[9]Philipson and Posner (2003).

[10]Cawley (2004).

[11]Cash et al. (2005).

[12]Yaniv et al. (2009).

[13]OECD (2012).

Table 2 OECD inequality index for overweight by education

	Men	Women
Australia	1.2	1.4
Austria	1.4	1.8
Canada	1.1	1.7
England	1.0	1.4
France	1.6	2.7
Hungary	1.0	1.7
Italy	1.3	2.9
Korea	0.7	5.0
Spain	1.2	3.2
Sweden	1.4	2.2
US	0.9	1.3

Source: OECD (2012)

health outcomes,[14] stress[15] and food insecurity.[16] For example, Lynch et al.[17] could show in a sample of Finish men that many of the poor health behaviours were rooted in poor childhood conditions, and related to low level of education and blue-collar employment. Economic constraints may force consumers to buy energy-dense food.[18]

2.2 *Effects of Obesity*

Overweight and obesity is an important risk factor in the rise of the burden of non-communicable diseases. In a review, Visschers and Seidell[19] assess the evidence for the association between obesity and other diseases. The association between obesity and the metabolic syndrome (hypertension dyslipidemia, insulin resistance, abdominal obesity), as well as an increased risk of Type 2 diabetes mellitus and cardiovascular diseases is well known. In addition obesity is associated to increased mechanical stress on the body as well as certain cancers.[20] The WHO estimates overweight and obesity is responsible for 44% of the diabetes, 23% of ischemic heart disease and 7–41% of certain cancer burdens.[21]

Being a risk factor for many important diseases, obesity is to be an important cost factor in terms of quality of life, but also in the health care system. In addition,

[14]Aue et al. (2016).

[15]Torres and Nowson (2007).

[16]Wilde (2011).

[17]Lynch et al. (1997).

[18]Wilde (2011).

[19]Visschers and Seidell (2001).

[20]Seidell (2005).

[21]WHO (2009).

people in the developed world spend enormous amounts of money on dieting or exercise to achieve weight loss.[22] According to a study from McKinsey & Company,[23] obesity ranks among the top three human-generated economic burdens in most developed economies. In the United Kingdom, for instance, obesity has the second-largest impact after smoking, generating an economic loss of more than $70 billion a year in 2012, or 3.0% of GDP. For Germany, total cost of overweight and obesity are estimated at 17 billion Euro in 2008, corresponding to 3.27% of the total German health care expenditures.[24]

2.3 Regulatory Approaches

Despite these costs, weight management (and individual health) is not an issue for regulation per se, but only when there are market failures. The literature has identified two types of market failures in this respect. First, there may be information deficits among consumers when choosing food. Second, there may be externalities in form of increased health care and insurance costs borne by others.[25]

Mazzocchi et al.[26] have analysed in detail policy options for these two types of market failure. First, information measures either address consumers directly via education programs and information campaigns or they work in the market environment when implemented via food labelling. Regulation can also address advertisement, including statements on the composition of a healthy diet (e.g. in France) or restricting advertisement of food to children.

Secondly, market interventions may be employed including taxes, subsidies, liability rules, as well as food standards for packaged food and food-away from home provision, e.g. in schools and at work. This contribution will look in detail at the intervention using taxes.

3 Fat Taxes: Rationale and Implementations in Europe

One common justification for regulation in the area of overweight and obesity refers to negative externalities of unhealthy diets. In the presence of negative externalities the social costs of a market activity are not covered by the private costs of the activity. In such a case, the market outcome is not efficient and may lead to overconsumption of the product. There seems little doubt that obesity and related

[22]Philipson and Posner (2003).

[23]Dobbs et al. (2014).

[24]Lehnert et al. (2015).

[25]Cawley (2004).

[26]Mazzocchi et al. (2009).

diseases create substantial external costs for society which contribute to an increased burden on national health insurances and might also lead to higher health insurance premiums for those taking out private health care. To counter externalities, one measure focused by policy makers and research is to change the market environment by taxes and subsidies. This chapter addresses taxation, also known under the term of fat tax.

3.1 Rationale of Fat Taxes

A fat tax is a tax that is placed upon unhealthy foods and aims to discourage unhealthy diets. A narrow definition refers to a tax on fat or saturated fat, whereas a broader definition includes other dietary components such as sugar, sweetened beverages, or junk food. In this chapter, we refer to the broader definition and include all taxes levied on food items that are considered at risk of oversupply in modern diets. The idea behind taxing unhealthy foods originates from economic theory where it is assumed that as the price of an item rises, the consumption of that item will typically fall. Thus increasing the price of unhealthy foods by taxation should reduce consumption of these foods. As the particular aim of the tax is to decrease the consumption of unhealthy foods but not primarily to generate state revenue, a fat tax belongs to Pigouvian taxes which are levied on market activities that generate negative externalities. Other examples of Pigouvian taxes are duties on cigarettes, alcohol, gambling and environmental emissions.[27]

Is a Fat Tax an Adequate Measure to Internalize Negative Externalities?

A negative externality occurs when an individual or firm making a decision does not have to pay the full costs of that decision. There seems little doubt that obesity creates substantial external costs for the economy. According to the studies cited above, diet-related diseases including obesity rank among the top risk factors for many non-communicable diseases. In view of this, it seems justifiable to internalize the external obesity costs, which would ensure that the costs associated with obesity are borne by those whose decisions create the costs. However, there is the question to what degree a fat tax is suitable in internalizing the external costs caused by obesity, and therefore to fulfil its central goal.

In general it can be assumed, that the growing obesity rate can, at least in part, be attributed to a greater consumption of fats and sugar. Nevertheless, it is frequently stressed that a further important factor influencing the growing numbers of overweight people is a lack of exercise. As mentioned in the introduction, people, particularly younger people, spend more time doing sedentary activities, such as

[27] Alemanno and Carreño (2013).

watching TV, surfing the internet, and playing computer games. Since it is not the consumption of unhealthy foods that causes external costs, but the overweight people themselves, and given that being overweight is not only caused by consuming unhealthy foods, some economists suggest focusing directly on the overweight by modifying the health payment system. For example, measures could be designed that provide stronger incentives for individuals to get into better shape and eat healthier diets.[28] This would also have the advantage that people with normal weight are not affected by measures targeting the overweight, as in the case of a fat tax.

Are Fat and Sugar Demerit Goods?

Another justification for implementing a fat tax could be that fat and sugar are considered demerit goods. A demerit good is a good for which consumption is regarded as unhealthy, degrading, or otherwise socially undesirable. Typical examples are alcoholic beverages, recreational drugs, and gambling. While a negative externality occurs when the consumption of a good has negative consequences on others who do not consume the good themselves, a demerit good is viewed as undesirable because its consumption has negative effects upon the consumer. For these goods people tend to under-estimate the private costs and over-estimate the private benefits, so that they are over-consumed if left to market forces. The question arises if unhealthy foods belong to demerit goods so that taxation can be justified from an economic point of view. Take fat as an example, in comparison to, say, drugs. Whereas drugs are unhealthy in general, fat is essential to a certain point, as it provides vital fatty acids and is a carrier of fat-soluble vitamins. Therefore, fat cannot fundamentally be defined as a demerit good. In contrast, sugar normally contains no essential nutrients so that its consumption reduces the nutrient density for a given energy intake. For this reason, added sugar could be attributed to demerit goods rather than fat, and therefore a taxation of added sugar seems to be more justified than a taxation of fat.

3.2 *Fat Tax Implementations in the European Union*

There are several examples of fat taxes around the world. For example, in January 2014 Mexico introduced a tax on high-calorie foods and sugar-sweetened beverages. The tax is set at one peso per litre (about 0.06 Euros) on soft drinks and at 8% sales tax on high-calorie-foods with more than 275 kcal per 100 g of foods. This means that foods such as potato chips, sweets and cereals are included. In the USA, several regions have excise taxes on sugar sweetened beverages. Currently this is the case in about 30 states. However, within the scope of this book, the following examples focus on taxes in EU member states. We refer to those fat taxes that are currently in

[28]Becker (2006).

Table 3 Current fat taxes in Europe

	Sweetened beverages	Energy drinks	Chocolate	Confectionery	Ice cream	Salty snacks	Saturated fat
Denmark	X[a]		X	X	X		X[b]
Finland	X		X	X	X		
France	X	X					
Hungary	X	X	X	X		X	

[a]Abolished in 2014
[b]Abolished in 2013

Table 4 Fat taxes in Denmark

	Sugar sweetened beverages/ juices (€ per litre[a])		Chocolate/ confectionery (€ per kg[a])		Saturated fats (€ per kg[a])
Before 2001	0.13				
2001	0.22				
2003	0.15				
2007	0.12		1.90		
2010	0.076[b]	0.145[c]	1.90[d]	2.38[e]	
2012	0.076[b]	0.212[c]	2.71[d]	3.18[e]	2.14
2013	0.079[b]	0.220[c]	2.81[d]	3.30[e]	Abolished
2014	Abolished				

Source: Own presentation based on ECORYS (2014)
[a]In 2015 exchange rates
[b]<0.5 g sugar/100 mL
[c]>0.5 g sugar/100 mL
[d]<0.5 g sugar/kg
[e]>0.5 g sugar/kg

place, have been recently introduced, or recently withdrawn. Table 3 gives an overview of the European countries that currently raise fat taxes.[29]

Denmark

Denmark has a long history with taxing unhealthier foods. As early as 1930, an excise duty on soft drinks and juices was introduced, followed by a tax on confectionery and chocolate in 1968. In 2011, Denmark became the first country to establish a real fat tax imposed on saturated fats. All tax regimes have been modified several times.

Table 4 shows that before 2001 sugar-sweetened beverages and juices were taxed with a rate of 13 Eurocents per litre. After a noticeable increase in 2001 to 22 Eurocents, the tax rate was lowered again in 2003 and 2007 to 12 Eurocents.

[29]The evidence on the tax types and levels are taken and summarized from ECORYS (2014).

As of 2010 a distinction was made between sugar-sweetened soft drinks (14.5 Eurocents) and light and sugar-reduced soft drinks with less than 0.5 g of sugar per 100 mL (7.6 Eurocents). After raising the tax rate in 2012 and again in 2013, it was reduced in July 2013 by 50%, and fully abolished in January 2014. The tax rates on chocolate and confectionery have also been changed several times. Until 2010 the Danes had to pay a rate of €1.90 per kg of final product. Since then, a difference has been made between products containing more than 5 g of sugar per kg (€2.38) and those with less than 5 g (€1.90). In 2012 and again in 2013, the rates were increased to a total of €3.30 and €2.81. A tax on saturated fats was introduced in October 2011. Foods that contain more than 2.3% saturated fat were taxed with a rate of €2.14 per kg of saturated fat. After being in place for around 14 months, the tax was abolished in January 2013.

Finland

Finland has had taxes on sweets since 1926. After abolishing the tax in 1999, it was reintroduced in 2011. Whereas previously confectionery and chocolate were affected by the tax, now ice cream is also involved. In addition, the Finns have a tax on beverages which was introduced in 1946, and was combined with the tax on sweets in 2011.

As represented in in Table 5, the tax on beverages was €0.045 per litre for all beverages until 2011. It was subsequently raised a few times and is now €0.11 per litre for sweetener-based beverages and mineral water, and €0.22 for sweetened beverages. The tax on chocolate, confectionary and ice cream was €0.75 per kg in 2011 and was raised to €0.95 one year later.

France

In France, a tax on sugar and non-sugar sweetened beverages was implemented in January 2012. It targets all beverages with added sugar or sweetener (regardless of the quantity) including light drinks. The official rationale underlying the tax was health related, but the collection of revenue was also considered to be a primary aim.

Table 5 Fat taxes in Finland

	Beverages (€ per liter)		Chocolate/confectionary/ice cream (€ per kg)
Before 2011	0.045		–
2011	0.075		0.75
2012	0.11		0.95
2014	0.11[a]	0.22[b]	0.95

Source: Own presentation based on ECORYS (2014)
[a]Sweetener based beverages and mineral water
[b]Sweetened beverages

Table 6 shows that at the time the tax was introduced in 2012, the suppliers had to pay €0.0716 per litre. As this rate is adjusted once a year in order to be in line with the growth rate of the consumer price index, it reached a value of €0.0731 in 2013 and €0.0745 in 2014. The total revenue generated from the tax was €375 million in 2013 and was used entirely for social security purposes.

Hungary

In 2011 Hungary introduced a tax on food and beverage products which are considered unhealthy because they exceed a certain content of sugar, fat, salt, and caffeine. The tax affects sugar sweetened beverages and their concentrates, syrups, energy drinks, confectionery, chocolate, salty snacks, condiments and flavoured beers. Table 7 lists a few examples for thresholds and tax rates. Since 2012, the rate for soft drinks has been €0.023/L if added sugar is more than 8 g/100 mL, the levy on confectionery €0.42/kg if added sugar is more than 25 g/100 g (the threshold for chocolate is different with 40 g/100 g), and the tax rate for salty snacks €0.8/kg if salt is more than 1 g/100 g. However, a range of exemptions are made, for example for products with more than 25% fruit and vegetable content.

Table 6 Fat taxes in France

	Sweetened beverages[a] (€ per litre)
2012	0.0716
2013	0.0731
2014	0.0745

Source: Own presentation based on ECORYS (2014)
[a]Added sugar or sweetener, regardless of the quantity

Table 7 Fat taxes in Hungary

	Sugar sweetened beverages[b] (€ per litre[a])	Energy drinks[c] (€ per litre[a])	Confectionery[d]	Salty snacks[f] (€ per kg[a])
			Chocolate[e] (€ per kg[a])	
2011	0.016	0.80	0.32	0.64
2012	0.023[b]	0.80	0.42	0.80

Source: Own presentation based on ECORYS (2014)
[a]In 2015 exchange rates
[b]Added sugar > 8 g/100 mL
[c]Methylxanthines > 15 mg/100 mL or taurin > 100 mg/100 mL
[d]Added sugar > 25 g/100 g
[e]Added sugar > 40 g/100 g
[f]Salt > 1 g/100 g

3.3 Lessons Learned from Fat Tax Implementations in Europe

The overview of the current fat taxes in Europe shows that all four countries have different tax regimes. In these regimes neither the subject of taxation nor the level of a tax rate is the same. The subject of taxation can be an ingredient such as saturated fat (Denmark), or it can be a product as a whole, such as a salty snack (Hungary). The taxed ingredients range from sugar and fat to salt, and concerned products include sweetened beverages, sweets and/or salty snacks. Also thresholds for taxes are different. In the case of sweetened beverages, which are taxed in all four countries, there are four different boundaries. In Denmark all sweetened beverages are taxed with two different rates: one for beverages with less than 0.5 g/100 mL sugar content, one for beverages with more than 0.5 g. The Fins also have two different tax rates, but, in contrast to Denmark, one for sweetener based beverages and another for sweetened beverages, wherein the quantity of sweetener or sugar is not considered. In France there is a uniform tax rate for sweetener-based or sugared beverages regardless of the quantities. And in Hungary they have the same concept as Denmark but the threshold for sugar content is, with 8 g/100 mL in comparison to 0.5 g/100 mL, clearly higher. In conclusion, the goal of the fat taxes in the countries is the same: to reduce the number of overweight people and the prevalence of diet-related diseases. However, the way to reach the goal is very different. As it is obviously not clear which way most likely leads to accomplishing the goal, there is a need for further research in this field.

4 Expected and Observed Effects of Fat Taxes on Consumers

4.1 Expected Effects

The central goal of implementing a fat tax is to reduce consumption of foods with a high percentage of components that are considered unhealthy (e.g. fat, sugar, salt) and thereby to improve nutrition and health. This section deals with the question of whether, and to what extent, such a tax is able to achieve this goal. As the implementation of a fat tax causes different reactions from the various market players, the final result is not clear and difficult to predict. Table 8 shows an overview of possible reactions, and their consequences, mentioned in the literature on fat taxes.

First of all the state revenue has to be mentioned. In Denmark the revenue from the tax on saturated fat was estimated at €160 million per year which is equivalent to

Table 8 Overview of the effects of a fat tax

Government...	
(a) Generates revenue	
Manufacturers may...	
(a) Reformulate their products	
(b) Bear a part of the tax burden	
(c) Experience higher administrative costs	
Consumers may...	
(a) Switch to cheaper versions of the product	
(b) Switch to other (healthier) food items (extent depends on price elasticities)	
Consequences:	– Food composition changes – Nutritional and energy supply changes (impact on health is unclear)
(c) Experience welfare losses (regressive effect)	
(d) Experience health effects (progressive effect?)	

Source: Own compilation based on ECORYS (2014)

about €74 per household per year.[30] Such means might be used for improving public health, as planned in Denmark, or for social security purposes as carried out in France. Either way, the revenue ultimately benefits the consumers, but there is redistribution between types of consumer groups and a part of the revenue is used for administrative purposes.

One possible reaction of manufacturers producing taxed foods could be that they reformulate their products to reduce the impact of the tax on the costs of the product. However, there are limitations to product reformulation as the taxed ingredients are often main flavour carriers and reformulating a product has to be compatible with the taste expectations of consumers. If reformulation is feasible, a reduction of the taxed ingredient may have positive health effects for consumers. An interview of fourteen European stakeholders regarding the impact of food taxes on product reformulation showed differences in opinions. While some stakeholders saw a reduction of innovations as a result of less capital available due to taxation, others think that product reformulation has continued or increased in response to taxation.[31] A second reaction of manufacturers or retailers could be that they add less than the tax rate to the consumer price and hence these firms bear a part of the tax burden themselves. The greater this part, the smaller the effect on consumption. Thirdly, manufacturers may face high administrative costs when a tax is implemented and these costs could be passed on to consumer prices in general, but not only to taxed products. In the case of the Danish tax on saturated fat, companies had to calculate and declare the quantities of saturated fat contained in each of their products, and to pay the corresponding taxes. A survey by the Danish Chamber of Commerce found that the fat tax's

[30]Smed and Robertson (2012).

[31]ECORYS (2014).

administrative costs caused by a range of financial, human, computer and logistical resources amounted to nearly 27 million Euros.[32]

Consumers on the other side may respond to price increases by moving to cheaper versions of the taxed product, either by buying private-label products instead of manufacturer brands, or by shifting from high-price supermarkets towards low-price discount stores. Such reactions may lower the effect of the tax. According to economic theory the most expected reaction is that consumers lower the demand for the product when the price rises (e.g. butter) and at the same time increase the demand for substitution products (e.g. margarine). The extent of these reactions is described by price elasticities, which are the percentage changes in consumption for a one percentage change in prices. However, the restructuring of the food basket can cause health effects that are not desired. For instance, a study by Mytton et al.[33] found that taxing saturated fat was offset by a rise in salt consumption and therefore the resulting health effects turned out to be unfavourable. Undesired health effects can also occur because the supply of essential nutrients that are combined with the taxed ingredient (e.g. essential fatty acids and important fat soluble vitamins) will decrease. A study by Allais et al.[34] found that a tax on cheese, butter and cream would decrease Vitamin D to the highest percentage among all vitamins if it were to be implemented in France. This is particularly critical because the supply of vitamin D is a relevant dietary issue. A further effect for consumers is that welfare losses occur when a tax is implemented. In the particular case of a food tax these losses are higher for lower income groups than for higher income groups, because they spend a greater proportion of their income on food. This regressive effect of a tax is unwanted from a social point of view. However, from a health perspective this fact may turn out to be a positive one, because the share of obese people is higher in lower socio-economic status groups (progressive health effect). Finally, it should be emphasized that all reactions listed in Table 8 are different for individual consumer (or manufacturer) groups. In most studies the reaction of an average consumer is considered, but to draw more meaningful conclusions on economic and health impacts of a fat tax, segmentations which focus on risky population groups (e.g. obese people, children) would be necessary. Furthermore, the strengths of effects are influenced by additional information campaigns or measures that are taken along with taxation, such as information on the negative impact of high-calorie foods on health.

In relation to the counterbalance effect in a health production framework, Smed et al.[35] warn for the unintentional effects of a fat tax, in particular for vulnerable parts of the population. Tiffin and Salois[36] (2014) have analysed the distributional impact of a fiscal food policy for the UK. As Smed et al. they can show that the effects of a

[32]Petkantchin (2013).

[33]Mytton et al. (2007).

[34]Allais et al. (2010).

[35]Smed et al. (2007).

[36]Tiffin and Salois (2014).

food tax concentrate on lower income households. This is because of the regressive nature of almost any food tax. This means while households of low economic status seem to be disproportionally affected by overweight and obesity, fat taxes may not be a successful means to address them.

4.2 Observed Effects from Different Types of Empirical Studies

There is a large body of literature trying to empirically investigate the aforementioned effects of a fat tax. Three different types of studies can be found. These include: (1) observation studies, (2) experimental studies and (3) simulation studies. Observation studies rely on actual experiences with fat taxes (e.g., Denmark's fat tax). These kinds of studies may provide the most convincing evidence of effects, nevertheless they have the drawback of eliminating other factors influencing the observed changes. In experimental studies, controlled trials are conducted in which prices are manipulated in simulated or closed environments such as analogue supermarkets or cafeterias. The disadvantage of this type of study is that it cannot be controlled to what extent compensatory behaviour occurs away from the study environment, or how well simulated environments (e.g. artificial budget constraints) are able to predict real choices. Simulation studies represent the major share of studies to be found in the literature. These studies use real household purchase data to estimate how price changes affect consumption. Using these data and applying econometric models, price elasticities are estimated and used to simulate a hypothetical fat tax, and to predict its effect on consumption. Some of these studies extend the changes in food demand to estimate the effects on health outcomes. The key limitations of these studies are that they are dependent on the availability of data and on the robustness of assumptions which are often made to simplify the model. In the following a selection of results is shown, taking examples from all three types of studies. For all examples we look at the effect on prices and consumption.

Observation Studies

Empirical observation studies on the effects of European fat taxes on price and demand changes were done in a study conducted by ECORYS.[37] Based on data provided by Euromonitor, price and demand changes for several products were observed over the period from 1999 to 2014. In doing so, the effects of the introduction (or abolition) of a food tax within this period could be viewed. The used databases covered the total revenue of various food sectors, the total volumes sold in a country and the number of inhabitants in a country. Using these variables,

[37]ECORYS (2014).

average prices per unit of the products were constructed by dividing the revenue by the volumes sold, and the per capita demand was calculated by dividing the total consumer demand by the total number of inhabitants in the country. Due to a lack of data proper statistical analyses could not be conducted, which meant that establishing direct causal relationships between price and demand was not possible. Instead, the authors of the study compared the observed actual price changes with expected price changes resulting from the tax under the assumption of a full leverage of the tax on consumer prices. Furthermore, they examined changes in consumption in the period that tax changes occurred. Both price and consumption changes were interpreted against the backdrop of long-term prices and consumption trends.

For Denmark the ECORYS's data analysis established that prices for soft drinks seemed to react in line with the tax changes during the whole period observed. When taxes were increased, e.g. for regular cola, prices increased and vice versa. In contrast, for juices the volatility of the market prices seemed to move separately from any of the tax changes. However, a tax reduction by 50% in 2013 was followed by a clear increase in demand for cola. Similarly for chocolate and confectionery all increases in tax rates were followed by increases in price, and these increases were larger than what could have been expected from tax effects alone. As expected from the price increases, the demand for chocolate and confectionary decreased. Regarding the tax on saturated fats, the tax seemed to have a strong impact on prices for fats and oils. The increase ranged from 5% for olive oil with a comparable low share of saturated fats, and almost 20% for cooking fats with a high share of saturated fats. After the abolition of the tax, prices decreased again. Following the introduction of the tax, the demand for most fats and oils showed either a continuing decline or a sudden drop.

In Finland, the prices for all taxed products (confectionery, chocolate, ice cream and soft drinks) have increased steadily since the tax was reintroduced in 2011 and this increase was more than what could be attributed to the tax. The rising prices were accompanied by a reduction in demand for both sweets and soft drinks.

With the introduction of the tax on sugar and non-sugar sweetened beverages in France, a clear price increase for both regular and low calorie cola was observed and this increase was higher than the price increase related directly to the tax. The rising prices had a substantial influence on the demand for cola. Whereas a steady increase of the demand for both regular and low calorie cola had been observed until 2011, this trend seemed to have been reversed with the introduction of the tax. Since 2011 both types of cola have been decreasing by 3% annually.

The public health product tax on various unhealthy products in Hungary, introduced in 2011, showed mixed effects on prices and demand. Whereas prices for confectionery and sugar-sweetened beverages increased more than could have been expected from the tax, the prices for salty snacks rose in line with the existing trend prior to the tax introduction, and the prices for energy drinks even decreased. Corresponding to the price developments, the demands for confectionery, sugar sweetened beverages, and salty snacks, had already showed decreasing trends prior to the tax introduction. The pure effect of the tax, therefore, is unclear. In contrast, the demand for energy drinks did not start to decline until 2012.

Table 9 Direction of price and consumption changes due to a fat tax worked out by ECORYS

	Consumer price increase	Consumption decrease
Denmark		
Sweetened beverages	Yes	Yes
Juices	Unclear	Unclear
Chocolate/confectionery	Yes	Yes
Saturated fats	Yes	Yes
Finland		
Beverages	Yes	Yes
Chocolate	Yes	Yes
Confectionery	Yes	Yes
Ice cream	Yes	Yes
France		
Sweetened and beverages	Yes	Yes
Hungary		
Sugar sweetened beverages	Yes	No
Energy drinks	No	Yes
Confectionery	Yes	No
Chocolate	Yes	No
Salty snacks	No	No

Source: Own compilation based on ECORYS (2014)

Overall the ECORYS study showed that tax changes were in most cases followed by price changes in the direction that was to be expected (see Table 9). Moreover, actual price increases were normally higher than expected price increases directly related to the tax tariffs. The only exception was Hungary, were the prices for salty snacks and energy drinks showed no increase, even a slight decrease, after the Public Health Product Tax was introduced. The demand reaction to the price changes also mostly showed expected results. With the exception of Hungary, tax-induced price increases showed demand decreases and vice versa.

While the ECORYS study did not control for factors apart from the tax effect affecting price and consumption changes, there are some empirical observation studies that rely on statistical methods in which further factors are considered. Using regression analysis, Bahl et al.[38] examined the table water/soft drink tax in Ireland which was in place from 1916 to 1992. Based on national level longitudinal data, the authors estimated the level of soft drink consumption, taking the prices of soft drinks, the prices of other goods, the level of income, and a variable of weather into account. Based on the regression results, they conducted a simulation and compared the simulation results with actual price and consumption changes. The study showed that holding weather and income levels constant, the tax rate reduction (abolition) itself would have driven down soft drink prices, and would have led to

[38]Bahl et al. (2003).

increased soft drink consumption. Jensen and Smed[39] conducted an *ex post* analysis of the tax on saturated fats in Denmark, which was in place from October 2011 until the end of 2012. By using weekly household purchasing data spanning the period from January 2008 until July 2012, they estimated three econometric models: a price setting model which analysed the tax effect on consumer price changes, and two consumption models: the first focused on the influence of the tax on purchases, and the second on demand effects in different store types. The analysis showed mixed results for the transmission of the tax to consumer prices. In discount stores the tax was either perfectly transmitted or it was used to increase the margin. In supermarkets the tax was fully passed through for some products and for others less than the full tax was transmitted to the consumer. Furthermore, the analysis showed that the level of consumption of fats dropped by 10–15% and it was observed that demand shifted from high price supermarkets towards low price discount stores. However, due to the relatively short data period with the tax being active and considering that hording effects were observed, meaning that consumers purchased large amounts of fat products before the tax was introduced. It should be noted that the results must be interpreted cautiously. Fletcher et al. (2010) analysed US soft drink taxes between 1989 and 2006. Using data on state soft drink sales, excise tax information and individual food intake data of the National Health Examination and Nutrition Survey (NHANES), they estimated the demand for soft drinks of children and adolescents. Considering influential factors such as individual and socio-economic characteristics, prices for soft drinks and for other beverages, as well as soft drink taxes, they found moderate reductions in soft drink consumption resulting from a soft drink tax. But these reductions were more than offset by increases in consumption of other high-calorie drinks, such as fruit juice and milk.

Overall, the observation studies based on statistical analyses came to the result that taxation had a more or less strong effect on consumer demand. With regard to the question how much the tax is passed on to the consumers, three possible scenarios were found: (1) a perfect transmission, (2) the tax was used by the stores to increase the margin or (3) the tax was less than fully passed on to the consumers, so that stores or manufacturers bore a part of the tax burden.

Experimental Studies

Experimental studies are conducted either in closed environments such as schools and cafeterias, or in laboratories in which participants are engaged in hypothetical purchases of products, often with a fixed hypothetical budget constraints. The closed environment studies mostly relate to price discounts on healthier foods such as low fat snacks[40,41]

---

[39]Jensen and Smed (2013).

[40]French et al. (1997).

[41]French et al. (2001).

and fruits and vegetables.[42,43] In general these studies found that consumers react to price reductions with an increase of consumption. However, a vending machine experiment by French et al. (2001) showed that price decreases for healthier products induced a large increase in total sales which is an unwanted side effect of a price reduction and may indicate an increase in total energy intake. There exist only a few studies that address price increases of unhealthier foods, and therefore are more comparable to the implementation of a fat tax. A study of Block et al.[44] analysed the effects of a 35% increase on the price of regular soft drinks in a hospital cafeteria. In comparison with the baseline, regular soft drink sales decreased by 26%. In a further experimental step, an educational campaign was offered that indicated weight loss could occur by reducing sugar-sweetened soda intake. The authors found that the combination of price increases with the educational campaign caused a decrease in sales by 36%. However, the education had no significant independent effect on sales. A laboratory experiment by Epstein et al.[45] focused on the question of whether price decreases of healthy foods have the same strength of effect as price increases of unhealthy foods. In an analogue of a convenience store, children were asked to purchase either a preferred high-energy-dense snack or a preferred fruit or vegetable. In one condition the price of the fruit or vegetable was held constant whereas the price for the snack was increased, and in the other condition the price for the snack was held constant whereas the price for the fruit or vegetable was decreased. It was found that the own-price elasticities for healthy and less healthy foods were nearly the same and amounted to −1.01 and −0.92. Giesen et al.[46] examined how price increases for unhealthy foods and calorie information influence lunch decisions in an analogue of a cafeteria. They randomly assigned 178 university students to four groups with budget (high/low) and calorie information (with/without). They found that a price increase for the high-calorie foods reduced the percentage of calories chosen for lunch but only in the absence of calorie information. In contrast, a laboratory experiment by Yang and Chiou[47] using 108 college students found that information on the negative impact of high-calorie foods strengthens the influence of price increases for high calorie beverages on their sales. When the information was not given, the price elasticity was −0.91, however when additional information was available, the elasticity turned to −1.27.

In general, all experimental studies found an impact of price instruments on food demand. Both discounts on healthier foods and price increases for unhealthier foods had nearly the same effect. Nevertheless, price decreases for healthier foods could cause an increase in total sales and thereby of calorie intake. Furthermore, the studies found that additional education campaigns or calorie information could strengthen

---

[42] Jeffery et al. (1994).

[43] Michels et al. (2008).

[44] Block et al. (2010).

[45] Epstein et al. (2012).

[46] Giesen et al. (2011).

[47] Yang and Chiou (2010).

the effect of price increases on unhealthier foods. All of the experimental studies fail to measure the effect of the tax intervention on total dietary choices and hence to assess the effect of the tax beyond the experimental environment.

Simulation Studies

This type of studies estimates consumers' reactions to price increases (price elasticities) which are used to simulate a hypothetical fat tax. They are mostly based on demand systems estimated using household purchase data. Using American data Chouinard et al.[48] estimated price elasticities for dairy products with different fat contents. They found that a 10% ad valorem tax on the percentage of fat would reduce fat consumption by less than a percentage point. As the demand for most dairy products was inelastic, the authors concluded that a fat tax would lead to relatively small consumer reactions, and instead to substantial state revenue. Furthermore, they stressed that a fat tax is regressive. In the case of Denmark, Smed et al.[49] investigated the nutritional effects of various taxation and subsidy schemes, focussing on the consumption of saturated fats, fibre and sugar. In general, they found that all scenarios have an effect on consumption, but a larger effect was detected when the tax or subsidy was levied directly on the nutrient content than when it was levied indirectly on the food commodities that contain the respective ingredient. However, they stressed that using the direct form places a relatively large administrative burden on the authorities. Furthermore, the authors found that the impact of price instruments was particularly strong for younger age groups and for lower social classes, which underlined the regressive nature of the fat tax. Therefore, although tax instruments may be effective in improving diets on average, it is questionable whether they reach the groups they are intended for. Tiffin and Salois[50] used UK data to investigate effects on nutrition consumption of a fiscal policy based on a combination of a tax on saturated fats and subsidies on fruits and vegetables. Using price elasticities they computed nutrient elasticities which show how consumption of nutrients changes when prices change. The authors found both positive and negative effects of the tax/subsidy scenario on nutrient supply. The tax resulted in a declined intake of energy intake, but also to a decreased consumption of important fat soluble vitamins, namely A, D and E. The subsidies on fruits and vegetables led to an increase of some key nutrients such as carotene, but also to an increase of sugar consumption. The authors concluded that such a fiscal policy may lead to negative health outcomes and therefore fail to achieve its goal. Finkelstein et al.[51] (2013) also focussed on the health outcome of a fiscal measure. Using US panel data they investigated how much body weight could be reduced when sugar-

[48]Chouinard et al. (2007).

[49]Smed et al. (2007).

[50]Tiffin and Salois (2014).

[51]Finkelstein et al. (2013).

sweetened beverages are taxed at a rate of 20%. In their analysis they took substitutions with other beverages, in addition with 12 major food categories into account. They found that the tax would result in a decrease in store-bought energy of 24.3 kcal per day per person, which would translate into an average weight loss of about 700 g during the first year, and an accumulated weight loss of 1.3 kg in the long run. For all these studies on ingredient taxation, only direct effects on consumer demand are estimated while possible reactions by industry are not accounted for.

To conclude, all of the aforementioned simulation studies found that consumers would reduce the demand of the respective food or nutrient when a fat tax was implemented. However, almost all authors mentioned some drawbacks. Firstly, the demand effect may be very small. Secondly, the tax may be not sufficiently directed to vulnerable groups and thirdly, not only the targeted nutrients may be reduced by the consumer, but also valuable nutrients such as fat soluble vitamins. Nevertheless, a positive effect on body weight was detected. Furthermore the state may generate substantial revenue.

4.3 Lessons Learned from Empirical Studies

Independently of whether observation, experimental or simulation studies were used for analysing the effects of a fat tax, they all found that consumers would reduce their consumption of the taxed food product. However, the level of the reduction is regarded differently in the literature. The restructuring of the food basket means that consumers' nutrient intake changes. This may lead to both positive and negative health outcomes. On the one hand, fat or sugar and therefore energy intake is expected to be reduced, which is positive for health as it could cause a reduction in body weight. On the other hand, important nutrients such as fat soluble vitamins could also be reduced, which might be negative for human health. However, studies on health outcomes which comprehensively analyse the influence of a fat tax on diet-related diseases, such as cardiovascular diseases or diabetes etc., are missing in the literature. As improving public health is the central goal of a fat tax, there is an urgent need for research in this field.

A central question regarding the fat tax is: how much of the tax is passed on to the consumer? Both the observation studies and the simulation studies found that the tax rates were at least in part transmitted to the consumer, and in some cases prices even increased more than what could have been expected from the tax effects alone. In summary it can be assumed that tax-induced price increases will reach the consumer, but to what extent cannot be precisely predicted.

In particular, the experimental studies focused on public health measures that could be taken in addition to the tax. They indicated that measures such as calorie information on foods packaging and concurrent education campaigns could be a promising action to strengthen the effect of a fat tax. In general, it can be said that previous empirical studies have mainly focused on the effects for consumers, but partly also on those for the state. However, the most important question regarding the consumers is, how their health will be affected by the tax. But this remains largely unclear. Furthermore, the effects for manufacturers, particularly in terms of reformulation of products and administrative costs, have rarely been examined.

5 Conclusions and Outlook

This chapter has reviewed the existing European experiences with a fat tax. This type of tax has a long standing history (as a luxury tax), currently being discussed as a way to meet public health objectives. In this context fat taxes have been introduced as a Pigouvian tax in order to address the emerging externalities of unhealthy food consumption behaviour. Nevertheless, the tax often bears a secondary objective of raising revenue for public health programmes and the like.

Empirical studies reviewed in this chapter mostly looked at direct consumer implications of a fat tax via food consumption and household expenditures. The results point to a general effectiveness of the tax with regard to price implications and consumption changes. Generally, a tax leads to a price increase and a consumption decrease. This holds true for a tax on however defined undesirable food items as well as for a tax on nutrients. The extent to which prices adjust in response to the tax depends on the analysis. Also the extent of consumption changes are quite different and can be substantial in some cases such as in the case of the French soda tax. In addition some studies, in particular those based on demand simulations, show that the tax is regressive in nature and leads to larger impacts in lower income households. Furthermore, attention is warranted with regard to unintentional side effects on nutrients not targeted by the tax, such as vitamins.

Only recently did studies focus on the ripple effects of fat taxes. These include reactions at the industry level in terms of product reformulation and innovation. Some studies point to effects regarding the competitiveness of different food products (e.g., brands and product categories) and retail outlets (e.g., discounters versus supermarkets) and further analyses are needed. For issues regarding the industry impact of nutrition policies, the reader is pointed to Requillart and Soler.[52] For instance Allais et al.[53] compare fat taxes with front-of-pack (FOP) labels in the French fromage blanc and dessert yogurt market under the assumption of oligopolistic price competition. They find a fat tax to be economically more efficient while both policy measures are deemed effective. When looking at the implementation of these taxes the evidence suggests that there are high administrative costs when working by nutrient. FOP only impacts consumers who have a preference for avoiding fat. However, taxing specific foodstuffs appears administratively more feasible but at the same time more distorting. If one wants to assess the efficiency

[52] Réquillart and Soler (2014).

[53] Allais et al. (2015).

and not only the effectiveness of a fat tax, regulatory costs would need to be studied in more detail.

A fat tax is often seen as an alternative or complement to information measures, because it is questionable if information measures are sufficient to handle the obesity issue. Indeed, experimental studies show that combining tax and information measures have the strongest effect. However, the biggest research gap in understanding the effectiveness of fat taxes as for other measures of regulation is that health impacts of the consumption changes are not studied. This is of high relevance in case of a fat tax, because valuable fatty acids and liposoluble vitamins such as Vitamin D are consumed in conjunction with fat. The issue is different for sugar that nutritionists don't assign nutritional value to.

"Permit but discourage" is the theme that accompanies fiscal measures on food consumption.[54] As experimental studies on taxes and subsidies of food items show, the measures are highly effective in a given environment, but much more knowledge is needed to estimate slippage effects. In addition, the stigmatizing effect of fat taxes needs to be considered when assessing the social effects of such tax measures.[55]

References

Alemanno A, Carreño I (2013) 'Fat taxes' in Europe and beyond – a legal and policy analysis under EU and WTO law. Eur Food Feed Law Rev 2:97–112

Allais O, Bertail P, Nichèle V (2010) The effects of a fat tax on French households' purchases: a nutritional approach. Am J Agric Econ 92(1):228–245

Allais O, Etilé F, Lecocq S (2015) Mandatory labels, taxes and market forces: an empirical analysis of fat policies. J Health Econ 43:27–44

Aue K, Roosen J, Jensen HH (2016) Poverty dynamics in Germany: evidence on the relationship between persistent poverty and health behaviour. Soc Sci Med 153:62–70

Bahl R, Bird R, Walker MB (2003) The uneasy case against discriminatory excise taxation: soft drink taxes in Ireland. Public Financ Rev 31(5):510–533

Becker G (2006) Taxing fat-BECKER. http://www.becker-posner-blog.com/2006/10/taxing-fat-becker.html. Accessed 29 Sept 2015

Block JP, Chandra A, McManus KD, Willett WC (2010) Point-of-purchase price and education intervention to reduce consumption of sugary soft drinks. Am J Public Health 100 (8):1427–1433

Bogart WA (2013) Regulating obesity? Government, society and questions of health. Oxford University Press, Oxford

Cash SB, Sunding DL, Zilberman D (2005) Fat taxes and thin subsidies: prices, diet and health outcomes. Acta Agric Scand Sect C Food Econ 2:167–174

Cash SB, Lacanilao RD, Adamowicz WL, Raine K (2007) An experimental investigation of the impact of fat taxes: prices effects, food stigma, and information effects on economic instrument to improve dietary health. University of Alberta, Consumer and Market Demand Network, Working paper

[54] Bogart (2013).

[55] Cash et al. (2007).

Cawley J (2004) An economic framework for understanding physical activity and eating behaviors. J Prev Med 27(3):117–125
Chouinard HH, Davis DE, LaFrance JT, Perloff JM (2007) Fat taxes: big money for small change. Forum Health Econ Policy 10(2):1–30
Deckelbaum RJ, Williams CL (2001) Childhood obesity: the health issue. Obes Res 9(4):239S–243S
Dobbs R, Sawers C, Thompson F, Manyika J, Woetzel J, Child P, McKenna S, Spatharou A (2014) Overcoming obesity: an initial economic analysis. McKinsey & Company, Discussion paper
Ecorys (2014) Food taxes and their impact on competitiveness in the agri-food sector. http://ec.europa.eu/DocsRoom/documents/5827/attachments/1/translations/en/renditions/pdf (Main Report); http://ec.europa.eu/DocsRoom/documents/6150/attachments/1/translations/en/renditions/pdf (Annexes). Accessed 29 Sept 2015
Epstein LH, Jankowiak N, Nederkoorn C, Raynor HA, French SA, Finkelstein E (2012) Experimental research on the relation between food price changes and food-purchasing patterns: a targeted review. Am J Clin Nutr 95(4):789–809
Finkelstein EA, Zhen C, Bilger M, Nonnemaker J, Farooqui AM, Todd JE (2013) Implications of a sugar-sweetened beverage (SSB) tax when substitutions to non-beverage items are considered. J Health Econ 32(1):219–139
Fletcher JM, Frisvold DE, Tefft N (2010) The effects of soft drink taxes on child and adolescent consumption and weight outcomes. J Public Econ 94(11–12):967–974
French SA, Jeffery RW, Story M, Hannan P, Patricia Snyder M (1997) A pricing strategy to promote low-fat snack choices through vending machines. Am J Public Health 87(5):849–851
French SA, Jeffery RW, Story M, Breitlow KK, Baxter JS, Hannan P, Patricia Snyder M (2001) Pricing and promotion effects on low-fat vending snack purchases: the CHIPS study. Am J Public Health 91(1):112–117
Giesen JCAH, Payne CR, Havermans RC, Jansen A (2011) Exploring how calorie information and taxes on high-calorie foods influence lunch decisions. Am J Clin Nutr 93(4):689–694
Grossman M (1972) On the concept of health capital and the demand for health. J Polit Econ 80 (2):223–255
Jeffery RW, French SA, Raether C, Baxter JE (1994) An environmental intervention to increase fruit and salad purchases in a cafeteria. Prev Med 23(6):788–792
Jensen JD, Smed S (2013) The danish tax on saturated fat – short run effects on consumption, substitution patterns and consumer prices of fats. Food Policy 42:18–31
Lehnert T, Streitchenia P, Konnopka A, Riedel-Heller SG, König H-H (2015) Health burden and cost of obesity and overweight in Germany: an update. Eur J Health Econ 16:957–967
Lynch JW, Kaplan GA, Salonen JT (1997) Why do poor people behave poorly? Variation in adult health behaviours and psychosocial characteristics by stages of the socioeconomic lifecourse. Soc Sci Med 44(6):809–819
Mazzocchi M, Bruce Traill W, Shogren JF (2009) Fat economics: nutrition, health and economic policy. Oxford University Press, Oxford
Michels KB, Bloom BR, Riccardi P, Rosner BA, Willett WC (2008) A study of the importance of education and cost incentives on individual food choices at the harvard school of public health cafeteria. J Am Coll Nutr 27(1):6–11
Mytton O, Gray A, Rayner M, Rutter H (2007) Could targeted food taxes improve health? J Epidemiol Community Health 61(8):689–694
OECD (2012) Obesity update. Paris. http://www.oecd.org/health/49716427.pdf. Accessed 9 Sept 2015
OECD (2014) Obesity update. http://www.oecd.org/els/health-systems/Obesity-Update-2014.pdf. Accessed 17 April 2018
Petkantchin V (2013) Nutrition taxes: the costs of Denmark's fat tax. http://www.institutmolinari.org/IMG/pdf/note0513_en.pdf. Accessed 29 Sept 2015
Philipson TJ, Posner RA (2003) The long-run growth in obesity as a function of technological change. Perspect Biol Med 46:S87–S107

Réquillart V, Soler L-G (2014) Is the reduction of chronic diseases related to food consumption in the hands of the food industry? Eur Rev Agric Econ 41(3):375–403

Seidell JC (2005) The epidemiology of obesity: a global perspective. In: Crawford D, Jeffrey RW (eds) Obesity prevention and public health. Oxford University Press, Oxford, pp 3–19

Sims LS (1998) The politics of fat: food and nutrition policy in America. Sharpe, Armonk

Smed S, Robertson A (2012) Are taxes on fatty foods having their desired effects on health? Br Med J 345:e6885. https://doi.org/10.1136/bmj.e6885

Smed S, Jensen JD, Denver S (2007) Socio-economic characteristics and the effect of taxation as a health policy instrument. Food Policy 32:624–639

Tiffin R, Salois M (2014) The distributional consequences of a fiscal food policy: evidence from the UK. Eur Rev Agric Econ 42(3):397–417

Torres SJ, Nowson CR (2007) Relationship between stress, eating behaviour, and obesity. Nutrition 23(11–12):887–894

Visschers TLS, Seidell JC (2001) The public health impact of obesity. Annu Rev Public Health 22:355–375

WHO (2009) Global health risks: mortality and burden of disease attributable to selected major risks. http://www.who.int/healthinfo/global_burden_disease/global_health_risks/en/. Accessed 12 Sept 2015

WHO (2015) Factsheet: obesity and overweight. http://www.who.int/mediacentre/factsheets/fs311/en/. Accessed 8 Sept 2015

Wilde P (2011) Food security policy in developed countries. In: Lusk JL, Roosen J, Shogren JF (eds) The Oxford handbook of the economics of food consumption and policy. Oxford University Press, Oxford, pp 321–343

Yang C-C, Chiou W-B (2010) Substitution of healthy for unhealthy beverages among college students. a health-concerns and behavioral-economics perspective. Appetite 54(3):512–516

Yaniv G, Rosin O, Tobol Y (2009) Junk-food, home cooking, physical activity and obesity: the effect of the fat tax and the thin subsidy. J Public Econ 93:823–830

Silke Thiele is a senior researcher and managing director of the ife Institute of Food Economics and gives lectures at the University of Kiel and at the University of Applied Sciences in Kiel. After she had studied Nutrition and Home Economics, she reached her doctoral and habilitation degree in food economics. Prior to her work at the ife Institute she was an assistant and interim professor at the University of Kiel. Her main research areas include demand analyses with respect to food and nutrients, identification of food purchase patterns, and measuring and analyzing determinants of diet quality. In addition, she is involved in various evaluation projects of the EU school fruit, vegetables and milk schemes.

Jutta Roosen is professor for Marketing and Consumer Research at Technical University of Munich. She studied Agricultural Economics at the University of Bonn and Washington State University (USA) and received her Ph.D. in Economics at Iowa State University (USA). Before joining the Technical University of Munich she served as faculty member at the Université cath. de Louvain (Belgium) and at the University of Kiel. Her main research interest are consumer decision making and the analysis of consumers' food and nutritional choices. Roosen is a member of the editorial boards of Agricultural Economics and Food Policy.

Substance Over Form: A Principle for European Food Information Regulation?

Harry Bremmers

Abstract The question that is addressed in this chapter is whether food fraud can be mitigated using principles, next to or instead of rules. In many ways, principles may be preferred, as they reduce the regulatory burdens and avoid formal compliance while at the same time violating the purpose of food information rules. Food fraud implicates not only a violation of substantive product and/or food processing norms, but also an information violation. With principles fraudulent behaviour can be obstructed, especially what we have depicted as 'fraud-by-effect': formal compliance while at the same time misleading the consumer. The adoption of the 'substance over form'-principle, well-known in financial accounting law and practice, can enrich the tool bag of instruments to protect the consumer.

1 Introduction

'Les mots et les choses- une archéologie des sciences humaines',[1] is the main work of Michel Foucault, famous French philosopher. In connection to the rules and principles that govern European food information law, it is of interest as analogy. In the work, Foucault describes the text found in an ancient encyclopaedia, that makes notice of a categorisation of 'animals', including among others animals belonging to the emperor, embalmed animals, tamed ones, porcelain figures, free animals, those that act madly, animals drawn with a very delicate camel brush, etc. If we would be able to suggest a common denominator for the conceptual content of 'principle' in law, it possibly would also cover—from a today's perspective—a weird collection of items which apparently only have the lingual expression in common (like principles of primary law, founding principles, principles for legal

[1]Foucault (1966).

H. Bremmers (✉)
Law and Governance Group, Wageningen University and Research (WUR), Wageningen, The Netherlands
e-mail: harry.bremmers@wur.nl

H. Bremmers, K. Purnhagen (eds.), *Regulating and Managing Food Safety in the EU*, Economic Analysis of Law in European Legal Scholarship 6,
https://doi.org/10.1007/978-3-319-77045-1_10

design, basic principles of law, food safety principles etc.).[2] In EU law, the use of the term 'principle' is 'diffuse'.[3] They are vested in primary law as 'constitutional principles',[4] like freedom, democracy, rule of law, and human rights protection, as well as in secondary law (like in food information law, the scientific domain of this contribution). A clear distinction between rules and principles[5] is made by Dworkin,[6] where principles are norms stating optimization requirements, leaving room for balancing one against another, whereas rules leave no room for partial realization. In this chapter we do not intend to contribute to the "rules-principles" discussion.[7] We note however that principles can supplement and/or provide a legitimate basis for rule-based regulation,[8] be used in practice to come to a legal solution by balancing in case rights are competing, but also to supplement substantive regulation in order to close legal gaps. For instance precaution, as a general obligation to reduce the probability of a harm to acceptable levels,[9] has been fundamental to numerous pieces of substantive and procedural regulation (for instance hygiene standards,[10] premarket approval of novel foods and of foods

---

[2]See in this context a summary of works on "principles" provided by Semmelmann (2014), p. 313, note 46. She states at p. 316 that "The absence of delineations of the concept of principle or of the generality of principles reflects their nature as exotic beings".

[3]Von Bogdandy (2010), p. 95.

[4]Von Bogdandy (2010), p. 96.

[5]Concepts like 'rule' or 'principle' are polluted through multiple interpretations and delineations; nevertheless, we use them to not being forced to define new concepts and with the danger to get into discussions that are out of the scope of this piece of work, that is intended to add a norm to the present stated principles governing food information for consumers practices. As 'working definition' of 'principle' is proposed 'a fundamental obligation to attend to, which is of higher level than specific rules' (see similar by Black 2007, p.192); rules are meant as immediate 'do's and don'ts', as in the vision of Dworkin and/or Alexy. In the context of this practical, not legal-fundamental, contribution, the here stated working 'definitions' are appropriate. We also limit ourselves to the principles which have been positively included in legal texts of (mainly) secondary European (food) law.

[6]Dworkin (1967).

[7]See extensively Shapiro (2007).

[8]We use the term rule-based as opposite to principle-based, and regulation in a broad meaning, not in the more narrow sense like in Orbach (2012), p. 10, but as Julia Black and also Havinga use the term "the sustained and focused attempt to alter the behavior of others according to defined standards or purposes with the intention of producing a broadly defined outcome, which may involve mechanisms of standard-setting, information gathering and behavior modification". It includes setting of norms, monitoring and compliance enforcement. Havinga (2006), p. 20, citing Black (2002).

[9]In the GFL, Article 3 point 9, 'risk' is described as a function of the probability of an adverse health effect and the severity of that effect, consequential to a hazard. The first element is influenced by precautionary measures.

[10]Regulation (EC) No 852/2004 of the European Parliament and of the Council of 29 April 2004 on the hygiene of foodstuffs; Regulation (EC) No 1829/2003 of the European Parliament and of the Council of 22 September 2003 on genetically modified food and feed, respectively.

containing or derived from genetically modified organisms,[11] the establishment of border controls,[12] of a rapid alert system, crisis management and policies in case of emergencies (Articles 50–57 GFL).

Next to their substantive function, principles may be relied on as a last-resort legitimation in case public interference to protect the public from harm is deemed to be necessary, despite the lack scientific evidence, and awaiting results of a thorough risk assessment. In this case, the precautionary principle provides a legitimate base for provisional risk management (Article 7(1) of the GFL). Alternative risk management options are to be weighted using the proportionality principle (Article 7 (2) of the GFL).

Principles may supplement or even replace substantive rules and in this way contribute to deregulation and the reduction of regulatory burdens, as is the case with a principles-based enforcement approach.[13] They also may be used to legitimise a public enforcement policy, for instance on financial markets[14] and—empirical object of this contribution—the food sector to ensure 'a high level of consumer protection'.[15]

In the past, food safety crises, like for instance BSE[16] and dioxin contaminations,[17] have triggered the effort to close loopholes[18] in the normative system that ensures food safety by expanding the predominantly prescriptive, detailed system of safety rules.

This constructive legal effort may be inspired by the belief that a substance-based system of strict rules is best suited to ensure consumer protection and—in doing so—also contributes to market functioning. It certainly is built on fear for public scrutiny in case soft, not-easy-to-enforce, general principles are applied to situations that can endanger public health. However, hard-core rules may induce formal compliance while at the same time avoiding the *purpose* of a rule.[19] This is also

[11]Regulation (EC) No 258/97 of the European Parliament and of the Council of 27 January 1991 concerning novel foods and novel food ingredients, and Regulation (EC) No 1829/2003 of the European Parliament and of the Council of 22 September 2003 on genetically modified food and feed, respectively.

[12]Regulation (EC) No 854/2004 of the European Parliament and of the Council of 29 April 2004 laying down specific rules for the organisation of official controls on products of animal origin intended for human consumption.

[13]See Black (2007), p. 192.

[14]Among others Black (2007), p. 192, point 7.

[15]Article 114 TFEU.

[16]First case transmissible spongiform encephalopathy in the UK was detected in 1987, subsequently leading to the death of hundreds of humans due to the Kreutzfeldt-Jacob disease.

[17]In 1999, in Belgium PCB's with dioxin infested animal feed and next entered the food chain to unacceptable levels. In 2004, in the Netherlands, dioxin migrated into the feed chain via potato peels which came in contact with contaminated clay.

[18]See for instance Regulation (EC) No 999/2001 of the European Parliament and of the Council of 22 May 2001 laying down rules for the prevention, control and eradication of certain transmissible spongiform encephalopathies.

[19]Black (2007), p. 192.

the case for the information requirements which govern a special segment of food safety law: food information to consumers. In the process of its development, the degrees of freedom for businesses, notably their fundamental right of 'freedom of speech/expression' (a fundamental right recognised in many state constitutions, as well as in the Charter of Human Rights) have been limited dramatically.[20] Despite all this, the occurrence of food safety incidents (like the horse meat crisis of 2013[21]) show that the system of hard-core, black-letter do's and don'ts is not apt to rule out unsafe foods brought in circulation by fraudulent food business operators. A reactive policy is to try to close the gaps in food (information) regulation by means of even more strict and detailed requirements. We doubt whether this is an effective strategy to protect the consumer and ask ourselves whether an extension of the principles underlying food information regulation can close the remaining gaps in food information law in a more effective way.

This contribution will first in Sect. 2 elaborate on the—in positive law text—stated principles and rules for food information provided to consumers, especially as enshrined in the Food Information to Consumers Regulation (FIC).[22] Next, in Sect. 3, we will identify legal gaps in food information law by elaborating on food fraud in two forms: by intent and by effect. In Sect. 4 we will introduce the (from financial markets regulation adopted) principle 'substance over form', as an alternative for increasing the density of rule-based regulation, to close off escapes for distrustful businesses. In the final remarks Sect. 5 we will discuss the caveats in the reliance on principles when fighting opportunism in information provision.

2 Food Information Regulation and Its Principles

Food information regulation encompasses the establishment of norms for the provision of food information to consumers (i.e., 'food information law') and for assurance of control and compliance. Substantive food information requirements have been laid down in hundreds of pieces of mandatory food information regulation. Just like in the General Food law, the primary responsibility for food information is vested on the food business operators, while compliance assurance is primarily a task of national enforcement authorities. The central piece of law governing information provision to (ultimately) the consumer is the FIC, which end 2014 replaced (among others) Directive 2000/13/EC on the labelling, presentation and advertising of

[20]van der Zee (2016).

[21]See Sawer et al. (2013).

[22]Regulation (EU) No 1169/2011 of the European Parliament and of the Council of 25 October 2011 on the provision of food information to consumers, amending Regulations (EC) No 1924/2006 and (EC) No 1925/2006 of the European Parliament and of the Council, and repealing Commission Directive 87/250/EEC, Council Directive 90/496/EEC, Commission Directive 1999/10/EC, Directive 2000/13/EC of the European Parliament and of the Council, Commission Directives 2002/67/EC and 2008/5/EC and Commission Regulation (EC) No 608/2004. OJ L 304, 22.11.2011, pp. 18–63.

foodstuffs.[23] In December 2016 it has replaced the Nutrition Labelling Directive 90/496/EEC[24] (abbreviated NLD). Scope, principles and horizontal rules for the businesses' non-commercial food information have been included in a single new act. It serves as a common basis for almost all horizontal food information (this is information regarding all foodstuffs, unless exempted, for instance mineral waters and foods for dietary uses like food for infants or for weight control), as well as vertical food information (that is: specific requirements for a single or a category of foods, like chocolate, orange juice or milk). The integration and improvement effort via the FIC focused at improving the normative system which was (but still remains, albeit to a lesser degree) scattered, complex at places, and incomplete. It also considered new scientific developments in food business and technology.[25] The EU food information law requirements stand next to the protection of the *commercial* interests of the consumer, as laid down in Directive 2005/29/EC on unfair business-to-consumer commercial practices (UCPD).[26] Producer protection is indirectly envisaged by ensuring the functioning of competitive markets via the informed choices of the consumer, but is neither a primary aim of the FIC, nor of the UCPD.[27]

As already indicated, with the FIC, public EU food information regulation has made significant steps forward towards integration, but is still far from an integrated system.[28] The present patchwork-like structure was induced by economic, historical and functional factors. Economic, because the food information system does not only serve the legitimate interests of consumers, but also tries to strike a balance with the aim of maintaining a free market. In some cases, specific requirements are necessary if both goals are conflicting. Historic, because manifest problems emerging at different times in recent history, required immediate legislative action (like

---

[23]Directive 2000/13/EC of the European Parliament and of the Council of 20 March 2000 on the approximation of the laws of the Member States relating to the labelling, presentation and advertising of foodstuffs. This is a follow-up of Directive 79/112/EEC of 1979.

[24]Council Directive 90/496/EEC of 24 September 1990 on nutrition labelling for foodstuffs.

[25]Like global sourcing and the use of multiple ingredients from all over the world, market gains of convenience foods, the consumers' call for complete information on allergens, a better legibility, the quest for information on the country of origin or place of provenance of foodstuffs, extended information on special treatments products have undergone (like imitating ingredients), the use of novel ingredients and substances (like nano-engineered material in foods and packaging material), as well as e-commerce.

[26]Directive 2005/29/EC of the European Parliament and of the Council of 11 May 2005 concerning unfair business-to-consumer commercial practices in the internal market ('Unfair Commercial Practices Directive', UCPD).

[27]Like is the case with Directive 2006/114/EC on misleading advertising, which focuses at messages in b-to-b relationships and comparative advertising.

[28]For instance, to it not only belong separate horizontal acts, but also (semi-)vertical requirements for primary foodstuffs (Regulation 1308/2013), for food supplements (Directive 2002/46/EC) and for special foods (Regulation 609/2013), separate requirements on additives (Regulation 1333/2008), enzymes (1332/2008), as well as specific rules on GM-food authorisation and labelling (among others Regulation 1829/2003), and many more.

origin labelling for unprocessed beef, Regulation 1760/2000, due to the occurrence of BSE).[29] Or, otherwise stated by Wright and Head, "institutional change often proceeds inconsistently, with new practices introduced alongside old ones".[30] Functional, because the European Union as legal entity consists of 28 Member States with not only common aims but also distinct sovereign, legal authority, where agreement requires compromises and exemptions.

The quest for systematisation and renewal of food information law has gained momentum due to the conclusion upon generic principles (Articles 3–7 of the FIC) and specific horizontal rules. The stated principles of food information law (Articles 3–8) are subdivided in general 'objectives' (Article 3) and principles governing mandatory food information (Article 4). The principles are complementary and in cases similar to the ones the General Food Law (GFL)[31] adheres to (i.e., a supply chain orientation (Article 4), risk analysis ('science-based food law'; Article 6), protection of human health (Article 5), free movement of goods (Article 6), precautionary action (Article 7) and protection of consumers' interests.[32] The latter requirement is laid down in Article 8 GFL: *Food law shall aim at the protection of the interests of consumers and shall provide a basis for consumers to make informed choices in relation to the foods they consume. It shall aim at the prevention of (a) fraudulent or deceptive practices, (b) the adulteration of food, and (c) any other practices which may mislead the consumer.*

Notably, the principles in the GFL reflect the purposes of food safety *law*, not principles of food safety as such, although material principles governing food safety can be derived from them. The principle stated in Article 8 reflects among others in Article 7 (1) of the FIC which requires that food information may not be misleading, and in Article 7 (2) which mandates that the information shall be accurate, clear and easy to understand for the consumer. Notably, putting forward the protection against misleading practices, the concept 'misleading' is delineated in Article 8 GFL using terms that are not specifically defined at the spot, nor in in food information law: 'fraudulent', 'deceptive', 'adulteration', 'other'.[33] This makes enforcement difficult and diverse, as national standards may be developed for specific cases.

---

[29]Regulation (EC) No 1760/2000 of the European Parliament and of the Council of 17 July 2000 establishing a system for the identification and registration of bovine animals and regarding the labelling of beef and beef products and repealing Council Regulation (EC) No 820/97.

[30]Wright and Head (2009), p. 194.

[31]Regulation (EC) No 178/2002 of the European Parliament and of the Council of 28 January 2002 laying down the general principles and requirements of food law, establishing the European Food Safety Authority and laying down procedures in matters of food safety.

[32]These are protection against fraudulent an deceptive practice, adulteration of food and misleading. Additionally, in Articles 9 and 10, the General Food Law gives for the procedures in information law crafting, making the principles of public consultation and information.

[33]In a competition law context (UCPD), 'misleading' is delineated as actions and omissions that negatively affect the commercial interests of consumers.

2.1 General Principles in the Food Information Regulation

General principles (stated as 'objectives' in the FIC) are the pursuance of a high level of consumers' health and interests by enabling them (1) to make informed choices including health, economic, environmental, social and ethical considerations, (2) ensuring the free movement of foodstuffs taking into account the legitimate interests of producers and promote the production of quality foods, (3) transitional periods to implementation of rules and regulations and (4) open and transparent public consultation. The last two principles entail formal procedural requirements in the act of designing (new) food information law. The first of the objectives signifies a broadening of consumer concerns, beyond food safety and technical food quality, with the inclusion of social and ethical dimensions. The second one confirms that producers have legitimate rights,[34] next to consumers. This is remarkable, since at the turn of centuries food law was (re)designed to better be able to protect the consumer against foodborne diseases, thereby limiting producers' rights.[35] The third principle assures temporization of implementation of the new requirements of the FIC. Food businesses are given time to change the mandatory information, due to the necessary redesign and the costs[36] involved. This principle has only merits to food businesses, if the rules that have to be implemented are stable over a considerable period of time. However, the Commission has been empowered to constitute implementing legislative acts in many instances,[37] the execution of which will potentially affect the content of food information law in the future.[38] Finally, transparency is a principle that has become prominent in EU policy since the midst of the 1990s.[39] It serves to regain and maintain trust of the European institutional environment by fostering consultations with actors on food law and policy issues as a basis for legal revisions.[40]

[34]See also recital 44 of Regulation 609/2013, Articles 11 and 52 of the Charter of Fundamental Rights, which notably are not on equal terms with the general objectives of the EU law, as enshrined in the TEU. See also case C544/10 ('Weintor') elaborated on in van der Meulen and van der Zee (2013).

[35]See the European Commission's White Paper on Food Safety (2000).

[36]See for instance DG Sanco (2004), pp. 5–6.

[37]Summed up in Article 51 of the FIC.

[38]The Commission has been granted substantial powers to supplement the present rules and regulations on a considerable amount of topics, like representing mandatory particulars with pictograms or symbols (Article 9 (4) FIC, revising the list of allergens in Annex II and via Article 21(2), rules for legibility, exemptions and additions (f.i. alcoholic beverages containing >1.2% alc./vol.), or with respect to ingredient listing via Article 6, providing and revising definitions on 'alcopops', on 'engineered nano-materials' via Article 18(2), on origin labelling (of among others meats other than beef, already amended) in Article 26, requiring additional particulars for certain foods in Annex III, etc.

[39]See European Commission (2000).

[40]Arienzo et al. (2008).

Remarkable from the previous elaboration is the inclusion of additional 'soft attributes' (i.e., social and ethical values) and the recognition of rights of food businesses. These will be addressed subsequently.

Soft Attributes

In EU food information law, mandatory requirements mainly serve to protect consumer's safety and health, while 'soft' attributes of food supply (like "fair farmer income" or "sustainable production") have to a large extent been left to voluntary (not-publicly-regulated)[41] regulation, or regulated to a minimum level (like is the case with organic production). At present, mandatory food information requirements are mainly bound to the immediate characteristics of the final product, so that transparency of process steps upward the supply chain is low. However, a shift towards a process orientation is apparent that reveals soft attributes, among others through the mandatory indication of hidden processing steps a food has undergone and extended information on the origin of a food and/or its constituents. Indications about processing steps in upper stages of the supply chain are for instance disclosed through mandatory additions to the name or an ingredient of a foodstuff. In the EU, the name of a food is accompanied by the treatment it has undergone, like 'smoked', 'dried' or 'irradiated', 'defrosted'; or also the applied technology, like 'nano' for 'engineered nanomaterials'.[42] Information on the origin of foodstuffs allows consumers to draw inferences with respect to the social, ethical and/or environmental conditions under which the product has been made. With the acceptance of the FIC, origin labelling has been substantially expanded,[43] beyond established rules for certain agricultural and fishery products and fresh unprocessed beef,[44] and indications on a voluntary basis.[45]

---

[41]Like 'fair-trade'-trademarks or extra requirements on organic products/production.

[42]Defined in Article 2(2) point (t) of the FIC as any intentionally produced material that has one or more dimensions of the order of 100 nm or less or that is composed of discrete functional parts, either internally or at the surface, many of which have one or more dimensions of the order of 100 nm or less, including structures, agglomerates or aggregates, which may have a size above the order of 100 nm but retain properties that are characteristic of the nano-scale.

[43]Such as mandatory indication of the origin of meats from pig, sheep, goat and poultry.

[44]For unprocessed beef, origin labelling is obligatory as a response to the BSE-crisis (Regulation (EC) 1760/2000, Commission Regulation (EC) 1825/2000; Also for some other primary products, like fruits and vegetables, the country-of-origin indication is mandatory on the basis of the marketing standards.

[45]In the EU, Protected Geographical Indications (PGI's) and Protected Designations of Origin (PDO's) can be applied for, as well as for Traditional Specialties Guaranteed.

Producers' Rights

Despite the assurance of producers' 'legitimate rights', its content is neither delineated in the FIC, nor anywhere else in European food law. Indirectly, producers' commercial interests are fostered by the maintenance of a 'level playing field' via antitrust and competition law (i.e., the abolishment of 'unfair' competition or agreements, concerted practices and power accumulations that endanger the smooth operation of the markets).[46] After the BSE-crisis, the consumer has been put central in food safety law, resulting in obligations of producers. The FIC puts the burden of providing fair food information on the shoulders of the food business (Article 8 of the FIC).[47] The do's and don'ts that substantiate it go to a large extend to the expense of the businesses freedom of expression in commercial messages. Limits to freedom of speech follow for instance from the Claims Regulation (Regulation 1924/2006), as only authorized claims may be made, under pre-specified conditions. The European food legislator is less prepared to refrain from don'ts compared to its US counterpart, which is more lenient if infringements on the constitutional rights of its people (including businesses) are manifest.[48] Another example of restriction can be found as to the mandatory information on engineered nanomaterials as ingredients. It is nearly impossible to define engineered nanomaterials and its technology in an all-inclusive way, so that refuge has to be taken by proclaiming it a 'dynamic' concept, the scope of which can change in course of time.[49] The EU-regulator seems to be barely aware of the signalling effect of references to new technologies of which the 'average'[50] or more than average consumer neither grasps the content, nor can assess the negative consequences of consumption and thus the intrusion on producers' rights. Disproportionate effects may occur to businesses that market certain foods, comparable to the induced negative-image effects of the regulation of GMO-foods.

On the basis of the general principles, the FIC formulates content standards for food information,[51] especially legibility and fairness.[52] Based on the general

[46]By means of installing and maintaining competition rules, Article 101 TFEU et seq.

[47]For as far as the business name is attached to the food or the business that provided the information is under control of another business (article 8(1) and 8(5) respectively).

[48]US Case Pierson-Shalala, 164 F.3d 650, 1999.

[49]van der Meulen et al. (2014).

[50]CJEU, case C-210/96, Gut Springenheide, ECLI:EU:C:1998:369, para 31. In the FIC, a gradual shift can be observed towards a more differentiated consumer concept. Among others in recital 2 'the health and well-being of citizens', recital 16 and Article 1 'differences in perception of consumers' and in recital 40 'young and vulnerable consumers'.

[51]Not in chapter II, concerning general principles of Food Information, but in chapter 3 which is headed "General food information requirements and responsibilities of food business operators".

[52]Article 7(1) FIC: [Food information] should not be misleading as to its characteristics, attributed properties, special characteristics assigned to the food (absence or presence of an ingredient for instance), suggesting a food can prevent, reduce the risk of or cure a disease (exemptions are foods for which claims have been authorized and mineral waters or food supplements), or substitution of a

requirement of legibility, a minimum font size ranging (depending on the size of the package) from 0.9 to 1.2 mm is mandatory. Fairness is fostered by putting forward three mandatory content categories (Article 4): (1) on the identity, composition, properties and/or other characteristics of a food, (2) information to protect the consumer's health (like on allergies and durability) and (3) nutrition information. New in European food information law is mandatory—instead of voluntary—nutrition information. The information on foods had to be adjusted/included end 2016 at the latest. As a consequence of this requirement, virtually all packages had to be redesigned to create space for mandatory information.[53] While balancing the fundamental rights of consumers and producers, the fact that nutrition-related diseases contribute significantly to social costs in the form of health-related diseases has induced this requirement,[54] but also has limited the free marketing space of businesses.

2.2 *Formal Principles of (Food Information) Law*

Next to the material principles and requirements of food information to consumers, formal 'crafting'-principles of (information) law can be discerned, addressing its projected structure. Formal principles with respect to the order in structuring the process of regulation of food information have not been included in formal legal texts, but can be derived from the general principles as laid down in the Treaties, notably the principle of legal certainty ('rule of law'), and, bottom-up, from the requirements thereon (like transparency and legibility). Food information law should not only be science-based in a technical sense (Article 6(2) of the GFL), but also from a logic-systematic viewpoint. Therefore the following formal principles regarding the envisaged legal structure may be discerned[55]:

- coherence: this reduces search costs and uncertainties about the appropriateness of a certain rule.

naturally present food or ingredient by an inferior one. 'Fairness' includes also the requirement that food information should be accurate, clear and easy to understand.

[53]Which has the advantage over voluntary (i.e. marketing) messages, but impedes producers' opportunities to express commercial messages.

[54]Capacci et al. (2012).

[55]These can be derived from the "verifying regulatory fitness questions" stated in the Better Regulation Policy of the Commission in the Staff Working Document (Better regulation Guidelines) COM(2015) 215 final, p. 32. In this document, a 'fitness check' is defined as 'an assessment of the effectiveness, efficiency, coherence, relevance and added-value of one single EU intervention'. Legislation is considered as one type of intervention, next for instance action plans or expenditures. Compare also with the Quality guidelines in Sustainability Reporting, as put forward by the Global Reporting Initiative, on https://www.globalreporting.org/Pages/default.aspx, last accessed 9 July 2015. See also the Interinstitutional Agreement of 22 December 1998 on common guidelines for the quality of drafting of Community legislation (OJ C 73, 17 March 1999).

- completeness: the legal framework should address all items that are considered relevant.
- clarity: the legal requirements should not only contribute to comprehension by the users of information, but also enable the *providers* of information on how to structure food information.

The level to which these 'crafting' principles are adhered to, is subject of the next subsections.

Coherence

The FIC mainly focuses on pre-packaged foods[56] that are directly or indirectly (via a mass caterer) sold to the final consumer. Some topics have been fully harmonized, other pieces of legislation have remained completely untouched. They co-exist in their original form without substantial harmonization of concepts, content and envisaged controls. For instance, relevant food information areas like gmo-foods,[57] claims,[58] supplements,[59] natural mineral waters,[60] and special foods[61] (former 'parnuts') and (vertical) common marketing requirements remained to a large extend next to the FIC in their original format. References in old legislation to new are often not updated,[62] nor are definitions and concepts adjusted systematically. In many cases, concepts keep their original content in the specific piece of law in which they are used.[63] This makes the system of food information law confusing (compared for instance with more integrated representation of 'labelling' in the US CFR[64]). The patchwork-like structure of food information law induces legal uncertainty,

[56]For non-prepacked foods, the only mandatory content requirement at the EU-level is the disclosure of allergens.

[57]Regulation (EC) 1829/2003.

[58]Regulation (EC) 1924/2006.

[59]Directive 2002/46/EC.

[60]Directive 2009/54/EC.

[61]Directive 2009/39/EC.

[62]Exceptions the amendments to the Claims Regulation (1924/2006) and the Regulation on the addition of vitamins and minerals to certain foods (1925/2006). Some specific directives and regulations have been repealed.

[63]Article 12 of Regulation (EC) 1760/2000 for instance states that 'labelling' in Section II has the meaning of: 'the attachment of a label to an individual piece or pieces of meat or to their packaging material, or in the case of non-prewrapped products the supply of appropriate information in written and visible form to the consumer at the point of sale'. The requirements for 'retail trade' in Ch. IV, Section IX of Annex III of Regulation (EC) 853/2004 states that 'labelling' includes any packaging, document, notice, label, ring, or collar accompanying or referring to such products, being raw milk/colostrum or products made with raw milk/colostrum. In other, related legislation on medicine [Directive 2001/83/EC Article 1], labelling is defined more restrictive, as "Information on the immediate or outer packaging".

[64]Code of Federal Regulations, Title 21.

transaction costs on the side of businesses and consumers as well (i.e., search costs), and regulatory burdens for authorities and food business operators. This may lead to 'regulatory stress': irritation and confusion about the normative system, inducing an attitude of self-protection.[65]

Completeness

It already was indicated that food information law leaves gaps, to the advantage of opportunistic businesses. Meticulous prescriptions may provide the consumer with a sense of protection and the regulator with a sense of achievement. Unintentionally, they inform businesses on the remaining loopholes to "play games with the rules",[66] enabling the compliance to regulation in an opportunistic way. We call this 'fraud-by-effect': despite obeying the formal rules, the purpose of law is violated. It appears not to prevent 'creative compliance',[67] the "structuring of transactions round the rules".[68]

Clarity

Although a major quality step has been taken by integrating European food information law, the present system remains unclear to especially small businesses.[69] Opportunistic business operators could hide behind an image of ignorance and in this way escape from being accused of fraudulent practices. Simulating mistake and hiding purpose can in practice be awarded with warnings and fines instead of being subjected to criminal charges.

3 Manifestations of 'Fraud'

Fraud as to food information is an ill-defined concept. Under the concept we range deliberate practices in purposeful violation of mandatory information requirements ('fraud-by-object') and practices which comply to formal requirements but nevertheless hinder consumers from making informed choices ('fraud-by-effect'). In the next subsections we illustrate the occurrence of both types of fraud and then ask ourselves, whether an extension of principles or rules can fight one or both manifestations.

---

[65]In this context note should be taken of the motivational posturing theory. Braithwaite et al. (2007).

[66]Mcnamara (2005), p. 3.

[67]Black (2007), p. 192.

[68]McDonald (2002).

[69]Bremmers et al. (2010).

3.1 'Fraud-by-Object'

We exemplify fraud-by-object by reference to the horse-meat crisis. Early 2013, in lasagne and other products than normally only contain beef, horsemeat and also pork was detected, without properly informing the consumers about the switch. This meat fraud crisis affected several countries of the EU (next to the UK and Ireland, notably also in the Netherlands, Germany, France and Romania). In view of the immense amount of requirements regarding the provision of safe food to the market, how can it be explained that on a large scale the labelling of horsemeat as beef stayed undetected for a long time?

From a 'principles'—perspective, the answer to the question may be found in three sources. First, the general principle laid down in Article 8 GFL (that food law shall aim at (among others) the prevention of fraudulent practices) is not specific enough (like most principles) and lacks a content-base as to what constitutes a 'fraudulent practice'. In the aftermath of the crisis the EP has discussed the need of a definition for 'food fraud'.[70] To support enforcement, a rule-based approach, based on common concepts and rules, was adopted. In the UK, the Food Standards Agency (FSA) has defined food fraud as "the deliberate placement on the market, for financial gain, with the intention of deceiving the consumer", subdividing it in the sales of foods that are dangerous or unfit for consumption and deliberate false description of a food.[71] The element 'deliberate' complicates the contestation of such practices, as the burden of proof with respect to the "malicious will" behind the act is put on the shoulders of the competent national authorities. The element 'dangerous or unfit for human consumption' clearly refers to the GFL (Article 14), so in essence is superfluous for enforcement purposes.

The US Food & Drug Administration has ranked "economically motivated adulteration" under the concept of food fraud.[72] The subjective motivational element complicates prosecution just as in the UK. In other jurisdictions, it depends on the boundaries of the concept 'food fraud' how, on a national level, rules will be enforced: along the route of food safety, as food information issue, and/or as a criminal law offence. The delimitation as 'intentional, economically motivated adulteration' points in the direction of the latter, though trespasses from one route to another are possible (see Fig. 1).

A second answer to the posed question might be vested in the simplistic attitude towards businesses, based on trust (supposing negligence instead of intent in case of

[70]European Parliament resolution of 14 January 2014 on the food crisis, fraud in the food chain and the control thereof (2013/2091(INI)).

[71]See http://www.food.gov.uk/enforcement/foodfraud, Also Spink and Moyer (2011).

[72]74 Federal register 64, 2009 (15497–15499): "fraudulent, intentional substitution or addition of a substance in a product for the purpose of increasing the apparent value of the product or reducing the costs of its production, i.e., for economic gain".

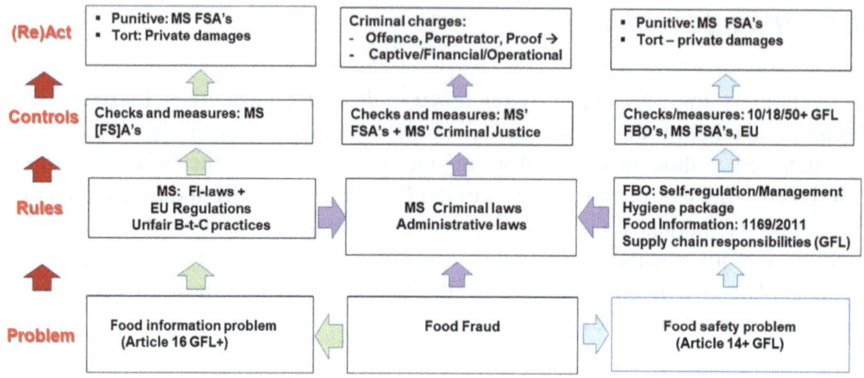

Fig. 1 Three enforcement routes for fighting food fraud

incidents), for instance as to the exchange of information in the supply chain. The requirement of traceability of a food or its ingredients is mandatory in Article 18 of the GFL. It requires information exchange one step upward and one step downward the supply chain.[73] This bilateral orientation is also implemented in food information law.[74] This orientation disregards the complexity in nowadays' ingredient procurement and processing. This complexity has at least three causes: the development from short to long supply routes, differentiated instead of uniform procurement (former short and vertically oriented supply chains have developed towards net-chains[75]) and global instead of local sourcing. The original manufacturer of a food or ingredient gets easily out of sight, especially if actors have the intention of cheating. For instance, during the horsemeat crisis incorrect information was processed from one actor to the other, as was also the case during the EHEC—and dioxin—crises and numerous other food safety incidents.[76]

A third answer could be found in the violation of the formal principles of legal crafting (see Sect. 2). The patchwork-like structure of food information

[73]However, for GMO foods/feed complete coverage of the supply chain is envisaged.

[74]See Article 1(3) of the FIC regarding its scope and Article 8 of the FIC.

[75]Lazzarini et al. (2001).

[76]As answer to the question what lessons have been learned was stated by the Commission, next to the need for tighter controls and of cross-border cooperation, that: "The most important is probably that large scale, cross-border fraudulent schemes that take advantage of the weaknesses of an increasingly globalised food supply can impact hugely on consumers and operators, on thus on the economy. Constant vigilance from operators and competent authorities towards economically motivated fraud, that can be perpetrated at any step of the food supply chain is needed." Citation adopted from http://ec.europa.eu/food/food/horsemeat/index_en.htm (Accessed 9th July 2015).

law induces thinking in simple dichotomies: food or medicine,[77] claim or not-a-claim,[78] safe or not-safe,[79] while some foods take a position somewhere along the scales. Envisaging short chains instead of complex ones and single business responsibilities instead of shared responsibilities[80] induces a feeling of certainty for the regulator but also lack of clarity for businesses as to compliance to food information regulation. Incidents also reveal a lack of robustness as to coherence and completeness.[81] As already indicated, at the EU food (information) law level, regulatory gaps are constantly filled with additional requirements (see Sect. 1), thus adding to the uncertainties of actors with regard to their information obligations. In the short run, formal compliance to incomplete or unclear standards can be exploited opportunistically. Can the endless process of constant additions and modifications be brought back to proportions by implementing an additional principle: substance over form? This is a question to be answered after addressing 'fraud-by-effect'.

3.2 *'Fraud-by Effect'*

An abundant amount of examples are available of information provision that complies with formal rules, but in effect puts the consumer on the wrong foot: claims made with respect to added vitamin E, where the vitamin has no function in the food; pictures of a fruit on a package, where the fruit content is barely absent; depicting a food as containing 'natural' ingredients (signalling the healthiness of the product); hidden references to medicinal properties of probiotics, etc. Also, it is still is possible to bring a food to the market with added water, without technical necessity.[82] It for instance is also possible to sell the sweetener stevia as a mix with 90% of a much less valuable ingredient (malt dextrin), if the formal labelling rules are not violated. The consumer may be set on the wrong foot by signalling high value with a high price to a package of sweetener, or be under the impression that a container of high-value stevia is acquired.[83] Although there is no formal trespassing of enforceable norms, in

[77]See in this respect the role of information in making this distinction in Directive 2001/83/EC of the EP and Council of 6 November 2001 on the Community code relating to medicinal products for human use, Article 1 (2).

[78]See the lists of authorised claims in the Annex of Regulation 1924/2006 and on ec.europa.eu/nuhclaims.

[79]See Article 14 of the GFL.

[80]See Article 17 of the GFL, Article 8 of the FIC.

[81]Like for instance bringing insect food to the market; till 2018 (the new novel foods regulation gaining effect) allowed freely to market in one MS but considered novel food in another.

[82]For added water in unprocessed beef, fish products and poultry, part of this loophole was closed with the provision in Annex VII, Part A, Point 1 of the FIC.

[83]The product was elected most misleading by Foodwatch Netherlands in 2013. http://www.foodnieuws.nl/foodwatch-wie-verdient-het-gouden-windei-2014/ (Accessed 9 July 2015).

effect in all these cases the less alerted consumer is making choices he would regret if facilitated better with information. A turnaround is emerging. In the Teekanne case (C-195/14) it was decided that a formally correct ingredient list cannot exempt food businesses from misleading the consumer, contrary to the legal doctrine till then.[84]

4 Substance Over Form

The problems with the 'filling-the-gaps'-strategy to improve food safety are multiple:

- it increases the pressure on enforcement authorities, and induces additional burdens for businesses.[85] Already the Commission has given advices on the instalment of tighter controls at the MS-level.[86]
- it induces short term and long-term uncertainties for businesses and thus negatively affects innovation and competitiveness[87];
- formal compliance to official rules may materially put consumers on the wrong foot.[88]

To find a better way of regulating food information supply, we draw on developments in another sector with regular crises and fraudulent practices: the financial sector. This sector went through a severe crisis in the period 2008–2014. In April 2007, the Financial Services Authority (abbreviated as FSA2) in the UK published[89] a new enforcement policy, a 'principles-based approach', as a supplement to the risk-based[90] and evidence-based[91] approaches it applied already, to regulate and control the financial institutions and markets. As stated by the FSA, their principles-based approach focuses more on outcome than on meticulous prescriptions for businesses on how to achieve a certain outcome. At the same time, it gives businesses the freedom and flexibility that is needed for improving their governance structures (i.e., with respect to information provision to actors on financial markets). It is based on confidence in the self-regulating capabilities of the financial services sector, rather than distrust. The financial crisis and the fraudulent practices of financial businesses that came to the surface, showed the weaknesses in the present regulation policy, but

[84]See Hagenmeyer (2014). Schebesta and Purnhagen (2016).

[85]Reduction of administrative burdens is an outspoken goal of the EU and its MSs; see in this respect Bremmers et al. (2007).

[86]COM (2013) 327 final – 2013/0169 (COD).

[87]Bremmers et al. (2010).

[88]Examples in Sect. 3.2.

[89]Financial Services Agency (2007).

[90]Issued set of rules by the Financial Action Task Force, to fight among others money laundering. Financial Action Task Force (2012).

[91]Using scientific evidence in enforcement matters.

also showed (as among others Black (2002, 2007) exemplifies) the opportunities of a *more* principles-based approach, that is, a further substantiation of the principles underlying the system of (enforcement) rules. This was notably the case in the USA, from where the financial crisis originated. The new approach was embraced as a response to the wave of accounting scandals, of which the Enron business failure[92] is one of the most prominent. By following the rules of the US Generally Accepted Accounting Principles (GAAPs), literally and to the letter, instead of focusing on "substance",[93] financial businesses could uphold fraudulent and misleading practices, to the expense of stakeholders (notably ultimately the tax payers). The shift towards a principles-based approach can also be discerned in accounting standards that were established in the EU for multinational companies (i.e., the International Financial reporting System, IFRS). This accounting approach is different from the requirements in the fourth[94] and seventh[95] European Directives, which formed the substantive core for financial disclosure for a long time. Two streams of financial reporting regulation have been developed on the basis of these Directives. One has solid roots in common law and relies on the provision of a 'true and fair view', rather than the rule of the black letter. In its ultimate consequence, if following the formal rules does not provide a sound insight in the financial position and performance of a business, it is *mandatory* to adjust the information.[96] The other root, also subsumed under the mentioned Directives, has partially been adopted by Germany[97] and notably by France,[98] where fiscal and financial reporting are traditionally connected. In many states, fiscal requirements are prepared to thwart fraud and reimburse taxes to the full. In doing so, there is little space for adjusting information to the needs of private actors.[99]

In the EU, the financial crisis substantiated that a significant number of financial institutions were out of control. Several banks (like ABN-AMRO, Fortis, Bank of Scotland, and other) had to be supported with public money, went bankrupt, or came in public hands. It led to the strengthening of standards as well as stricter controls to

---

[92]Leading to the conviction of fraudulent board members in May 2006.

[93]That is, the purpose (intent) of financial information, namely facilitating actors to make informed choices on financial markets.

[94]Fourth Council Directive of 25 July 1978 based on Article 54(3)(g) of the Treaty on the annual accounts of certain types of companies (78/660/EEC).

[95]Seventh Council Directive 83/349/EEC of 13 June 1983 based on the Article 54(3)(g) of the Treaty on consolidated accounts.

[96]For instance, a financial lease may from a juridical perspective not be classified as transferring property from the lessor to the lessee; economically (from a 'property right'-perspective) such an asset is, as to its enclosed utilities, under control of the lessee. With the consequence that it has to be published on the balance sheet of the lessee, and not the lessor's.

[97]The Maβgeblichkeitsprinzip entails that fiscal privileges are only granted if in the reports for private stakeholders the fiscal rules in that respect are followed.

[98]Where the principle 'unité', integration of fiscal and commercial reporting, was upheld.

[99]The acceptance of the International Financial Reporting System and the acceptance of the Accounting Regulation of 2013 have, due to international connectivity of large companies.

ensure financial sustainability. Steering on outcome (in the form of content-based indicators) was complemented with intensified monitoring by public authorities. Unless a public takeover took place, the responsibility for good governance was left in the hands of the private sector, but with strict targets and control mechanisms as safety assurance. The developments in the financial sector are not completely comparable to the food safety industry, but there are some parallel moves.

The parallel development of financial and food safety regulation is visible in several MSs, especially at the enforcement level. In the Netherlands, food safety authorities and other public institutions felt the cuts in their financial means because of the financial crisis. It has instigated them to cut back on product inspections by applying a principles- and risk-based approach. This, next to a tendency towards deregulation, has induced reliance on the self-steering capabilities of businesses. In practice this means that if the processes are in control (via public or private systems) there is no need to intervene or check on content (like with laboratory tests for assessing the safety of products). However, fraud and other incidents have seriously affected the base of trust for relying on the self-steering capabilities of food businesses. The developments in the Netherlands show that with respect to the implementation of rules a cost-effective steering on principles-based outcomes is envisaged, while at the same time the core of substantive law is gradually expanded: not only or primarily by the national regulator(s), but notably by the EU. This is the result of the awkward position in which regulators are. Incidents bring authorities in an awkward position: on the one side they are pressed towards stricter controls and on the other side they are forced to stay within the limits of their budgets. This creates opportunities for businesses to simulate an image of compliance, while at the same time the purpose of law is violated.

The implementation of a principle 'substance-over–form' could provide an outcome under specific circumstances. For food information provided by businesses this would implicate that if the consumer is misled despite following the formal information rules, the information should be adjusted. This has as advantage for the substantive core of food information law:

- that the aim is envisaged, not the formal requirement;
- that the perception of the consumer is a landmark for compliance-assurance;
- that the continuous flow of additional food information requirements is canalized and eventually reversed.

By embracing the 'substance-over-form'-principle, the complexity of the business environment is recognized. Moreover, by recognising the 'substance-over-form'-principle improved coherence (by simplifying the rule-system), completeness (by removing opportunities for opportunism) and clarity (by envisaging purpose rather than obeying formalities) can be reached. The adherence to the principle might provide an effective standard in case of 'fraud-by-object' and 'fraud-by-effect'. In both cases, legal gaps are closed. 'Fraud-by-object' is obstructed by installing an additional rule, while 'fraud-by-effect' provides enforcement authorities a legal escape where legal gaps remain.

5 Final Remarks

In our view, a principles-based approach goes beyond a mere outcome-based enforcement policy. A principles-based approach embraces a conclusive set of principles and so covers the crafting of law as well as compliance assurance. As to food information, the enforcement-based principles-based approach should be supported by a general principle 'substance over form', as a fundamental and complementary norm to the present rule-based requirements, as regulators "cannot foresee all situations".[100] Coming back to the 'informed choice' consumers are to be enabled to make, the substance-over-form principle requires an image of a consumer that is individualistic instead of average. It also requires a turn in the mentality of EU legislative authorities, as the scattered rule-based food information law will continue to show loopholes or induce quasi-compliance.

The application of the substance-over-form principle in practice requires a difference in business information governance. No longer is the average consumer landmark for assessing whether information is appropriate, but the specific perceptions of the targeted consumer.[101] Insights from social sciences can be used to assess the effects of information on consumers' choice behaviour, compared to the -at present- technological-sciences-orientation of food (information) law. It induces a responsibility to take account of the behavioural effects of food information.[102] Substance over form is not only meant to be leading for the responsibilities of businesses, but should also be a guiding for better regulation. When new law is crafted, not only the social, economic and environmental effects should be assessed, but also the behavioural effects, as is envisaged in (more) responsive regulation. A dense and detailed system of rules does not necessarily induce better regulation of food supply. In this sense, the substance-over-form principle can replace obsolete and/or ineffective regulation and ultimately improve the supply of safe food as well as empower consumers to make really informed choices.

References

Arienzo A, Coff C, Barling D (2008) The European Union and the regulation of food traceability: from risk management to informed choice? In: Coff C, Barling D, Korthals M (eds) Ethical traceability and communicating food. Springer, Dordrecht, pp 23–41

Black J (2002) Critical reflections on regulation. London School of Economics, London

Black J (2007) Making a success of principles-based regulation. Law Financ Mark Rev 1:191–206

---

[100]Herbert Hart (1961), p. 129 in the context of the "due care" requirement. The fact that the future is intrinsically uncertain, has motivated also to include the precautionary principle in food law (see Sect. 1).

[101]Compare at this place Regulation 2005/29 recital 18.

[102]See in this context Regan et al. (2015).

Braithwaite V, Murphy K, Reinhart M (2007) Taxation threat, motivational postures and responsive regulation. Law Policy 29(1):137–158
Bremmers H, van der Meulen B, Poppe K, Wijnands J (2007) Administrative burdens in the European food industry. LEI (WUR), The Hague
Bremmers H, van der Meulen B, Poppe K, Wijnands J (2010) Managerial responses to transaction cost disequilibrium in food supply chains and networks. J Chain Netw Sci 10(1):51–58
Capacci S, Mazzocchi M, Shankar B, Brambila MJ, Verbeke W, Pérez-Cueto F, Kozioł-Kozakowska A, Piórecka B, Niedzwiedzka B, D'Addesa D, Saba A, Turrini A, Aschemann-Witzel J, Bech-Larsen T, Strand M, Smillie L, Wills J, Traill B (2012) Policies to promote healthy eating in Europe: a structure review of policies and their effectiveness. Nutr Rev 70 (3):188–200
Dworkin R (1967) The model of rules. Univ Chicago Law Rev 35:14–46
European Commission (2000) White paper on food safety. European Commission, Brussels
Financial Action Task Force (2012) International standards on combating money laundering and the financing of terrorism and proliferation: the FATF recommendations. OECD, Paris
Financial Services Agency (2007) Principles-based regulation - focusing on the outcomes that matter. Financial Services Agency, London
Foucault M (1966) Les Mots et les Choses. Editions Gallimard, Paris
Global Reporting Initiative. Quality Guidelines Sustainability Reporting. https://www.globalreporting.org/Pages/default.aspx. Accessed 9 July 2015
Hagenmeyer M (2014) Does the consumer have to read the ingredients list? Eur Food Feed Law Rev 4:263–264
Hart H (1961) The concept of law. Clarendon Press, Oxford
Havinga T (2006) Private regulation of food safety by supermarkets. Law Policy 28(4):515–533
Lazzarini S, Chaddad F, Cook M (2001) Integrating supply chain and network analyses: the study of Netchains. J Chain Netw Sci 1(1):7–22
McDonald L (2002) Principles-based approach to standard setting. http://www.fasb.org/project/principles-based_approach.shtml. Accessed 7 May 2015
Mcnamara D (2005) Improving governance performance: rules-based vs principles-based approaches. Leadersh Acumen 16:1–6
Orbach B (2012) What is regulation? Yale J Regul Online 30(1):1–10
Regan Á, Marcu A, Shan LC, Wall P, Barnett J, McConnon Á (2015) Conceptualising responsibility in the aftermath of the horsemeat incident: an online study with Irish and UK consumers. Health Risk Soc 17(2):149–167
Sanco DG (2004) The impact of mandatory nutrition labelling in the European Union. DGSanco, Brussels
Sawer P, Toma B, Allen P (2013) Horse meat scandal: how horses slaughtered in Romania end up on British plates. The Telegraph, 10 February 2013 at http://www.telegraph.co.uk/foodanddrink/foodanddrinknews/9859915/Horse-meat-scandal-How-horses-slaughtered-in-Romania-end-up-on-British-plates.html. Accessed 7 July 2015
Schebesta H, Purnhagen K (2016) The behaviour of the average consumer: a little less normativity and a little more reality in the court's case law? Reflections on Teekanne. Eur Law Rev 4:590–598
Semmelmann C (2014) Legal principles in EU law as an expression of a European legal culture between unity and diversity. In: Helleringer G, Purnhagen K (eds) Towards a European legal culture. Nomos, Baden Baden, pp 303–329
Shapiro S (2007) The "Hart-Dworkin" debate: a short guide for the perplexed. Public law and legal theory. Working Paper Series. University of Michigan Law School, No. 77
Spink J, Moyer D (2011) Defining the public health threat of food fraud. J Food Sci 76(9):R157–R163
van der Meulen B, van der Zee E (2013) Through the wine gate: first steps towards human rights awareness in EU food (labelling) law. Eur Food Feed Law Rev 1:41–52
van der Meulen B, Bremmers H, Purnhagen K, Gupta N, Bouwmeester H, Geyer L (2014) Governing nano foods. Principles-based responsive regulation. EFFoST Critical Reviews #3. Elsevier, The Hague

van der Zee E (2016) Legal limits on food labelling law: comparative analysis of the EU and the USA. Eur Bus Law Rev 27(3):295–323

von Bogdandy A (2010) Founding principles of EU law: a theoretical and doctrinal sketch. Eur Law J 16(2):95–111

Wright J, Head B (2009) Reconsidering regulation and governance theory: a learning approach. Law Policy 31(2):192–216

Harry Bremmers acquired an MSc degree in business economics at Tilburg University and in Dutch law at the Erasmus University Rotterdam, in the Netherlands. Here he was employed as assistant professor till 1993. In Rotterdam, he graduated as Phd in 1994 on a legal-economic subject (Effects of environmental law on financial reporting). In 1993–2010 he occupied a full-time position at the Business Administration group of the Social Sciences department of Wageningen University, the Netherlands. Since 2010 he occupies the position of associate professor at the Law & Governance group of Wageningen University and Research, Netherlands. He participated in several national and international projects at the interplay of law and economics and has published on a broad range of legal and economic topics. He is specialized in food information law.

European Food Law and the Precautionary Principle: Paradoxical Effects of the EU's Precautionary Food Policies

Lucas Bergkamp and Jaap C. Hanekamp

Abstract The precautionary principle has been invoked to support stringent European food law. By its nature, the principle is particularly relevant to food security. This chapter discusses how precaution has been applied in EU food law generally, and finds that its application has been both controversial and selective. We then turn to two specific cases in which the precautionary principle played a prominent role: antibiotic residues in food and micronutrient malnutrition. On this basis, we revisit the precautionary principle's role in EU food law. We conclude that the precautionary principle is best understood as a political tool, rather than an intellectual concept.

1 Introduction

In the European Union, the core regulatory framework for food is Regulation 178/2002/EC on general principles of food law (the "General Food Law").[1] Under this regulation, 'food' (or 'foodstuff') denotes 'any substance or product, whether processed, partially processed or unprocessed, intended to be, or reasonably expected to be ingested by humans.'[2] The regulation applies broadly to 'all stages

[1]Regulation (EC) No 178/2002 of the European Parliament and of the Council of 28 January 2002 laying down the general principles and requirements of food law, establishing the European Food Safety Authority and laying down procedures in matters of food safety, OJ L31, 1.2.2002, p. 1.

[2]Article 2, Regulation 178/2002.

L. Bergkamp (✉)
Hunton Williams Kurth LLP, Brussels, Belgium
e-mail: lbergkamp@hunton.com

J. C. Hanekamp
University College Roosevelt, Middelburg, The Netherlands

Environmental Health Sciences, University of Massachusetts Amherst, Amherst, MA, USA
e-mail: j.hanekamp@ucr.nl

H. Bremmers, K. Purnhagen (eds.), *Regulating and Managing Food Safety in the EU*, Economic Analysis of Law in European Legal Scholarship 6,
https://doi.org/10.1007/978-3-319-77045-1_11

of the production, processing and distribution of food.'[3] Its general objective is to provide 'a high level of protection of human life and health and the protection of consumers' interests'.[4] It tries to accomplish this objective, by setting general rules for all products, including dietary supplements and fortified foods that are placed on the EU market. General requirements deal with food safety, presentation, traceability, and related responsibilities of food business operators. Importantly, the regulation also establishes the European Food Safety Authority ('EFSA') and defines its tasks and powers.

EU food law also pursues several specific objectives. As Article 5(1) of the General Food Law states, EU food law pursues one or more of the general objectives of a high level of protection of human life and health and the protection of consumers' interests, including fair practices in food trade, taking account of, where appropriate, the protection of animal health and welfare, plant health and the environment." Whenever the EU pursues a "high level of protection," the precautionary principle comes into play. The area of food law is a prime example.

Although the General Food Law does not say so explicitly, EU food law has also pursued the objective of food security, in particular through the Common Agricultural Policy (CAP).[5] In 1996, the World Food Summit stated that food security is achieved when 'all people, at all times, have physical and economic access to sufficient, safe and nutritious food to meet their dietary needs and food preferences for an active and healthy life.'[6] Food security, of course, is an urgent issue in the developing world, but this does not mean that it is not an issue in the EU. Security of food supply has been a driving force behind the Common Agricultural Policy. The Treaty of Rome (1957) states that common agricultural policy among the Member States should 'increase agricultural productivity', 'assure the availability of supplies' and 'ensure that supplies reach consumers at reasonable prices'.

Since the adoption of the Maastricht Treaty, the precautionary principle has been part of EU law.[7] Although the pertinent treaty provision refers only to protection of the environment[8] the European Court of Justice ruled that the principle applies also to protection of human health and safety.[9] Thus, the principle can be invoked in the area of food law, insofar as it is concerned with the protection of human health or the environment. Unfortunately, the principle is not defined in the treaty nor in any other EU law instrument, except indirectly and in vague terms ("the possibility of harmful effects on health is identified but scientific uncertainty persists").[10] It appears to require that precaution be applied in EU policy making.

[3]Article 1(3), Regulation 178/2002.

[4]Article 1(1), Regulation 178/2002.

[5]Reform the CAP, http://www.reformthecap.eu/issues/policy-objectives/food-security-in-the-eu.

[6]Rome Declaration on World Food Security (1996).

[7]Article 130R(2), Maastricht Treaty.

[8]See also the Rio Declaration from 1992; Graham (2001).

[9]GC, case T-74/00, Artegodan GmbH v. Commission, ECLI:EU:T:2002:283.

[10]Article 7(1), Regulation 178/2002. See also Szajkowska (2010).

Precaution should be distinguished from prevention; the precautionary principle has been implemented in ways that go beyond prevention. *Prevention* refers to measures to avoid damage, so that no after-the-fact remediation is necessary. Prevention addresses known risks: the damage to be avoided is caused by a specific process in a causal chain of events that is well understood (e.g., injuring one's finger in a food processor, food poisoning as a result of consuming food-borne pathogens such as *Salmonella enteritidis*, and so forth). Thus, prevention involves measures to reduce or eliminate an already identified risk before it can materialize.

Precaution, on the other hand, implies action taken to protect against *possible* danger, failure, or injury, before it is reasonably certain that the danger will, or even can, materialise. Precaution, as understood by the EU, takes prevention a step further. It justifies decisions not to postpone some intervention to prevent *potential* damage on the ground that scientific evidence cannot exclude a *potential* or possible hazard that, if it exists, may be stopped from causing harm by the intervention.[11] Taking precautionary measures means that regulation of some sort is imposed at an early stage before there is causal proof, or that more stringent regulation is introduced than would otherwise be justifiable. Precautionary regulation thus may concern the timing or the stringency of regulatory interventions, or both.[12]

In 2000, the Commission issued a Communication on the Precautionary Principle (COM(2000)1 final). In this document, the principle is considered to cover "those specific circumstances where scientific evidence is insufficient, inconclusive or uncertain and there are indications through preliminary objective scientific evaluation that there are reasonable grounds for concern that the potentially dangerous effects on the environment, human, animal or plant health may be inconsistent with the chosen level of protection." In the General Food Law, the precautionary principle is presented as a way to enhance the protection of consumer health. As Recital 21 puts it, "in those specific circumstances where a risk to life or health exists but scientific uncertainty persists, the precautionary principle provides a mechanism for determining risk management measures or other actions in order to ensure the high level of health protection chosen in the Community." On the other hand, the Regulation also recognizes that precautionary measures can "give rise to barriers to the free movement of food or feed," and, therefore, "it is necessary to adopt a uniform basis throughout the Community for the use of this principle." (recital 20). This, of course, does not eliminate trade barriers resulting from precautionary measures. It just means that they are uniformly applied throughout the EU and at the EU's external borders.

Under the General Food Law, the precautionary principle is presented as one of the grand principles for EU food safety policy, and, as such, carries substantial weight. Article 7(1) states that in "specific circumstances where, following an assessment of available information, the *possibility* of harmful effects on health is identified but scientific uncertainty persists, provisional risk management measures

[11]Raffensperger and Tickner (1999).

[12]Wiener, The Reality of Precaution 2011.

necessary to ensure the high level of health protection chosen in the Community may be adopted, pending further scientific information for a more comprehensive risk assessment." To provide some protection against excessive precautionary measures, pursuant to Article 7(2), precautionary measures must be "proportionate and no more restrictive of trade than is required to achieve the high level of health protection chosen in the Community, regard being had to technical and economic feasibility and other factors regarded as legitimate in the matter under consideration." Thus, precautionary measures must be proportional and the least trade-restrictive means. But whether, in a specific case, these standards limit the range of options available to regulators, is also a function of how the nature and magnitude of the hazard is described.

As this analysis suggests, European food policy conceives of precaution in terms of (1) lack of scientific certainty (or the presence of scientific uncertainty) with respect to (2) possible harmful effects on health as a result of which (3) provisional measures should be taken in order to (4) guarantee a high level of health protection. By design, precaution is linked to a laudable objective, namely strong health protection, which has been wholeheartedly endorsed by the EU. Indeed, the European Commission's Directorate on Health and Food Safety is clear about its ambitions where it presents its mission as "[t]o make Europe a healthier, safer place, where citizens can be confident that their interests are protected." Suggesting that it is willing to go far in taking precautionary measures, it states that a "zero-risk society may not be possible but we are doing as much as we can to reduce and manage risks for our citizens."[13]

But, as the General Food Law acknowledges, precaution comes at a price. Precautionary regulation, like any policy approach, involves trade-offs. Precautionary regulation may conflict not only with free trade (which is not problematic if the restrictions are justified), but also with innovation and other objectives of food policy, such as food security. Conceived in this manner, a precautionary measure may provide additional health protection by eliminating or reducing possible threats, at the possible expense of, for instance, less innovation or less food security. If this is the right way to frame the issue of precautionary food policy, it inherently balances conflicting interests.

This contribution analyses EU food policy from this vantage point, and attempts to understand whether the EU's precautionary approach produces a high level of food safety, and, if so, what the disadvantages of any such policy might be. To understand the nature of food precautionary policies, we first provide a brief overview of EU precautionary measures in the area of food law (Sect. 2). We then proceed to analyse two specific cases in-depth. The cases involve antibiotics in food (Sect. 3) and micro-nutrients (Sect. 4), and attempt to draw some general conclusions. In Sect. 5, our focus shifts to the economic aspects of precaution in the area of food. On the basis of this analysis, in Sect. 6, we develop a theory of precautionary

[13]European Commission, Directorate-General Health and Food Safety, http://ec.europa.eu/dgs/health_food-safety/about_us/who_we_are_en.htm.

food policy that challenges the assumption that precaution implies enhanced food safety and health protection, and discuss what this means for our understanding of the effects of precaution in food policy on food safety and consumer protection, as well as food security and innovation. Conclusions are set forth in Sect. 7.

2 Precaution and EU Food Law

Over the last several decades, the EU has taken a series of precautionary measures in relation to food-related hazards. For instance, precautionary measures were taken in response to the BSE crisis, dioxin in poultry meat, and several other food scares.[14] Other food policy measures did not have a clear relation with health incidents. Already in the 1980s, the EU banned beef hormones.[15] It also prohibited the use of antibiotics in animal feed,[16] and the use of chlorine wash (and other pathogen reduction treatments) for poultry meat.[17] And, of course, the EU has long restricted, and in many cases effectively banned, the cultivation of genetically modified organisms (GMOs), including seeds, and restricted the marketing of food containing genetically modified material.[18]

In the debate on the trade agreement between the EU and the United States (US), known as the "Transatlantic Trade and Investment Partnership" (TTIP), several of these precautionary measures feature prominently.[19] In the past, the US has questioned these measures and in some cases asserted claims against the EU for violating international trade law by applying these restrictions on US food exports to the EU. Accordingly, the US has sought withdrawal or relaxation of these measures. In the TTIP negotiations, it now seeks the inclusion in TTIP of a mechanism for regulatory convergence over time, so that these measures can be revisited and their scientific basis can be tested.[20] On the other hand some NGOs are heavily invested in these measures, and are asking for guarantees that they remain in place unaltered.[21]

Interestingly however the EU has not been precautionary with respect to all possible hazards, or even all food-related hazards. Unlike the US, the EU has been relaxed about certain known and obvious risks arising from the consumption of

[14]See e.g. Hanekamp et al. (2003).

[15]Sien (2007); Council Directive 96/22/EC.

[16]Forrester and Hanekamp (2006).

[17]SCVPH (1998); Council Decision 2009/121/EC.

[18]See Vogel (2012).

[19]Bergkamp and Kogan (2013).

[20]TTIP: what to expect from EU/U.S. regulatory convergence? Enhanced Compatibility, maybe, https://blog.coleurope.eu/2015/04/20/ttip-what-to-expect-from-euu-s-regulatory-convergence-enhanced-compatibility-maybe/.

[21]Susan Cohen Jehoram, 6 things you need to know about the TTIP, 13 May 2016, http://www.greenpeace.org/international/en/news/Blogs/makingwaves/6-things-about-ttip/blog/56429/.

foods. For instance, the use of raw milk for the production of cheese is permitted, even though there have been incidents in Europe involving contamination of raw milk cheese with listeria and other bacteria, which resulted in death and disease.[22] These bacteria could have been killed by pasteurizing the milk from which the cheese is made. In the case of raw milk cheese however the EU did not impose any such measure, while the US did regulate the risk.

This brief overview of the application of the precautionary principle in the area of EU food policy begins to suggest that precautionary food regulation can be simultaneously controversial and selective. In the remainder of this chapter we analyse precautionary food policy measures on the basis of their stated rationales and objectives, not with respect to other motives. It should be noted here that precautionary food policy measures are not always consistently based on the precautionary principle. In Sects. 3 and 4, below, we analyse two cases, antibiotic residues and micronutrients, from this perspective. In analysing these cases however, we actively search for the counter-productive or paradoxical effects of precautionary measures and add critical notes where useful.

3 Antibiotic Residues in Food

During a lifetime, an individual, consumes on average 30 tons of food, in endless dietary varieties. Digestion splits all food in all of these different diets into the same basic elements: nutrients, non-nutritive naturally occurring components, man-made contaminants and additives.[23] Food, thus, is chemistry. Interestingly, the focus of regulatory policy is virtually exclusively on synthetic (man-made) chemicals potentially present in food. The amounts of synthetic pesticide residues in plant foods, however, are low compared to the amounts of natural pesticides produced by plants themselves. Of all dietary pesticides that humans eat, roughly 99.99% are natural. These are chemicals produced by plants to defend themselves against fungi, insects, and other animal predators.[24]

An issue that caught the regulators' attention is the use of antibiotics in food-producing animals and their potential detrimental health effects if they end up in foods digested by human beings. Protecting the general public from toxic chemicals, particularly carcinogens, has been a principal goal of public policy, including food policy.[25] Following blatant misuses of antibiotics, precautionary zero-tolerance is deemed to be an appropriate response in some cases. This means that the use of certain veterinary products that may show up in foods as residues is banned. Below,

[22]Carrique-Mas et al. (2003), Quaglia et al. (2008), Dominguez et al. (2009) and Oliver et al. (2009).

[23]De Vries (1997).

[24]Ames et al. (1990).

[25]See further Hanekamp (2015).

we first discuss the toxicological issues and then the policy issues. Antibiotics resistance is not discussed.

In the EU, zero-tolerance levels are in force for compounds without a Maximum Residue Level, ("MRL"). An MRL represents the upper concentration limit for a pesticide or veterinary medicine residue in or on food or feed based on good agricultural practices ensuring the lowest possible consumer-exposure.[26] If a substance is not authorized or not subject to an MRL, it should not be present in food products at all,[27] even if the concentration is negligible. This means that the concentration of such an unauthorized/substance in food or feed must always be below the detection limit, and, of course, it may not be intentionally added.

For all intents and purposes, the regulatory regime for these compounds is an application of the so-called toxicological "linear no-threshold model" (LNT model). The LNT model has been developed for addressing genotoxic carcinogens, i.e., those chemicals that interfere with the genetic material in the cell. This model assumes that an adverse effect can occur at any dose greater than zero and, thus, results in a regulatory "no-dose no-disease" approach. "Zero dose" is regarded as the only safe regulatory route[28] despite the fact that the LNT model reflects a physico-chemical reality that is contradictory to the Second Law of Thermodynamics; entropy (the progression to thermodynamic equilibrium) drives the inexorable diffusion (spread) of chemicals throughout the world whatever their origins. Indeed, the explicit goal of zero-tolerance is not risk- but precaution-based, since the absence of an MRL is translated into "dangerous at any dose" other than zero.[29]

As a result of increasing analytical capabilities that can detect chemicals at ever-lower levels, zero-tolerance has created massive problems. Technologically advanced analytical equipment can now measure compounds in parts per billion and even parts per trillion. Indeed, we have entered the realm of atto- (part per quintillion; 10^{-18}) and zeptomoles (part per sextillion; 10^{-21}) of detectable analytes.[30] At these extremely low detection limits toxicological effects do not occur and zero-tolerance no longer supports food safety.

The epitome of this evolution was the trade-dispute between the European Union and some Asian countries in the first half of the 2000s over the parts-per-billion-presence of chloramphenicol, or CAP, in shrimp. CAP is an antibiotic used for the treatment of bacterial infections in humans, and is a prototypical broad-spectrum antibiotic frequently used in the developing world.[31] Once the EU found out about the low-level presence of CAP in the shrimp imports from Asia, it closed its borders for fish products from the countries concerned. In addition, it ordered laboratory

---

[26]MRLs are set forth in the now defunct Annex IV of Council Regulation EEC No 2377/90.

[27]Directive 2001/82/EC of 6 November 2001 on the Community Code relating to veterinary medicinal products, OJ L 311, 28.11.2001, p. 1.

[28]Calabrese and Baldwin (2003) and The Health Council of the Netherlands (2010).

[29]Hanekamp and Bast (2007).

[30]Pagnotti et al. (2011).

[31]Hanekamp et al. (2003), Hanekamp and Kwakman (2004) and Hanekamp and Calabrese (2007).

analyses of numerous batches of imported products to test for the presence of CAP. Some European countries even had food products containing low-levels of CAP destroyed for precautionary reasons.

Perfectly safe and nutritious food was thus destroyed to hold up the precautionary paradigm of zero tolerance. In 2009, the failure of this policy was, to some extent, corrected by the designation of Minimum Required Performance Limit (MRPLs) as targets for regulatory levels of concern for banned antibiotics,[32] which serve as so-called Reference Points for Action.[33] However, this MRPL approach has not eliminated the fallacious drivers for zero-tolerance. Fundamentally, the policy remains based on the misconception that risks arise from exposure to low-level concentrations of chemicals, such as CAP.[34] It also assumes that an unambiguous causal link can be established between the detection of some banned compound and an illegal activity in food production. However, as our own findings show,[35] CAP has been found as a natural component in plant material used as animal feed, through which it is transferred to cattle for meat production.[36]

It is this kind of precautionary policy that creates direct conflicts between precaution, on the one hand, and food security, sound science, and common sense, on the other hand. The wholesale destruction of food considered to be contaminated by trace amounts of molecules that have a natural background level is not only problematic from a scientific viewpoint, but also detrimental to food security and, thus, to human health. Precaution has created this problem by singularly focussing on the risks of low-level exposures to certain chemicals singled out for regulation, while disregarding the potential natural background of these chemicals, and the issue of food security of the less affluent countries within and outside the Europe.[37] Food safety has become an absolute and dominant public value that must be maximized, as DG Health and Food Safety emphasizes, and, therefore, always trumps food security. This precautionary regulatory culture has created a substantial and growing market for food safety research, which is subsequently fed into the policy process. Precautionary food safety research, however, does not necessarily live up to conventional standards of scientific rigor and robustness. Of course, where scientific conclusions err on the side of caution, they also err on the side of regulating.

Already in 1999 the European Commission's DG SANCO was made aware of the risks of absolutes in policy-making. A report commissioned by DG SANCO, but subsequently ignored, addressed the future of scientific advice on food and public

[32]Regulation No 470/2009 of 6 May 2009 laying down Community procedures for the establishment of residue limits of pharmacologically active substances in foodstuffs of animal origin, repealing Council Regulation (EEC) No 2377/90 and amending Directive 2001/82/EC of the European Parliament and of the Council and Regulation (EC) No 726/2004 of the European Parliament and of the Council, OJ L 152/11 (16.6.2009).

[33]EFSA (2013).

[34]Hanekamp and Bast (2015).

[35]Hanekamp et al. (2003).

[36]Berendsen et al. (2010) and Berendsen et al. (2013).

[37]Hanekamp and Kwakman (2009).

health, and recommended scientific analysis integrating nutritional, health, and social-economic considerations.[38] It states:

> To have scientific analysis on a European basis is important because currently many policy makers simply consider that the answer to tobacco problems is to 'educate' the individual consumer not to start smoking. This naïve approach is evident in many other dimensions of public health, e.g. those relating to inappropriate diets in pregnancy; the substantial problems of low birth weight babies; the continuing challenge of iodine deficiency within the EU; the widespread anaemia in children and adult woman; the major issues relating to the health of Asians and other immigrant communities within the EU; the challenge of coping with escalating rates of adult chronic diseases and the huge and growing impact of the poor health of Europe's elderly. In societal terms the health impact of societal deprivation, social exclusion and poverty is now becoming a major European issue which requires much more objective scientific analyses than are currently available.

The authors recommended that a European Food and Public Health Authority be established, but it was never to be. Instead, the European Food Safety Authority (EFSA) was established in 2002. Unfortunately, precaution has drawn resources away from the kind of research proposed in the 1999 report, to spend it on studies and analyses of ever smaller and more remote potential food safety hazards deemed to exist by default. The question arises whether such a precautionary food policy approach serves the public interest in an effective and efficient food regulatory framework.

4 Micro-Nutrition and Health

Interest in micronutrient malnutrition has increased only over the last few years, although James et al. already reported on this issue back in 1999, as the quote in the preceding section testifies. One of the main reasons for this increased interest is the growing understanding that micronutrient malnutrition contributes substantially to the global burden of disease. Micronutrient malnutrition is not a problem occurring only in developing countries. In Europe alone, 10% of the population lacks in iron, and 57% of the European population has an insufficient iodine intake.[39] A leading researcher in the field of micronutrients has stated that "[i]t is becoming clear that unbalanced diets will soon become the largest contributor to ill health, with smoking following close behind."[40] The solution to this problem is a "metabolic tune-up through an improved supply of micronutrients" that will have "great health benefits, particularly for those with inadequate diets, such as many of the poor, young, obese and elderly."[41]

---

[38]James et al. (1999).

[39]Allen et al. (2006).

[40]Ames (2005).

[41]Ames (2005).

Despite the overarching significance of this problem, the EU adopted a policy that, in effect, restricts the supply of micro-nutrients. This policy is embodied in the Food Supplements Directive 2002/46/EC (FSD) and the Nutrition and Health Claims Regulation 1924/2006EC (NHCR) regarding commercial communications on foods and foodstuffs. The FSD is intended to protect human health against the potential toxicity of excess intake of micronutrient food supplements, while the latter regulates nutrition and health claims made in commercial communications, whether through the labelling, presentation or advertising of foods.

4.1 The Food Supplements Directive

Although not explicitly based on the precautionary principle, the FSD reflects a one-sided regulatory outlook aimed at avoiding only false negatives. The FSD's main concern is controlling risks arising from overexposure to food supplements. Data regarding the health effects of micronutrients consumption, and the risks of under-consumption of such nutrients, are either not considered at all or at best an after-thought.[42] The lack of empirical grounding is based on the FSD's assumption, unambiguously stated in the third recital, that an "adequate and varied diet could, under normal circumstances, provide all necessary nutrients for normal development and maintenance of a healthy life in quantities which meet those established and recommended by generally acceptable scientific data." Even if that were true in theory, reality shows us a very different picture, as discussed further below.

The reference to an adequate and varied diet as a primary source of all necessary nutrients suggests that food supplements are superfluous products, *if only* European consumers would "eat healthy." The truism that we can obtain everything we need from a balanced diet holds only if we, in fact, eat such a balanced diet consistently. At bottom the EU seems to be saying, tautologically, that an adequate diet is adequate. How such adequacy can be achieved, and what an adequate diet would actually be like, remains indeterminate. Further, factors impinging on the individual nutritional status are only partly related to the dietary intake on which the EU is focused. Mal-absorption (genetic or otherwise) and increased nutritional requirements (e.g. during a disease period) also greatly affect the nutritional status of individuals. However, the EU does not bother to discuss these aspects and fails to take them into account in policy making. In other words, the FSD is based on the normative non-empirical idea that people should consume an adequate and varied diet, rather than rely on food supplements.

As such, the FSD carries distinct overtones of one-sided precaution. It focuses only on the risk of excess intake of micronutrient food supplements, to the detriment of controlling the risk of insufficient intake of such supplements. This one-sided precautionary approach has been sanctioned by the European courts. In two cases

[42]See Expert Group on Vitamins and Minerals (2003).

concerning the FSD, the European Court of Justice opined as follows (Cases C-154/04 and C-155/04, ECLI:EU:C:2005:449):

> In those circumstances and in view of the need for the Community legislature to take account of the precautionary principle when it adopts, in the context of the policy on the internal market, measures intended to protect human health [...], the authors of Directive 2002/46 [FSD] could reasonably take the view that an appropriate way of reconciling the objective of the internal market, on the one hand, with that relating to the protection of human health, on the other, was for entitlement to free movement to be reserved for food supplements containing substances about which, at the time when the directive was adopted, the competent European scientific authorities had available adequate and appropriate scientific data capable of providing them with the basis for a favourable opinion, whilst giving scope, in Article 4(5) of the directive, for obtaining a modification of the positive lists by reference to scientific and technological developments.
>
> It is also necessary to state in that regard that, by virtue of Article 7 of the General Food Law, the Community legislature is entitled to adopt the provisional risk management measures necessary to ensure a high level of health protection and may do so whilst awaiting further scientific information for a more comprehensive risk assessment, as is stated in the 10th recital to Directive 2002/46.

Under the FSD thus constructed, food supplements, including those that have been legitimately marketed in one or more Member States in accordance with the relevant national regulations, may be placed on the EU market only if an appropriate, precautionary scientific risk characterisation is presented. Whether or not micronutrient supplement intake might add to the overall health of European citizens is, from the regulatory point of view, irrelevant. Note that this asymmetry is not a coincidental and rare effect of precaution; rather, it is inherent to precautionary culture.[43] The precautionary approach assumes what actually should be proven, namely, that the health effects of a regulation aimed at limiting only false-negatives is superior to the alternatives, *including* the zero-alternative of doing nothing.[44] This conjecture is accompanied by a closely related, but equally unproven assumption that there are no negative health effects from proposed regulation; health is improved by regulation, while the adverse, counter-productive side-effects of regulation are denied.[45]

4.2 *The Nutrition and Health Claims Regulation*

The NHCR harmonizes the use of health claims in commercial communications concerning food and food products in the EU. It is aimed at establishing a precautionary high level of protection for consumers through the scientific assessment of health claims. In this case, precaution requires that misleading information on food products is effectively eliminated. To ensure that no misleading information that might potentially damaging to the European public's health becomes available, all

---

[43]Hanekamp (2015).

[44]Coase (1960).

[45]Wildavsky (1997).

health claims must be scientifically vetted by EFSA's Panel on Dietetic Products, Nutrition and Allergies (NDA Panel).[46]

To connect dietary patterns (including supplementation and fortification) with human health and to assess benefits and risks of food constituents, a series of methods, such as observational epidemiologic studies, intervention trials (Randomised Controlled Trials—RCTs), models and simulations, *in* and *ex vivo* animal and human studies, and *in vitro* research, are commonly utilized by researchers around the world. Some of these methods are mechanistic in nature, e.g. an animal study on metabolic pathways, while other methods are phenomenological, e.g. an RCT on the effectiveness of a certain intervention. From a political, regulatory and mainstream scientific perspective, the RCT is regarded as the "gold standard" for establishing causal links between food and health. Accordingly, in the "organisation of pertinent scientific data," Regulation 353/2008 establishes a "hierarchy of study design" with RCT at the top of this ostensibly scientific pyramid. RCTs thus are granted regulatory preference and constitute the overriding factor with respect to the approval or rejection of health claims for foods or food products. In this manner, the EU legislature has standardised the scientific inquiry into nutrition and health claims, with the EFSA as the risk assessment body. As a precautionary means to protect public health and shield the consumer from misleading information, any health claim "requires the evidence to be convincing."[47]

What the EU legislature and EFSA did not mention is that RCTs are limited in determining causal relations. An RCT does not directly investigate causation. Rather, it investigates correlation and then infers causation on that basis. In other words, *how* and *why* a food constituent has the effect it has, is not clarified by a RCT. It shows only that a particular result is actually obtained. Of course, in many cases RCTs in the field of nutritional science are undertaken based on evidence already gathered through other research, since it would be inefficient to run RCTs at random. Nonetheless, RCTs do not establish causal relations, and do not elucidate the 'how' and the 'why' of the observed effect(s) of the food constituent under investigation in the trial. These limits of RCTs have been recognized, yet hardly internalised in the field of science and regulation.[48]

The logic of RCTs is that the trial circumstances are ideally constructed for ensuring that the effect of the agent can be unambiguously identified under '*ceteris paribus*' conditions. But RCTs are by no means ideal for all purposes. For instance, they may not provide a sound basis for extrapolating or generalising—the very aspects that have made RCTs the regulatory "gold standard." To conduct sound policy, however, we do not need to know that "it works somewhere," i.e. within some RCT study-design, as that knowledge is trivial. We need evidence for "it-will-

[46]Bast et al. (2013).

[47]EFSA (2010).

[48]Cartwright (2011).

work-for-us" claims, i.e. that the agent will produce the desired outcome in our situation.[49] Thus, although RCTs may well help to identify a link between some agent in some members of the investigated study population, they do little if anything to establish that the agent under scrutiny has the same effects in all other cases.

Ironically, due to its heavy reliance on RCTs, it is hard to determine whether the European regulation concerning health claims in fact works and protects consumers from misleading information. In some sense, running an RCT as the primary way to find a causal relation, to paraphrase Leamer, is much like trying to learn the laws of electricity by playing the radio.[50] The scientific absolutism stipulated in the NHCR also tends to result in "scientism"—the view that the only real knowledge is scientific knowledge, in particular empirical scientific knowledge.[51] This, in turn, tends to render all nutritional data contentious, including data from the EFSA itself, with the ostensible "gold standard" of the RCT as the sole exception.

Taken to its logical extreme, much highly relevant and useful research in the area of nutritional science becomes trivial in the regulatory area. As a consequence of the regulatory preference for RCTs, the normal peer-review process is skewed or even partly circumvented. By concentrating chiefly on RCTs, the NHCR may well cause correct claims to be prohibited, and incorrect claims to be permitted. The method employed, rather than scientific knowledge itself, decides between "right" and "wrong." This scientific regime may well result in the banning of innovative products for precautionary reasons. As the 2001 study "Late Lessons from Early Warnings" of the European Environment Agency put it, "their very novelty might be taken as a warning sign."[52]

Reflecting the lopsidedness of the precautionary principle, the Nutrition and Health Claims Regulation, in line with Article 7(1) of the General Food Law Regulation, conceives of health claims information primarily as a risk factor. As applied to micronutrients, the NHCR disregards the potential benefits of health claims to the consumer. Such benefits are real, in view of the known, widespread micronutrient deficiencies and the adverse effects thereof. While this approach is justified as precautionary, the regulatory disregard of the potential benefits from foods and food-products may well increase the risks for the public and impede innovation. This in turn contravenes the very goal of precaution. In other words, it is risky to be risk averse.

The problems identified by our analysis have been recognized by other authors. As Robert Heaney pointed out, there is a "general agreement to the effect that nutrition is important, despite the fact that the still growing number of failed trials of individual nutrients might suggest that no nutrient actually made much of a difference, a conclusion that is absurd on its face and ought to have alerted us to

[49]Cartwright (2011) and Cartwright and Hardie (2012).

[50]Leamer (1983).

[51]Bast et al. (2013).

[52]Harremoës et al. (2001), p. 170.

the possibility that there was something wrong with how we were investigating the matter."[53] Clearly, Heaney has the NHCR in mind here. To drive his point home, he adds: "To provide the proof needed to sustain revised intake recommendations, we shall have to find a design better suited to nutrients than the randomized controlled trial as currently implemented, and we need to develop a series of global indices, nutrient by nutrient, which better capture the polyvalent nature of most nutrients." Preventing misinformation, of course, is as much a matter of *providing* correct information as it is of *not suppressing* correct information. It is ironic, but not surprising, that the NHCR produces the very thing—misinformation—it tries to combat. Although the EU legislature did not enact the NHCR in the name of precaution, it is the precautionary thinking behind this regime that causes these paradoxical effects.[54]

5 Economic Effects of Precautionary Food Policy

The cases discussed in Sects. 3 and 4 show that precaution, as applied in the field of food law, causes unintended and counter-productive effects. In both cases, the precautionary principle tries to prevent possible "negative externalities," i.e. adverse effects on persons that are not reflected in the pricing of a good or service. The externality concept lies also at the heart of the precautionary principle.[55] Opinions differ on how exactly the precautionary principle prevents negative externalities. Kysar has argued that proponents of the precautionary principle, who "emphasize the limits of human knowledge and the frequency of unpleasant surprises from technology and industrial development," prefer "an *ex ante* stance of precaution whenever a proposed activity meets some threshold possibility" of causing harm.[56] According to Purnhagen, the precautionary principle would be "a counterbalance to the loss aversion and availability bias of regulators, who may too hastily" adopt less or non-protective regulatory measures.[57] No sound empirical bases for these claims, however, has been established. It has also been argued that there is a separate, economically distinguishable "precautionary effect." This effect would arise from a decrease in current consumption stemming from scientific uncertainty, which conversely would reduce risks in the future and for future generations.[58] Such economic effects have also been asserted in the context of the precautionary outlook on the two cases discussed above.

[53]Heaney (2008), pp. 1591–1595.

[54]See further Hanekamp et al. (2015).

[55]Treich (2001).

[56]Kysar (2006)

[57]Purnhagen (2014).

[58]Gollier et al. (2000).

Precautionary food policy has a tenuous relation with empirics and facts. While a conventional economics approach needs empirical evidence and probabilities for rational decision-making, precaution-driven decision-making is not dependent on empirical evidence and probabilities, and, through open or hidden assumptions, can operate under conditions of uncertainty based on the mere existence of possibilities or scenarios.[59] Indeed, the growing influence of *possibilistic* (as opposed to *probabilistic*) thinking invites speculation about what can possibly go wrong, not what is likely to go wrong. In possibilistic thinking, the distinction between what can possibly go wrong and what is likely to happen moves into the background, and worst possible outcomes or worst case scenarios become the basis for policy-making. As Furedi observes, in possibilistic thinking, the key question "what can possibly go wrong" invites the answer "everything."[60] Precaution is thus seen as a means to cope with history before it happened.[61] Or put differently, to construct rather than predict the future.

In 2002, Majone noted that little analysis had been done by economists on the precautionary principle's potential significant economic consequences.[62] Not much has changed since Majone made this observation, but there is some empirical evidence on precautionary effects on economies, both from before and after Majone's remarks. There is empirical evidence of the adverse economic consequences of the EU's GMO policies on the economies of EU Member States. Due to almost complete unavailability of GM seeds, agricultural yields have not been as high as they could have been, average farmer income has been lower, food-related diseases have occurred more frequently, pesticide use has been more intense than it could have been, and the consumption of certain foods may have been less than optimal.[63] Further, there is empirical evidence of the injurious impact on Africa of the EU's precautionary approach towards genetically modified food. Turvey and Mojduszka show how the implementation of the precautionary principle adversely affects welfare, and that "the unintended consequences could be very high when inaction is taken based upon the precautionary principle." In the case of Africa, the precautionary principle resulted in the acceptance of "widespread famine, starvation and death with certainty, in favor of an unproven, undocumented, and undefined future risk."[64] They argue that "environmentalists, policy makers, politicians and other groups have grasped the precautionary principle as a *cause celebre* to justify particular positions they deem important without taking full council on the externality of deferment on others." In order to prevent such perverse effects, they recommend that proponents of the precautionary principle "look beyond the mere measurement of scientific uncertainty to consider fully and completely the

---

[59]Bergkamp (2014).

[60]Furedi (2009).

[61]Hanekamp (2015).

[62]Majone (2002).

[63]Bradford (2012), Smyth and Phillips (2014) and Park et al. (2011).

[64]Turvey and Mojduszka (2005).

opportunity and societal costs of" precautionary measures. Of course, the fact that precautionary measures impose high costs, does not mean that such measures therefore should be rejected, but one would want to be comfortable that substantial benefits will flow from them, which could otherwise not be obtained. A general reference to hypothetical risks would not suffice.

Another example involves the EU requirements regarding aflatoxins. Aflatoxins, naturally occurring mycotoxins that are produced by the fungi *Aspergillus flavus* and *Aspergillus parasiticus*, are potentially hepatotoxic compounds that may cause liver cancer in human beings and be present on foods such as nuts. Otsuki et al. have analysed how the extremely low EU standards for aflatoxins caused a substantial drop in African exports of nuts, cereals, and dried/preserved fruits. According to calculations by Otsuki et al., the standard for aflatoxin in milk was based on daily consumption nearly 8 times higher than the per capita consumption of milk, and the new EC standard would reduce the deaths from aflatoxins by only 2.3 persons per billion per year.[65] These authors note that this reduction in deaths applied to a population of 500 million is immeasurable relative to the estimated 33,000 liver cancer deaths in the EU each year. As Turvey and Mojduszla note, "[w]hether or not the precautionary principle would actually save 2.3 lives is uncertain in its own right, but the negative effects of trade on African nations would be quite certain.[66] These certain costs should feature in any precautionary analysis. As noted in the prior paragraph, it cannot be excluded that, despite such high costs, precautionary measures are justified if the expected benefits exceed the costs, but this should be established.

Precautionary measures may generate benefits, if it subsequently appears that they have been imposed with respect to real, rather than phantom, risks. To determine whether risks are real, research is needed, but the problem is that the interest in research often disappears after a regulatory measure has been put into place. Independent of whether they produce benefits, precautionary measures also impose costs, and these costs will be higher if the suspected risk subsequently appears not to exist or is less serious than initially feared. In other words, precautionary action always has a price. This price includes not only the direct monetary costs of the design and implementation of, and compliance with, the precautionary measure itself, but also the risks or impacts associated with the measure, and the opportunity costs associated with the prohibited or restricted activity, which would have produced some advantages for people for some time. The key question in the debate is how much society is willing to pay (in a broad sense) for precaution. As Munthe put it: "how much of increased expenditure, new threats, actual harms and lost goods should be accepted as a result of precautionary measures? And in what type of circumstances would it actually be acceptable to pay this price?"[67] Note, however,

---

[65]Otsuki et al. (2001).

[66]Turvey and Mojduszka (2005).
See further Bast and Hanekamp (2017).

[67]Munthe (2011).

that if the concept of "price" is taken as a "net price" (i.e. costs minus benefits) it may become so broad that it encompasses any and all possible negative effects, including ethical and emotional effects such as fear. In the extreme, the precautionary approach's possibilistic outlook[68] may be reflected in its entirety in the price of precautionary measures.

In the food area, as elsewhere, the economics of precautionary regulation can also be captured in the value of statistical life ("VSL"). In effect, the VSL reflects trade-offs between money and fatality risks, and provides the cost per life or year saved by a regulatory intervention. VSLs serve as a reference point for assessing the benefits of risk reduction efforts.[69] Even if a benefit-cost assessment cannot be applied to precautionary regulation, policies that on balance harm individual health presumably should not be adopted.[70] The VSL's measure of the risk-money trade-off for small risks of death, which are the risks typically addressed by precautionary regulations, can serve as a basis for establishing the monetary cost of predicted reductions in mortality risks resulting from health, safety, and environmental policies. It is known that the cost-effectiveness of life-saving interventions shows a wide range, from "those that save more resources than they cost, to those costing more than 10 billion dollars per year of life saved."[71] Given scarcity of resources, it is unlikely that a regulator could justify a life-saving intervention at the high end of this range as being in the public interest. Where regulation is based on the precautionary principle, this problem is aggravated, since the costs of regulation are immediate and certain, but the benefits of regulation are less certain and more remote.

At least four types of risk-risk trade-offs influence the net effect of a policy or regulation on a population's risk exposure.[72] First, a policy may reduce risks of one type while increasing risks of another type. Second, policies to reduce risks may create incentives for individuals to undertake less individual effort to reduce their exposure to risks (the so-called "moral hazard"). Third, risk-reduction policies may result in regulatory expenditures that directly increase fatalities (cost-induced fatalities).[73] Fourth, the costs of risk-reduction policies decrease income available to finance other health and safety expenditures. Precautionary regulation, including precautionary food policy, may involve all four types of risk/risk trade-offs. For instance, a prohibition of pesticides to protect the environment may increase the price of vegetables, thus reducing consumption and harming human health.[74] Second, a government policy aimed at ensuring an adequate and balanced diet may make individuals less inclined to pay attention to their diets. Third, precautionary food policy increases the price of food and makes people poorer, thus increasing

---

68 Furedi (2009).

69 Viscusi (2015).

70 Viscusi and Aldy (2003).

71 Tengs et al. (1995).

72 Viscusi and Aldy (2003).

73 See Keeney (1994, 1997).

74 Ames et al. (1990).

their overall exposure to risks. Fourth, the resources available to government to manage risks are drained by precautionary policies, and thus result in underspending on risks that are more immediate and more serious than the remote, uncertain risks addressed by precautionary policies.

6 The Problems of Precautionary Food Policy Revisited

Precautionary policy is deemed to be necessary to tackle uncertain and remote risks, which might be the foreboding of certain future risks. The axiom underlying the precautionary principle is that under conditions of uncertainty, precautionary policies add to the protection of human health and/or the environment by reducing or eliminating potential hazards or threats before they become real risks. Precautionary policies might include bans on activities or products, other types of restrictions (e.g. concentration limits), or yet other regulatory instruments, such as mitigation strategies or research. Precautionary policy is a response to the alleged reluctance on the part of government to take protective environmental and/or public health measures where absolute proof of harm is lacking. Taken to its logical extreme, such a conservative regulatory attitude would result in the indefinite continuation of the status quo, because it is always possible to identify some remaining uncertainties, which, in turn, would justify postponing regulatory interventions. Even if more and more evidence of harm comes to the fore and scientific consensus on a cause-effect relation exists, there is always some remaining uncertainty that can be invoked as a justification for not intervening. This, of course, is a caricature of conventional policy, but it is the one to which the precautionary principle responds. In response to this problem, precautionary intervention "errs on the safe side."[75] The precautionary principle is intended to provide guidance early on, before there is a risk of harm. It encourages regulation in cases in which scientific research and knowledge of the harmful effects of a proposed activity or product is still incomplete, or premature. Paradoxically, science and knowledge are also the most important available probes in matters of risk, uncertainty and precaution.

The analysis and the two cases presented in this chapter show that, in the real world, matters are more complicated than the simplistic rhetoric of the precautionary principle suggests. If it is assumed that the precautionary principle is intended as an intellectually coherent concept, rather than a malleable political slogan, a series of objections can be made to the prescriptions following from it. These objections are not unique to the application of the precautionary principle in the area of food policy, but apply more generally. As we attempted to show in this chapter, some more or less specific problems arise in the food area (such as the security of supply), which may not be as prominent in other areas. At the same time, the precautionary principle can be applied in a holistic fashion to address a wide range of problems. A case in

[75]Rolston III (1988).

point is the judgment of a Dutch court on the state's obligations with respect to climate change. Based on the seriousness of the potential threats posed by climate change, which the Court found to include reduced food production, the court ruled that the state of The Netherlands is required to take measures to ensure that emissions of greenhouse gases are reduced by at least 25% by 2020, compared to 1990.[76] This ruling was based, in part, on the precautionary principle. It confirms that the precautionary principle is able to open up a broad range of possibilities for regulatory and judicial activism in the service of the social good. Below, we review the principal problems associated with precautionary policy-making.

First, precautionary policies, by necessity, have to be selective, since it is impossible to deal with all potential hazards on a precautionary basis, as the number of hazards is literally infinite. We are surrounded by hazards, and there is no hope of eliminating or reducing all of them. Science cannot test for every possible consequence of even one specific action because this would entail an unbounded search space of possible consequences. Science can only investigate specific consequences.[77] If science cannot even completely investigate all possible consequences of one activity, it, of course, can never investigate all possible consequences of all possible acts. Worse yet, the precautionary principle distorts the selection of threats for regulation by focusing on uncertain and remote risk. Thus, the uncertain and remote risks of "overdosing" on food supplements or micro-nutrients is prioritized over the certain and immediate risks of "under-dosing" on food supplements and micro-nutrients.[78]

Second, the two cases presented in this chapter show that the choices made under the heading of precaution, in fact, reflect political preferences. Over and above the problem of scientific uncertainty, which more often than not is grossly overstated, non-epistemic determinants drive precautionary responses. No prior distribution of probabilities reflects factual data alone. It will always, in part, reflect non-epistemic determinants corresponding to a given socio-economic and ideological context.[79] Therefore, how low the probability of minimal or acceptable risk is set is contingent on more than scientific evidence. Precautionary decisions may be informed by green romanticism and the belief that 'tampering with nature' should be avoided.[80] The cases discussed in Sects. 3 and 4 show how green romanticism and the "appeal to nature" fallacy[81] shape precautionary policies: the use of antibiotics interferes with natural food safety, and a natural, adequate and varied diet contains all necessary nutrients for normal development and maintenance of a healthy life in quantities that

[76]District Court of The Hague, judgment of 24 June 2015, Urgenda versus State of The Netherlands; Hanekamp and Bergkamp (2016) and Bergkamp and Hanekamp (2015).

[77]Mckinney and Hammer Hill (2000).

[78]Likewise, prescribed minimum doses will tend to be on the low side.

[79]Mckinney and Hammer Hill (2000).

[80]Bramwell (1989), Veldman (1994), Sjöberg (2000) and Hanekamp et al. (2005); see further Hanekamp (2015).

[81]Baggini (2002), pp. 181–182.

meet those established and recommended by generally acceptable scientific data, so that supplementation is not necessary or not morally justified.[82]

Third, even if limited to the binary choice of regulating or not regulating a specific potential hazard, the precautionary principle does not provide guidance, since there are always potential hazards on both sides of the equation. Each choice carries with it certain foreseen and unforeseen risks. Unquantified worst-case scenarios without probabilities can be thought up for each choice, which implies that we have no way to choose. The precautionary principle does not provide improper guidance, it provides no guidance at all.[83] In both its design and application, the precautionary principle is not some exogenous panacea, but an endogenous (i.e., societal embedded) and fallible human pursuit. It could be viewed as a form of "technology," in a broad sense, and, as such, it involves risks; risks that are as real as the risks it targets against.

Fourth, as a related matter, precaution cannot be equated with safety. This follows from the proposition that there are risks on all sides of the societal and regulatory equation, which implies that risk aversion itself is risky. The "safe course" is not safe; it is an alternative course involving other and new, including unforeseen, risks, which evoke a secondary precautionary response, which, again, gives rise to other and new, including unforeseen, risks, et cetera, *ad infinitum*. In other words, even if an effect of human activity is possibly catastrophic, that suspicion alone cannot rationally compel us to impose a precautionary remedy, unless we know for sure that the remedy itself is not worse than the ostensible problem it addresses. It is one thing to detect a certain detrimental phenomenon, such as cancer; it is another thing to assign to this phenomenon a cause, such as a low-level exposure to certain man-made chemicals, like CAP. Thus, precaution and prevention are two different things.

Fifth, the economics of precaution show that the regulatory and societal expenditures associated with precautionary regulation are real and can be assessed, but the benefits, i.e. the return on the precautionary investments, cannot be assessed because of the uncertainty and remoteness of the possible threats that are targeted by such regulation. This means that, in some cases, no VSL can be calculated for a precautionary measure, because there is no way to tell whether the measure will save a life. In other cases, where there is a sufficient level of certainty around the target risk, the VSL of a precautionary measure is astronomically high, or even negative, i.e. the regulation causes additional deaths. An example in the area of food policy is the case of the EU-levels for aflatoxin. As Otsuki et al. have demonstrated, the prior precautionary EU limits resulted in an extremely slight reduction of deaths from exposure to aflatoxins by only 2.3 persons per billion per year.[84] On the cost side of the equation, these levels did cause a substantial drop in imports into to the EU and an

[82]The information on food supplements may not create the impression that a normal balanced diet does not provide the necessary nutrients etc., so in the negative, not the positive.

[83]Sunstein (2005).

[84]Otsuki et al. (2001).

increase in prices, which, in turn, caused additional deaths in both the EU and the exporting countries. Thus, the costs of these precautionary levels greatly exceed their benefits. Once the VSL of a particular measure reaches levels over EUR 10 million, it should be reconsidered because it might have a net negative value, even directly in terms of lives saved. Fortunately, the new EU regulation is now in line with the Codex maximum aflatoxin level,[85] although the EU regulation, compared to the Codex standard, covers more products and imposes separate maximum levels for aflatoxin B1. The new EU levels are based on Good Agricultural Practice (GAP), which allow for substantial reduction of aflatoxin contamination, but not to the precautionary levels the EU previously imposed.

7 Conclusions

Despite its intellectual incoherence and unboundedness, the precautionary principle has become a cornerstone of EU food policy. With the precautionary principle now being part of the EU constitutional landscape, there is substantial vested interest in precautionary science and precautionary regulation, also in the food area. Natural, organic, and traditional foods, and foods that are free from GMOs, bisphenol-A, aspartame, phthalates, dioxin, cholesterol, saturated fats, sugar, and other substances, have benefitted from EU precautionary food policy measures. Given the substantial vested interests in precautionary food policy, the debate about the intellectual merits is increasingly becoming moot. At the risk of beating a dead horse we revisited the intellectual foundations of the precautionary principle in the food policy area.

A common justification for the precautionary principle is the lack of timely and sufficiently stringent regulation in the face of novel, uncertain, and remote risks that may have serious or irreversible consequences. The precautionary principle is not a stand-alone concept; it is part and parcel of the grand idea of sustainable development.[86] This may have given it additional credibility and further impetus, and propelled precautionary regulation to become a sizeable industry. When the principle is invoked, the proposed policy will by default be desirable because it is presumed to be protective of health and the environment. Precautionary measures can be put in place before risks become a reality, early in the putative causal chain, when threats are still remote and uncertain. Given the asserted uncertainty, traditional science is forced to play second fiddle because, by definition, it has not been able to resolve the uncertainty. The earlier regulation of a novel risk is enacted, the less likely it is that traditional science will have much to say about the risk, and the less relevant it becomes to decision-making. The gap is filled by precautionary science, the science of mere possibilities and scenarios. By intervening earlier in

[85]Codex (2010); Commission Regulation (EU) No 165/2010.

[86]Hanekamp (2015).

putative causal chains, causality itself becomes a mockery. At the same time, conventional cost-benefit analysis loses much of its relevance, and is unable to protect society against ineffective and disproportionally costly regulations. Insofar as the precautionary principle promises safety, its promise is false; as discussed in Sect. 6, precautionary regulation involves risks too, and thus may increase rather than decrease over-all risk levels.

Given its incoherence and irrational prescriptions, the precautionary principle is best understood as a political tool rather than an intellectual concept. As a political tool it has its champions and foes. Precautionary regulation creates winners and losers. In light of the analysis presented in this chapter, it is easy to see who benefits from the availability of the precautionary principle and precautionary regulation, and who loses. The first group of winners are those that favour strict regulation of risks. Interestingly, this group includes both people at the left end of the political spectrum, who desire to strictly regulate industry and the risks it creates, and people at the right, who desire to take strict precautionary measures to combat terrorism, fight crime, and address other social ills.[87] Generally, expanded regulatory powers and additional regulatory program imply larger government, and thus government agencies tend to benefit too. The losers of course are those that are in favour of economic and individual freedom and limited government. They are faced with expanded government powers, more regulations, more or larger agencies, additional regulatory burdens for enterprise, and more limited economic freedom.

A second group of winners are the suppliers of precautionary science, alternative analytical tools, and similar programs and procedures that can be used to support precautionary science. How the precautionary principle has affected science itself, is an issue that is insufficiently recognized at EU level, due in part to the Commission misleading insistence that the principle comes into play only at the risk management phase, not the risk assessment phase.[88] In fact, precautionary science and technology is big business, as the enormous amounts of public funding for sustainable and other precautionary projects testify. This funding facilitates the establishment of separate precautionary scientific schools, which can displace traditional scientific disciplines, as happened in the area of endocrine disrupters. The precautionary principle has effectively politicized science and created factions that are no longer on speaking terms. Hanekamp and Pieterman (2009) have dubbed this movement the "precautionary coalition." In their words: "We can first ascertain that uncertainty, even distrust, has become an important source for scientific investigation as such. Today, there are a vast number of academic disciplines that focus on the problems man produces through science, technology and industry. Rachel Carson, or indeed the Club of Rome could not have foreseen this tremendous increase in the number of concerned scientists having a professional career focused on elucidating the impact of man on the planet. However, it is not only at the level of academic studies that the focus on technological risks has gained prominence. All those academics hold

[87] See e.g. Stern and Wiener (2006).

[88] Commission (2000).

positions in institutions that are expressly created to further the social, political, and economic awareness of the problems technology poses for our environment and our health. (...) In order to be accepted among fellow professionals, within such institutional context, individuals have to take their duty to warn against possible problems – that could be potential disasters – very seriously. They similarly have an interest in keeping their job and in promoting the interests of their organization. (...) Because of their training, their self-esteem and their job satisfaction the scientific professionals in these organizations must believe that what they do is essential to the welfare of society." Conventional scientists and providers of conventional cost-benefit analyses, and similar services are the losers. In the precautionary culture, there is little need for conventional science with its cautious, tentative, and limited conclusions, void of policy recommendations. As conventional scientists are believed to lack the courage to venture into the uncertain terrain of possible hazards and unwilling to provide clear guidance on the right course action to protect the planet, they are marginalized.

A third group are consumer interest groups and other non-governmental organizations that represent the public interest. Under the precautionary principle, there is a tendency for politicians, as Morris puts it, "to give more weight to the misanthropic views of environmentalists and other undemocratic pressure groups who claim to speak for the public."[89] Indeed, misanthropism is a well-known driver within the precautionary realm.[90] These groups have also claimed a place at the negotiation table, and a vote on any policy proposals, invoking concepts of "stakeholder dialogue" and "new governance." The losers are non-activist citizens who do not feel represented by any of these groups. This unorganized "silent majority" is confronted with policy outcomes they do not support or indeed even understand. For them, the only solution would be to become politically engaged, but that is the one thing they do not want to do. As a result, in the precautionary stakeholder dialogue society they are voiceless.

Is there a way out of this conundrum? The most critical and volatile issues arising in current society cannot be solved by a precautionary response. They require effective marshalling of expert scientific knowledge and judgment. The same holds true for the economic valuation of precautionary regulation: all regulations must produce benefits at acceptable costs. A way out of the precautionary conundrum is to reiterate the values of objective science, knowledge, education, responsibility, and critical judgment.[91] In a democracy, to effect change, one must persuade with transparent valid and sound arguments. This article attempted to persuade readers that the EU food policy debate would benefit greatly from being freed from the precautionary muzzle. Sound science (not scientism), risk assessment, and risk management based on cost-benefit analysis can, and should, serve as the cornerstones of excellent EU food regulations for the twenty-first century.

---

[89]Morris (2002).

[90]Hanekamp (2015).

[91]See e.g. Hottois (2000).

References

Allen L, De Benoist B, Dary O, Hurrell R (eds) (2006) Guidelines on food fortification with micronutrients. World Health Organization, Geneva

Ames BN (2005) Increasing longevity by tuning up metabolism. EMBO Rep 6:S20–S24

Ames BN, Profet M, Gold LS (1990) Dietary pesticides (99.99% all natural). Proc Natl Acad Sci U S A 87:7777–7781

Baggini J (2002) Philosophy: key texts. Palgrave Mac Millan, London

Bast A, Hanekamp JC (2017) Toxicology: what everyone should know. A book for researchers, consumers, journalists and politicians. Academic Press, London

Bast A, Briggs W, Calabrese E, Fenech M, Hanekamp JC, Heaney R, Rijkers G, Schwitters B, Verhoeven P (2013) Scientism, legalism and precaution - contending with regulating nutrition and health claims in europe. Eur Food Feed Law Rev 6:401–409

Berendsen B, Stolker L, de Jong J, Nielen M, Tserendorj E, Sodnomdarjaa R, Cannavan A, Elliott C (2010) Evidence of natural occurrence of the banned antibiotic chloramphenicol in herbs and grass. Anal Bioanal Chem 397:1955–1963

Berendsen B, Pikkemaat M, Römkens P, Wegh R, van Sisseren M, Stolker L, Nielen M (2013) Occurrence of chloramphenicol in crops through natural production by bacteria in soil. J Agric Food Chem 61:400–4010

Bergkamp L (2014) The quiet revolution in EU administrative procedure: judicial vetting of precautionary risk assessment - case T-333/10, ATC and others v commission, 16/09/2013 ('animal trading'). Eur J Risk Reg 5:102–110

Bergkamp L, Hanekamp J (2015) Climate change litigation against states: the perils of court-made climate policies. Eur Energy Environ Law Rev 24:102–114

Bergkamp L, Kogan L (2013) Trade, the precautionary principle, and post-modern regulatory process: regulatory convergence in the transatlantic trade and investment partnership. Eur J Risk Reg 4:493–507

Bradford A (2012) The brussels effect. Northwest Univ Law Rev 107(1)

Bramwell A (1989) Ecology in the 20th century. A history. Yale University Press, New Haven, London

Calabrese EJ, Baldwin LA (2003) Toxicology rethinks its central belief. Hormesis demands a re-appraisal of the way risks are assessed. Nature 421:691–692

Carrique-Mas JJ, Hökeberg I, Andersson Y, Arneborn M, Tham W, Danielsson-Tham ML, Osterman B, Leffler M, Steen M, Eriksson E, Hedin G, Giesecke J (2003) Febrile gastroenteritis after eating on-farm manufactured fresh cheese – an outbreak of listeriosis? Epidemiol Infect 130:79–86

Cartwright N (2011) The art of medicine. A philosopher's view of the long road from RCTs to effectiveness. Lancet 377:1400–1401

Cartwright N, Hardie J (2012) Evidence-based policy. A practical guide to doing it better. Oxford University Press, Oxford

Coase RH (1960) The problem of social cost. J Law Econ 3:1–44

Codex Alimentarius (2010) Codex general standard for contaminants and toxins in food and feed. Codex Stan 193-1995

Commission of the European Communities (2000) Communication from the commission on the pre-cautionary principle. Brussels

Commission Regulation (EC) 353/2008 of April 2008 establishing implementing rules for applications for authorisation of health claims as provided for in Article 15 of Regulation (EC) No 1924/2006 of the European Parliament and of the Council. O J Eur Union L109:11–20

Commission Regulation (EU) No 165/2010 of 26 February 2010 amending Regulation (EC) No 1881/2006 setting maximum levels for certain contaminants in foodstuffs as regards aflatoxins. O J Eur Union L50:8–12

Council Directive 96/22/EC of 29 April 1996 concerning the prohibition on the use in stockfarming of certain substances having a hormonal or thyrostatic action and of beta-agonists, and repealing Directives 81/602/EEC, 88/146/EEC and 88/299/EEC. O J Eur Comm L125:3–8

Council Regulation (EEC) No. 2377/90 of 26 June 1990 laying down a Community procedure to set up maximum residue limits of veterinary medicinal products in foodstuffs of animal origin. 1990. O J Eur Comm L224:1–8

De Vries J (ed) (1997) Food safety and toxicity. CRC Press, New York

Directive (EU) 2015/412 of the European Parliament and of the Council of 11 March 2015 amending Directive 2001/18/EC as regards the possibility for the Member States to restrict or prohibit the cultivation of genetically modified organisms (GMOs) in their territory. O J Eur Union L68:1–8

Directive 2002/46/EC of the European Parliament and of the Council of 10 June 2002 on the approximation of the laws of the Member States relating to food supplements. O J Eur Union L183:51–57

Dominguez M, Jourdan-Da Silva N, Vaillant V, Pihier N, Kermin C, Weill FX, Delmas G, Kerouanton A, Brisabois A, de Valk H (2009) Outbreak of Salmonella enterica serotype Montevideo infections in France linked to consumption of cheese made from raw milk. Foodborne Pathog Dis 6(1):121–128

EFSA (2010) Guidance on human health risk-benefit assessment of foods. EFSA J 8(7):1673

EFSA Panel on Contaminants in the Food Chain (CONTAM) (2013) Guidance on methodological principles and scientific methods to be taken into account when establishing Reference Points for Action (RPAs) for non- allowed pharmacologically active substances present in food of animal origin. EFSA J 11(4):3195

Expert Group on Vitamins and Minerals (2003) Safe upper levels for vitamins and minerals

Forrester I, Hanekamp JC (2006) Precaution, science and jurisprudence: a test case. J Risk Res 9 (4):297–311

Furedi F (2009) Precautionary culture and the rise of possibilistic risk assessment. Erasmus Law Rev 2(2):197–220

Gollier C, Bruno J, Treich N (2000) Scientific progress and irreversibility: an economic interpretation of the precautionary principle. J Pub Econ 75(2):229–253

Graham JD (2001) Decision-analytic refinements of the precautionary principle. J Risk Res 4 (2):127–141

Hanekamp J, Bergkamp L (2016) The 'best available science' and the Paris agreement on climate change. Eur J Risk Reg 7:35–41

Hanekamp JC (2015) Utopia and gospel: unearthing the good news in precautionary culture. Dissertation, Tilburg University, The Netherlands

Hanekamp JC, Bast A (2007) Hormesis in a precautionary regulatory culture: models preferences and the advancement of science. Hum Exp Toxicol 26:855–873

Hanekamp JC, Bast A (2015) Antibiotics exposure and health risks: chloramphenicol. Environ Toxicol Pharmacol 39(1):213–220

Hanekamp JC, Calabrese EJ (2007) Chloramphenicol, European legislation and hormesis. Dose Response 5:91–93

Hanekamp JC, Kwakman J (2004) Beyond zero-tolerance: a novel and global outlook on food-safety and residues of pharmacological active substances in foodstuffs of animal origin. Environ Liabil 1:33–39

Hanekamp JC, Kwakman JHJM (2009) Towards intended normal use (part I): a European appraisal of the chloramphenicol case and some thoughts on the potential of global harmonization of antibiotics regulation. In: Boisrobert C, Stjepanovic A, Oh S, Lelieveld H (eds) Ensuring global food safety: exploring global harmonization. Academic Press, New York, pp 193–208

Hanekamp JC, Pieterman R (2009) Risk communication in precautionary culture–the precautionary coalition. Hum Exp Toxicol 28:15–20

Hanekamp JC, Frapporti G, Olieman K (2003) Chloramphenicol, food safety and precautionary thinking in Europe. Environ Liabil 6:209–221

Hanekamp JC, Verstegen SW, Vera-Navas G (2005) The historical roots of precautionary thinking: the cultural ecological critique and 'The Limits to Growth'. J Risk Res 8(4):295–310

Hanekamp JC, Bast A, Calabrese EJ (2015) Nutrition and health – transforming research traditions. Crit Rev Food Sci Nutr 55(8):1074–1080

Harremoës P, Gee D, MacGarvin M, Stirling A, Keys J, Wynne B, Vaz SG (2001) Late lessons from early warnings: the precautionary principle 1896–2000. Environmental issue report no 22. European Environment Agency, Copenhagen

Heaney RP (2008) Nutrients, endpoints, and the problem of proof. J Nutr 138(9):1591–1595

Hottois G (2000) A philosophical and critical analysis of the European convention of bioethics. J Med Philos 25:133–146

James P, Kemper F, Pascal G (1999) A European food and public health authority. The future of scientific advice in the EU

Joined Cases C-154/04 and C-155/04. See http://eur-lex.europa.eu/LexUriServ/LexUriServ.do?uri=CELEX:62004CJ0154:EN:HTML. Accessed 29 May 2015

Keeney R (1997) Estimating fatalities induced by the economic costs of regulations. J Risk Uncertain 14:5–23

Keeney RL (1994) Mortality risks induced by the costs of regulations. J Risk Uncertain 8:95–110

Kysar DA (2006) It might have been: risk, precaution, and opportunity costs. J Land Use Environ Law 22:1–57

Leamer EE (1983) Let's take the con out of econometrics. Am Econ Rev 73(1):31–43

Majone G (2002) What price safety? The precautionary principle and its policy implications. J Common Mark Stud 40(1):89–109

Mckinney WJ, Hammer Hill H (2000) Of sustainability and precaution: the logical, epistemological, and moral problems of the precautionary principle and their implications for sustainable development. Ethics Environ 5(1):77–87

Morris J (2002) The relationship between risk analysis and the precautionary principle. Toxicology 27:127–130

Munthe C (2011) The price of precaution and the ethics of risk. The international library of ethics, law and technology, vol 6. Springer, New York

Oliver SP, Boor KJ, Murphy SC, Murinda SE (2009) Food safety hazards associated with consumption of raw milk. Foodborne Pathog Dis 6(7):793–806

Otsuki T, Wilson JS, Sewadeh M (2001) Saving two in a billion: quantifying the trade effect of European Food Safety Standards on African exports. Food Policy 26:495–514

Pagnotti VS, Chubatyi ND, McEwen CN (2011) Solvent assisted inlet ionization: an ultrasensitive new liquid introduction ionization method for mass spectrometry. Anal Chem 83:3981–3985

Park J, McFarlane I, Phipps R, Ceddia G (2011) The impact of the EU regulatory constraint of transgenic crops on farm income. New Biotechnol 28(4):396–406

Purnhagen K (2014) The behavioural law and economics of the precautionary principle in the EU and its impact on internal market regulation. J Consum Policy 37:453–464

Quaglia NC, Dambrosio A, Normanno G, Parisi A, Patrono R, Ranieri G, Rella A, Celano GV (2008) High occurrence of Helicobacter pylori in raw goat, sheep and cow milk inferred by glmM gene: a risk of food-borne infection? Int J Food Microbiol 124:43–47

Raffensperger C, Tickner J (eds) (1999) Protecting public health and the environment: implementing the precautionary principle. Island Press, Washington

Regulation (EC) No 178/2002 of the European Parliament and of the Council of 28 January 2002 laying down the general principles and requirements of food law, establishing the European Food Safety Authority and laying down procedures in matters of food safety. O J Eur Comm L31:1–24

Regulation (EC) No 470/2009 of the European Parliament and of the Council of 6 May 2009 laying down Community procedures for the establishment of residue limits of pharmacologically active substances in foodstuffs of animal origin, repealing Council Regulation (EEC) No 2377/90 and amending Directive 2001/82/EC of the European Parliament and of the Council

and Regulation (EC) No 726/2004 of the European Parliament and of the Council. 2009. O J Eur Comm L152:11–22
Regulation 1924/2006 of the European Parliament and of the Council of 20 December 2006 on nutrition and health claims on foods. O J Eur Union L404:9–25
Rolston H III (1988) Environmental ethics. Duties to and ethics in the natural world. Temple University Press, Philadelphia
Rome Declaration on World Food Security (1996) See http://www.fao.org/docrep/003/w3613e/w3613e00.HTM. Accessed 8 June 2015
Scientific Committee on Veterinary Measures Relating to Public Health (SCVPH) (1998) On benefits and limitations of antimicrobial treatments for poultry carcasses
Sien IAR (2007) Beefing up the hormones dispute: problems in compliance and viable compromise alternatives. Georget Law J 95:565–590
Sjöberg L (2000) Perceived risk and tampering with nature. J Risk Res 3(4):353–367
Smyth SJ, Phillips PWB (2014) Risk, regulation and biotechnology: the case of GM crops. GM Crops Food 5(3):170–177
Stern J, Wiener JB (2006) Precaution against terrorism. J Risk Res 9(4):393–447
Sunstein CR (2005) Laws of fear: beyond the precautionary principle. Cambridge University Press, Cambridge
Szajkowska A (2010) The impact of the definition of the precautionary principle in EU food law. Common Mark Law Rev 47:173–196
Tengs TO, Adams ME, Pliskin JS, Safran DG, Siegel JE, Weinstein MC, Graham JD (1995) Five-hundred life-saving interventions and their cost-effectiveness. Risk Anal 15 (3):369–390
The Health Council of the Netherlands (2010) Guideline to the classification of carcinogenic compounds. Report No. A10/07E, The Hague, the Netherlands
Treich N (2001) What is the economic meaning of the precautionary principle? Geneva Pap Risk Insur Issues Pract 26(3):334–345
Turvey CG, Mojduszka EM (2005) The precautionary principle and the law of unintended consequences. Food Policy 30:145–161
Veldman M (1994) Fantasy, the bomb and the greening of Britain. Romantic protest, 1945–1980. Cambridge University Press, Cambridge
Viscusi WK (2015) The role of publication selection bias in estimates of the value of a statistical life. Am J Health Econ 1(1):27–52
Viscusi WK, Aldy J (2003) The value of a statistical life: a critical review of market estimates throughout the world. J Risk Uncertain 27(1):5–76
Vogel D (2012) The politics of precaution: regulating health, safety, and environmental risks in Europe and the United States. Princeton University Press, Princeton
Wildavsky A (1997) But is it true? A citizen's guide to environmental health and safety issues. Harvard University Press, Cambridge

Lucas Bergkamp is a partner in the Brussels office of Hunton Williams Kurth LLP, and assists clients with managing complex risk management issues. Trained as a lawyer and medical doctor, Lucas practices at the interface of regulatory law, policy, and science. He focuses on meeting client needs for smart and cost-effective solutions to environmental, health and safety, life sciences, and other product-related regulatory issues. In addition, he assists client with related transactional work and mitigation of liability exposure.

Lucas is recognized as a leading regulatory lawyer in many legal directories and by many organizations, including Chambers Europe and Legal 500. He has published numerous articles and written several books on regulatory law, and co-authored books on chemical regulation, environmental liability, civil liability for terrorism-related risk, and EU legislative and regulatory processes. From 1996 to 2005, Lucas was Professor of Law at the Erasmus University Rotterdam.

Jaap C. Hanekamp Jr. received his degree in chemistry at Utrecht University, The Netherlands, in 1989. He received his first Ph.D., also in chemistry, from the same institution in 1992, and completed his post-doctoral degree in chemistry at the University of California Riverside. Dr. Hanekamp received his second Ph.D. in philosophy and theology at the University of Tilburg, The Netherlands, in 2015. Since receiving his advanced degree in chemistry, Dr. Hanekamp has served on scientific review committees tasked with auditing the scientific quality of work performed by various Dutch national public health and environmental agencies, and has also served as a scientific auditor mediating between various Dutch and European industries and Dutch and European governmental institutions on scientific and legislative issues, and has prepared reports based on his findings. Since 2007, Dr. Hanekamp has been an Associate Professor at the University College Middleburg in The Netherlands, where he teaches chemistry and the philosophy of science. Also since 2007, Dr. Hanekamp has been Director of HAN-Research, an independent scientific and technological research advisory company that is involved in the evaluation of food, chemical and product safety, and public health and environmental issues. Since 2011, Dr. Hanekamp has also served as Adjunct Faculty Member at the University of Massachusetts Amherst, in the department of Public Health and Environmental Health Sciences. Dr. Hanekamp is the author of more than 60 articles published in peer-reviewed scientific journals.

Enforcement of European Food Laws

Franziska Weber

Abstract Taking the substantive law dimension as a given, this contribution assesses the enforcement policy of European food laws from a law and economics point of view. In this exercise the roles of the European Food Safety Authority and the national enforcement authorities in the Member States are being evaluated. National authorities are primarily responsible to ensure businesses' compliance with food laws and handle situations of non-compliance. Aside of the public law dimension, the private law enforcement dimension is explored also. Overall, when critically assessing the current system against the law and economics criteria as developed by Steven Shavell for the choice between regulation or liability laws, the EU enforcement system can be seen in a rather positive light. Both, the strong role given to public regulators, same as the supplementary role given to private litigation can be supported by economic arguments. In the light of a resource-saving enforcement strategy placing some emphasis on self-regulation, also called "private regulation" within this volume, is likewise warranted.

1 Introduction

Europe has traditionally been strongly involved in the Member States' (MS) agriculture policies. Following some food scandals in the late 1990s the European Commission increasingly took action to harmonize food and feed policy within the European Union (EU). This framework, the starting point of which is the so-called "General food law regulation" (GFL) of 2002,[1] has been further developed over the past years. The main objective of the GFL is to secure a high level of

I wish to thank two anonymous referees for their helpful comments.

[1]See Regulation (EC) No 178/2002 laying down the general principles and requirements of food law (General Food Law Regulation).

F. Weber (✉)
Institute of Law and Economics, Faculty of Law, University of Hamburg, Hamburg, Germany
e-mail: franziska.weber@uni-hamburg.de

H. Bremmers, K. Purnhagen (eds.), *Regulating and Managing Food Safety in the EU*, Economic Analysis of Law in European Legal Scholarship 6,
https://doi.org/10.1007/978-3-319-77045-1_12

protection of public health and consumer interests with regard to food products and, at the same time, the free movement of legally produced and marketed food. The GFL regulation defines "food" in its Art. 2 as meaning "any substance or product, whether processed, partially processed or unprocessed, intended to be, or reasonably expected to be ingested by humans". It further states general principles, establishes the European Food Safety Authority (EFSA) and sets out procedures to deal with emergencies. Broadly speaking, EU food legislation covers product characteristics, the production process (including premises) and product presentation.[2] As the latest development as of 13 December 2014 the rules contained in a new regulation on the provision of food information to consumers apply.[3]

This contribution addresses the enforcement dimension rather than the substantive aspects of European food law when assessing the enforcement structure of EFSA in liaison with national enforcement authorities. It is in fact the national authorities' task to ensure businesses' compliance with EU food laws and handle situations of non-compliance. There is, hence, a strong public law element, which may depending on the MS we are discussing be complemented by private law enforcement of differing shapes.

After setting out the basic enforcement structure of EU food law enforcement (Sect. 2.1), law and economics arguments favouring private as opposed to public law enforcement regarding enforcement in the food industry will be presented (Sect. 2.2) that allow critical reflections on the current European food laws enforcement landscape (Sect. 2.3). Section 3 concludes.

2 The Law and Economics of Food Law Enforcement in Europe

In order to assess the enforcement of European food law a basic understanding of the bodies and mechanisms involved in this exercise is the key.

2.1 Sketching the Landscape

The enforcement dimension of European food law is characterized by an interaction of EU and MS level. In essence, the EU controls the MS. National authorities and private actors control businesses. The primary responsibility to ensure compliance with legal rules in the food sector is put on businesses.[4] Food may not be brought to

[2]As classified by van der Meulen (2013), p. 71.

[3]See Regulation (EU) No 1169/2011 of the European Parliament and of the Council of 25 October 2011 on the provision of food information to consumers.

[4]See van der Meulen (2013), pp. 71, 80.

the market if it is unsafe (Article 14 GFL Regulation). Businesses are to assess this on a case-by-case basis. It is then the public authorities' task to ensure this compliance and solve matters of non-compliance. Any infringement of EU food law triggers an enforcement action. This is the approach taken for most products. Business can, in essence, place them on the market, when they feel that the safety requirements are met ("abuse principle"). For some food products, however, entrance to the market is barred, unless safety is proven to the satisfaction of the authorities *ex ante* ("prohibition principle").[5]

At European Level

The EU policy in the food law context is based on risk analysis—consisting of risk assessment, risk communication and risk management.[6] EFSA is a cornerstone in food safety assessment. The GFL Regulation sets out how EFSA is to provide scientific advice and scientific and technical support in all areas impacting food safety.[7] It is to constitute an independent source of information on all matters in this field and to ensure the transmission of information to the general public. Therefore, it collects and publishes scientific and technical data on food safety matters. The core activity of EFSA in line with EU policy is thus to be responsible for the risk assessment but also the identification of emerging risks. EFSA is involved in the coordination of European networks of organisations operating in the field of food safety.[8]

At Member States Level

The sanctioning powers are vested at MS level. MS are to enforce food law and ensure that food and feed business operators comply at all stages of production, processing and distribution. They are to maintain a system of "official controls and other activities appropriate to the circumstances".[9] Enforcement is done by way of public and private means. Whereas private enforcement operates on an *ex post* basis only, namely once litigation is initiated, public enforcement has an *ex ante* (e.g. monitoring) and *ex post* (e.g. imposition of fines) dimension.

---

[5]The system operates via positive lists.

[6]See Article 3(10) and Recital 17 GFL Regulation.

[7]See Chapter III GFL Regulation. Since its enactment the regulation has been amended a number of times.

[8]Article 22 ff.

[9]Article 15 f. Regulation 882/04.

Public Law Enforcement

The responsibility of the MS to ensure food safety emanates from Article 17 GFL Regulation. They are called upon to test compliance of products marketed within the internal market.[10] As said, one needs to differentiate between the abuse approach and the prohibition approach. Article 17(2) GFL Regulation requires MS to enforce food law and monitor and verify that the relevant requirements of food law are fulfilled by food and feed business operators at all stages of production, processing and distribution. This includes public communication on food and feed safety and risk, food and feed safety surveillance and other monitoring activities covering all stages of production, processing and distribution. More specifically, Article 4 of Regulation 882/2004 "official controls"—which is considered a twin regulation to the GFL regulation—requires MS to set up a competent authority with certain tasks and competences (investigation, methods and techniques, sampling and analysis, reporting, penalties, contingency plans).[11] In essence, the standards for the national operations are set at European level. MS are to lay down their compliance efforts in a Multi-Annual National Control Plan.[12] Additionally, MS are required to lay down the rules on measures and penalties applicable to infringements of food law, which must be effective, proportionate and dissuasive.[13] One aspect to be taken into consideration by the public authority is the nature of the non-compliance and the operator's past record with regard to non-compliance (Article 54 Regulation 882/2004). The sanctions can in essence be administrative injunctions or fines and criminal sanctions (fines and imprisonment) depending on the respective MS.[14] Food products may have to be recalled or (parts of) businesses can be closed down. Article 54 Regulation 882/2004 expresses a whole list of actions and ends with "any other measure the competent authority deems appropriate". The approach taken depends on the type of food product.

Private Law Enforcement

In addition to the public law enforcement side, there is a private law enforcement structure. There is no provision in EU food law as such that grants the individual

[10]See Article 17(1) GLF Regulation.

[11]See Regulation (EC) No 882/2004 of the European Parliament and of the Council of 29 April 2004. A new Regulation (EU) 2017/625 of the European Parliament and of the Council of 15 March 2017 on official controls and other official activities performed to ensure the application of food and feed law, rules on animal health and welfare, plant health and plant protection products has recently entered into force. The new rules will gradually become applicable with the main application date being 14 December 2019. These rules have been published after this contribution was written (June 2015) and will be reflected in future analyses.

[12]See Article 40 Regulation 882/04.

[13]See Article 17 GFL Regulation, Article 55 Regulation 882/04.

[14]See van der Meulen (2013), p. 72.

consumer a remedy that can be invoked in court despite the protection of consumers' health and other consumers' interests being the first and foremost objectives of EU food law.[15] Aside of the regulatory dimension, food and consumer law, however, encompasses various fields that can induce liability. Liability can, for instance, ensue in the context of consumer protection laws, such as product liability law and general contract law.[16]

There is extensive regulation on food labelling to consumers,[17] which restricts the private autonomy of contracting parties. Some quality labels result from private regulation. Consumers may be successful in seeking redress via contract law remedies. Furthermore, infringements of food safety requirements constitute a basis for tort liability[18]: An obvious source may be product liability law, where a lot of harmonization on substantive matters has been going on at Union level.[19] With a view to legislation setting out which information needs to be provided to consumers, there is a link to unfair commercial practices law.[20] Again a lot of harmonization regarding unfair commercial practices law has been going on at European level, leaving the details of the enforcement dimension to the respective MS.[21]

Consumers' rights are said to being increasingly mentioned in EU food law.[22] Consumers' actions are essentially invoked in the MS. Here we, hence, have both dimensions, the public structure, but depending on the country a stronger or less strong involvement of private parties to initiate private liability claims. In addition to individual civil litigation, mass litigation is available to different extents in the different MS. European involvement in the matter of collective actions due to a lack of consensus has not produced any binding legislation.[23] In how far businesses

[15]See van der Meulen (2013), p. 88.

[16]See also Article 21 GFL Regulation.

[17]This was amended and expanded with Regulation 1169/2011 on the provision of food information to consumers.

[18]See van der Meulen (2013), p. 88.

[19]Council Directive 85/374/EEC of 25 July 1985 on the approximation of the laws, regulations and administrative provisions of the Member States concerning liability for defective products, OJ L 210, 7.8.1985, pp. 29–33; see also Article 21 GFL Regulation.

[20]See Directive 2005/29/EC of the European Parliament and of the Council of 11 May 2005 concerning unfair business-to-consumer commercial practices in the internal market.

[21]Directive 2005/29/EC of the European Parliament and of the Council of 11 May 2005 concerning unfair business-to-consumer commercial practices in the internal market, OJ L 149, 11.6.2005, pp. 22–39.

[22]See van der Meulen (2013), p. 88.

[23]In the context of harmonization efforts at European level, rather recently Commission Recommendation of 11 June 2013 on common principles for injunctive and compensatory collective redress mechanisms in the Member States concerning violations of rights granted under Union Law, OJ L 201, 26.7.2013, pp. 60–65 and Communication from the Commission to the European Parliament, the Council, the European Economic and Social Committee and the Committee of the regions "Towards a European Horizontal Framework for Collective Redress", COM(2013) 401 final have been adopted.

can take action against their competitors lastly also depends on the respective rules governing competition law.

With the primary responsibility of compliance with product safety standards being placed upon businesses, an emergence of co-regulation by which self-regulatory schemes and public regulators interact can be observed in the MS.[24] In this way market players play an even stronger role in ensuring EU food safety compliance. Again, the intensity varies depending on the MS concerned.

To align the European and the MS interests, there is, for instance, an intensive training programme managed by the Commission Services.[25] National authorities are to report back certain activities to the European Commission. When a national authority, by way of example, adopts measures to restrict the placing on the market of a product or force the withdrawal or recall of food or feed, it is to immediately notify the Commission.[26] The Commission has a role to play when it comes to adopting emergency measures. Furthermore, according to Article 45 Regulation 882/2004 Commission officials are involved in auditing the action taken at MS level in verifying whether the Multi-Annual National Control Plan is observed. Article 34 (and following) of the same regulation sets out how the competent authorities in the different MS are to assist each other if a matter concerns various MS.

2.2 An Economic Appraisal

From an economic point of view the established goal of law enforcement is to create incentives to comply with the law by way of deterring illegal behaviour with an adequate sanction.[27] In the deterrence framework, expected liability matters to the potential wrongdoer *ex ante*, that is, before a wrong is committed.[28] This approach stems from criminal law enforcement and is meanwhile applied more broadly as a benchmark allowing a systematic answer regarding the structure of an enforcement response.[29] The underlying assumption of this model is that (potential) wrongdoers are rational utility maximisers, and therefore weigh possible benefits against the costs of their behaviour.[30] It is assumed that only if the costs of committing a wrong

[24]See Martinez et al. (2007), pp. 299–314. They argue how this approach is strongest in the UK. Fagotto (2014), pp. 83–109 regarding the role and importance of private food safety standards.

[25]See Article 51 Regulation 882/2004.

[26]See van der Meulen (2013), p. 87.

[27]See Ogus (2004), p. 46.

[28]See Shavell (2004), p. 515.

[29]Becker's model is the most often cited; see Becker (1968), pp. 169–217; see also Schäfer (2000), p. 184.

[30]These days behavioural economics that strongly questions the rational choice perspective is, furthermore, gaining more and more importance.

outweigh the benefits, a rational individual will comply with the law.[31] Factors that influence the cost side of the wrongdoer are the magnitude of the sanction and the probabilities of detection and conviction. Those, in turn, depend on the law enforcement mechanism that is put in place. As a consequence, potential wrongdoers will respond differently to public and private law enforcement or a combination of both. Deterrence can be achieved by way of both. *Steven Shavell* has developed criteria with a view to the suitability of liability rules—i.e. private law enforcement—vis-à-vis regulation—i.e. public law enforcement—in a regulated environment.[32] He determines how risky activities should be controlled on the basis of four core criteria:

1. Is there an information advantage of a public authority over private parties or vice versa? This would make one of the options more attractive depending on the regulated environment.
2. Is there an insolvency risk with the defendants? If the defendants were facing a private liability suit that was beyond their assets, they could not be deterred fully by private law enforcement. Public law enforcement works differently. In the regulatory context, they would have needed to comply with certain standards in order to be allowed to carry out a certain activity in the first place.[33]
3. Another aspect concerns the question whether the responsible parties would face a suit for the harm done in court at all. Reasons for why this may not be the case in *Shavell's* words are dispersed harm, a long lapse of time before harm eventuates and difficulties in attributing the harm to the responsible party. More commonly these days one focuses on the rational victim's cost benefit analysis. He will not act if costs outweigh the benefits, for instance when harm is very small and the investment to enforce the law is costly.[34] This is the so-called 'rational apathy'. If harm to the society is large, for example in a case of small and widespread harm, no enforcement action may happen because of a divergence between the individual and social incentive to sue.[35] This harms society and reduces incentives to comply. Before switching to other enforcement mechanisms like public regulation to cure this problem, one can look for solutions within private law enforcement. Any form of grouping claims can, for instance, lead to cost reductions for the participating individuals and thereby reduce rational apathy.[36] There are, however, also cases, in which instead of the suing party the defendant turns out to be the victim—the victim of a 'frivolous lawsuit'. Such an action is not based

[31]Note that for this contribution we only address the external costs (such as fines and damage payments) that would induce compliance. However, there can be other elements than the external legal rules that may induce behaviour as well, such as social norms as well as intrinsic motivation.

[32]See Shavell (1984), pp. 357–374.

[33]This approach, hence, only fits with products that need to be cleared before entering the Internal market.

[34]See van den Bergh (2007), p. 184.

[35]See Landes and Posner (1975), p. 33.

[36]See Keske et al. (2010), p. 59.

on merits. No societal resources should be spent on such a case. Frivolous actions become particularly worrisome if they are followed by a wrong decision. Error costs refer to courts taking mistaken decisions,[37] but can be expanded to anyone who decides a legal matter. Error costs can generally be divided into two groups: Error I costs are those that occur when an individual who is guilty might mistakenly be found not liable ('mistaken acquittal'). Error II costs on the other hand occur if an innocent individual might mistakenly be found liable ('mistaken conviction'). Both cases dilute deterrence. Another reason why a victim refrains from taking action is the so-called 'free-riding' problem. We can imagine a situation in which many victims suffer from a food law infringement but all gain as soon as one of them complains. For each individual it is beneficial to wait for someone else to do so and then profit from the result.[38] Again a socially desirable action may not happen. We can see how this is clearly interrelated with the remedy sought. One can again think of designs of group litigation that reduce the free-riding mentality, if strictly only those who contribute to the proceedings are allowed to profit from them.[39] In the end collective actions may cure some aspects of individual litigation but need to be designed well not to fall flaw to their own problems.[40]

4. And lastly, mechanisms differ as to their regulatory costs. These refer, in essence, to any costs incurred in administering law enforcement (e.g. maintenance of infrastructure, personnel, procedures to impose remedies).

What does this more specifically mean for the choice between public and private enforcement in the context of food regulation?

Private Law Enforcement

The first crucial parameter is the question in whose hands the relevant information regarding legal violations is. Before a civil court, claimants must provide most of the evidence and may not rely on the inquisition of the judge—the core of the principle of party presentation. Therefore, if the individual misses information, lawsuits may be impeded if lawyers or civil judges cannot generate it either. Many food law violations as a matter of fact are difficult to detect for private individuals. They may not even notice that harm has occurred. Another problem may be the wrongdoer's

[37] See Posner (2000), p. 291. He refers to system costs as 'direct costs' for operating the legal dispute-resolution machinery.

[38] See Landes and Posner (1975), p. 29.

[39] See van den Bergh (2013), p. 14.

[40] For some aspects regarding the design and incentive problems between the representative and the represented parties, see Keske et al. (2010).

identity and location.[41] Also such cases are imaginable regarding businesses operating in the food sector. When it comes to expert knowledge regarding a scientific matter, this could well enter a civil court procedure by way of appointing an expert.

The insolvency risk of the wrongdoer is also labelled the problem of the "judgment-proof wrongdoer". As to insolvency, law and economics literature argues that private law generally provides only purely monetary sanctions that cannot sufficiently deter a judgment-proof offender.[42] This is generally true. However, a civil law injunction is different because that prospect can be a powerful deterrent for a trader.[43] With mass damage in food law cases, like the BSE scandal, one can easily imagine how compensation claims would surmount a wrongdoer's assets.[44] It is, hence, a valid consideration.

As to the other impediments in civil procedure the following can be remarked. In a civil procedure primarily court and lawyer's fees are incurred. Depending on the cost rule (e.g. loser-pays rule), the parties have to bear them to differing extents. Both parameters will determine the cost side in an individual's calculation. The individual will weigh them up against possible benefits from initiating a legal action. Needless to say a substantial damage payment will impact this calculation differently than a minor compensation payment. In one case an individual will initiate a lawsuit, whereas in the other case rational apathy may come into play. The severity of the 'rational apathy' problem primarily depends on litigation fees (for instance, reduced by alternative dispute resolution tools), allocation rules for civil procedure costs, the confidence of winning and the remedy sought. In the context of food regulation both type of damage to individual consumers are imaginable. So the danger of under-enforcement due to rational apathy must be considered, particularly in cases of small and widespread harm.[45] To remedy this disincentive, the enforcement mechanism may offer options for risk sharing (e.g. legal aid or legal insurance).[46] One can consider how far procedures can be joined to reduce the individual's costs. Thus these are ways to improve the risk allocation, i.e. by sharing it.

Regarding the potential for frivolous lawsuits in general, it can be assumed that a single lawsuit will not generate huge reputational harm. Things might look differently for lawsuits involving two competitors[47] or if claims were bundled.[48] One can particularly think of competitors being inclined to take up such type of action in the

[41]See van den Bergh (2007), p. 201; Cseres (2012), p. 192; for tort law scenarios, see Shavell (1993), p. 274; the hit-and-run offender is a classical example of an attempt to conceal someone's identity.

[42]See Shavell (2004), p. 473. An insolvent trader cannot be deterred by purely monetary sanctions. In practice, this is where insurances and funds come into play. In contract law, the judgment-proof problem is mitigated, according to Shavell (2004), p. 586, as people tend to know about each other.

[43]See Faure et al. (2009), p. 176.

[44]There is obviously an inter-linkage with the insurance market.

[45]See Shavell (1997), p. 577.

[46]See Shavell (1997), p. 576; Visscher and Schepens (2010).

[47]Compare the situation of competitors in antitrust cases, Renda et al. (2007), p. 563.

[48]See Schäfer (2000), p. 184.

food sector. This danger depends upon the potential gains that can be achieved. It can be countered by systems filtering out such cases quickly or imposing sanctions on such undesirable behaviour.

Free-riding may occur in cases of injunctions or reforms resulting from a judgment that provides benefits to people other than the claimant. The allocation of risks to all who profit from a remedy would have to be guaranteed to avoid the risk of inaction due to a free-rider problem. Free riding may be less likely if risks to the individual are reduced. The decisive factors for the free-riding problem seem to be the effect of the remedy and the costs of the procedure. If a competitor reaped benefits from an intervention, he might be inclined to act (in a way instead of consumers but at the same time to their benefit).

Each country's procedural law will, furthermore, stipulate for how long a wrongdoer can be held responsible for the harm he/she caused and how causality can be determined. These questions would not be relevant if compliance with food regulation was a precondition to being admitted to being a market participant at all—i.e. for Europe products falling under the prohibition principle.

Regarding the incurred administrative costs, these, in the civil court, are the time, effort and legal expenses that private parties bear, as well as the public expenses of conducting civil trials.[49] Few studies exist that measure these costs accurately. Litigation costs of small claims are normally lower than those of large claims.[50] As has been stressed by *Shavell*, one of the strengths of the private liability system is that it induces compliance even when no or very few cases are brought to court.[51] Costs are reduced because (to a large extent) they are only incurred if a case is actually litigated.

Public Law Enforcement

If law infringements are difficult to discover, an agency's lower costs of information discovery can be beneficial.[52] This is very relevant in the context of food safety. When information becomes highly technical or scientific, a public authority might be better equipped to gather or produce it.[53] Technological developments such as information systems (databases) shift the efficiency arguments in favour of the public sector. Economies of scale generally support using the public law system in this context, particularly if duplication of enforcement costs among private parties were to occur.[54] This is true for the *ex ante* aspects of regulating in the context of risk

[49]See for instance: Shavell (1984), p. 364.

[50]See Duggan (2003), p. 48.

[51]See Shavell (1984), p. 364.

[52]See for consumer law and competition law: van den Bergh (2007).

[53]See Shavell (1993), p. 270; Hood et al. (2001), p. 73.

[54]See Landes and Posner (1975), p. 29: An example would be competition authorities that do not only have more resources, but also wide investigate powers that an individual could not make use

assessments and compliance checks throughout the life of a food product. When it comes to enforcing its regulations public authorities may likewise have advantages in locating wrongdoers, by making use of their investigative powers and the ability to cooperate with other authorities (also across borders). For instance, tracking online traders that offer food products (digital investigation) requires certain particular investigative powers that are unavailable to individuals. The public authority has tools at its disposal that the individual lacks. Administrative law enforcement allows for continuous information gathering through monitoring or market studies to detect infringements.

Regarding insolvent wrongdoers, *Shavell* points us to regulatory enforcement because parties need to comply in order to be able to engage in a certain activity.[55] This is certainly the case if a product's access to the market is otherwise barred, if it has to be cleared by a public authority. It is not true with a view to food products for which a responsibility is put on businesses to ensure compliance when placing a product on the market. This means that they may commit regulatory breaches in this process and we would again need to look at the sanctioning mechanisms. Also administrative law has primarily monetary sanctions, like fines, in its power. However, sanctions such as license revocation available to a public agency might be effective with regard to a judgment-proof wrongdoer.[56] Here, an important advantage would be given with criminal law enforcement as the system's various available sanctions include non-monetary ones, primarily imprisonment, that serve to remedy the issue of a judgment-proof defendant.[57] Imprisonment is essential as a deterrent[58] and is the desirable sanction when the probability of detection and conviction is low and the likelihood of defendants being judgment-proof is high.[59]

Public enforcement similar to group litigation involves means to reduce the costs of the individual. With widely dispersed harm, a case can also be made for public enforcement to uphold the threat of a lawsuit, as the individual clearly does not have an incentive to sue. Risk allocation is improved with the state assuming part of the risk.[60] Individuals can report to public authorities or they can act, formulate regulations, investigate and enforce them on an own motion.

Depending on the case, some form of reporting—with potential rational apathy problems—may be necessary to make the authority aware of an infringement. Because many violations may be hidden or can only be detected with high costs

of. Also economies of scope can speak in favour of the involvement of a public authority, see Trebilcock (2003), p. 84.

[55]See Shavell (1984), p. 361.

[56]See Trebilcock (2003), p. 84; Faure et al. (2009), p. 178, elaborate on the issue of licenses and how this can possibly have a higher deterrent effect for traders than imprisonment.

[57]See Bowles et al. (2008), p. 402; Shavell (1985), p. 1247; Shavell (2004), p. 544.

[58]See Shavell (2004), p. 532.

[59]See Bowles et al. (2008), p. 405.

[60]Ultimately, of course, tax payers' money finances the whole system.

and with technical expertise, pro-active *ex ante* monitoring by public authorities may be necessary since a reactive approach would not suffice to detect violations.[61]

Frivolous lawsuits seem to be less of an issue within administrative law enforcement, at least in the classical sense. The public official decides which investigations into non-compliance to carry out. The challenge effectively becomes to design the selection process well, possibly designing some ways of challenging a public official's decision not to investigate a certain matter.

Within an administrative procedure the danger of error costs depends on the complexity of the issues to be solved, and on the resources, expertise and experience of the public authority.[62] The occurrence of error costs is more likely in administrative enforcement compared with criminal law enforcement, because the decisionmaking process is less elaborate.[63]

It is common to public authorities that the action they take is beneficial for the whole society. If an agency is involved, free-riding is rather unlikely because individuals are forced to contribute to the litigation expenses through taxes.[64] However, a discrepancy might exist in terms of who contributes and who profits from an action.

In stark contrast to civil litigation the benefits for individuals within administrative law enforcement usually do not include compensation.[65] The possibility of obtaining compensation is an important motivation.[66] This has the potential to reduce the incentive for an individual to involve a public agency. Public agencies traditionally have remedies like injunctions, revocation of licenses or fines at their disposition. For an authority to obtain necessary information monitoring may be an alternative source of information, as will cooperation with e.g. consumer advice centres or other organisations working with food laws. If the authority works on the basis of giving out permits, as a consequence of checking whether companies fulfil the necessary requirements harm may not occur in the first place.

As has been stressed by *Shavell*, one of the strengths of the private liability system is that it only incurs costs whenever a case is brought. Regulation will always lead to costs. Safety regulation (enforced through administrative law) would work to a large extent *ex ante*, would not be triggered by actual harm and could therefore potentially lead to high costs.[67] This assessment varies with the type of cases at hand. The *ex ante* dimension may not always be more important than the *ex post* dimension if, for

---

[61]See Faure et al. (2009).

[62]See van den Bergh (2007), p. 195. See also Ogus (2004), p. 44 where he distinguished the burden of proof and procedural safeguards between criminal law and administrative law from high to low.

[63]See Faure et al. (2009), p. 176.

[64]See van den Bergh (2008), p. 305.

[65]However, in some cases the individual can use the outcome of the administrative law enforcement in a subsequent private law suit.

[66]See Shavell (1993), p. 267: other incentives for an individual are the desire to avoid future harm, the retributive motive, and possibly a fear of reprisal.

[67]See Shavell (1984).

instance, a lot of compliance checks have to be carried out. The main costs with public enforcement occur in the form of monitoring and investigation: particularly, the use of investigative powers.[68]

Interim Conclusions

Arguing along the four steps that Shavell suggests the following conclusions can be drawn:

The theoretical assessment identifies public law enforcement as the primary player in the context of food law. This is particularly true because of the information advantage that is vested in public enforcement. Specialized knowledge is necessary in the context of food safety regulation, for its formulation and during compliance checks. At the same time, experts from the authorities may also be able to intervene in court proceedings, providing expert advice. One has to distinguish different shapes that information can have. Some information may be in the hands of private individuals that would make use of it in order to obtain compensation. To avoid that this information is lacking in the overall enforcement response, either private individuals may be able to litigate in court or systems must in a position to share such information with public authorities. In how far individuals are inclined to share information with a public authority may depend on the remedies they could obtain there, the benefits they would have or possibly the sanctions they would face if they did not share.

Public law enforcement scores better than private law enforcement regarding the judgment proof-wrongdoer. However, we have seen that only criminal law may provide for deterrence in all cases.

There are potential incentive problems regarding the rational expectation that a case will be initiated in the civil court and successfully litigated. The problems of rational apathy and free-riding have been referred to. Public law enforcement may be a cure to many of these problems. Some cases can be solved by allowing for forms of collective action.

The advantage of civil litigation is that (most of the) costs are only incurred whenever an actual case is litigated. A regulatory approach leads, on the other hand, to constant administrative costs. Identifying the costs in detail is challenging. These costs are particularly high if a lot of responsibilities are placed on the public authority to carry out (*ex ante*) checks. They can be reduced if responsibility is placed upon the operators in the market. In this case, non-compliance with the regulation triggers an enforcement response just as liability rules do. Hence, again (to a large extent) costs in these scenarios only occur once there are reasons to expect non-compliance.

The outcome provides a mixed picture and leads to the conclusion that aiding the key public players by some supplementary private law enforcement may be warranted. This may at the same time serve as a disciplining mechanism. As the

[68]See Wittmann (1977), p. 207.

name suggests, public officials work in the public interest. When it comes to assessing public servants' behaviour and predictability, a rather severe issue in a public authority is the risk of capture that induces under-enforcement.[69] An official that is "captured" starts working in the interests of the group (e.g. a certain lobby) instead of the public interest. Regulation to separate competences either by different entities or different units may be warranted,[70] and the possibility of appeals and reviews (as generally given within administrative procedural law) may reduce the occurrence of this risk. Another measure is the case selection procedure and ways to challenge the authority's refusal to investigate. Involving court judges in one way or another could mitigate the problem. One way would be to allow some civil litigation. Another possibility may be to have public agencies litigate some cases in the courts. The courts would then be a neutral decision-maker that eliminates "captured" decisions. Another related concern with a pure reliance on public regulators is that when deciding which policies to adopt they may be looking too much at costs rather than at the benefits.[71]

Having in mind a resource-saving enforcement approach, making use of private-regulatory techniques in the food market could also be desirable. One of the presumed advantages of self-regulation is that it generates better information (since traders—experts—would be better informed than bureaucrats).[72] Thus such a system would, given the information advantage, be able to solve cases of non-compliance at lower costs than a court system or a system relying purely on public regulation. Moreover, such a system is often privately financed (by industry), which may have substantial advantages in providing incentives for cost reduction.[73] Then again, the risk of capture is embedded in self-regulation. According to some authors, self-regulation runs the risk of being the 'ultimate form' of regulatory capture, as there is obviously a tight link with the industry.[74] It may be crucial for governments to play an 'active role' in monitoring self-regulatory activities.[75] Self-regulatory entities enforcing codes of conducts are also typically much more limited in their sanctioning powers. Again an interlinkage with other, more powerful, enforcers is crucial to incentivize compliance with self-regulatory schemes. Such schemes will not work with businesses operating in the food market that do not care about their reputation as they exert very limited binding power.

---

[69]See Ogus (1994), p. 57. For the food sector more specifically, see Henson and Caswell (1999).

[70]See Cafaggi and Micklitz (2009), p. 406: 'In theory the use of public agencies to monitor and directly sanction would seem to be more effective than separating administrative monitoring from judicial enforcement. But especially in relation to cooperative enforcement, when the enforcer has to conclude agreements with the infringer, the resort to an independent judiciary may ensure transparency and reduce capture. Thus the higher the use of cooperative enforcement, the more necessary it is to resort to separation between monitoring and enforcement.'

[71]Martinez et al. (2007), p. 312.

[72]See on the advantages of self-regulation inter alia Ogus (1995).

[73]This may, however, also lead to biased decision-making.

[74]See Stephen and Love (2000), p. 990.

[75]See Miller (1985), p. 903.

The nature of food regulation requires an interaction of public and private law enforcement, with a strong emphasis on publicly controlled or checked scientific investigation. Public enforcement is a cure where incentive problems impede individual civil litigation (to which establishing collective actions is also a potential cure). Private law enforcement can be reverted to when private information is needed. How effective public regulators in the food context can be depends not the least on the resources that are allocated and the number of checks that can hence be carried out. Involving private players (like competitors) may be a resource-saving strategy. The same is true for making use of self-regulatory means for the type of traders for which they are effective. For rogue traders where the regulator's powers are not sufficient, one may have to consider the criminal law dimension to provide accurate deterrence. The most powerful response to judgment proof wrongdoers is likewise to be found with criminal sanctions.

2.3 Application to the European Approach

Assessing this outcome against the European enforcement strategy with a view to food law, that has been set out in the beginning, the following picture can be drawn:

There is a clear need to generate scientific information—a task coordinated by EFSA. This information is made available to all players in the European food market (businesses, national regulators, consumers, consumer associations). EFSA is therefore an important information generator, serving to reduce information asymmetries between consumers and producers and between different producers.

The sanctioning powers are allocated to the MS level. The sanctions available to such public authorities are indeed very wide. Deterrence is therefore likely. Sanctions may even be criminal in nature, responding to concerns expressed as the "judgment-proof-problem". As said, the catalogue of sanctions that MS authorities may apply is open. They could theoretically prescribe any other remedies (e.g. compensation). To fine-tune the picture a more careful analysis of each MS' precise enforcement system would be needed. The activities of public authorities cure rational apathy or free-riding problems. Wide investigative powers and the possibility to cooperate with other authorities across boarders ensure that much information can be generated in the process. The question is whether they also get all the necessary information that is in private hands.

Private action is possible on an individual basis in the context of liability claims (via contract law, tort law and unfair commercial practices law). It is worthwhile exploring whether mass damage cases for harmed individuals are possible. This is the case only in very few MS. As regards mass actions Europe is so far rather reluctant. However, action can be taken by competitors in the context of unfair commercial practices or competition law. The existence of this dimension is crucial for cases that the public authority neglects.

As said there are various means by which it can be ensured that the risk of capture is kept low. Public officials need to be disciplined. The national approaches vary but clearly the Commission builds up some oversight in auditing the action taken at MS level.

In essence, both enforcement dimensions—the public and the private one—are represented with a focus on public law enforcement. This integration, i.e. mix, is supported by *Shavell's* categorisation. Many variations exist in the MS. This is true for the amount of powers and types of sanctions granted to public authorities but particularly for the extent to which there is a private law dimension. In terms of aiding the public regulators and thereby ensuring an adequate level of deterrence, enabling private litigation is to some extent needed. Well-designed collective actions may enhance this approach further in the future. Competitors are generally empowered to file cases. Lastly, the benefits of self-regulation are reaped in some of the MS with a view to bona fide traders. As a public regulator is a given in every MS, different forms of co-regulation will emerge.

3 Conclusion

EU food law enforcement has a European and a MS dimension. In the context of this contribution attention was paid to the overall European approach, rather than to the specificities of different European MS. Furthermore, the assessment was carried out primarily from the perspective of deterrence-induced compliance and only partly from the compensation perspective. It turns out that when critically assessing the current system against the law and economics criteria as developed by *Steven Shavell* for the choice between regulation or liability laws, the current system can be seen in a rather positive light. It ensures a strong public law enforcement dimension, not least due to the requirements made by EU legislation. Furthermore, in each MS enforcement is complemented by a private law dimension to differing degrees. To ensure that it is a credible complement, more attention in the future may have to be drawn to allowing mass litigation. Furthermore, MS differ in the extent to which they employ self-regulation. A lot of such standard setting has a European or even international basis though. MS also differ as to the sanctioning powers granted, with some imposing criminal fines and imprisonment. For rogue traders operating in the food sector such deterrent sanctions may indeed be necessary.

Whereas this was a purely theoretical exercise, a next step could be taken with an empirical assessment of which instruments and regulatory measures are effective and which are not. Clearly, to provide a more comprehensive picture the enforcement landscape of the respective MS would need to be investigated in more detail.

References

Becker G (1968) Crime and punishment: an economic approach. J Polit Econ 76:169–217

Bowles R, Faure MG, Garoupa N (2008) The scope of criminal law and criminal sanctions: an economic view and policy implications. J Law Soc 35(3):389–416

Cafaggi F, Micklitz H-W (2009) Administrative and judicial enforcement in consumer protection: the way forward. In: Cafaggi F, Micklitz H-W (eds) New frontiers of consumer protection – the interplay between private and public enforcement. Intersentia, Antwerp, pp 401–445
Cseres KJ (2012) Consumer protection in the European Union. In: van den Bergh RJ, Pacces AM (eds) Regulation and economics (vol. 9, encyclopedia of law and economics), 2nd edn. Edward Elgar, Cheltenham, pp 163–222
Duggan AJ (2003) Consumer access to justice in common law countries: a survey of the issues from a law and economics perspective. In: Rickett CEF, Telfer TGW (eds) International perspectives on Consumers' access to justice. Cambridge University Press, Cambridge, pp 46–67
Fagotto E (2014) Private roles in food safety provision: the law and economics of private food safety. Eur J Law Econ 37(1):83–109
Faure MG, Ogus AI, Philipsen NJ (2009) Curbing consumer financial losses: the economics of regulatory enforcement. Law Policy 31(2):161–191
Henson S, Caswell J (1999) Food safety regulation: an overview of contemporary issues. Food Policy 24(6):589–603
Hood C, Rothstein H, Baldwin R (2001) The government of risk: understanding risk regulation regimes. Oxford University Press, New York
Keske S, Renda A, van den Bergh R (2010) Financing and group litigation. In: Tuil M, Visscher L (eds) New trends in financing civil litigation in Europe - a legal, empirical and economic analysis. Edward Elgar, Cheltenham, pp 57–92
Landes WM, Posner RA (1975) The private enforcement of law. J Leg Stud 4:1–46
Martinez MG, Fearne A, Caswell JA, Henson S (2007) Co-regulation as a possible model for food safety governance: opportunities for public-private partnerships. Food Policy 32:299–314
Miller JC (1985) The FTC and voluntary standards: maximizing the net benefits of self-regulation. Cato J 4(3):897–903
Ogus AI (1994) Regulation: legal form and economic theory. Clarendon Press, Oxford
Ogus AI (1995) Rethinking self-regulation. Oxf J Leg Stud 15:97–108
Ogus AI (2004) Enforcing regulation: do we need the criminal law? In: Sjörgen H, Skogh G (eds) New perspectives on economic crime. Edward Elgar, Cheltenham, pp 42–56
Posner RA (2000) An economic approach to legal procedure and judicial administration. In: Parisi F (ed) The economic structure of the law: the collected economic essays of Richard A. Posner. Edward Elgar, Cheltenham, pp 290–349
Renda A et al (2007) Making antitrust damages actions more effective in the EU: welfare impact and potential scenarios. Report for the European Commission/Contract DG COMP/2006/A3/012
Schäfer H-B (2000) The bundling of similar interests in litigation. The incentives for class action and legal actions taken by associations. Eur J Law Econ 9(3):183–213
Shavell S (1984) Liability for harm versus regulation of safety. J Leg Stud 13(2):357–374
Shavell S (1985) Criminal law and the optimal use of nonmonetary sanctions as a deterrent. Columbia Law Rev 85:1232–1262
Shavell S (1993) The optimal structure of law enforcement. J Law Econ 36:255–288
Shavell S (1997) The fundamental divergence between the private and the social motive to use the legal system. J Leg Stud 16:575–612
Shavell S (2004) Foundations of economic analysis of law. The Belknap Press of Harvard University Press, Cambridge
Stephen FH, Love JH (2000) Regulation of the legal profession. In: Bouckaert B, De Geest G (eds) Encyclopedia of law and economics volume III. The regulation of contracts. Edward Elgar, Cheltenham, pp 987–1017
Trebilcock MJ (2003) Rethinking consumer protection policy. In: Rickett CEF, Telfer TGW (eds) International perspectives on Consumers' access to justice. Cambridge University Press, Cambridge, pp 68–98

van den Bergh R (2007) Should consumer protection law be publicly enforced? In: van Boom WH, Loos MBM (eds) Collective enforcement of consumer law. Europa Law Publishing, Groningen, pp 179–203

van den Bergh R (2008) Enforcement of consumer law by consumer associations. In: Faure MG, Stephen FH (eds) Essays in the law and economics of regulation - in honour of Anthony Ogus. Intersentia, Antwerpen, pp 279–306

van den Bergh R (2013) Private enforcement of European competition law and the persisting collective action problem. Maastricht J 1:12–34

van der Meulen BMJ (2013) The structure of European food law. Laws 2:69–98

Visscher LT, Schepens T (2010) A law and economics approach to cost shifting, fee arrangements and legal expense insurance. In: Tuil ML, Visscher LT (eds) New trends in financing civil litigation in Europe: a legal, empirical and economic analysis. Edward Elgar, Cheltenham, pp 7–32

Wittmann D (1977) Prior regulation versus post liability: the choice between input and output monitoring. J Leg Stud 6:193–212

Franziska Weber is a Junior professor of Civil Law and Law & Economics at the Institute of Law & Economics, University of Hamburg, since October 2013. Besides she is a Research Affiliate at Erasmus University Rotterdam (The Netherlands). She wrote her dissertation entitled "Towards an optimal mix of public and private enforcement in consumer law?" within the EDLE (European Doctorate in Law and Economics)-Program at the Universities of Rotterdam, Bologna and Hamburg. She is a comparative jurist and eligible to the bar in Germany and in Spain.

The Economics of Harmonization of Food Law in the EU

Michael Faure

Abstract This chapter applies the economics of federalism to the harmonization of food law in the EU. The economic criteria for centralization (more particularly transboundary externalities, the risk of a race to the bottom and a reduction of transaction costs) are used to ask the question whether some centralization of food law may be warranted. The question is also asked whether harmonization of food law could serve the goal of market integration.

In addition to sketching the economic principles of centralization the evolution of EU food law is sketched and compared to the economic theory. It is sketched how EU food law now represents a hybrid system. Still, an important Law and Economics scholarship argues that even though there may be strong arguments for some intervention at the EU level, currently directives go much too far in prescribing requirements concerning food, which may not always reflect the diverging preferences of citizens as far as food safety is concerned.

1 Introduction

This chapter will focus on one of the important regulatory challenges of food safety in the internal market, being the question to what extent and under which particular circumstances harmonization of food law in the EU is needed. A theoretical approach will be used to answer that question, more particularly the economics of federalism. Hence, the goal is not so much to focus on current EU food safety law (as that will be done in many other chapters) but rather to analyze from a theoretical perspective whether in a federal system, like the EU, food safety should be regulated at a decentralized (Member State) or rather at a centralized (EU) level.

The economics of federalism has developed an interesting theory which allows to address this question by examining the criteria for centralization. Starting point is indeed

M. Faure (✉)
METRO, Maastricht and Erasmus School of Law, Rotterdam, The Netherlands
e-mail: michael.faure@maastrichtuniversity.nl

H. Bremmers, K. Purnhagen (eds.), *Regulating and Managing Food Safety in the EU*, Economic Analysis of Law in European Legal Scholarship 6,
https://doi.org/10.1007/978-3-319-77045-1_13

that through a decentralized approach a beneficial competition between jurisdictions can emerge which can guarantee that legislation is provided corresponding to the preferences of citizens. This competitive process may lead to differentiated legal rules which equally can have the advantage of mutual learning, thus increasing the quality of regulation. However, this presumption in favour of decentralization disappears when particular conditions are met. For example in the case of transboundary externalities there may be a strong argument in favour of centralization. As food travels at first blush the risk of transboundary externalities may be large. However, it needs careful examination whether states would indeed be able, e.g. by adopting low quality food safety law, to externalize risks to others. A second reason justifying centralization may be the danger of a race to the bottom. If there were empirical evidence that states would engage in a destructive race, trying to attract food industry with low quality legislation, this would again be an argument in favour of centralization. The probably most compelling argument in the European context may be an internal market one, being that non-harmonized food safety standards could endanger the free flow of products between Member States as a result of mutual distrust or the danger that barriers to entry would be created. Other arguments could still justify centralization (like a reduction of transaction costs or providing a minimum level of protection) although they may be less convincing.

The goal of this chapter is to discuss the emergence of an EU-wide food safety law from the perspective of the economics of federalism, thus attempting to provide a theoretical basis to EU harmonization of food safety law. However, public choice theory has also pointed at the fact that decisions about (de)centralization will obviously not only be taken on the basis of objective criteria, but may sometimes be the result of lobbying by influential interest groups. To the extent that a deviation would be observed between the ideal division of labour from an economic perspective and the actual division of labour, it is often the result of lobbying by interest groups, who can equally gain advantage by allocating powers to particular levels of governance. This issue will only be touched upon since it will be elaborated in more detail in the next chapter, focusing in detail on capture issues by Alessandra Acuri.

The chapter will be set up as follows: after an introduction (Sect. 1) the basic principles of the economics of federalism will be summarized (Sect. 2); criteria for harmonization of food law in the EU will be critically reviewed (Sect. 3) and a few policy consequences will be discussed (Sect. 4). Section 5 concludes.

2 Basic Economic Principles[1]

2.1 Tiebout

The question of whether regulation should be promulgated at a central (European or federal) level or at a more decentralized level (or, to generalize, what kind of regulation should be set at which level) has been addressed in the economics of

[1]This section builds further on Faure (2003).

federalism. The starting point for the analysis is usually Tiebout's theory about the optimal provision of local public goods.[2] Tiebout argued that when people with the same preferences cluster together in communities, competition between local authorities will, under certain restrictive conditions, lead to allocative efficiency. If there are, for example, in one community citizens who greatly prefer sporting facilities and in another a majority of citizens with a preference for opera, the first community will probably construct sporting facilities, whereas the second may build an opera house. If someone living in the second community preferred sporting facilities to the opera house, he could then move to the first community, which apparently provides services more to his taste. The idea is that well-informed citizens will move to the community that provides the local services that are best adapted to their personal preferences. Through this so-called "voting with the feet", competition between local authorities will lead citizens to cluster together according to their preferences.[3] In practice, it is clear that different communities do indeed offer a variety of different services. The idea is that the citizen can have an effect on this provision of local public goods either by influencing the decision-making (vote) or by moving (exit).[4]

2.2 *Competing Legal Orders*

This basic idea applies not only to community services, but also, for example, to fiscal decisions[5] and environmental choices.[6] In addition, this idea of citizens moving to the community that provides services which best correspond with their preferences can also be applied with respect to legal rules. Thus, it has been argued by *van den Bergh* that competition between legislators will lead to legal systems competing with each other to provide legislation that corresponds best to the preferences of citizens.[7] Also *Ogus* argues that the various lawmakers in the nation-states will create a competitive market for the supply of law.[8] The idea therefore is that in an optimal world, citizens will cluster together in states that provide legal rules that correspond to their preferences. Well-informed citizens who are dissatisfied with the legislation provided could move (voting with the feet) to the community that provides legislation that corresponds best to their preferences. This idea, assuming that different legal systems offer different legal rules to satisfy the demands of the citizens, thus explains the variety and differences between legal systems.[9] Moreover, it also shows that differences between the various legal rules

[2]Tiebout (1956), p. 416. For a discussion see Rose-Ackerman (1992), p. 169 f.

[3]Compare Mueller (1997), p. 255.

[4]This follows the well-known book by Hirschman (1970).

[5]See, e.g., Inman and Rubinfeld (1994), p. 147; Kirchgässner and Pommerehne (1996); Oates (1972).

[6]So Oates and Schwab (1988), p. 333.

[7]van den Bergh (1998).

[8]Ogus (1999), p. 405 and see Ogus (2001), p. 27.

[9]van den Bergh (1998), p. 134; van den Bergh (2000a), p. 437.

of different countries should not necessarily be judged negatively, as is often the case in Europe today. The idea of competing legal systems can probably best be seen “in action” in international private law where parties can choose the legal system that best suits their needs in a choice of law regime.[10] *Frey* and *Eichenberger* have proposed an extreme form of this competition between legal orders by suggesting the emergence of Functional Overlapping Competing Jurisdictions (FOCJ), whereby citizens may choose different governmental authorities for different functions of government.[11]

Obviously, this system, assuming that competition between legal orders leads to allocative efficiency in the provision of legal rules, works only if certain conditions are met. One condition is that citizens have adequate information on the contents of the legal rules provided by the various legislators, in order to be able to make an informed choice. In addition, exit is often costly, so people may stay even if the (legal) regime does not best suit their needs.[12] Moreover, a location decision is obviously made under the influence of a set of criteria, in which the legal regime may not be decisive.[13] Usually the job location and residence are so important that in reality there is little left for people to choose.[14] Finally, as we will discuss below, this system of competition between legal orders works only if the decisions in one legal order have no external effects on others.

2.3 “Bottom up Federalism”

In economic literature, the Tiebout model is used to argue that, from an economic point of view, decentralization should be the starting point, since competition between legislators will lead to allocative efficiency. van den Bergh also uses this theory to provide criteria for centralization/decentralization within the European Union. Taking *Tiebout* as a starting point and assuming that competition between decentralized legislators will lead to an optimal provision of legal rules, the crucial question is: why centralize? van den Bergh criticizes that part of the current discussion in the European legal literature which seems to focus on the question why there should be decentralization (referred to by van den Bergh as “top down federalization”). According to economic theory, that is the wrong question. Starting

[10] Although the choice for a particular legal regime may not always be related to the quality of the legal system but, say, to the quality of the court or arbitration system. The latter explains, according to Ogus, the popularity of English law in choice of law clauses in contracts (Ogus 1999, p. 408).

[11] Frey and Eichenberger (1996a), p. 315; see also Frey and Eichenberger (1996b), p. 335; Casella and Frey (1992), p. 639.

[12] As Ogus states, there should be no barriers to the freedom of establishment and to the movement of capital (Ogus 1999, p. 407). For these conditions, see also van den Bergh (2000a), p. 438.

[13] That is one of the reasons why Frey and Eichenberger argue in favour of FOCJ: the choice for one legal or institutional regime should not be exclusive; there may be ‘overlapping’ jurisdictions depending upon the different functions (Frey and Eichenberger 1996a, pp. 316–318).

[14] Rose-Ackerman (1992), p. 169.

from Tiebout's model, there is reason to believe in what van den Bergh calls a "bottom up federalization", assuming that in principle the local level is optimal, since the local level has the best information on local problems and on the preferences of citizens. Decision-making should be moved to a higher level only when there is a good reason.[15] Economic theory has indeed suggested that there may be a variety of reasons why the local level is not best suited to take decisions and that there are occasions when central decision-making can lead to more efficient results.

I will now apply these criteria in favour of centralization and relate them to the harmonization of food law in Europe.

3 Criteria for Harmonization of Food Law

In the Law and Economics literature with respect to environmental federalism various criteria have been advanced for centralization.[16] I will in turn discuss transboundary externalities (Sect. 3.1), designing optimal jurisdictions (Sect. 3.2), the danger of a race to the bottom or a race to the top (Sect. 3.3), the internal market (Sect. 3.4), reducing transaction costs (Sect. 3.5) and providing a minimum level of protection and justifications for centralization (Sect. 3.6). For each criterion in favour of centralization the general economic justification based on the literature will be provided and then the arguments will be applied to the specific case of food. Section 3.7 summarizes the arguments.

3.1 Transboundary Externalities

General

The presumption in favour of local or decentralized legal rules generally holds on the condition that the decentralized rules do not have transboundary effects. In some cases regulation introduced by one state could have transboundary effects to other jurisdictions. In that case a problem would arise since decision-makers (like in the European context, Member States) would have no incentives to impose stringent rules upon their own citizens if the consequences of harmful actions were mainly felt outside of their own jurisdiction. This is the case in so-called transboundary externalities. From a public choice perspective one understands that politicians may be tempted to draft legislation that benefits their own citizens (voters) and throw costs (externalization) on citizens in other jurisdictions. When those transboundary externalities would emerge there is a strong argument in favour of centralization.[17]

[15] A major American supporter of this "presumption in favour of decentralization" is Revesz. See, e.g., Revesz (2000a), p. 1; Revesz (2000b), p. 37.

[16] See in this respect more particularly van den Bergh (2000a).

[17] See further on this interstate externalities argument in favour of centralization (with many nuances) Revesz (2000a), p. 1; Revesz (2000b), p. 37.

Food

It is not so clear to what extent the transboundary externalities argument could be considered as a justification for a centralization of food safety. The argument is especially advanced in cases where measures can be taken in one jurisdiction which clearly throw consequences on others, in other words where jurisdictions would be able to externalize harm. The typical example of a transboundary externality argument is the one relating to environmental harm. The risk that states might externalize harm to other jurisdictions in the case of environmental pollution (like transboundary rivers) is very clear and therefore constitutes in that case a clear argument in favour of centralization of decision-making.[18] However, with the issue of food safety one has to be careful. Food products undoubtedly cross borders, but it is not immediately clear, for example in the case of the EU, whether that makes the risk created by food necessarily a transboundary externality. In the case of European private law van den Bergh provided the example where a producer in the Netherlands were to produce products which comply with the Dutch (supposedly low) product liability and product standards and would then export those products to say, Belgium and France, where (hypothetically) the required level of product safety would be much higher. In that particular case a transboundary externality problem, justifying centralization would only exist if the consumers in Belgium and France had no possibility of filing a law suit against the Dutch manufacturer. Generally, manufacturers of defective (also food) products remain liable to damages for harm suffered in export markets.[19] The question in this example would therefore be whether a particular jurisdiction (in this example the Netherlands) would have the possibility to externalize harm resulting from poor food safety to other jurisdictions. In the product liability case, as mentioned, Law and Economics scholars held that the risk of such a transboundary externalization of unsafe foods is relatively limited since consumers in other (EU) jurisdictions would be able to hold the exporters liable.[20]

However, there are a few issues which call for attention. One is that particularly in the case of food there is a serious risk of wide-spread damage. Individual damage to consumers may in some cases be small, but the total social costs could be large. It is well-known that more particularly in those cases tort suits are often not brought.[21] Moreover, in the case of poor food quality, in many cases damage may be instant, but there could also be long-term damage, as a result of which latency problems could occur.[22] It is well-known that in case of damage with a so-called "long tail"[23] the tort system will often fail to provide adequate incentives for internalization of the

---

[18]The basic paper is by Oates and Schwab (1988), p. 333.

[19]See generally van den Bergh (1998), p. 141.

[20]For a further analysis of the centralization of product liability see Faure (2000).

[21]It is related to the well-known problem of rational disinterest or rational apathy which may arise in so-called mass damage claims. See Schäfer (2000).

[22]Latency refers to the long time lapse between the moment of the tort on the one hand and the moment that the damage occurs on the other.

[23]Referring more particularly to the fact that the damage may only appear a long time after the tort.

externality.[24] In those cases there may be a risk that through poor food safety legislation jurisdictions would be able to externalize harm to other jurisdictions, which would thus justify centralization.

3.2 Designing Optimal Jurisdictions

General

Another issue which is related to the fact that many problems to be regulated are not merely local is the fact that when problems cross national borders one could advance an economies of scale argument to shift powers to a higher legal order that has competence to deal with the issue over a larger territory. The simple foundation for this is that if the problem to be regulated crosses the borders of competence of the national jurisdiction, decision-making powers should be shifted to a higher regulatory level, preferably to an authority which has jurisdiction over a territory large enough to deal adequately with the problem.[25] In the words of Susan Rose-Ackerman: "Economic theory provides a straightforward but unrealistic answer to regional problems: draw optimal' jurisdictional boundaries'".[26] The basis for this economics of scale argument is related to the argument that the transaction costs of regulation will be lower if regulation is made at a higher level.

Food

This economics of scale argument is undoubtedly a rather strong one, favouring centralization for the particular area of food safety. There is, especially in the EU context overwhelming literature pointing at the fact that within the EU there is a strong reliance on food supply from other EU Member States.[27] That would hence justify centralization at EU level. However, one has to be slightly careful with this argument: centralization may undoubtedly reduce transaction costs, but (1) there are benefits in differentiation as well, which may not be neglected and (2) harmonization in itself also creates transaction costs which should be accounted for as well.[28]

---

[24]See on that point generally Shavell (1984).

[25]So Ogus (1999), p. 414 and see Esty (1996), p. 625.

[26]See Rose-Ackerman (1995), p. 38.

[27]See Leibovitch (2008), p. 435.

[28]We will come back to this point below in Sect. 3.5.

3.3 *Race to the Bottom–Race to the Top*

Race to the Bottom

General

There may be an economic argument for centralization, in that there is a risk that a "race to the bottom" would emerge between countries to attract foreign investments. As a result of this, prisoner's dilemmas could arise, whereby countries would fail to enact or enforce effective legislation. Centralization can be advanced as a remedy for these prisoner's dilemmas. This race to the bottom argument could in theory play a role in the case of product safety as well.[29] It would mean that local governments would use lenient legislation as a competitive tool to attract industry.[30] The result would be an overall reduction of environmental quality below efficient levels. This should correspond with the traditional game theory result that prisoner's dilemmas create inefficiencies.

The race to the bottom argument has had supporters as well as opponents. Law and economics scholars tend to stress the benefits of competition between states and point out the dangers of centralization,[31] whereas some legal scholars tend to attach more belief to the race to the bottom rationale for centralization.[32]

As we will indicate below this race to the bottom argument has not as such been explicitly discussed in the European legal debate. It only shows up in the argument that the conditions of competition should be harmonized. That will be discussed below. From a Law and Economics perspective the race to the bottom is only a rationale for centralization if it can be established that states could attract industry with lenient tort rules.[33] Let us examine, again with a few examples, whether that is a realistic scenario.

Food

In the Law and Economics literature the danger of a race to the bottom has been especially discussed in the environmental context, whereby the question arose whether states would engage in a destructive competition, lowering environmental standards in order to attract industry. The answer, in the environmental context as to whether there is empirical evidence of such a race to the bottom occurring is nuanced, in the sense that it depends upon the specific time and place. Early literature argued that, especially since the costs of environmental regulation would only be a small proportion of total investment costs, the differences in stringency of environmental regulations would

[29]For a detailed discussion of this argument, see Esty and Geradin (1998), pp. 16–19.

[30]Compare Rose-Ackerman (1992), pp. 166–170.

[31]See Revesz (1992), p. 1210; Revesz (1996), p. 2341.

[32]See Esty and Geradin (1997), p. 265; Esty and Geradin (1998), p. 5.

[33]See van den Bergh (2000a), p. 445.

only lead to small costs differences as a result of which this would not affect investment decisions.[34] Other literature, however, pointed at the fact that, especially given relocation costs, states may not always be able to attract industry towards relocation with lower environmental standards,[35] but intrajurisdictional competition could lead to a so-called "regulatory chill", meaning that jurisdictions would refrain from imposing more stringent environmental regulations out of fear that this might affect industry decisions concerning their location.[36] More recent empirical literature also shows, especially in the American context, that differences in the stringency of environmental regulation do affect location decisions.[37]

In the European context it was originally argued that the (before 2004) than Member States would not engage in a race to the bottom, by lowering their environmental quality in order to attract industry. This would run counter to the state's interest since it may lead to lower environmental quality in their own jurisdiction, for which citizens would have no demand.[38] However, again also in this domain more recent evolutions, especially after EU enlargement show that there may be a race to the bottom, especially as far as the Central and Eastern European Member States are concerned. The race to the bottom would not so much consist of a lowering of environmental standards (as all have to accept the environmental acquis imposed through environmental directives) but in a reduced enforcement in some Member States.[39] In other words, it can still be attractive for industry to relocate to the new Member States if they would have lower enforcement levels than other Member States.

How does this environmental case compare to the case of food safety? Also in this case the argument could be made that there may be little incentives for jurisdictions (more particularly EU Member States) to attract industry with lenient food safety regulation. After all, if they were to do so the primary victims of such legislation may be their own citizens, presuming that the food products would also be marketed in their own jurisdiction. This could hence violate the interests of their own constituency. And as was mentioned above, in the case of food producers that largely depend upon export markets, lenient food safety regulation may not be very beneficial to them as they do remain liable for damage caused in export markets.[40] The race to the bottom could only justify centralization if it could be proven that without centralization a risk of destructive competition between jurisdictions would emerge.[41]

---

[34]See in that respect for example Jaffe et al. (1995), p. 132.

[35]It is a point strongly stressed by Revesz (1992), p. 2010; Revesz (1996), p. 2341.

[36]See *inter alia* Esty (1996) and see Esty and Geradin (1997), p. 265.

[37]For an overview see *inter alia* Faure (2011).

[38]See for example Faure et al. (1996), p. 141.

[39]See on this point especially Faure and Johnston (2009).

[40]But in that case, as mentioned above, the transboundary externality argument could justify centralization.

[41]In the words of Susan Rose-Ackerman: "If state and local laws seem designed to protect local business rather than reflect genuine differences in tastes across jurisdiction, the federal government should take a hard look to determine the possible interference with interstate commerce" (Rose-Ackerman 1992, p. 173).

The race to the bottom would only constitute a rationale for centralization if there were empirical evidence that states would engage in such a competition in order to attract industry with low quality food legislation. It is not so clear in the European context to what extent this has been the case. Of course, in the aftermath of the BSE-crisis some have strongly criticized the attitude of the British institutions in rejecting scientific evidence that there may have been a problem in order to protect the interests of the British beef industry.[42]

Race to the Top

General

There is in fact also a reverse danger: some jurisdictions may not be striving for lower quality legislation, but may to the contrary be involved in a so-called race to the top. At first blush it would seem curious that states would try to compete with other jurisdictions by imposing ever more stringent regulations upon their industry. However, the argument is that it may be relatively attractive for states to be located in a high standard jurisdiction. The high standards may also generate technological improvements and thus competitive advantages.[43] This corresponds strongly with what is often referred to as the "Porter hypothesis", developed by Michael Porter: stringent (environmental) legislation would, according to this hypothesis, not endanger the competitiveness of industry, but would to the contrary improve the competitiveness and hence the profitability of industry. The logic of this so-called "Porter hypothesis" is that stringent regulation would lead to technological innovation which would in turn lead to improved competitiveness.

That may explain why some jurisdictions may not engage in a race to the bottom, but rather in a race to the top. There is, however, another (potentially more negative) normative twist to this: a side effect of this race to the top is undoubtedly that states can, by imposing more stringent regulations, also create barriers to market entry, more particularly for firms from outside the state's jurisdiction. That explains why industry will often, together with (consumer and environmental) NGOs lobby in favour of stringent environmental and consumer legislation: this may benefit industry (by creating barriers to market entry) and NGOs (by serving the goals of their constituency). It is a phenomenon described in many publications of David Vogel and referred to as "trading up".[44]

---

[42]See for example Vos (2000) and Vos and Wendler (2006).

[43]See generally Ogus (1999), p. 415.

[44]See *inter alia* Vogel (1995).

Food

If a race to the top were to occur as far as food safety is concerned the difficulty is always to determine whether this is a wealth maximizing increase of food safety standards, corresponding with preferences of citizens and leading to technological innovations and increased competitiveness of the food industry or whether it should rather be considered as an attempt to create barriers to market entry. It is obvious that more particularly in the area of food safety there is always a danger that states would engage in such a race to the top which de facto leads to barriers to market entry, hence to trade restrictions, often aiming at the protection of national interests. Many have argued that the French refusal to comply with the ruling of the Court of Justice against France which continued to refuse to import British beef, although experts had stated that it was safe, is precisely an example of such a (destructive) race to the top.[45]

Both a race to the bottom as well as a race to the top can be arguments in favour of centralization. Within the EU context the argument is particularly strong as the example of the BSE-crisis showed. From an economic perspective the crucial question is whether a distinction can be made between a genuine demand for high food safety quality, corresponding with preferences of citizens on the one hand and an unjustified ban on imports, creating inefficient barriers to trade on the other. That obviously requires consensus on the scientific evidence available concerning the safety risks posed by particular food and that is precisely what EU policy after the BSE-crisis has been aiming at. That therefore largely fits within the economic logic.[46]

3.4 *Internal Market*

General

An argument often used in the EU context to justify harmonization has been the need to create a level playing field for industry. It was often referred to as "harmonizing conditions of competition". That argument looks like the earlier discussed race to the bottom risk, but can also be distinguished from it. The argument justified for EU harmonization "to harmonize conditions of competition" has been strongly criticized in the economic literature.[47]

The argument as it is usually presented in Europe, cannot, as was stated above, be fitted into the economic criteria for centralization, since it suggests that removing any difference in legal systems would be necessary to cure the race to the bottom risk,

[45]See *inter alia* Leibovitch (2008), p. 441.

[46]See Vos (2000), pp. 227–255; Vos and Wendler (2006), pp. 65–138.

[47]See for example Revesz (2001), p. 19.

which is neither supported by economic theory, nor by empirical evidence. Also, even if one were to take the (political) "common market" goal as a starting point and legal rules were to be harmonized on that ground, this would still *not* create a level playing field since differences in, for example, energy resources, access to raw materials and atmospheric conditions will still lead to differing marketing conditions that favour trade.[48]

There is, in addition, a strong counter-argument, in that there are many examples showing that economic market integration is possible (without the distortions predicted by the race to the bottom argument) with unstandardized legal orders. Public choice scholars have often advanced the Swiss federal model as an example where economic market integration goes hand in hand with differentiated legal systems.[49] It is apparently possible to create a common market without the total harmonization of all legal rules and standards. That is not to say that there may not be other arguments in favour of the harmonization of tort law in Switzerland. Notably the reduction of transaction costs argument (to be discussed below) may well constitute a powerful reason to prefer one Federal Swiss tort law instead of 26 different cantonal systems. Therefore, clear steps towards harmonization of tort law can be seen in Switzerland as well.[50]

Food

Although a complete harmonization of all possible legal rules is, as argued above, not necessary to create market integration, it may be clear that more particularly in the area of food safety the free flow of products may be endangered if food safety standards between the Member States were to differ. That could therefore be an argument in favour of harmonization. A comparable argument has been made in the context of product safety. There it was equally held that differences in product safety standards may endanger interstate trade.[51] An agreement between Member States on "essential safety requirements" is necessary in order to promote a free flow of products in the Union.

Law and Economics scholars would normally argue in favour of harmonizing "essential safety requirements" which would guarantee that food products correspond with a minimum level of safety which all consumers in the EU would require. Those requirements could be set by national expert committees and would lead to mutual recognition. That is the model which is usually promoted from an economic perspective since it would promote a competition between different national and European standards.[52] However, it is made clear in the abundant literature on food

---

[48]So van den Bergh (2000b), p. 6.

[49]Frey (1994), p. 338.

[50]See Winiger (2001), p. 299; and see Koziol (1996), p. 592 f.

[51]Faure (2003), p. 54.

[52]See in this respect for example Ogus (1994), pp. 177–179.

safety that a system of mutual recognition, as it existed before the BSE-crisis, may not suffice if (as apparently was the case in the area of food safety) the differences between Member States were de facto large.[53] The different national provisions on food still created substantial obstacles to creating a single market for food stuffs.[54] The main goal of the legislation originally issued by the EU, before the BSE-crisis, was therefore to ensure the free movement of food stuffs.[55] The creation of the internal market for food in Europe was therefore originally based on the principle of mutual recognition.[56] There is convincing empirical evidence that the harmonization of food laws within the EU did indeed increase the trade between the Member States. Henry de Frahan and Vancauteren (2006) report that the harmonization in food regulation has increased intra-EU imports of all food products by around 2/3 and of fruits and vegetables by around 1/3 in the period 1990–2001.[57] It can therefore be concluded that from an economic perspective alignment of food safety legislation between Member States is beneficial and even a condition for promoting trade between the Member States. However, it was equally held that a mere system of mutual recognition may not be sufficient, especially if differences between food safety standards in the Member States were still large (as the BSE-crisis showed). That is why after the BSE-crisis EU food policy went one step further by improving the centralization of the gathering of the scientific evidence concerning food safety risks in the creation of the European Food Safety Authority (EFSA) in 2002.[58] However, the literature equally holds that this economic goal of creating the single market may not be sufficient for equally guaranteeing a high level of safety to consumers.[59]

3.5 *Reducing Transaction Costs*

The argument of reducing transaction costs may generally be one of the main motivators for harmonization from an economic perspective. For example the argument discussed above, that optimal jurisdictions have to be designed to be able to deal with the problem in an adequate manner[60], in fact is an argument of transaction costs reduction. The same can be said about the just-mentioned argument that some approximation of legislation may be necessary to allow the creation of an internal market. That could also be rephrased as the need to reduce transaction costs

[53]See in that respect de Frahan and Vancauteren (2006), p. 339.

[54]See Alemanno (2007), p. 4.

[55]Not so much the protection of consumer health (Alemanno 2007, p. 5; Vos 2002, p. 9).

[56]van der Meulen (2013), p. 75.

[57]de Frahan and Vancauteren (2006), p. 354.

[58]Leibovitch (2008), pp. 432–434.

[59]Alemanno (2007), p. 1.

[60]See Sect. 3.2.

(resulting from differences in food safety standards) which would create transaction costs as a result of distrust between Member States, thus leading to barriers to entry. Those could again result from a race to the top between Member States, equally discussed before.[61] The desire to reduce transaction costs through centralization may hence be a central motif behind any harmonization initiative.

Although the goal of reducing transaction costs is of course one that one could hardly disagree with, from an economic perspective there are two reasons to be slightly careful with blindly following this argument (which would in fact justify harmonization of any type of rules).

A first problem is that one can, from an economic perspective, not only look at the benefits of transaction costs reduction (resulting from harmonized rules), but one should equally look at the benefits from differentiation and at the costs of harmonization as well.

Starting point for the economic analysis, as explained above,[62] is indeed that differentiated legal rules have the major advantage of better fitting the preferences of individuals.[63] That issue may play a role in the area of food safety as well. Preferences of citizens concerning the desired quality of food may to an important extent depend upon differing cultures, but also upon the level of development. After all, there is a price to be paid to achieve a particular level of food safety and it may well be that for example the willingness of people in the Netherlands to pay that price would be different than for example in Hungary or Greece. Harmonization may have benefits, but it may have the disadvantage of neglecting the differences in preferences.

Another problem is that there may indeed be many transaction costs savings in harmonized legal rules, but the costs of harmonization may be substantial as well. Given differences between legal cultures some have argued that these differences are indeed prohibitive for harmonization. It is more particularly Legrand who has argued that the differences between the legal systems in Europe and more particularly between the common law and the continental civil law systems are so different that harmonization would be impossible.[64] In economic terms that would mean that the costs of harmonization are prohibitive. Legrand may have a point with respect to the area of European private law. There one can indeed notice that in any domain where attempts towards harmonization have been undertaken (like in the Environmental Liability Directive and in the European Product Liability Directive) harmonization is always at best partial and important issues are always left out of the scope of the Directive and have to be decided by Member State law.[65] The problem of high transaction costs in harmonizing may to some extent play a role in the area of food safety as well, to the extent that preferences in that respect between the various

[61] See Sect. 3.3.

[62] See *supra* 2.

[63] See for a further and detailed analysis of the argument, van den Bergh (1998), pp. 129–152.

[64] See Legrand (1997), p. 111.

[65] See with respect to the failure to completely harmonize product liability law, Faure (2000) and with respect to the Environmental Liability Directive see De Smedt (2007).

citizens in the Member States would substantially differ. That would make a harmonization more costly and complex. However, to the extent that the harmonization would focus on minimum requirements on which all European citizens could agree (like avoiding food that would create a danger to health) the problem of high transaction costs related to differing preferences might be less serious.

In sum, one cannot only focus on the benefits in transaction costs saving. Those can, as indicated above, undoubtedly be substantial. But one also has to balance those against the benefits of differentiated legal rules (which will be lost in case of total harmonization) and against the costs of harmonization.[66]

3.6 Minimum Level of Protection

General

It could of course be argued that the question of centralization/harmonization within the EU should not only be addressed from an economic perspective and that also other, non-economic arguments could justify the harmonization of food safety law. Those non-economic arguments have also strongly influenced the European policy debate.

Obviously, the question whether EU law should go beyond the economics of federalism and provide a minimum protection level to its citizens goes beyond the area of economics. However, a slight problem with this reasoning, at least from an economic perspective, is that one would then go towards legislation that would not necessarily correspond with the preferences of citizens. Especially if preferences were heterogeneous that might be problematic. Of course preferences of citizens for low standards at low costs may in some situations be overruled, for example if it is held that these low standards would infringe widely held perceptions of human rights.[67] Also in other areas, for example as far as environmental protection is concerned, some call for centralized minimum quality standards for reasons of "equity, justice or pure paternalism".[68] This then amounts to the political question whether a particular policy area (like food safety) is considered that important that there are reasons to disrespect differing preferences of citizens that would justify a harmonization at a higher level of protection.

[66]See for the arguments in favour of centralization of food safety regulation, Leibovitch (2008), pp. 434–436.

[67]"Rights may, in this instance, justifiably 'trump' efficiency". So Ogus (1999), p. 418.

[68]See Cohen (1996), p. 170.

Food

In the literature with respect to EU food law it is often been stressed that economics (more particularly the internal market) may not be the only argument in favour of harmonization, but that the creation of a high level of food safety may play a role as well.[69] The new general food law clearly states that a high level of protection of human life and health should be pursued.

Although consumer health is hence now strongly stressed at EU-level,[70] at EU-level at the same time free movement is still included as an important objective as a result of which the literature holds that the EU thus continues to pursue two potentially conflicting objectives of market liberalization and health protection.[71] Another issue is that the point about centralization disregarding heterogeneous preferences is also mentioned in the food safety literature: there can be issues of "cultural and national pride" as well as differing "local tastes on food safety regulation" which could still be sources of disagreement.[72] This underscores the argument made in the economic literature that one should always take into account that there are costs related to harmonization as well.

3.7 *Summary*

Having reviewed the economic literature on federalism, discussing the criteria for centralization, there seem to be several strong arguments that can be made in favour of harmonization of food law. The risk of an externalization of harm resulting from food safety laws may exist to the extent that consumers in export states would not be able to sue manufacturers liable for bringing defective food products on the market. That may be a, but probably not the strongest, argument in favour of centralization. The same could be said about the race to the bottom. Only if there were empirical evidence that states were, with lenient food safety legislation able to attract industry, would the race to the bottom constitute a justification for centralization. However, food products often cross borders and transaction costs could thus be reduced if a higher level jurisdiction could design food safety law. That may also be important since there could be a serious risk of a race to the top, in some cases leading to the creation of barriers to entry. However, it should equally be recognized that the reduction of transaction costs (resulting from differentiated legal rules) may jeopardize trade (and thus the single market) but that a harmonization does not come

[69]See for example Broberg (2008), pp. 5, 62 who discusses food safety as an objective in its own right.

[70]And food safety objectives can, under certain conditions, even override all other policy objectives (see Ugland and Veggeland 2006, p. 619).

[71]Ugland and Veggeland (2006), p. 618.

[72]Leibovitch (2008), p. 442.

without costs. Those costs do not only constitute in the complexities related to harmonizing often different legal rules, but are also related to the reduction of the benefits of differentiation, i.e. rules that match differing preferences of citizens.[73]

In sum, there seem, also from an economic perspective, in this policy area, to be strong arguments in favour of centralization. That is especially related to the costs emerging from differentiated rules with respect to food safety. The latter could endanger the single market and may lead to a race to the top. Recall that the creation of a single market is as such not an economic, but rather a political objective. But given this political objective (at EU-level) it is clear that differentiated food safety standards may endanger the reaching of that particular goal. However, the potential benefits of centralization (in reducing those transaction costs) should then be weighed in the first place against the costs of harmonization and against the loss of benefits in no longer having differentiated food safety laws, corresponding to the preferences of citizens.

4 Policy Consequences

After having provided this economic approach to the centralization of food safety law we will now briefly come back to the evolutions at EU-level and address the literature in this domain, comparing it to the economic arguments. Again, it should be repeated that the goal of this chapter is not to discuss EU food safety law in detail, as that will be done in other chapters, but rather to verify whether the evolutions at policy level and the rhetoric used in the food safety literature correspond with the economic criteria for centralization.

First the evolution of EU food law will be reconsidered in the light of the economic literature discussed in the previous sections (Sect. 4.1); next an analysis of the current highbride division of labour between the European and the Member State level will be discussed (Sect. 4.2).

4.1 Evolution of EU Food Law

There is a lot of literature describing in detail how EU food law has evolved over roughly the past 25 years. It is obviously neither possible nor indicated within the frame of this chapter which focuses on the economics of federalism to review that evolution in detail. I will just summarize the highlights as they appear from the literature in order to relate this briefly to the economic criteria we have discussed in the previous section.[74]

---

[73]See also Leibovitch (2008), pp. 434–443.

[74]For a more detailed account of EU food law see *inter alia* Vos (1999) and Vos and Wendler (2006).

One highlight in many of the publications on EU food law is that there has been a shift from the policy goals to be achieved from first a strong focus on the promotion of free trade and the avoidance of market distortions towards a stronger focus on a genuine protection of consumer health. A second focus in the literature is related to the importance of the BSE-crisis, which may have functioned as an important wakeup call and which has initiated a lot of the subsequent EU legislation. A third issue often mentioned in the literature is the importance of the creation of EFSA as well as the integrated policy approach in the general food law. A fourth element often stressed is that notwithstanding the important developments that have taken place over the past twenty years, there still is no European full integration of food policy, Member States still playing an important role (Sect. 4.1.4). I will briefly discuss these four elements from the literature, also in the light of the Law and Economics literature on federalism discussed in Sect. 3.

From Internal Market Towards Consumer and Health Protection

Ugland and Veggeland sketch that the original approach in EU food legislation was mainly based on the objective of ensuring free movements of food stuffs.[75] However, given different national traditions of Member States there was no coordinated approach to food legislation and a reorientation was considered necessary as a tool of the completion of the internal market. Different institutional and legal tools were used for the development of EU food law whereby originally the promotion of the so-called four freedoms (free movement of labour, services, capital and goods) played an important role, supported by the case law of the court.[76] At the end of the last century also the essential requirement of promoting and protecting public health became increasingly important.[77] But an institutional core responsible for food safety issues at EU-level was lacking.[78] After the BSE-crisis it was held that in that period the market (integration) still had more priority than the protection of public health.[79] As a result of the BSE-crisis new European legislation was created that ensured that food safety objectives would be integrated in all sectors and also in situations of uncertainty, thus applying the precautionary principle. Under conditions food safety objectives can therefore override all other policy objectives.[80] However, the general food law still declares the "protection of human life and health and the protection of consumers' interests" as one of the objectives,[81] but the same article equally refers to the objective of achieving "the free movement in the

[75]Ugland and Veggeland (2006), p. 612.

[76]See on this evolution also van der Meulen (2013), pp. 73–78; Leibovitch (2008), pp. 432–434.

[77]Ugland and Veggeland (2006), p. 612.

[78]Ugland and Veggeland (2006), p. 613; Joerges and Vos (1999).

[79]Ugland and Veggeland (2006), p. 615.

[80]Ugland and Veggeland (2006), p. 619.

[81]Article 5(1) of the general food law.

Community of food and feed manufactured or marketed according to the general principles and requirements". There has hence been a shift from first primarily harmonizing because of internal market objectives towards harmonization for providing a higher level of protection. The EU "does continue to pursue the two potentially conflicting objectives of market liberalization and health protection".[82] The way in which these conflicts should in theory be solved is by having a central organ (EFSA) deciding on whether particular food would comply with the general principles of the general food law.

Rephrasing this in terms of the economic analysis provided in Sect. 3, it seems that first the goal of the realization of the internal market was leading EU policy[83] and thus the goal to reduce transaction costs for trade.[84] The mutual recognition policy used in the last century was hence also meant as a tool to avoid that some Member States would race to the top, thereby creating barriers to market entry.[85] Those goals apparently still play a role, but the protection of health and safety clearly refers to providing a minimum level of protection as well.[86] This is, as was mentioned above, rather a political objective than one which is routed in the economics of federalism.

The BSE-Crisis

Almost all commentators writing on EU food law refer at some moment to the BSE-crisis. From an economics of federalism perspective it is interesting for many reasons. First, the crisis showed some of the problems inherent in a disintegrated food safety policy based on mutual recognition.[87] Second, as was already mentioned above, the crisis equally highlighted that a differentiated system of the scientific evaluation of risks related to food stuffs may lead to different kinds of protectionism. The British were blamed for not being transparent in their communication concerning risks of beef that was exported to France (thus potentially creating an externalization of risk and potentially a race to the bottom) whereas the French were equally blamed (by the European Commission and the Court of Justice) for still banning British beef also when scientists had objectively established that it was safe (thus creating barriers to entry). The BSE-crisis therefore illustrated the importance of having an independent scientific evaluation of the risks inherent to particular food stuffs. The BSE-crisis made clear that, given the commercial interests involved, there will always be a risk that national agencies will, also as a result of lobbying by the interest groups involved, rather serve the interests of industry than the promotion

---

[82]Ugland and Veggeland (2006), p. 618.

[83]See Sect. 3.4.

[84]See Sect. 3.5.

[85]See Sect. 3.3.

[86]See Sect. 3.6.

[87]Ugland and Veggeland (2006), p. 612.

of public health. Finally, the crisis equally made clear that the separate evaluation of risk (risk assessment) by agencies in Member States led to a large amount of distrust among European consumers, thus endangering interstate trade. The crisis, in other words, underscored the importance of centralization of food safety issues on the basis of many of the criteria discussed in the previous section. It can be summarized in one line: the existence of a differentiated system of risk assessment for food gave rise to a variety of transaction costs (resulting both from attempts towards externalization as well as the creation of barriers to entry), all of which created high transaction costs and thus jeopardized interstate trade. The BSE-crisis therefore understandably provided a strong call for further harmonization.

EFSA

As already mentioned, the BSE-crisis gave rise to many actions at the EU-level.[88] The European Food Safety Authority (EFSA) which was created in 2002 took over the responsibility of the then still existing scientific committees and has a primary task to provide scientific advice through risk assessment. EFSA has no decision-making powers, but it is the exclusive organ for performing risk assessments at EU-level concerning food safety.[89] With the creation of EFSA the Commission hoped to eliminate barriers to trade in food between the Member States.[90] The goal of the EFSA is to engage in scientific risk assessment, but the risk management still is in the hands of the Member States.[91] The reason for that set-up of the EFSA was to keep scientific analysis (risk assessment) separate from political responsibilities (risk management).[92]

EFSA's methodology for risk assessment works on the basis of various key principles such as administrative independence, scientific independence, transparency and participation of the public.[93] EFSA, however, lacks regulatory competences. It merely provides advice. Monitoring and enforcement tasks lay at the European level with the Food and Veterinary Office (FVO) and with national bodies within the Member States. EFSA is hence considered as the "scientific point of reference for the whole Union".[94]

---

[88]For a summary see *inter alia* Alemanno (2010); van der Meulen (2013), pp. 69–98; Vos (2000), pp. 227–255.

[89]Ugland and Veggeland (2006), p. 618.

[90]Alemanno (2006).

[91]Leibovitch (2008), p. 434.

[92]See Abels and Kobusch (2010).

[93]Abels and Kobusch (2010), pp. 16–17.

[94]See further Alemanno (2007), pp. 20–26.

Incomplete Centralization

As the description of the tasks of EFSA already illustrate, the current situation is that there has been a harmonization of scientific risk assessment concerning food within EFSA. However, the literature equally stresses that, as the previous analysis already made clear, there is certainly no full harmonization or centralization in the sense as discussed in Sect. 3. A first point is that EFSA is indeed, as mentioned, the "scientific point of reference" for the whole Union, but it lacks regulatory powers. The agency lacks formal authority to reach binding resolutions on potentially contiguous scientific issues.[95] Second, EFSA's opinions will undoubtedly have some authoritative value for national decision-makers, but they are not binding.[96]

The division of labour between the EFSA and the Member States as far as risk assessment and risk management is concerned is quite refined. Risk assessment is basically taking place in the EFSA as a result of the general food law.[97] Risk management is according to Article 17 of the General Food Law allocated to the Member States with a few exceptions. A few management functions in relation to crisis situations have been entrusted by the General Food Law to the Commission.[98] That makes not EFSA, but the European Commission (DG Sanco), primarily responsible for managing food safety risks,[99] although there still is responsibility for risk management with the Member States as well. Leibovitch summarizes it as follows: "The EFSA gives scientific assessments, but does not handle any of the risk management. Instead, the EU institutions and the Member States themselves are responsible for risk management, a division of authority that poses an obstacle to greater centralization".[100]

There are a number of reasons why the EFSA was set up this way. One important reason mentioned in the literature is simply the element of "path dependency". This refers to the fact that history matters in organizational design. Institutions (in this case national institutions at Member State level) will often reject institutional changes.[101] In addition differing cultures may also have played an important role in the resistance of the Member States against a full integration of European food safety policy.[102] To some extent these differing cultures hence led to a continuation of the mutual recognition principle rather than opting for a full harmonization, for example by providing regulatory powers to EFSA.[103]

---

[95] So Alemanno (2007), p. 23.

[96] Alemanno (2007), p. 25.

[97] See Vos and Wendler (2006), p. 74.

[98] Vos and Wendler (2006), p. 74.

[99] Vos and Wendler (2006), p. 88.

[100] Leibovitch (2008), p. 434.

[101] So Abels and Kobusch (2010), pp. 10–11.

[102] Alemanno (2007), pp. 31–32.

[103] Alemanno (2007), pp. 30–31.

Again, this resistance of Member States can be understood in the light of the economic literature discussed above. Cultural differences and resistance by institutions could on the one hand refer to genuine differing preferences which may make harmonization undesirable. It is also possible that the resistance does not follow from differing preferences, but for example from vested interests and institutions refusing to give up acquired powers. Whatever the reason is, the fact that important decision-making powers are de facto still left with the Member States underscores once more the fact that harmonization is apparently not costless and that also in this case the costs of harmonization were apparently prohibitive, in the end leading to a hybrid solution of combining scientific risk assessment by EFSA at the EU-level with final decision-making concerning risk management by Member States.[104] The question of course arises whether the current system of collaboration between the EU and the Member States is optimal from an economic point of view.

4.2 *Analysis of the Hybrid System*

The brief sketch of the evolution of EU food law indicates that currently there still is some shift of powers (as far as scientific risk assessment is concerned) to the EU-level, although it is more advisory than regulatory and that important powers are still left with the Member States. There is in the literature considerable criticism on the current model (the main focus of the criticism being that the centralization at EU-level does not go far enough and that too many powers are still kept with the Member States). Some have compared the current regulatory regime in the EU with the situation in the US and have clearly stated that for a variety of reasons the EU clearly did not want the EFSA to be a full blown regulatory agency with competences such as the Food and Drug Administration (FDA) in the US.[105] The Member States clearly still wanted to preserve an opportunity for incorporating national perspectives into the risk assessment.[106] The Member States still have strong national competent authorities that were apparently not willing to give up their powers completely to EFSA.[107] The EU was hence, so it is often concluded, not ready yet for a complete centralization: Member States are not obligated to follow EFSA's recommendations, since a mandatory character of EFSA recommendations would be considered as an infringement on their sovereignty.[108] Member States

[104]It should be stressed that the details of the European food regulatory system and the combination with the international and Member State level are far more complicated than sketched here. They entail for example also early warnings, emergency measures and a rapid alert system. Those can, however, in the framework of this chapter, not be further discussed in detail. See for example Vos and Wendler (2006), pp. 91–92 and see Alemanno (2010), pp. 207–208.

[105]Abels and Kobusch (2010), p. 9.

[106]See *inter alia* Alemanno (2008).

[107]For an overview of the functioning of those national regulatory authorities see *inter alia*, Abels and Kobusch (2010), pp. 16–29.

[108]Leibovitch (2008), p. 440.

remain quite important in the regulation of food safety, but especially in the enforcement, monitoring and verification. However, it is important to sketch that in 1997 the Food and Veterinary Office (FVO) was instituted as part of the European Commission. It has *inter alia* as task to audit the performance of national agencies in the Member States.[109] Some are therefore critical and argue that as a result of many (mostly political and cultural) reasons centralization did not go far enough. Some qualify the hybrid nature of the current system (advice on risk assessment by the EFSA and decision-making on risk management by the individual Member States) as only half a step towards a coherent risk assessment of food safety in the EU.[110]

It is hard to judge whether from an economic perspective the current form of centralization does not go far enough, as is stressed in some literature. On the one hand one can argue that the economic criteria mentioned in Sect. 3 indeed strongly point towards the importance of centralization of powers for food safety. At the same time the economic framework also points at the costs of harmonization and at the importance of respecting differences in national preferences. It is for example unclear whether some of the resistance against a further going centralization at EU-level by Member States is the result of differing preferences of citizens concerning food safety (which would constitute a valid economic justification for keeping some powers at Member State level) or whether the resistance is only the result of path dependency and vested interests by institutions (which would obviously not be a strong economic argument to keep some powers at Member State level). The economic approach seems indeed to support a further integration of food safety, in the style of a US-type FDA. That could undoubtedly lead to a further lowering of transaction costs and facilitate interstate trade.

On the other hand it should also be stressed that compared with the situation before the BSE-crisis and the subsequent EU legislation that emerged at the beginning of this century, substantial changes have taken place. In addition to the creation of EFSA we could point at issues not further discussed here, for example concerning traceability and labelling, hygiene rules and the crisis management system.[111] The BSE-crisis led to a fundamental change of the regulatory landscape concerning food safety in the EU[112] and it seems likely that even though the lack of a complete centralization is criticized in the literature, the EU and Member State agencies are now more resilient and able to response to crisis than they were before the BSE-crisis. Alemanno argues, using the case of Melamine contamination from China as a stress test that the new institutions functioned reasonably well in reaction to that crisis.[113] However, he equally held that this was not a major crisis as a result of which he holds that "the jury is still out on the ability of the EU import safety regime to address a full-scale crisis".[114]

[109] van der Meulen (2013), pp. 85–86.

[110] See Alemanno (2008), pp. 16–17.

[111] For further details see Leibovitch (2008), pp. 444–451; Vos and Wendler (2006), pp. 87–92.

[112] Ugland and Veggeland (2006), p. 620.

[113] Alemanno (2010).

[114] Alemanno (2010), p. 215.

Recently van den Bergh also provided a critical analysis of EU food law. He basically argues that there is indeed an economic argument in favour of centralization, for example when addressing rules combatting the BSE disease:

> Another example is the area of food law. Again, centralization may be warranted when substantial negative externalities require a centralized response and preferences of consumers are sufficiently homogeneous, such as a general desire for food safety. In this way rules combatting the BSE disease may be supported.[115]

However, van den Bergh is much more critical of many directives providing minimum requirements concerning specific food stuffs. In that respect he argues:

> However, many EU directives look like recipes in a (poor quality) cook book. Examples include the rules on the composition of chocolate, jam and fruit juices. It may be doubted whether the best brains in Brussels should spend their precious time on fixing the amount of cocoa butter, vegetable fats and milk and chocolate, deciding the amount of sugar in fruit juices and nectars, defining tomato juice as fruit juice and determining the fruit content in jam, jellies and marmalade.
>
> He therefore concludes:
>
> Again, this does not imply that there is no need for EU legislation, but rules should be restricted to cases where the benefits of centralization outweigh its advantages. The directives on the composition of food stuffs cannot be explained by welfare considerations, but rather as the result of a political compromise between pressure groups from industry and attempts to shelter the "fortress Europe" from imports of Africa (palm oil).

5 Concluding Remarks

This chapter addressed the economics of harmonization of food law in the EU. Economists have developed criteria to decide whether for particular issues powers should be allocated to a decentralized (local or Member State) level or rather to a centralized level. Starting point for this economic literature is the insight that regulation should best be made as close as possible to where the problem emerges, hence close to the citizen. That hence provides, at least as a starting point, a strong presumption in favour of decentralization or at least a system of differentiated legal rules. The need for centralization should therefore be justified.

That starting point is, so we argued, in principle not different for the case of food safety. Especially since the desired level of safety can strongly depend upon national preferences, cultural values, but also economic development, it is likely that the preferred level of food safety between the 28 EU Member States might differ. This is a logical consequence of the fact that also the level of economic development between the Member States strongly differs. Adopting a particular level of food safety also comes at a price which may therefore lead to differing preferences as far as the desired level of food safety is concerned.

---

[115]See van den Bergh (2016).

However, notwithstanding this starting point we argued that there are strong criteria in favour of centralization of food safety. Food products within the EU concern an important part of EU trade. The most important justification for centralization is that differentiated legal rules could, for a variety of reasons, discussed in this chapter, lead to high transaction costs, that may jeopardize the economic advantages of trade. That is hence, as we argued, a strong economic case in favour of shifting decision-making powers concerning food safety to the EU-level. This could particularly prevent the abuse of the food safety argument by Member States who would simply aim to erect barriers to market entry for reasons of national protectionism.

The BSE-crisis gave rise to an important move towards food safety harmonization in Europe, with the creation of EFSA that plays an important role in the scientific assessment of food safety risks. However, Member State institutions, for a variety of reasons, still retain some powers as well. The institutional design of EFSA is such that (*inter alia* through information exchange between EFSA and national authorities) in principle conflicts between national authorities and EFSA should be minimized, but the risk can never be totally excluded. The literature concerning food safety law argues that food safety is a domain where centralization should in fact go further than is currently the case as a result of which a European institution with further going powers than EFSA currently has should be created. Economic analysis seems to support those calls to an important extent. Some of the resistance against further harmonization from Member States does not seem to follow from differing national preferences (although that is not totally clear), but to be the result from vested interests that oppose the necessary institutional reforms.

Whereas in some domains, like European private law, Law and Economics scholars have traditionally been skeptical of the need for European harmonization.[116] In this area of food safety economic arguments justifying centralization are considerably stronger. To an important extent the calls in the literature for further harmonization of food safety at EU-level can therefore be supported from an economic perspective.

Acknowledgement I am grateful to Ellen Vos (Maastricht), Kai Purnhagen (Wageningen) and Roger van den Bergh (Rotterdam) for useful comments on an earlier version of this paper.

References

Abels G, Kobusch A (2010) Regulation of food safety in the EU: changing patterns of multilevel governance. Paper presented at the conference of the ECPR standing group on regulatory governance, June 2010, pp 8–9

Alemanno A (2006) Food safety and the single European market. In: Ansell CK, Vogel D (eds) What's the beef? The contested governance of European food safety. The MIT Press, Cambridge, pp 237–248

[116]See in that respect more particularly, van den Bergh (1998).

Alemanno A (2007) The evolution of European food regulation. Why the European food safety authority is not a EU-style FDA? Working Paper. http://papers.ssrn.com/sol3/papers.cfm?abstract_id=1007451
Alemanno A (2008) The European food safety authority at five. Eur Food Feed Law Rev:2–29
Alemanno A (2010) The European food import safety regime under a 'stress test': the melamine contamination of the global food supply chain. Erasmus Law Rev 3(4):203–215
Broberg MP (2008) Transforming the European Community's regulation of food safety. Swedish Institute for European Policy Studies (SIEPS)
Casella A, Frey B (1992) Federalism and clubs. Towards an economic theory of overlapping political jurisdictions. Eur Econ Rev 36(2/3):639–646
Cohen M (1996) Commentary. In: Eide E, van den Bergh R (eds) Law and economics of the environment, vol 170. Juridisk Forlag, Oslo
de Frahan BH, Vancauteren M (2006) Harmonization of food regulations and trade in the single market: evidence from disaggregated data. Eur Rev Agric Econ 33(3):337–360
De Smedt K (2007) Environmental liability in a federal system: a law and economics analysis. Intersentia, Antwerp
Esty DC (1996) Revitalising environmental federalism. Mich Law Rev 95:625–653
Esty DC, Geradin D (1997) Market access, competitiveness and harmonisation: environmental protection in regional trade agreements. Harv Environ Law Rev 21:265–336
Esty DC, Geradin D (1998) Environmental protection policies and international comparativeness: a conceptual framework. J World Trade:5–46
Faure M (2000) Product liability and product safety in Europe: harmonisation or differentiation? Kyklos 53:467–508
Faure M (2003) How law and economics may contribute to the harmonization of tort law in Europe. In: Zimmermann R (ed) Grundstrukturen des Europäischen Deliktsrechts. Nomos, Baden-Baden, pp 31–82
Faure M (2011) Does environmental law matter? In: Faure M, Smits J (eds) Does law matter? On law and economic growth. Intersentia, Antwerp, pp 385–416
Faure M, Johnston JS (2009) The law and economics of environmental federalism: Europe and the United States compared. Va Environ Law J 27(3):205–274
Faure M, Lefevere JGJ, van den Bergh R (1996) The subsidiarity principle in European environmental law: an economic analysis. In: Eide E, van den Bergh R (eds) Law and economics of the environment. Juridisk Forlag, Oslo, pp 121–166
Frey BS (1994) Direct democracy: politico-economic lessons from Switzerland. Am Econ Rev 84 (2):338–342
Frey BS, Eichenberger R (1996a) FOCJ: competitive governments for Europe. Int Rev Law Econ 16(3):315–327
Frey BS, Eichenberger R (1996b) To harmonise or to compete? That's not the question. J Public Econ 60(3):335–349
Hirschman AO (1970) Exit, voice and loyalty, responses to decline in exit, voice and loyalty: responses to decline in firms, organizations and states. Harvard University Press, Cambridge
Inman RP, Rubinfeld DL (1994) The EMU and fiscal policy in the new European Community: an issue for economic federalism. Int Rev Law Econ 14:147–161
Jaffe AB, Peterson SR, Portney PR, Stavins RN (1995) Environmental regulation and the competitiveness of US manufacturing: what does the evidence tell us? J Econ Lit 33(1):132–163
Joerges C, Vos E (1999) EU committees: social regulation, law and politics. Hart Publishing, Oxford
Kirchgässner G, Pommerehne WW (1996) Tax harmonisation and tax competition in the European Community: lessons from Switzerland. See also in (1996). J Public Econ 60:351–371
Koziol H (1996) Das niederländische BW und der Schweizer Entwurf als Vorbilder für ein künftiges europäisches Schadenersatzrecht. ZEuP:587–599
Legrand P (1997) The impossibility of legal transplants. Maastricht J Eur Comp Law 4:111–124

Leibovitch EH (2008) Food safety regulation in the European Union: toward an unavoidable centralization of regulatory powers. Tex Int Law J 43:429–450
Mueller DC (1997) Federalism and the European Union: a constitutional perspective. Public Choice 90(1/4):255–280
Oates WE (1972) Fiscal federalism. Harcourt Brace Jovanovich, New York
Oates WE, Schwab RM (1988) Economic competition among jurisdiction: efficiency enhancing or distortion inducing? J Public Econ 35:333–354
Ogus AI (1994) Regulation, legal form and economic theory. Clarendon Press, Oxford
Ogus AI (1999) Competition between national legal systems: a contribution to economic analysis to comparative law. Int Comp Law Q 48(2):405–418
Ogus AI (2001) The contribution of economic analysis of law to legal transplant. In: Smits J (ed) The contribution of mixed legal systems to European law. Intersentia, Antwerp, pp 27–37
Revesz R (1992) Rehabilitating interstate competition: rethinking the race for the bottom rational for federal environmental regulation. N Y Univ Law Rev 67:1210–1254
Revesz R (1996) Federalism and interstate environmental externalities. Univ Pa Law Rev 144 (6):2341–2416
Revesz R (2000a) Environmental regulation in federal systems. In: Somsen H (ed) Yearbook of European environmental law. Oxford University Press, Oxford, pp 1–35
Revesz R (2000b) Federalism and environmental regulation: an overview. In: Revesz RL, Sands P, Stewart RB (eds) Environmental law: the economy and sustainable development. Cambridge University Press, Cambridge, pp 37–79
Revesz R (2001) Federalism and regulation: some generalizations. In: Esty DC, Geradin D (eds) Regulatory competition and economic integration, comparative perspectives. Oxford University Press, Oxford
Rose-Ackerman S (1992) Rethinking the progressive agenda: the reform of the American regulatory state. Free Press, New Haven
Rose-Ackerman S (1995) Controlling environmental pollution: the limits of public law in Germany and the United States. Edward Elgar, Cheltenham
Schäfer H-B (2000) The bundling of similar interests in litigation. The incentives for class action and legal actions taken by associations. Eur J Law Econ 9(3):183–213
Shavell S (1984) Liability for harm versus regulation of safety. J Leg Stud 13:357–374
Tiebout CM (1956) A pure theory of local expenditures. J Polit Econ 64(5):416–424
Ugland T, Veggeland F (2006) Experiments in food safety policy integration in the European Union. J Common Mark Stud 44(3):607–624
van den Bergh R (1998) Subsidiarity as an economic demarcation principle and the emergence of European private law. Maastricht J Eur Comp Law 5(2):129–152
van den Bergh R (2000a) Towards an institutional legal framework for regulatory competition in Europe. Kyklos 53:435–466
van den Bergh R (2000b) Economics in a legal strait-jacket: the difficult reception of economic analysis in European law. Paper presented at the workshop empirical research and legal realism: setting the agenda, Haifa, 6–9 June 1999
van den Bergh R (2016) Farewell Utopia? Why the European Union should take the economics of federalism seriously. Maastricht J Eur Comp Law 23(6):937–964
van der Meulen BMJ (2013) The structure of European food law. Laws 2(2):69–98
Vogel D (1995) Trading up: consumer and environmental regulation in the global economy. Harvard University Press, Cambridge
Vos E (1999) Institutional frameworks of community health and safety legislation: committees, agencies and private bodies. Hart Publishing, Oxford
Vos E (2000) EU food safety regulation in the aftermath of the BSE-crisis. J Consum Policy 23:227–255
Vos E (2002) Institutional frameworks of community health and safety regulation. Hart Publishing, Oxford

Vos E, Wendler F (2006) Food safety regulation at the EU level. In: Vos E, Wendler F (eds) Food safety regulation in Europe. A comparative institutional analysis. Intersentia, Antwerp, pp 65–70

Winiger B (2001) L'architecture de l'Avant-projet de Loi sur la responsabilité civile. Revue de droit suisse 12:299–326

Michael Faure LL.M. became academic director of the Maastricht European institute for transnational legal research (METRO) and professor of Comparative and International Environmental Law at the law faculty of Maastricht University in September 1991. He still holds both positions today. In addition, he is academic director of the Ius Commune Research School and member of the board of directors of Ectil. Since the first of February 2008, he is half time professor of comparative private law and economics at the Rotterdam Institute of Law & Economics (RILE) of the Erasmus University Rotterdam and academic director of the European Doctorate in Law and Economics (EDLE) programme.

Since 1982 he is equally attorney at the Antwerp Bar. He publishes in the areas of environmental (criminal) law, tort and insurance and economic analysis of (accident) law.

Pre-Market Approval and Its Impact on Food Innovation: The Novel Foods Example

Martin Holle

Abstract Pre-market approval is a high barrier to market entry. Its impact on innovation and competitiveness of food businesses depends to a large extent on the requirements and duration of the authorisation process. The higher the number of unknown variables in the equation, the more reluctant businesses are with their decision to invest in innovation. The European authorisation process for Novel Foods contains a number of elements that make it difficult for companies to form a reliable plan for their route to market. Key issues are the lack of binding time lines for regulatory decisions, of effective protection of the applicant's proprietary scientific data and of a transparent process for the consideration of so-called "other legitimate factors". These shortcomings are not addressed by Regulation (EU) No. 2015/2283 (the new Novel Foods Regulation) and can only be eliminated if the European Commission, Member States and the European Food Safety Authority tackle these issues in the implementation of the Regulation.

1 The Concept of Novel Foods

The appearance of new foods has always been a phenomenon in food markets. In Roman times black pepper was imported from India. Potatoes were brought from South America to Europe in the Middle Ages. The increasing globalisation of food trade in the nineteenth and twentieth century made exotic, non-indigenous foods widely available to European consumers with the variety of products on offer steadily increasing. Those foods, like any food on the market, had to be safe for human consumption. For centuries, due to the lack of better methods to determine food safety, the fact that imported foods were consumed by the populations of the countries of origin served as prima facie evidence that those foods were safe to eat (today this is known as "history of safe consumption"). It was only the development

M. Holle (✉)
Hamburg University of Applied Sciences, Faculty of Life Sciences, Hamburg, Germany
e-mail: martin.holle@haw-hamburg.de

H. Bremmers, K. Purnhagen (eds.), *Regulating and Managing Food Safety in the EU*, Economic Analysis of Law in European Legal Scholarship 6,
https://doi.org/10.1007/978-3-319-77045-1_14

of more sophisticated methods in the assessment of the toxicological and microbiological safety of foods that triggered additional requirements imported foods had to comply with. Still, these safety standards were basically the same for all foods on the market, regardless of their origin, and they were only enforced ex-post.

1.1 Emerging Systems of Pre-Market Assessment of Foods and Food Ingredients

The appearance of man-made substances like synthetic dyes in foods eventually led to regulatory concepts of pre-market approval for certain categories of foods and food ingredients. Examples are the Federal Food, Drug and Cosmetic Act of 1938 in the United States or Article 4a of the German Food Act of 1958, prohibiting the use of colourants and other additives in foods without prior authorisation. Similar provisions were established in the European Economic Community with the Directives on the authorisation of colouring matters (62/645/EEC), preservatives (64/54/EEC), antioxidants (70/357/EEC) and emulsifiers, stabilisers, thickeners and gelling agents (74/329/EEC) for use in foodstuffs. All of them had in common that they referred to substances or food ingredients that were of synthetic origin and/or were not consumed as foods as such. Conventional foodstuffs with technological properties like egg yolk, flour or non-modified starches were excluded from the scope (cf. Art. 9 of Directive 74/329/EEC).

Further progress in food technology led to the creation of a new category of food ingredients that were obtained from plant or microbial sources. In contrast to additives, their intended use was not the improvement of the technological but the enhancement of the nutritional properties of foods. In the early 1970s high hopes were put in particular into the development of new protein sources that were supposed to end food shortages in developing countries.[1] As the creation of these new food ingredients involved substances which had not been eaten by a human population before and were not obtained by processes that could be considered minor variations of existing techniques, a new safety framework had to be created that took these developments into account. It was developed by the United Nations' Protein Advisory Group (PAG). The PAG had already issued a guidance note on human testing of supplementary food mixtures in 1966[2] and complemented it by additional guidelines on the production of single-cell protein for human consumption,[3] the preclinical testing of novel sources of protein[4] and on nutritional and safety aspects of protein sources for animal feeding.[5] Those guidelines subsequently got

[1]See e.g. Gounelle de Pontanel (1973).

[2]Protein Advisory Group (1966).

[3]Protein Advisory Group (1972).

[4]Protein Advisory Group (1974a).

[5]Protein Advisory Group (1974b).

updated in 1983.[6] The guideline on preclinical testing of novel sources of food for the first time spelled out a set of criteria to define what constitutes a Novel Food:

> Novel foods are defined as those not previously eaten by a human population, and that cannot be considered to be minor processing variants of conventional food. This guideline is directed towards commonly used foods processed by new techniques and to raw materials not so far used as human food either directly or by inclusion in food products. Similar attention needs to be applied to new varieties of conventional foods or those that have been genetically changed. Clear examples for application of the guidelines are new foods developed by isolation from conventional sources by unusual techniques and yeasts, bacteria, moulds, or algae, i.e. the so-called single-cell proteins. It is recommended that all new foods, including proteins, be evaluated with respect to their safety for use and nutritional value before application as a human food source.[7]

This definition became the blueprint for the categories of Novel Foods specified in Article 1(2) of the European Novel Foods Regulation (EC) No. 258/97. It already included most of the classes specified there like foods derived from or consisting of genetically modified organisms, isolates, foods that have not been previously consumed by the European population and foods produced by new technologies. The recommendation of the guideline to always evaluate the safety as well as the nutritional value of a Novel Food prior to its use as a food source was also adopted by the European legislator and was spelled out in Article 3 of Regulation (EC) No. 259/97.

A voluntary system for the assessment of Novel Foods was established in the UK since the 1980s.[8] In 1987 the Advisory Committee on Novel Foods and Processes (ACNFP) was created to assist with the scientific assessment of the safety and nutritional adequacy of Novel Foods. Section 18 of the Food Safety Act 1990 enabled the Secretary of State to issue regulations on the prohibition of commercial operations with regard to Novel Foods. These statutory powers, however, were not frequently used as businesses usually respected the findings of the ACNFP.

1.2 The Regulation of Novel Foods in the European Union

On European level, the need to regulate Novel Foods was for the first time formally recognised in the European Commission's White Paper "Completing the Internal Market"[9] which included a proposal for a "general directive on new foodstuffs obtained by a biotechnological process" in the working programme for 1987–1992. In 1992 the Commission presented its first draft of a Regulation on novel foods and novel food ingredients.[10] The proposal used a significantly wider definition of a Novel Food than the PAG guidelines and included any product which had no history of food use or was

---

[6]United Nations (1983).

[7]United Nations (1983).

[8]House of Commons (1999).

[9]COM (85) 310 final of 14 June 1985.

[10]COM (92) 295 final of 7 July 1992.

subject to new processing techniques. Due to strong criticism from the Member States and other stakeholders the proposal had to be redrafted several times and eventually got adopted as Regulation (EC) No. 258/97 in 1997. Article 1(2) defined Novel Foods as

> foods and food ingredients which have not hitherto been used for human consumption to a significant degree within the Community and which fall under the following categories:
>
> (a) foods and food ingredients containing or consisting of genetically modified organisms within the meaning of Directive 90/220/EEC;
> (b) foods and food ingredients produced from, but not containing, genetically modified organisms;
> (c) foods and food ingredients with a new or intentionally modified primary molecular structure;
> (d) foods and food ingredients consisting of or isolated from micro-organisms, fungi or algae;
> (e) foods and food ingredients consisting of or isolated from plants and food ingredients isolated from animals, except for foods and food ingredients obtained by traditional propagating or breeding practices and having a history of safe food use;
> (f) foods and food ingredients to which has been applied a production process not currently used, where that process gives rise to significant changes in the composition or structure of the foods or food ingredients which affect their nutritional value, metabolism or level of undesirable substances.

The European legislator thus kept the core principle that a Novel Food is a food that was not consumed by humans before, but at the same time introduced several important modifications. On one hand, it limited the definition to a closed catalogue of products listed in subsections (a) to (f) of Article 1(2). On the other hand its scope was extended to foods that were not consumed in the European Community to a significant extent. The latter became a major roadblock for the introduction of foods from third countries and for the extension of the use of ingredients from food supplements to conventional foods (cf. Sect. 1.3 below).

The categories specified in Article 1(2) of Regulation (EC) No. 258/97 got further elaborated by Commission Recommendation 97/618/EC which assigned them to six classes of products (see Table 1).

Class 1 comprised single chemically defined substances and mixtures thereof which were of non-GM origin. More complex Novel Foods like intact plants, animals or microorganisms as well as food components like complex carbohydrates, fats, proteins or dietary fibre were attributed to class 2. Plants, animals and

Table 1 Classes of Novel Foods in the implementation of Regulation (EC) No. 258/97

		(a)	(b)	(c)	(d)	(e)	(f)
Class 1	Pure chemicals or simple mixtures from non-GM sources			x	x	x	
Class 2	Complex Novel Food from non-GM sources				x	x	
Class 3	GM plants and their products	x	x				
Class 4	GM animals and their products	x	x				
Class 5	GM microorganisms and their products	x	x				
Class 6	Foods produced using a novel process						x

Source: Commission Recommendation 97/618/EC

microorganisms of GM-origin formed the classes 3–5. Class 6 includes all processes that had not been used before in food production. Depending on the character of the food and its production a Novel Food could be attributed to more than one class at a time, leading to an accumulation of safety requirements.

The class of the Novel Food determined the scope and depth of the scientific assessment and consequently the level of supporting information that had to be supplied by the applicant. With Regulations (EC) No. 1829 and 1830/2003 genetically modified food and feed got subject to a specific legal framework as of 19 April 2004 and henceforth were excluded from the scope of the Novel Foods Regulation. The Novel Foods framework also does not apply to food additives within Regulation (EC) No. 1333/2008, flavourings for use in foods within Regulation (EC) No. 1334/2008 and extraction solvents used in the production of foods within Directive 2009/32/EC. Despite the fact that each of these categories has its own legal definition, areas of overlap remain and create demarcation problems. It is quite easy to envisage the case of an extract from an exotic food not consumed in the EU to date which is used for flavouring purposes. The borderline between Novel Foods and additives has already been tested with the application for ice-structuring protein (below Sect. 1.3).

For the Novel Food categories specified in Article 1(2) (d) and (e) (see above), Article 3(4) and (5) of Regulation (EC) No. 258/97 allowed a simplified authorisation, based on a notification to the European Commission in case the Novel Food was substantially equivalent to existing foods or food ingredients with regard to composition, nutritional value, metabolism, intended use and the level of undesirable substances contained. This had to be demonstrated on the basis of generally recognised scientific evidence or on the basis of an opinion delivered by one of the competent national risk assessment authorities. In practice, the European Commission in most of the cases required the assessment of the substantial equivalence by the competent body of a Member State because for such a complex and very specific evaluation comprehensive generally accepted scientific data is rarely available. Another reason might have been the fact that the European Commission itself simply was not equipped with the resources to conduct such assessments.

Article 8(1) of Regulation (EC) No. 258/97 defined the test criteria for the assessment of substantial equivalence, which included

(a) any characteristic or food property such as:
- the composition,
- the nutritional value or nutritional effects,
- the intended use of the food,

which renders a novel food or food ingredient no longer equivalent to an existing food or food ingredient.

(b) the presence in the novel food or food ingredient of material which is not present in an existing equivalent foodstuff and which may have implications for the health of certain sections of the population;

(c) the presence in the novel food or food ingredient of material which is not present in an existing equivalent foodstuff and which gives rise to ethical concerns.

In a guidance document the European Commission further specified the criteria for the assessment of substantial equivalence.[11] According to the guidance,

[11] European Commission (n.d.-b).

substantial equivalence could be demonstrated either with regard to an existing authorised Novel Food already on the market, a product that was not identical but closely resembled that Novel Food or a product that was equivalent to a conventional food on the market; equivalence was excluded for food supplements and additives as well as to a large degree for extracts with regard to their source material.[12] The novel and the existing products had to be of the same or at least very similar taxonomic origin, had to have "a high degree of compositional similarity" and should not contain substances that were not contained in the original food.[13] New uses, specifically if they extended into a wider range of the population or involved higher levels than in the conventional diet, were not deemed acceptable for the notification procedure.[14]

The European Commission's guidance drew from the experiences made in the numerous notification procedures and summarised the decisions taken at various crossroads of the process. It is not legally binding and goes beyond the legal requirements set out in the Regulation.

According to the law, the food business operator could place the Novel Food on the market once he had submitted the notification to the European Commission. This, however, would happen at the operator's own risk because at no point in time the product would be deemed approved. If based on the notification the Commission came to the conclusion that the Novel Food was not substantially equivalent to conventional foods, this would mean a public recall of the product as it was on the market without authorisation. But also Member States could voice their objections to the classification as substantially equivalent even though this was not specifically foreseen in the Regulation. In many cases, the Commission therefore sought the views of the Member States before it positively accepted a notification and formally distributed it.

With Regulation (EU) No. 2015/2283 a major review of the Novel Food definition took place. The two key issues that dominated the political debate were the new techniques of cloning and nanotechnology and how they should be regulated. While both technologies were already covered by the Novel Food definition in Article 1 (2) of Regulation (EC) No. 258/97 (under subsections e and f respectively) the European Parliament in particular pushed for the introduction of a general ban of food produced from cloned animals in the revised Regulation.[15] After the first proposal had failed for lack of agreement between Commission, Parliament and Council, the Commission decoupled the issue of cloning from the revision process of the Novel Food Regulation by issuing separate proposals for Directives on cloning techniques and the use of food from cloned animals.[16] Until agreement is reached, the Novel Food Regulation continues to apply to food from animal clones. This is confirmed by recital 14 of Regulation (EU) No. 2015/2283. The revised Regulation

[12]European Commission (n.d.-b).

[13]European Commission (n.d.-b).

[14]European Commission (n.d.-b).

[15]USDA (2011).

[16]COM(2013) 892 and 893 final.

in its Article 3(2) also contains the following new categories of Novel Foods that were not established in Regulation (EC) No. 258/97:

- food consisting of, isolated from or produced from material of mineral origin (iii)
- food consisting of, isolated from or produced from cell culture or tissue culture derived from animals, plants, micro-organisms, fungi or algea (vi)
- food consisting of engineered nanomaterials (viii)
- vitamins, minerals and other substances as defined in the legislation on food supplements, fortification and on foods for particular nutritional uses if a new production process was used or they contain or consist of engineered nanomaterials (ix)
- food used exclusively in food supplements prior to 15 May 1997 if they are intended to be used in foods other than food supplements (x).

These changes on one hand take into account the technological progress that has been achieved since the entry into force of the first Novel Food Regulation in 1997, e.g. in cell and tissue engineering. On the other hand it expresses a significant level of distrust of the regulator in food business operators as most of the new categories were already covered under the less specific wording of the classes under the previous regulation, like nanotechnology. Additionally, it aims to legalise an administrative practice concerning the different treatment of conventional foods and food supplements exercised by the Commission and the Member States contra legem under Regulation (EC) No. 258/97. As shown above, this regulation applied to novel foods and food ingredients without further specification. Because food supplements are foods according to Article 2 of the General Food Law (Regulation (EC) No. 178/2002), by virtue of this definition no distinction could be made between these two groups. Thus, the approach to disregard a significant level of consumption in food supplements for the determination of the material degree of consumption of the same food or ingredient in the area of conventional foods, legally stood on shaky ground. With the new category under Article 3(2)(x) of Regulation (EU) No. 2015/2283 a legal basis was created for a principle that so far had been applied by habit, even if the inconsistency with the food definition of the General Food Law persists.

Another novelty of the revised Novel Food Regulation are the specific rules for traditional foods from third countries in section II of the regulation which allow the authorisation of such foods in the European Union based on a history of safe use in a third country and under a simplified procedure. These provisions are a reaction of the European legislator to the raising concerns that the EU Novel Food regime created a substantial trade barrier to exotic traditional foods and was potentially inconsistent with WTO rules.[17]

To determine the Novel Food status of a product, the European Commission and Member States produced a number of guidance documents to assist food business operators with the assessment.[18] In order to demonstrate "human consumption to a

[17]Hermann (2009), p. 499 ff. Broberg (2009) and Neville Craddock Associates (2005).

[18]European Commission (n.d.-a) and Food Standards Agency (2013).

significant degree" within the European Union prior to 15 May 1997 evidence of sale should be provided.[19] Whether the level of consumption is considered significant depends on factors like the geographical reach of the sales, the quantities consumed, the number of units sold, the availability on the market (currently and over a longer period of time), the target group of the product, its intended use and the application of new production processes.[20]

1.3 Practical Issues in the Application of the EU Definition of Novel Food

In the about two decades of application of the European pre-market authorisation procedure, like so often, life has proven to be much more colourful and diverse than the lawmakers had envisaged. Product innovation is a creative process that does not always follow the lines drawn by the legislator. Almost inevitably this created a certain tension with the category-based approach taken by the Novel Food Regulation. The most frequent points of discussion in the authorisation process were the determination of the Novel Food status and the additional requirements that should be taken into account beyond the assessment of the safety of the product.

Product Categorisation

According to Article 4(1) of Regulation (EU) No. 2015/2283 on novel foods it is the food business operators' responsibility to verify whether or not a food falls within the scope of the Regulation. In spite of the rather detailed description of categories, this often remains a difficult task and the consequences of a wrong classification can be severe. If the manufacturer or importer concludes that the food is not novel and places it on the market, but his view is not shared by the authorities, he is in breach of Article 6(2) of Regulation (EU) No. 2015/2283 and the product very likely will have to be withdrawn from the market. The situation is even more tricky if the food in question is used as an ingredient of other foods, which will further increase the potential damage caused by an incorrect classification. To allow food business operators to mitigate those risks, Article 4(2) of Regulation (EU) No. 2015/2283 gives them the option to consult the competent authorities of the Member State where the food should first be placed on the market. This Member State in turn can consult the European Commission and the other Member States. While at first glance this might look like a compelling proposition, in real life companies might hesitate to initiate such a consultation process.

[19] Food Standards Agency (2013).

[20] European Commission (n.d.-a).

The reason for the possible reluctance of food business operators to ask for official guidance is the complete lack of control on the process and the outcome as the Regulation does neither give any time lines nor any procedural rights to the questioner. Once the question has been raised, the answer must be awaited. The consultation process may eventually include all 28 Member States and the Commission. With such a large number of regulators involved, the likelihood that objections will be raised is substantial. As there is no legally defined procedure how to handle such objections, the most obvious solution is to opt for the least common denominator, which typically is to ask for an authorisation, just "to be on the safe side". Due to the informal nature of the consultation, it is not possible to challenge its conclusion before the European Courts. In summary, it must be asserted that regardless of the legislator's best intentions, for a food business operator asking for advice is high risk while for regulators there is no incentive for innovation-friendly decision making, because overruling objections during consultation may look to the public like jeopardising consumer safety for the sake of economic interests.

Next to the process of determining the Novel Food status itself, practical issues occur when it comes to the delineation between conventional and Novel Foods as well as between Novel Foods and other regulated product categories like additives, food supplements or fortified foods.

Uncertainties in the context of a food category often arise if a commonly consumed food or part of it is subject to treatments like extraction or other forms of selective enrichment of specific compounds. If the result of such a treatment is a substantially increased level of certain compounds which is significantly higher than what can be consumed from a conventional diet, the case is usually quite obvious, as certainly those compounds have not been consumed in the EU prior to 15 May 1997. An example are plant sterols, which naturally occur in small amounts in many nuts, seeds, fruit and vegetables. The estimate daily intake from these sources is around 60 mg[21] while the intended use in yellow fat spreads that was the subject of the Novel Foods authorisation led to daily intakes of 1.5–3 g.

Raspberry ketone extracts have been used as flavourings under Regulation (EC) No. 1334/2008. Similar to food supplements, the question arises if such a use can be considered consumption to a material degree. Given the typically rather low amount of active ingredient that is used for flavouring purposes, the level of consumption in the overall population in this case should be lower than for food supplements. However, if the amounts added for nutritional purposes were similar to the levels used in flavourings, it might become difficult to argue that a separate approval as a Novel Food would be required. The whole issue gets even trickier in the case of raspberry seed oil. Raspberry seeds are consumed as a part of a conventional diet. However, the amounts are low as they only form a minor component of the whole raspberry. Consequently, the levels consumed from an oil would be significantly higher than the intake from the normal diet. To decide whether raspberry seed oil requires a Novel Food authorisation thus depends on

[21]Piironen et al. (2003).

whether "consumption to a material degree" refers to the whole raspberry or to the raspberry seed oil. Ostensibly it appears that the case is similar to the one on the authorisation of plant sterols. A closer look reveals though that a number of oils from plant seeds that are not typically consumed as such are already on the market as conventional foods, e.g. grape seed oil or apricot kernel oil. So before raspberry seed oil is classified as a Novel Food, the question must be answered why it is so substantially different from other seed oils that it should be treated differently. And what about raspberry juice extracts with a wide range of different compositions?

The examples show that the classification of a food or food ingredient never is a simple task. In particular small and medium sized enterprises (SMEs) could easily underestimate the complexity of the assessment and will not have the resources to deal with an in-depth expert discussion on this matter. But even for large multinational companies the risks of navigating uncharted waters are high.

Borderline to Other Legal Regimes

A very good illustration of the borderline issues that arise in the product classification between the Novel Food Regulation and other legal frameworks provides the case of lycopene. Lycopene prepared from natural foods by the use of physical methods has been used for a long time as a colourant. It was authorised for this purpose already under Directive 94/36/EC and it is still today under Regulation (EC) No. 1333/2008. The levels permitted are in a range from 5 to 500 mg/kg (the latter only for some applications where a low level of intake can be expected like e.g. coatings), with most permitted uses being in the range between 10 and 40 mg/kg. Lycopene can be naturally derived from tomatoes, by fermentation from a fungus called Blakeslea trispora or synthecially. In all three cases, the lycopene is chemically identical. However, under Directive 94/36/EC only lycopene from natural sources was permitted for use as a food colourant.

In 2003 a food business operator intended to place lycopene on the market that was produced by fermentation of strains of the fungus Blakeslea trispora. This Lycopene is biosynthesised through the same pathway as lycopene produced in the tomato and is considered nutritionally equivalent to natural dietary lycopene.[22] From a toxicological point of view, lycopene from different sources (natural from tomatoes, synthetic and from Blakeslea trispora) are comparable, which resulted in the determination of a common ADI (acceptable daily intake) for lycopene from all sources by the European Food Safety Authority in 2008 (EFSA 2008). Because of the origin from a fungus, the European Commission categorised the lycopene in class 2.2 "Complex Novel Food from non-GM sources; the source of the Novel Food has no history of food use in the Community". While there's certainly no doubt about the fact that Blakeslea trispora has not been consumed as a food within the EU prior to 1997, it is at least questionable why the Commission denied the lycopene

[22]European Food Safety Authority (2005).

derived from it the substantial equivalence to lycopene obtained from tomatoes, given the similarities in nutritional properties and toxicology.

The motivation for the demand to go through the full authorisation process becomes clearer from the arguments that were brought up by the Member States during the procedure. The vast majority of the objections raised referred to the fact that lycopene was now to be used for nutritional rather than technological purposes and thus affected the question of the comparable "intended use" according to Article 3(4) of Regulation (EC) No. 258/97. Doubts were raised about the nutritional benefit of adding lycopene to the diet. Other concerns were the increase of the overall intake of lycopene from the diet and in particular the potential added intake of up to 20 mg per day from use in food supplements proposed by the applicant.[23] Against an estimated daily intake from conventional foods between 0.5 and 8 mg/kg this indeed appears to be excessive. On the other hand it must be noted that 20 mg is the amount contained in a 200 ml glass of tomato juice.[24] So far no safety concerns have been voiced with regard to potentially excessive consumption of such juice. It can of course be argued that for food supplements the risk of over-consumption is much higher than for conventional foods and drinks, in particular if formats like pills or powders are used. But this risk is inherent to these formats. It applies to any supplement in the market and thus is not specific to Novel Foods. In addition, lycopene oleoresin as a food supplement has been used in the UK since before 1997 to a significant degree[25] and apparently no food safety issues had occured. However, according to the administrative practice agreed between the Commission and the Member States, consumption of a food that occured only in the sector of food supplements was not considered sufficient to support a significant degree of consumption in the food sector as a whole. This distinction, that now got legalised in Regulation (EU) No. 2015/2283, was questionable at the time when the lycopene assessments were performed. Food supplements are foods by virtue of the definitions in Article 2 of Regulation (EC) No. 178/2002 and of Article 2(a) of Directive 2002/46/ EC. And also in Regulation (EC) No. 258/97 no distinction between conventional foods and food supplements was made. The reason that it was nevertheless applied were the huge differences in the size of the national food supplement markets and the varied safety levels administered there.

The opposite movement could be observed with the application for ice structuring proteins (ISP). The benefit of the novel ingredient was its ability to modify the texture of ice cream in such a way that less fat and sugar could be used in the product and the organoleptic properties like smoothness and mouthfeel could be improved[26] Although the end point of the application of ISP in the food product certainly was a nutritional benefit (less sugar, less fat) one may nevertheless wonder whether ISP itself was added for nutritional or rather for technological purposes if the initial effect of the ingredient

[23]European Food Safety Authority (2005).

[24]European Food Safety Authority (2005).

[25]European Food Safety Authority.

[26]ACNFP (2007); European Food Safety Authority.

was to modify the texture of the ice cream.[27] Quite likely this was discussed between the European Commission and the Member States before the application was channeled into the Novel Foods regime. It is difficult though to identify a rationale behind the different treatment of lycopene and ISP against the background that both ingredients can be used for technological as well as nutritional purposes. As none of the regulator's considerations on this aspect have been made publicly available, the probably most likely assumption from an outside perspective is that for lycopene there was a need to control its overall intake from various sources while for ISP the possible applications were limited to the ice cream category. Or, to phrase it differently, for ISP it did not really matter under which legal regime it got assessed, provided that the safety could be demonstrated, while for lycopene the extended use requested under Novel Foods had to be aligned with the usage already existing in the additives sector. Politically, this might make sense. However, working backwards from the desired outcome meant that some definitions and principles of the Novel Food Regulation got squeezed in order to meet political objectives. The result was a haziness at the fringes of the Regulation that created a considerable amount of uncertainty and commercial risks for food businesses operating in the sector. More examples that confirm the wavering classification practice of the EU are the Novel Food authorisations for a dextran preparation produced by Leuconostoc mesenteroides (similar to starch, added with the purpose to bind water and to improves softness, crumb texture and loaf volume in bread), tagatose/trehalose/isomaltulose (sweetening properties, but additives regulation does not apply to mono—and disaccharides) and phosphated distarch phosphate (food additive as a freeze-thaw-stable thickener but also a source of dietary fibre) on one hand and Stevia rebaudiana authorised as a sweetener under the additives regime (after an earlier application as a Novel Food was unsuccessful due to insufficient safety data) on the other.

The increasing relevance of food products in the marketplace that deliver proven health benefits brings along the need to determine more clearly the demarcation line between (novel) foods and medicinal products. In the search for more "functional" foods, research is often focussing on active materials that are absorbed from the gastrointestinal tract and where the intrinsic activity could be described as a pharmacological mechanism of action. For such ingredients the potential adverse effect profile must be characterised in a way approaching that of drug safety assessment. On the other hand, it must be taken into account that the desired end-point of functional food intake and drug therapy are subtly different in that functional foods are not designed to be curative. Therefore, in general, it may be expected that dose levels and/or efficacy of any active functional food ingredient will be lower than that of a drug.

Article 2(2) of Directive 2001/83/EC on the Community code relating to medicinal products for human use stipulates that "in cases of doubt, where, taking into account all its characteristics, a product may fall within the definition of a 'medicinal product' and within the definition of a product covered by other Community

[27] Cf. FDA (2002).

legislation" the provisions on medicinal products should prevail. In Article 1 point 2 of Directive 2001/83/EC a medicinal product is defined as:

> (a) Any substance or combination of substances presented as having properties for treating or preventing disease in human beings;
>
> or
>
> (b) Any substance or combination of substances which may be used in or administered to human beings either with a view to restoring, correcting or modifying physiological functions by exerting a pharmacological, immunological or metabolic action, or to making a medical diagnosis.

This very broad definition and in particular the inclusion of any modification of physiological functions by a metabolic action creates difficulties when it comes to the determination of an exact borderline between foods and drugs. This is illustrated by the provision of Article 5 of Regulation (EC) No. 1924/2006 on nutrition and health claims made on foods which reads:

> General conditions
>
> 1. The use of nutrition and health claims shall only be permitted if the following conditions are fulfilled:
> (a) the presence, absence or reduced content in a food or category of food of a nutrient or other substance in respect of which the claim is made has been shown to have a beneficial nutritional or physiological effect, as established by generally accepted scientific data;

It is apparent from the legislative texts in Article 2(2) of Directive 2001/83/EC and Article 5 of Regulation (EC) No. 1924/2006 that both provisions refer to a physiological effect of a substance. Therefore the physiological effect itself cannot be a criteria to differentiate disease risk reduction claims for foods from medicinal claims. According to the jurisdiction of the European Court of Justice a case-by-case evaluation needs to be made:

> For the purposes of determining whether a product must be classified as a medicinal product or as a foodstuff within the meaning of the Community regulations, the competent national authority must decide on a case-by-case basis, taking account of all the characteristics of the product, in particular its composition, its pharmacological properties, to the extent to which they can be established in the present state of scientific knowledge, the manner in which it is used, the extent of its distribution, its familiarity to consumers and the risks which its use may entail.[28]

This case-by-case evaluation requested by the European Court does not allow for certain substances a priori to be classified as drugs or a disease risk reduction claim to be classified as a medicinal claim. An individual assessment must be made based on the criteria developed by the Court. Of the criteria mentioned the effect of the substance plays a central role. A substance would be considered a drug if it has pharmacological properties. However, the term "pharmacological properties" needs

[28]CJEU, case C-211/03, HLH Warenvertriebs GmbH a.o./Federal Republic of Germany, ECLI:EU:C:2005:370.

to be used with utmost caution. Pharmacological or biological activity is an expression describing the beneficial or adverse effects of a drug on living matter. When the drug is a complex chemical mixture, this activity is exerted by the substance's active ingredient but can be modified by the other constituents. The main kind of biological activity is beneficial effect or toxicity of a substance. Activity is generally dose-dependent and it is not uncommon to have effects ranging from beneficial to adverse for one substance when going from low to high doses.

From this characterisation it becomes evident that the scientific definition of "pharmacological properties" does not allow a clear distinction between foods and drugs or disease risk reduction claims and medicinal claims. Even the mere action of providing a thirsting person with water will result in an improvement of the electrolytic metabolism in the cells of the body and thus in an improvement of physiological functions like concentration and efficiency. This shows that food is administered to human beings also with a view to restoring, correcting or modifying physiological functions.

Because of the broad interpretation of the definition of "pharmacological effect" (covering any beneficial or adverse effect on the organism) there is always a danger that food business operators intending to place new functional foods on the market will be caught in a vicious circle: Article 5(1) of Regulation (EC) No. 1924/2006 requires for the permission of a disease risk reduction claim that the active substance is present in the product in a quantity that will produce the claimed physiological effect as accepted by generally accepted scientific evidence. This evidence usually will have to show a statistically significant physiological effect of the active substance. If there is no statistically significant effect, the claim is considered to be not substantiated and therefore prohibited. But if the substance shows a significant effect, it is regarded as pharmacological which means the claim is categorised as medicinal and prohibited for a food. In addition, also the substance itself can be classified as a medicinal product.

That this is not an unlikely scenario is demonstrated by the cases of melatonin and of monacolin K. For both substances a health claim got authorised under Regulation (EC) No. 1924/2006. As the European Commission pursuant to Article 17(1) of Regulation (EC) No. 1924/2006 is obliged to consider "any relevant provisions of Community law" one would expect that such an authorisation includes the decision whether the food or substance for which the health claim is made is classified as a food or a drug. Consequently, the approval of a health claim would imply that the product or substance on which the claim is based is regarded as a food (at least if used in the amounts specified in the conditions of use of the claim). Surprisingly, this is not the case. Recital 17 of Regulation (EC) No. 432/2012 states that "inclusion in the list of permitted claims [...] does not constitute an authorisation to the marketing of the substance on which the claim is made, a decision on whether the substance can be used in foodstuffs, or a classification of a certain product as a foodstuff." The provision was introduced at the instigation of some Member States that were concerned that due to the qualified majority decisions in the Standing Committee procedure they could lose the discretion given to them in the application of Directive 2001/83/EC to determine whether a certain substance or product is classified as a food or a drug. Based on the principle expressed in recital 17, Germany decided to continue to classify melatonin as a drug. For monacolin K the German authorities ruled that daily doses of more than 5 mg per day are considered to have a pharmacological effect. The decision effectively removes such products from the market, because according to the conditions of use for the authorised health claim the beneficial effect can only be achieved with a daily intake of 10 mg and food businesses are prevented from recommending this to consumers in Germany.

The precedence of the law on medicinal products is confirmed by recital 18 of Regulation (EU) No. 2015/2283. Borderline issues will therefore continue to be a source of uncertainty for applicants also under the new Regulation.

Consumed to a Significant Degree

Human consumption to a significant degree within the European Union prior to 15 May 1997 is one of the key criteria in the determination of the Novel Food status of a food or food ingredient. In the application of this principle, quite a number of considerations must be made, like consumption by whom, by how many people, across which territory and what if the food has been subject to further processing.

To help with the assessment, the European Commission produced an "Information and Guidance Document" on the core elements that need to be considered.[29] Determining the degree of consumption prior to 15 May 1997 is in essence a fact finding mission that comprises all available information including e. g. sales data, import lists, shipping notes, invoices, catalogues but also recipes and cookbooks. In the light of the long period of time that has passed since 1997, it is getting increasingly difficult for food business operators to present the evidence required. First of all, the documentation needed frequently predates the time for which electronic records are kept. Regularly, the legal time periods for financial record keeping will also have expired. And even if sales documents or invoices are still available, they often do not contain the information that is required to support the case like information on the composition or the intended use of the product.[30] A further complication is added by the precondition that the product must have been legally on the market before 1997. This is virtually impossible to prove as there is no pre-market authorisation requirement for foods and authorities thus do not certify the legality of a food product. So even if there is evidence that the product was on the market in the past, it does not tell anything about its legal classification. This becomes particularly relevant for products that are considered foods in some Member States but medicinal products in others, e.g. in the field of botanicals.

These challenges did not go away under Regulation (EU) No. 2015/2283 but will even be enhanced by the fact that new Novel Foods categories were introduced which may subject some products that were legally placed on the market after 15 May 1997

[29] European Commission (n.d.-b).

[30] Coppens (2015).

but before the entry into force of the new Regulation on 1 January 2018 to the Novel Foods regime and require an ex-post authorisation (cf. Sect. 4 below).

Novel Production Process

Article 1(2)(f) Regulation (EC) No. 258/97 included in the remit of the Novel Food definition "foods and food ingredients to which has been applied a production process not currently used, where that process gives rise to significant changes in the composition or structure of the foods or food ingredients which affect their nutritional value, metabolism or level of undesirable substances". This definition lacked precision because it did not specify whether "a production process not currently used" referred to food production in general or to the production of the specific food. However, Recommendation 97/618/EC clarified that it meant processes that are not currently used in food production as such. It mentioned as examples "new types of heat processing, non-thermal preservation methods, new processes to chill or freeze products, to dehydrate products, and the application of new processes catalysed by enzymes". In Article 3(2)(a)(vii) of Regulation (EU) No. 2015/2283 it is now spelled out that foods are considered to be novel if they result from "a production process not used for food production within the Union before 15 May 1997". An example of such a process is high-pressure pasteurisation in the production of fruit preparations which got authorised as a Novel Food by Commission Decision 2001/424/EC.

Uncertainties continue to persist when it comes to the question how similar or different a new production process is compared to the existing state of technology. An example of this is the process of ohmic heating, a method of heat treatment that can be applied for a number of purposes including extraction, fermentation, dehydration and evaporation as well as sterilisation and pasteurisation. Its difference to other heating methods is that electric current is passed through the food by the means of electrodes that are in direct contact with the food creating the advantage of a rapid and more uniform heating of the product.[31] The process of ohmic heating itself has been known for a very long time but its use in food processing has not been established prior to 15 May 1997. It is thus a novel production process. In the next step of the assessment it must be checked whether the application of the process leads to significant changes in the composition or structure of the food or food ingredients. Obviously, a heat treatment will result in changes of the structure of the food. Whether these changes are "significant" is debatable and will amongst others depend on the duration and temperature of the heat treatment. The heating will possibly also affect the nutritional value of the product, which is another indicator for the novelty of the process. According to the guidance provided by the European Commission in Recommendation 97/618/EC such new types of heat treatment should be within the remit of Novel Foods. Similar issues can occur in other innovative fields of food processing

[31]Knirsch et al. (2010), p. 436 f.

technology like pulsed electric field treatment, high power ultrasonics dense phase carbon dioxide processing or cold plasma processing.[32]

Additional Requirements

Primary purpose of the Novel Food Regulation is to ensure the safety of new foods placed on the market. But already Article 3 of Regulation (EC) No. 258/97 set out additional criteria that had to be considered in the authorisation by stipulating that Novel Foods and food ingredients must not present a danger to the consumer, mislead the consumer or differ from foods or food ingredients which they are intended to replace to such an extent that their normal consumption would be nutritionally disadvantageous for the consumer. So on top of the toxicological and microbiological safety of the food the economic interests of the consumers and aspects of public health should be considered. As a consequence, an applicant had to produce information that allows to determine the dietary and nutritional significance of the Novel Food. Generating projections for the expected intake levels of a specific food ingredient across the whole European Union requires considerable effort and is a huge project even for major food companies. More importantly, as every kind of modelling is based on assumptions, an area of ambiguity exists and only the result of the assessment by EFSA will tell if the applicant's suppositions were shared by the Scientific Panel. At times the assessment of the nutritional aspects got even stretched further during the authorisation process and included not only the safety but also the efficacy of the product. The most prominent example is the authorisation procedure for the use of added phytosterols in a number of food categories. Here the Scientific Committee on Food and EFSA respectively took a view on the level of the cholesterol-lowering effect of the ingredient. While avoiding the authorisation of a product with no proven effect is certainly a legitimate consideration in the context of Article 3 of Regulation (EC) No. 258/97 it is disputable if a comprehensive assessment of efficacy must be conducted even if evidence for a dose-response relationship has been provided by the applicant. Unlike for medicinal products, a risk-benefit analysis is not appropriate for a Novel Food because side effects are generally not acceptable in a food. Hence, the assessment of nutritional properties of a Novel Food should be limited to its safety, potential adverse effects on the diet and whether consumers could be mislead. In contrast, it is not the task of the risk assessor to determine in which dose range the best possible effect is achieved. Why such considerations nevertheless played a role in the case of phytosterols can probably best be explained by the lack of a harmonised European framework on nutrition and health claims at the time the applications were made.

With the entry into force of Regulation (EC) No. 1924/2006 the efficacy part of the assessment shifted to the applications for authorisation of health claims, resulting in two separate evaluations for safety and for health effects of the same food or food

[32]For an overview on the innovation pipeline in food processing cf. Doona et al. (2010).

ingredient which were not always conducted in a coordinated fashion. Regulation (EU) No. 2015/2283 tries to accommodate the changed situation by introducing rules on parallel applications for authorisation of Novel Foods and health claims. The solution offered, however, is far from satisfactory for applicants as the authorisation procedure for the Novel Food is put on hold until the assessment of the health claim has been completed by EFSA. This makes it rather unlikely that such a combined application authorisation procedure is concluded in much less than 3 years.

Regulation (EU) No. 2015/2283 further extends the list of factors that must be looked at by the European Commission in the decision-making on the authorisation or its rejection. Pursuant to Article 12 on top of the safety, the nutritional adequacy and the consumer's economic interests, the Commission is obliged to consider any relevant provision of European Union law, in particular the precautionary principle, and any other legitimate factors relevant to the application. In this way, the bar for new authorisations is raised significantly because aspects so diverse as consumer acceptance, animal welfare or local food traditions could become part of the assessment. At the same time, because of the reference to the precautionary principle, any scientific uncertainty works to the disadvantage of the applicant. What might become subject of the evaluation can be very difficult to predict as there is no fixed catalogue of criteria and a campaign by a non-governmental organisation may be enough to trigger additional demands of regulators in the authorisation procedure (cf. Sect. 2.2. below).

2 Regulatory Considerations in the Approval Process

The legal frame for the European Commission's decision on a Novel Food application is defined by its obligation expressed in Articles 114 and 169 TFEU to promote the interests of consumers and to ensure a high level of consumer protection by safeguarding health, safety and economic interests of consumers on one hand and by its duty to warrant the functioning of the internal market on the other. With the adoption of a European Regulation on Novel Foods in 1997 national provisions got harmonised and a level playing field for all food business operators was created. At the same time, the European Commission took over the responsibility to ensure a high level of consumer protection with regard to this product category. Pursuant to Article 3 of Regulation (EC) No. 258/97 the Commission had to make sure that the Novel Foods it authorised for placing on the market were safe, did not mislead the consumer and were not nutritionally disadvantageous. Since the entry into force of the General Food Law in 2002, the food safety standards codified in there, in particular the precautionary principle, had to be taken into account. With Article 12 of Regulation (EU) No. 2015/2283 the list of criteria to be considered in the authorisation process got extended by all provisions of EU law that are relevant to the application and any other legitimate factors. While the safety aspects are the focal point of the scientific risk assessment performed by EFSA, the consideration of other

EU legislation and other legitimate factors are typically part of the risk management decision by the European Commission.

2.1 Safety

Food safety is at the heart of the Novel Food authorisation process. The pre-market authorisation serves the aim expressed in Articles 114 and 169 TFEU to assure a high level of protection for consumers' health and safety. For foods the concept of safety is spelled out more in detail in Regulation (EC) No. 178/2002 on the general principles and requirements of food law. According to Article 14 of this Regulation, food should not be injurious to health or unfit for human consumption. When determining the safety of a food its normal conditions of use and the information available to the consumer must be taken into account. The safety assessment should look at:

- the probable immediate, short-term and long-term effects of the food on the health of a person consuming it, but also on subsequent generations;
- the probable cumulative toxic effects;
- the particular health sensitivities of a specific category of consumers where the food is intended for that category of consumers.

In addition, based on the precautionary principle established in Article 7 of Regulation (EC) No. 178/2002, regulators can deny the authorisation of a Novel Food if the risk assessment identifies a possibility of harmful effects on health even if scientific uncertainty on the relevance of these findings persists.

The safety assessment is conducted by EFSA based on the criteria defined in Article 3 of Regulation (EC) No. 258/97 and Articles 10, 11, 14 and 17 of Regulation (EU) No. 2015/2283 respectively. While Article 3(1) of Regulation (EC) No. 258/97 was quite short and crisp in just demanding that the Novel Food had to be safe, not misleading and not nutritionally disadvantageous to the consumer, Regulation (EU) No. 2015/2283 introduced two separate sets of safety requirements, one for traditional foods from third countries and one for all other Novel Foods. Commission Implementing Regulation (EU) 2017/2469 and the complementing EFSA guidance (EFSA 2016b) on the preparation and presentation of applications pursuant to Article 10 of Regulation (EU) No. 2015/2283 contain more specific elements that should be addressed by applicants in the standard authorisation procedure.

For traditional foods from third countries the applicant must demonstrate the history of safe food use in a third country based on documented data. Pursuant to Article 17(2) of Regulation (EU) No. 2015/2283 EFSA assesses the history of safe use in the third country, the safety of the food and potential nutritional disadvantages from its consumption if it is intended to replace another food in the diet. The general administrative and scientific requirements for this assessment are laid out in Commission Implementing Regulation (EU) 2017/2468.

More details are provided by an EFSA guidance which asks for a specification of the typical composition of the food based on at least five independently produced batches, a detailed description of the production process and qualitative as well as quantitative data on the physical, chemical, biochemical and microbiological properties of the food.[33] In addition, information on the extent of use of the traditional food in the population, its preparation and handling, the role in the diet and precautions to be taken should be given.[34]

To demonstrate the extent of use in the third country the applicant must provide documentation on:

- the place of production and volume of the traditional food produced per year in the third country or countries;
- the geographical areas (e.g. region, country, continent) where it has been consumed;
- the quantity of consumption, information on the serving size(s), average, high and if available maximum intake levels per person;
- if available, intake estimates based on food consumption surveys or other estimates; a clear distinction should be made between the intakes of a part of a botanical as such, preparations made of it (e.g. tea), or e.g. an intake of essential oil;
- the length and continuity of its use over time.[35]

This extensive safety assessment programme can be considerably reduced if existing conventional foods exist in the market with a composition which is very similar to the Novel Food. In that event, key nutrients and toxicants as well as the nutritional properties will be compared for their similarities and differences. If no relevant divergences are identified, the Novel Food can be considered as safe as its conventional counterpart and no supplementary safety data is required.[36] The approach was used e.g. in the procedures for the authorisation of dextran produced from the bacteria Leuconostoc mesenteroides[37] and for fruit preparations produced with the use of high-pressure pasteurisation.[38]

2.2 *Community Law and "Other Legitimate Factors"*

Next to the scientific safety assessment provided by EFSA the European Commission is obligated to take into account all EU legislation and any other legitimate factor that is pertinent to the authorisation of the Novel Food. This opens up a wide space of discretion for the regulator which is only limited by the applicant's fundamental rights and the general principles of European Community Law,

[33]European Food Safety Authority (2016a).

[34]European Food Safety Authority (2016a).

[35]European Food Safety Authority (2016a).

[36]ACNFP (n.d.).

[37]Decision 2001/122/EC.

[38]Decision 2001/424/EC.

including in particular the right to good administration and the principle of proportionality[39] which has also been acknowledged in Article 296 TFEU.

In a field where the EU institutions are granted a large degree of discretion and where they must undertake complex assessments, however, the control by the courts is restricted to "examining whether it is vitiated by a manifest error of assessment or a misuse of powers or whether the legislature has manifestly exceeded the limits of its discretion".[40]

Correspondingly, there is also only a limited liability in case damages are caused by an unlawful decision. According to the jurisprudence of the European Court of Justice, liability will only arise if the Commission "manifestly and gravely disregarded the limits on the exercise of its powers".[41]

The level of justification the European Court demands for the decision taken by the regulator is equally low. Although it is acknowledged that the rationale for a decision "must be appropriate to the measure at issue and must disclose in a clear and unequivocal fashion the reasoning followed by the institution which adopted the measure in such a way as to enable the persons concerned to ascertain the reasons for it and to enable the competent Community court to exercise its power of review",[42] the Court also held that "it is not necessary for the reasoning to go into all the relevant facts and points of law, since the question whether the statement of reasons meets the requirements of Art. 190 of the Treaty [now Art. 296 TFEU] must be assessed with regard not only to its wording but also to its context and to all the legal rules governing the matter in question".[43] Even if the rationale given for a decision must take into account the individual interests of its addressees in obtaining explanations,[44] it is not necessary that the reasoning specifies all the relevant facts and legal considerations on which the act of the institution is based. It is rather sufficient if its adoption happens in circumstances familiar to the addressee which allow him to comprehend the scope of the measure affecting him.[45] According to the European Courts it suffices if the applicant can conclude the reasons for the European

[39]CJEU, case C-189/01, Jippes/Minister van Landbouw, Natuurbeheer en Visserij, ECLI:EU:C:2001:420, para 81; CJEU, joined cases C-133/93, C-300/93 and C-362/93, Crispoltoni and others, ECLI:EU:C:1994:364, para 41; CJEU, case C-331/88, The Queen/Ministry of Agriculture, Fisheries and Food, ex parte FEDESA and others, ECLI:EU:C:1990:391, para 13.

[40]CJEU, case C-601/11 P, France/Commission, ECLI:EU:C:2013:465, para 142; CJEU, case C-236/01, Monsanto Agricoltura Italia and others, ECLI:EU:C:2003:431, para 135.

[41]CJEU, case C-312/00 P, Commission/Camar and Tico, ECLI:EU:C:2002:736, para 54; GC, case T-291/04, Enviro Tech/Commission, ECLI:EU:T:2011:760, para 124.

[42]CJEU, joined cases C-341/06 P and C-342/06 P, Chronopost, ECLI:EU:C:2008:375, para 88.

[43]CJEU, joined cases C-341/06 P and C-342/06 P, Chronopost, ECLI:EU:C:2008:375, para 88; CJEU, case C-501/00, Spain/Commission, ECLI:EU:C:2004:438, para 73; CJEU, case C-367/95 P, Commission/Sytraval, ECLI:EU:C:1998:154, para 63.

[44]GC, case T-390/08, Bank Melli Iran/Council, ECLI:EU:T:2009:401, para 82.

[45]GC, case T-296/12, Health Food Manufacturers' Association and others/Commission, ECLI:EU:T:2015:375, para 150; GC, case T-539/10, Acino/Commission, ECLI:EU:T:2013:110, para 130; case T-390/08, Bank Melli Iran/Council, ECLI:EU:T:2009:401, para 82.

Commission's decision from the overall context of the authorisation process, including e.g. discussions and correspondence with EFSA, Member States or the Commission regarding the application, opinions of EFSA and any other relevant materials known to him.[46]

Compared to the legal interests codified in EU legislation "other legitimate factors" are largely political criteria. They express the prerogative of the risk manager to consider in his decision not only the science and the law but also wider aspects of public interest. Examples of such factors are given in recital 19 of Regulation (EC) No. 178/2002 and include societal, economic, traditional, ethical and environmental factors as well as the feasibility of controls. The regulator can also factor into his decision matters like consumer acceptance of a new food, animal welfare, the protection of local specialties or traditional methods of production.[47] So even if a product from a scientific point of view does not pose a health risk, the European Commission could still decide not to authorise a Novel Food for reasons of public health (if e.g. the consumption of the food could lead to a significant increase of the daily fat intake) or because of the rejection of a new technology by the population for ethical reasons (like the use of stem cells from animal embryos for the in-vitro production of meat).

While defining "other legitimate factors" as "any factor legitimate to the matter"—like an EU official did it[48]—may be a step too far, it must be acknowledged that a plethora of public interest considerations can be relevant for a decision. In its ruling on the action for annulment of Regulation (EU) No. 432/2012 the General Court held that even a political need to examine tensions between different legal regimes can constitute a legitimate other factor to postpone or accelerate the adoption of a list of authorised health claims.[49]

Because of their mostly political nature, it is very difficult for the applicant in a Novel Foods authorisation procedure to anticipate which of the other legitimate factors may become relevant. Even if some of them may be obvious like the increased public scrutiny in case of the use of genetically modified organisms or nanotechnology, many of them could still hit the applicant out of the blue, e. g. if a policy change happens during the authorisation process. Unlike for the science-based risk assessment approach applied with regard to the safety of the product, there are no guidelines or hard criteria food business operators can benchmark against when it comes to other legitimate factors. The political debate largely takes place behind closed doors in the Standing Committee to which the applicant has no direct access. The publicly available minutes of those meetings only contain a laconic summary of the results but not the considerations that were the basis of the decisions.

---

[46]Cf. EGC, case T-539/10, Acino/Commission, ECLI:EU:T:2013:110, para 130.

[47]Cf. Szajkowska (2012).

[48]European Commission (2013).

[49]EGC, case T-296/12, Health Food Manufacturers' Association and others/Commission, ECLI: EU:T:2015:375, para 106.

This lack of transparency combined with the broad discretion attributed to the regulator leaves food businesses highly exposed to commercial and reputational risks. As an applicant it is thus not sufficient to rely on sound science to win the day. In order to manage it, every Novel Food application must be complemented by a political strategy that includes an analysis and management of all relevant stakeholders in the field. The human and financial resource required to execute such a plan is significant and can be close to the cost of producing the application itself.

3 Impact on Food Business Operators

Without any doubt, a pre-market authorisation requirement is a limitation to a food business's freedom to operate. While such a restriction can be justified by other legitimate legal interests like the protection of consumer's health, the principle of proportionality requires that such restrictions are not more severe than necessary to achieve their objective. But this is not only a legal matter of balancing fundamental rights of food business operators and consumers but also an economic question of maintaining and improving the European food industry's competitiveness in a globalised market. In general, businesses can live with legal restrictions if they create a level playing field and are applied consistently. What they do not like is legal uncertainty and unclear time lines for decisions. Bringing an innovation to market is a complex exercise that requires thorough planning and substantial investment of human and financial resources without knowing in advance to what degree this investment will pay off in the future. Deviations from the plan often turn out to be costly, in particular if they negatively affect the marketability of the product or lead to a delay in the launch date. Before taking a decision, any company's senior management will therefore try to eliminate as many uncertainties as possible from the scenario. The more difficult it is to predict whether a new product will be authorised at all or whether the process to obtain approval will take 1, 2 or 3 years, the closer the investment decision comes to a leap in the dark and the less inclined a business leadership will be to take it. Unfortunately for food business operators in the EU the road to Novel Foods approval is paved with ambiguities and indefinite time lines so that a lot of entrepreneurial spirit is needed to embark on such a venture.

3.1 *The Role of Innovation for the Competitiveness of Food Manufacturers*

R&D intensity in the food and beverages sector typically is at a low to medium level compared to other industry sectors.[50] However, this overall picture must be treated with caution as it is distorted by the fact that over 99% of the food and drink

[50]EU Commission (2015).

companies are small and medium sized enterprises (SMEs)[51] which typically do neither have the need nor the resources to do high end research and development. The picture might further be skewed by the use of patenting activities as a major indicator of research activity in the European Commission's statistics. As a matter of nature, patents on food innovations are rare because formulations, recipes or clinical data identifying new health benefits are usually not patentable.

The total R&D expenditures of the 28 food and drink companies leading in innovation amounted to € 2517 million in 2014 with an average R&D intensity (R&D spend in % of net sales) of 2.6%. This is below the EU's industry-wide target of 3% but well in line with the spend in non-EU food and drink companies. Two food companies are amongst the EU's top 66 high-performing R&D driven innovators.[52]

The food and drink industry is part of the Fast Moving Consumer Goods (FMCG) sector. In the European Union the FMCG markets overall are characterised by a low to stagnant growth and an increasing level of sales on promotion.[53] In the years 2011–2013 of 12.000 product innovations 76% did not last longer than a year and only very few reached sales of more than € 10 million in their first year.[54] In the food business radical innovations are rare. Most new products are minor improvements of existing products, seasonal variants or line extensions.[55] Only around 2% of the total number of innovations can be considered breakthrough.[56]

It is game-changing, breakthrough innovation though that gives food manufacturers the best short-term opportunities to create growth in the largely saturated markets of the developed world.[57] Players that do not innovate are limited to competing solely on price, which favours those companies that produce with the lowest cost input.[58] Thus, it is crucial for food business operators to bring new products to the market as quickly as possible. If a pre-market approval is required, the duration of the authorisation process has a significant impact on the speed to market of an innovation and hugely affects the company's ability to generate return on its investment in new product development. In comparison with other jurisdictions, the European Union's approval procedure under Regulation (EC) No. 258/97 was the slowest by a large margin. While the authorisation of a spreadable vegetable fat with added phytosterol esters as a Novel Food took 3 months in the United States, 14 months in Australia and Switzerland and 18 months in Japan, the European Union needed 31 months to complete the process.[59]

[51]Janssen (2011) and Brookes (2007).

[52]European Commission (2015).

[53]Nielsen Holdings (2014) and Statista (2013).

[54]Nielsen Holdings (2014).

[55]Lagnevik et al. (2004).

[56]Lagnevik et al. (2004) and Janssen (2011).

[57]PwC (2014) and Nielsen Holdings (2014).

[58]Winger and Wall (2006).

[59]Wendelin (2009).

In the example of the plant sterols case the lengthy European approval procedure created a major disadvantage for the applicant, because during that time a competitor was able to market products with a similar composition and the same functional benefit without any regulatory constraints by using plant stanols rather than plant sterols as an ingredient which were on the market in a Member State of the European Union prior to 15 May 1997. In the two and a half years it took to complete the authorisation process for plant sterol esters in the European Union, the applicant's competitor sold plant stanol-based ingredients and foods worth € 100 million.[60]

The example shows that speed to market matters, a factor which often is massively underestimated by regulators. In the long run, jurisdictions with lengthy authorisation procedures are at a disadvantage in global competition because food businesses will prefer to launch their innovations first in those markets where they can expect a return on their investment in the shortest period of time. On top of that growth rates in the food sector are higher in emerging and developing markets than in the advanced, relatively saturated markets of the highly industrialised countries of the European Union or the United States. It can therefore be expected that a lot of original innovation will shift to those markets if the regulatory environment in Europe cannot provide by and large reliable timings and a reasonable level of legal certainty.

3.2 *Innovation Under the Novel Foods Regulation*

The business decision to start the development of a new product is based on the expectation that a reasonable return on investment will be achieved. Business leaders must demonstrate to the owner or shareholders of the company that the expected return exceeds alternative investment options and in any event is not lower than the cost of capital. The typical internal rate of return anticipated for an innovation in the foods sector is in a range of 20–25%, with 15% being a kind of bottom line below which investment is unlikely to happen.[61]

The return on investment of an innovation can be severely affected by the regulatory environment. Major factors are in particular uncertainties in the legal classification of a product, delays in the authorisation process and the level of exclusivity granted to the initial applicant.[62]

Grey Areas in the Product Classification

The Novel Food categories specified in Article 1(2) of Regulation (EC) No. 258/97 and Article 3(2) a) of Regulation (EU) No. 2015/2283 respectively play a pivotal role in

[60]Raisio (1998) and Raisio (1999).

[61]Brookes (2007).

[62]Brookes (2007).

determining the scope of the Regulation and thus for the decision whether a food requires an authorisation or not. Unfortunately, the definitions are rather generic and leave substantial room for grey areas in which the classification becomes a very difficult exercise. This might concern the categorisation of the food, the technology applied or the borderline to other legal regimes, e.g. for additives or for fortification (cf. Sect. 1.3).

Product Categorisation

Categorisation of a newly developed product can be a difficult task and consultations with authorities may cut both ways. That is why many potential applicants may prefer to get clarity on the classification internally first before they go out to external parties. Despite the existence of guidance documents by the Commission and some Member States, a certain lack of coherence in the treatment of similar foods or food ingredients can be observed in the authorisation practice, which is mainly driven by political considerations rather than by a lack of assessment criteria. So for companies doing their own assessment it is as important to build an arguable case for a certain categorisation as it is to demonstrate the safety of the product.

Eventually, from a business perspective, the applicant will always find himself between a rock and a hard place as he must choose between the chance to obtain a more favourable classification at the cost of certainty and an authoritative response from Commission and Member States at the level of the least common denominator which could result in a rejection or in restrictions of use being imposed. If this dilemma will disappear with the move to a centralised procedure in Regulation (EU) No. 2015/2283 remains to be seen. While formally the power for decision on the status of a food or food ingredient shifts to the European Commission, Article 4 (2) of the Regulation foresees an advisory role of Member States when a company is uncertain about the classification of a product. This raises the concern that if a Member State disagrees with a company's classification as a conventional food it may still be able to force the business into an authorisation procedure.[63] Only practical implementation will show whether Member States will primarily execute the Commission's views or if they will reserve themselves some discretion. No matter which way the regulatory practice will turn, food businesses will remain to struggle with the core question what constitutes significant similarities or differences to an existing conventional food on the market.

Novel Technology in Food Production

The example of ohmic heating in Sect. 1.3 above shows how even relatively simple and straightforward technologies are at risk of getting caught in the net of Novel Foods. It demonstrates the legislator's policy choice to subject new technologies in food

[63]European Parliament (2014).

processing to a pre-market authorisation as widely as possible. From a scientific perspective this is not always comprehensible because there is no obvious reason why e.g. heating by electric current would be considered a substantially higher risk than heating by microwaves. The uncertainty created by the very broad definition of what could be considered a novel production process eventually can bring innovations in food technology to a halt because businesses are not prepared to invest in a long, costly and rather unpredictable authorisation process, in particular if there are other markets in the world that embrace innovation and offer better economic growth perspectives. This negative impact of the Novel Foods requirements on the competitiveness of the European food industry has been acknowledged in a study commissioned by the Directorate Enterprise and Industry of the European Commission and was described as more restricting than any other food safety requirement, including HACCP and traceability.[64] Further strain is added by the fact that the Novel Food Regulation does not distinguish effects that may pose a safety risk from effects that may be beneficial for consumers. According to the legal definition, for the assumption of novelty it does not matter whether a significant change in the nutritional composition of the food is for the better or the worse. In both cases the Regulation applies. In a time where unhealthy eating has been identified as a major contributor to public health issues it would be expected that regulators seize any opportunity to stimulate innovation that leads to a healthier composition of the foods on offer in the market place. Unfortunately, this chance so far has been missed in the area of Novel Foods.

Borderline to Other Legal Regimes

Borderline issues are very difficult to handle for a food business because different legal classifications can seriously change the legal requirements the product must meet but also the way in which it can be marketed. Sales channels, positioning and pricing of a conventional food are very different from a food supplement or a product for special dietary needs. And for an ingredient supplier it makes a huge difference whether the product can only be sold as an additive or also for nutritional purposes, like it was the case for lycopene.

The challenge for regulators in the lycopene case was not so much its use in conventional foods and in food supplements per se but how to deal with a potential increase of intake levels for lycopene in the population from all sources and uses. Due to the lack of an appropriate single procedure for a comprehensive safety assessment, regulators decided to rather stretch the legal boundaries of the Novel Food Regulation than to manage the safety based on the principle of substantial equivalence and supported by the assessments that had already been performed earlier in the food additive sector and in other jurisdictions like the United States. Still, two different panels of EFSA had to deal with the safety assessment (the NDA panel for the Novel Food applications and the AFC panel for the food additive uses). Even with close

[64]Wijnands et al. (2006).

collaboration between the two panels, compared to the notification route, the authorisation process was long and cumbersome. It took 3 years for the application for lycopene from Blakeslea trispora (Commission Decision 2006/721/EC), three and a half years for synthetic lycopene (Commission Decision 2009/348/EC) and four and a half years for lycopene from tomato oleoresin (Commission Decision 2009/355/EC).

For the food business operator who requested the authorisation such time scales are close to prohibitive because every year the process drags on means a loss in revenue for the company and reduces the probability to achieve the return on investment that formed the foundation of the business case. It was estimated that compared to a fast authorisation procedure of approximately 6 months in some other jurisdictions, a delay of the process by 2–3 years will cause the internal rate of return on investment to drop from 24–25% to 17–18%, which is close to the point where the investment does not pay off anymore.[65] If the authorisation is delayed even further, the business case becomes negative.

The lycopene case demonstrates that the European legal framework for Novel Foods is not geared up to handle applications that are at the intersection of different legal regimes and/or can be used for multiple purposes. The risk of delays for complex applications is therefore high. Unfortunately, this has not changed under Regulation (EU) No. 2015/2283. Other than in the field of food additives, where the Food Improvement Agent Package introduced a common authorisation procedure for food additives, food enzymes and food flavourings with Regulation (EC) No. 1331/2008, in the revision of the Novel Food Regulation the opportunity to plug into this process was missed. Even if the political motives for keeping Novel Foods separate may be valid ones, it leads to a complication of the authorisation process for foods and food ingredients for multiple uses and creates a disincentive to innovate in this area. Art. 3 (2) (a) (ix) of Regulation (EU) No. 2015/2283 even extends the group of foods subject to Novel Food authorisation to vitamins, minerals and other substances to be used in food supplements, for food fortification or in products intended for other specific nutritional purposes if a new production process or nanotechnology is applied to them. This provokes potential clashes with the provisions in Articles 4 and 5 of Directive 2002/46/EC, chapter II and III of Regulation (EC) No. 1925/2006 and of Article 9 of Regulation (EU) No. 609/2013 (which e.g. contains a clause on engineered nanomaterials as well), in particular as the European Commission had issued specific guidance on the process to follow for these food categories.[66] For the area of novel sources of food supplements, however, the potential impact could to a large degree get absorbed if EFSA implemented its suggestion voiced in the European Parliament's workshop on Novel Foods to run both assessments simultaneously.[67] For other sectors, specifically if they touch the borderline to medicinal products, grey areas will remain.[68]

[65]Brookes (2007).

[66]European Commission (2012).

[67]European Parliament (2015).

[68]European Parliament (2014).

Another complication is created by Article 28 of Regulation (EC) No. 2015/2283 regarding the authorisation in case of a parallel application for the authorisation of a health claim. In that event, the Regulation foresees that the Novel Foods application will be stayed until the health claim application has been assessed. To phrase it differently, for the avoidance of potential extra work for risk assessors and regulators food business operators must accept a substantial delay of their application of about 18–24 months. Given the limited resources at EFSA the European legislator had probably not much choice to pursue a different approach. Still, with companies being willing to pay for the use of extra resources needed for a fast-tracked application, alternative and more innovation-friendly solutions could have been found. As the legal framework stands today, innovative food companies will probably think twice before they submit an application that is at risk of getting lost in the thicket of overlapping legal regimes.

Other Requirements

The most difficult part for applicants to deal with are those requirements of the Regulation that are not spelled out in detail. While there is a reasonable level of clarity on the data needed to demonstrate the safety of a product, this is far less the case when it comes to the nutritional adequacy or what are considered "significant" changes in the product's composition or its nutrional values. Unlike in the authorisation process for medicinal products, applicants for a Novel Food authorisation cannot agree with the Commission or EFSA in a binding manner in advance what the scope of the assessment and an acceptable study design would be. Food businesses thus could face the situation that either significant investments in clinical studies could turn out to be in vain or that they must spend much more money than originally anticipated in the business case if EFSA or the European Commission hold that additional data is required on a certain aspect of the application. Despite the fact that the cost of Novel Food applications are substantially lower than those of dossiers for the authorisation of medicinal products, the financial uncertainties associated with the Novel Food process are considerably higher and more difficult to mitigate because in most cases the extra cost cannot be subsequently recovered by exploiting the advantages of protected intellectual property like a patent.

Even more difficult to predict are the "other legitimate factors" that might come into play during the risk management phase of the authorisation process. Because of their largely political nature, applicants must monitor the political landscape surrounding their market and product category very closely. In particular if the novel product could be associated with public health concerns (e.g. intake of fat, sugar or salt for indulgence foods) or controversial technologies (e.g. cloning or nanotechnology) a well-prepared policy and public relations strategy is essential. Such factors lead to a substantial increase in the cost and the risk of failure of the authorisation process.

Duration of the Authorisation Process

In the authorisation procedures completed under Regulation (EC) No. 258/97 the average time from application to the approval decision was around 3 years,[69] and the only legal deadlines were the 3 months' period for the completion of the initial assessment by the national authorities, the 60 days' period for comments on this report by the other Member States and the 60 days' period for the circulation of notifications of substantial equivalence. However, in practice these time limits were not enforced as the Regulation did not foresee any legal consequences in case the deadline was exceeded.

Regulation (EU) No. 2015/2283 introduced a time limit of 9 months for the scientific assessment of an application by EFSA and a 7 months' deadline for the submission of a proposal for an implementing act by the European Commission to the Standing Committee. With this it deviates significantly from the "ideal" procedure described in the Commission's own impact assessment in which EFSA's evaluation could have taken as little as 6 months and the presentation of draft decision to the Standing Committee just 3 months, thereby reducing the overall duration of the authorisation process to little more than a year.[70] This timing in the Regulation only was achieved for traditional foods from third countries.

At first glance it still appears that the time required for the authorisation process almost got halved compared to the practice under Regulation (EC) No. 258/97. A closer look reveals that this is not quite true. First of all, the clock only starts once the validity of the application has been confirmed by the European Commission. Even if the Regulation requires that the verification of the validity should happen "without delay" there is no strict time line set and no consequences attached to any possible deferment. With the centralisation of the scientific assessment on European level, the step of an initial national evaluation was removed. In principle, this should accelerate the procedure. It is nonetheless remarkable that under Regulation (EC) No. 258/97 Member States had 3 months to complete the assessment while EFSA now is given 9 months' time. Certainly it can be argued that the initial assessment by a Member State was complemented by EFSA's second opinion in case of reasoned objections and thus was of a kind of preliminary nature. On the other hand the authorisations handled so far demonstrate that Member States took the initial assessment very seriously and as a result there were hardly any differences in the outcomes of national and EFSA assessments. Given the fact that the deadline can be extended if additional information is required by the applicant, 9 months seem rather generous for a safety assessment in which the pertinent data is already presented by the applicant. The time frame is consistent though with the timings set in Regulation (EC) No. 1331/2008 on the common authorisation procedure for food additives, food enzymes and food flavourings. Once EFSA has published its opinion, the European Commission is obliged to present a draft implementing act proposing

[69]European Parliament (2015), Wendelin (2009) and Brookes (2007).

[70]European Commission (2008).

either the approval or the rejection of the application to the Standing Committee on Plants, Animals, Food and Feed (Section Novel Food and Toxicological Safety of the Food Chain). The time limit only applies to the submission of the proposal, not to its adoption. As a consequence, the decision on the application can take much longer than suggested by the deadline. Based on the administrative practice of the Standing Committees this is a likely scenario. First of all, those meetings are held in alternating intervals, with no meetings taking place from end of November to early February. So if a proposal is not ready for the November meeting, it will only be discussed in February, causing a delay of almost 3 months. Secondly, decisions on proposals are never taken in the meeting in which they are first presented to allow for Member States to exchange their views. As the following meeting will only happen about 2 months later, this time must be added to the decision process, bringing its minimal total duration to 4–6 months. And finally, some time must be added for the formal adoption of the implementing act by the European Commission and its publication in the Official Journal. Taking all this into account, it seems fair to assume that the typical duration of the authorisation process under Regulation (EU) No. 2015/2283 will be approximately 2 years, provided it is about a straightforward application and does not concern politically controversial subjects like nanotechnology. This might be regarded as an improvement, but still the applicant is very much at the mercy of the European institutions when it comes to the timings of the authorisation process, with only very limited options to accelerate the procedure. Even though an individual applicant enjoys legal standing in proceedings before the European Court of Justice, taking action for failure to act pursuant to Article 265 TFEU as a last resort to force a decision on an application would not be an easy ride. According to Article 265(2) and (3) TFEU such an action can only be taken against acts other than recommendations or opinions and requires that the relevant European institution did not define its position within an indicated timeframe. Based on these preconditions, a delay in the delivery of an EFSA opinion cannot be sanctioned. In contrast, an action for failure to act could be taken against the Commission once the 7 months' period for submission of a draft implementing act has expired. But even if the action was successful, it would not lead to the desired authorisation as the adoption of the implementing act depends on the opinion of the Standing Committee. And, as said earlier, opinions cannot be the subject of an action for failure to act. Even if the Standing Committee did not express any opinion at all, there is no way to force the Commission to act. Article 30(3) of Regulation (EU) No. 2015/2283 and Article 5(4) of Regulation (EU) No. 182/2011 state that in such cases the Commission "may adopt the draft implementing act", hence leaving the decision at the Commission's discretion. According to the jurisprudence of the European Court of Justice an action for failure to act can only be taken if the respective European institution had an obligation to act. This is not the case if there was only a right, but no duty to act.[71] One might argue such an obligation is created by Article 10(4) of Regulation (EU) No. 2015/2283 which states that the authorisation

[71]CJEU, case 247/87, Star Fruit Co./Commission, ECLI:EU:C:1989:58, para 12.

procedure should end with the adoption of an implementing act. It is questionable though whether the provision indeed intends to create a legal obligation of the Commission. The comitology procedure as set out in Article 5 of Regulation (EU) No. 182/2011 gives the Commission some discretion to adopt an implementing act or not. This finding is confirmed by Article 10(6) of Regulation (EU) No. 2015/2283 which allows the Commission to terminate the procedure at any stage if it considers the adoption of an implementing act as not justified.

In summary it must therefore be concluded, that hardly any of the deadlines included in the Regulation are enforceable which leaves the timing of the authorisation procedure very much to the discretion of the Commission.

For traditional foods from third countries the situation for food business operators looks slightly more positive. Pursuant to Articles 14 and 15 of Regulation (EU) No. 2015/2283 it is sufficient to notify the intention to place such a food on the market in the European Union together with information on the composition, the origin and the history of safe use of the food. The notification then is circulated to the Member States. If no duly reasoned objections are raised within a time period of 4 months, the Commission is obliged to authorise the placing on the market. If in this case the Commission should not act, legal action could be taken before the European Court of Justice. Notwithstanding the stronger position of the applicant in the accelerated procedure, its effectiveness still must stand the test of time. So far, experience from the notifications of substantial equivalence under Regulation (EC) No. 258/97 has shown that in 83% of the notification cases reasoned objections were made by one or more Member States.[72] As a result, the full authorisation procedure had to be applied.

In particular the requirement to demonstrate a history of safe use in a third country stipulated by Article 14 of Regulation (EU) No. 2015/2283 may be difficult to meet. According to the EFSA guidance on this provision, applicants will have to present comprehensive information on: "the extent of use of the traditional food, the population group for which the traditional food has been a part of their diet, information on its preparation and handling, its role in the diet, information on precautions".[73] In addition, it is necessary to do a comprehensive literature review of human studies related to the consumption of the traditional food. To demonstrate the extent of use, the applicant should provide documentation where in the third country the food is produced and what the volume of the annual production is. Further he should produce data on the quantity of consumption (preferably spelled out by different population groups) and intake estimates based on food consumption surveys. It seems difficult to envisage, how a small scale cooperative of farmers in a developing country that wants to sell their agricultural products in Europe would cope with this EFSA "wish list". And even a big multinational company might find that in many countries no reliable consumption data will be available.

[72] European Parliament (2015).

[73] European Food Safety Authority (2016a).

Exclusivity

Exclusivity of an authorisation gives the initial applicant a head start compared to his competitors. The first mover advantage allows to establish the product in the market relatively unhampered from competition and gives the innovator the chance to recoup his innovation costs through an attractive margin of profit. The longer the period of exclusivity lasts, the more attractive an investment in innovation will be. On the other hand any legal framework granting some level of exclusivity to first movers has to take into account that lack of competition is disadvantageous to consumers because it drives up prices. Every regulation thus must strike a balance between the interests of the innovator to recover his R&D investment and the interests of consumers to pay a competitive price.

Under Regulation (EC) No. 258/97 the authorisation was exclusively granted to the applicant without any time limitations to that exclusivity. However, by providing to secondary market entrants the low-threshold option of notifying substantial equivalence with the original product according to Article 3(4) and Article 5 of Regulation (EC) No. 258/97 the exclusivity initially granted to the first applicant got significantly devalued. According to the law, a product that is substantially equivalent to a food that has already been authorised can be placed on the market straight away provided that it has been notified to the European Commission. In practice such notifications by competitors are made prior to the placing on the market in order to take into account potential objections. They typically happen within 3–6 months after the initial authorisation was granted.[74] This fast response of competitors is facilitated by EFSA's transparency obligations according to Articles 38 and 41 of Regulation (EC) No. 178/2002 which gives the competition a good understanding of the initial applicant's intentions to market a certain product well in advance of its launch.

The availability of the simplified notification procedure to the followers in the market resulted in a very short period of exclusivity and led to an erosion of returns and profit for the initial applicant.[75] In fact, the internal rate of return of the followers could be up to 2–4% higher than the return for the business who originally made the R&D investment and went through the troubles of the authorisation process.[76] It must be noted though, that the said impact is likely referring to manufacturers or importers of a finished product that is sold directly to the final consumer like e.g. noni-juice rather than to an ingredient supplier like a producer of plant sterols who is able to sell his product on to multiple businesses for a number of different purposes and therefore is less impacted by competition.

Articles 26 and 27 of Regulation (EU) No. 2015/2283 introduced a data protection concept which is almost an exact copy of the provisions in Article 21 of Regulation (EC) No. 1924/2006 on nutrition and health claims. During the 5 year protection period the data may not be used for the benefit of subsequent applications

[74] Brookes (2007).

[75] Brookes (2007).

[76] Brookes (2007).

unless this is authorised by the initial applicant. According to recital 30 its intention is "to stimulate research and development within the agri-food industry" and "to protect the investment made by applicants". Unfortunately, however, it has already been demonstrated in the context of nutrition and health claims that these data protection provisions only have a very limited effect. The reason lies in the narrow interpretation the European Commission gave to the term "exclusive right of reference". In its Decision 2009/980/EU regarding the authorisation of a claim on the health benefits of water-soluble tomato concentrate the Commission held that such an exclusive right of reference can only be established in unpublished data. Thus, any publication prior to the submission of the application forfeits the applicant's right to data protection. Although this interpretation has the advantage of providing a clear cut-off point it does not outweigh the drawbacks that come with it. Requiring the data to be unpublished is likely to result in the delay of its publication to the scientific community at congresses or in scientific journals. Often such a practice will not be in line with scientific standards, in particular in cases where results of clinical trials are concerned, because it reduces transparency and may result in the duplication of studies, which could be considered unethical. It might also lead to an increase of animal testing. Furthermore it creates a new barrier to international trade as it is contradictory to the assessment concepts used in other jurisdictions like the United States, where only published and peer-reviewed data is considered, and inconsistent with other data protection regimes in EU law.[77] It is therefore unlikely that the ambition expressed in recital 30 of the Regulation will be achieved.

Market Access for Traditional Foods from Third Countries

Traditional foods from third countries seem to be one of the main beneficiaries of the new regime introduced by Regulation (EU) No. 2015/2283. Instead of having to undergo a full safety assessment the demonstration of a history of safe use will suffice to gain entry to the European market. The trouble is that thus far nobody knows exactly how a history of safe use is proven to the regulator. At first sight it seems that there are issues of data availability, data quality and data reliability. The Commission's Implementing Regulation and the complementing EFSA guidance certainly set requirements many applicants find difficult to meet due to limitations of the available data on the food in question or the financial and human resources of the potential applicant, which, unlike in conventional Novel Food applications, frequently could be small to medium-sized import businesses. Certainly rural communities and other small scale producers in developing countries who want to market their indigenous food in the European Union will continue to struggle with market entry if no additional support is provided to them.

Another unknown factor is the risk of Member States raising reasoned objections during the notification process. History shows, that the risk is real, because 83% of

[77]Holle (2014).

notifications in the past received reasoned objections.[78] Even in the case of a simple vegetable oil obtained from the seed of the tropical Allanblackia tree nine Member States felt the need to object. To what extent the risk materialises will largely depend on the level of agreement that can be achieved between Commission, Member States and EFSA on the common standards that form the basis of the assessment. With the least common denominator being the classic European formula for achieving consensus, the expectation is that the requirements will rather be on the high side.

4 Concluding Remarks

Irrespective of the superficial friendliness towards innovation expressed in recital 24 of Regulation (EU) No. 2015/2283, its true character is conservative and hardly supportive of novelty. The main reasons are the choice of 15 May 1997 as the point of reference for the definition of novelty, unresolved borderline issues with other legal frameworks, the lack of binding deadlines, the ineffective protection of newly developed scientific evidence and the untransparent consideration of other legitimate factors in the authorisation process.

Under Regulation (EC) No. 258/97 a Novel Food was defined as a food or food ingredient not used for human consumption to a significant degree within the European Community prior to the entry into force of the Regulation on 15 May 1997. Even though the date appears to be arbitrary and is acknowledged to lack any scientific rationale,[79] at the time the definition made sense, because it allowed any food that had already been marketed to a relevant degree in one or more Member States to stay on the market without being subject to an assessment as a Novel Food. It was also relatively easy to prove whether a food had been on the market prior to the cut-off date or not as trade documents were still readily available. More than 18 years on, though, any applicant is likely to struggle to provide such evidence, because even the longest compulsory periods for record-keeping of commercial activities have expired. As recital 19 of Regulation No. 2015/2283 puts the onus of proof on the food business operator, the retention of 15 May 1997 as the cut-off date in effect creates a constantly growing hurdle to enter the European market. Registers like the European Commission's Novel Food Catalogue, the Nettox-list of 334 major European food plants and plant parts consumed to a significant degree in the EU prior to 15 May 1997[80] or national lists like in Belgium[81] may ease that burden a bit but are of limited help as they are neither comprehensive nor legally binding.

On top of that, the introduction of new categories of Novel Foods in Regulation No. 2015/2283 generates major issues for products that have been developed and/or

[78]European Parliament (2015).

[79]European Parliament (2014).

[80]Pilegaard et al. (2007).

[81]FPS Health (2013).

imported between 1997 and today and were not considered Novel Foods under Regulation (EC) No. 258/97. Foods that could legally be placed on the market as conventional products in the beginning of 2015 might thus have become Novel Foods by the date of application of the revised Novel Food Regulation in 2018. This also affects innovative techniques like "tissue engineering", e.g. for the creation of cultured meat or other foods and food ingredients from animal or plant cells.[82] As a result, these products will have to undergo an authorisation process by 2 January 2020 the latest.

Insufficient protection of the economic value of the scientific data generated by the applicant for the purpose of the authorisation process forces food business operators to either rely on other forms of protection of intellectual property like patents, plant breeders' rights or trade secrets. These are either difficult to obtain in the foods sector (the composition of a food or its functional benefit as such are not patentable) or will require some opaqueness around them (trade secrets). Both developments are contrary to the best practices of science and research. Applicants will have to make the choice whether they move back from open innovation to more secretive in-house development or if they just do without any protection and rely on their strength in the marketplace to recover the cost of their R&D. Admittedly, the second option will only be available to the big players in the market. Small and medium sized companies will always have to rely on external partners like universities and support by publicly funded research projects to have at least a fair chance to bring a Novel Food to market. But then all this kind of research is subject to publicity requirements and thus not eligible for data protection under Article 26 of Regulation (EU) No. 2015/2283. The revision of the Novel Food Regulation in this way might put the last nail in the coffin for original research activities by SMEs; very likely they will increasingly have to rely on second-to-market strategies and the import of traditional foods from third countries.

But even the relatively straightforward business of importing exotic foods with a history of safe use from outside the EU does not provide a safe harbour for businesses. The key question that remains to be answered is what constitutes a "history of safe consumption" and how it would be proven. EFSA already indicated that it may be difficult to obtain robust data on a history of safe consumption from third countries and that such data might not meet the food safety standards applied in the European Union.[83] Combined with the Member States' "history of objecting"[84] it is probably fair to expect that many notifications of traditional foods from third countries may struggle to take the hurdle of a proven history of safe consumption and would have to go through the full authorisation procedure, a view that is shared by representatives of EFSA.[85]

The saying "hope is just delayed disappointment" adequately summarises the expectations regarding the potential speed-up of the authorisation process under the

[82]Cf. Lanza et al. (2013) and Fu et al. (1999).

[83]European Parliament (2014).

[84]Trollope (2015).

[85]European Parliament (2014).

newly introduced centralised procedure. As meeting the few deadlines that were introduced cannot be enforced by the applicant and the major causes for delays in the process have not been addressed, it is unlikely that under Regulation (EU) No. 2015/2283 the duration of the authorisation procedure is significantly shortended. Even if—as a UK retailer phrased it in a different context—"every little helps", the acceleration envisaged is probably not substantial enough to have a major impact on businesses' investment decisions. Combined with the remaining other uncertainties applicants are confronted with in the process, they will still need a lot of stamina. It is most likely thus that food business operators will only embark on that journey if they are confident that they can secure an acceptable return on their investment via other means than the first mover advantage or data protection.

"Other legitimate factors" are the most unpredictable and variable part of the overall equation. While the outcome of a science based safety assessment can reasonably be predicted based on the available data, it is almost impossible to anticipate the political turns and twists of the risk management process. Unfortunately, the European regulator so far has done little to create transparency in this field.

With the adoption of Regulation (EU) No. 2015/2283 the legal framework is set for the years to come. From a commercial perspective not much of the law helps to improve the business case for launching innovative food products in the European Union. If the intended balance of supporting innovation while maintaining a high level of consumer protection expressed in the recitals of the Regulation should still be achieved, all hopes now lie with the implementation. It is up to Commission, Member States and EFSA, despite the shortcomings of the legal foundation, to establish effective and reliable procedures. This could be achieved by measures like the voluntary introduction of deadlines at more stages of the authorisation procedure, concurrent assessments of safety, nutritional properties and health claims, acknowledgement of unpublished scientific data as eligible for data protection and the development of robust and precise criteria for the determination of a history of safe consumption, just to mention a few. All this could be achieved without having to change a single iota of the legal text. It just requires the political will to do it.

References

Advisory Committee on Novel Foods and Processes (ACNFP) (2007) Annual Report 2007. Food Standards Agency, London

Advisory Committee on Novel Foods and Processes (ACNFP) (n.d.) Guidelines on the use of human studies in the pre-market safety assessment of novel foods. http://acnfp.food.gov.uk/committee/acnfp/acnfppapers/inforelatass/guidetastehuman/guidlinespre-market. Accessed 31 Mar 2018

Broberg M (2009) European Food Safety Regulation and the Developing Countries. Regulatory problems and possibilities. DIIS Working Paper 2009:09. Copenhagen. http://subweb.diis.dk/graphics/Publications/WP2009/WP2009-09_European_Food_Safety_Regulation_web2.pdf. Accessed 31 Jan 2016

Brookes G (2007) Economic impact assessment of the way in which the EU novel foods regulatory approval procedures affect the EU food sector. Briefing paper for the Confederation of the Food and Drink Industries of the European Union (CIAA) & the Platform for Ingredients in Europe (PIE)

Coppens P (2015) Potential impact of 2013 Regulation on Innovation in the Food Sector. In: Proceedings of the Workshop on Novel Foods. Brussels, 7 October 2014. European Parliament. IP/A/ENVI/2014-07. Document PE 518.774

Doona CJ, Kustin K, Feeherry FE (eds) (2010) Case studies in Novel Food processing technologies. Innovations in processing, packaging and predictive modelling. Woodhead Publishing, Oxford

European Commission (2008) Draft report on impact assessment for a regulation replacing regulation (EC) No. 258/97 on novel foods and novel food ingredients. COM (2007) 872 final

European Commission (2012) Administrative Guidance on Submissions for Safety Evaluation of Substances Added for Specific Nutritional Purposes in the Manufacture of Foods. European Commission, Health and Consumers Directorate-General. February 2004. Revised: April 2012

European Commission (2013) Food safety risk analysis. How it is applied in the EU and in the Codex Alimentarius Commission. Presentation at the conference food safety risk analysis – fifty years with codex alimentarius in the European Region. Pulawy, 19–20 September 2013. http://cceuro.pl/index.php/conference-on-food-safety-risk-analysis-fifty-years-with-codex-alimentarius-in-the-european-region.html. Accessed 12 Feb 2016

European Commission (2015) Economics of Industrial research and Innovation. The 2015 EU R&D Scoreboard. http://iri.jrc.ec.europa.eu/scoreboard15.html. Accessed 8 Feb 2016

European Commission (n.d.-a) Human Consumption to a Significant Degree. Information and Guidance Document. http://ec.europa.eu/food/safety/docs/novel-food_guidance_human-consumption_en.pdf. Accessed 22 Feb 2016

European Commission (n.d.-b) EU Guidelines for the presentation of data to demonstrate substantial equivalence between a novel food or food ingredient. http://www.aecosan.msssi.gob.es/AECOSAN/docs/documentos/seguridad_alimentaria/evaluacion_riesgos/NOVEL_FOOD_SUBSTANTIAL_EQUIVALENCE_UE_2013.pdf. Accessed 8 Feb 2016

European Food Safety Authority (2005) Opinion of the Scientific Panel on Dietetic Products, Nutrition and Allergies on a request from the Commission related to an application on the use of α-tocopherol-containing oil suspension of lycopene from Blakeslea trispora as a novel food ingredient (Request N° EFSA-Q-2004-169). Adopted on 21 April 2005. EFSA J 212:1–29

European Food Safety Authority (2008) Use of lycopene as a food colour. Scientific opinion of the panel on food additives, flavourings, processing aids and materials in contact with food (Questions No EFSA Q-2007-001, Q-2007-081, Q-2008-076). Adopted on 30 January 2008. EFSA J 674:1–66

European Food Safety Authority (2016a) Guidance on the preparation and presentation of the notification and application for authorisation of traditional foods from third countries in the context of regulation (EU) 2015/2283. EFSA J 14(11):4590

European Food Safety Authority (2016b) Guidance on the preparation and presentation of an application for authorisation of a novel food in the context of regulation (EU) 2015/2283. EFSA J 14(11):4594

European Parliament (2014) European Parliamentary Research Service. Complementary Impact Assessment reviewing and updating the European Commission's 2008 Impact Assessment for a Regulation on Novel Foods. Document PE 528.801

European Parliament (2015) Directorate General for Internal Policies. Proceedings of the Workshop on Novel Foods. Brussels, 7 October 2014. IP/A/ENVI/2014-07. Document PE 518.774

Food Standards Agency (2013) Novel foods checklist. http://www.food.gov.uk/sites/default/files/multimedia/pdfs/novel-foods-checklist.pdf. Accessed 1 Feb 2016

FPS Health (2013) Belgian Federal Public Service. Health, Food chain safety and environment. Indicative list of plants/plant parts/substances and their novel food status (non-exhaustive list). Last updated 28 October 2013. http://www.health.belgium.be/eportal/foodsafety/foodstuffs/novelfoods/?fodnlang=en#.VpzytFK4JG0. Accessed 11 Jan 2016

Fu T-J, Singh G, Curtis R (1999) Plant cell and tissue culture for the production of food ingredients. In: Proceedings of the symposium on plant cell and tissue culture for food ingredient production

held on April 13–17, 1997 at the American Chemical Society National Meeting in San Francisco, CA, New York
Gounelle de Pontanel H (1973) Proteins from hydrocarbons. In: The proceedings of the 1972 symposium at Aix-en-Provence and relevant guidelines of the UN Protein Advisory Group, London and New York
Hermann M (2009) The impact of the European Novel Food regulation on trade and food innovation based on traditional plant foods from developing countries. Food Policy 34:499–507
Holle M (2014) The protection of proprietary data in Novel Foods. How to make it work. Eur Food Feed Law Rev 5:280–284
House of Commons (1999) Select committee on agriculture minutes of evidence. Memorandum submitted by Professor Janet Bainbridge, Chairman of the Advisory Committee on Novel Foods and Processes (ACNFP) (R29). https://publications.parliament.uk/pa/cm199900/cmselect/cmagric/71/9121413.htm. Accessed 31 Mar 2018
Janssen KL (2011) Driving the food market. Proactive consumer involvement to support radical product innovation. Dissertation, Nijmegen
Knirsch MC, dos Santosa CA, Vicente AAM d OS, Vessoni Pennaa TC (2010) Ohmic heating – a review. Trends Food Sci Technol 21(9):436–441
Lagnevik M, Sjoholm I, Lareke A, Ostberg J (2004) The dynamics of innovation clusters: a study of the food industry. Edward Elgar, Cheltenham
Lanza R, Langer R, Vacanti JP (2013) Principles of tissue engineering, 4th edn. Academic, London
Neville Craddock Associates (2005) The EU Novel Food Regulation. Impact on the potential export of exotic traditional foods to the EU: suggestions for revision. Discussion paper prepared for UNCTAD and CBI. http://www.underutilized-species.org/Documents/PUBLICATIONS/cbi_unctad_paper_on_eu_nfr.pdf. Accessed 31 Jan 2016
Nielsen Holdings NV (2014) Breakthrough innovation report. European edn. http://www.nielsen.com/content/dam/nielsenglobal/eu/nielseninsights/pdfs/Breakthrough_Innovation_Report_EU_FINAL.pdf. Accessed 11 Jan 2016
Piironen V, Toivo J, Puupponen-Pimiä R, Lampi A-M (2003) Plant sterols in vegetables, fruits and berries. J Sci Food Agric 83:330–337. https://doi.org/10.1002/jsfa.1316
Pilegaard K, Eriksen FD, Soerensen M, Gry J (2007) EuroFIR-NETTOX plant list. European Food Information Resource Consortium, Norwich
PricewaterhouseCoopers (2014) 17th Annual Global CEO Survey. Fit for the future. Capitalising on global trends. http://read.pwc.com/i/243985-pwcs-17th-annual-global-ceo-survey. Accessed 12 Jan 2016
Protein Advisory Group of the United Nations System (1966) WHO/FAO/UNICEF PAG Meeting - Geneva, Switzerland, 17–19 Aug 1966. Note on human testing of supplementary food mixtures. New York
Protein Advisory Group of the United Nations System (1972) Production of single-cell protein for human consumption. PAG guideline No. 12. New York
Protein Advisory Group of the United Nations System (1974a) Preclinical testing of novel sources of protein. PAG guideline No. 6. PAG Bulletin (FAO/WHO/UNICEF) IV(3):17–31. New York
Protein Advisory Group of the United Nations System (1974b) Nutritional and safety aspects of protein sources for animal feeding. PAG guideline No. 15. New York
Raisio (1998) Annual Report 1998. http://www.raisio.com/pt/web/raisio-oyj/vuosikertomukset. Accessed 11 Jan 2016
Raisio (1999) Annual Report 1999. http://www.raisio.com/pt/web/raisio-oyj/vuosikertomukset. Accessed 11 Jan 2016
Statista (2013) Year-on-year change in volume of FMCG sales and volume of FMCG sales on promotion in Europe in 2013, by selected countries. http://www.statista.com/statistics/375570/fmcg-sales-volume-change-vs-sales-on-promotion-european-countries/. Accessed 11 Jan 2016
Szajkowska A (2012) Regulating food law. Risk analysis and the precautionary principle as general principles of EU law. Wageningen Academic Publishers, Wageningen

Trollope K (2015) State of play on Novel Foods. In: Proceedings of the Workshop on Novel Foods. Brussels, 7 October 2014. European Parliament. IP/A/ENVI/2014-07. Document PE 518.774

U.S. Food and Drug Administration (FDA) (2002) Agency Additional Correspondence Letter GRAS Notice No. GRN 000117. http://www.fda.gov/Food/IngredientsPackaging Labeling/GRAS/NoticeInventory/ucm352955.htm. Accessed 19 Feb 2016

United Nations (1983) Food and Nutrition Bulletin 5(1), Tokyo. http://archive.unu.edu/unupress/food/8F051e/8F051E00.htm#Contents. Accessed 28 Dec 2015

United States Department of Agricuture (USDA) (2011) Global Agricultural Information Network (GAIN). EU Novel Foods Proposal failed to win Approval. Gain Report E60023. http://gain.fas.usda.gov/Recent%20GAIN%20Publications/EU%20Novel%20Foods%20Proposal%20failed%20to%20win%20Approval_Brussels%20USEU_EU-27_4-15-2011.pdf. Accessed 4 Jan 2016

Wendelin MP (2009) European regulation on Novel Food: grey areas and future perspectives. Vienna

Wijnands JHM, van der Meulen BMJ, Poppe KJ (eds) (2006) Competitiveness of the European Food Industry. An economic and legal assessment. LEI, The Hague. http://bookshop.europa.eu/en/competitiveness-of-the-european-food-industry-pbNB7807110/. Accessed 15 Dec 2015

Winger R, Wall G (2006) Food product innovation A background paper. Agricultural and Food Engineering Working Document 2. Food and Agricultural Organization of the United Nations, Rome

Martin Holle is Professor of Food Law and Administrative Law at Hamburg University of Applied Sciences. He did his PhD thesis (doctor iuris) on constitutional aspects of food regulation at Mainz University and obtained a Master in Administrative Sciences at the German University of Administrative Sciences. Martin held various national and international positions as a Legal Counsel with Unilever, advising the company in all matters of Food and Advertising Law. He is a scientific member of the German Food Code Commission and member of the advisory board of the German Scientific Association for Food Law.

Agricultural Biotechnology: Regulation in the United States and the European Union

Margaret Rosso Grossman

Abstract Biotechnology has played an increasingly important role in agriculture since the commercialization of genetically engineered crops, now planted globally on 185 million hectares. Animal applications of biotechnology include transgenic and cloned animals. In the US and the EU, legislative measures described in this chapter govern authorisation of GE crops, with a focus on food and feed safety and protection of the environment; transgenic and cloned animals are also subject to regulation. The US and the EU share some regulatory priorities, including scientific risk assessment, and face similar issues (a lengthy regulatory process and coexistence of GE and other crops). Significant differences in regulation, particularly in risk management, exist. Moreover regulatory barriers caused by asynchronous approvals of GE crops have reduced trade between the US and EU. Innovative genetic technologies, which may escape regulation under current laws, may require amendments to US and EU regulatory measures. This chapter suggests that despite differences in approach, regulatory systems should facilitate the development of new products of biotechnology and help to make these products available to global producers and consumers.

1 Introduction

For centuries, humans have bred plants and animals, using selection and crossbreeding, to achieve desirable traits. Discovery of the process of heredity in the 1800s led to more sophisticated plant breeding, which has helped to improve crop yields and continues to offer new crop varieties.[1] The "domestication and artificial selection of animals" began

This Chapter is based on work supported by USDA, National Institute of Food and Agriculture, Hatch Project No. ILLU-470-348.

[1]NAS (2004), p. 17.

M. R. Grossman (✉)
Department of Agricultural and Consumer Economics, University of Illinois at Urbana-Champaign, Urbana, IL, USA
e-mail: peggyg@illinois.edu

H. Bremmers, K. Purnhagen (eds.), *Regulating and Managing Food Safety in the EU*, Economic Analysis of Law in European Legal Scholarship 6,
https://doi.org/10.1007/978-3-319-77045-1_15

as long as 8000 years ago, and conventional animal breeding continues to play an important role in agriculture.[2] Since the 1960s and 1970s, genetically-based biotechnology has resulted in more rapid selection for desirable traits.[3]

Biotechnology has been defined as "that set of techniques by which living creatures are altered for the benefit of humans and other animals."[4] More specifically, genetic engineering is "a process by which humans introduce or change DNA, RNA, or proteins in an organism to express a new trait or change the expression of an existing trait."[5] Biotechnology has been called the "fastest adopted crop technology in the world."[6]

Developments in biotechnology have made a significant impact in crop production. In 2016, producers in 26 countries grew about 185.1 million hectares of genetically engineered (GE) crops. Major GE crops were soybeans (50% of global acreage), corn, cotton, and canola.[7] Global value of biotech seed in 2016 was $15.8 billion; "farm-gate revenues" were 10 times the seed value.[8]

Producers in 19 developing countries planted 54% of the world's GE crop area; 7 industrial countries planted 46 percent. The US planted 73 million hectares; Brazil, Argentina, Canada, and India planted more than 10 million hectares. Eighteen countries grew 50,000 hectares or more, and 8 other countries grew fewer GE crops.[9] It is noteworthy, however, that "countries that have adopted GM crops are planting them on increasingly larger acreages year after year as opposed to broader diffusion of the technology to previously non-adopting countries."[10]

Between 1994 and 2016, 40 nations approved GE crops for food, feed, or cultivation. Approvals involve 26 crops and 392 biotech "events." Most approvals are for direct use or processing of food and feed, with fewer varieties approved for cultivation.[11] Countries are often slow to approve crops for cultivation, showing reluctance to make the decision that "signifies a willingness to adopt . . . [GE] crop technologies."[12] As the US National Academies of Science, Engineering, and Medicine noted in a recent report, "[f]or a variety of scientific, economic, social, and regulatory reasons, most genetically engineered (GE) traits and crop varieties

---

[2]NAS (2002), p. 4.

[3]NAS (2002), p. 4; NASEM (2016), p. 5.

[4]NAS (2002), p. 4.

[5]NASEM (2016), p. 1.

[6]ISAAA (2017), p. 2. These crops are termed genetically engineered (GE) or, especially in the EU, genetically modified (GM). This Chapter will use both terms.

[7]ISAAA (2017), pp. 1–4. In 1996, total plantings were 1.7 million hectares. The US grew sugar beets, alfalfa (8.46 million hectares), and small amounts of papaya, squash, and potato.

[8]ISAAA (2017), pp. 12–13.

[9]ISAAA (2017), pp. 2–4.

[10]Gliem et al. (2016), p. 112.

[11]ISAAA (2017), p. 10. The 3768 separate approvals do not include GM flowers. There were 1238 approvals for feed, 1777 for food, and 753 for cultivation.

[12]Gliem et al. (2016), p. 102. A study of corn found more approvals for import, often for feed, than for cultivation (pp. 108–109).

that have been developed are not in commercial production."[13] A few herbicide and insect resistant crops are cultivated (soy, cotton, corn, canola) along with a small, but growing, number of other crops.

Cloned and transgenic animals are less common. Livestock companies in a number of countries clone domestic animals, including cattle and pigs. Few cloned animals have entered the food chain, but products of clones and their progeny are sold as food in the US and a few other countries. Transgenic animals are not yet marketed for food. The AquAdvantage salmon, the first GE animal approved for food in the US, has not been sold commercially in the US since its 2015 approval.[14]

Despite the enthusiasm for products of biotechnology by governments, industry, farmers, and consumers in some countries, genetic engineering has engendered controversy. Regulation of biotech products differs. Some countries relied at first on existing laws and regulations, while others created new regulatory systems. Some focus regulatory attention on the product; others allow the process of biotechnology to trigger regulation. Costly and time-consuming regulatory barriers can limit innovation and impede new technology. Long approval times result in asynchronous approvals, when GE crops approved in one nation are not yet approved by trading partners. Low-level presence of unapproved GE varieties have caused rejection of crop shipments. Standards for approval vary. Most nations apply similar scientific assessments of risk, but socio-economic considerations that play a role in risk management may burden the approval process.[15] Moreover, innovative biotechnology, with new techniques and more complex products, will present more challenges. Some products may fall outside the purview of agency regulation, perhaps because they do not fit the traditional definition of a GE crop. Different risk characteristics may call for different approaches to risk assessment and regulation.[16]

In light of both the promise of biotechnology and the controversy engendered by its products, this chapter discusses on the regulatory systems in the United States and the European Union. The emphasis is regulation and not the science of biotechnology. The chapter focuses on measures that govern genetically engineered crops and food, transgenic animals, and cloned animals and their products. The chapter gives more attention to GE crops, because of their prominence in the market place, their perceived benefits, and a longer experience in the regulatory systems of the US and the EU. The chapter focuses on the US and EU regulatory systems, with emphasis on recent developments and controversial issues. A comparison of the two regulatory systems identifies a few commonalities, different approaches to risk management, regulatory barriers to trade, and the challenge of innovative technologies.

---

[13]NASEM (2016), p. 5.

[14]See discussion of AquAdvantage salmon below and Grossman (2016b).

[15]See ISAAA (2017), pp. 15–16.

[16]NASEM (2016), pp. 493–494.

2 Genetically Engineered Crops

Despite considerable controversy about GE crops, studies have demonstrated that these products offer significant benefits, but pose some issues. Benefits include insect resistance and herbicide tolerance, as well as good economic outcomes and management flexibility for producers.[17] GE seeds command higher prices than conventional seeds, but "farmers realize economic benefits from growing GE crops through higher crop yields, and/or lower pesticide costs, and management time savings."[18]

Research indicates that global socio-economic and environmental effects of GE technology have been positive. The global farm income benefit in 2015 was $15.4 billion, with a total increase in farm income since 1996 of $167.8 billion. Yield gains from insect-resistant maize have generated significant additional income; insect-resistant cotton resulted in lower costs and higher yields; herbicide-tolerant soybeans and canola increased farm income significantly.[19] The US shared in these farm income benefits ($72 billion since 1996),[20] followed by Argentina, India, China, and Brazil. Developing countries farmers gained $86.1 billion. The EU gained relatively little: $251.3 million in Spain; $23.6 million in other EU countries.[21]

GE traits have led to "a significant reduction in the environmental impact associated with insecticide and herbicide use" on global GE crop areas.[22] Since 1996, pesticide use declined by 8.1%, and environmental impacts of herbicides and insecticides declined by 18.6%. Insect resistant traits have led to the most environmental gain. Overuse of glyphosate, however, has fostered weed resistance in some areas.[23] Recent research indicated that from 1990 to 2015, the intensity of herbicide use increased more in non-GE crops—maize, rice, wheat, and cotton—than in GE crops.[24] No GE wheat is approved for cultivation. GE crops can also lead to lower emission of greenhouse gas, through reduced fuel use (chemical applications and soil cultivation) and increased carbon sequestration (no-till and reduced till).

---

[17]NASEM (2016), p. 21. See also Smyth (2017), pp. 79–81. Health benefits include reduced pesticide poisoning in developing countries (p. 4).

[18]Fernandez-Cornejo et al. (2014), p. 47.

[19]Brookes and Barfoot (2017), pp. 9–10.

[20]In 2017, biotech varieties were 92% of corn, 94% of soy, and 96% of upland cotton. NASS (2017), pp. 29–31. Most corn and cotton seeds have stacked traits that provide both insect resistance and herbicide tolerance. Producers planted significant amounts of GE canola and sugar beets, with fewer acres of GE alfalfa, sweet corn, squash, and papaya. Greene et al. (2016). By 2013, about 98% of US sugar beets and 95% of canola were GE (herbicide tolerant) varieties. Only 13% of harvested alfalfa acres were GE; alfalfa is planted every 6–7 years, and (after litigation beginning in 2007) deregulation occurred only in 2011. Fernandez-Cornejo et al. (2016).

[21]Brookes and Barfoot (2017), pp. 10–11.

[22]Brookes and Barfoot (2017), p. 13.

[23]Brookes and Barfoot (2017), pp. 13–15. Resistance occurs where producers did not follow management strategies, including refuges of non GM crops and high-dose applications to kill partially-resistant insects. NASEM (2016), p. 13.

[24]Kniss (2017), p. 1.

GE crops and their food and feed products have caused no known health effects. No adverse effects on livestock have been detected, and there is "no substantial evidence that foods from GE crops were less safe than foods from non-GE crops," and no higher health risk from GE foods than from their conventional counterparts.[25] An important research report noted, however, that "any new food—GE or non-GE—may have some subtle favorable or adverse health effects that are not detected even with careful scrutiny and that health effects can develop over time."[26] Nonetheless, commentators have emphasized the safety of GE crops and their products: "To our knowledge, no GM product has been explicitly rejected for health or environmental safety reasons by any regulator anywhere."[27] Moreover, "[b]iotech crops have now had an unblemished record of safe use and consumption for over 20 years."[28]

2.1 *Regulation in the United States*

Authorisation

US law is designed to ensure that GE crops and their food products are safe for agriculture, the environment, and health.[29] The Coordinated Framework for Regulation of Biotechnology, published in 1986 and updated in 1992,[30] established US policy, which applied existing federal law, later supplemented by new laws and regulations. US policy relies on a "risk-based, scientifically sound approach" to regulation of genetically engineered crops and their products.[31] Regulation depends on characteristics of the product (for example, plant pest) or its intended use (for example, food).[32] Under the Coordinated Framework, the US Department of Agriculture (USDA) ensures that GE crops are safe to grow; the US Environmental Protection Agency (EPA) ensures that they are safe for the environment; the US Food and Drug Administration (FDA, along with the EPA) ensures that they are safe to eat. A brief summary of agency responsibilities follows.[33]

---

[25]NASEM (2016), pp. 2, 19.

[26]NASEM (2016), p. 19. A recent study of 25 research articles that found negative effects of GM food and feed concluded that the articles appeared in low-ranking journals and had "methodological flaws that invalidate any conclusions of adverse effects." Sánchez and Parrott (2017), p. 1.

[27]Gliem et al. (2016), p. 99.

[28]ISAAA (2017), p. 1. As commentators noted, a global ban on GE crops (although unlikely) would increase food prices and impose other significant welfare losses; a ban is also likely to affect land use and to increase greenhouse gas emissions, adding more than a billion tons of carbon dioxide to the atmosphere. Mahaffey et al. (2016).

[29]This section relies in part on Grossman (2016a), pp. 306–314, and Grossman (2012).

[30]OSTP (1986, 1992).

[31]OSTP (1992), p. 6753.

[32]NASEM (2016), p. 467. Although US regulation focuses on the product, whether USDA and EPA regulate is based in part on process (p. 25).

[33]For more detail, see Grossman (2012).

The Plant Protection Act of 2000[34] gives the USDA authority to regulate plant pests.[35] Most GE varieties could harbour a plant pest. Therefore they are considered "regulated" articles and cannot be sold commercially until they are evaluated and authorised—that is, classified as "nonregulated." Regulations enacted by the USDA's Animal and Plant Health Inspection Service (APHIS) govern authorisation.[36] Under the APHIS science-based regulatory framework, developers of GE plants must submit extensive data and carry out field trials to assess safety.[37] If field trials indicate that a new GE variety is not a plant pest or a threat to agriculture or the environment, the developer can petition APHIS for a determination of nonregulated status so that the variety can be sold commercially. APHIS reviews the data and complies with the National Environmental Policy Act (preparing an environmental assessment and, if required, an environmental impact statement).[38] If the GE variety poses no environmental or agricultural risk, APHIS will make a determination of nonregulated status. If the variety also meets the requirements of the FDA and the EPA, it can move freely in commerce. By December 2017, APHIS had issued 123 determinations of nonregulated status. Recent determinations included several Simplot potatoes, an apple that resists browning, and glyphosate-resistant bentgrass.[39]

The EPA has authority, under the Federal Insecticide, Fungicide, and Rodenticide Act (FIFRA),[40] to regulate GE crops that produce pesticidal substances (for example, the insecticide *bacillus thuringiensis* (*Bt*)), called plant incorporated protectants (PIPs).[41] FIFRA provides that no pesticide can be sold or used until it is registered, a process that requires the developer to demonstrate that the pesticide will not "cause unreasonable adverse effects on the environment."[42] Field tests, conducted by the developer under experimental use permits, help to establish the safety of the PIP. If the developer complies with EPA requirements, the EPA may register the GE plant.

The EPA also governs pesticide residues in GE foods, under authority of the Food, Drug and Cosmetic Act (FDCA).[43] A food with a pesticide residue is considered adulterated; it cannot be sold in interstate commerce unless the residue

[34] 7 USC §§ 7701–7772 (replacing the Plant Pest and Plant Quarantine Acts).

[35] 7 USC § 7711.

[36] 7 CFR part 340.

[37] APHIS regulations required a permit for trials that posed special risks; other trials required only notification and compliance with APHIS performance standards. The 2017 proposed regulation would require permits for regulated organisms. See discussion below.

[38] NEPA, 42 USC § 4332(2)(C), requires federal agencies to prepare an environmental impact statement for "major federal actions significantly affecting the quality of the human environment."

[39] APHIS, USDA (2017a) (data base of petitions).

[40] 7 USC §§ 136-136y.

[41] PIPs are considered pesticides because they are introduced in plants as way of "preventing, destroying, repelling, or mitigating any pest." 7 USC § 136(u). The EPA defines PIP as "a pesticidal substance that is intended to be produced and used in a living plant, or in the produce thereof, and the genetic material necessary for [its] production." 40 CFR § 174.3.

[42] 7 USC § 136a(c)(5). Unreasonable adverse effects are defined in § 136(bb).

[43] 21 USC §§ 301–399f.

meets an established tolerance (a legal limit on the maximum amount in food) or is exempt from the tolerance requirement.[44] The EPA may establish a pesticide tolerance for food only if scientific data establishes that the tolerance is safe.[45] But the EPA may also grant exemptions from the tolerance requirement if the pesticidal protein is not toxic or allergenic and data shows a reasonable certainty that aggregate exposure will not cause harm to human health. EPA regulations grant exemptions to most PIPs in GE crops.[46]

The FDA governs food safety under the FDCA. In 1992, the agency issued a Policy Statement on GE foods. The FDA indicated that developers of new foods have legal responsibility to evaluate food safety and to comply with the FDCA. In fact, the FDA did not routinely conduct premarket safety review of new plant foods, and it did not plan to review GE foods unless changes in structure, function, or composition made it necessary to review and approve a new GE food to protect public health.[47] The FDCA and FDA regulations prohibit adulteration and misbranding of food and govern food additives.[48] The FDA relied on these measures to ensure the safety of GM foods. Its focus was on the food product—its characteristics and intended use—rather than the process of development.

Implementing this policy, the FDA does not require premarket approval of all GE foods, but relies on the concept of substantial equivalence, a comparative approach that ascertains whether a GE crop or food shares characteristics—nutritional components—with its conventional counterpart.[49] The agency requires premarket review if foods lack substantial equivalence because their nutritional components (for example, allergens, toxins) differ or pose more risk.

The FDA also regulates food additives, which are considered unsafe (and therefore adulterated)[50] until they have been granted premarket approval or are exempt from approval. The FDCA definition of food additive excludes substances that are "generally recognized as safe" (GRAS).[51] Because most new plant foods have been accepted as safe, the FDA decided that most GM foods would be considered GRAS.[52] Therefore, most GE foods escape premarket review as food additives. Manufacturers themselves make the GRAS determination and may, but need not,

[44]21 USC § 346a.

[45]Safe means "a reasonable certainty that no harm will result from aggregate exposure to the pesticide chemical residue, including all anticipated dietary exposures and all other exposures for which there is reliable information." 21 USC § 346a(b)(2).

[46]40 CFR §§ 174.501–174.535 (listing permanent and temporary exemptions from the requirement of a tolerance).

[47]FDA (1992).

[48]21 USC §§ 342, 348.

[49]FDA (1992), p. 22,992 (referring to OECD and FAO/WHO documents on substantial equivalence).

[50]21 USC § 342(a), defining as adulterated any food additive that is unsafe under § 348.

[51]21 USC § 321(s). A GRAS determination requires the same level of scientific evidence required for approval of a food additive.

[52]FDA (1992), pp. 22,990.

notify FDA of their decision. FDA's GRAS policy is controversial. In 2016 the FDA issued a new GRAS rule, which amends the regulatory criteria for determining when a substance is GRAS. The new rule establishes a format for voluntary GRAS notices and emphasizes the stringent scientific requirements for a GRAS determination.[53]

The FDA issues guidance documents (less formal than regulations and not binding on the agency or the public) to guide industry. The agency recommends that developers consult with FDA about new GE products, and these guidance documents facilitate consultation. Early food safety evaluations are carried out during field tests, before new GE proteins can enter the food supply. Biotechnology consultations precede commercialization of new foods. These voluntary consultations, which involve submission of comprehensive data, allow the FDA to identify and resolve any scientific or regulatory issues. Food companies seek consultations, perhaps to avoid liability, and by November 2017 the FDA had completed 178 consultations.[54]

As this summary indicates, US agency decisions about GE crops and their products are generally technical decisions that focus on whether products meet statutory requirements. US law allows little consideration of socioeconomic issues.[55] The FDA and the EPA (in considering pesticide tolerances) focus on food safety and the reasonable certainty of no harm. The EPA, however, can consider economic costs and benefits in determining whether a pesticide has an "unreasonable adverse effect on the environment."[56]

Labels for GE Food

Since 1992, the US FDA relied on language in the FDCA to conclude that food from GE crops did not need special labels.[57] The FDCA provides that a food is "misbranded" if its label is "false or misleading."[58] Whether a label is misleading is determined in part by "the extent to which the labeling ... fails to reveal [material] facts."[59] Because the FDA focused on the food product and did not consider the process used for new plant varieties to be "material" information, the FDA concluded that it had no legal or scientific basis to require labels for GE food unless the food itself differed materially from similar foods.[60] The FDA applied similar

[53]FDA (2016) and Grossman (2017). In May 2017, several public interest groups challenged the GRAS rule, alleging that the rule, a "secret GRAS system," allows potentially unsafe food additives to enter the food supply without FDA review. Center for Food Safety (2017).

[54]FDA (2017a) (Biotechnology Consultations).

[55]NASEM (2016), pp. 472–473.

[56]7 USC 136(bb). See NASEM (2016), pp. 474–477 (details of risk assessment).

[57]The discussion is guided by Grossman (2016c) and the references therein.

[58]21 USC § 343(a).

[59]21 USC § 321(n).

[60]A federal district court decision upheld the FDA's conclusion. Alliance for Bio-Integrity v. Shalala, 116 F. Supp. 2d 166 (D DC 2000).

reasoning to GE animals and did not require GE labelling for the AquAdvantage salmon, authorized in 2015 (see discussion below). The FDA did, however, provide guidance for voluntary labelling of GE food.[61]

Some NGOs and consumers demanded labels for GE food, and several states enacted labelling laws. In part to preempt state labelling laws, Congress enacted the 2016 National Bioengineered Food Disclosure Standard,[62] which requires labelling of most bioengineered food and food with bioengineered ingredients—food with genetic material modified with DNA techniques and for which the modification could not be "obtained through conventional breeding or found in nature."[63]

The GE Disclosure Standard assigns responsibility for regulation and enforcement to the USDA. By 29 July 2018, the USDA must establish a standard for disclosure with requirements to carry out that standard. Regulations must determine when a food is bioengineered (among other issues, the GE threshold for labelling) and the form of disclosure (text on the label, a symbol, a QR code or digital link).[64] Small manufacturers will face less burdensome obligations and a later compliance date, and very small manufacturers and restaurant foods are exempt.[65] In June 2017, USDA published questions for consideration by stakeholders. These questions focus on terminology and definitions, types of disclosure, application of exemptions, and compliance. USDA will consider comments from consumers and industry. The agency planned to publish a draft regulation in Fall 2017, but by early April 2018, no regulation had been proposed.[66]

The food industry seems to have accepted the law, especially because it preempts inconsistent state labelling laws, but some advocacy groups are critical, especially because the law allows digital disclosure instead of text on the food package. The GE Disclosure Standard negates the FDA's decision that GE technology does not require disclosure, and USDA regulations may conflict with some FDA labelling requirements, especially the requirement that disclosures must appear on food labels. The law contains inartful language and may leave regulatory gaps and incomplete disclosure. USDA regulations will determine whether US consumers will be adequately informed about GE food.[67]

Recent Developments

In recent years, the regulation of biotechnology in the US has attracted renewed attention. In January 2011, President Obama issued an Executive Order that focused

---

[61]FDA (2015a) (Guidance, Voluntary Labeling).

[62]National Bioengineered Food Disclosure Standard (2016), Public Law 114–216.

[63]7 USC § 1639(1).

[64]A study of technological challenges that affect electronic or digital access to disclosure, required by law, identified obstacles for retailers and consumers. Deloitte (2017).

[65]7 USC § 1639b.

[66]AMS, USDA (2017).

[67]Grossman (2016c), pp. 504–507.

on improved regulation and called for regulatory agencies to strive, among other goals, for scientific integrity and to use the "most innovative and least burdensome tools" for regulation.[68] In a March 2011 memorandum, the Office of Science and Technology Policy (OSTP) set out principles, consistent with the Executive Order, for regulating emerging technologies, including genetic engineering and related techniques. Agencies "share a fundamental desire for regulation and oversight that ensure the fulfillment of legitimate objectives such as the protection of safety, health, and the environment. Regulation and oversight should avoid unjustifiably inhibiting innovation, stigmatizing new technologies, or creating trade barriers."[69]

The September 2016 National Strategy for Modernizing the Regulatory System for Biotechnology Products applies this policy to biotechnology.[70] The goal of the National Strategy is "to ensure that the Federal regulatory system is equipped to efficiently assess the risks, if any, associated with future products of biotechnology while supporting innovation, protecting health and the environment, promoting public confidence in the regulatory process, increasing transparency and predictability, and reducing unnecessary costs and burdens."[71] Support for science in the assessment of biotechnology products is critical.

The National Strategy indicates that the major regulatory agencies for biotechnology in the US plan to improve cooperation, predictability, and efficiency. Plans include more interagency communication to ensure timely decisions about regulatory jurisdiction, collaboration in scientific oversight, and review of regulatory structures and requirements. Individual agencies also plan to review and update various policies and guidance for regulating products of biotechnology.[72]

In connection with the National Strategy, the updated Coordinated Framework for the Regulation of Biotechnology, finalized in January 2017, sets out principles for regulation of biotechnology products.[73] Among these is the principle that regulation will continue to focus on the intended uses of products rather than the process of development. Risk should be determined by characteristics of the product, the environment, and uses of the product. Under the risk-based approach, "the regulatory system should distinguish between those biotechnology products that require a certain level of Federal oversight and those that do not."[74] Developments in science may result in changes in regulation to address perceived risks.

[68]Obama (2011), pp. 1–2.

[69]OSTP (2011), p. 1. The memorandum distinguished risk assessment and risk management: "Federally mandated risk management actions should be appropriate to, and commensurate with, the degree of risk identified in the assessment" (p. 2).

[70]Language in the National Strategy is similar. The policy of the US government is to adopt regulatory approaches "to protect health and the environment while reducing regulatory burdens and avoiding unjustifiably inhibiting innovation, stigmatizing new technologies, or creating trade barriers." US White House (2016), p. 13.

[71]US White House (2016), p. 8.

[72]US White House (2016), pp. 16–18.

[73]US White House (2017). In 2015, the Executive Office of the President had directed the agencies to update the Coordinated Framework (p. 5).

[74]US White House (2017), p. 8.

The 2017 Coordinated Framework delineates the current responsibilities of the USDA, EPA, and FDA in regulation of products of biotechnology. The document sets out the statutory authority for each agency and the "protection goal" related to each source of authority.[75] It discusses each agency's responsibility, under relevant statutes, for assessment of GE foods and other products. It provides a detailed table that identifies numerous biotechnology product areas (including food from GE plants and animals) and the responsibility and coordination among regulatory agencies for oversight of organisms derived from GE plants, GE animals, GE microbes and cells.[76] Because some GE products face regulation from more than one agency, the 2017 Coordinated Framework also describes the ways in which the agencies cooperate in the regulation of biotechnology products. Eight hypothetical case studies, intended for those who develop GE products subject to regulation, provide practical examples of the process of regulation and agency roles.[77]

In January 2017, USDA's APHIS proposed to amend its 1987 rule that governs the release and commercialization of GE organisms.[78] In the proposal, withdrawn in November 2017,[79] APHIS discussed a number of bases for the proposed rule. Advances in understanding of GE organisms indicate that most GE techniques do not lead to plant pest risk. In contrast, some techniques that use no plant pests as donor or recipient organisms, vectors, or vector agents could pose plant pest risks, but these might not be defined as regulated articles under the 1987 rule. APHIS noted the importance of evaluating GE plants as noxious weeds, as well as plant pests, because some GE plants (for example, switchgrass used to produce ethanol) may become weedy.[80] Moreover, to protect the food supply, APHIS emphasized the importance of regulating GE biological control agents and GE plants that produce plant-made industrials and pharmaceuticals.

APHIS identified two situations in which a GE plant should be a regulated organism. One is "when APHIS has reached a determination that the plant and trait combination associated with the GE plant causes it to act as a plant pest or noxious weed."[81] The other is "when APHIS is presented with a GE plant with a novel plant and trait combination, and has not yet evaluated this plant and trait combination for its plant pest and noxious weed risk."[82] As APHIS had proposed, if a plant falls within the regulatory definition of GE organism, a developer who wants

[75]US White House (2017), Table 1, pp. 9–10.

[76]US White House (2017), Table 2, pp. 28–35.

[77]US White House (2017), pp. 39–51.

[78]APHIS, USDA (2017b), proposing to amend 7 CFR part 340 (Docket APHIS-2015-0057). The 1987 rule had been amended several times, and in 2015 APHIS withdrew its 2008 proposed amendment. The 2017 proposed rule responds to a request from the USDA Office of the Inspector General and a directive from Congress to amend some aspects of APHIS regulations.

[79]APHIS, USDA (2017c).

[80]APHIS, USDA (2017b), pp. 7009–7011. APHIS is developing a Weed Risk Assessment System for Genetically Engineered Plants.

[81]APHIS, USDA (2017b), p. 7018.

[82]APHIS, USDA (2017b), p. 7018.

to release the organism into the environment must ask APHIS to conduct an evaluation of the organism as a plant pest or noxious weed. If APHIS agrees that the organism is unlikely to pose such a risk, it would no longer be regulated. If the evaluation indicates that a risk may exist, the developer must obtain a permit to release, to import, or to move the organism interstate, and comply with regulatory requirements under that permit.[83]

Various stakeholders submitted public comments on the proposed rule, with substantial disagreement. Some comments asserted that the proposal would expand regulation of GE organisms; others, that it would narrow the scope of regulation. Some comments objected that the proposed risk assessment would hinder innovation; others claimed that it lacked rigor. In light of public comments, and perhaps the changed political climate in the United States, APHIS withdrew the proposal, effective 7 November 2017. The agency plans to consider public comments and new scientific knowledge about GE organisms and to engage stakeholders in a search for alternative policy approaches.[84]

Also in January 2017, the FDA published a request for comments about genome editing in new plant varieties used for foods.[85] In the National Strategy discussed above, the FDA had indicated its intention to "clarify its policy for the regulation of products derived from genome editing techniques," that is, modification by "targeted DNA sequence alterations."[86] The FDA plans to continue to offer consultation with developers of new food varieties, but seeks data about food safety risks from new technology, along with data relevant to safety assessment and the regulatory status of these new organisms. FDA's request does not propose new regulatory measures.

2.2 *Regulation in the European Union*

Authorisation

The marketing of GMOs (the term used in EU documents), both for cultivation and for food and feed, has engendered controversy in the EU. Unlike the US, which relied at first on existing legislation to govern biotechnology, the European Community enacted new measures to govern the new technology. Indeed, according to one European scholar, since the 1990s, EU regulation of GMOs and their risks "has imposed a procedural straight-jacket which is decidedly stricter than that provided for in other countries."[87] Although a number of GMOs and their products have been authorized for

[83]APHIS, USDA (2017b), pp. 7014–7015.

[84]APHIS, USDA (2017c). APHIS provided no time frame for developing a new regulatory proposal.

[85]FDA (2017b) (Notification, Genome editing).

[86]FDA (2017b), p. 6565.

[87]de Sadeleer (2015), p. 557. New crops based on conventional breeding do not require review and approval, but can be recalled under the General Food Law if health or safety issues appear post-market. NASEM (2016), p. 478.

food and feed, EU farmers may cultivate only one *Bt* maize (MON 810). In 2016, only Spain, Portugal, the Czech Republic, and Slovakia cultivated GM maize, with a total of 136,000 ha—95% (129,000 ha, 35% of Spain's maize) in Spain.[88]

Directives enacted in 1990 regulated contained use[89] and deliberate release (placing on the market) of GMOs, followed by Directive 2001/18 with "a stricter risk assessment and an emphasis on the precautionary principle" for the deliberate release and marketing of GMOs.[90] Risk assessment determines whether the GMO is "safe for human health and the environment."[91] The General Food Law (Regulation 178/2002) again emphasized the precautionary principle as "a mechanism for determining risk management measures"[92] to protect health. The General Food Law indicated that because "scientific risk assessment alone" cannot always provide enough information, risk management decisions may consider "societal, economic, traditional, ethical and environmental factors."[93]

New regulations in 2003 governed approval of GM food and feed at the EU level (Regulation 1829/2003) and traceability and labelling of GM food and their products (Regulation 1830/2003). Regulation 1829/2003 offers a single process for authorizing GMOs both for cultivation and for feed and food.[94]

The EU authorisation procedure[95] begins with submission of an application dossier, with required information about the GMO and GM food, to the competent authority of a Member State. Regulation 1829/2003 governs requirements, including submission of scientific data, for authorisation. The European Food Safety Authority (EFSA), consulting with Member States, conducts a safety assessment of GMOs to be cultivated and imported for food or processing. The authorization process for cultivation is more complicated.[96]

EFSA published guidelines for risk assessment for food safety and the environment.[97] EFSA guidelines for food safety require extensive scientific and technical data from product applicants. Assessment of food safety includes, among other elements, the comparison of the GM plant and its food and feed products with conventionally bred comparators.[98] The applicant must provide data to show that

---

[88]ISAAA (2017), p. 9.

[89]Contained use is now governed by Directive 2009/41.

[90]Winter (2016), p. 121. For recent criticism of EU regulation (lacking characteristics of legal certainty, non-discrimination, and scientific adaptability), see Zetterberg and Björnberg (2017).

[91]Directive 2001/18, preamble (47). See de Sadeleer (2015), pp. 535–537.

[92]Regulation 178/2002, preamble (112); see also preamble (20), Articles 6, 7.

[93]Regulation 178/2002, preamble (19).

[94]For detail on these measures, see Grossman (2009), pp. 280–295.

[95]On the role of EFSA, see de Sadeleer (2015), pp. 539–541.

[96]An October 2016 draft proposal (SANTE/11248/2016 Annex) would amend Annexes II and III of Directive 2001/18 to strengthen environmental risk assessment, making it "needlessly more burdensome." FAS, USDA (2016), p. 19 (referring to SANTE/11248/2016).

[97]EFSA (2010b, 2011). Environmental assessment involves a Member State environmental risk assessment, as well as an EFSA assessment for the whole EU. EFSA (2010b).

[98]EFSA (2011), 3.1.3.

consumption of the food is as safe as its comparators, that it is not "nutritionally disadvantageous," and that it will not mislead consumers.[99]

If EFSA's scientific assessment finds the food poses no risk to health or the environment, the European Commission, after public consultation on the EFSA opinion, prepares a draft decision for authorisation. Under the EU's comitology procedure, Member States, acting as the Standing Committee on Plants, Animals, Food and Feed, have the opportunity to decide, by a qualified majority, to authorize the food or not. If the Standing Committee issues no opinion (or if a simple majority is against the draft), the Commission draft decision is submitted to Member States in the Appeal Committee. If the Appeal Committee makes no decision, the European Commission will decide whether to authorise the product. Authorisation is for 10 years and subject to EU requirements for traceability and labelling.[100]

Member States, acting in the Standing Committee and the Appeal Committee, have failed to approve or reject the Commission's draft decisions for GMOs. As required by the GMO authorisation process and the Charter of Fundamental Rights, the Commission believes it "has little choice but to give the authorization."[101]

In the EU, the average authorization time for GMOs is 47 months; the timeline set out by the authorization process totals 12 months.[102] EuropaBio and other organizations filed a case with the EU Ombudsman in October 2014, alleging maladministration for failure to act within a reasonable time in making 20 GE authorization decisions under Regulation 1829/2003. Although the Commission had finally acted on these products before the Ombudsman's January 2016 opinion, the Ombudsman believed delays were a "systemic problem" and therefore constituted maladministration.[103] The Ombudsman noted that Member States, both in the Standing Committee on Plants, Animals, Food and Feed and in the Appeal Committee, failed to deliver opinions on the Commission's draft decisions about authorizing GMs for cultivation or food. The Commission delayed both in submitting its draft decisions to the Standing Committee[104] and making a decision within a reasonable time after a failure of the Appeal Committee to reach a qualified majority.[105]

Asynchronous approvals, due in part to the EU's long regulatory process, raise the issue of low-level presence of GE material unapproved in the EU. For food, no threshold for low-level presence of unapproved varieties has been defined, so the tolerance for low-level presence of unapproved GE food is zero, which makes imports difficult.[106] Imported feed is critical for the EU livestock industry, and Regulation

[99]EFSA (2011), 3.3.3. A similar process applies to feed. If a product will be used as both food and feed, a single decision is made. Regulation 1829/2003, art. 27.

[100]Regulation 1829/2003; Regulation 1830/2003.

[101]European Commission (2015b) (Memo/15/4779).

[102]FAS, USDA (2016), p. 23 (GAIN FR1624). In the US and Brazil, the average is 25 months.

[103]EU Ombudsman (2016).

[104]Regulation 1829/2003, Article 7(1) imposes a time limit of within 3 months after the EFSA decision.

[105]EU Ombudsman (2016), para 20–21.

[106]FAS, USDA (2016), pp. 17–18, 32–33. The EU threshold for labelling is 0.9%. See below.

619/2011 set a tolerance for feed: a limit of 0.1% (the lowest level at which GE presence can be validated quantitatively). The tolerance applies if the GE material is from biotech varieties authorized in a third country, varieties unapproved in the EU with an authorisation procedure pending for over 3 months and no adverse findings by EFSA, and varieties approved in the EU but for which authorisation has expired.[107]

Member State Discretion

The EU process had given limited discretion to Member States, especially for restrictions on cultivation of GMOs. Several measures included safeguard clauses, which allowed Member States to restrict or prohibit the use of a GMO if new or additional information indicated that the product "constitutes a risk to human health or the environment."[108] A few Member States invoked these safeguard clauses, generally without success.[109] Since 2003, Directive 2001/18 allowed Member States to restrict planting in certain areas by adopting coexistence measures—"appropriate measures to avoid the unintended presence of GMOs in other products."[110] The Commission provided coexistence guidelines in 2003 and 2010, but effective coexistence measures proved difficult in practice.[111]

Under a 2015 measure, a Member State can now restrict and even prohibit cultivation of GE crops on its territory.[112] Directive 2015/412 noted the strong Member State interest in governing the cultivation of GMOs: "Experience has shown that cultivation of GMOs is an issue which is more thoroughly addressed at Member State level. Issues related to the placing on the market and the import of GMOs should remain regulated at Union level to preserve the internal market. Cultivation may however require more flexibility in certain instances as it is an issue with strong national, regional and local dimensions, given its link to land use, to local agricultural structures and to the protection or maintenance of habitats, ecosystems and landscapes."[113]

The so-called GMO opt-out enacted in Directive 2015/412 applies only to cultivation, "not to the free circulation and import" of GM seeds and products.[114]

[107]Commission Regulation 619/2011, Article 2 and preamble (14). Some private operators set a 0.01 threshold for seed. See ICF-GHK (2013), pp. 33–34. In 2009, according to the Foreign Agricultural Service, "the EU denied the entry of 180,000 metric tons of U.S. soy because the shipment contained traces of three biotech corn types that the EU had not approved for food, feed, or import, although these products were allowed for use in the United States." This event led to the 2011 regulation. FAS, USDA (2016), p. 32.

[108]For example Directive 2001/18, Article 23.

[109]de Sadeleer (2015), pp. 543–545.

[110]Directive 2001/18, Article 26a, added by Regulation1829/2003, art. 43. On early coexistence measures in the EU, see Grossman (2007).

[111]European Commission (2010), repealing Recommendation 2003/556/EC.

[112]See Bodiguel (2016).

[113]Directive 2015/412, preamble (6).

[114]Directive 2015/412, preamble (16).

The Directive amended the coexistence provision in Directive 2001/18, adding a new Article 26b. It first indicated that, beginning in April 2017, Member States where GMOs are cultivated should take measures to avoid cross-border contamination to neighbouring Member States where cultivation is prohibited.[115]

The opt-out provision in Article 26b offers two methods for Member States to restrict cultivation on their territories. The first, applicable during the authorisation process for a GMO, allows a Member State to demand that the applicant adjust the geographical scope of the authorisation to exclude territory in that State. The applicant's response can adjust the geographical scope or confirm the initial scope of the application.[116] If no demand was made or the initial scope is confirmed, then the Member State can "adopt measures restricting or prohibiting the cultivation in all or part of its territory of a GMO, or a group of GMOs."[117] Member State measures must be "reasoned, proportional and non-discriminatory" and based on compelling grounds (or a combination of grounds), which include, but are not limited to, "environmental policy objectives; town and country planning; land use; socioeconomic impacts;[118] avoidance of GMO presence in other products . . .; agricultural policy objectives; public policy."[119] Because uniform scientific risk assessment to protect health and the environment in the EU is critical, Member States grounds cannot conflict with the EU's health and environmental risk assessments.[120] The Member State must inform the Commission of its grounds and measures and refrain from adopting its measures for 75 days. Measures "shall not affect the free circulation of authorized GMOs as, or in, products."[121]

As of December 2016, 19 Member States had invoked the opt-out provision, but none of those States cultivated GE crops.[122] The opt-out, which returns power from the EU to the Member States, "is a radical solution to a long running controversy."[123] It might be viewed, as scholars have indicated, as an "optional deactivation of the EU competence," "reverse harmonization"[124] or a widened scope of the

---

[115]Directive 2015/412, Article 1, amending 2001/18, Article 26a.

[116]Directive 2001/18, Article 26b(1)-(2). See European Commission (2017b) (Member State demands).

[117]Directive 2001/18, Article 26b(3).

[118]See Directive 2015/412, preamble (15). Socio-economic impacts, both quantitative and qualitative impacts, include "costs of coexistence, the lack of benefit, and consumer protection." Winter (2016), p. 127.

[119]Directive 2001/18, Article 26b(3) (enumeration omitted).

[120]Directive 2001/18, preamble (14): Member State grounds can include "the maintenance and development of agricultural practices which offer a better potential to reconcile production with ecosystem sustainability, or maintenance of local biodiversity, including certain habitats and ecosystems, or certain types of natural and landscape features, as well as specific ecosystem functions and services."

[121]Directive 2001/18, Article 26b(8).

[122]FAS, USDA (2016), pp. 9–10.

[123]Winter (2016), p. 121.

[124]Salvi (2016), pp. 209–210.

safeguard clauses.[125] Increased authority for Member States to restrict or prohibit cultivation may help to address hostility to GMOs, but leaves "the issues of legitimacy, credibility and efficiency that characterize the European decision making process ... unresolved."[126]

Although the decision to prohibit cultivation has been returned to the Member States, the decision to limit the use of authorized GM food and feed has not. In October 2015, the EU rejected a Commission proposal to amend Regulation 1829/2003 to allow Member States to restrict or prohibit GM use on their territory for nonscientific reasons (societal or political concerns).[127] Member States, trading partners, and industry interests (for example, EuropaBio) expressed doubts about the proposal, and Parliament rejected it.[128] Parliament believed that the proposal was not workable and inconsistent with the internal market and obligations under the WTO. The Commission did not withdraw the proposal, but it seems unlikely that Member States will vote.[129]

The Commission may find another means of increasing the regulatory role of Member States: a February 2017 proposed amendment to the comitology procedure, which would apply both for GM authorisation and for other areas of regulation.[130] Precipitated by the Commission's legal obligation in 2015 and 2016 to adopt authorisations for 17 "sensitive products and substances,"[131] the proposed amendment would give more responsibility to the Member States, particularly in the Appeal Committee. Voting rules for the Appeal Committee would count only positive or negative votes (not abstentions), and Member State votes would be made public. If the Appeal Committee has no opinion, the Commission could call a further meeting at Ministerial level; the Commission could also request an advisory opinion from the Council.[132]

Labelling in the EU

Labelling of GM products is an important part of EU regulation. Labels help to facilitate traceability of food, feed, and food-producing animals, as required by the 2002 General Food Law. Directive 2001/18 emphasized traceability and required labelling as an important step of placing a GMO on the market. More specific requirements in Regulation 1830/2003 establish a uniform system of traceability.

[125] de Sadeleer (2015), p. 557. Questions remain if the opt out or national measures interfere with the free movement of goods, under Article 34 TEFU. The EU Court of Justice may eventually make this decision. de Sadeleer (2015), pp. 547–551.

[126] Salvi (2016), p. 210.

[127] European Commission (2015c), COM (2015) 177 final.

[128] Salvi (2016), pp. 208–209.

[129] FAS, USDA (2016), p. 18.

[130] European Commission (2017c), COM (2017) 85.

[131] Products were GMOs and glyphosate. European Commission (2017a) (Memo/17/273).

[132] European Commission (2017c), COM (2017) 85; European Commission (2017a) (Memo/17/273).

Each GMO is associated with a unique identifier.[133] Those who sell or receive a product in the market must transmit (and retain for 5 years) two types of information: a statement that the products contains or consists of GMOs and the unique identifiers assigned to the GMOs. Labels on pre-packaged products and displays of bulk products must indicate that the product contains GMOs.

Regulation 1830/2003 requires labels for products consisting of or containing GMOs, with language such as "This product contains genetically modified organisms." Similarly, Regulation 1829/2003 requires labels for GM food or feed that "contain or consist of GMOs; or … are produced from or contain ingredients produced from GMOs," but not for food produced with GMOs or products from animals fed with GM feed.[134] The regulation prescribes language for labels.

Traceability and labelling requirements may not apply if a product has only a small amount of GM material. Directive 2001/18 and Regulation 1829/2003 provide that labelling is not required if the adventitious or technically unavoidable presence of authorized GM material does not exceed 0.9%.[135] Few foods in the EU are labelled, however. Producers have sometimes changed the composition of foods to avoid GM ingredients, and many large supermarkets and other retailers do not sell GM foods.

3 Genetically Engineered and Cloned Animals

Developments in biotechnology have been relevant for animal agriculture, as well as for crops, and are equally, if not more, controversial. Transgenic animals and clones are at the centre of these developments. Both cloning and transgenics have technical and practical limitations, and both face "lack of public understanding and acceptance," perhaps from risk of "the unknown rather than with a genuine hazard."[136]

Transgenic animals result when human intervention introduces a new gene or modifies an existing gene. Transgenics have the potential to develop disease-resistant animals, to improve food safety and quality, to decrease the environmental impact of livestock production, and to increase the efficiency of production of meat, milk, and wool.[137]

Cloning, in contrast, creates a genetically identical copy of an existing animal, often one with desirable production traits. Since 1996, when the cloned sheep Dolly

[133]Commission Regulation 65/2004.

[134]Regulation 1829/2003, Article 12. Labelling must also mention characteristics of food that is different from its conventional counterparts or that may "give rise to ethical or religious concerns" (Article 13).

[135]Regulation 1830/2003, Article 4 (traceability); Directive 2001/18, Article 21; Regulation 1829/2003, Article 12.

[136]CAST (2009), p. 12.

[137]CAST (2009), pp. 5–12.

was born, at least 15 domestic species, ranging from mouse to horse, buffalo, and camel, have been cloned.[138] The high cost of cloning makes it unlikely that clones will be produced for milk or meat in the near future. Cloning may be most useful in cattle, and some clones have high value—for example, a clone of a genetically superior bull, whose value may be more than $100,000.[139] Moreover, a cloning technique, gene transfer, can create transgenic animals more precisely than many other technologies.[140]

In 2002, the National Academy of Sciences issued a report to analyse "whether the food and other products of animal biotechnology, whether genetically engineered, or from clones, are substantially different from those derived by more traditional, extant technologies."[141] The report focused on several concerns, defined as uneasy states of "blended interest, uncertainty, and apprehension."[142] These concerns related to food safety, the environment, animal health and welfare, and policy and societal issues. In general, the NAS found that food safety assessment for GE animals, despite new proteins that could cause allergenicity or change nutritional attributes, would be "qualitatively the same" as for non-GE animals. Most safety concerns would be low.[143] Cloning posed a low level of food safety concern in the cloned animals, though evaluation of composition of their food products would be wise. Offspring, produced by natural mating, showed no safety concerns.[144] Environmental effects raised the most significant concerns, particularly among species (for example, aquatic organisms or insects) that might escape confinement and become feral.[145]

[138]Economist (2017), p. 19.

[139]CAST (2009), p. 4.

[140]CAST (2009), p. 5.

[141]NAS (2002), p. 4.

[142]NAS (2002), p. 2.

[143]NAS (2002), pp. 7–8, and chap. 4. Food from animals genetically engineered for pharmaceuticals and other non-food products may raise food safety issues. Lack of data on the composition of food products left some uncertainty. See also NAS (2004).

[144]NAS (2002), pp. 8–9. Low levels of concern accompanied techniques common in 2002 (blastomere nuclear transfer, embryo splitting), and somatic cell cloning showed no evidence of food safety concern. In 2008, FDA's Center for Veterinary Medicine indicated no concern. CVM, FDA (2008).

[145]NAS (2002), pp. 9–11 and chap. 5. Fitness in the environment will determine whether a GE animal—for example, GE salmon—will become established in the wild. The report noted the lack of regulatory framework to govern biotechnology in arthropods (p. 14).

3.1 GE Animals

US Regulation

The FDA's 1992 Statement of Policy on GE foods focused on plant varieties, rather than animals or new animal drugs.[146] In 1993, however, the FDA decided to govern both GE animals and insects, later defining GE animals as "animals modified by rDNA techniques, including the entire lineage of animals that contain the modification."[147] The FDA governs GE animals under the new animal drug provisions of the FDCA and its regulations.[148] FDA's Guidance 187, last revised in 2015, aids the agency and product developers in complying with approval requirements. An rDNA construct in a GE animal falls within the definitions of drug and new animal drug in the FDCA.[149] A new animal drug is considered unsafe until approved by the FDA. Therefore a GE animal, regulated as a new animal drug, must obtain premarket approval. Premarket approval requires proof of safety and efficacy, with technical information required by the FDA to rule out allergenicity and toxicity. If tissues from the GE animals are "as safe as those from animals of the same or comparable type that are commonly and safely consumed," the FDA is likely to conclude that food from the GE animal is safe.[150] Approval of the GE animal also requires examination of any significant environmental impacts under provisions of the National Environmental Policy Act,[151] a procedural statute that requires analysis of environmental impacts and public disclosure.

In November 2015, the FDA approved the AquAdvantage salmon, the first genetically engineered animal to be approved for commercial sale under the new animal drug provisions. AquAdvantage is genetically modified to consume 25% less feed and to reach market weight in 16 to 18 months, rather than 3 years. Eggs would be produced in Canada and the salmon grown out in Panama. The FDA approval process took more than 20 years and involved both food safety and environmental

[146] FDA (1992), pp. 22, 985. This discussion of GE animals is derived from Grossman (2016b).

[147] CVM, FDA (2015), p. 3 (Guidance 187). Guidance 187 focuses on animals with heritable rDNA constructs, including food animals. Nonheritable modifications include, for example, gene therapy, and may be addressed in a later FDA guidance.

[148] 21 USC § 360b; 21 CFR parts 510, 514. In 2002 the NAS indicated some lack of clarity about the meaning of the FDCA new animal drug provisions in the context of transgenic animals. Policy questions existed about the meaning of safe, environmental impacts, degree of precaution, application of new animal drug regulatory standards. NAS (2002), p. 111.

[149] The FDCA defines drugs as "articles (other than food) intended to affect the structure or any function of the body of man or other animals." A new animal drug is "any drug intended for use in animals other than man, including any drugs intended for use in animal feed . . . the composition of which is such that such drug is not generally recognized [among experts] as safe and effective." 21 USC §§ 321(g), 321(v).

[150] CVM, FDA (2015), p. 25 (Guidance 187). The FDA indicated that its focus on toxicity and allergenicity is consistent with the recommendations for food safety assessment in the Codex Alimentarius Commission's 2008 Guideline. CAC (2008).

[151] NEPA, 42 USC § 4332(2)(C).

assessments. After extensive regulatory evaluation by the FDA's Center for Veterinary Medicine, the agency concluded that AquAdvantage is no different, either in composition or allergenicity, from other Atlantic salmon and is therefore safe to eat.[152] The FDA did not require labels for grown-out salmon because it is not "materially different" from other Atlantic salmon. Voluntary labelling was permitted, and the FDA provided guidance to industry for voluntary labelling of food from GE salmon.[153]

Strong objections followed the FDA's decision to authorize AquAdvantage. A lawsuit challenged the authorization, and numerous grocery chains and restaurants announced that they would not sell or serve the GE salmon. In an appropriations law, Congress prescribed that the FDA "shall not allow the introduction or delivery for introduction into interstate commerce of any food that contains genetically engineered salmon until FDA publishes final labeling guidelines for informing consumers of such content."[154] In response, the FDA banned the import of GE salmon, so AquAdvantage is unlikely to be sold in the US in the near future.[155] Moreover, the recent GE Disclosure Standard, discussed above, applies to GE animals, as well as plant foods.

The FDA recently published a Draft Revised Guidance 187. If finalized, after public comments, the guidance will expand the scope of regulation beyond animals genetically engineered with modified rDNA technology to include animals developed with genome editing and other new molecular technologies.[156] That is, it will apply to any "intentionally altered genomic DNA in both the founder animal . . . and the entire subsequent lineage of animals that contains the genomic alteration," with a primary focus on heritable genomic alterations.[157] The Guidance recommendations for food safety, like the earlier Guidance, focus on comparison with an existing animal that is safe to eat.

The FDA's regulation of GE animals under the new animal drug provisions of the FDCA has been subject to criticism as inappropriately complicated, and the FDA's lengthy review of AquAdvantage characterized as "grotesquely incompetent." The FDA's approach has discouraged development of new GE animals,[158] and Draft Guidance 187 has engendered controversy among scientists.

---

[152]FDA (2015b), Final Rule: New Animal Drugs. For details, see Grossman (2016b).

[153]FDA (2015c) (Draft Guidance on Labeling).

[154]Consolidated Appropriations Act 2016, § 761(a).

[155]In Canada, 4.5 tons of AquAdvantage salmon were sold for consumption, with no label requirement, in August 2017. Waltz (2017).

[156]The "regulated article" is the "intentionally altered genomic DNA of the animal." CVM, FDA (2017), pp. 4–5 (Draft Guidance 187).

[157]CVM, FDA (2017), p. 3.

[158]Miller (2017), including quotation in prior sentence. Miller suggests that the FDA could avoid lengthy pre-market review by using the GRAS concept to GE animals; "adding a GRAS gene to a GRAS organism is likely to yield a GRAS outcome," thus eliminating some pre-market review.

EU Regulation

A number of EU countries are developing GM animals in connection with medical and pharmaceutical research. Fewer countries focus on improved animal breeding. But no transgenic animal is commercialized for food use in the EU, and by 2016, EFSA had received no application for release or marketing of GM animals.[159] Moreover, the EU has experienced public resistance both to GM animals and clones and their products. Ethical and animal welfare issues lead to low market acceptance for consumers, policy makers and industry, including the livestock industry.[160]

Because developers of transgenic food animals may apply for authorisation to market food in the EU, the European Commission asked EFSA to develop risk assessment guidelines, focusing on food and feed safety, animal health and welfare, and the environment. In 2012, EFSA published its risk assessment guidance on food and feed, as well as animal health and welfare aspects.[161] EFSA recommended comparing GM animals and their products with conventional counterparts with a history of safe use. It also recommended post-market monitoring and surveillance. In 2013, EFSA published its guidance on environmental risk assessment of GE animals, setting out a multi-step assessment process, as well as the analysis of a number of possible risks.[162] The EFSA guidance, however, did not consider traceability, labelling or coexistence, nor did it focus on societal, political and economic concerns. Risk managers consider these factors in deciding if GE animals and their products can be commercialized.[163]

Although the Novel Foods Regulation applies to some food from animals (for example food from clones), GM animals are excluded. The Novel Foods Regulation does not apply to "genetically modified foods falling within the scope of Regulation (EC) No 1829/2003.[164] Food from GM animals falls within the General Food Law definition of food: "any substance or product, whether processed, partially processed, or unprocessed, . . . intended to be, or reasonably expected to be ingested by humans," including live animals "prepared for placing on the market for human consumption."[165] Moreover, GM animals fit within the definition of genetically modified organism in Regulation 1829/2003, which references Directive 2001/18: "an organism, with the exception of human beings, in which the genetic material has been altered in a way that does not occur naturally by mating and/or natural recombination."[166]

---

[159]FAS (2016), pp. 42–43.

[160]FAS (2016), pp. 45–46.

[161]EFSA (2012a).

[162]EFSA (2013). The document focuses on risk assessment under both Regulation 1829/2003 and Directive 2001/18.

[163]EFSA (n.d.).

[164]Regulation 2015/2283, Articles 2(2)(a), 3(2)(a)(v).

[165]Regulation 178/2002, Article 2. Live animals are not defined as food unless they are intended for human consumption (Article 2(b)).

[166]Regulation 1829/2003, Article 2(5); Regulation 2001/18, Article 2(2) and Annex IA.

Thus, Regulation 1829/2003 governs authorization of food, included imported food, from GM animals in the EU. An application to place food from a transgenic animal on the market will follow a procedure similar to that used for food from GM plants, with a risk assessment carried out by EFSA, a draft decision from the Commission, and participation by Member States. Like other GM foods, products of GM animals must be labelled as such.[167]

3.2 *Cloned Animals*

US Approach to Cloning

The US approach to cloning is far less complicated than the new animal drug process used for transgenic animals. Indeed, since 2008, meat and milk from cloned animals and their progeny have been approved for sale in the United States. Even earlier, in the 1990s, meat and milk from clones (1000 cattle and sheep) entered the food chain.[168] Beginning in 2001, in an exercise in precaution while risk assessments occurred, the US had a voluntary moratorium on marketing of cloned animals and their progeny. After 2008, no moratorium applied to sexually-reproduced offspring of clones. In the US, cloned animals, expensive to produce, are normally used as breeding animals and do not enter the food chain. Nonetheless, industry has created a supply chain management program, which tracks clones through an animal registry for consumer information, not for food safety.[169]

In the years after the 2002 National Academy of Sciences report discussed above, the FDA's Center for Veterinary Medicine reviewed the cloning process. The assessment was intended to determine whether cloning, called somatic cell nuclear transfer (SCNT), carried any risks to animals when compared to other assisted reproductive technologies. The assessment also analysed the safety of foods from clones and their progeny when compared with their conventional counterparts. As a precautionary measure, the FDA had asked that companies keep meat or milk from animal clones and progeny off the market until the risk assessment was complete.[170]

In 2008, the Center for Veterinary Medicine released its report, *Animal Cloning: A Risk Assessment*. In terms of risks to animals, the report concluded that reproductive anomalies occurred in cattle and sheep (rather than goats and swine). The anomalies were not different from anomalies from other assisted reproductive technologies and natural mating, but they occurred more often.[171]

[167]Regulation 1829/2003; Regulation 1830/2003.

[168]CAST (2009), p. 3.

[169]BIO (2010).

[170]CVM, FDA (2015) (Guidance 187), p. 2.

[171]CVM, FDA (2008a), pp. 9–10.

In terms of food safety, the CVM found no "subtle hazards [or allergenic effects] that might indicate food consumption risks in healthy clones of cattle, swine, or goat."[172] Relative to conventionally-bred counterparts, clones posed no increased food consumption risks. Progeny of clones and their products also posed no food consumption risks. The CVM conclusions corroborated the food safety analysis in the 2002 NAS report.[173]

Relying on the CVM risk assessment, the FDA published its 2008 Guidance for Industry. The FDA reiterated the CVM's conclusions in the risk assessment, and stated that "because food from clones would be subject to the same requirements as food from their conventionally bred counterparts, we do not believe that meat or milk from cattle, swine, and goat clones would require any additional controls compared with meat or milk from cattle, swine, or goats currently entering the food supply today."[174] The FDA recommended, however, that "edible products from clones from animals other than cattle, swine, or goat (e.g., sheep) not be introduced into the human food supply."[175] Moreover, the FDA indicated that if SCNT or animal clones "meet the statutory definition of new animal drug" under the FDCA, the FDA does not intend to regulate or enforce against food or non-food species (so called "enforcement discretion").[176] The FDA's guidance did not require labels for clones or their progeny.

After the FDA's actions, the USDA focused on managing the marketing of products from clones and their progeny.[177] Recognizing that rules for livestock cloning "may impact trade and technology transfer," the US Foreign Agriculture Service and several other nations issued a Joint Statement on Animal Cloning for Livestock Production. The statement insisted that regulations should be based on science and "no more trade-restrictive than necessary."[178] It recognized that scientific evidence found no food safety risks from clones and that progeny of clones are not clones. Regulatory restrictions on food from clone progeny (bans or labels) would be impossible to apply and could harm international trade.

Cloning in the EU

The EU has been less hospitable to clones than the US and other nations. At a request from the European Commission, EFSA evaluated cattle and pig clones, with a focus on food safety, animal health, animal welfare, and the environment. EFSA's 2008 scientific opinion found no indication that milk and meat from clones and their

---

[172]CVM, FDA (2008a), p. 15.

[173]CVM, FDA (2008a), p. 16.

[174]CVM, FDA (2008b) (Guidance 179), p. 2. Clones are, however, inconsistent with organic production. AMS, USDA (2011).

[175]CVM, FDA (2008b) (Guidance 179), p. 3.

[176]CVM, FDA (2008b) (Guidance 179), p. 3.

[177]Knight (2008).

[178]FAS (2011) (Argentina, Brazil, New Zealand, Paraguay).

progeny differed from products of conventionally-bred animals and that cloned animals posed no new environmental risks. EFSA indicated, however, that cloning affects animal welfare, with adverse health outcomes on clones and dams, but not for sexually-reproduced progeny of clones.[179] A 2009 EFSA statement confirmed the validity of its 2008 conclusions, and in a 2010 update on the state of play, EFSA again confirmed its earlier conclusions.[180] In 2012, EFSA issued another update on the state of play. Limited data continued to restrict EFSA's conclusions to cattle and pigs. On the basis of peer-reviewed scientific literature, other data supplied to EFSA, and discussions with experts, EFSA again confirmed its conclusions from 2008, 2009, and 2010. "With respect to food safety, there are no indications that differences exist between food products derived from healthy clones or their offspring—in particular milk and meat—from those of healthy, conventionally bred animals."[181] EFSA again found no unique threats to the environment, but acknowledged continued animal health and welfare concerns, as well as lower cloning efficiency in cattle and pigs than *in vitro* reproduction.[182]

In December 2013, the European Commission proposed two Directives on cloning along with its proposal for the new Novel Foods Regulation.[183] Under the existing Novel Foods measure, Regulation 258/1997, animal clones were regulated as food "produced from non-traditional breeding techniques," but lawmakers had requested separate legislation on cloning.[184] Both proposed Directives would have governed clones, but not progeny of clones or products of those progeny. No labelling of products from the offspring of clones would be required because of the difficulty of documenting a link between food-producing animals and their meat.[185]

One proposal was a Directive on the cloning of several species of animals kept and reproduced for farming purposes.[186] The Directive would not apply to animals used exclusively for other purposes such as research or production of pharmaceuticals. Noting that EU legislation requires Member States to avoid causing unnecessary suffering for farm animals,[187] the preamble focused on cloning's effect on the

[179]EFSA (2008).

[180]EFSA (2009, 2010a).

[181]EFSA (2012b), p. 2.

[182]EFSA (2012b), p. 18.

[183]European Commission (2013e), COM (2013) 894 final (Novel Foods proposal).

[184]European Commission (2013c), COM (2013) 892 final, p. 2. A Commission impact assessment accompanying the proposals set out several policy options: no change (continue use of Novel Foods Regulation); pre-market approval of food from clones and their progeny; labelling of food from clones and their progeny (requiring identification and traceability of animals); and temporary suspension of cloning and import of clones. European Commission (2013b), SWD (2013) 519 final, pp. 28–47.

[185]European Commission (2013a) (Memo/13/1169), p. 3.

[186]European Commission (2013c), COM (2013) 892 final. The legal basis for the Directive was Article 43 TEFU (agriculture), and would have been enacted under the co-decision procedure, with both Parliament and Council reaching agreement. Another objective was "to ensure uniform conditions of production for farmers" (p. 2).

[187]Council Directive 98/58/EC protects the welfare of farm animals.

welfare of farm animals, including reproductive dysfunctions, low efficiency of breeding, and clone abnormalities identified by EFSA. The Directive would have required Member States to enact measures to "provisionally prohibit" both the cloning of animals and the placing on the market of clones and embryo clones and to establish penalties for violations of the prohibition. After 5 years, the Commission would report on cloning, on the basis of Member State experience.

A companion Directive would have prevented the placing on the market of food from animal clones.[188] Intended to address consumer perspectives about food from animal clones, its preamble noted that EFSA found no differences in food safety between food from healthy clones and conventionally bred animals, but identified animal welfare and ethical concerns that made EU citizens reluctant to eat food from animal clones. The Directive is thus intended to ensure that food from animal clones, including clones from other countries, does not enter the food chain. It therefore would require Member States to enact national provisions to keep food from animal clones off the market and to prescribe penalties for infringement of those provisions. After 5 years, the Commission would report on application of the Directive, on the basis of Member State experience.

The EU did not adopt either Directive. The response of Parliament, delivered in 2015, approved the cloning directive, but with significant amendments. Parliament stated that cloning for food production "jeopardises the defining characteristics of the European farming model, which is based on product quality, food safety, consumer health, strict animal welfare rules and the use of environmentally sound methods."[189] Parliament would have made the measure a Regulation and favoured a clear prohibition of cloning and import of clones and their products. No further legislative steps occurred since 2015.[190]

In the absence of specific EU legislation to govern clones and their products, food from clones will be covered by the Novel Foods Regulation 2015/2283, which enters fully into force 1 January 2018 and repeals Regulation 258/97.[191] The new Regulation indicates that food from cloned animals had been governed under Regulation 258/97 as food from animals obtained by non-traditional breeding practices. Therefore, "until specific legislation on food from animal clones enters into force, food from animal clones should fall under the scope of this Regulation as food from animals obtained by non-traditional breeding practices and should be appropriately labelled for the final consumer in accordance with the Union legislation in force."[192]

[188]European Commission (2013d), COM (2013) 893 final. The legal basis was Article 352(1) Lisbon Treaty and would have required consent of Parliament and unanimous decision of the Council.

[189]European Parliament (2015), para 2g. A ban on cloning may conflict with obligations under the WTO, including GATT Article XI and SPS Articles 2 and 5. But see GATT Article XX and SPS Article 5.7. Carreño (2014), p. 364.

[190]See Eur-Lex (n.d.).

[191]Under Regulation 258/97, Member State food assessment agencies reviewed new foods first. Regulation 2015/2283 introduces a more efficient centralized procedure, with an EFSA risk assessment.

[192]Regulation 2015/2283, preamble (14); Article 1(2)(e).

Cloned animals fit the definition of "novel food" in the Novel Foods Regulation: "food consisting of, isolated from or produced from animals or their parts, except for animals obtained by traditional breeding practices which have been used for food production within the Union before 15 May 1997 and the food from those animals has a history of safe food use within the Union."[193] Food from cloned animals must therefore comply with the authorization procedure, now coordinated by the Commission, set out in the Regulation.[194] The procedure may include an opinion from EFSA about the safety of the food.

Novel foods are subject to general labelling provisions in EU food law,[195] and specific labelling requirements may accompany authorization of a novel food.[196] A 2015 Commission study focused on labelling of products from cloned animals and their offspring. That report identified "consumer resistance and industry indifference" in the EU and thus did not expect significant growth of cloning in the near future.[197] Indeed, a ban on cloning for food seems more likely. Nonetheless, possible imports of live animals, products of cloned animals, and genetic materials make labelling relevant.

An EU labelling requirement, however, would affect both the EU livestock industry and producers in third countries. Current law, especially the General Food Law (Regulation 178/2002), does not require tracing or labelling of meat and dairy products to individual animals. Therefore a labelling requirement would impose new obligations and costs on both producers and others in the supply chains for meat and dairy: ancestry recording, identification of individual animals, provision of information through the supply chain, and verification of status for each animal. The impact of labelling would be minimal if the definition of "clone offspring" includes only the first generation offspring. Identifying clone offspring in subsequent generations would impose additional documentation and costs (for example, expensive DNA verification), both for importers and for the EU livestock industry. Indeed, the expense and complexities of labelling, as well as the impact on consumer perception, suggest that clones and their offspring are unlikely to be sold in the EU, but trading partners in countries where cloning is used would still bear the expense of providing required information to import animals and their products, raising prices for consumers.[198]

---

[193]Regulation 2015/2283, Article 3(2)(a)(v). See also Article 3(2)(a)(vi), defining novel food as "food consisting of, isolated from or produced from cell culture or tissue culture derived from animals, plants, micro-organisms, fungi or algae." Like some procedures in the US, the Regulation indicates that food operators should determine if their product must comply with the regulation. In case of uncertainty, operators should consult the relevant Member State, which may consult other States and the Commission (Article 4(1)-(3)).

[194]Regulation 2015/2283, Articles 10–13. Articles 14–20 set out a procedure to facilitate use of traditional food with a 25-year history of safe consumption in third countries.

[195]For example, Regulation 1169/2011.

[196]Regulation 2015/2283, preamble (33) and Article 9(2)(c), (3)(b).

[197]European Commission (2015a), p. 1.

[198]European Commission (2015a), pp. 1–6. See also ICF GHK (2012). Requirements for an effective system could resemble identification and tracking of individual animals in the National Animal Identification System, developed to monitor animal health and eventually abandoned by the US Department of Agriculture. Grossman (2006).

4 Regulation in the US and the EU: Some Comparisons

4.1 A Few Commonalities

Scientific Risk Assessment

Despite many differences in approach to GE crops, GE (transgenic) animals, cloned animals, and their food products in the EU and the US, some principles apply in both regulatory systems. Most significant is a reliance on a "broadly similar" scientific risk assessment conducted by expert scientists.[199] For food safety, recommendations from the Codex Alimentarius Commission (CAC) have influenced EU and US guidelines for risk assessment.[200] For environmental safety, without an international scientific expert equivalent to the CAC, risk assessment is guided by other policies, including documents from the Organisation for Economic Co-operation and Development. To some extent, both the US and the EU employ the concept of substantial equivalence, comparing GE varieties with a conventionally-bred counterpart.[201] Of course, differences exist in the stringency of testing, the agencies charged with risk assessment, transparency to the public, and political pressures.

Moreover, in the US, the agency that evaluates risk (for example, the USDA) makes the authorization decision. In the EU, that decision is not assigned to risk assessors, but to Member States and the Commission, who are more politically accountable.[202] In the process of risk management, non-scientific issues (discussed below) often influence regulatory decisions. One commentator noted that at the EU level, scientific expertise, directed to human health and environmental impacts, predominates. In the Member States, however, socioeconomic impacts and other considerations are relevant.[203] The Member States and the EU have often reached a regulatory deadlock: "Member states are still trying to determine *if* they should approve GMOs; the EU is trying to determine *how* they should approve GMOs."[204]

Lengthy Regulatory Process

Another commonality is the slow pace and high cost of regulation. Even after long experience with GE crops and food products, regulatory time frames have not decreased and in some instances have increased.[205] Moreover, regulation is costly.

---

[199]NASEM (2016), p. 455.

[200]Codex (2003a) (risk analysis); Codex (2003b) (GE plants); Codex (2008) (GE animals). Compliance with the Codex risk analysis also complies with the SPS agreement. NASEM (2016), p. 457.

[201]NASEM (2016), p. 492.

[202]See NASEM (2016), p. 502.

[203]Stapleton (2016), p. 531.

[204]Stapleton (2016), pp. 530–531. Stapleton believes that Directive 2015/412, which allows Member States to opt out of cultivation, helps to resolve the deadlock.

[205]Gliem et al. (2016), pp. 110–112.

Between 2008 and 2012, the mean cost of complying with regulations was $35 million of a total product development cost of $136 million.[206] High costs to develop new GE products often can be justified by significant economic and agricultural benefits. Unfortunately, "[d]elays in authorising GE crops postpone their benefits and cause economic losses in foregone profits. Losses are further exaggerated by asynchronous approval processes, which cause market disruptions, and lead to strained trading relations that in some cases have escalated to formal international disputes. Potential environmental and human health benefits are also delayed."[207]

In a recent study of approval times, researchers calculated time taken for similar steps in the process of regulatory oversight in the US (including applications for cultivation) and the EU (applications for import or food and feed). Similar steps in regulatory oversight were "bureaucratic" decision-making (assessment of scientific evidence submitted by the developer) in the US and "risk assessment" (the EFSA analysis) in the EU. The researchers' analysis did not include the time spent for political risk management decisions in the EU. For the 26 GE events considered, the process took 686 days in the US and 995 days in the EU.[208] In a global analysis, the researchers found that the mean time for the entire approval process in the US was 1321 days from 1988 to 1997, but increased to 2467 days for 1998 to 2015. The increased time might be explained by a number of disruptive incidents and controversies (for example, the accidental release of unapproved varieties). The mean time in the EU between 1995 and 2015 was 1758 days.[209] Researchers found it surprising that EU time to adoption has shortened over the years, although risk assessments have taken more time.[210]

Lengthy regulation has discouraged innovation in both the US and the EU. The FDA's long delay in establishing a process for regulating transgenic animals[211] did not encourage new developments. Moreover, neither the complex new animal drug process used by the FDA to govern transgenic animals nor the 20-year regulatory process for AquAdvantage salmon has encouraged commercialization of new transgenic animals. The USDA's long timeline for deregulating GM traits affects small companies that cannot afford the high cost of regulatory delays. In the EU, the lengthy regulatory process and general opposition to GE products has led some companies to move their biotechnology research out of the EU. In addition, the EU share of global agricultural research and development decreased from one-third to less than 10% in last 20 years.[212] Industry interests allege that the Commission's delay in authorizing GE products, characterized as maladministration by the European Ombudsman, creates "concrete market disruption and material damage."[213]

[206]Smart et al. (2017), p. 183.

[207]Smart et al. (2017), p. 183 (references omitted).

[208]Smart et al. (2017), p. 192.

[209]Smart et al. (2017), pp. 187, 192. The US study included 95 observations; EU, 65 observations of completed applications.

[210]Smart et al. (2017), pp. 192–193. In the EU, developers' scientific investigations can use data submitted by other notifies.

[211]CAST (2009), p. 12.

[212]Smyth et al. (2016), p. 189.

[213]EuropaBio (2016) (referring to products with applications dating from 2011 and 2012). See EU Ombudsman (2016).

Coexistence

Both the US and the EU have faced the issue of coexistence—the unintended mixing of GE crops with traditional and organic crops. The issue of coexistence has been contentious, perhaps more in the EU, where few GE crops are grown, than in the US. As the discussion above indicated, Commission recommendations on coexistence guided Member State efforts to ensure that GE material did not "contaminate" other crops. The 2015 Directive that allows Member States to restrict or prohibit the use of GE crops in their territory may avoid some coexistence problems.

In the US, where GE varieties predominate for some major crops, efforts to address coexistence are ongoing, both by government and in the private sector. The USDA Advisory Committee on Biotechnology and 21st Century Agriculture (AC21) has developed recommendations to strengthen coexistence in an increasingly complex agricultural landscape.[214] The Government Accountability Office indicated that the USDA should work toward enhanced oversight and a better understanding of the impacts of the mixing of crops.[215]

Despite efforts by producers and supply chains to avoid pollen drift and commingling of crops, the risk of adventitious presence still exists.[216] The prevalence of GE varieties, planted on almost half of US cropland, and the adventitious presence of GE crops have economic consequences for producers of traditional (non-GE) and organic varieties. Practices required to avoid cross-pollination (for example, buffer strips, delayed planting) and to segregate and test non-GE and organic varieties raise costs for producers and the grain industry. Pollen drift and commingling also have economic consequences for non-GE producers. Some organic farmers have reported economic losses ($6.1 million in 2014) from commingling with GE varieties.[217] Failure of coexistence results in significant trade disruption, especially in the context of asynchronous approvals of GE varieties, discussed below.

Labelling

One of the significant differences between US and EU law is scheduled to disappear, at least in part, in the near future. Although the EU has long required both traceability and labelling of GE food, the US FDA did not require labels. Labels were not needed to protect human health, and the FDA did not believe that it had the legal authority to require labels for information that is not "material," even in the face of consumer preference.[218]

---

[214]USDA, AC21 (2016).

[215]US Government Accountability Office (2016).

[216]NASEM (2016), p. 501. Indeed, adventitious presence has been considered normal. Farming "is practiced in the open air" subject to the vagaries of nature, and "100% purity is impossible." Grossman (2007), p. 329.

[217]Greene et al. (2016), pp. 25–28.

[218]The Canadian Parliament defeated a GM labelling law in May 2017.

The National Bioengineered Disclosure Standard, enacted in 2016 with regulations expected in 2018, will require labels for most GE food and food with GE ingredients. It will apply to transgenic animals, but not to clones and their progeny. The definition of biotechnology in the law will determine whether labelling will apply to products developed by new genetic technologies. The law assigns responsibility to the USDA, and the agency will establish the threshold for labelling, as well as the required language or symbols for product labels. It would be helpful if the USDA imposed the EU labelling threshold of 0.9%; proposed regulations will provide more information. It seems unlikely, however, that USDA regulations will require the same type of labelling language that is required in EU measures.[219]

4.2 *Risk Management*

The different approaches of the US and EU to regulation of agricultural biotechnology might be characterized as "why not" (the US, with an emphasis on substantial equivalence and scientific assessment) and "why" (the EU, with emphasis on the precautionary principle and Member State and consumer preferences).[220] In the EU, the "why" shows up most clearly in the risk management stage of the approval process—the political decision made by Member States and the Commission after EFSA has determined that a product is safe. Both the precautionary principle and socio-economic considerations are relevant.

Precautionary Principle

GE regulatory systems might be considered either permissive (why not) or precautionary (why).[221] The precautionary principle, articulated in the 1992 Rio Declaration on Environment and Development, indicated that "[w]here there are threats of serious or irreversible damage, lack of full scientific certainty shall not be used as a reason for postponing cost-effective measures to prevent environmental degradation."[222] Other international instruments, including the Cartagena Protocol on Biosafety,[223] espoused the principle in different formulations.[224]

The US has not formally adopted the precautionary principle, but its principles for risk analysis reflect precaution, especially in the US approach to food safety and

[219]The Codex Alimentarius Commission has no rules for labelling, but listed a number of relevant Codex texts. CAC (2011).

[220]Young (2003), pp. 461–466.

[221]NASEM (2016), pp. 455–456.

[222]United Nations (1992), principle 15.

[223]United Nations (2000), preamble and Article 1.

[224]For comparison of US and EU approaches to precaution, see Anker and Grossman (2009).

environmental protection. For example, the FDCA, which governs authorization of GE foods, requires scientific proof of safety of food additives, even those considered GRAS. The USDA's obligation to analyse environmental impacts of GE crops under the National Environmental Policy Act is another example of a precautionary approach.

Precaution is far more explicit in the EU regulation of GE crops and food. The precautionary principle is a core value in the General Food Law, which invokes the principle as a factor in risk management in cases of scientific uncertainty about harmful effects on health.[225] Directive 2001/18 (deliberate release) and Regulation 1830/2003 (traceability and labelling)[226] also refer to the principle. More recently the 2015 Novel Foods Regulation requires decisions for authorization to take account of the precautionary principle.[227] The precautionary principle influences risk management, and measures imposed after approval of new GE products (for example, traceability and labelling; post market monitoring) might be seen as applications of the precautionary principle.[228]

Some history may explain the EU's reliance on precaution. The EU regulatory system was influenced, in part, by several food security issues, including bovine spongiform encephalopathy (BSE or mad cow disease) and variant Creutzfeldt Jakob disease in the UK in the 1980s and 1990s and dioxin contamination of animal feed in Belgium in the late 1990s. Regulatory failures in response to earlier crises "contributed to a more precautionary approach to risk management for new technologies in food production, especially at the moment when GMOs appeared on the agenda."[229]

Nonetheless, stringent application of the precautionary principle to reject GE crops and their products can pose disadvantages in the EU and elsewhere. These include loss of benefits, including higher yields and increased income, to farmers; discouragement of development of nonproprietary GE traits by developers who cannot afford to commercialize their products; and regulatory delays that impede commercialization of beneficial crops (including, for example, golden rice).[230]

---

[225] Regulation 178/2002, Articles 6, 7, which do not mention consumer preferences. Preamble (112) refers to "a risk to life or health."

[226] "Traceability should also facilitate the implementation of risk management measures in accordance with the precautionary principle." Regulation 1830/2003, preamble (3). See European Commission (2000).

[227] Regulation 2015/2283, Article 12(1)(B), referring to Regulation 178/2002 (General Food Law), Article 7. "Novel foods should be safe and if their safety cannot be assessed and scientific uncertainty persists, the precautionary principle may be applied." Regulation 2015/2283, preamble (20).

[228] Anker and Grossman (2009), p. 21. One European lawyer commented that "[b]ehind the concept of a precautionary system . . . , there is a rigid political choice on the part of the European legislator which rather encourages suspicion regarding the application of biotechnologies in agriculture, in a manner that is very different from that of other countries." Lucifero (2016), p. 155.

[229] Stapleton (2016), p. 518. Perhaps the EU moratorium reflects application of the precautionary principle. CAST (2013), p. 12.

[230] CAST (2013), pp. 12–13.

Socioeconomic Issues

In the US, regulatory approval of GE crops and their products is generally based on science, with little formal consideration of consumer preference and other socioeconomic issues. Nonetheless, as the NAS noted (in the context of animal biotechnology), "even when the social and economic aspects of the technology are beyond the regulatory jurisdiction of an agency, they can affect the questions regulatory agencies are pressed to address by various groups, and sometimes can dominate the public debate in ways that have unavoidable spillover effects on the regulatory process."[231]

In the EU, in contrast, socioeconomic issues play a significant role in the approval process, generally at the risk management stage, after EFSA has ruled out harm to health and the environment. Indeed, the EU has been identified as the "driving force behind efforts to have social attitudes reflected in international regulation and trade agreements" perhaps because "food safety failures had left a legacy of consumer mistrust and skepticism surrounding many food production processes and methods."[232] Researchers have identified an international consensus that socioeconomic considerations, as well as other issues and factors, should (and sometimes must) play a role in assessing GE products for agriculture.[233]

No international agreements require consideration of socioeconomic considerations, though some agreements allow it.[234] The Cartagena Protocol on Biosafety, which espoused the precautionary principle, also encouraged the use of socioeconomic considerations: "The Parties, in reaching a decision on import under this Protocol or under its domestic measures implementing the Protocol, may take into account, consistent with their international obligations, socio-economic considerations arising from the impact of living modified organisms on the conservation and sustainable use of biological diversity, especially with regard to the value of biological diversity to indigenous and local communities."[235]

This language in the Cartagena Protocol, it has been argued, helped to justify "the movement away from science-based regulation" in the EU.[236] The General Food Law, for example, indicates that scientific risk assessment is not always the only basis for risk management decisions. "[O]ther factors relevant to the matter under consideration should legitimately be taken into account including societal,

[231]NAS (2002), p. 116.

[232]Phillipson (2016), p. 92.

[233]Binimelis and Myhr (2015), pp. 61–62.

[234]NASEM (2016), p. 464. Trade agreements discourage consideration of socioeconomic concerns.

[235]United Nations (2000), Article 26(1), Socio-Economic Considerations.

[236]Smyth (2017), p. 82. Smyth argues that the Cartagena Protocol undermines agriculture research in developing countries. Moreover, he asserts that the EU offers preferred tariff rates to developing countries that ratify the Protocol and discourages developing countries from adopting GE crops by threating loss of access to EU markets (pp. 82–84). His rather draconian recommendations are to help developing countries to leave the Cartagena Protocol and to "develop a means of fencing Europe out of global commodity trade" (p. 85).

economic, traditional, ethical and environmental factors and the feasibility of controls."[237] The 2015 Novel Foods Regulation acknowledges the legitimacy of socioeconomic considerations. It identifies the free movement of food as a factor that "contributes significantly to the health and well-being of citizens, and to their social and economic interests."[238] Authorisation of a novel food takes into account scientific evaluation, the precautionary principle, and "any other legitimate factors relevant to the application."[239] These "legitimate factors" would seem to include consumer preferences, animal welfare, and other socioeconomic considerations.

Insofar as GE crops and their products are concerned, the inclusion of socioeconomic considerations burdens the approval process.[240] The "conscious attempt to move away from purely science-based regulations has resulted in impacts for the regulation and trade of products in biotechnology."[241] Incorporation of socioeconomic considerations delays the regulatory process for a minimum of two years, due in part to the lack of clear methods for making socioeconomic assessments.[242] Delays are likely to decrease both private and public research and development. Moreover, the importance of socioeconomic considerations in GE crop approval "has driven investment risk so high that firms are no longer willing to take this level of risk and have reallocated their agricultural investment resources into countries that have functioning regulatory systems."[243] For developing countries, the inclusion of socioeconomic considerations in the approval of GE crops "is a clear and costly impediment to successfully improving food security" and is "the biggest barrier that presently exists to innovation and improving food security in developing countries."[244]

Socioeconomic considerations also raise difficult issues of compatibility with various international agreements, including trade agreements.[245] In terms of trade, the WTO focuses on science, so "consideration of socioeconomic issues receives little support in resolving trade disputes between countries."[246] The WTO Sanitary and Phytosanitary (SPS) Agreement does not reflect consumer socioeconomic concerns about biotechnology.[247] In the 2003 WTO dispute precipitated by the EU's moratorium on GE approvals and alleging violation of the SPS Agreement, the WTO dispute resolution panel focused on the science-based approval of GE

[237] Regulation 178/2002, preamble (19).

[238] Regulation 2015/2283, preamble (1).

[239] Regulation 2015/2283, Article 12(1)(d).

[240] ISAAA (2017), p. 112.

[241] Phillipson (2016), p. 92. Mandatory labelling, which facilitates consumer choice but is not based in science, is another socioeconomic issue. NASEM (2016), p. 462.

[242] Smyth et al. (2016), p. 189.

[243] Smyth et al. (2016), pp. 189–190.

[244] Smyth et al. (2016), p. 190.

[245] Phillipson (2016), pp. 94–95.

[246] NASEM (2016), p. 461.

[247] Smyth (2017), p. 82.

products and did not apply either the precautionary principle or provisions of the Cartagena Protocol on Biosafety.[248]

Insofar as GE animals and clones are concerned, socioeconomic considerations seem to weigh heavily. In the US, the NAS evaluated science-based concerns connected with animal biotechnology, but it recognized the implications of other factors and the impact of technologies on "social, political, economic, religious, and spiritual conditions or values"—clearly socioeconomic considerations.[249] At that time, the NAS recognized a lack of clarity among regulatory agencies about the regulatory role of social or economic impacts of new technologies.[250]

In the EU, "[c]onsumer and producer choice regarding GM and cloned animals is at least as important as in the case of food and products from GM plants."[251] Socioeconomic considerations, particularly animal welfare, seem to have led to rejection of cloning and distrust of transgenic animals in the EU. Trade implications, however, remain relevant: "Taking ethical and social aspects into account in the assessment of importing cloned and GM animals can lead to trade conflicts under WTO law. If the EU chooses to take these aspects into consideration, it should bear this in mind when drawing up measures."[252]

4.3 Regulatory Barriers: Asynchronous Approvals and Low-Level Presence

At present, regulatory barriers to products of biotechnology apply mostly to GE crops and their food and feed products. No transgenic animals are sold for food in the US (despite FDA's 2015 approval of AquAdvantage salmon) or in the EU. Clones of cattle and swine, allowed for food in the US, are too expensive for the food market, and the progeny that result from normal breeding are sold for food, but not necessarily identified. Therefore this discussion focuses on GE crops and their products.

A number of regulatory barriers, some discussed above, impede the international market for GE crops and their products. The high cost of development and especially the cost of complying with regulatory requirements is a barrier to innovation. Regulatory requirements are critical to ensure the safety of new products, but inefficiencies, both in the EU and the US, are time consuming and delay commercialization. The focus on various socioeconomic considerations in the risk-management process imposes additional delay. These factors and others lead to

---

[248]NASEM (2016), p. 461 (citing the 2006 Panel Report in WTO Dispute DS291). The moratorium dated from 24 June 1999. The last GE approval (carnations) before the moratorium was in October 1998; last food approval, in April 1998.

[249]NAS (2002), p. 13.

[250]NAS (2002), p. 14.

[251]COGEM (2011), p. 106.

[252]COGEM (2011), p. 103.

contentious problems created by asynchronous approval of GE products and the low or zero thresholds applied when traces of GE material are detected in non-GE products.[253]

The US, the EU, and other nations implement their own legal procedures for authorizing the cultivation and import of GE crops and their products. Because many GE varieties are approved first in the US, approvals in the EU and other nations often lag behind those in the US. Moreover, not all GE crop developers seek approval in other jurisdictions. This condition of asynchronous approvals, caused by regulatory differences and long delays in GE approvals, has increased costs and created barriers to trade. Between 2000 and 2013, US exports of grain, feed, and oilseeds fell, and US agricultural exports to the EU did not keep pace with market growth in the EU or export growth from the US.[254]

Asynchronous approvals cause significant trade risks, "The primary risk … [is] that small amounts of grain with biotech events approved in an exporting country but not in an importing one, known as low-level presence (LLP), may be contained in an international shipment of agricultural commodities."[255] Commercial grain contracts normally allow some impurities, but many countries impose a zero or extremely low tolerance for unapproved GE varieties, even when the presence is adventitious.[256] Grain shipments that exceed the importing country's tolerance can be rejected, with economic losses falling first on the trading partners, but also on shippers, importing traders and processors, and producers and others in the grain industry in the exporting country. Economic impacts from trade disruptions often continue for years, and researchers have found that greater asynchronies between pairs of countries lead to less trade.[257]

Numerous incidents involving GE crops produced in the US had trade implications. Some involved asynchronous approvals; others resulted from adventitious presence of crops not yet approved in the US. Herculex™ corn (DAS 59122-7), developed by Dow AgroSciences and Pioneer Hi-Bred, was approved in 2007 for import in the EU, after an authorization process beginning in 2000. Despite stewardship efforts in the US corn industry, traces of Herculex corn appeared in shipments to the EU before approval, violating the EU's policy of zero tolerance. The result was a 3-year disruption in the corn market, with a 30–40% decrease in exports of US corn gluten feed to the EU.[258] Similarly, in 2006 traces of Bayer's LibertyLink™ rice (LL601), not yet approved in the US, appeared in samples of commercial long-grain rice including exports. Although the rice did not pose environmental or food safety concerns and soon received a determination of

[253]ISAAA (2017), pp. 112–113.

[254]FAS, USDA (2014).

[255]CAST (2016), p. 3.

[256]For certified seed, the normal purity level is 99.5% (allowing .25% weed seed and .25% other crop varieties). Grain contracts often allow 3–5% impurity. Smyth (2017), pp. 82–83.

[257]CAST (2016), pp. 3, 5.

[258]Smyth (2017), p. 83.

nonregulated status, financial consequences were significant. The EU required certification that imported rice was free of LL601, but by 2012 US rice imports to the EU had been reduced by 60%. Moreover, Bayer faced over 1000 lawsuits from producers and others and paid over $2 billion in settlements.[259] Indeed, issues with asynchronous approval affect trade worldwide. Syngenta's Viptera® corn (MIR 162) was sold and planted in the US in 2011 before China has approved the variety. China rejected shipments in 2013, resulting in lower corn prices and significant losses to producers. Thousands of producers and grain handlers have filed individual and class action lawsuits against Syngenta, and total damages may reach $5 billion.[260] In June 2017, a jury found Syngenta negligent and awarded $217.7 million to a class of 7000 Kansas farmers.[261] Cases in other states were scheduled for trial, but in September 2017, Syngenta agreed to a $1.4 billion global settlement of cases involving more than 100,000 farmers in Minnesota and elsewhere.[262]

As the discussion above suggests, low level presence of GE varieties does not raise a food or feed safety issue, at least when the GE variety has been approved in the exporting country. Instead, "it is an issue of noncompliance with the importing country's regulations for a product with at least one existing completed full safety assessment and a history of safe use."[263] Low level presence of GE material in critical livestock feed imported to the EU (GE corn, soybeans, soybean meal) led to the practical solution of an EU feed threshold in 2011.[264] A zero tolerance applies for other products.

As a recent report indicated, low-level presence "can cause abrupt, large-scale trade disruptions, sustained changes in international trade patterns, and significant economic losses that are borne by both importers and exporters."[265] A more tolerant acceptance of low levels of GE varieties that have been tested in accordance with recommendations of the Codex Alimentarius Commission might avoid some trade disruptions.[266] One organization has recommended a threshold of 5% as a "technically feasible, cost effective, and practical threshold," at least for GE food, feed, and grain for processing, if the GE variety has passed Codex review in the exporting country.[267]

Careful industry stewardship can help to avoid low level presence caused by commingling of GE with traditional and organic crops. Both the American Soybean Association and the National Corn Growers Association developed stewardship programs. The ASA asked seed companies not to sell unapproved varieties and provided

---

[259]Smyth (2017), p. 83. See Grossman (2012), pp. 93–95 for a discussion of StarLink™ corn and LL601 rice.

[260]Karnowski (2017). See also Redick (2017), pp. 45–54.

[261]Tidgren (2017). Syngenta planned to appeal the verdict.

[262]Feeley and Fisk (2017).

[263]GAABT (2015), p. 6.

[264]Commission Regulation 619/2011.

[265]CAST (2016), p. 8.

[266]CAST (2016), p. 8.

[267]GAABT (2015), p. 4. If requested by the importing government, a safety dossier should be submitted for unauthorized GE events.

advice for identity preservation of unapproved GE beans. The NCGA's "know before you grow" program provided information to minimize trade disruption and recommended against export of varieties not approved in the EU.[268] Industry stewardship may also involve delayed commercialization of new GE crops. That is, seed firms may delay commercial use until major import markets have approved a new crop, temporarily depriving producers and consumers of the benefits of the new crop.[269]

This aspect of stewardship illustrates an incomplete development of what has been termed the "Brussels Effect." That is, stricter EU regulation of GE crops and their products has forced some US companies and producers to adjust their behaviour to the requirements of EU regulation: "U.S. producers of GMO varieties continue to feel the (limited) Brussels Effect due to their inability to altogether ignore the EU market and their dependence on multinational companies who prefer to cater to a single global standard and remain sensitive to potential risks and liabilities they may face in the EU."[270] Thus, some US producers plant only crops that have been approved for import in the EU.

Despite efforts at stewardship in the US, it seems likely that trade disruptions caused by asynchronous approval will increase in the future. A recent report indicated that "the potential for sustained regulatory asynchrony and chronic trade disruptions in the future is magnified by the tendency of major importers—the European Union, China, and several other Asian countries—to adopt approval systems that are not synchronized with those of key exporting countries—Argentina, Brazil, Canada, and the United States."[271]

4.4 *Innovative Technologies*

Regulation of genetic technology, both in the US and the EU, is based on measures that may define the regulated article or product in terms of genetic modification with DNA techniques. In recent years, however, new "genetic-engineering technologies challenge most existing regulatory systems by blurring the distinction between genetic engineering and conventional plant breeding while enabling increasingly profound alterations of plant metabolism, composition, and ecology."[272] Although these technologies offer precision and diversity, they raise difficult regulatory issues. One issue is whether these crops "will fall within the definition of GE crops used by

[268] Grossman (2016a), p. 328.

[269] CAST (2016), p. 5.

[270] Bradford (2012), p. 35. Requirements for the Brussels Effect include market power, regulatory capacity and preference for strict rules, inelastic targets of regulation (no relocation possible), and legal, technical, and economic nondivisibility of standards (pp. 11–19).

[271] CAST (2016), p. 3.

[272] NASEM (2016), p. 26. For an explanation and comparison of new techniques in agricultural biotechnology see High Level Group of Scientific Advisors 2017.

various regulatory agencies as a regulatory trigger and therefore be subject to premarket safety reviews."[273] This issue may be critical, especially if the definition of genetic engineering is based on the process of development, rather than the product. Another significant question is whether traditional types of risk assessment and regulation address risk characteristics of crops produced with new technologies. Moreover, some new technologies create products with no markers that indicate what technology was used to develop the product.[274]

An example of lack of a "regulatory trigger" is the CRISPR/Cas9 technology, which makes genome editing more precise. In 2016, the USDA decided not to regulate a white mushroom modified with CRISPR/Cas9 technology to resist browning. The technology deleted genes related to an enzyme that causes browning. The mushroom contained no introduced DNA from plant pests, which trigger USDA regulation under the Plant Protection Act and USDA regulations.[275] The absence of possible plant pests led to USDA's decision not to regulate. USDA has also declined to regulate about 30 products developed with other innovative techniques (for example, zinc-finger nuclease) that do not pose a risk of plant pests.[276]

In the EU, as in the US, legislation that governs agricultural biotechnology was enacted before these new technologies were commercialized. Thus, differences of opinion exist about whether plants produced with techniques such as cisgenesis or intragenesis fit within the parameters of EU legislation that governs GMOs. If these techniques do not produce GMOs, as defined in legislation, then GMO legislation may not apply; the decision about applicability may fall to the Court of Justice.[277] Insofar as foods are concerned, the Novel Foods Regulation would seem to apply to novel foods that are not regulated as GMOs.[278] The regulatory status of innovative technologies is likely to affect commercialization of new varieties. If a technique results in a product that is not considered a GM variety, development costs and regulatory delays will be minimal, and the techniques will be attractive for a broader range of applications and for developers that lack the resources of major corporations.[279]

---

[273]NASEM (2016), p. 493.

[274]Smyth (2017), p. 81. Some technologies, considered mutagenesis, are not regulated as GM crops in the US.

[275]Firko (2016). Arctic apples, which do not brown when cut, were developed by gene silencing, which shut down genes for the browning enzyme.

[276]Waltz (2016). Other techniques include cisgenesis and intragenesis, which are faster and more precise than genetic engineering and perhaps more acceptable to consumers. Miraglia and Brera (2016), p. 312. Cisgenesis involves modification of an organism with a gene from a sexually compatible species and does not change the DNA sequence in the recipient organism. It is especially useful for organisms, like trees, with a long reproduction cycle. Miraglia and Brera (2016), pp. 309–310. Intragenesis is a modification "that leads to a combination of different gene fragments from donor organism(s) of the same or a sexually compatible species as the recipient." Miraglia and Brera (2016), p. 310, quoting EFSA. Simplot's Innate potato, approved for cultivation in the US, is intragenic.

[277]Miraglia and Brera (2016), pp. 316–317.

[278]Regulation 2015/2283, Articles 2, 3.

[279]Lusser et al. (2011), pp. 8, 49–50.

In any event, the EU is giving serious consideration to these new technologies.[280] The Commission "supports the need for continuous progress in plant breeding techniques, which can help to overcome some limitations of traditional breeding and enlarge the portfolio of products developed in the EU."[281] Since 2007, a working group has assessed various new breeding techniques, including cisgenesis, intragenesis, and others. So far, EFSA has assessed the risks of cisgenesis/intragenesis and zinc finger nuclease 3. EFSA concluded that its existing guidance documents on evaluation of food and feed products and environmental risk assessments were appropriate for these techniques. More recently, the Commission indicated the need for "a broad EU reflection on new breeding techniques," and a spokesperson indicated that the EU should "move away from a GMO-centered discussion" of innovative plant reproduction, and not "treat all new techniques as 'hidden' GMOs."[282]

In the US, the government supports and promotes the application of new technologies in agriculture "as a matter of policy" and as a means to enhance US competitiveness.[283] Principles for regulating new technologies, including genetic technologies, articulated in 2011,[284] helped to inspire recent efforts to modernize the regulatory system, which focused on three activities: the 2016 National Strategy for regulation of biotechnology, the 2017 update to the Coordinated Framework, and an independent study of risks (or lack of risks) and risk assessment (including genetic engineering, genome engineering, and targeted manipulation of genetic information) carried out by the National Academies of Sciences, Engineering, and Medicine.[285] As discussed above, the National Strategy recommends that regulation focus on products that require federal oversight, and the Coordinated Framework focuses on agency responsibility and coordination. Both the USDA and the FDA plan to clarify agency policy on regulation of products of new technologies.

The National Academies report viewed the updated Coordinated Framework and the National Strategy as starting points, but recommended "a consistent, efficient, and effective decision-making framework that continues to balance innovation and safety."[286] In terms of regulation, the National Academies report found that the Coordinated Framework is flexible and can govern many types of biotechnology products, but that the authority of the FDA, USDA, and EPA may result in "gaps or redundancies in regulatory oversight."[287] Because not all products of innovative biotechnologies will fit within existing agency jurisdictions, regulators may need to use "the flexibility available under their statutes to minimize gaps in jurisdiction"

280 Member States have mixed views about innovative genetic technologies. Some States are open to new techniques; others are uncertain; most have no official position. Little public awareness of innovative biotechnologies exists. FAS, USDA (2016), p. 41.

281 European Commission (n.d.).

282 Michalopoulos (2017). See High Level Group of Scientific Advisors (2017).

283 Bergeson (2017), p. 33.

284 OSTP (2011) and Obama (2011).

285 NASEM (2017).

286 NASEM (2017), p. 11.

287 NASEM (2017), p. 6. Other agencies may also have jurisdiction, but the Coordinated Framework does not provide specific details.

and use the most suitable regulatory system for the new product.[288] Agencies may be unprepared, in capacity and expertise, for an increased number of new products.[289] Moreover the US regulatory system is complex and fragmented, posing uncertainty and other difficulties for product developers and the general public. Regulatory oversight that is too complex will deter innovation, but oversight must match "scope, scale, complexity, and tempo of future technological developments and increase[] public confidence in the safety of products entering the marketplace."[290]

Another National Academies report recommended that regulatory focus be on the product of biotechnology: the risk of novel characteristics to health or environment, the uncertainty of severity of harm, and potential for exposure. If a new product has no intended traits that have health or environment concerns and no intended alterations that raise concerns, it should face no further testing. Products with potential for health or environmental effects or with differences from comparators that cannot be interpreted should face further safety testing.[291] Taking an approach more like the EU, the National Academies recommended that, in addition to issues of safety, policymakers address socioeconomic issues and emphasize communication to the public.[292]

Already in 2012, scholars recognized that innovative plant breeding techniques do not always fit within existing "product definitions, regulatory frameworks and risk assessment approaches" used for GE products.[293] In basic agreement with the National Academies recommendations, they identified a number of significant challenges. First, regulatory frameworks must remain "fit for purpose"—that is, process-based and other narrow definitions of GE products may not apply to plants developed with new technologies. Second, regulation and risk assessment must be "proportional to the level of risk" to health and the environment, especially when products of new technology (for example, cisgenesis) resemble conventionally-bred plants. Third, regulatory measures should not only prevent harm, but also stimulate innovation and help to encourage consumer acceptance of new products. Fourth, regulatory frameworks must facilitate international harmonization, particularly in light of problems caused by asynchronous authorisations. Finally, regulatory systems must ensure that products with "equal potential to cause harm" will face similar risk assessments; this means that assessments must focus on characteristics of the plant, not the process of development.[294]

[288]NASEM (2017), p. 11.

[289]NASEM (2017), p. 8.

[290]NASEM (2017), p. 11.

[291]NASEM (2016), pp. 26–27. A European expert on risk regulation may agree with this approach: "Safe GMOs are subject to onerous prior risk assessment and approval regimes, as well as reporting and labelling requirements." Bergkamp (2017), p. 61. He asserted that generally "regulators should think twice before regulating the risks associated with new technologies. Innovation is important to any society, and innovation requires risk-taking" (p. 62). He suggested that regulators ask "whether we are better off without the proposed restrictions, or with a more modest regime. Not all risks can and should be regulated; some risks are well worth taking" (p. 63).

[292]NASEM (2016), p. 26.

[293]Podevin et al. (2012), p. 1057.

[294]Podevin et al. (2012), pp. 1058–1060.

5 Conclusion

Since the initial commercialization of GE crops in 1996, global cultivation has increased 110-fold, and producers are planting an increasing variety of GE crops.[295] In the US, over half of cultivated cropland is planted to GE crops, and in some developing countries, millions of small farmers profit from GE varieties of cotton and other crops. Global socioeconomic and environmental benefits include increased income for farmers and reduced application of herbicides and pesticides. Consumption of GE products has caused no known health problems for humans or animals. During the past several decades, animal applications of biotechnology have resulted in both transgenic and cloned animals, but transgenic animals are not sold for food, and clones are seldom in the food chain.

Global regulation of GE crops has developed since the 1990s, and legislative measures focus on the safety of GE crops for food and feed and for the environment. Both in the US and in the EU, authorisation of new varieties and their products is time-consuming and costly. Although the US and the EU share some regulatory priorities, including scientific risk assessments, approaches to risk management differ, with more EU reliance on the precautionary principle and consideration of socioeconomic issues and consumer preferences. Most GE crops are authorised first in the US, with later (sometimes much later) authorisation in the EU and other countries. The resulting asynchronous approvals have led to reduced trade between the US and the EU, with significant losses for producers and others in the grain industry.

In recent years, researchers have developed innovative technologies—perhaps triggered in part by stringent regulation of GE products—to produce new crop varieties. Some of these technologies, which do not meet statutory definitions of GE crops, may escape regulation under existing legislative measures in the US and the EU. Thus, in the near future, policymakers in both the US and the EU are likely to make critical decisions about the types of risk assessment and the level of regulation appropriate for these new products.

GE crops developed with DNA technology and crops developed using innovative technologies pose challenges for regulators and stakeholders. These include "regulatory barriers that limit scientific innovation and restrict technology development," trade disruptions caused by asynchronous approvals and unrealistic thresholds for low level presence of GE material, and the widespread lack of understanding of biotechnology by consumers and other stakeholders.[296] Regulatory systems that protect human and animal health and the environment are critical, both for GE crops and for products of new technologies. But risk management decisions should also ensure that, wherever possible, the products of GE technology will be available to producers and consumers who choose to use those products.[297] It can be hoped that regulatory systems will facilitate, rather than hinder, international trade in

[295] ISAAA (2017), p. 2.

[296] ISAAA (2017), p. 115.

[297] ISAAA (2017), p. 113.

agricultural products, including products of biotechnology, particularly in light of increased global populations and the predicted agricultural impacts of global warming. Meeting the challenges of agricultural biotechnology will require significant flexibility and perhaps amendment of regulatory measures, both in the US and in the EU.

References

Literature

Agricultural Marketing Service (AMS), USDA. 2011. Policy Memorandum: NOP Statements on Cloning and Organic Livestock Production. Policy Memo 11-11.

AMS, USDA. 2017. Proposed Rule Questions Under Consideration. <https://www.ams.usda.gov/rules-regulations/gmo-questions> (accessed 30 August 2017).

Alliance for Bio-Integrity v. Shalala, 116 F. Supp. 2d 166 (D DC 2000).

Animal and Plant Health Inspection Service (APHIS), USDA (2017a) Petitions for determination of nonregulated status. <https://www.aphis.usda.gov/aphis/ourfocus/biotechnology/permits-notifications-petitions/petitions/petition-status> Accessed 4 Dec 2017

Anker, Helle Tegner and Margaret Rosso Grossman. 2009. Authorization of Genetically Modified Organisms: Precaution in US and EC Law. *European Food and Feed Law Review* 4(1): 3-22.

Bergeson, Lynn L. 2017. Enlisting Modern Technologies to Ensure a Safe Food Supply. *Natural Resources and Environment* 31(3): 31-34.

Bergkamp, Lucas. 2017. The Reality of Risk Regulation. *European Journal of Risk Regulation* 8(1): 56-63.

Binimelis, R. and A.I. Myhr. 2015. Socio-economic considerations in GMO Regulations: opportunities and challenges. In *Know Your Food: Food ethics and innovation*, ed. Diana Elena Dumitras, Ionel Mugurel Jitea and Stef Aerts. 61-67. Wageningen, the Netherlands: Wageningen Academic Publishers.

Biotechnology Industry Organization (BIO). 2010. All about Animal Cloning. <https://www.bio.org/sites/default/files/files/Cloning_onepager.pdf>.

Bodiguel, Luc. 2016. Local Governance of GMOs: From Hope to Pragmatism. In *GMO's in the EU Law*, ed. Maria Pia Ragionieri. 263-277. Assago: Wolters Kluwer.

Bradford, Anu. 2012. The Brussels Effect. *Northwestern University Law Review* 107(1): 1-67.

Brookes, Graham and Peter Barfoot. 2017. *GM crops: global socio-economic and environmental impacts 1996-2015*. UK: PG Economics Ltd.

Carreño, Ignacio. 2014. European Commission Proposes to Revise the EU's Legislative Framework on Novel Foods and Animal Cloning. *European Journal of Risk Regulation* 5(3): 362-365.

Center for Food Safety v. Price. 2017. Case 1:17-cv-03833 (SD NY, filed 22 May 2017).

Council for Agricultural Science and Technology (CAST). 2009. Animal Productivity and Genetic Diversity: Cloned and Transgenic Animals. Issue Paper 43. Ames, Iowa: CAST.

CAST. 2013. Impact of the Precautionary Principle on Feeding Current and Future Generations. Issue Paper 52. Ames, Iowa: CAST.

CAST. 2016. The Impact of Asynchronous Approvals for Biotech Crops on Agricultural Sustainability, Trade, and Innovation. QTA2016-2. Ames, Iowa: CAST.

Codex Alimentarius Commission (CAC). 2003a. Principles for the Risk Analysis of Foods Derived from Modern Biotechnology. Doc CAC/GL/44-2003. Rome: World Health Organization and Food and Agriculture Organization.

CAC. 2003b. Guideline for the Conduct of Food Safety Assessment of Foods Derived from Recombinant-DNA Plants. Doc CAC/GL/45-2003 (Annex 3, 2008). Rome: World Health Organization and Food and Agriculture Organization.

CAC. 2008. Guideline for the Conduct of Food Safety Assessment of Foods Derived from Recombinant-DNA Animals. Doc CAC/GL/68-2008. Rome: World Health Organization and Food and Agriculture Organization.

CAC. 2011. Compilation of Codex Texts Relevant to Labelling of Foods Derived from Modern Biotechnology. Doc CAC/GL/76-2011. Rome: World Health Organization and Food and Agriculture Organization.

Commissie Genetische Modificatie (COGEM). 2011. *Genetically Modified Animals: A Wanted and Unwanted Reality*. COGEM Topic Report CGM/120111-01. Bilthoven, The Netherlands: COGEM.

Deloitte. 2017. *Study of Electronic or Digital Link Disclosure: A Third-Party Evaluation of Challenges Impacting Access to Bioengineered Food Disclosure*. Washington DC: USDA.

Economist. 2017. The sheep of things to come. 18 February 2017: 17-20.

EuropaBio. 2016. Maladministration on GMOs by the EU Commission Distorting Markets. Press Release (8 April 2016).

European Commission. n.d.. New plant breeding techniques. <http://ec.europa.eu/food/plant/gmo/legislation/plant_breeding_en> (accessed 9 June 2017).

European Commission. 2013a. FAQ: Commission tables proposals on animal cloning and novel food. Memo/13/1169 (18 December 2013).

European Commission. 2015a. *Study on the labelling of products from cloned animals and their offspring*. Final Report, Executive Summary. Brussels: Directorate General for Agriculture and Rural Development.

European Commission. 2015b. Review of the decision-making process on GMOs in the EU: Questions and Answers, Memo/15/4779 (22 April 2015).

European Commission. 2017a. Comitology Procedure Reforms: Questions & Answers. Memo/17/273 (14 February 2017).

European Commission. 2017b. Restrictions of geographical scope of GMO applications/authorisations: Member States demands and outcomes. <http://ec.europa.eu/food/plant/gmo/authorisation/cultivation/geographical_scope_en> (last updated 1 September 2017).

European Food Safety Authority (EFSA). n.d.. Genetically modified animals. <http://www.efsa.europa.eu/en/topics/topic/genetically-modified-animals> (accessed 31 August 2017).

EFSA. 2008. Scientific Opinion: Food Safety, Animal Health and Welfare and Environmental Impact of Animals derived from Cloning by Somatic Cell Nucleus Transfer (SCNT) and their Offspring and Products Obtained from those Animals. *EFSA Journal* 6: 767, 1-49.

EFSA. 2009. Further Advice on the Implications of Animal Cloning (SCNT). *EFSA Journal* 7(6): RN 319, 1-15.

EFSA. 2010a. Update on the state of play of animal cloning. *EFSA Journal* 8(9): 1784.

EFSA. 2010b. Guidance on the environmental risk assessment of genetically modified plants. *EFSA Journal* 8(11): 1879.

EFSA. 2011. Guidance for risk assessment of food and feed from genetically modified plants. *EFSA Journal* 9(5): 2150.

EFSA. 2012a. Guidance on the risk assessment of food and feed from genetically modified animals and on animal health and welfare aspects. *EFSA Journal* 10(1): 2501.

EFSA. 2012b. Update on the state of play of Animal Health and Welfare and Environmental Impact of Animals derived from SCNT Cloning and their Offspring, and Food Safety of Products Obtained from those Animals. *EFSA Journal* 10(7): 2794.

EFSA. 2013. Guidance on the environmental risk assessment of genetically modified animals. *EFSA Journal* 11(5): 3200.

Eur-Lex. n.d.. Procedure 2013/0433/COD. <http://eur-lex.europa.eu/procedure/EN/2013_433> (accessed 29 May 2017).

European Union Ombudsman. 2016. Case 1582/2014/PHP (decided January 2016).

Feeley, Jef and Margaret Cronin Fisk. 2017. Syngenta Agrees to Pay More Than $1.4 Billion in Corn Accord. <www.bloomberg.com> (27 September 2017).

Fernandez-Cornejo, Jorge, Seth Wechsler, Mike Livingston and Lorraine Mitchell. 2014. *Genetically Engineered Crops in the United States*. ERS, USDA, ERR 162.

Fernandez-Cornejo, Jorge, Seth Wechsler and Daniel Milkove. 2016. *The Adoption of Genetically Engineered Alfalfa, Canola, and Sugarbeets in the United States*. ERS, USDA, EIB 163.

Firko, Michael. 2016. Letter to Yinong Yang. Re: Request for confirmation that transgene-free, CRISPR-edited mushroom is not a regulated article. Riverdale MD: Biotechnology Regulatory Services, APHIS, USDA (13 April 2016).

Food and Drug Administration (FDA) (2017a) Biotechnology consultations on food from GE plant varieties. <https://www.accessdata.fda.gov/scripts/fdcc/?set=Biocon> Accessed 4 Dec 2017

Foreign Agricultural Service (FAS), USDA (2011) Joint statement on animal cloning for livestock production. <https://www.fas.usda.gov/jointstatement-animal-cloning-livestock-production> Buenos Aires

FAS, USDA. 2014. Why Trade Promotion Authority Is Essential for U.S. Agriculture and the Transatlantic Trade and Investment Partnership. <https://www.fas.usda.gov/sites/default/files/2014-04/tpa-ttip.pdf>.

FAS, USDA. 2016. EU-28 Agricultural Biotechnology Annual 2016. GAIN Rep. No. FR1624.

Gleim, Savannah, Stuart J. Smyth and Peter W.B. Phillips. 2016. Regulatory System Impacts on Global GM Crop Adoption Patterns, *The Estey Journal of International Law and Trade Policy* 17(2): 96-116.

Global Alliance for Ag Biotech Trade (GAABT). 2015. *Practical Approach to Address Low Level Presence (LLP) of Agricultural Biotechnology-derived Plant Products in Food, Feed, and Grain for Processing (FFP)*. Washington, DC: GAABT.

Greene, Catherine, Seth J. Wechsler, Aaron Adalja and James Hanson. 2016. *Economic Issues in the Coexistence of Organic, Genetically Engineered (GE), and Non-GE Crops*. ERS, USDA, EIB 149.

Grossman, Margaret Rosso. 2006. Animal Identification and Traceability under the US National Animal Identification System. *Journal of Food Law & Policy* 2(2): 231-315.

Grossman, Margaret Rosso. 2007. The Coexistence of GM and Other Crops in the European Union. *Kansas Journal of Law and Public Policy* 16(3): 325-392.

Grossman, Margaret Rosso. 2009. Protecting Health, Environment and Agriculture: Authorisation of Genetically Modified Crops and Food in the United States and the European Union. *Deakin Law Review* 14(2): 257-304.

Grossman, Margaret Rosso. 2012. Genetically Modified Crops and Their Products in the United States: A Review of the Regulatory System. *Jahrbuch des Agrarrechts* XI: 69-96.

Grossman, Margaret Rosso. 2016a. Genetic Technology and Food Security: A View from the United States. In *Genetic Technology and Food Security*, ed. Roland Norer. 289-332. Cham, Heidelberg, New York, Dordrecht, London: Springer.

Grossman, Margaret Rosso. 2016b. Genetically Engineered Animals in the United States: The AquAdvantage Salmon. *European Food and Feed Law Review* 11(3): 190-200.

Grossman, Margaret Rosso. 2016c. The United States Bioengineered Food Disclosure Standard: Labels for Genetically Engineered Food. *European Food and Feed Law Review* 11(6): 502-507.

Grossman, Margaret Rosso. 2017. US FDA Enacts Final Rule for GRAS Substances. *European Food and Feed Law Review* 12(2): 169-172.

High Level Group of Scientific Advisors, European Commission. 2017. New Techniques in Agricultural Biotechnology. Brussels: European Commission.

ICF GHK, DG Sanco. 2012. *Impact in the EU and third countries of EU measures on animal cloning for food production*. London: ICF GHK.

ICF GHK, European Commission. 2013. *State of play in the EU on GM-free food labelling schemes and assessment of the need for possible harmonization*. Brussels: European Commission.

International Service for the Acquisition of Agri-Biotech Applications (ISAAA). 2017. Global Status of Commercialized Biotech/GM Crops: 2016. Report and Executive Summary. ISAAA Brief No. 52. Ithaca NY: ISAAA.

Karnowski, Steve. 2017. 1st farmer lawsuit against Syngenta goes to trial. *The Detroit News* (24 April 2017.

Knight, Bruce I. 2008. Animal Cloning: Transitioning from the Lab to the Market. Speech to Advisory Committee on Biotechnology and 21st Century Agriculture, Washington, DC (5 March 2008).

Kniss A (2017) Long-term trends in the intensity and relative toxicity of herbicide use. Nat Commun 8:14865. 1–7. https://doi.org/10.1038/ncomms14865

Lucifero, Nicola. 2016. Placing GM Foods on the Market. Biotechnology between Food Safety and Consumer Protection. In *GMO's in the EU Law*, ed. Maria Pia Ragionieri. 123-156. Assago: Wolters Kluwer.

Lusser, Maria, Claudia Parisi, Damien Plan and Emilio Rodriguez-Cerezo. 2011. *New plant breeding techniques. State-of-the-art and prospects for commercial development.* (JRC Scientific and Technical Report EUR 24760). Luxembourg: European Union.

Mahaffey, Harry, Farzad Taheripour and Wallace E. Tyner. 2016. Evaluating the Economic and Environmental Impacts of a Global GMO Ban. *Journal of Environmental Protection* 7: 1522-1546.

Michalopoulos S (2017) Commission: EU needs 'broad reflection' on new breeding techniques and beyond. EurActive (4 May 2017)

Miller, Henry I. 2017. Will Genetically Engineered Animals Finally Bring Home the Bacon? *Forbes* (15 February 2017).

Miraglia, Marina and Carol Brera. 2016. Back to the Future with Cisgenesis and Intragenesis. In *GMO's in the EU Law*, ed. Maria Pia Ragionieri. 303-323. Assago: Wolters Kluwer.

National Academy of Sciences (NAS). 2002. *Animal Biotechnology: Science Based Concerns.* Washington, DC: National Academies Press.

NAS. 2004. *Safety of Genetically Engineered Foods: Approaches to Assessing Unintended Health Effects.* Washington, DC: National Academies Press.

National Academies of Sciences, Engineering, and Medicine (NASEM). 2016. *Genetically Engineered Crops: Experiences and Prospects.* Washington, DC: National Academies Press.

NASEM. 2017. *Preparing for Future Products of Biotechnology.* Washington, DC: National Academies Press.

National Agricultural Statistics Service (NASS), USDA. 2017. *Acreage.*

Obama, Barack. 2011. Executive Order 13563—Improving Regulation and Regulatory Review, 3 Code of Federal Regulations 13,563 (18 January 2011).

Phillipson, Martin. 2016. Regulatory Impacts on Trade in Products of Biotechnology—the Issues. *The Estey Journal of International Law and Trade Policy* 17(2): 91-95.

Podevin, Nancy, Yann Devos, Howard Vivian Davies and Kaare Magne Nielsen. 2012. Transgenic or not? No simple answer! New biotechnology-based plant breeding techniques and the regulatory landscape. *EMBO Reports* 13(12): 1057-1061.

Redick, Thomas P. 2017. Liability Prevention for Agricultural Biotechnology. *Drake Journal of Agricultural Law* 22(1): 31-64.

Salvi, Laura. 2016. The EU Regulatory Framework on GMOs and the Shift of Powers towards Member States: An Easy Way Out of the Regulatory Impasse? *European Food and Feed Law Review* 11(3): 201-210.

de Sadeleer, Nicolas. 2015. Marketing and Cultivation of GMOs in the EU: An Uncertain Balance between Centrifugal and Centripetal Forces. *European Journal of Risk Regulation* 6(4): 532-558.

Sánchez MA, Parrott WA (2017) Characterization of scientific studies usually cited as evidence of adverse effects of GM food/feed. Plant Biotechnol J. https://doi.org/10.1111/pbi.12798

Smart, Richard D., Matthias Blum and Justus Wesseler. 2017. Trends in Approval Times for Genetically Engineered Crops in the United States and the European Union. *Journal of Agricultural Economics* 68(1): 182-198.

Smyth SJ (2017) Genetically modified crops, regulatory delays, and international trade. Food Energy Secur 6:78–86. https://doi.org/10.1002/fes3.100

Smyth, Stuart J., José Falck-Zepeda and Karinne Ludlow. 2016. The Costs of Regulatory Delays for Genetically Modified Crops. *The Estey Journal of International Law and Trade Policy* 17(2): 173-195.

Stapleton, Patricia A. 2016. From Mad Cows to GMOs: The Side Effects of Modernization. *European Journal of Risk Regulation* 7(3): 17-531.

Tidgren, Kristine A. 2017. Additional Syngenta Trials Have Been Scheduled in Kansas MDL. <https://www.calt.iastate.edu/blogpost/>.

United Nations. 1992. Rio Declaration on Environment and Development, 18 December 1992, UN Doc. A/Conf.151/5/Rev.1, reprinted in 31 ILM 874.

United Nations. 2000. Cartagena Protocol on Biosafety to the Convention on Biological Diversity. Montreal, 29 January 2000, entered in force 11 Sept. 2003. <http://www.cbd.int/biosafety/protocol>.

USDA, Advisory Committee on Biotechnology and 21st Century Agriculture (AC21). 2016. *A Framework for Local Coexistence Discussions.* <https://www.usda.gov/sites/default/files/documents/ac21-report-final-local-coexistence.pdf>.

US Government Accountability Office. 2016. *Genetically Engineered Crops: USDA Needs to Enhance Oversight and Better Understand Impacts of Unintended Mixing with Other Crops.* GAO-16-241.

Waltz, Emily. 2016. Gene-edited CRISPR mushroom escapes US regulation. *Nature* 532: 293 (21 April 2016).

Waltz, Emily. 2017. First genetically engineered salmon sold in Canada. *Nature* 548: 148 (10 August 2017).

Winter, Gerd. 2016. Cultivation Restrictions for Genetically Modified Plants. *European Journal of Risk Regulation* 7(1): 120-143.

Young, Alasdair R. 2003. Political Transfer and "Trading Up"?: Transatlantic Trade in Genetically Modified Food and U.S. Politics. *World Politics* 55: 457-484.

Zetterberg, Charlotta and Karin Edvardsson Björnberg. 2017. Time for a New Regulatory Framework for GM Crops? *Journal of Agricultural and Environmental Ethics* 30: 325-347.

US Statutes, Regulations, and Regulatory Documents

Statutes and Regulations

Consolidated Appropriations Act, 2016. Pub. L. 114-113, 129 Stat. 2242 (18 December 2015).

Federal Insecticide, Fungicide, and Rodenticide Act (FIFRA). 7 United States Code [USC] §§ 136-136y.

Food, Drug, and Cosmetic Act (FDCA). 21 USC §§ 301-399f, supplemented by the Food Safety Modernization Act, 2011, 21 USC §§ 2201-2252.

National Bioengineered Food Disclosure Standard. Pub. L. 114-216, 130 Stat. 834-839 (2016), amending the Agricultural Marketing Act of 1946 by adding Subtitles E and F, codified at 7 USC §§ 1639-1639c, §§ 1639i-1639j, § 6524.

National Environmental Policy Act (NEPA). 42 USC §§ 4321-4347.

Plant Protection Act of 2000. 7 USC §§ 7701-7772 (replacing the Plant Pest and Plant Quarantine Acts).

7 Code of Federal Regulations [CFR] part 340. Introduction of organisms and products altered or produced through genetic engineering which are plant pests or which there is reason to believe are plant pests.

21 CFR parts 510, 514. New animal drugs; New animal drug applications.

40 CFR part 174. Procedures and requirements for plant-incorporated protectants.

Agency Policy and Proposals

Animal and Plant Health Inspection Service (APHIS), USDA. 2017b. Proposed rule, Importation, Interstate Movement, and Environmental Release of Certain Genetically Engineered Organisms. 82 Federal Register 7008-7039 (19 January 2017); 82 Federal Register 10,312 (10 February 2017) (extending comment period to 19 June 2017).
APHIS, USDA (2017c) Proposed rule; withdrawal, importation, interstate movement, and environmental release of certain genetically engineered organisms. Fed Regist 82:51582–51583. (7 Nov 2017)
Center for Veterinary Medicine (CVM), FDA (2008a) Animal cloning: A risk assessment. FDA, Rockville, MD. Announced at 73 Federal Register 2923 (16 Jan 2008)
CVM, FDA (2008b) Guidance for Industry 179: use of animal clones and clone progeny for human food and animal feed
CVM, FDA. 2015. Guidance for Industry 187: Regulation of Genetically Engineered Animals Containing Heritable Recombinant DNA Constructs (2009, slightly revised 2011, 2015).
CVM, FDA. 2017. Draft Guidance for Industry: Regulation of Intentionally Altered Genomic DNA in Animals. Guidance 187. Announced at 82 Federal Register 6561 (19 January 2017).
FDA. 1992. Statement of Policy: Foods Derived from New Plant Varieties. 57 Federal Register 22,984-23,005 (29 May 1992).
FDA. 2015a. Guidance for Industry: Voluntary Labeling Indicating Whether Foods Have or Have Not Been Derived from Genetically Engineered Plants.
FDA. 2015b. Final Rule, New Animal Drugs in Genetically Engineered Animals. 80 Federal Register 73,104 (24 November 2015).
FDA (2015c) Draft guidance for industry: voluntary labeling indicating whether food has or has not been derived from genetically engineered Atlantic Salmon. Announced at 80 Federal Register 73,193 (24 Nov 2015)
FDA. 2016. Final rule, Substances Generally Recognized as Safe. 81 Federal Register 54,960-55,055 (17 August 2016), amending 21 CFR parts 170, 570, and others.
FDA (2017b) Notification. genome editing in new plant varieties used for foods: request for comments. Fed Regist 82:6564–6566. (19 Jan 2017)
Office of Science and Technology Policy (OSTP). 1986. Coordinated Framework for Regulation of Biotechnology Products. 51 Federal Register 23,302 (26 June 1986) (drafted in cooperation with administrative agencies).
OSTP. 1992. Exercise of Federal Oversight Within Scope of Statutory Authority: Planned Introductions of Biotechnology Products into the Environment. 57 Federal Register 6753 (27 February 1992).
OSTP (2011) Principles for regulation and oversight of emerging technologies (11 Mar 2011)
US White House. 2016. National Strategy for Modernizing the Regulatory System for Biotechnology Products (Biotechnology Working Group, Emerging Technologies Interagency Policy Coordination Committee).
US White House. 2017. Modernizing the Regulatory System for Biotechnology Products: Final Version of the 2017 Update to the Coordinated Framework for the Regulation of Biotechnology.

EU Legislation and Commission Documents

Legislation (in Chronological Order)

Regulation (EC) 258/97 of the European Parliament and of the Council of 27 January 1997 concerning novel foods and novel food ingredients. 1997 OJ (L 43) 1-6 (14 February 1997).

Council Directive 98/58/EC of 20 July 1998 concerning the protection of animals kept for farming purposes. 1998 OJ (L 221) 23-27 (8 August 1998).
Regulation (EC) 178/2002 of 28 January 2002 [General Food Law] laying down the general principles and requirements of food law, establishing the European Food Safety Authority and laying down procedures in matters of food safety. 2002 OJ (L 31) 1-24 (1 February 2002).
Directive 2001/18/EC of the European Parliament and of the Council of 12 March 2001 on the deliberate release into the environment of genetically modified organisms and repealing Council Directive 90/220/EEC. 2001 OJ (L 106) 1-38 (17 April 2001).
Regulation (EC) 1829/2003 of the European Parliament and of the Council of 22 September 2003 on genetically modified food and feed. 2003 OJ (L 268) 1-23 (18 October 2003).
Regulation (EC) 1830/2003 of the European Parliament and of the Council of 22 September 2003 concerning the traceability and labelling of genetically modified organisms and the traceability of food and feed products produced from genetically modified organisms and amending Directive 2001/18/EC. 2003 OJ (L 268) 24-28 (18 October 2003).
Commission Regulation (EC) 65/2004 of 14 January 2004 establishing a system for the development and assignment of unique identifiers for genetically modified organisms. 2004 OJ (L 10) 5-10 (16 January 2004).
Directive 2009/41/EC of the European Parliament and of the Council of 6 May 2009 on the contained use of genetically modified micro-organisms. 2009 OJ (L 125) 75-97 (21 May 2009).
European Commission. 2010. Commission Recommendation of 13 July 2010 on guidelines for the development of national co-existence measures to avoid the unintended presence of GMOs in conventional and organic crops. 2010 OJ (C 200) 1-5 (22 July 2010).
Commission Regulation (EU) 619/2011 of 24 June 2011 laying down the methods of sampling and analysis for the official control of feed as regards presence of genetically modified material for which an authorisation procedure is pending or the authorisation of which has expired. 2011 OJ (L 166) 9-15 (25 June 2011).
Regulation (EU) 1169/2011 of the European Parliament and of the Council of 25 October 2011 on the provision of food information to consumers. 2011 OJ (L 304) 18-63 (22 November 2011).
Directive (EU) 2015/412 of 11 March 2015 amending Directive 2001/18/EC as regards the possibility for the Member States to restrict or prohibit the cultivation of genetically modified organisms (GMOs) in their territory. 2015 OJ (L 68) 1-8 (13 March 2015).
Regulation 2015/2283 of the European Parliament and of the Council of 25 November 2015 on novel foods, amending Regulation (EU) No 1169/2011 of the European Parliament and of the Council and repealing Regulation (EC) No 258/97 of the European Parliament and of the Council and Commission Regulation (EC) No 1852/2001. 2015 OJ (L 327) 1-22 (11 December 2015).

Commission and Parliament Documents

European Commission. 2000. Communication from the Commission on the precautionary principle. COM (2000) 1 final (2 February 2000).
European Commission. 2013b. Staff Working Document: Impact Assessment [accompanying the Commission's cloning proposals]. SWD (2013) 519 final; Executive summary: SWD (2013) 520 final (18 December 2013).
European Commission. 2013c. Proposal for a Directive of the European Parliament and of the Council on the cloning of animals of the bovine, porcine, ovine, caprine and equine species kept and reproduced for farming purposes. COM (2013) 892 final (18 December 2013).
European Commission. 2013d. Proposal for a Council Directive on the placing on the market of food from animal clones. COM (2013) 893 final (18 December 2013).
European Commission. 2013e. Proposal for a Regulation of the European Parliament and of the Council on novel foods. COM (2013) 894 final (18 December 2013).

European Commission. 2015c. Proposal for a Regulation of the European Parliament and of the Council amending Regulation (EC) No 1829/2003 as regards the possibility for the Member States to restrict or prohibit the use of genetically modified food and feed on their territory. COM (2015) 177 final (22 April 2015).

European Commission. 2017c. Proposal for a Regulation of the European Parliament and of the Council amending Regulation (EU) No 182/2011 laying down the rules and general principles concerning mechanisms for control by Member States of the Commission's exercise of implementing powers. COM (2017) 85 final (14 February 2017).

European Parliament. 2015. Cloning of animals kept and reproduced for farming purposes. European Parliament legislative resolution P8_TA(2015)0285 (8 September 2015).

Margaret Rosso Grossman Ph.D., J.D. (University of Illinois), is Bock Chair Emerita and Professor of Agricultural Law Emerita in the Department of Agricultural and Consumer Economics, University of Illinois (USA). Her research focuses on agricultural and environmental law in the United States and Europe. Grossman is the author of 130 law review articles and book chapters published in the United States, United Kingdom, Canada, Australia, the Netherlands, Germany and Italy. She is author or editor of books published in Europe and the United States, and she has presented papers and lectures in numerous European countries as well as in Australia, China and Taiwan. Professor Grossman received three Fulbright Senior Scholar Awards and a German Marshall Fund Research Fellowship. The American Agricultural Law Association awarded her the Distinguished Service Award, the Professional Scholarship Award (twice), and the Excellence in Agricultural Law Award. She received the Silver Medal of the European Council for Agricultural Law. She is a Fellow of the Wageningen School of Social Sciences, Wageningen University, the Netherlands.

MIX
Papier aus verantwortungsvollen Quellen
Paper from responsible sources
FSC® C105338

If you have any concerns about our products,
you can contact us on
ProductSafety@springernature.com

In case Publisher is established outside the EU,
the EU authorized representative is:
Springer Nature Customer Service Center GmbH
Europaplatz 3, 69115 Heidelberg, Germany

Printed by Libri Plureos GmbH
in Hamburg, Germany